Driving Green Marketing in Fashion and Retail

Theodore K. Tarnanidis
International Hellenic University, Greece

Evridiki Papachristou
International Hellenic University, Greece

Michail Karypidis
International Hellenic University, Greece

Vasileios Ismyrlis
Hellenic Statistical Authority, Greece

A volume in the Advances in Marketing, Customer Relationship Management, and E-Services (AMCRMES) Book Series

IGI Global
PUBLISHER of TIMELY KNOWLEDGE

Published in the United States of America by
IGI Global
Business Science Reference (an imprint of IGI Global)
701 E. Chocolate Avenue
Hershey PA, USA 17033
Tel: 717-533-8845
Fax: 717-533-8661
E-mail: cust@igi-global.com
Web site: http://www.igi-global.com

Library of Congress Cataloging-in-Publication Data

CIP DATA PROCESSING

2024 Business Science Reference

ISBN(hc): 9798369330494
ISBN(sc): 9798369351178
eISBN: 9798369330500

This book is published in the IGI Global book series Advances in Marketing, Customer Relationship Management, and E-Services (AMCRMES) (ISSN: 2327-5502; eISSN: 2327-5529)

British Cataloguing in Publication Data
A Cataloguing in Publication record for this book is available from the British Library.

For electronic access to this publication, please contact: eresources@igi-global.com.

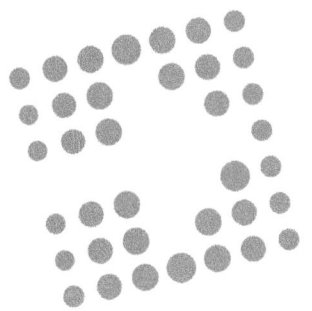

Advances in Marketing, Customer Relationship Management, and E-Services (AMCRMES) Book Series

Eldon Y. Li
National Chengchi University, Taiwan & California Polytechnic State University, USA

ISSN:2327-5502
EISSN:2327-5529

Mission

Business processes, services, and communications are important factors in the management of good customer relationship, which is the foundation of any well organized business. Technology continues to play a vital role in the organization and automation of business processes for marketing, sales, and customer service. These features aid in the attraction of new clients and maintaining existing relationships.

The Advances in Marketing, Customer Relationship Management, and E-Services (AMCRMES) Book Series addresses success factors for customer relationship management, marketing, and electronic services and its performance outcomes. This collection of reference source covers aspects of consumer behavior and marketing business strategies aiming towards researchers, scholars, and practitioners in the fields of marketing management.

Coverage

- Social Networking and Marketing
- Data mining and marketing
- CRM and customer trust
- Electronic Services
- Customer Relationship Management
- Database marketing
- Mobile CRM
- Cases on CRM Implementation
- Ethical Considerations in E-Marketing
- Telemarketing

IGI Global is currently accepting manuscripts for publication within this series. To submit a proposal for a volume in this series, please contact our Acquisition Editors at Acquisitions@igi-global.com or visit: http://www.igi-global.com/publish/.

The Advances in Marketing, Customer Relationship Management, and E-Services (AMCRMES) Book Series (ISSN 2327-5502) is published by IGI Global, 701 E. Chocolate Avenue, Hershey, PA 17033-1240, USA, www.igi-global.com. This series is composed of titles available for purchase individually; each title is edited to be contextually exclusive from any other title within the series. For pricing and ordering information please visit http://www.igi-global.com/book-series/advances-marketing-customer-relationship-management/37150. Postmaster: Send all address changes to above address.

Titles in this Series

For a list of additional titles in this series, please visit:
www.igi-global.com/book-series/advances-marketing-customer-relationship-management/37150

AI Innovation in Services Marketing
Ricardo Correia (Instituto Politécnico de Bragança, Portugal & CiTUR, Portugal) and Dominyka Venciute (ISM University of Management and Economics, Lithania)
Business Science Reference • © 2024 • 299pp • H/C (ISBN: 9798369321539) • US $285.00

Ethical Marketing Through Data Governance Standards and Effective Technology
Shefali Saluja (Chitkara Business School, Chitkara University, India) Varun Nayyar (Chitkara University, India) Kuleep Rojhe (Chitkara University, India) and Sandhir Sharma (Chitkara Business School, Chitkara University, ndia)
Business Science Reference • © 2024 • 328pp • H/C (ISBN: 9798369322154) • US $285.00

Enhancing and Predicting Digital Consumer Behavior with AI
Thomas Heinrich Musiolik (Woxsen University, India & University of Europe for Applied Sciences, Germany) Raul Villamarin Rodriguez (Woxsen University, India) and Hemachandran Kannan (Woxsen University, India)
Business Science Reference • © 2024 • 445pp • H/C (ISBN: 9798369344538) • US $395.00

Marketing and Big Data Analytics in Tourism and Events
Tareq Nael Hashem (Applied Science Private University, Jordan) Ahmad Albattat (Management and Science University, Malaysia) Marco Valeri (Niccolò Cusano University, Italy) and Anukrati Sharma (University of Kota, India)
Business Science Reference • © 2024 • 294pp • H/C (ISBN: 9798369333105) • US $295.00

Impact of Teleworking and Remote Work on Business Productivity, Retention, Advancement, and Bottom Line
Harish Chandra Chandan (Independent Researcher, USA)
Business Science Reference • © 2024 • 311pp • H/C (ISBN: 9798369313145) • US $290.00

AI-Driven Marketing Research and Data Analytics
Reason Masengu (Middle East College, Oman) Option Takunda Chiwaridzo (University of Science and Technology Beijing, Beijing, China) Mercy Dube (Midlands State University, Zimbabwe) and Benson Ruzive (Modern College of Business and Science, Oman)
Business Science Reference • © 2024 • 490pp • H/C (ISBN: 9798369321652) • US $290.00

Marketing Innovation Strategies and Consumer Behavior
Belem Barbosa (University of Porto, Portugal)
Business Science Reference • © 2024 • 469pp • H/C (ISBN: 9798369341957) • US $325.00

IGI Global
PUBLISHER of TIMELY KNOWLEDGE

701 East Chocolate Avenue, Hershey, PA 17033, USA
Tel: 717-533-8845 x100 • Fax: 717-533-8661
E-Mail: cust@igi-global.com • www.igi-global.com

Table of Contents

Preface xiv

Chapter 1
Consumers' Choice Behavior Towards Sustainable Fashion Based on Social Media Influence 1
Neetu Singh, Symbiosis Institute of Design, Symbiosis International University (Deemed), India

Chapter 2
Defeating Global Glut of Clothing: An Examination of Sustainable Fashion Consumption of Young Consumers 26
Nurul Hidayana Mohd Noor, Universiti Teknologi MARA, Malaysia

Chapter 3
Impact of Green Marketing on Consumer Behavior: An Investigation Towards Purchasing Decisions, Loyalty, and Willingness to Pay a Premium Price 50
Saumendra Das, GIET University, India
Nayan Deep S. Kanwal, University Putra Malaysia, Malaysia
Udaya Sankar Patro, Rayagada Autonomous College, India
Tapaswini Panda, Model Degree College, Rayagada, India
Debasis Pani, GIACR College, India
Hassan Badawy, Luxor University, Egypt

Chapter 4
IoT Driven by Machine Learning (MLIoT) for the Retail Apparel Sector 63
Kutubuddin Sayyad Liyakat Kazi, BMIT, Solapur, India

Chapter 5
Navigating the Landscape of Green Marketing Trends and Identifying Greenwashing Red Flags 82
Pournima Somesh, Christ University, India
M. Ritika, Christ University, India
Harmandeep Singh, Christ University, India

Chapter 6
Purchase Intention of Sustainable Fashion: The Relationship With Price 95
Paulo Botelho Pires, Porto Business School, Portugal
Cláudia Morais, School of Economics and Management, University of Porto, Portugal
Catarina Delgado, School of Economics and Management, University of Porto, Portugal
José Duarte Santos, CEOS.PP, ISCAP, Polytechnic of Porto, Portugal

Chapter 7
The Consumer in the Fashion Industry: An Empirical Study to Understand if It Is Sustainable....... 112
Francesco Pacchera, Tuscia University, Italy
Cecilia Silvestri, Tuscia University, Italy
Alessandro Ruggieri, Tuscia University, Italy

Chapter 8
The Influence of Environmentally Mindful Marketing Tactics on the Perceptual Framework and Predispositions of Generation Z Shoppers in the Indian App.......... 131
Sanjana S. Hothur, Christ University, India
Senthilmurugan Paramasivan, Christ University, India
Mallika Sankar, Christ University, India
Shikha Bhagat, Christ University, India
Roshna Thomas, Christ University, India

Chapter 9
The Role of Social Responsibility on Consumer Engagement Through Fashion Brands' Instagram 148
Sara Santos, Research Centre in Digital Services, Portugal
Paulo Silva, Research Centre in Digital Services, Portugal
Margarida Caramelo Lopes, ESEV, Instituto Politécnico de Viseu, Portugal

Chapter 10
Treating Textile Effluents for Sustainable Fashion and Green Marketing.......... 166
Michail Karypidis, International Hellenic University, Greece
Theodore Tarnanidis, International Hellenic University, Greece
Evridiki Papachristou, International Hellenic University, Greece

Chapter 11
Unveiling the Viral Thread: A Comprehensive Analysis of Virality Coefficients in Indian Fashion Brand Dynamics.......... 180
N. Ravi Kumar, Presidency College, India
Prasad Kulkarni, Euclea Business School, UAE
V. Kalaiarasai, PSG College of Arts and Science, India

Chapter 12
Virtual Try-On Application and Fashion Purchase Intentions Among Gen Z Consumers in Malaysia.......... 194
Logaiswari A. P. Indiran, Universiti Teknologi Malaysia, Malaysia
Afifi Alifia Salsabila Putri, Universiti Teknologi Malaysia, Indonesia
Chen Fu, Universiti Teknologi Malaysia, Malaysia
Jadel Autor Dungog, Iligan Institute of Technology, Mindanao State University, Philippines

Chapter 13
Exploring Contemporary Green Marketing Theories: Insights From the Research 213
Ashish Ashok Uikey, Symbiosis International University (Deemed), India

Chapter 14
Analyzing the Impact of Digital Fashion, Gaming, and the Metaverse on Social Presence in Digital Worlds Through a Literature Review 226
Tia Bilali, International Hellenic University, Greece
Evridiki Papahristou, International Hellenic University, Greece

Compilation of References 251

About the Contributors 304

Index 311

Detailed Table of Contents

Preface.. xiv

Chapter 1
Consumers' Choice Behavior Towards Sustainable Fashion Based on Social Media Influence............ 1
Neetu Singh, Symbiosis Institute of Design, Symbiosis International University (Deemed), India

Social media is now a marketing platform effectively utilizing influencer marketing to connect with the target consumers. The young Generation Z consumer is extremely active on social media attracted by the lure of influencers, opinion leaders, and active creators, and they utilize social media to gain knowledge about their brands. Fashion brands nowadays have been trying to meet the consumer demand for sustainable products by utilizing social media and influencer marketing to develop, advertise, and showcase corporate social responsibility (CSR) around green sustainable fashion products. The consumer seeks cognitive information from their social media experience, fulfilling aesthetic and entertainment gratification, received through appealing images, social media videos, stories, influencer content, and interaction enabling information gathering, entertainment, and allowing consumers to transform their knowledge into intent by purchasing green, sustainable fashion brands.

Chapter 2
Defeating Global Glut of Clothing: An Examination of Sustainable Fashion Consumption of Young Consumers.. 26
Nurul Hidayana Mohd Noor, Universiti Teknologi MARA, Malaysia

The purpose of the study was to examine the determinants of sustainable fashion consumption among young consumers. The empirical study adopted quantitative methodology using a survey approach for collecting data. The sample of 500 young consumers was collected using stratified random and purposive sampling techniques. This study uses five main identified determinants of sustainable fashion consumption: pro-environmental attitude, environmental knowledge, subjective norm, price incentive, perceived behavioural control, and environmental value. The final data of 481 young consumers were analysed using structural equation modeling (SEM). Findings confirm that environmental value acts as a mediator. The input of this study is expected to be a valuable indicator for stakeholders such as the government, fashion designers, retailers, and manufacturers. The study contributes to the scarce literature by recognising the mediating effect of environmental value.

Chapter 3
Impact of Green Marketing on Consumer Behavior: An Investigation Towards Purchasing Decisions, Loyalty, and Willingness to Pay a Premium Price 50
Saumendra Das, GIET University, India
Nayan Deep S. Kanwal, University Putra Malaysia, Malaysia
Udaya Sankar Patro, Rayagada Autonomous College, India
Tapaswini Panda, Model Degree College, Rayagada, India
Debasis Pani, GIACR College, India
Hassan Badawy, Luxor University, Egypt

This study examines the influence of green marketing on consumer behavior, including purchasing habits, brand allegiance, and inclination to pay a premium. This research provides a clear definition of green marketing and examines different marketing strategies used by firms to advertise environmentally friendly products and services. A quantitative study approach was used, using a sample of 200 consumers who had previously made purchases of ecologically sustainable items or services. The acquired data was analyzed using regression analysis and qualitative statistics. Research findings demonstrate a substantial impact of environmental marketing on customer behavior. Consumers are inclined to choose ecologically friendly items and are prepared to pay a higher price for them when they are exposed to marketing strategies that promote environmental consciousness. Green marketing also enhances client loyalty. The results have substantial ramifications for organizations who are marketing eco-friendly goods and services.

Chapter 4
IoT Driven by Machine Learning (MLIoT) for the Retail Apparel Sector 63
Kutubuddin Sayyad Liyakat Kazi, BMIT, Solapur, India

Despite the challenges faced, the future of the apparel retail industry looks promising, with endless opportunities for growth and development. Automated body measurements and size suggestions for customers is a game-changer in the world of online shopping. It offers convenience, accuracy, inclusivity, and sustainability, benefiting both customers and retailers. With the constant advancements in technology, it is safe to say that this system will continue to evolve and improve, making the online shopping experience even more seamless and personalized in the future. MLIoT is transforming the retail apparel sector by providing retailers with real-time insights, automation, and personalization.

Chapter 5
Navigating the Landscape of Green Marketing Trends and Identifying Greenwashing Red Flags...... 82
Pournima Somesh, Christ University, India
M. Ritika, Christ University, India
Harmandeep Singh, Christ University, India

Through this chapter, the authors intend to provide information to the fashion and retail industry about the latest trends and their drawbacks, further increasing the awareness of environmentally conscious consumers. The objective of the study is first to examine the prevalent green marketing strategies adopted by fashion and retail businesses. Further, it also evaluates the actual reality and effectiveness behind the strategies used by brands to understand if they are creating an illusion of sustainability or are genuinely committed through case studies of various retail brands. Lastly it investigates consumer attitudes and perceptions of green marketing in fashion and retail. This research employs an approach to explore driving factors for green marketing in the fashion and retail industry. Utilizing secondary data, a comprehensive review of existing literature on sustainable practices, consumer behaviour, and industry trends was done.

Chapter 6
Purchase Intention of Sustainable Fashion: The Relationship With Price 95
Paulo Botelho Pires, Porto Business School, Portugal
Cláudia Morais, School of Economics and Management, University of Porto, Portugal
Catarina Delgado, School of Economics and Management, University of Porto, Portugal
José Duarte Santos, CEOS.PP, ISCAP, Polytechnic of Porto, Portugal

In today's world, the idea of sustainable fashion is gaining traction. Finding a link between pricing and the purchase of sustainable clothes is the aim of this study. Regression models and t-tests of two independent samples (two-tailed tests) were applied by means of the application of a questionnaire. The study found that consumers' willingness to pay for price increases is related with non-linear (quadratic or exponential) product pricing. The results of this study suggest that consumers are willing to pay higher prices for sustainable clothing. Through an understanding of the relationship between price and consumer behavior, businesses can more effectively align their pricing strategies with the demands of environmentally conscious consumers.

Chapter 7
The Consumer in the Fashion Industry: An Empirical Study to Understand if It Is Sustainable 112
Francesco Pacchera, Tuscia University, Italy
Cecilia Silvestri, Tuscia University, Italy
Alessandro Ruggieri, Tuscia University, Italy

The production and consumption of textile products worldwide generate severe environmental impacts as well as economic and social repercussions. Companies are embarking on a new path towards sustainable production and consumption patterns to respond to increasingly environmentally conscious consumers. This study aims to investigate the characteristics of a sustainable consumer in the fashion industry and their level of awareness regarding sustainability at the time of purchase. To this end, a questionnaire was developed to analyse consumer behaviour in the fashion sector, while various statistical techniques were used to analyse the data. The results show that a cluster of consumers can be defined as sustainable, and that socio-demographic variables and price influence the purchase of sustainable products. Sustainability knowledge is also crucial for adopting sustainable consumption behaviour.

Chapter 8
The Influence of Environmentally Mindful Marketing Tactics on the Perceptual Framework and Predispositions of Generation Z Shoppers in the Indian App 131
Sanjana S. Hothur, Christ University, India
Senthilmurugan Paramasivan, Christ University, India
Mallika Sankar, Christ University, India
Shikha Bhagat, Christ University, India
Roshna Thomas, Christ University, India

Green marketing decisively helps businesses distinguish themselves from their competition, strengthen their image, and obtain the attention of consumers who increasingly prefer environmentally conscious businesses. By elevating a business's reputation and image, green marketing creates an effect on how people consider a brand and enhances customer loyalty and retention. The "green generation," or Generation Z, is well-known for its sustainable product preferences and ecological concerns. The study analysed how green marketing techniques relate to and affect Gen Z customers' purchasing habits in India's garment industry. The study targeted 300+ Gen Z consumers through an online cross-sectional survey to get information on their perceptions of green brands, green marketing tactics, purchase intentions, and buying patterns. This study found that green marketing tactics used by fashion firms have a favorable impact and the ability to affect various aspects of customer behavior.

Chapter 9
The Role of Social Responsibility on Consumer Engagement Through Fashion Brands' Instagram 148
Sara Santos, Research Centre in Digital Services, Portugal
Paulo Silva, Research Centre in Digital Services, Portugal
Margarida Caramelo Lopes, ESEV, Instituto Politécnico de Viseu, Portugal

At a time when consumers are becoming more aware of social and environmental responsibility, they are increasingly recognising the fashion industry's impact on the world. Based on this growing awareness, the response from fashion brands is to strategically use digital platforms to highlight their commitment to the issue of sustainability. Brands that consciously share this content on online platforms adopt an effective communication strategy, attracting greater engagement with their audience. In particular, the analysis in this study focuses on the Instagram presence of three notable brands: Naz, Isto, and Tentree. The results of this study affirm the positive impact of social responsibility on consumer engagement when it comes to the Instagram accounts of these fashion brands. This underlines the significant role that social responsibility plays in influencing consumer perceptions and interactions in the digital sphere.

Chapter 10
Treating Textile Effluents for Sustainable Fashion and Green Marketing 166
Michail Karypidis, International Hellenic University, Greece
Theodore Tarnanidis, International Hellenic University, Greece
Evridiki Papachristou, International Hellenic University, Greece

One of the main causes of water pollution is the textile industry, which involves dyeing and finishing processes. Aquatic life and human health can be threatened by the variety of chemicals and dyes contained in the effluent generated by these processes. The impact of these effluents on the environment has been minimized by the development of several effluent treatments. This presentation discloses the available solutions for liquid effluent treatment from textile dyeing and finishing providing a fast, clear, and deep understanding of methods such as the physicochemical and biological treatments as well as the recent advanced oxidation processes. Thus, utilizing a combination of these technologies in a treatment plant can frequently lead to more effective outcomes. Ultimately, this investigation will assist researchers and academic practitioners in enhancing and aligning green marketing models with sustainability trends in the textile, apparel, and fashion industries.

Chapter 11
Unveiling the Viral Thread: A Comprehensive Analysis of Virality Coefficients in Indian Fashion Brand Dynamics.. 180
N. Ravi Kumar, Presidency College, India
Prasad Kulkarni, Euclea Business School, UAE
V. Kalaiarasai, PSG College of Arts and Science, India

The research examined and clarified the complex dynamics that underlie the virality of Indian fashion brands. It also quantified and analyzed virality coefficients, exploring the elements and processes that facilitated the expansion of these brands' reach across various channels. The study used bibliometric analysis, classifying academic papers on the dynamics of Indian fashion brands by year, nation, and subject area by using data from the Scopus database. The basis for further research into the virality coefficients was laid by the visual mapping of keyword co-occurrences, the identification of clusters, and the extraction of variables using the VOSviewer software. Advanced textual analysis techniques were used for topic modeling at the same time, including lemmatization, TF-IDF matrix generation, and latent Dirichlet allocation (LDA). The Python programming language made it easier to see hidden motifs in the literature.

Chapter 12
Virtual Try-On Application and Fashion Purchase Intentions Among Gen Z Consumers in Malaysia 194
Logaiswari A. P. Indiran, Universiti Teknologi Malaysia, Malaysia
Afifi Alifia Salsabila Putri, Universiti Teknologi Malaysia, Indonesia
Chen Fu, Universiti Teknologi Malaysia, Malaysia
Jadel Autor Dungog, Iligan Institute of Technology, Mindanao State University, Philippines

Online shopping, integral to modern life, lacks the tactile experience of physical retail, a significant shortfall in fashion. This gap is being addressed by incorporating virtual reality (VR) and augmented reality (AR) technologies to meld the digital and in-store experiences. This research critically examines the impact of virtual try-on (VTO) applications on Gen Z's fashion purchasing intentions in Malaysia, assessing factors like virtual presence and perceived ease of use. A quantitative approach, involving a survey with 94 participants, was taken. The study presents a novel model merging the technology acceptance model (TAM) with virtual presence. Results indicate Gen Z's overwhelming endorsement of VTO, with perceived usefulness as their main buying intention driver. These insights offer valuable direction for VTO developers, marketing strategists, and policymakers aiming to promote VTO in fashion retail.

Chapter 13
Exploring Contemporary Green Marketing Theories: Insights From the Research 213
Ashish Ashok Uikey, Symbiosis International University (Deemed), India

This chapter offers an in-depth exploration and analysis of various theories underpinning green marketing research to understand and predict consumer behavior towards environmentally friendly products and services. The discussion navigates through diverse theoretical frameworks like the theory of planned behavior, theory of reasoned action, attitude-behavior-context theory, value-belief-norm theory, etc. While these theories offer valuable perspectives, they also exhibit limitations in predicting and comprehensively explaining green consumer actions. To bridge these gaps, future research directions propose integrating theories; accounting for cultural, social, and economic influences; exploring emerging technological advancements to refine green marketing strategies. The integration and exploration of these theories offer a robust foundation for businesses to develop effective strategies aligning with diverse consumer motivations and contexts, fostering sustainable consumption patterns for a greener future.

Chapter 14
Analyzing the Impact of Digital Fashion, Gaming, and the Metaverse on Social Presence in Digital Worlds Through a Literature Review 226
Tia Bilali, International Hellenic University, Greece
Evridiki Papahristou, International Hellenic University, Greece

This research explores the concept of social presence in the context of the evolving relationship between technology, fashion, and digital environments, specifically focusing on the intersections of fashion in the metaverse and fashion in gaming. The study employs a scoping literature review methodology, utilising desk research to gather and synthesise evidence. The convergence of the physical and digital realms, facilitated by technologies of metaverse and gaming, have brought a new way of social presence and more materials to support it. The methodology used is a systematic literature review with the concept based on the reality virtuality continuum and the concept of social presence, with effects on user experience, engagement, and purchase behaviour. This research provides information and attempts to deepen the meaning of the existence of digital fashion in games and metaverse through by measuring it with social presence response.

Compilation of References 251

About the Contributors 304

Index 311

Preface

Sustainability in fashion retail is the focus of this book, which is rapidly becoming the key to future fashion retail strategies. Sustainable fashion marketing processes and techniques involve using strategies that align with environmentally conscious practices that promotes environmental and socially responsible products, practices, and brand values more transparently. Successful marketers in the fashion industry adapt to these trends and leverage emerging technologies or socially responsible practices that engage with increasingly informed and conscious consumers. The internationalization of markets demands for businesses to combine the internet-enabled sphere in combination with innovative digital models.

The book's chapters give theoretical and practical insight into the positive impact of going green on fashion retailers and marketers' strategies in response to the changing hyper environment. Therefore this book focuses on the effort of clothing/fashion businesses to best articulate the spectrum of green and sustainable digital marketing techniques based on the use o pioneering practices. By integrating these green and sustainable digital marketing techniques, fashion brands can effectively communicate their commitment to eco-friendly mechanisms towards the growing audience of environmentally conscious consumers. The book focuses on the ongoing trends of green and sustainable (digital) marketing techniques in the fashion industry. Additionally, we are optimistic that readers will find this book essential for enhancing their current work and education. All the contributors of the accepted chapters deserve our final words of appreciation.

TARGET AUDIENCE

This publication is an important reference source for academics and researchers, undergraduate students, postgraduate students, consultants, technology developers and policymakers interested in exploring green and sustainable marketing techniques in fashion.

Coverage

This publication covers a wide range of academic areas, but they are not limited:

- Social Media Influence
- Sustainable Fashion
- AI, AGI and Machine Learning in Green Marketing
- Big Data and Analytics and Visualization

- Virtual Try-Ons and Augmented Reality (AR)
- Green Marketing Trends
- Consumer in the Fashion Industry
- Consumer Engagement and purchasing behavior
- Social Media Challenges and Brand strategies
- Green Advertising

Theodore K. Tarnanidis
International Hellenic University, Greece

Evridiki Papachristou
International Hellenic University, Greece

Michail Karypidis
International Hellenic University, Greece

Vasileios Ismyrlis
Hellenic Statistical Authority, Greece

Chapter 1
Consumers' Choice Behavior Towards Sustainable Fashion Based on Social Media Influence

Neetu Singh
https://orcid.org/0000-0002-0338-9846
Symbiosis Institute of Design, Symbiosis International University (Deemed), India

ABSTRACT

Social media is now a marketing platform effectively utilizing influencer marketing to connect with the target consumers. The young Generation Z consumer is extremely active on social media attracted by the lure of influencers, opinion leaders, and active creators, and they utilize social media to gain knowledge about their brands. Fashion brands nowadays have been trying to meet the consumer demand for sustainable products by utilizing social media and influencer marketing to develop, advertise, and showcase corporate social responsibility (CSR) around green sustainable fashion products. The consumer seeks cognitive information from their social media experience, fulfilling aesthetic and entertainment gratification, received through appealing images, social media videos, stories, influencer content, and interaction enabling information gathering, entertainment, and allowing consumers to transform their knowledge into intent by purchasing green, sustainable fashion brands.

INTRODUCTION

In an environmentally conscious era, consumers have demanding requirements in many areas. Being aware of environmental issues, nowadays, consumers seek eco-friendly products. People have started looking for "Green Products" everywhere (Hasan et al., 2022; Khan et al., 2022). In terms of fashion apparel, consumers' purchasing decisions were previously based upon comfort, style, aesthetic appeal, etc., but now more on the eco-friendliness of products. Sustainable fashion can be described as eco-friendly clothing (Elisa & Cecilia, 2016; Wagner et al., 2019), slow fashion focusing on style orientation rather than fashion orientation (Gupta et al., 2019), consumers' long-term relationship with their clothing (Pettersson McIntyre, 2021) and the positive role of biosphere and altruistic values influencing sustainable

DOI: 10.4018/979-8-3693-3049-4.ch001

clothing consumption as opposed to the negative role of hedonistic values promoting overconsumption and excess (Geiger & Keller, 2018). Many clothing companies have started providing clothes made from eco-friendly fabrics, and the demand for these green products is increasing (Bielawska & Grebosz-Krawczyk, 2021). The criteria to judge any material as "environmentally friendly" are renewability, the ecological footprint of the resource, and the usage of any chemical to grow/process to make the product ready for use. If textile-producing companies embrace these trends, they capitalize by increasing profits and sleep better, knowing they are playing their part in protecting our environment. Adopting friendly practices such as reusing and recycling wastewater is an excellent start for accomplishing these goals. Current business models are directly linked to sales and production volumes, with sustainable consumption leading to reduced volumes and decreasing profitability in production, not as an opportunity for a new kind of green business (Meyer, 2001). Green brands such as H&M, Zara have been implementing environmental conservation and environmentally sustainable practices through their products (Albino et al., 2009; Y. S. Chen, 2010).

Social media usage is among the most popular activities, with 4.59 billion people in 2022, projected to increase to six billion in 2027(Stacy, 2023b). Worldwide, 64% of consumers are showing deep concern for the environment and sustainability, with 79% of consumers centralized around developing economies such as China, India, and Indonesia and 55% of consumers in developed countries like the U.S. and Europe (Faelli Francois, Blasberg John, Johns Leah, 2023). Generation Z consumers have emerged as protagonists concerned more about sustainability than their older counterparts, with 72% of Gen Z consumers and 68% of boomers extremely concerned about the environment (Schneider Benjamin & Lee Diana, 2022). Social media hence provides an effective forum to promote green product awareness amongst consumers and to ratify to the consumers whether the brands are stringently following the green sustainability route through their fashion or just using it as a ploy to increase sales and profitability (Cronin et al., 2011) Generation Z consumers are known digital natives primarily because they were born in a digital age spending at least 8 hours online on social media, internet, and media second only to the time spent sleeping (Deloitte, 2022; Djafarova & Bowes, 2021) with their purchase decisions influenced by opinion leaders, bloggers, influencers, peers, and older peers from their social networks (Djafarova & Bowes, 2021; Liu, 2022). A 2022 study done by McKinsey and Co. on European consumers during the Covid-19 crisis identified that 67% of consumers considered the usage of sustainable materials from their fashion brands, while 63% consider a brand promotion of sustainability as a deciding factor in choosing a fashion brand (McKinsey & Company, 2020). Sustainability overlaps with the notion of CSR(Corporate Social Responsibility), responsible for producing ethical, social, and environmentally responsible production of apparel respecting judicial and ethical guidelines, fair treatment of employees, and prevention of harmful environmental and social activities through organizational activities (Jermsittiparsert et al., 2019; MOHR et al., 2001). Companies like Patagonia, People Tree, and Eileen Fischer are renowned for producing sustainable apparel, while fast fashion brands like Zara, H&M, Primark & Gap, earlier known to focus on costing and production processes, have now integrated sustainability into their apparel (Arrigo, 2013; Cachon & Swinney, 2011). Thus, companies, through their CSC(Corporate Social communication), need to communicate socially responsible practices, mainly ethical labor conditions, and sustainable production practices, and communicate to the consumers about mindful clothing consumption and disposal habits (Shen, 2014; Shen et al., 2014; Strähle & Chantal, 2016).

Nudging through social media, therefore, proves to be an effective tool for promoting eco-friendly behavior, with verbal nudging showing a significant influence and visual nudges to a lesser extent influencing consumers' choice of eco-friendly sustainable fashion apparel (Goldsmith et al., 2015; Roozen et al., 2021). When a brand is unable to prove its green credentials, the consumers receive it with cynicism and uncertainty (Carlson et al., 1993), which is why social media also provides an adequate forum informing consumers about different sustainable consumption patterns, displaying a brand green credentials, passing information about sourcing production and distribution techniques and whether they meet the sustainability goals set by the young consumer or not (Kang & Kim, 2017; Karimi Alavijeh et al., 2018; McNeill & Venter, 2019). Social media is more than just an interactive platform for conversation with family and friends. They are now commercial spaces with brands and services actively marketing their products and services (Siregar et al., 2023; Wang & Huang, 2023). Globally The top 5 social media platforms are Facebook (3 billion), YouTube (2.5 billion), Instagram(2 billion), Tiktok (1.2 billion), and Snapchat (750 million) (Shelley, 2023; Stacy, 2023a), with both social media marketing and social media influencer marketing gaining precedence during the COVID-19 pandemic (Danielle & Forbes, 2021). Though Instagram is not the largest, it is indeed the most influential, accounting for more than 50% of social media, with customers interacting through functions of "Likes" and "Comments" (Testa et al., 2021). Posts on Instagram can also be of multiple natures, such as a single photo, numerous photo formats, and videos. Images of text, text-embedded photos, or a reel can be shared with various people across Instagram, influencing consumer engagement (Gandomi & Haider, 2015).

THEORETICAL BACKGROUND

Theories Promoting Sustainable Green Fashion on Social Media Platforms

Generation Z tops millennials on social media shopping and purchasing; however, empirical evidence corroborating intention with actual purchase behavior needs to be substantiated, with 68% of Gen Z consumers searching for products and only 22% ultimately completing a purchase (Balakrishnan et al., 2014; Lee & Watkins, 2016; Pymnts, 2023). The green apparel industry is in its nascent stage, constituting less than 10% of the total market (Charm et al., 2020; Jacobs et al., 2018), and despite consumers ethical considerations indicating affinity for green apparel, they rarely transform their intentions into purchase leading researchers to explore the attitude-behavior gap influencing their decision making (McNeill & Moore, 2015; Wiederhold & Martinez, 2018). Instagram and TikTok are popular social networks for browsing clothing, apparel, and beauty products (Pymnts, 2023). The theory of planned behavior suggests that consumer cognitions influence the behavioral intentions toward purchasing green fashion. Exposure to media messages, social media or influencer content, and magazine or blog content influences consumers' cognitions, evoking behavioral intention toward green apparel and predicting consumers' likelihood to enact the purchase behavior (de Lenne & Vandenbosch, 2017). Cognitions can be a composite of attitudes, norms, and self-efficacy beliefs. Attitudes are the consumer's belief in favorable outcomes when buying sustainable/green apparel (Armitage & Christian, 2003; Hiller Connell & Kozar, 2012). Subjective norms exist in the form of social pressure toward sustainable apparel purchases. In contrast, descriptive norms ratify consumers' belief that their social environment values and engage in purchasing sustainable apparel (Zheng & Chi, 2015). Self-efficacy indicates consumers' belief in accomplishing sustainable apparel purchase behavior (Kumar et al., 2022; Terry & O'Leary, 1995).

Uses and Gratifications theory (UGT) is an often repeated theory in understanding consumer motivations and gratifications received from mass-mediated consumption (Katz et al., 1973). Consumers' media usage is motivated by personal and functional needs arising out of a combination of psychological, sociological, and environmental factors along with gratification, which implies the expectations they have from a media medium (Bae, 2018) and how their needs are categorized as cognitive, affective, personal, integrative .social integrative and escape are satisfied (Katz et al., 1973). Thus, the difference between gratification sought versus that obtained describes the level of satisfaction consumers feel while using social media, making UGT the premise of multiple media and communication strategies, especially those exploring the adoption and usage of mobile, e-commerce, and social media influence (Jones & Kang, 2020; Joo & Sang, 2013; Whiting & Williams, 2013). Thus, while using social media platforms like Facebook, Instagram, YouTube, Twitter, etc., consumers derive different gratifications arising out of activities such as passing time, showing love/affection, following passions such as fashion, games, etc., and demonstrating sociability through peer engagement, word of mouth, and community reach (Quan-Haase & Young, 2010; Sheldon & Bryant, 2016).

Personality trait theory is one of the leading theories founded by (Allport, 1961), analyzing personalities and the combination of psychological patterns of thinking, feelings, behaving, and interacting, which eventually controls consumers' social media behavior (Shang et al., 2016). This mode describes personalities under the Big Five Model, categorizing behaviors as "agreeableness, neuroticism, extraversion, openness to experience (intellect) and conscientiousness" (Leong et al., 2017; Tommasel et al., 2015). Investigating the role of personality traits or the Big Five Model on consumers' social media activities resulting in positive Word of Mouth for environmentally sustainable fashion brands can provide valuable insights on consumers' optimistic environmental awareness and the same resulting in positive WOM (word of mouth) for sustainable fashion (Salem & Alanadoly, 2021). Studies have revealed that agreeableness, extraversion, and openness to experience are associated with social media activities, while conscientiousness and neuroticism are not (Salem & Alanadoly, 2021). People with agreeableness interacted most on social media platforms, reacting positively to it and being influenced by informative posts (Gil De Zuniga et al., 2017). Dominant extraversion depicts a high level of socialization resulting in social media-specific activity, while (Bornstein, 2018; Brick & Lewis, 2016) individuals open to experience are open to new experiences and curious to dabble in new ideas and adopt new communication styles. Conscientious individuals are analytical thinkers and, because of moral obligations, have their own opinions and beliefs (Esmaeelinezhad & Afrazeh, 2018; Lynn et al., 2017). However, researchers contradicted this information (Gil De Zuniga et al., 2017; Lynn et al., 2017), validating conscientious individuals' ability to share information through social networks. The final personality type of individuals with neuroticism uses social media to gather information, avoiding group activities. The social media activities of all personality types prove that their search and share activities promote eco-friendly, sustainable behavior, resulting in generating interest and positive WOM (Word of Mouth) for green fashion amongst peers and social media connections through knowledge-sharing (Karavasilis et al., 2015; Oladayo,Oladimeji, 2017).

As consumers are getting more and more motivated to purchase green fashion in countries like China, Bangladesh, and India (Khare et al., 2022; Khare & Kautish, 2021; W. Zhao et al., 2017), the roles of social media marketing influencing green fashion have been defined as influencing sustainable fashion, increasing brand publicity, increasing brand transparency, educating consumers about green fashion, customer engagement, customer relationship management (CRM), enabling social interaction between consumers and growing consumer trust and empowerment (Strähle & Chantal, 2016). We can categorize social media communication about a brand as brand-related or non-brand-related (Table 1)

Table 1. Categories of social media brand communication on social media platforms

Brand Related Communication	Non-Brand Related Communication
Brand-to-consumer communication	Brand activism
Consumer engagement	Brand sufficiency and Anti-consumption
User Generated Content and Electronic Word of Mouth	Celebrities as Influencers
Influencer marketing strategies	

Brand-Related Communication

An essential aspect of social media marketing is its ability to reach existing and potential customers, thereby enabling brand-related communications to retain existing customers and engage new potential customers through eWOM (electronic word of mouth)((Chloe) Ki et al., 2022). Concerning green fashion, social media enables awareness about the fashion system, environment, and social impacts and works as a marketing tool for green brands to reach otherwise inaccessible consumers. Brand-related communication on social media regarding sustainable green fashion is categorized as follows.

Brand-to-Consumer Communication

Current literature points out the development of companies proposing sustainability as their core value and innovative business models. Most brands undertaking sustainability efforts through their supply chain, consumption, and disposal practices to respond to stakeholders' concerns are now engaging in social media communication with their stakeholders to communicate the same, interacting with consumers, building brand-consumer relationships, and facilitating consumer decision-making effectively through a larger platform.(Kong et al., 2021; Todeschini et al., 2017).Fashion brands exceptionally now propose sustainability as their core value, with a large number of them facing backlash for greenwashing practices or deceptively convincing consumers about their environmental practices (Schmuck et al., 2018). Therefore, companies must use social reports, disclosure initiatives, and participation in environmentally friendly discourses through advertising, magazines, and events (Guercini et al., 2020; Jestratijevic et al., 2020). Social media communication of sustainable fashion brands has, therefore, now become a predominant part of their marketing activity (K. H. Kim & Kim, 2020), raising brand awareness, engaging consumers, and developing brand loyalty (Hollebeek et al., 2014). Current research has identified the significance of three motives, functional, hedonic, and authenticity, behind brand-related content generated on social media (Lou & Yuan, 2019; Xu & Chen, 2006). Functional aspects enable consumers to judge the "utilitarian or functional perspectives including topicality, novelty, understandability and reliability" (Rungruangjit & Charoenpornpanichkul, 2022, p. 3) hedonic aspect enables them to assess the interestingness and relevance of content, while authenticity reflects upon the trustworthiness of the brand (Becker-Leifhold, 2018) and the brand influencer as perceived by the consumers resulting in their trust or mistrust through likes or dislikes (Hollebeek et al., 2014; Pornsrimate & Khamwon, 2021). Consumers' degree of knowledge about sustainability and purchase motivation for organic apparel are positively correlated, while in contrast, low acceptance of green apparel is due to poor awareness of environmental issues and the negative impact of the clothing manufacturing supply chain on the environment (D'Souza et al., 2015; J. Kim et al., 2020). Thus, information sharing about environmental issues such as energy saving, conservation, environment friendliness, green products, organic materials, recycling and reuse, green apparel, supply chain, and its impact on the environment when shared with customers would create awareness and build consumer knowledge creating customer perceptions about brand's CSR efforts, also associated with brand attachment and positive purchase intentions (Y. Kim et al., 2016; Kong et al., 2016; Yoo et al., 2018).

Consumer Engagement

While social media is a platform to communicate a variety of messages, it is essential to understand effective engagement techniques to keep the consumer explicitly involved while conveying messages of sustainability. Content type and brand intentions impact social media followers' e-Wom intentions. Studies exploring information exposure and green apparel acquisition behavior of consumers revealed that consumers do not purchase eco-friendly apparel due to environmental concerns, giving predominance to other attributes such as price and functionality during their purchase considerations (Sonnenberg et al., 2014). Social media predicts the consumption of fashion brands that are congruent with the consumer's actual self and not their ideal self (Wallace et al., 2020). Thus, brands must align themselves with corporate social responsibility (CSR) aspects and promote happiness and well-being amongst their followers on social media to generate interest in green fashion apparel. Social and environmentally friendly brands share a variety of brand-related information like brand business models, product attributes, or consequences to the consumer and society as a whole (Viciunaite, 2022). Brands engaging in online debates on sufficiency encourage consumers to proactively assess their consumption patterns and improve sufficiency behavior in the short term (Frick et al., 2021).

Current research indicates that consumers engage with social sustainability messages on social media when the message is consistent with the principles of the brand, as is the case of sustainable fashion brands (J. Kim et al., 2020). Research categorizes Fashion brands as Sustainable fashion brands(SFB), Sustainably aware fashion brands (SAB), and Traditional fashion brands(TFB). Sustainable fashion brands (SFB) are founded on principles of sustainability; sustainably aware fashion brands (SAB) do not find origins in sustainability but undertake public sustainability efforts, while Traditional fashion brands (TFB)do not affiliate with a public sustainability effort (Testa et al., 2021). Brands such as Stella McCartney, Patagonia, Reformation, and Ever Lane are the world's top sustainable fashion brands grounded and created on sustainability principles. Brands like H&M, Mango, Zara, and Levis are becoming increasingly sustainably aware and incorporating sustainability in their supply chain and products, while traditional fashion brands like forever21 and Chanel are. Alexander Mc Queen, Free People, and Teva follow traditional fashion brand guidelines, focusing on the product and not hopping onto the sustainability bandwagon (Lucy, 2023; Turker & Altuntas, 2014).

Both likes and comments received on brand posts define consumer engagement with the brand. A thematic content analysis of these brands via written, spoken, and pictorial content analysis done on social media via content analysis (Neuendorf, 2017) found high consumer engagement on single photo shoots, while video shoots generated fewer comments with a high number of likes. Similarly, multiple photo shoots received lower likes and higher comments on the post. Thus, to engage consumers effectively, brands need to explore content that generates both likes and comments and image curation for a highly engaged consumer response. A visual content analysis of imagery depicting sustainability by brands Patagonia and Stella McCartney depicts different sustainability representations by both brands even though they are associated with solid sustainability characteristics. Patagonia strategically uses nature and animal imagery to support fashion items, drawing attention to the recycling and reusing of old clothing (Baumgardner & Richards, 2004). McCartney reflects the designer's personality and positioning strategy through images showing fashion shows, photoshoots, and fashion events (Chu et al., 2020; K. H. Kim & Kim, 2020). Both these brands managed to engage the audience, with Patagonia getting greater digital engagement with the highest likes while McCartney got more comments on their post (Milanesi et al., 2022). However, to ensure that the consumer does not feel exposed to green washing by the brands, brands must delve deep into the sourcing techniques, production processes, and consumption and recycling processes and share this information on social media to engage and make the consumer aware of genuine sustainability practices of their brands.

User Generated Content and Electronic Word of Mouth

Before making a purchase, consumers seek peer advice and opinions regarding products or services (WOM) or Word of Mouth (Hu et al., 2012), which have now become digital, incorporating technology such as digital comments ratings, reviews, online comments, and discussions posted on social media platforms, texts, blogs, and video logs also known as e WOM(Electronic Word of Mouth)communication (Haines et al., 2023). Social media facilitates communication not just between consumers but also between brands and consumers (Quach & Thaichon, 2017), customer-retailer conversations, product/service-related queries, complaints, critical or sarcastic conversations, positive/negative referrals, sharing of product details, product usage and warnings against certain products are all categories of content explicitly created on digital media which is publically available for end users, defined as User-generated content (UGC) (Peeroo et al., 2017). UGC on social media platforms like Facebook, Instagram, and Twitter entails content created in the form of social media posts, texts, blogs and video logs, ratings, and reviews of products encourage online interactions and social relationships amongst consumers by advocating, sharing, socializing and co-creating brand knowledge, influencing consumer trust, brand attitudes, emotional engagement and generating e WOM or positive word of mouth through electronic media (Brodie et al., 2013; Hung et al., 2011; A. J. Kim & Johnson, 2016; Morrison et al., 2013). UGC dimensions for fashion brands are "promotional self-presentation, brand centrality, marketer-directed communication, response to online marketer action, factually informative communication about the brand and brand sentiment" (Smith et al., 2012, p. 104). The fashion industry is under scanner for unsustainable fast fashion practices causing global pollution (Brenot et al., 2019), with consumers becoming extremely conscious of the detrimental effects of fashion and seeking sustainable green fashion choices instead (McNeill & Moore, 2015; Papadopoulou et al., 2022). However, the easy availability of fast fashion at affordable prices fuels consumers' desire to purchase trendy clothing. In contrast, sustainable green fashion is touted as expensive, unstylish, and lacking variety with fashion trends, limited variety, supply chain challenges, promotion, and marketing issues posing deterrents towards its adoption (Dhir et al., 2021; Velasco-Molpeceres et al., 2022).

However, current research analyzing almost 73,713 comments on social media regarding sustainable fashion between the period 2010-2019 (Haines et al., 2023) showed a growth of 468% on social media sites, corroborating that consumers are getting increasingly conscious and attracted towards green sustainable fashion (Fletcher, 2010; Joy et al., 2012). Consumers decision to purchase green and sustainable apparel is motivated by eco-consciousness (Kautish et al., 2021), environmental awareness (Jeong & Ko, 2021), understanding of sustainable fashion (Shen et al., 2012), empathy for sustainable fashion(Cowan & Kinley, 2014; Khare & Sadachar, 2017) and social influence (Moser, 2015). Savvy brand marketers on the social web model encourage consumer participation on social media to generate e WOM rather than propagate through generic broadcast messaging (Hajli, 2014; Kautish Pradeep, 2016). Hence, in addition to offering green apparel online, brands need to engage the consumers effectively by increasing consumer participation through online communities, group memberships encouraging participation, creating engagement, and finally, e WOM (Chatterjee, 2020).

Influencer Marketing Strategies

Social media influencers are individuals or celebrities who have established high credibility in the minds of their connections and followers attained through live streaming, blogging, or posting on YouTube, Instagram, or Pinterest, disseminating information about fashion and non-fashion brands (Jin et al., 2019; Lou & Yuan, 2019).In 2022 influencer marketing reached $16.4 billion, with more than 75% of brands dedicating budgets to influencer marketing with a 1% increase in influencer marketing spending resulting in an engagement of 0.46%, resulting in positive ROI (Leung et al., 2022). Social media fashion influencers (SMFI)are celebrities who sit in front rows of fashion shows or are the first to adopt fashion and motivate their followers to pursue it. Ryan and Deci (2000) describe the self-determination theory (SDT) as the intrinsic and extrinsic motivation behind live streamers, online brand communities, fashion influencers, and sustainable product consumers. Hence, while intrinsic motivation is the enjoyment received from a process, extrinsic motivation is the need for reward or punishment. It is hence the inherent needs of the consumer during social media interaction manifesting as competency-need to feel adequate, relatedness-need to care and connect, and autonomy-the desire to engage in action controlling one's behaviors which create the correct experiential value for online consumers and attracting them towards social media fashion influencers to seek information. Applying the theory of information relevance (Y. C. Chen et al., 2014; Zhang & Choi, 2022), considering the utilitarian and functional perspective, factors such as novelty, understandability, reliability, and interestingness of content attract consumers towards influencer-driven content.

Moreover, fashion enables consumers' self-expression and helps their sense of self-concept by identifying with fashion brand traits and engaging in frequent buying behavior, resulting in consumers seeking fashion influencers' opinions and a successful marketing strategy for fashion brands. Finally, applying the influencer credibility model, numerous studies have determined a congruence between influencers, attractiveness, trustworthiness, and expertise influencing their followers purchase intentions (AlFarraj et al., 2021; Koay et al., 2022; Rungruangjit, 2022), brand love and brand engagement (Pornsrimate & Khamwon, 2021), and the parasocial interaction of digital influencers affecting the buying intent (Gong & Li, 2017). Parasocial Interaction theory (PSI), in this case, refers to the media consumption behavior of consumers where they imagine the influencers as ordinary people they interact with in their day-to-day life and develop an intimate connection with them (Hartmann, 2016; Horton & Richard Wohl, 1956).

Non-Brand Related Communication

Brand Activism, Anti-Consumption, Sufficiency

Excessive consumption affects consumer well-being negatively, which is why anti-consumption or reduction in consumption enables happiness and satisfaction at a micro level by fostering self-determination and self-actualization and at a macro level by protecting the environment (Hoffmann & Lee, 2016).

Current initiatives to reduce consumption are low and "seem very much at odds with current business practices," hindering business practices (Bocken & Short, 2016, p. 43). Lowering consumption or anti-consumption is at the heart of the sufficiency strategy (Vita et al., 2020), described as an absolute reduction of consumption, shifting models towards those which are lesser resources centric, product longevity, extending product lifecycle and sharing practices amongst individuals (Sandberg, 2021). Brands, while using sustainability as messaging, are now using social media to reduce consumption (demarketing), an example of which would be Patagonia's "Don't buy this jacket" campaign (J. Kim et al., 2020; Kong et al., 2021; Reich & Soule, 2016). Brand activism is an emerging phenomenon, and brands use their platform to address environmental issues and impact societal goals (Vredenburg et al., 2020). Brands Sustainability strategies of brands focusing on environmentally friendly methods, anti-consumption, and sufficiency should be a part of social learning initiatives towards consumer learning and may change consumers' attitudes and purchase intentions (Buenstorf & Cordes, 2008; L. Zhao et al., 2019).

Based on institutional theory, corporate activism is a company's stand on social, political, and economic issues toward social change by influencing the attitudes and behaviors of consumers in an institutional environment (Bulmer et al., 2024; Eilert & Nappier Cherup, 2020). Corporate activism, therefore, is a response to barriers that hinder solutions to an issue, which in this case is environmental, and addresses them through influence and change management strategies through "top-down" or "bottom-up" approaches (Eilert & Nappier Cherup, 2020). When brands meet activist messaging purpose and values with their corporate practices, they engage in authentic brand activism, contrary to brands that disassociate their activist messaging from their purpose (Bulmer et al., 2024; Vredenburg et al., 2020). When consumers interpret brands and their company's moral misconduct, it results in hateful feelings, resulting in anti–brand activism (Romani et al., 2015). Social media is a treasure cove of information to understand sustainable fashion consumption by advertising, sharing information, and educating consumers about changing consumption patterns and sufficiency through story telling (Gorge et al., 2015; Hwang et al., 2016), influencers or role models and publicly questioning acts of overconsumption through rigorous social media content.

Brands focusing on sustainability gain predominance in consumers' minds above others (Remi, 2020). with their efforts bolstering consumer willingness to purchase products from brands pursuing social or environmental causes, especially with 43% of millennials and 44% of Gen Z consumers optimistic that efforts to protect the environment would sustain the planet's health (Deloitte, 2022). The social media platforms of sustainable brands do not elucidate "sustainability" through their content. Current research shows a difference in consumer "acting and awareness" (Testa et al., 2021, p. 580) regarding sustainability (Amel et al., 2009), which can be due to consumers already engaging with sustainable brands on social media to demonstrate their activism, negating the use of continuous sustainability content by the brand. In contrast, the sustainably aware brands incorporating supply chain, distribution, consumption, recycling sustainability through their products and traditional fashion brand content received more engagement from consumers when they shared sustainability-related posts because it surprised the followers and engaged them more (Testa et al., 2021).

Social media also enables consumers to share their green methods while allowing them to interact with one another and start a conversation about the brand through advocacy posts, shared messages, videos, video imagery, and text-based stories (Voorveld, 2019). Therefore, brands use platforms like Instagram to create official accounts to publish evocative, visually appealing narratives and content to strengthen their brand and its eco-activism and foster a brand community (B. Kim et al., 2021; Rietveld et al., 2020). For example, Swedish brand H&M invited influencers to social media to talk about their

Conscious Exclusive collection, made entirely from recyclable material. They even undertook a social media campaign for World Recycling Week, combining social media with their recycling campaign, asking for old clothes to be recycled in return for consumer discounts (Andrea, 2016). Patagonia is another brand focusing highly on indigenous rights, cultural issues, traditional ecological knowledge, and environmentally sustainable issues. It uses Instagram to engage with its consumers through visual imagery. Corporate Social Responsibility or a brand's ability to influence the consumers responsibly involves "the dynamic community of customers who communicate through social media – an environment in which control of the relationship has shifted to the customer, who has the power to influence others in his or her social network" (Heller Baird & Parasnis, 2011, p. 27).

It primarily focusses on (i) creating influential CSR associations in the consumer's minds on social media and (ii) propagation of the brand CSR agenda has a positive influence not only on the brand corporate brand reputation but also on consumer attitude and purchase intentions (Fernández et al., 2022; Pérez-Curiel et al., 2021). Numerous brands utilize social media, e.g., Instagram, Twitter, and TikTok, to capture consumers' interest and promote their sustainability goals (Vladimirova et al., 2023). Brands Used apparel collection(UAC) programs running on social media encourage consumers to donate old clothing, which results in recycling, upcycling, or reuse following principles of closed-loop supply chain (Chow & Li, 2018). The UAC programs of fashion retailers such as H&M, Uniqlo, Patagonia Inc., and Eileen Fischer on social media have shown effective consumer involvement in brands' sustainability practices. Green social media marketing primarily aims to analyze customer data better, systemize workflow, enhance customer engagement, and create compelling sales and marketing strategies.

Celebrity vs. Influencer Marketing on Social Media

The growing popularity of social media enables individuals to amass several million followers on social media platforms. Brands are now recognizing the potential of these influencers as they are overtaking the popularity of traditional celebrities too on social media; current research has identified a substantial difference in the perception of consumers regarding celebrities and influencers (Gräve, 2017; Zeren & Gökdağlı, 2020) with companies increasingly abandoning traditional celebrities in favor influencers on Instagram, Youtube, etc. (Schouten et al., 2020).When consumers share beliefs, interests, values, or characteristics with somebody they admire, they are more likely to emulate their beliefs, attitudes, and behaviors in their personal lives, too (Kelman, 2006). Consumers are attracted to celebrity endorsers and wishfully aspire to be like them (Kamins, 1990), which is in sharp contrast to influencer marketing, where a sense of perceived similarity (Gräve, 2017). Influences are, therefore, more relatable and approachable, creating a sense of camaraderie with their followers through directly connecting with them on social media, which strongly impacts consumer brand attitudes and purchase behaviors (Djafarova & Rushworth, 2017). Perceptions of trust similarity and peer kinship drive consumer response towards influencers where they regularly follow the lifestyle of the influencers following product recommendations which they perceive as credible, spreading positive WOM (word of mouth) through recommendation (Erz & Heeris Christensen, 2018; Gannon & Prothero, 2018). Hence, celebrities offer wishful identification to consumers attracted to the glitz and glamour. Still, influencers provide genuine, authentic, and "ordinary" person relatability, enabling the consumer to trust the influencers on social media (Schouten et al., 2020, 2021).

IMPLICATIONS

Green, sustainable brands should be aware of the potential of social media to promote sustainable buying behavior amongst consumers. On exploring the visual and textual social media cue of brand marketing via social media, the results clearly stated that the image and captions shown by the brand were consistent with the brand's identities and sustainability goals, with users showing more engagement with posts containing expressive and directive acts (L. Zhao et al., 2022). Thus, implementing a successful CRM strategy through social media should be the primary objective of green fashion brands. Green fashion brands, therefore, should engage with influencers and social media platforms, posting more vivid videos) and interactive content to influence consumers (De Vries et al., 2012; Muk, 2013). Social media posts influence consumers' attitudes toward sustainable apparel, descriptive norm perceptions, and self-efficacy beliefs, which are cognitions that directly influence consumers' purchase intentions (de Lenne & Vandenbosch, 2017). The practical implications of this research will enable green brands to tailor target consumer-centric social media activities to reach out to a wide variety of consumers, encouraging green fashion consumption and benefit marketers to improve their marketing strategy on Social media platforms.

REFERENCES

Albino, V., Balice, A., & Dangelico, R. M. (2009). Environmental strategies and green product development: An overview on sustainability-driven companies. *Business Strategy and the Environment*, *18*(2), 83–96. Advance online publication. doi:10.1002/bse.638

AlFarraj, O., Alalwan, A. A., Obeidat, Z. M., Baabdullah, A., Aldmour, R., & Al-Haddad, S. (2021). Examining the impact of influencers' credibility dimensions: Attractiveness, trustworthiness and expertise on the purchase intention in the aesthetic dermatology industry. *Review of International Business and Strategy*, *31*(3), 355–374. doi:10.1108/RIBS-07-2020-0089

Allport, G. W. (1961). Pattern and growth in personality. In Journal of the American Academy of Child Psychiatry. Holt, Rinehart & Winston.

Amel, E. L., Manning, C. M., & Scott, B. A. (2009). Mindfulness and Sustainable Behavior: Pondering Attention and Awareness as Means for Increasing Green Behavior. *Ecopsychology*, *1*(1), 14–25. doi:10.1089/eco.2008.0005

Andrea, L. (2016). *How H&M Became The World's 2nd Largest Fashion Retailer*. Referralcandy.Com. https://www.referralcandy.com/blog/hm-word-of-mouth-marketing

Armitage, C. J., & Christian, J. (2003). From attitudes to behaviour: Basic and applied research on the theory of planned behaviour. Current Psychology. doi:10.1007/s12144-003-1015-5

Arrigo, E. (2013). Corporate responsibility management in fast fashion companies: The Gap Inc. case. *Journal of Fashion Marketing and Management*, *17*(2), 175–189. Advance online publication. doi:10.1108/JFMM-10-2011-0074

Bae, M. (2018). Understanding the effect of the discrepancy between sought and obtained gratification on social networking site users' satisfaction and continuance intention. *Computers in Human Behavior*, *79*, 137–153. Advance online publication. doi:10.1016/j.chb.2017.10.026

Balakrishnan, B. K. P. D., Dahnil, M. I., & Yi, W. J. (2014). The Impact of Social Media Marketing Medium toward Purchase Intention and Brand Loyalty among Generation Y. *Procedia: Social and Behavioral Sciences*, *148*, 177–185. doi:10.1016/j.sbspro.2014.07.032

Baumgardner, J., & Richards, A. (2004). Feminism and Femininity: Or How We Learned to Stop Worrying and Love the Thong. In All About the Girl: Power Culture and Identity (pp. 59–63). doi:10.4324/9780203492567

Becker-Leifhold, C. V. (2018). The role of values in collaborative fashion consumption - A critical investigation through the lenses of the theory of planned behavior. *Journal of Cleaner Production*, *199*, 781–791. doi:10.1016/j.jclepro.2018.06.296

Benjamin, S., & Lee, D. (2022, October 11). *BoF Insights | Gen-Z and Fashion in the Age of Realism | BoF*. Business of Fashion. https://www.businessoffashion.com/reports/retail/gen-z-fashion-in-the-age-of-realism-bof-insights-social-media-report/

Bielawska, K., & Grebosz-Krawczyk, M. (2021). Consumers' Choice Behaviour Toward Green Clothing. *European Research Studies*, *24*(2), 238–256. doi:10.35808/ersj/2124

Bocken, N. M. P., & Short, S. W. (2016). Towards a sufficiency-driven business model: Experiences and opportunities. *Environmental Innovation and Societal Transitions*, *18*, 41–61. doi:10.1016/j.eist.2015.07.010

Bornstein, M. H. (2018). *The SAGE Encyclopedia of Lifespan Human Development*. SAGE Publications, Inc. doi:10.4135/9781506307633

Brenot, A., Chuffart, C., Coste-Manière, I., Deroche, M., Godat, E., Lemoine, L., Ramchandani, M., Sette, E., & Tornaire, C. (2019). Water footprint in fashion and luxury industry. In *Water in Textiles and Fashion* (pp. 95–113). Elsevier. doi:10.1016/B978-0-08-102633-5.00006-3

Brick, C., & Lewis, G. J. (2016). Unearthing the "Green" Personality: Core Traits Predict Environmentally Friendly Behavior. *Environment and Behavior*, *48*(5), 635–658. Advance online publication. doi:10.1177/0013916514554695

Brodie, R. J., Ilic, A., Juric, B., & Hollebeek, L. (2013). Consumer engagement in a virtual brand community: An exploratory analysis. *Journal of Business Research*, *66*(1), 105–114. doi:10.1016/j.jbusres.2011.07.029

Buenstorf, G., & Cordes, C. (2008). Can sustainable consumption be learned? A model of cultural evolution. *Ecological Economics*, *67*(4), 646–657. doi:10.1016/j.ecolecon.2008.01.028

Bulmer, S., Palakshappa, N., Dodds, S., & Harper, S. (2024). Sustainability, brand authenticity and Instagram messaging. *Journal of Business Research*, *175*, 114547. doi:10.1016/j.jbusres.2024.114547

Cachon, G. P., & Swinney, R. (2011). The value of fast fashion: Quick response, enhanced design, and strategic consumer behavior. *Management Science*, *57*(4), 778–795. Advance online publication. doi:10.1287/mnsc.1100.1303

Carlson, L., Grove, S. J., & Kangun, N. (1993). A Content Analysis of Environmental Advertising Claims: A Matrix Method Approach. *Journal of Advertising*, *22*(3), 27–39. doi:10.1080/00913367.1993.10673409

Charm, T., Dhar, R., Haas, S., Liu, J., Novemsky, N., & Teichner, W. (2020). *Understanding and shaping consumer behavior in the next normal | McKinsey*. https://www.mckinsey.com/business-functions/marketing-and-sales/our-insights/understanding-and-shaping-consumer-behavior-in-the-next-normal# doi:10.1080/0144929X.2019.1587001

Chen, Y. C., Shang, R. A., & Li, M. J. (2014). The effects of perceived relevance of travel blogs' content on the behavioral intention to visit a tourist destination. *Computers in Human Behavior*, *30*, 787–799. Advance online publication. doi:10.1016/j.chb.2013.05.019

Chen, Y. S. (2010). The drivers of green brand equity: Green brand image, green satisfaction, and green trust. *Journal of Business Ethics*, *93*(2), 307–319. Advance online publication. doi:10.1007/s10551-009-0223-9

Chow, P.-S., & Li, C. K. Y. (2018). Towards Closed-Loop Fashion Supply Chains—Reflections from Retailer-Facilitated Used Apparel Collection Programs. In *Contemporary Case Studies on Fashion Production, Marketing and Operations* (pp. 219–239). Springer. doi:10.1007/978-981-10-7007-5_13

Chu, S.-C., Chen, H.-T., & Gan, C. (2020). Consumers' engagement with corporate social responsibility (CSR) communication in social media: Evidence from China and the United States. *Journal of Business Research*, *110*, 260–271. doi:10.1016/j.jbusres.2020.01.036

Cowan, K., & Kinley, T. (2014). Green spirit: Consumer empathies for green apparel. *International Journal of Consumer Studies*, *38*(5), 493–499. Advance online publication. doi:10.1111/ijcs.12125

Cronin, J. J. Jr, Smith, J. S., Gleim, M. R., Ramirez, E., & Martinez, J. D. (2011). Green marketing strategies: An examination of stakeholders and the opportunities they present. *Journal of the Academy of Marketing Science*, *39*(1), 158–174. Advance online publication. doi:10.1007/s11747-010-0227-0

D'Souza, C., Gilmore, A. J., Hartmann, P., Apaolaza Ibáñez, V., & Sullivan-Mort, G. (2015). Male eco-fashion: A market reality. *International Journal of Consumer Studies*, *39*(1), 35–42. Advance online publication. doi:10.1111/ijcs.12148

Danielle, W., & Forbes, C. A. (2021). *Influencer Marketing's Surprising Rise Of The 'Everyperson.'* Forbes.Com. https://www.forbes.com/sites/forbesagencycouncil/2021/02/04/influencer-marketings-surprising-rise-of-the-everyperson/?sh=7660272e3b23

de Lenne, O., & Vandenbosch, L. (2017). Media and sustainable apparel buying intention. *Journal of Fashion Marketing and Management*, *21*(4), 483–498. doi:10.1108/JFMM-11-2016-0101

De Vries, L., Gensler, S., & Leeflang, P. S. H. (2012). Popularity of Brand Posts on Brand Fan Pages: An Investigation of the Effects of Social Media Marketing. *Journal of Interactive Marketing*, *26*(2), 83–91. Advance online publication. doi:10.1016/j.intmar.2012.01.003

Deloitte. (2022). *The Deloitte Global 2022 Gen Z and Millennial Survey*. Author.

Dhir, A., Sadiq, M., Talwar, S., Sakashita, M., & Kaur, P. (2021). Why do retail consumers buy green apparel? A knowledge-attitude-behaviour-context perspective. *Journal of Retailing and Consumer Services, 59*, 102398. Advance online publication. doi:10.1016/j.jretconser.2020.102398

Djafarova, E., & Bowes, T. (2021). 'Instagram made Me buy it': Generation Z impulse purchases in fashion industry. *Journal of Retailing and Consumer Services, 59*, 102345. doi:10.1016/j.jretconser.2020.102345

Djafarova, E., & Rushworth, C. (2017). Exploring the credibility of online celebrities' Instagram profiles in influencing the purchase decisions of young female users. *Computers in Human Behavior, 68*, 1–7. doi:10.1016/j.chb.2016.11.009

Eilert, M., & Nappier Cherup, A. (2020). The Activist Company: Examining a Company's Pursuit of Societal Change Through Corporate Activism Using an Institutional Theoretical Lens. *Journal of Public Policy & Marketing, 39*(4), 461–476. Advance online publication. doi:10.1177/0743915620947408

Elisa, W., & Cecilia, H.-M. (2016). Relationship Marketing in Green Fashion—A Case Study of hessnatur. In S. S. Muthu & M. A. Gardetti (Eds.), *Green Fashion* (1st ed., pp. 21–47). Springer Singapore. doi:10.1007/978-981-10-0245-8

Erz, A., & Heeris Christensen, A.-B. (2018). Transforming Consumers Into Brands: Tracing Transformation Processes of the Practice of Blogging. *Journal of Interactive Marketing, 43*, 69–82. doi:10.1016/j.intmar.2017.12.002

Esmaeelinezhad, O., & Afrazeh, A. (2018). Linking personality traits and individuals' knowledge management behavior. *Aslib Journal of Information Management, 70*(3), 234–251. Advance online publication. doi:10.1108/AJIM-01-2018-0019

Fernández, P., Hartmann, P., & Apaolaza, V. (2022). What drives CSR communication effectiveness on social media? A process-based theoretical framework and research agenda. *International Journal of Advertising, 41*(3), 385–413. Advance online publication. doi:10.1080/02650487.2021.1947016

Fletcher, K. (2010). Slow Fashion: An Invitation for Systems Change. *Fashion Practice, 2*(2), 259–265. doi:10.2752/175693810X12774625387594

Francois, F., John, B., & Leah, J. L. Z. (2023). *Selling Sustainability Means Decoding Consumers | Bain & Company*. Bain & Company. https://www.bain.com/insights/selling-sustainability-means-decoding-consumers-ceo-sustainability-guide-2023/

Frick, V., Gossen, M., Santarius, T., & Geiger, S. (2021). When your shop says #lessismore. Online communication interventions for clothing sufficiency. *Journal of Environmental Psychology, 75*, 101595. doi:10.1016/j.jenvp.2021.101595

Gandomi, A., & Haider, M. (2015). Beyond the hype: Big data concepts, methods, and analytics. *International Journal of Information Management, 35*(2), 137–144. doi:10.1016/j.ijinfomgt.2014.10.007

Gannon, V., & Prothero, A. (2018). Beauty bloggers and YouTubers as a community of practice. *Journal of Marketing Management, 34*(7-8), 592–619. Advance online publication. doi:10.1080/0267257X.2018.1482941

Geiger, S. M., & Keller, J. (2018). Shopping for Clothes and Sensitivity to the Suffering of Others: The Role of Compassion and Values in Sustainable Fashion Consumption. *Environment and Behavior*, *50*(10), 1119–1144. doi:10.1177/0013916517732109

Gil De Zuniga, H., Diehl, T., Huber, B., & Liu, J. (2017). Personality Traits and Social Media Use in 20 Countries: How Personality Relates to Frequency of Social Media Use, Social Media News Use, and Social Media Use for Social Interaction. *Cyberpsychology, Behavior, and Social Networking*, *20*(9), 540–552. Advance online publication. doi:10.1089/cyber.2017.0295 PMID:28922034

Goldsmith, E. B. E., Ronald, G., & Todd, B. (2015). Social Influence and Sustainable Behavior. In *Social Influence and Sustainable Consumption* (1st ed., pp. 127–154). Springer Cham. doi:10.1007/978-3-319-20738-4_8

Gong, W., & Li, X. (2017). Engaging fans on microblog: The synthetic influence of parasocial interaction and source characteristics on celebrity endorsement. *Psychology and Marketing*, *34*(7), 720–732. doi:10.1002/mar.21018

Gorge, H., Herbert, M., Özçağlar-Toulouse, N., & Robert, I. (2015). What Do We Really Need? Questioning Consumption Through Sufficiency. *Journal of Macromarketing*, *35*(1), 11–22. doi:10.1177/0276146714553935

Gräve, J.-F. (2017). Exploring the Perception of Influencers vs. Traditional Celebrities. *Proceedings of the 8th International Conference on Social Media & Society - #SMSociety, 17*, 1–5. 10.1145/3097286.3097322

Guercini, S., Milanesi, M., Mir-Bernal, P., & Runfola, A. (2020). Surfing the Waves of New Marketing in Luxury Fashion: The Case of Online Multi-brand Retailers. In Springer Proceedings in Business and Economics (pp. 203–210). doi:10.1007/978-3-030-47595-6_25

Gupta, S., Gwozdz, W., & Gentry, J. (2019). The Role of Style Versus Fashion Orientation on Sustainable Apparel Consumption. *Journal of Macromarketing*, *39*(2), 188–207. Advance online publication. doi:10.1177/0276146719835283

Haines, S., Fares, O. H., Mohan, M., & Lee, S. H. (2023, November 08). (Mark). (2023). Social media fashion influencer eWOM communications: Understanding the trajectory of sustainable fashion conversations on YouTube fashion haul videos. *Journal of Fashion Marketing and Management*, *27*(6), 1027–1046. Advance online publication. doi:10.1108/JFMM-02-2022-0029

Hajli, N. (2014). A study of the impact of social media on consumers. *International Journal of Market Research*, *56*(3), 387–404. Advance online publication. doi:10.2501/IJMR-2014-025

Hartmann, T. (2016). Mass Communication and Para-Social Interaction: Observations on Intimacy at a Distance. In Schlüsselwerke der Medienwirkungsforschung (pp. 75–84). Springer Fachmedien Wiesbaden. doi:10.1007/978-3-658-09923-7_7

Hasan, M. M., Cai, L., Ji, X., & Ocran, F. M. (2022). *Eco-Friendly Clothing Market: A Study of Willingness to Purchase Organic Cotton Clothing in Bangladesh*. Sustainability. doi:10.3390/su14084827

Heller Baird, C., & Parasnis, G. (2011). From social media to social customer relationship management. *Strategy and Leadership*, *39*(5), 30–37. doi:10.1108/10878571111161507

Hiller Connell, K. Y., & Kozar, J. M. (2012). Social Normative Influence: An Exploratory Study Investigating its Effectiveness in Increasing Engagement in Sustainable Apparel-Purchasing Behaviors. *Journal of Global Fashion Marketing*. doi:10.1080/20932685.2012.10600847

Hoffmann, S., & Lee, M. S. W. (2016). Consume Less and Be Happy? Consume Less to Be Happy! An Introduction to the Special Issue on Anti-Consumption and Consumer Well-Being. *The Journal of Consumer Affairs*, *50*(1), 3–17. doi:10.1111/joca.12104

Hollebeek, L. D., Glynn, M. S., & Brodie, R. J. (2014). Consumer Brand Engagement in Social Media: Conceptualization, Scale Development and Validation. *Journal of Interactive Marketing*, *28*(2), 149–165. doi:10.1016/j.intmar.2013.12.002

Horton, D., & Richard Wohl, R. (1956). Mass Communication and Para-Social Interaction. *Psychiatry*, *19*(3), 215–229. doi:10.1080/00332747.1956.11023049 PMID:13359569

Hu, N., Bose, I., Koh, N. S., & Liu, L. (2012). Manipulation of online reviews: An analysis of ratings, readability, and sentiments. *Decision Support Systems*, *52*(3), 674–684. Advance online publication. doi:10.1016/j.dss.2011.11.002

Hung, K., Li, S. Y., & Tse, D. K. (2011). Interpersonal Trust and Platform Credibility in a Chinese Multibrand Online Community. *Journal of Advertising*, *40*(3), 99–112. doi:10.2753/JOA0091-3367400308

Hwang, C., Lee, Y., Diddi, S., & Karpova, E. (2016). "Don't buy this jacket": Consumer reaction toward anti-consumption apparel advertisement. *Journal of Fashion Marketing and Management*, *20*(4), 435–452. doi:10.1108/JFMM-12-2014-0087

Jacobs, K., Petersen, L., Hörisch, J., & Battenfeld, D. (2018). Green thinking but thoughtless buying? An empirical extension of the value-attitude-behaviour hierarchy in sustainable clothing. *Journal of Cleaner Production*, *203*, 1155–1169. Advance online publication. doi:10.1016/j.jclepro.2018.07.320

Jeong, D., & Ko, E. (2021). The influence of consumers' self-concept and perceived value on sustainable fashion. *Journal of Global Scholars of Marketing Science: Bridging Asia and the World*. doi:10.1080/21639159.2021.1885303

Jermsittiparsert, K., Siam, M. R. A., Issa, M. R., Ahmed, U., & Pahi, M. H. (2019). Do consumers expect companies to be socially responsible? The impact of corporate social responsibility on buying behavior. *Uncertain Supply Chain Management*, 741–752. doi:10.5267/j.uscm.2019.1.005

Jestratijevic, I., Rudd, N. A., & Uanhoro, J. (2020). Transparency of sustainability disclosures among luxury and mass-market fashion brands. *Journal of Global Fashion Marketing*, *11*(2), 99–116. doi:10.1080/20932685.2019.1708774

Jin, S. V., Muqaddam, A., & Ryu, E. (2019). Instafamous and social media influencer marketing. *Marketing Intelligence & Planning*, *37*(5), 567–579. Advance online publication. doi:10.1108/MIP-09-2018-0375

Jones, A., & Kang, J. (2020). Media technology shifts: Exploring millennial consumers' fashion-information- seeking behaviors and motivations. *Canadian Journal of Administrative Sciences / Revue Canadienne Des Sciences de l'Administration*, *37*(1), 13–29. doi:10.1002/cjas.1546

Joo, J., & Sang, Y. (2013). Exploring Koreans' smartphone usage: An integrated model of the technology acceptance model and uses and gratifications theory. *Computers in Human Behavior*, *29*(6), 2512–2518. Advance online publication. doi:10.1016/j.chb.2013.06.002

Joy, A., Sherry, J. F. Jr, Venkatesh, A., Wang, J., & Chan, R. (2012). Fast fashion, sustainability, and the ethical appeal of luxury brands. *Fashion Theory*, *16*(3), 273–295. Advance online publication. doi:10.2752/175174112X13340749707123

Kamins, M. A. (1990). An investigation into the "match-up" hypothesis in celebrity advertising: When beauty may be only skin deep. *Journal of Advertising*, *19*(1), 4–13. Advance online publication. doi:10.1080/00913367.1990.10673175

Kang, J. Y. M., & Kim, J. (2017). Online customer relationship marketing tactics through social media and perceived customer retention orientation of the green retailer. *Journal of Fashion Marketing and Management*, *21*(3), 298–316. Advance online publication. doi:10.1108/JFMM-08-2016-0071

Karavasilis, G., Nerantzaki, D.-M., Pantelidis, P., Paschaloudis, D., & Vrana, V. (2015). What Generation Y in Greece thinks about Green Hotels. *World Journal of Entrepreneurship, Management and Sustainable Development*, *11*(4), 268–280. doi:10.1108/WJEMSD-02-2015-0010

Karimi Alavijeh, M. R., Esmaeili, A., Sepahvand, A., & Davidaviciene, V. (2018). The effect of customer equity drivers on word-of-mouth behavior with mediating role of customer loyalty and purchase intention. *The Engineering Economist*, *29*(2). Advance online publication. doi:10.5755/j01.ee.29.2.17718

Katz, E., Haas, H., & Gurevitch, M. (1973). On the Use of the Mass Media for Important Things. *American Sociological Review*, *38*(2), 164. Advance online publication. doi:10.2307/2094393

Kautish, P., Khare, A., & Sharma, R. (2021). Influence of values, brand consciousness and behavioral intentions in predicting luxury fashion consumption. *Journal of Product and Brand Management*, *30*(4), 513–531. doi:10.1108/JPBM-08-2019-2535

Kelman, H. C. (2006). Interests, Relationships, Identities: Three Central Issues for Individuals and Groups in Negotiating Their Social Environment. *Annual Review of Psychology*, *57*(1), 1–26. doi:10.1146/annurev.psych.57.102904.190156 PMID:16318587

Khan, M. M., Fatima, F., Ranjha, M. T., & Akhtar, S. (2022). Willingness to Pay For Sustainable Green Clothing. *Indonesian Journal of Social and Environmental Issues*, *3*(2), 167–178. doi:10.47540/ijsei.v3i2.565

Khare, A., & Kautish, P. (2021). Cosmopolitanism, self-identity, online communities and green apparel perception. *Marketing Intelligence & Planning*. Advance online publication. doi:10.1108/MIP-11-2019-0556

Khare, A., & Sadachar, A. (2017). Green apparel buying behaviour: A study on Indian youth. *International Journal of Consumer Studies*, *41*(5), 558–569. Advance online publication. doi:10.1111/ijcs.12367

Khare, A., Sadachar, A., & Chakraborty, S. (2022). Influence of celebrities and online communities on Indian consumers' green clothing involvement and purchase behavior. *Journal of Fashion Marketing and Management*, *26*(4), 676–699. Advance online publication. doi:10.1108/JFMM-02-2021-0033

Kim, A. J., & Johnson, K. K. P. (2016). Power of consumers using social media: Examining the influences of brand-related user-generated content on Facebook. *Computers in Human Behavior*, *58*, 98–108. doi:10.1016/j.chb.2015.12.047

Kim, B., Hong, S., & Lee, H. (2021). Brand Communities on Instagram: Exploring Fortune 500 Companies' Instagram Communication Practices. *International Journal of Strategic Communication*, *15*(3), 177–192. Advance online publication. doi:10.1080/1553118X.2020.1867556

Kim, J., Kang, S., & Lee, K. H. (2020). How social capital impacts the purchase intention of sustainable fashion products. *Journal of Business Research*, *117*, 596–603. Advance online publication. doi:10.1016/j.jbusres.2018.10.010

Kim, K. H., & Kim, E. Y. (2020). Fashion marketing trends in social media and sustainability in fashion management. *Journal of Business Research*, *117*, 508–509. doi:10.1016/j.jbusres.2020.06.001

Kim, Y., Yun, S., Lee, J., & Ko, E. (2016). How consumer knowledge shapes green consumption: An empirical study on voluntary carbon offsetting. *International Journal of Advertising*, *35*(1), 23–41. Advance online publication. doi:10.1080/02650487.2015.1096102

Koay, K. Y., Cheung, M. L., Soh, P. C.-H., & Teoh, C. W. (2022). Social media influencer marketing: The moderating role of materialism. *European Business Review*, *34*(2), 224–243. doi:10.1108/EBR-02-2021-0032

Kong, H. M., Ko, E., Chae, H., & Mattila, P. (2016). Understanding fashion consumers' attitude and behavioral intention toward sustainable fashion products: Focus on sustainable knowledge sources and knowledge types. *Journal of Global Fashion Marketing*, *7*(2), 103–119. doi:10.1080/20932685.2015.1131435

Kong, H. M., Witmaier, A., & Ko, E. (2021). Sustainability and social media communication: How consumers respond to marketing efforts of luxury and non-luxury fashion brands. *Journal of Business Research*, *131*, 640–651. doi:10.1016/j.jbusres.2020.08.021

Kumar, N., Garg, P., & Singh, S. (2022). Pro-environmental purchase intention towards eco-friendly apparel: Augmenting the theory of planned behavior with perceived consumer effectiveness and environmental concern. *Journal of Global Fashion Marketing*. doi:10.1080/20932685.2021.2016062

Lee, J. E., & Watkins, B. (2016). YouTube vloggers' influence on consumer luxury brand perceptions and intentions. *Journal of Business Research*, *69*(12), 5753–5760. Advance online publication. doi:10.1016/j.jbusres.2016.04.171

Leong, L. Y., Jaafar, N. I., & Sulaiman, A. (2017). Understanding impulse purchase in Facebook commerce: Does Big Five matter? *Internet Research*, *27*(4), 786–818. Advance online publication. doi:10.1108/IntR-04-2016-0107

Leung, F. F., Gu, F. F., Li, Y., Zhang, J. Z., & Palmatier, R. W. (2022). Influencer Marketing Effectiveness. *Journal of Marketing*, *86*(6), 93–115. doi:10.1177/00222429221102889

Liu, F. (2022). Driving Green Consumption: Exploring Generation Z Consumers' Action Issues on Sustainable Fashion in China. *Studies in Social Science & Humanities, 1*(5), 25–49. doi:10.56397/SSSH.2022.12.03

Lou, C., & Yuan, S. (2019). Influencer Marketing: How Message Value and Credibility Affect Consumer Trust of Branded Content on Social Media. *Journal of Interactive Advertising, 19*(1), 58–73. Advance online publication. doi:10.1080/15252019.2018.1533501

Lucy, B. (2023). *Top 10 Sustainable Clothing Companies 2023*. Sustainability. https://sustainabilitymag.com/articles/top-10-sustainable-clothing-companies

Lynn, T., Muzellec, L., Caemmerer, B., & Turley, D. (2017). Social network sites: Early adopters' personality and influence. *Journal of Product and Brand Management, 26*(1), 42–51. doi:10.1108/JPBM-10-2015-1025

McKinsey & Company. (2020). *Survey: Consumer sentiment on sustainability in fashion | McKinsey*. Mckinsey.Com. https://www.mckinsey.com/industries/retail/our-insights/survey-consumer-sentiment-on-sustainability-in-fashion

McNeill, L., & Moore, R. (2015). Sustainable fashion consumption and the fast fashion conundrum: Fashionable consumers and attitudes to sustainability in clothing choice. *International Journal of Consumer Studies, 39*(3), 212–222. doi:10.1111/ijcs.12169

McNeill, L., & Venter, B. (2019). Identity, self-concept and young women's engagement with collaborative, sustainable fashion consumption models. *International Journal of Consumer Studies, 43*(4), 368–378. Advance online publication. doi:10.1111/ijcs.12516

Meyer, A. (2001). What's in it for the customers? Successfully marketing green clothes. *Business Strategy and the Environment, 10*(5), 317–330. doi:10.1002/bse.302

Milanesi, M., Kyrdoda, Y., & Runfola, A. (2022). How do you depict sustainability? An analysis of images posted on Instagram by sustainable fashion companies. *Journal of Global Fashion Marketing, 13*(2), 101–115. doi:10.1080/20932685.2021.1998789

Mohr, L. A., Webb, D. J., & Harris, K. (2001). Do Consumers Expect Companies to be Socially Responsible? The Impact of Corporate Social Responsibility on Buying Behavior. *The Journal of Consumer Affairs, 35*(1), 45–72. doi:10.1111/j.1745-6606.2001.tb00102.x

Morrison, M. A., Cheong, H. J., & McMillan, S. J. (2013). Posting, Lurking, and Networking: Behaviors and Characteristics of Consumers in the Context of User-Generated Content. *Journal of Interactive Advertising, 13*(2), 97–108. doi:10.1080/15252019.2013.826552

Moser, A. K. (2015). Thinking green, buying green? Drivers of pro - Environmental purchasing behavior. *Journal of Consumer Marketing, 32*(3), 167–175. Advance online publication. doi:10.1108/JCM-10-2014-1179

Muk, A. (2013). What factors influence millennials to like brand pages? *Journal of Marketing Analytics, 1*(3), 127–137. doi:10.1057/jma.2013.12

Neuendorf, K. A. (2017). The Content Analysis Guidebook. In *The Content Analysis Guidebook* (2nd ed.). SAGE Publications, Inc., doi:10.4135/9781071802878.n1

Oladayo, S. (2017). *Sustainable and Ethical Fashion Consumption: the role of Consumer Attitude and Behaviou.* Hamburg School of Business Administration.

Papadopoulou, M., Papasolomou, I., & Thrassou, A. (2022). Exploring the level of sustainability awareness among consumers within the fast-fashion clothing industry: A dual business and consumer perspective. *Competitiveness Review, 32*(3), 350–375. Advance online publication. doi:10.1108/CR-04-2021-0061

Peeroo, S., Samy, M., & Jones, B. (2017). Facebook: A blessing or a curse for grocery stores? *International Journal of Retail & Distribution Management, 45*(12), 1242–1259. doi:10.1108/IJRDM-12-2016-0234

Pérez-Curiel, C., Jiménez-Marín, G., & García-Medina, I. (2021). The Role of Social Media in the Fashion Industry: The Case of Eco Luxury in Today's Consumption. In *Firms in the Fashion Industry* (pp. 97–115). Springer International Publishing. doi:10.1007/978-3-030-76255-1_7

Petersson McIntyre, M. (2021). Shame, Blame, and Passion: Affects of (Un)sustainable Wardrobes. *Fashion Theory, 25*(6), 735–755. doi:10.1080/1362704X.2019.1676506

Pornsrimate, K., & Khamwon, A. (2021). How to convert Millennial consumers to brand evangelists through social media micro-influencers. *Innovative Marketing, 17*(2), 18–32. doi:10.21511/im.17(2).2021.03

Pradeep, K. (2016). Digital and Internet Marketing: Crucial Business Management Landscape. In *E-Governance in India: Problems, Prototypes and Prospects* (pp. 91–118). Nova Science Publishing. https://www.researchgate.net/publication/316137040_Digital_and_Internet_Marketing_Crucial_Business_Management_Landscape

Pymnts. (2023). *Gen Z Tops Millennials on Social Media Shopping and Spending*. Pymnts.Com. https://www.pymnts.com/news/social-commerce/2023/gen-z-tops-millennials-on-social-media-shopping-and-spending/

Quach, S., & Thaichon, P. (2017). From connoisseur luxury to mass luxury: Value co-creation and co-destruction in the online environment. *Journal of Business Research, 81*, 163–172. Advance online publication. doi:10.1016/j.jbusres.2017.06.015

Quan-Haase, A., & Young, A. L. (2010). *Uses and Gratifications of Social Media: A Comparison of Facebook and Instant Messaging*. doi:10.1177/0270467610380009

Reich, B. J., & Soule, C. A. A. (2016). Green Demarketing in Advertisements: Comparing "Buy Green" and "Buy Less" Appeals in Product and Institutional Advertising Contexts. *Journal of Advertising, 45*(4), 441–458. doi:10.1080/00913367.2016.1214649

Remi, R. (2020). *Sustainability sells: Why consumers and clothing brands alike are turning to sustainability as a guiding light.* Business Insider, India. https://www.businessinsider.in/international/news/sustainability-sells-why-consumers-and-clothing-brands-alike-are-turning-to-sustainability-as-a-guiding-light/articleshow/73259499.cms

Rietveld, R., van Dolen, W., Mazloom, M., & Worring, M. (2020). What You Feel, Is What You Like Influence of Message Appeals on Customer Engagement on Instagram. *Journal of Interactive Marketing*, *49*(1), 20–53. Advance online publication. doi:10.1016/j.intmar.2019.06.003

Romani, S., Grappi, S., Zarantonello, L., & Bagozzi, R. P. (2015). The revenge of the consumer! How brand moral violations lead to consumer anti-brand activism. *Journal of Brand Management*, *22*(8), 658–672. doi:10.1057/bm.2015.38

Roozen, I., Raedts, M., & Meijburg, L. (2021). Do verbal and visual nudges influence consumers' choice for sustainable fashion? *Journal of Global Fashion Marketing*, *12*(4), 327–342. doi:10.1080/20932685.2021.1930096

Rungruangjit, W. (2022). What drives Taobao live streaming commerce? The role of parasocial relationships, congruence and source credibility in Chinese consumers' purchase intentions. *Heliyon*, *8*(6), e09676. doi:10.1016/j.heliyon.2022.e09676 PMID:35756134

Rungruangjit, W., & Charoenpornpanichkul, K. (2022). Building Stronger Brand Evangelism for Sustainable Marketing through Micro-Influencer-Generated Content on Instagram in the Fashion Industry. *Sustainability (Basel)*, *14*(23), 15770. doi:10.3390/su142315770

Ryan, R. M., & Deci, E. L. (2000). Self-determination theory and the facilitation of intrinsic motivation, social development, and well-being. *The American Psychologist*, *55*(1), 68–78. Advance online publication. doi:10.1037/0003-066X.55.1.68 PMID:11392867

Salem, S. F., & Alanadoly, A. B. (2021). Personality traits and social media as drivers of word-of-mouth towards sustainable fashion. *Journal of Fashion Marketing and Management*, *25*(1), 24–44. Advance online publication. doi:10.1108/JFMM-08-2019-0162

Sandberg, M. (2021). Sufficiency transitions: A review of consumption changes for environmental sustainability. *Journal of Cleaner Production*, *293*, 126097. doi:10.1016/j.jclepro.2021.126097

Schmuck, D., Matthes, J., & Naderer, B. (2018). Misleading Consumers with Green Advertising? An Affect–Reason–Involvement Account of Greenwashing Effects in Environmental Advertising. *Journal of Advertising*, *47*(2), 127–145. doi:10.1080/00913367.2018.1452652

Schouten, A. P., Janssen, L., & Verspaget, M. (2020). Celebrity vs. Influencer endorsements in advertising: The role of identification, credibility, and Product-Endorser fit. *International Journal of Advertising*, *39*(2), 258–281. doi:10.1080/02650487.2019.1634898

Schouten, A. P., Janssen, L., & Verspaget, M. (2021). Celebrity vs. Influencer endorsements in advertising: the role of identification, credibility, and Product-Endorser fit. In *Leveraged Marketing Communications* (1st ed., pp. 208–231). Routledge. doi:10.4324/9781003155249-12

Shang, K.-C., Chao, C.-C., & Lirn, T.-C. (2016). The application of personality traits model on the freight forwarding service industry. *Maritime Business Review*, *1*(3), 231–252. doi:10.1108/MABR-09-2016-0021

Sheldon, P., & Bryant, K. (2016). Instagram: Motives for its use and relationship to narcissism and contextual age. *Computers in Human Behavior*, *58*, 89–97. doi:10.1016/j.chb.2015.12.059

Shelley, W. (2023). [*Social Media Sites & Platforms*. Search Engine Journal. https://www.searchengine-journal.com/social-media/social-media-platforms/

Shen, B. (2014). Sustainable Fashion Supply Chain: Lessons from H&M. *Sustainability (Basel)*, *6*(9), 6236–6249. doi:10.3390/su6096236

Shen, B., Wang, Y., Lo, C. K. Y., & Shum, M. (2012). The impact of ethical fashion on consumer purchase behavior. *Journal of Fashion Marketing and Management*, *16*(2), 234–245. doi:10.1108/13612021211222842

Shen, B., Zheng, J.-H., Chow, P.-S., & Chow, K.-Y. (2014). Perception of fashion sustainability in online community. *Journal of the Textile Institute*, *105*(9), 971–979. doi:10.1080/00405000.2013.866334

Siregar, Y., Kent, A., Peirson-Smith, A., & Guan, C. (2023). Disrupting the fashion retail journey: Social media and GenZ's fashion consumption. *International Journal of Retail & Distribution Management*, *51*(7), 862–875. Advance online publication. doi:10.1108/IJRDM-01-2022-0002

Smith, A. N., Fischer, E., & Yongjian, C. (2012). How Does Brand-related User-generated Content Differ across YouTube, Facebook, and Twitter? *Journal of Interactive Marketing*, *26*(2), 102–113. doi:10.1016/j.intmar.2012.01.002

Sonnenberg, N., Jacobs, B., & Momberg, D. (2014). The Role of Information Exposure in Female University Students' Evaluation and Selection of Eco-Friendly Apparel in the South African Emerging Economy. *Clothing & Textiles Research Journal*, *32*(4), 266–281. Advance online publication. doi:10.1177/0887302X14541542

Stacy, D. J. (2023a). *Biggest social media platforms 2023*. Statista.Com. https://www.statista.com/statistics/272014/global-social-networks-ranked-by-number-of-users/

Stacy, D. J. (2023b). *Number of worldwide social network users 2027*. Statista.Com. https://www.statista.com/statistics/278414/number-of-worldwide-social-network-users/

Strähle, J., & Chantal, G. (2016). The Role of Social Media for a Sustainable Consumption. In *Green Fashion Retail* (1st ed., pp. 225–247). Springer Singapore. doi:10.1007/978-981-10-2440-5_3

Terry, D. J., & O'Leary, J. E. (1995). The theory of planned behaviour: The effects of perceived behavioural control and self-efficacy. *British Journal of Social Psychology*, *34*(2), 199–220. Advance online publication. doi:10.1111/j.2044-8309.1995.tb01058.x PMID:7620846

Testa, D. S., Bakhshian, S., & Eike, R. (2021). Engaging consumers with sustainable fashion on Instagram. *Journal of Fashion Marketing and Management*, *25*(4), 569–584. doi:10.1108/JFMM-11-2019-0266

Todeschini, B. V., Cortimiglia, M. N., Callegaro-de-Menezes, D., & Ghezzi, A. (2017). Innovative and sustainable business models in the fashion industry: Entrepreneurial drivers, opportunities, and challenges. *Business Horizons*, *60*(6), 759–770. doi:10.1016/j.bushor.2017.07.003

Tommasel, A., Corbellini, A., Godoy, D., & Schiaffino, S. (2015). Exploring the role of personality traits in followee recommendation. *Online Information Review*, *39*(6), 812–830. Advance online publication. doi:10.1108/OIR-04-2015-0107

Turker, D., & Altuntas, C. (2014). Sustainable supply chain management in the fast fashion industry: An analysis of corporate reports. *European Management Journal*, *32*(5), 837–849. doi:10.1016/j.emj.2014.02.001

Velasco-Molpeceres, A., Zarauza-Castro, J., Pérez-Curiel, C., & Mateos-González, S. (2022). Slow Fashion as a Communication Strategy of Fashion Brands on Instagram. *Sustainability (Basel)*, *15*(1), 423. doi:10.3390/su15010423

Viciunaite, V. (2022). Communicating Sustainable Business Models to Consumers: A Translation Theory Perspective. *Organization & Environment*, *35*(2), 233–251. doi:10.1177/1086026620953448

Vita, G., Ivanova, D., Dumitru, A., García-Mira, R., Carrus, G., Stadler, K., Krause, K., Wood, R., & Hertwich, E. G. (2020). Happier with less? Members of European environmental grassroots initiatives reconcile lower carbon footprints with higher life satisfaction and income increases. *Energy Research & Social Science*, *60*, 101329. doi:10.1016/j.erss.2019.101329

Vladimirova, K., Henninger, C. E., Alosaimi, S. I., Brydges, T., Choopani, H., Hanlon, M., Iran, S., McCormick, H., & Zhou, S. (2023). Exploring the influence of social media on sustainable fashion consumption: A systematic literature review and future research agenda. *Journal of Global Fashion Marketing*, 1–22. doi:10.1080/20932685.2023.2237978

Voorveld, H. A. M. (2019). Brand Communication in Social Media: A Research Agenda. *Journal of Advertising*, *48*(1), 14–26. Advance online publication. doi:10.1080/00913367.2019.1588808

Vredenburg, J., Kapitan, S., Spry, A., & Kemper, J. A. (2020). Brands Taking a Stand: Authentic Brand Activism or Woke Washing? *Journal of Public Policy & Marketing*, *39*(4), 444–460. doi:10.1177/0743915620947359

Wagner, M., Curteza, A., Hong, Y., Chen, Y., Thomassey, S., & Zeng, X. (2019). A design analysis for eco-fashion style using sensory evaluation tools: Consumer perceptions of product appearance. *Journal of Retailing and Consumer Services*, *51*, 253–262. Advance online publication. doi:10.1016/j.jretconser.2019.06.005

Wallace, E., Buil, I., & Catalán, S. (2020). Facebook and luxury fashion brands: Self-congruent posts and purchase intentions. *Journal of Fashion Marketing and Management*, *24*(4), 571–588. doi:10.1108/JFMM-09-2019-0215

Wang, P., & Huang, Q. (2023). Digital influencers, social power and consumer engagement in social commerce. *Internet Research*, *33*(1), 178–207. doi:10.1108/INTR-08-2020-0467

Whiting, A., & Williams, D. (2013). Why people use social media: A uses and gratifications approach. *Qualitative Market Research*, *16*(4), 362–369. doi:10.1108/QMR-06-2013-0041

Wiederhold, M., & Martinez, L. F. (2018). Ethical consumer behaviour in Germany: The attitude-behaviour gap in the green apparel industry. *International Journal of Consumer Studies*, *42*(4), 419–429. Advance online publication. doi:10.1111/ijcs.12435

Xu, Y., & Chen, Z. (2006). Relevance judgment: What do information users consider beyond topicality? *Journal of the American Society for Information Science and Technology*, *57*(7), 961–973. Advance online publication. doi:10.1002/asi.20361

Yoo, J.-J., Divita, L., & Kim, H.-Y. (2018). Predicting consumer intention to purchase clothing products made from sustainable fabrics: Implications for the fast-fashion industry. *Clothing Cultures*, *5*(1), 47–60. doi:10.1386/cc.5.1.47_1

Zeren, D., & Gökdağlı, N. (2020). Influencer Versus Celebrity Endorser Performance on Instagram. In *Strategic Innvotive Marketing and Tourism* (pp. 695–704). Springer Science and Business Media B.V. doi:10.1007/978-3-030-36126-6_77

Zhang, X., & Choi, J. (2022). *The Importance of Social Influencer-Generated Contents for User Cognition and Emotional Attachment: An Information Relevance Perspective*. Sustainability. doi:10.3390/su14116676

Zhao, L., Lee, S. H., & Copeland, L. R. (2019). Social media and Chinese consumers' environmentally sustainable apparel purchase intentions. *Asia Pacific Journal of Marketing and Logistics*, *31*(4), 855–874. Advance online publication. doi:10.1108/APJML-08-2017-0183

Zhao, L., Lee, S. H., Li, M., & Sun, P. (2022). *The Use of Social Media to Promote Sustainable Fashion and Benefit Communications: A Data-Mining Approach*. Sustainability. doi:10.3390/su14031178

Zhao, W., Lun, R., Gordon, C., Fofana, A. B. M., Espy, D. D., Reinthal, M. A., Ekelman, B., Goodman, G. D., Niederriter, J. E., & Luo, X. (2017). A Human-Centered Activity Tracking System: Toward a Healthier Workplace. *IEEE Transactions on Human-Machine Systems*, *47*(3), 343–355. Advance online publication. doi:10.1109/THMS.2016.2611825

Zheng, Y., & Chi, T. (2015). Factors influencing purchase intention towards environmentally friendly apparel: An empirical study of US consumers. *International Journal of Fashion Design, Technology and Education*, *8*(2), 68–77. Advance online publication. doi:10.1080/17543266.2014.990059

ADDITIONAL READING

Chow, P.-S., & Li, C. K. Y. (2018). Towards Closed-Loop Fashion Supply Chains—Reflections from Retailer-Facilitated Used Apparel Collection Programs. In *Contemporary Case Studies on Fashion Production, Marketing and Operations* (pp. 219–239). Springer. doi:10.1007/978-981-10-7007-5_13

Elisa, W., & Cecilia, H.-M. (2016). Relationship Marketing in Green Fashion—A Case Study of hessnatur. In S. S. Muthu & M. A. Gardetti (Eds.), *Green Fashion* (1st ed., pp. 21–47).

Goldsmith, E. B. E., Ronald, G., & Todd, B. (2015). Social Influence and Sustainable Behavior. In Social Influence and Sustainable Consumption. Springer. doi:10.1007/978-3-319-20738-4_8

Pérez-Curiel, C., Jiménez-Marín, G., & García-Medina, I. (2021). The Role of Social Media in the Fashion Industry: The Case of Eco Luxury in Today's Consumption. In *Firms in the Fashion Industry* (pp. 97–115). Springer International Publishing. doi:10.1007/978-3-030-76255-1_7

Schouten, A. P., Janssen, L., & Verspaget, M. (2021). Celebrity vs. Influencer endorsements in advertising: the role of identification, credibility, and Product-Endorser fit. In *Leveraged Marketing Communications* (1st ed., pp. 208–231). Routledge. doi:10.4324/9781003155249-12

Strähle, J., & Chantal, G. (2016). The Role of Social Media for a Sustainable Consumption. In Green Fashion Retail. Springer Singapore.

Zeren, D., & Gökdağlı, N. (2020). Influencer Versus Celebrity Endorser Performance on Instagram. In *Strategic Innvotive Marketing and Tourism* (pp. 695–704). Springer Science and Business Media B.V. doi:10.1007/978-3-030-36126-6_77

KEY TERMS AND DEFINITIONS

CRM: Customer Relationship Management combines practices, strategies, and technologies companies use to manage and analyze customer interactions.

eWOM: Electronic word of mouth is the positive referral shared about a brand with peers or fellow community members by writing, liking, sharing, or recommending fashion brands-related messages through digital channels, social media platforms, websites, blogs, and video logs.

ROI: Return on Investment is a metric that describes how well an investment has performed. It is a percentage of total profit (or loss) divided by the initial cost.

SAB: Sustainably aware fashion brands do not find origins in sustainability but undertake public sustainability efforts incorporating sustainability into some aspects of the supply chain.

SDT: Social Determination Theory is the intrinsic and extrinsic motivation behind live streamers, online brand communities, fashion influencers, and sustainable product consumers. Hence, while intrinsic motivation is the enjoyment received from a process, extrinsic motivation is the need for reward or punishment.

SFB: Sustainable fashion brands work on sustainability principles with product sourcing, production, marketing, and disposal during the supply chain, done sustainably.

SMFI: Social Media Fashion Influencers are celebrities or bloggers with a high number of followers who create fashion content through their social media channels and have the power to influence their followers to adopt new fashion trends, styles, and movements.

TFB: Traditional fashion brands) do not affiliate with a public sustainability effort. They focus on product and functional characteristics and market them accordingly.

UGC: User Generated Content, content explicitly created on digital media that is publicly available for end users, resulting in electronic word of mouth.

UGT: Uses and Gratification theory in studies of mass media behavior, understanding the intent of consumer motivations and the resultant gratifications received during mass media consumption.

WOM: Word of Mouth is a social communication in marketing literature meant to transfer information about a product or brand from person to person as either a recommendation or peer review.

Chapter 2
Defeating Global Glut of Clothing:
An Examination of Sustainable Fashion Consumption of Young Consumers

Nurul Hidayana Mohd Noor
https://orcid.org/0000-0003-2262-2524
Universiti Teknologi MARA, Malaysia

ABSTRACT

The purpose of the study was to examine the determinants of sustainable fashion consumption among young consumers. The empirical study adopted quantitative methodology using a survey approach for collecting data. The sample of 500 young consumers was collected using stratified random and purposive sampling techniques. This study uses five main identified determinants of sustainable fashion consumption: pro-environmental attitude, environmental knowledge, subjective norm, price incentive, perceived behavioural control, and environmental value. The final data of 481 young consumers were analysed using structural equation modeling (SEM). Findings confirm that environmental value acts as a mediator. The input of this study is expected to be a valuable indicator for stakeholders such as the government, fashion designers, retailers, and manufacturers. The study contributes to the scarce literature by recognising the mediating effect of environmental value.

INTRODUCTION

Sustainable consumption refers to the attitude and behavior that every youth needs to contribute positively to environmental conservation and guarantee a sustainable future. The youth, who are also future heirs, need to be exposed to sustainable consumption to increase their understanding of the importance of environmental conservation. Excessive clothing waste occurs due to fast fashion changes with a constant trend in new fashion designs (Paço et al., 2021). In the past decade, the rhythm of fashion has accelerated toward the life cycle of fast fashion. The concept is dominated by consumption and fast-changing

DOI: 10.4018/979-8-3693-3049-4.ch002

trends. Consumers bought more clothes because of the reasonable prices and threw them away after just one season (Muthu, 2019). Therefore, fast fashion contributes a large amount of the waste disposal the fashion industry produces (Akter et al., 2022; Niinimäki et al., 2020). Mukendi et al. (2020) describe the polarization among consumers about eco-fashion helping to reduce the use of clothing materials and foster responsibility towards the environment.

Nevertheless, Lee et al. (2020) found that many consumers need help understanding or knowing about environmental issues. The consumers are also found to have no guilt when disposing of expensive items. Hosted and Zabkar (2021) also found that consumers are less interested in environmental ethics and social awareness. While Rausch and Kopplin's (2021) study found that fashion designers are aware of the adverse effects of non-recyclable materials, they also found that if the consumers know that the materials are made from recycled materials, they will not buy them. They are more interested in buying new products. At this point, they believe that the used clothes can be given to developing countries for emergency aid or sold for recycling.

Disposing of clothes will have a long-term impact on the environment because the clothing is dyed with chemicals that can be toxic to the environment and human health (Lee et al., 2020; Niinimäki et al., 2020). Sustainable fashion is an alternative to dealing with the unsustainable aspects of fast fashion (Akter et al., 2022). Clothing retailers like Zara, H&M, and Uniqlo have introduced garment collecting and recycling initiatives to support sustainable fashion. Sustainable fashion can be defined as "the variety of means by which a fashion item or behaviour could be perceived to be more sustainable, including (but not limited to) environmental, social, slow fashion, reuse, recycling, cruelty-free and anti-consumption and production practices" (Mukendi et al., 2020, p.20).

Sustainable fashion consumption is essential to support the United Nations Sustainable Development Goal (SDG) 12, "Responsible Consumption and Production." It refers to the efficient use of natural resources, minimizing the use of hazardous substances, and reducing pollution and waste production. SDG 12 encourages all parties to consider environmental impact and efficient use of resources at each stage of product production and usage (Akter et al., 2022; Yusof et al., 2022).

This study utilized the theory of planned behavior (TPB). Previous research has demonstrated that the TPB can explain behavior and intention. The TPB was initially used in social psychology, health and sports, education, marketing, organizational behavior, and another field. According to this theory, any desired behavior is influenced or initiated by someone's intention. This intention is triggered based on attitude, subjective norm, and perceived behavioral control. These three factors are hypothesized to determine the intention to perform the desired behavior (Ajzen, 1991). Although the TPB has been widely used in several research studies, different results were found. TPB has repeatedly criticized for not considering sufficient construction of human behavior. There needs to be more prediction and actual behavior, which opens opportunities for further research to consider other variables to increase the utilization of the TPB.

Therefore, this study contributes to the current literature by extending the TPB by adding several new variables to the original model. This study aims to determine the role of pro-environmental attitude, environmental knowledge, subjective norm, price incentive, and perceived behavioral control in influencing sustainable fashion consumption among young Malaysian consumers. This study also aimed to assess a conceptual framework emphasizing the mediating influence of environmental value. This study also provides a new understanding of the function of the mediator effect since few studies have explored this matter in the literature. To the best of our knowledge, the role of environmental value has yet to be studied in the context of sustainable fashion.

An additional aim was to explain the determinants of sustainable fashion consumption for young consumers known as Generation Z. According to Tapscott (2008), the demographics of the population can be categorized into six generations, namely, 1) pre-baby boomers (born in 1945 and before), 2) the baby boomers (born between 1946 - 1964), 3) generation X (born between 1965 – 1976), 4) generation Y (born between 1977 – 1997), 5) Zoomers or generation Z (born between 1998 to 2009), and 6) generation A (born in 2010). This study focuses on Generation Z consumers aged 18-25. According to the Stats Geoportal data disclosed by the Department of Statistics of Malaysia, Malaysia has a population of around 2.9 million young people. The younger generation has been found to normalize the idea of clothing recycling, and they like to reinvent their clothing and accessories.

LITERATURE REVIEW AND THEORETICAL FRAMEWORK

Extending Theory of Planned Behavior (TPB)

The theory of planned behavior (TPB) provides a framework for studying human action and behavior. Specifically, the intention is influenced by three determinants, namely a) attitude that leads to a desired or unwanted behavior, b) subjective norms, which are perceptions of social pressure or people around, and c) notions of perceived behavioral control to increase self-confidence to control the behavior. Based on Figure 1, all three constructs contribute to initiating intentions and subsequently implementing behavior (Ajzen, 1991). Actual behavior will be able to be implemented when an individual can identify and fully control the desired behavior, where it is triggered by solid intentions (Ajzen & Manstead, 2007). This theory also suggests that an intention to do behavior could be influenced directly by the perceived behavior control when self-efficacy beyond realistic action causes an individual to continue performing the desired behavior.

Some previous research has successfully utilised the TPB to show the impact of TPB predictors on behavioural changes (e.g., Nguyen, 2023). For example, Djafarova and Foots' (2022) research findings show that young consumers' awareness and desire towards ethical and environmental issues significantly influence ethical consumption. Similarly, the results of Rotimi et al. (2023) show positive relationships between all the TPB factors on garment recycling. Conversely, some research results show the difference or gap between favorable attitudes and actual practice. Tiwari et al. (2023) and Sujood et al. (2023) have discovered that perceived behavioral control did not influence intention. The gap revealed that not all predictors always translate into action. The expert also revealed that the TPB model was not considered suitable for explaining behavior since it only focuses on limited variables and ignores other important variables such as feeling or emotion. Thus, it is necessary for this study to extend the TPB utilization and to address the gap that occurs in this theory. Research in the future is expected to expand and enrich the discussion about the TPB. Like previous studies (e.g., Annamdevula et al., 2023; Sann et al., 2023), our current study aims to extend the TPB by examining the intervening influences of environmental value on the relationships between pro-environmental attitude, environmental knowledge, subjective norm, price incentive, perceived behavioral control, and young consumer sustainable fashion consumption.

Figure 1. A framework of the TPB (adapted from Ajzen, 1991)

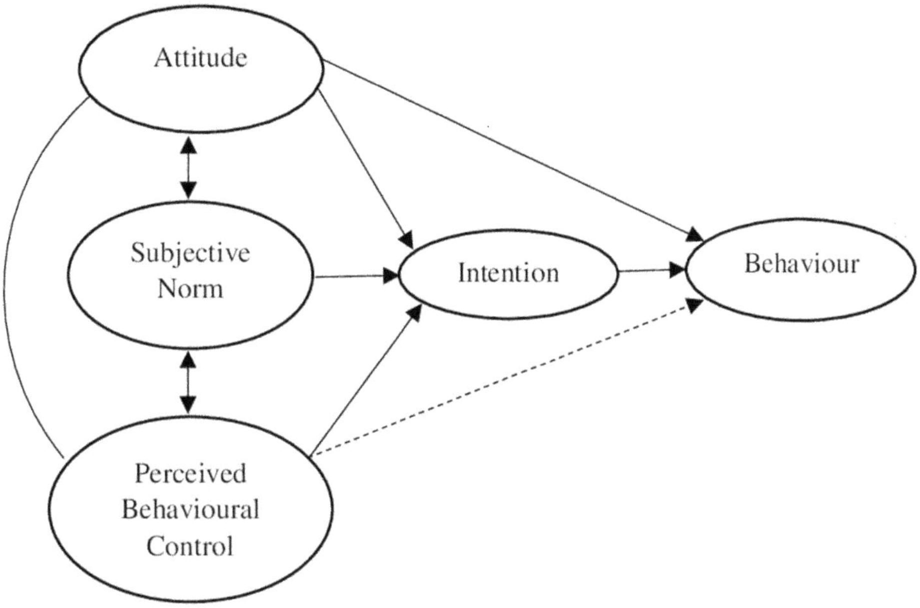

Sustainable Fashion Consumption

The basis of a sustainable fashion business model is the conservation of natural resources, the low environmental impact of the materials used, the reduction of the carbon footprint, and respect for the economic and working environment (Pal & Gander, 2018). The fashion industry already has many famous designers, models, and celebrities championing sustainable fashion. These include Lucy Tammam, Stella McCartney, Amour Vert, Edun, Shalom Harlow, and Summer Rayne Oakes. Sustainable fashion is gradually gaining its place in the industry. There is also growth in organizing competitions, festivals, events, classes, and blogs. For example, Portland Fashion Week features only 100 percent (%) eco-friendly designs. Sustainable Fashion Day has also been held in Madrid for four years. In Argentina, Verde Textile offers products with zero environmental impact and 100% social commitment. Heavy Eco is the first fashion company established in prison to produce sustainable clothing. Consumers need to understand the effects of materials and fabrics when shopping sustainably. Understanding the impact of the materials that make up our clothes is essential (Rahman & Koszewska, 2020). A good rule of thumb is to avoid synthetic fibers like polyester because their composition involves fossil fuels that take years to break down.

Consumers should also pay attention to natural fabrics such as organic cotton (Paço et al., 2021). The best thing is to look for clothes with sustainable certificates to ensure that the fabrics and materials they use have a limited impact on the planet (Lee et al., 2020). Examples are the Global Organic Textile Standard for cotton and wool, the Leather Working Group Certificate for leather or stickers, and the Forest Stewardship Council Certificate for rubber fibers. In addition, one way to tell if a company is genuinely interested in reducing its environmental impact is to see if it is committed to sustainable scientific standards (Lee et al., 2020).

For example, the Burberry brand is required to comply with the Paris Agreement to reduce emissions. Sustainability companies like Mara Hoffman and Sheep Inc. Champion agricultural techniques such as direct seeding or cover crops to improve soil quality and protect biodiversity. In Malaysia, local fashion brand Wanzar promotes casual women's fashion made from 100% organic cotton fabric. It is a sustainable initiative to ensure and offer eco-friendly fashion collections. This collection will also please many fashion fans who are part of the consumer group that cares about the environment in Malaysia. Using sustainably sourced organic cotton, the fashion brand also encourages tailoring through fashion designs that are versatile and reusable for long periods. The consumers are always encouraged to read the label, ask about the production of the brand, invest in high-quality clothing that will last longer, choose clothes made with biodegradable and natural fibers, and recycle clothes to give new life to unused accessories (Koszewska, 2021; McEachern et al., 2020).

Fashion designers should be part of promoting sustainable consumption, but unfortunately, public awareness of the importance of conserving nature is less applied in most Asian countries (Claxton & Kent, 2020). Fashion designers and textile manufacturers in Malaysia also need more emphasis on protecting the environmental interests in producing textile products. Thus, the civic awareness campaign must continue motivating people to care for the natural environment (Ortega-Egea & Garca-de-Frutos, 2019). The designer must also know the importance of producing textile and clothing products that can be used, reused, or recycled (Claxton & Kent, 2020; Pal &Gander, 2018). Meanwhile, some studies suggest that manufacturers need to find effective ways to encourage consumers to buy textile products that can be recycled. A study by Ahmad and Zhang (2020) also found that many consumers nowadays are more positive and tend to buy environmentally friendly and recyclable textile or clothing products. A study also found that consumers have begun to realize the advantages of sustainable clothes (Koszewska, 2021). Besides, green marketing campaigns and awareness indirectly influence consumers (Ortega-Egea & García-de-Frutos, 2019).

Pro-Environmental Attitude and Sustainable Fashion Consumption of Young Consumers

Attitude can be defined as an individual's positive or negative evaluation of specific behavioral performance (Ajzen, 1991). According to Schiffman and Kanuk (2007), the components of attitude are cognitive, affective, and behavior. The cognitive dimension refers to the perceptual component or object evaluation .Affective dimensions reflect emotions and feelings related to preferences concerning objects, persons, or actions. The behavioral dimension refers to intention and shapes actions toward the object. Environmental attitudes can be defined as beliefs, influences, and behavioural intentions that a person has regarding activitiesor problems related to the environment (Khare, 2023).The attitude towards the environment is a tendency described by evaluating the assertion or the environment; it is believed to be one of the components that affect its quality, from severaldegrees of kindness and reluctance (Tran et al., 2022). Information about the climate can influencebuyers' mentality. The higher the attitude, the higher the knowledge. The attitude had a positive impact on sustainable fashion consumption. Attitudes are articulations that reflect different preference towards something, the buyer's perspective in buying sustainable fashion. Customer awareness of climate and well-being will influence people's attitudes, causing an increasing demand forsustainable fashion (Bairrada et al., 2023). Razzaq et al. (2018) research shows that attitude and caring significantly influence sustainable fashion consumption. In line with the discussion in the literature on this subject, this study hypothesises that:

H1: A pro-environmental attitude is positively associated with young consumers' behavior towards sustainable fashion consumption.

Environmental Knowledge and Sustainable Fashion Consumption of Young Consumers

Knowledge is recognized in consumer research as a characteristic that affects all decision-making process phases (Ewe &Tjiptono, 2023). Knowledge is a relevant and significant construct that affects how consumers collect information, how information is used in decision-making, and how consumers evaluate products and services (Dhir et al., 2021). Empirical studies have found that someone who has sufficient environmental knowledge will affect responsibilities toward the environment (Grazzini et al., 2021). Khare (2019) explained that there is a positive correlation between knowledge and sustainable fashion consumption. In addition, according to Lee et al. (2020), knowledge of environmental sustainability is a basis of eco-practices such as saving electricity, reusing, reducing, and recycling (3R), and others. Therefore, critical and efficient action towards nature must be disclosed to the younger generation. Knowledge is not something to be stored and transmitted orally. Instead, it is something made and delivered by applying. A high level of knowledge enables society to recognise social progress happening around them, and as a result, they will feel high responsibility to promote sustainable fashion consumption (Grazzini et al., 2021).

Furthermore, their level of education also made them prioritise their income towards sustainable consumption practices (Dhir et al., 2021). However, due to a self-centered lifestyle, many people must pay more attention to sustainability. Thus, previous studies have encouraged the promotion of education from childhood to further increase society's sensitivity toward sustainability (Jorgenson et al., 2019). The application of sustainable practice should also be emphasised toward the community (Dhir et al., 2021; Rausch &Kopplin, 2021). Liu et al. (2021) emphasize that changes in value, attitudes, skills, and behavior towards sustainable fashion will be achieved through effective education, primarily through an in-depth understanding of the issues of a sustainable environment. Thus, the following hypothesis can be proposed.

H2: Environmental knowledge is positively associated with behavior towards sustainable fashion consumption of young consumers.

Subjective Norm and Sustainable Fashion Consumption of Young Consumers

Subjective norms are acceptance and focus on influences such as a friend, peers, or family members that significantly impact individual behavior (Chang & Watchravesringkan, 2018). Subjective norms refer to social sharing and the implementation of certain attitudes from people essential to the individual (Khare, 2023). The two components of subjective norms, according to Ajzen (1991), namely 1) normative beliefs, which are individual beliefs about the extent to which others who are considered essential to them think that they should do or not do certain behaviors, and 2) motivation to fulfill that drives a person directs behavior to achieve goals. This includes drives, hopes, and desires. In addition to positive attitudes, situational factors such as social norms prevailing in the consumer's social environment can also affect sustainable fashion consumption (Hosta &Zabkar, 2021).

Religion is significant in a social structure. Social influence can occur from interpersonal influences such as family, neighbors, or friends and external influences such as mass media or social media. If social expectation encourages a person to perform the behavior, they tend to implement it. Grazzini et al. (2021) found that friends, family, and coworkers are significant components of the norm that can influence the behavior of sustainable fashion consumption. Based on the study of Brandão and da Costa (2021), consumers aware of sustainable fashion's existence in the market will rely less on the advice and recommendations of social groups such as friends, family, and mass media. Based on this argument, the following hypothesis is stated:

H3: Subjective norm is positively associated with young consumers' behavior towards sustainable fashion consumption.

Price Incentive and Sustainable Fashion Consumption of Young Consumers

Consumers need help looking for sustainable fashion due to relatively high prices that affect purchase intention. Sadiq et al. (2021) agree that some consumers need help finding stores that sell cheap and inexpensive sustainable fashion and clothing in the market. Price incentive is often used as a marketing tactic to increase purchase intent and drive product sales (Wang et al., 2019). Price incentives include promotions, limited time offers, and special deals. Product sales can be boosted using tactics of loss aversion; consumers tend to avoid the risk of loss when the purchase reward is offered as a profit, which is used to affect purchase intention (Rajapaksa et al., 2019). Empirical studies show that price incentives positively influence sustainable fashion purchase decisions (Chang et al., 2019).

A study by Schwartz et al. (2019) found that online clothing purchases are motivated by low prices and promotions. Even if customers consider themselves loyal, e-coupon offers can change their buying habits. Price-sensitive buyers also tend to bear the cost of searching for discounted goods. The study also found a positive response to price and online coupon promotions among consumers (Chang et al., 2019). In addition, the market begins to create a strategy to increase sustainable fashion purchases among consumers. Comfort is often associated with the fit of clothing, which is a visual and physical satisfaction with clothing and its function (Park & Lin, 2020). A study by Bozo and Abreu (2019) found that consumers only buy sustainable clothing products if they meet their needs with good aesthetic, functional, and financial benefits. Purchase intention is also influenced by the fabric used to produce the garment, representing the clothing quality (Hayes & Venkatraman, 2016). Big fashion competitors such as Uniqlo and H&M often produce clothes from natural materials such as organic cotton and recycled textiles to make clothes that allow consumers to compare their perception with actual product performance (Park & Lin, 2020). Therefore, this study brings forth the following hypothesis:

H4: Price incentive is positively associated with behavior towards sustainable fashion consumption of young consumers.

Perceived Behavioral Control and Sustainable Fashion Consumption of Young Consumers

Perceived behavioral control refers to the extent to which an individual decides to behave despite being influenced by the environment (Azjen, 1991). People cannot perform a behaviour if they do not believe they have no opportunity to do so, even if they are optimistic about the behaviour and believe the other person will allow it (Abrar et al., 2021). This perceived behavioral control can influence a person's behavior directly or indirectly through behavioral intentions. This behavior depends on the experience and obstacles expected to occur to perform such behavior. Perceived behavioural control refers to the extent to which a person can behave depending on the difficulty and pleasure of acting based on one's experiences and beliefs (Chi et al., 2021). For example, an individual purchases sustainable fashion (attitude towards behavior), followed by the subjective norm of their social environment.

The desire to purchase sustainable fashion will be determined by the perceived behavioral control, whether the individual purchase sustainable apparel. Thus, perceived behavioral control often reflects actual behavioral control (Saricam & Okur, 2019). How easy or difficult it is to perform the behavior depends on internal and external factors such as knowledge, skills, resources, and opportunities for a person to behave (Brandão & Costa, 2021). If a person has control over a particular factor, the individual's intention will increase. On the other hand, if the individual does not have control over the factor, then the intention for the person to do the behavior becomes weak. Thus, the following hypothesis is proposed:

H5: Perceived behavioral control is positively associated with behavior towards sustainable fashion consumption of young consumers.

The Mediating Role of Environmental Value

Environmental value is a discipline of study that debates the value system that needs to exist to justify human actions and whether the actions taken are good or bad for the environment (Li et al., 2019). Environmental value is a concept that refers to the efforts to justify human behavior in the environment that can be applied as a guideline to how humans should interact with the environment. Discussions regarding the environmental value led to categorizing whether behavior is good or bad. Human behavior that cares about sustainable interaction with nature can ensure the survival of nature in the future. Increasing environmental value is essential in building national capacity toward sustainable development (Rendtorff, 2020). Human values serve as guiding principles in human life. A study by Ng et al. (2022) found that the environmental value through practical impacts sustainable behavior and lifestyle. According to Legere and Kang (2020), attitude change and persistent egocentrism should continue in the community because they can minimizes the destruction of the environment. Ecocentrism is this pro-environmental attitude and value that will subsequently change the community's lifestyle in ensuring the responsibility of preserving the environment can be borne together for future generations (Fang et al., 2022; Williams & Hodges, 2022).

Moreover, some studies have categorised the main factors influencing consumer behaviour into two values: individualism and collectivism (Lin et al., 2022). In a way, individualism represents how immense a person focuses on independence. On the other hand, collectivism implies cooperation, assistance, and consideration of group goals relative to individuals. Collectivist individuals tend to be more friendly to the environment, while individuals who are individualists tend to be more unsociable. In this study, we proposed an intermediary role of environmental values. The intermediate variable is a variable that can theoretically affect the relationship between the independent variable and the dependent variable. As such, this study developed the following hypotheses:

H6a: Environmental value mediates the influence of pro-environmental behavior towards sustainable fashion consumption of young consumers.
H6b: Environmental value mediates the influence of environmental knowledge towards sustainable fashion consumption of young consumers.
H6c: Environmental value mediates the influence of subjective norm towards sustainable fashion consumption of young consumers.
H6d: Environmental value mediates the influence of price incentive towards sustainable fashion consumption of young consumers.
H6e: Environmental value mediates the influence of perceived behavioral control towards sustainable fashion consumption of young consumers.

This study assumes that the relationships between pro-environmental attitude, environmental knowledge, subjective norm, price incentive, perceived behavioral control, and sustainable fashion consumption could be mediated by environmental value. Figure 2 shows a conceptual model for this study, formed based on the research hypothesis.

Figure 2. Conceptual model

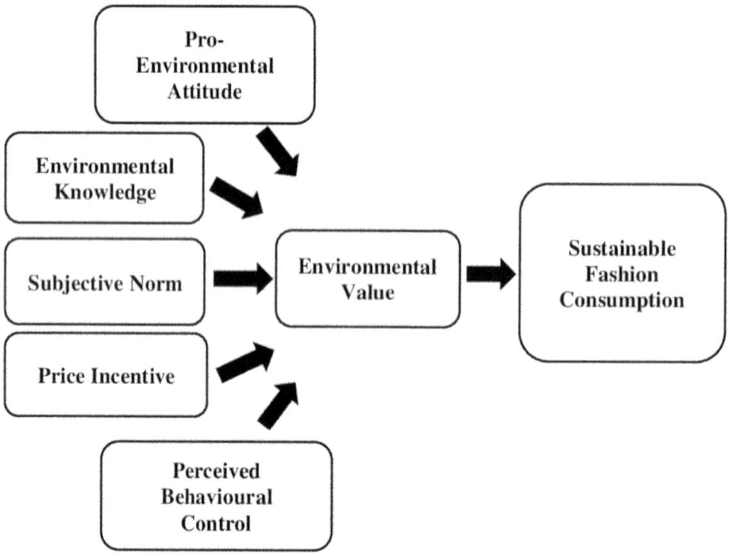

METHODOLOGY

This study used a cross-sectional survey design by applying a quantitative approach. The study population is young Malaysian consumers in the Klang Valley area. The Klang Valley is in the middle of Selangor and Kuala Lumpur. It is the center of industry and commerce in Malaysia. The study population included young consumers in Malaysia. According to Tapscott (2008), generation Z was born between 1998 and 2009 to define the young consumers' age group. Thus, this study has focused on those aged

18-25. From the Stats Geoportal data disclosed by the Department of Statistics of Malaysia, Malaysia has around 5.8 million young generation population. Selangor and Kuala Lumpur areas have 1,000,000 and 272,600young generation population, respectively (Department of Statistics of Malaysia, 2023).

Based on the Monte Carlo study, the minimum sample size required to reduce bias in all structural equation modeling estimates is 200 (Loehlin, 1998). Thus, using a combination of stratified random and purposive sampling techniques, the sample size of this study was 500 young consumers. The survey was administered using the Google form. It was sent to potential respondents through electronic mailing lists and social networks. Research data was collected using a modified questionnaire adapted from previous studies such as Deng (2015), Brandão and da Costa (2021), and Carlson et al. (2019). The questionnaire contains four main sections, namely 1) demographic information, 2) independent variables (i.e., pro-environmental attitude, environmental knowledge, subjective norm, price incentive, and perceived behavioral control), 3) mediating variable (i.e., environmental value), and 4) dependent variable (i.e., sustainable fashion consumption) (see Table 1).

A Likert scale from 1 (strongly disagree) to 5 (strongly agree) was used to measure each item in the questionnaire. In addition, Cronbach's alpha value was calculated for all variables. Cronbach's alpha is explained as excellent when the value is more than 0.9 and assumed as good ($0.8 \leq \alpha < 0.9$), acceptable ($0.7 \leq \alpha < 0.8$), questionable ($0.6 \leq \alpha < 0.7$), poor ($0.5 \leq \alpha < 0.6$), and unacceptable ($\alpha < 0.5$) (Montshiwa & Moroke, 2014). The reliability requirement for the variables was good and acceptable, and their respective values are depicted in Table 1.

Table 1. Measurement of the variable

Variable	Items		Cronbach's Alpha	Source
Pro-Environmental Attitude	PEA1	For me, having a sustainable clothing consumption behavior is: Good	0.860	Deng (2015)
	PEA2	Wise		
	PEA3	Pleasant		
	PEA4	Positive		
	PEA5	Satisfactory		
	PEA6	Favorable		
	PEA7	Desirable		
Environmental Knowledge	K1	Chemical pollutants are produced while manufacturing synthetic or manufactured fibers such as polyester.	0.760	Brandão & da Costa (2021)
	K2	Disposable diapers have substantially contributed to the number of textile products discarded in landfills.		
	K3	Phosphate-containing laundry detergents can be a source of water pollution.		
	K4	The fashion industry has contributed to a decline in the ecological environment.		

Table 1 continued

Variable	Items		Cronbach's Alpha	Source
Subjective Norm	N1	People who are important to me think I should have sustainable clothing consumption behavior.	0.753	Brandão & da Costa (2021)
	N2	People who are important to me would approve of my sustainable clothing consumption behavior.		
	N3	Most influential people to me would have a sustainable clothing consumption behavior.		
Price Incentive	P1	Based on the price, sustainable clothing is very economical.	0.852	Brandão & da Costa (2021)
	P2	Sustainable clothing is good value for the money.		
	P3	The price for sustainable clothing is acceptable.		
	P4	Sustainable clothing is a bargain.		
Perceived Behavioral Control	PCB1	I have great control over purchasing sustainable fashion.	0.809	Deng (2015)
	PCB2	I am confident that I can buy sustainable fashion.		
	PCB3	It would be easy for me to buy sustainable fashion.		
Environmental Value	V1	Performing pro-environmental behavior is fun.	0.777	Carlson et al. (2019)
	V2	Performing pro-environmental behavior is entertaining.		
	V3	Performing pro-environmental behavior is helpful for me.		
	V4	Performing pro-environmental behavior is functional for me.		
	V5	Participating in pro-environmental behavior could help me build a better relationship with my friend.		
Sustainable Fashion Consumption	S1	I had a sustainable clothing consumption behavior.	0.845	Brandão & da Costa (2021)
	S2	I frequently buy sustainable clothing.		
	S3	I tried to have a sustainable clothing consumption behavior.		

The data analysis technique used in this research was the Structural model equation modelling (SEM). SEM is a second-generation multivariate analysis technique that allows researchers to test the relationship between complex variables to obtain a comprehensive model picture. In SEM, there are two types of models, namely, the measurement model (i.e., confirmatory factor analysis) and the structural model. Before structural model analysis, a model can be considered good if empirical data conceptually and theoretically support the model. The goodness of fit test is used for path analysis, which uses the following measurements (Hair et al., 2010):

- Goodness-of-fit Index (GFI) (≥ 0.90)
- Tucker-Lewis Index (TLI) (≥ 0.90)
- Comparative Fit Index (CFI) (≥ 0.90)
- Normed Fit Index (NFI) (≥ 0.90)
- Root Mean Square Error of Approximation (RMSEA) (<0.08)
- Chi-Square/degree of freedom ratio ($\chi 2/df$) (<5.0)

This study further assessed convergent and discriminant validity. Convergent validity shows whether a test designed to assess a particular construct correlates with other tests that assess the same construct. According to Hair et al. (2010), convergent validity is established when composite reliability (CR) and average variance extracted (AVE) are more significant than 0.70 and 0.50, respectively.

Next, the Fornell-Larcker (1981) criterion and cross-loading examination were referred to in determining the discriminant validity. Discriminant validity is established when the square root of AVE is greater than the correlation and the correlation value between the constructs is more than 0.50 and below 0.85 (Fornell & Larcker, 1981). The discriminant validity assessment ensures that the constructs have the most robust relationships with their indicators (Hair et al., 2010). Structural model analysis was used to test the mediation effect in the final step. PROCESS macro confirmed the mediational model (Hayes & Preacher, 2013).

FINDINGS

Demographic Profiles

The data were collected from 500 participants. The final valid responses include 481 young consumers. Based on Table 2, 246 females (51.1%) and 235 males (48.9%) participated in the survey. Regarding age group, most respondents were 21-25 years old (n=311, 64.7%), and the rest were 18-20 years old (n=170, 35.3%). Most participants live in Selangor (n=245, 50.9%), and the rest live in Kuala Lumpur (n=236, 49.1%). From the education level, a majority of 81.7% of the participants obtained undergraduate qualifications (n=393). This is followed by the postgraduate level (n=54, 11.2%) and *Sijil Tinggi Pelajaran Malaysia*/Foundation (n=34, 7.1%). Next, most of the respondents in this study were private sector employees (n=251, 52.2%). Most respondents live in small- or middle-sized towns (n=312, 64.9%). Finally, when asked about the frequency of purchasing sustainable fashion clothing items, most bought 6-10 apparel each year (n=227, 47.2%).

Measurement Model

The confirmatory factor analysis (CFA) outcome revealed that the model met the recommended fit requirements (Chisq/df = 2.811, CFI = 0.94, GFI = 0.91, TLI = 0.96, RMSEA = 0.032). The convergent validity is tested based on the Average Variance Extracted (AVE) and composite reliability (CR). The values of AVE must be greater than 0.50, and the value of CR must be greater than 0.70 (Fornell & Larcker, 1981). The results show that all values meet the requirements (see Table 3).

Next, the Fornell-Larcker (1981) criterion and cross-loading examination were referred to in determining the discriminant validity. Discriminant validity is established when the square root of AVE is greater than the correlation and the correlation value between the constructs is more than 0.50 and below 0.85 (Fornell & Larcker, 1981). The discriminant validity assessment ensures that the constructs have the most robust relationships with their indicators (Hair et al., 2010). Discriminant validity is also established when the square root of AVE is greater than the correlation (Fornell & Larcker, 1981). Based on Table 4, this study has met the prescribed criteria. Thus, the variables are unrelated to each other.

Table 2. Demographic profile

Profile		Frequency (n)	Percentage (%)
Gender	Male	235	48.9
	Female	246	51.1
Age	18-20	170	35.3
	21-25	311	64.7
Area of Living	Selangor	245	50.9
	Kuala Lumpur	236	49.1
Highest Academic Qualification	*Sijil Pelajaran Malaysia* (Secondary School)	0	0
	Sijil Tinggi Pelajaran Malaysia/Foundation	34	7.1
	Undergraduate	393	81.7
	Postgraduate	54	11.2
	Other	0	0
Current Status	Public Sector	78	16.2
	Private Sector	251	52.2
	Unemployed	5	1
	Self-employment	100	20.8
	Full-time Students	47	9.8
	Other	0	0
Living Environment	Rural area or village	41	8.5
	Small- or middle-sized town	312	64.9
	Large town	128	26.6
Frequency of Purchasing Sustainable Fashion Clothing	Less than five apparels per year	167	34.7
	6-10 apparels per year	227	47.2
	More than ten apparels per year	87	18.1

Table 3. Measurement of variation

Variable	Items	Item Loadings	AVE	CR
Pro-Environmental Attitude	PEA1	0.710	0.850	0.750
	PEA2	0.706		
	PEA3	0.711		
	PEA4	0.714		
	PEA5	0.709		
	PEA6	0.710		
	PEA7	0.714		
Environmental Knowledge	K1	0.617	0.860	0.780
	K2	0.667		
	K3	0.712		
	K4	0.759		

Table 3 continued

Variable	Items	Item Loadings	AVE	CR
Subjective Norm	N1	0.823	0.839	0.800
	N2	0.876		
	N3	0.899		
Price Incentive	P1	0.667	0.805	0.715
	P2	0.698		
	P3	0.700		
	P4	0.742		
Perceived Behavioral Control	PCB1	0.712	0.830	0.740
	PCB2	0.700		
	PCB3	0.715		
Environmental Value	V1	0.693	0.810	0.788
	V2	0.645		
	V3	0.612		
	V4	0.654		
	V5	0.634		
Sustainable Fashion Consumption	S1	0.735	0.870	0.821
	S2	0.721		
	S3	0.667		

Structural Model

As shown in Table 5, it was discovered that pro-environmental attitude (β=0.327, p>0.001), environmental knowledge (β=0.327, p>0.001), and perceived behavioural control (β=0.327, p>0.001) have a significant influence on sustainable fashion consumption. Thus, H1, H2, and H5 were accepted. This means young consumers' sustainable fashion consumption increases per unit associated with pro-environmental attitude, environmental knowledge, and perceived behavioural control when other predictors are constant. On the other hand, the results found that subjective norm (β= 0.012, p<0.001) and price incentive (β= 0.018, p<0.001) insignificantly influence young consumers' sustainable fashion consumption. Thus, H3 and H4 were not accepted.

The results also confirmed that environmental knowledge significantly influences young consumers' sustainable fashion consumption (β =0.469, p<0.001). This means young consumers' sustainable fashion consumption increases per unit associated with environmental value when other predictors are constant. Moreover, direct relationships between pro-environmental attitude (β=0.311, p>0.001), environmental knowledge (β=0.265, p>0.001), subjective norm (β=0.371, p<0.001), price incentive (β=0.396, p<0.001), perceived behavioral control (β=0.319, p>0.001), and environmental value are also significantly tested. This indicated that an increase in the environmental value per unit is associated with a pro-environmental attitude, environmental knowledge, subjective norm, price incentive, and perceived behavioral control when other predictors are constant.

Table 4. Discriminative validity assessment

No.		1	2	3	4	5	6	7
1	PEA	**0.922**						
2	EK	0.604	**0.927**					
3	SN	0.620	0.726	**0.916**				
4	PI	0.693	0.653	0.700	**0.897**			
5	PBC	0.754	0.676	0.701	0.707	**0.911**		
6	EV	0.760	0.720	0.658	0.611	0.688	**0.900**	
7	SFC	0.742	0.680	0.700	0.654	0.722	0.768	**0.933**

Note: Values in the diagonal show the square root of AVE; Pro-Environmental Attitude, PEA; Environmental Knowledge, EK; Subjective Norm, SN; Price Incentive, PI; Perceived Behavioral Control, PBC; Environmental Value, EV; Sustainable Fashion Consumption, SFC.

Table 5. Direct, indirect, and total effects in the structural model

Standardized Direct Effects			Std. Estimate β
Sustainable Fashion Consumption		**Pro-Environmental Attitude**	**0.418*** **
Sustainable Fashion Consumption		Environmental Knowledge	0.324***
Sustainable Fashion Consumption		Subjective Norm	0.012
Sustainable Fashion Consumption		Price Incentive	0.018
Sustainable Fashion Consumption		Perceived Behavioral Control	0.388***
Sustainable Fashion Consumption		Environmental Value	0.469***
Environmental Value		Pro-Environmental Attitude	0.311***
Environmental Value		Environmental Knowledge	0.265***
Environmental Value		Subjective Norm	0.371***
Environmental Value		Price Incentive	0.396***
Environmental Value		Perceived Behavioral Control	0.319***
Standardized Indirect Effects (Mediation Effect via Environmental Value)			
Sustainable Fashion Consumption		Pro-Environmental Attitude	0.146***
Sustainable Fashion Consumption		Environmental Knowledge	0.124***
Sustainable Fashion Consumption		Subjective Norm	0.174***
Sustainable Fashion Consumption		Price Incentive	0.186***
Sustainable Fashion Consumption		Perceived Behavioral Control	0.150***
Standardized Total Effects (Direct Effect + Indirect Effect)			
Sustainable Fashion Consumption		Pro-Environmental Attitude	0.564***
Sustainable Fashion Consumption		Environmental Knowledge	0.448***
Sustainable Fashion Consumption		Subjective Norm	0.186***
Sustainable Fashion Consumption		Price Incentive	0.204***
Sustainable Fashion Consumption		Perceived Behavioral Control	0.538***

Note: ***Paths are significant at the 1% level ($p < 0.01$). ***Indirect effects are significant at the 1% level with bootstrap at 5000 and bias-corrected percentile method

Next, the mediation effect was tested. Path coefficients representing unstandardised regression weights and standard errors in mediation analysis can be defined as paths a, b, c, and c'. Path a represents the direct influence of independent variables on a mediator. At the same time, path b represents the direct influence of the mediator on a dependent variable. Path c' indicates the direct influence of independent variables on the dependent variables. Indirect effect or mediation weight is calculated by multiplying paths a and b. The c path coefficient represents the total effect of the direct and indirect path (c= c' + ab). The model would have partial mediation if all analyzed paths were significant ($p<0.01$). In contrast, if all analyzed paths were significant ($p<0.01$), however, path c' is insignificant, meaning the model has complete mediation.

As shown in Table 5, the results confirm that the relationship between pro-environmental attitude ($\beta=0.146$, $p>0.001$), environmental knowledge ($\beta=0.124$, $p>0.001$), perceived behavioral control ($\beta=0.150$, $p>0.001$), and young consumers sustainable fashion consumption are partially mediated by environmental value. Hence, H6a, H6b, and H6ewere accepted. In other words, pro-environmental attitude, environmental knowledge, and perceived behavioral control have a significant impact on sustainable fashion consumption, and they also have a significant impact on environmental value, which has a significant impact on young consumers' sustainable fashion consumption.

On the other hand, results confirm that the relationship between subjective norm ($\beta=0.174$, $p>0.001$), price incentive ($\beta=0.186$, $p>0.001$), and young consumers' sustainable fashion consumption are fully mediated by environmental value. Hence, H6c and H6d were accepted. The results mean that subjective norm and price incentive cannot directly impact sustainable fashion consumption without the appearance of environmental value. The total effects were also calculated for mediating paths, adding indirect and direct effects (Hayes & Preacher, 2013).

DISCUSSION

Consistent with the previous studies such as Abrar et al. (2021), Bairrada et al. (2023), Chi et al. (2021), and Khare (2023), the findings confirm the role of pro-environmental attitude, environmental knowledge, and perceived behavioral control on sustainable fashion consumption. Like Legere and Kang (2020) and Li et al. (2019), the results also confirmed that the environmental value significantly influences young consumers' sustainable fashion consumption. Furthermore, results show that environmental value mediates the relationship between pro-environmental attitude, environmental knowledge, subjective norm, price incentive, perceived behavioural control, and sustainable fashion consumption. The environmental value supports preserving and conserving the environment (Li et al., 2019; Williams &Hodges, 2022). Religion is the main element in forming values, beliefs, and norms. For instance, Islam supports sustainable development as implemented by the authority without eliminating the value of community health and safety and protecting the environment is the primary duty of human beings. Value creates appreciation and moral obligations toward preserving the environment and ecosystem (Fang et al., 2022; Rendtorff, 2020).Empirical studies have found that environmental education is one of the efforts to produce a knowledgeable and ethical society (Dhir et al., 2021). Environmental education allows everyone to acquire the values, attitudes, and skills required to protect and improve the environment (Jorgenson et al., 2019).

This study highlights and proves the influence of pro-environmental attitude, environmental knowledge, subjective norm, price incentive, and perceived behavioral control on young consumers' sustainable fashion consumption behavior. The result of this study also validates the direct influence of perceived behavioral control on behavior, which has been highlighted in the TPB model. TPB has mentioned that the perceived behavior control could directly influence the behavior without solid desire or intention. Moreover, the results also advance the TPB by highlighting the significance of the mediating role of environmental value. To the best of the authors' knowledge, the current article is among the pioneer empirical studies to develop a sustainable fashion consumption model by including this mediating variable: environmental value. Most studies assess the enablers of sustainable fashion consumption and individual characteristics (e.g., socio-economic status, personalities, and values) on the decision to purchase sustainable fashion, and the examination of causal path relationships needs to be addressed. Thus, past studies have provided a partial picture of the enablers and barriers of sustainable fashion consumption. Environmental value could jointly shape the individual's behavior toward buying sustainable fashion. However, no empirical investigation on this subject exists using environmental value as a mediator of the relationships between pro-environmental attitude, environmental knowledge, subjective norm, price incentive, perceived behavioral control, and sustainable fashion consumption of young consumers. This study hopes to contribute new insights to the current environmental and sustainability studies literature.

PRACTICAL AND MANAGERIAL IMPLICATIONS

As practical implications, various parties, including the government, responsible bodies, textile producers, fashion designers, consumer associations, society, and non-governmental organizations (NGOs), must play a vital role in improving sustainable fashion consumption among young consumers. It is recommended that the primary and secondary school curriculum apply environmental education to sustainable production and consumption (Jorgenson et al., 2019). This initial stage is crucial for shaping individual behavior. In this aspect, the teacher is essential in guiding and encouraging the younger generation to practice a sustainable way of life.

The government also needs to step up more campaigns to educate young consumers and the public on the importance of sustainable fashion through various channels such as newsletters, television, social media, radio, and exhibitions (Ortega-Egea & García-de-Frutos, 2019). The campaign needs to be intensified throughout the country. In addition, the government can also encourage the purchase of sustainable fashion through legislation. For example, parents must buy sustainable school uniforms. The government must also cooperate with the producers and retailers to form an eco-friendly certification scheme and guidelines for explicit advertising. In addition, the government and its agencies need to develop more apps or platforms to promote Preloved selling. The Carousell is said to be more preferred by Malaysians than other platforms due to its user interface, and we need more platforms such Carousell.

Retailers and designers must explore new ways and technologies of designing and using new raw materials to make their collections. H&M Malaysia, for instance, has provided a discount voucher for recycling old clothes at H&M. Under the "Let's Close the Loop" campaign initiative, customers will receive a 15% discount voucher for one medium-sized bag of clothes. H&M is limited to only two medium-sized bags per person in a day. In addition, retailers also need to reduce the price of sustainable fashion or clothes to ensure affordabilityto most consumers (Schwartz et al., 2019). In this case, the government also contributes by subsidising the price of sustainable products (Chang et al., 2019).

The relevant agencies need to cooperate with NGOs to develop more collection centers or ease the process of cloth collection. For example, *Rumah Amal Limpahan Kasih (RLAK)* has provided a service to collect used clothes without charge, but it is limited to the Klang Valley area only. More initiatives need to be implemented. Moreover, consumer associations and NGOs should proactively promote environmentally friendly products and encourage sustainable fashion consumerism practices. These associations must educate users on how to avoid or minimize their non-recycling purchase's impact on the environment—for example, implementing DIY workshops to transform old clothes into new things like bags, blankets, and even new clothes since not everyone is good at sewing and very diligent about DIY. Moreover, these associations also need to educate the consumers to boycott products that negatively impact the environment.

Top artists or influencers will be fashion models for young consumers (Cheah et al., 2019; Fan et al., 2023). For example, K-pop culture has emerged as a new phenomenon in the era of globalization that has become a trend in society worldwide. Hence, local artists and celebrities, including social media influencers and iconic leaders, must be trendsetters for sustainable clothing.

FUTURE RESEARCH

This study has several limitations that may affect its findings. The study data were collected through a questionnaire in the form of self-reporting from one source, which allows the occurrence of common method bias (MacKenzie & Podsakoff, 2012). However, some steps have been taken to reduce the possibility of this problem. For example, the control over the procedure in the questionnaire administration includes ensuring aspects such as the confidentiality guarantee, the order of questionnaire items broken into specific parts, and specific instructions given for each section. Harman's method single-factor test is also an indicator used to inspect for common method bias. Data from various sources can further strengthen the findings of this study. Next, this research only took samples in two areas (i.e., Selangor and Kuala Lumpur). Samples from other cities that are wider can be compared with the results of this study. Furthermore, this study is cross-sectional. The relationship pattern examined is a momentary portrait that describes the relationships that occur during data collection, and the dynamics of changing consumer behavior can change at any time. Accordingly, the relationship between variables cannot be interpreted as causal. Future researchers interested in confirming this study's findings should use a longitudinal design. Hence, all respondents' answers are based on their genuine attitudes and behavior, not momentary emotions.

CONCLUSION

Today's consumers chase fast fashion, which can produce more unsold items and waste. This creates a more significant push to move from a linear economy to a cyclical economy and build a more sustainable culture where we care about our consumption. Waste such as textile products can be reused to produce other textiles with various uses. It is necessary to raise awareness among young consumers about purchasing recyclable products or items made from recycled materials. Society needs to realize the importance of recycling for environmental sustainability. Otherwise, adverse effects such as air pollution, water pollution, and carbon dioxide emissions will occur. Zero waste is a philosophy that encourages the reuse of materials where any waste sent to landfills is minimal. Sustainable fashion consumption is vital to zero waste; all parties must work together (Grazzini et al., 2021). With the cooperation of all parties, environmental pollution can inevitably be overcome (Rafie et al., 2021).

REFERENCES

Abrar, M., Sibtain, M. M., & Shabbir, R. (2021). Understanding purchase intention towards eco-friendly clothing for generation Y & Z. *Cogent Business & Management*, *8*(1), 1997247. doi:10.1080/23311975.2021.1997247

Ahmad, W., & Zhang, Q. (2020). Green purchase intention: Effects of electronic service quality and customer green psychology. *Journal of Cleaner Production*, *267*, 122053. doi:10.1016/j.jclepro.2020.122053

Ajzen, I. (1991). The theory of planned behavior. *Organizational Behavior and Human Decision Processes*, *50*(2), 179–211. doi:10.1016/0749-5978(91)90020-T

Ajzen, I., & Manstead, A. S. (2007). Changing health-related behaviors: An approach based on the theory of planned behavior. In M. Hewstone, H. Schut, J. De Wit, K. Van Den Bos, & M. Stroebe (Eds.), *The scope of social psychology: Theory and applications* (pp. 43–63). Psychology Press.

Akter, M. M. K., Haq, U. N., Islam, M. M., & Uddin, M. A. (2022). Textile-apparel manufacturing and material waste management in the circular economy: A conceptual model to achieve sustainable development goals (SDG) 12 for Bangladesh. *Cleaner Environmental Systems, 4*. 100070.doi.org/10.1016/j.cesys.2022.100070

Annamdevula, S., Nudurupati, S. S., Pappu, R. P., & Sinha, R. (2023). Moral obligation for recycling among youth: Extended models of the theory of planned behavior. *Young Consumers*, *24*(2), 165–183. doi:10.1108/YC-05-2022-1520

Bairrada, C. M., Coelho, A. F. D. M., & Moreira, J. R. M. (2023). Attitudes towards ethical consumption in clothing: Comparing Peruvian and Portuguese consumers. *Journal of International Consumer Marketing*. 1-17.doi.org/10.1080/08961530.2023.2200221

Brandão, A., & da Costa, A. G. (2021). Extending the theory of planned behavior to understand the effects of barriers towards sustainable fashion consumption. *European Business Review*, *33*(5), 742–774. doi:10.1108/EBR-11-2020-0306

Buzzo, A., & Abreu, M. J. (2019). Fast fashion, fashion brands & sustainable consumption. In S. Muthu (Ed.), *Fast fashion, fashion brands, and sustainable consumption, textile science and clothing technology*. Springer. doi:10.1007/978-981-13-1268-7_1

Carlson, J., Wyllie, J., Rahman, M. M., & Voola, R. (2019). Enhancing brand relationship performance through customer participation and value creation in social media brand communities. *Journal of Retailing and Consumer Services*, *50*, 333–341. doi:10.1016/j.jretconser.2018.07.008

Chang, H. J., & Watchravesringkan, K. T. (2018). Who are sustainably minded apparel shoppers? An investigation of the influencing factors of sustainable apparel consumption. *International Journal of Retail & Distribution Management*, *46*(2), 148–162. doi:10.1108/IJRDM-10-2016-0176

Chang, K. C., Hsu, C. L., Hsu, Y. T., & Chen, M. C. (2019). How green marketing, perceived motives, and incentives influence behavioral intentions. *Journal of Retailing and Consumer Services*, *49*, 336–345. doi:10.1016/j.jretconser.2019.04.012

Cheah, J.-H., Ting, H., Cham, T. H., & Memon, M. A. (2019). The effect of selfie promotion and celebrity endorsed advertisement on decision-making processes: A model comparison. *Internet Research, 29*(3), 552–577. doi:10.1108/IntR-12-2017-0530

Chi, T., Gerard, J., Yu, Y., & Wang, Y. (2021). A study of US consumers' intention to purchase slow fashion apparel: Understanding the key determinants. *International Journal of Fashion Design, Technology and Education, 14*(1), 101–112. doi:10.1080/17543266.2021.1872714

Claxton, S. M., & Kent, A. (2020). The management of sustainable fashion design strategies: An analysis of the designer's role. *Journal of Cleaner Production, 268*, 122112. doi:10.1016/j.jclepro.2020.122112

Deng, X. (2015). Understanding Chinese consumers' ethical purchasing decision-making process: A combination of qualitative and quantitative study. *Geoforum, 67*, 204–213. doi:10.1016/j.geoforum.2015.03.018

Department of Statistics of Malaysia. (2023). *Population based on age group. Department of Statistics of Malaysia*. Retrieved at https://statsgeo.mycensus.gov.my/geostats/mapv2.php#

Dhir, A., Sadiq, M., Talwar, S., Sakashita, M., & Kaur, P. (2021). Why do retail consumers buy green apparel? A knowledge-attitude-behavior-context perspective. *Journal of Retailing and Consumer Services, 59*, 102398. doi:10.1016/j.jretconser.2020.102398

Djafarova, E., & Foots, S. (2022). Exploring ethical consumption of generation Z: Theory of planned behavior. *Young Consumers, 23*(3), 413–431. doi:10.1108/YC-10-2021-1405

Ewe, S. Y., & Tjiptono, F. (2023). Green behavior among Gen Z consumers in an emerging market: Eco-friendly versus non-eco-friendly products. *Young Consumers, 24*(2), 234–252. doi:10.1108/YC-06-2022-1533

Fan, F., Chan, K., Wang, Y., Li, Y., & Prieler, M. (2023). How influencers' social media posts have an influence on audience engagement among young consumers. *Young Consumers, 24*(4), 427–444. doi:10.1108/YC-08-2022-1588

Fang, W. T., Hassan, A. A., & LePage, B. A. (2022). Environmental ethics: Modelling for values and choices. In W. T. Fang, A. A. Hassan, & B. A. LePage (Eds.), The living environmental education: Sound Science towards a cleaner, safer, and healthier future (pp. 151–174). Academic Press.

Fishbein, M., & Ajzen, I. (1975). *Belief, attitude, intention, and behavior: An introduction to theory and research*. Addison–Wesley.

Fornell, C., & Larcker, D. F. (1981). Structural equation models with unobservable variables and measurement error: Algebra and statistics. *JMR, Journal of Marketing Research, 18*(3), 382–388. doi:10.1177/002224378101800313

Grazzini, L., Acuti, D., & Aiello, G. (2021). Solving the puzzle of sustainable fashion consumption: The role of consumers' implicit attitudes and perceived warmth. *Journal of Cleaner Production, 287*, 125579. doi:10.1016/j.jclepro.2020.125579

Hair, J. F. Jr, Matthews, L. M., Matthews, R. L., & Sarstedt, M. (2017). PLS-SEM or CB-SEM: Updated guidelines on which method to use. *International Journal of Multivariate Data Analysis, 1*(2). 107–123. doi.org/10.1504/IJMDA.2017.087624

Hayes, A. F., & Preacher, K. J. (2013). Conditional processing modeling: Using structural equation modeling to examine contingent causal processes. In G. R. Hancock & R. O. Mueller (Eds.), *Structural equation modeling: A second course* (pp. 219–266). IAP Information Age Publishing.

Hayes, S. G., & Venkatraman, P. (Eds.). (2016). *Materials and Technology for Sportswear and Performance Apparel* (p. 370). CRC Press.

Hosta, M., & Zabkar, V. (2021). Antecedents of environmentally and socially responsible sustainable consumer behavior. *Journal of Business Ethics*, *171*(2), 273–293. doi:10.1007/s10551-019-04416-0

Jorgenson, S. N., Stephens, J. C., & White, B. (2019). Environmental education in transition: A critical review of recent research on climate change and energy education. *The Journal of Environmental Education*, *50*(3), 160–171. doi:10.1080/00958964.2019.1604478

Khare, A. (2023). Green apparel buying: Role of past behavior, knowledge, and peer influence in the assessment of green apparel perceived benefits. *Journal of International Consumer Marketing*, *35*(1), 109–125. doi:10.1080/08961530.2019.1635553

Koszewska, M. (2021). Clothing labels: Why are they important for sustainable consumer behavior? *Journal of Consumer Protection and Food Safety, 16*. 1–3.doi.org/10.1007/s00003-021-01319-z

Lee, E. J., Bae, J., & Kim, K. H. (2020). The effect of sustainable certification reputation on consumer behavior in the fashion industry: Focusing on the mechanism of congruence. *Journal of Global Fashion Marketing*, *11*(2), 137–153. doi:10.1080/20932685.2020.1726198

Lee, E. J., Choi, H., Han, J., Kim, D. H., Ko, E., & Kim, K. H. (2020). How to "Nudge" your consumers towards sustainable fashion consumption: An fMRI investigation. *Journal of Business Research*, *117*, 642–651. doi:10.1016/j.jbusres.2019.09.050

Legere, A., & Kang, J. (2020). The role of self-concept in shaping sustainable consumption: A model of slow fashion. *Journal of Cleaner Production*, *258*, 120699. doi:10.1016/j.jclepro.2020.120699

Li, D., Zhao, L., Ma, S., Shao, S., & Zhang, L. (2019). What influences an individual's pro-environmental behavior? A literature review. *Resources, Conservation and Recycling*, *146*, 28–34. doi:10.1016/j.resconrec.2019.03.024

Lin, M. T. B., Zhu, D., Liu, C., & Kim, P. B. (2022). A meta-analysis of antecedents of pro-environmental, behavioral intention of tourists and hospitality consumers. *Tourism Management*, *93*, 104566. doi:10.1016/j.tourman.2022.104566

Liu, Y., Liu, M. T., Perez, A., Chan, W., Collado, J., & Mo, Z. (2021). The importance of knowledge and trust for ethical fashion consumption. *Asia Pacific Journal of Marketing and Logistics*, *33*(5), 1175–1194. doi:10.1108/APJML-02-2020-0081

Loehlin, J. C. (1998). *Latent variable models: An introduction to factor, path, and structural analysis*. Erlbaum.

MacKenzie, S. B., & Podsakoff, P. M. (2012). Common method bias in marketing: Causes, mechanisms, and procedural remedies. *Journal of Retailing*, *88*(4), 542–555. doi:10.1016/j.jretai.2012.08.001

McEachern, M. G., Middleton, D., & Cassidy, T. (2020). Encouraging sustainable behavior change via a social practice approach: A focus on apparel consumption practices. *Journal of Consumer Policy*, *43*(2), 397–418. doi:10.1007/s10603-020-09454-0

Montshiwa, V. T., & Moroke, N. D. (2014). Assessment of the reliability and validity of student-lecturer evaluation questionnaire: A case of Northwest University. *Mediterranean Journal of Social Sciences*, *5*(14), 352. doi:10.5901/mjss.2014.v5n14p352

Mukendi, A., Davies, I., Glozer, S., & McDonagh, P. (2020). Sustainable fashion: Current and future research directions. *European Journal of Marketing*, *54*(11), 2873–2909. doi:10.1108/EJM-02-2019-0132

Muthu, S. S. (Ed.). (2019). *Consumer behavior and sustainable fashion consumption*. Springer. doi:10.1007/978-981-13-1265-6

Ng, P. M. L., & Cheung, C. T. Y. (2022). Why do young people do things for the environment? The effect of perceived values on pro-environmental behavior. *Young Consumers*, *23*(4), 539–554. doi:10.1108/YC-11-2021-1411

Nguyen, T. T., Dang, H. Q., & Le-Anh, T. (2023). Impacts of household norms and trust on organic food purchase behavior under adapted theory of planned behavior. *Journal of Agribusiness in Developing and Emerging Economies*. Advance online publication. doi:10.1108/JADEE-10-2022-0218

Niinimäki, K., Peters, G., Dahlbo, H., Perry, P., Rissanen, T., & Gwilt, A. (2020). The environmental price of fast fashion. *Nature Reviews. Earth & Environment*, *1*(4), 189–200. doi:10.1038/s43017-020-0039-9

Ortega-Egea, J. M., & García-de-Frutos, N. (2019). Greenpeace's Detox campaign: Towards a more sustainable textile industry. In M. M. Galen-Ladero & H. M. Alves (Eds.), *Case studies on social marketing. Management for professionals*. Springer. doi:10.1007/978-3-030-04843-3_4

Paço, A., Leal Filho, W., Ávila, L. V., & Dennis, K. (2021). Fostering sustainable consumer behavior regarding clothing: Assessing trends on purchases, recycling, and disposal. *Textile Research Journal*, *91*(3-4), 373–384. doi:10.1177/0040517520944524

Pal, R., & Gander, J. (2018). Modelling environmental value: An examination of sustainable business models within the fashion industry. *Journal of Cleaner Production*, *184*, 251–263. doi:10.1016/j.jclepro.2018.02.001

Park, H. J., & Lin, L. M. (2020). Exploring attitude–behavior gap in sustainable consumption: Comparison of recycled and upcycled fashion products. *Journal of Business Research*, *117*, 623–628. doi:10.1016/j.jbusres.2018.08.025

Rafie, S. K., Abu, R., Abdul, S. K. S., & Mutalib, A. Z. H. S. (2021). Environmental sustainability practices in rural libraries. *International Journal of Service Management and Sustainability*, *6*(1). 165–176. doi.org/10.24191/ijsms.v6i1.12885

Rajapaksa, D., Gifford, R., Torgler, B., Garcia-Valiñas, M., Athukorala, W., Managi, S., & Wilson, C. (2019). Do monetary and non-monetary incentives influence environmental attitudes and behavior? Evidence from an experimental analysis. *Resources, Conservation and Recycling*, *149*, 168–176. doi:10.1016/j.resconrec.2019.05.034

Rausch, T. M., & Kopplin, C. S. (2021). Bridge the gap: Consumers' purchase intention and behavior regarding sustainable clothing. *Journal of Cleaner Production, 278*, 123882. doi:10.1016/j.jclepro.2020.123882

Razzaq, A., Ansari, N. Y., Razzaq, Z., & Awan, H. M. (2018). The impact of fashion involvement and pro-environmental attitude on sustainable clothing consumption: The moderating role of Islamic religiosity. *SAGE Open, 8*(2). doi:10.1177/2158244018774611

Rendtorff, J. D. (2020). Sustainability, basic ethical principles, and innovation. In J. D. Rendtorff (Ed.), *Handbook of business legitimacy: Responsibility, ethics, and society* (pp. 1631–1658). Springer International Publishing. doi:10.1007/978-3-030-14622-1_48

Rotimi, E. O. O., Johnson, L. W., Kalantari Daronkola, H., Topple, C., & Hopkins, J. (2023). Predictors of consumers' behavior to recycle end-of-life garments in Australia. *Journal of Fashion Marketing and Management, 27*(2), 262–286. doi:10.1108/JFMM-06-2022-0125

Sadiq, M., Bharti, K., Adil, M., & Singh, R. (2021). Why do consumers buy green apparel? The role of dispositional traits, environmental orientation, environmental knowledge, and monetary incentive. *Journal of Retailing and Consumer Services, 62*, 102643. doi:10.1016/j.jretconser.2021.102643

Sann, R., Jansom, S., & Muennaburan, T. (2023). An extension of the theory of planned behavior in Thailand cycling tourism: The mediating role of attractiveness of sustainable alternatives. *Leisure Studies*, 1–15.doi.org/10.1080/02614367.2023.2182346

Saricam, C., & Okur, N. (2019). Analyzing the consumer behavior regarding sustainable fashion using the theory of planned behavior. *Consumer Behavior and Sustainable Fashion Consumption*, 1–37.doi.org/10.1007/978-981-13-1265-6_1

Schiffman, L. G., & Kanuk, L. L. (2007). *Consumer behavior* (9th ed.). Pearson Prentice Hall.

Schwartz, D., Milfont, T. L., & Hilton, D. (2019). The interplay between intrinsic motivation, financial incentives, and nudges in sustainable consumption. In K. Gangl & E. Kirchler (Eds.), *A research agenda for economic psychology* (pp. 87–103). Edward Elgar Publishing. doi:10.4337/9781788116060.00012

Sujood, S. S., Bano, N., & Al Rousan, R. (2023). Understanding intention of Gen Z Indians to visit heritage sites by applying the extended theory of planned behavior: A sustainable approach. *Journal of Cultural Heritage Management and Sustainable Development*. Advance online publication. doi:10.1108/JCHMSD-03-2022-0039

Sussman, R., & Gifford, R. (2019). Causality in the theory of planned behavior. *Personality and Social Psychology Bulletin, 45*(6), 920–933. doi:10.1177/0146167218801363 PMID:30264655

Tapscott, D. (2008). *Grown up digital: How the net generation is changing your world*. McGraw Hill Professional.

Tiwari, A., Kumar, A., Kant, R., & Jaiswal, D. (2023). Impact of fashion influencers on consumers' purchase intentions: Theory of planned behavior and mediation of attitude. *Journal of Fashion Marketing and Management*. Advance online publication. doi:10.1108/JFMM-11-2022-0253

Tonglet, M., Phillips, P. S., & Read, A. D. (2004). Using the theory of planned behavior to investigate the determinants of recycling behavior: A case study from Brixworth, U K. *Resources, Conservation and Recycling, 41*(3), 191–214. doi:10.1016/j.resconrec.2003.11.001

Tran, K., Nguyen, T., Tran, Y., Nguyen, A., Luu, K., & Nguyen, Y. (2022). Eco-friendly fashion among generation Z: Mixed-methods study on price, value image, customer fulfillment, and pro-environmental behavior. *PLoS One, 17*(8), e0272789. doi:10.1371/journal.pone.0272789 PMID:35972928

Wang, Y., Xiang, D., Yang, Z., & Ma, S. S. (2019). Unraveling customer sustainable consumption behaviors in sharing economy: A socio-economic approach based on social exchange theory. *Journal of Cleaner Production, 208*, 869–879. doi:10.1016/j.jclepro.2018.10.139

Williams, A., & Hodges, N. (2022). Adolescent Generation Z and sustainable and responsible fashion consumption: Exploring the value-action gap. *Young Consumers, 23*(4), 651–666. doi:10.1108/YC-11-2021-1419

Yuriev, A., Dahmen, M., Paillé, P., Boiral, O., & Guillaumie, L. (2020). Pro-environmental behaviors through the lens of the theory of planned behavior: A scoping review. *Resources, Conservation and Recycling, 155*, 104660. doi:10.1016/j.resconrec.2019.104660

KEY TERMS AND DEFINITIONS

Environmental Knowledge: Individuals' awareness of environmental issues and general knowledge of facts, concepts, and relationships concerning the natural environment and its major ecosystems.

Environmental Value: A concept that refers to the efforts to justify human behavior in the environment. It can be applied as a guideline for how humans should interact with the environment.

Perceived Behavioral Control: An individual's perceived ease or difficulty of performing the behavior.

Price Incentive: Motivations such as sales and discounts to either supply a good or service or to buy that good or service.

Pro-Environmental Attitude: Environmentally friendly actions such as recycling or taking alternative modes of transportation often require individuals to prioritize the minimal damage to the environment, even benefitting the environment.

Subjective Norm: A social psychological concept that refers to the perceived social pressure or expectation to engage in a particular behavior.

Sustainable Fashion Consumption: Sustainable fashion consumption involves conserving natural resources, using materials with a low environmental impact, reducing one's carbon footprint, and respecting the economic and working environment.

Theory of Planned Behavior: A framework for studying human action and behavior. Specifically, the intention is influenced by three determinants, namely a) attitude that leads to a desired or unwanted behavior, b) subjective norms, which are affected or perceptions of social pressure or people around, and c) notions of perceived behavioral control to increase self-confidence to control the behavior.

Young Consumers: Generation Z was born between 1998 and 2009 to define the young consumers' age group.

Chapter 3
Impact of Green Marketing on Consumer Behavior:
An Investigation Towards Purchasing Decisions, Loyalty, and Willingness to Pay a Premium Price

Saumendra Das
https://orcid.org/0000-0003-4956-4352
GIET University, India

Nayan Deep S. Kanwal
University Putra Malaysia, Malaysia

Udaya Sankar Patro
https://orcid.org/0009-0009-9198-3578
Rayagada Autonomous College, India

Tapaswini Panda
https://orcid.org/0009-0003-8327-9990
Model Degree College, Rayagada, India

Debasis Pani
https://orcid.org/0009-0002-1706-5751
GIACR College, India

Hassan Badawy
https://orcid.org/0000-0001-6536-150X
Luxor University, Egypt

ABSTRACT

This study examines the influence of green marketing on consumer behavior, including purchasing habits, brand allegiance, and inclination to pay a premium. This research provides a clear definition of green marketing and examines different marketing strategies used by firms to advertise environmentally friendly products and services. A quantitative study approach was used, using a sample of 200 consumers who had previously made purchases of ecologically sustainable items or services. The acquired data was analyzed using regression analysis and qualitative statistics. Research findings demonstrate a substantial impact of environmental marketing on customer behavior. Consumers are inclined to choose ecologically friendly items and are prepared to pay a higher price for them when they are exposed to marketing strategies that promote environmental consciousness. Green marketing also enhances client loyalty. The results have substantial ramifications for organizations who are marketing eco-friendly goods and services.

DOI: 10.4018/979-8-3693-3049-4.ch003

1. INTRODUCTION

The urgency for businesses to implement environmentally friendly practices has risen as a result of the present global environmental crisis, which has intensified the focus on sustainability. As a result, green marketing has emerged as a crucial tactic used by businesses to advertise their green goods and services. Green marketing is the practice of promoting goods and services that are friendly to the environment. It comprises a number of marketing initiatives, including branding, packaging, and advertising. Consumer behavior is changing in favor of environmentally friendly items as a result of growing consumer awareness of how their shopping decisions affect the environment. A variety of environmentally friendly products are being offered by businesses in response to the growing demand for sustainable goods and services brought about by environmentally concerned consumers. However, how green marketing affects customer behavior will determine its effectiveness (Martinez, 2015; Moser, 2015).

This study paper's goal is to examine how green marketing affects customer behavior, including decisions about what to buy, brand loyalty, and willingness to pay extra for environmentally friendly goods. By examining customer views of green products, the efficacy of green promotions, and the function of green retail in influencing consumer behavior, this study investigates the connection between green marketing and consumer behavior.

2. AN OVERVIEW OF GREEN MARKETING

The technique of advertising products or services that are favorable to the environment is known as "green marketing." a marketing plan that emphasizes a product or service's positive impact on the environment and incorporates diverse marketing tactics including branding, packaging, and advertising. Green marketing aims to enhance a company's reputation by promoting green products and programs. In recent years, green marketing has gained popularity as a vital technique for businesses to advertise their eco-friendly goods and services (Galati et al., 2023). The ability of green marketing to enhance a company's reputation and brand image is one of its primary advantages. Businesses may show their dedication to sustainability and environmental preservation by supporting environmentally friendly goods and activities. This draws in customers who are concerned about the environment and look for goods and services that reflect their values (Das et al., 2024).

Green marketing also has the potential to provide firms a competitive edge. The demand for environmentally friendly goods and services rises as people become more ecologically aware. Offering a variety of organic goods may help businesses stand out from the crowd and draw in a new demographic of customers prepared to spend extra for such goods (González-Rodríguez et al., 2020). Green marketing provides advantages, but there are drawbacks as well. The common misconception that organic products are more expensive than non-organic items is one of the key issues. For consumers who are price conscious and do not want to pay extra for organic products, this might be a hurdle. Another issue is that the green marketing sector sometimes lacks regulation and standards, which can result in businesses making deceptive or incorrect environmental claims. Green marketing is an important strategy for companies to promote their environmentally friendly products and services. It can improve a company's reputation, create a competitive advantage and attract green consumers (Zaidi et al., 2022).

Green marketing is not a new concept, but it has become very important in today's business world due to the growing environmental awareness of consumers. The creation and promotion of ecologically friendly products is central to the idea of green marketing. It is a sustainable marketing approach that emphasizes promoting products and services with minimal environmental impact (Zhang et al., 2018). Green marketing aims to meet customer needs while preserving the environment. Interest in green marketing has grown over the past few years and this trend is expected to continue. Consumer behavior is changing dramatically due to growing consumer awareness of environmental issues (Kanwal et al., 2024). Consumers are now increasingly aware of the environmental impact of their actions, leading to changes in purchasing behavior. Green products are increasingly popular with consumers and companies are paying attention to this trend (Venugopal, Das & Badawy, 2023; Panda et al., 2023).

The rise of green marketing has prompted companies to adopt new strategies to attract green consumers. This has led to the development of a wide range of environmentally friendly products and services. Companies are currently investing heavily in research and development to develop green products in line with green marketing principles (Majeed et al., 2022). Science and marketing professionals are very interested in how green marketing affects customer behavior. The link between green marketing and consumer behavior has been the subject of several research. According to these research, green marketing has a favorable impact on customer behavior, including buying decisions, brand loyalty, and willingness to pay extra for environmentally friendly goods (Venugopal & Das, 2023).

3. LITERATURE REVIEW

The practice of creating and selling environmentally friendly goods and services is known as "green marketing." Companies may use it to stand out in the market and connect with customers who are becoming more environmentally sensitive. Product design, packaging, advertising, and promotion are just a few examples of how green marketing is practiced. The ability to draw in environmentally conscious customers is one of the key advantages of green marketing. Consumers are more inclined to acquire items and services that are ecologically friendly, according to research (Das et al., 2023). In fact, consumers are becoming more conscious of how their choices affect the environment and are seeking for solutions to lower their carbon footprints. Additionally, green marketing enhances a business's reputation and fosters client loyalty. Companies that show a commitment to environmental sustainability are more likely to gain the trust and loyalty of customers (Venugopal, Das & Vakamullu, 2023; González-Viralta et al, 2023).

4. GREEN MARKETING STRATEGY

Companies use various strategies to promote environmentally friendly products and services. One of the most common strategies is to highlight the environmental benefits of your products. This can be achieved through advertising, packaging, and labeling. Businesses can also promote sustainable business practices such as renewable energy and waste reduction. Another strategy adopted by companies is to offer sustainable packaging (Chekima et al., 2016). This includes using recycled materials, reducing packaging waste, and developing easy-to-recycle packaging. Companies can also promote sustainable consumption by encouraging consumers to use their products responsibly and sustainably. This can be achieved through education and information campaigns, such as promoting energy-efficient household appliances and encouraging consumers to recycle waste (Waghray, Das, & Ahmed, 2024).

5. THE IMPACT OF GREEN MARKETING ON CONSUMER BEHAVIOR

Consumer behavior is significantly impacted by green marketing. According to research, customers who are exposed to environmental marketing are more likely to choose products that are good for the environment (Ahmed et al., 2023). Additionally, consumers are becoming more and more prepared to pay more for organic goods (Narayanan & Singh, 2023). Customer loyalty is enhanced via green marketing. Companies that show a commitment to environmental sustainability are more likely to gain the trust and loyalty of customers (Sharma, 2021). Customers do believe that environmentally friendly businesses are moral, ethical, and reliable. According to Venugopal et al (2023), green advertising significantly influences customers' views and inclinations to buy organic products. According to the survey, customers who identify as environmentally concerned are more likely to respond favorably to green advertising and buy green goods. According to a different study (Zhang, Xiao & Zhou, 2020; Tsai et al., 2020) most of the customer's willingness to pay extra for a product or service is significantly influenced by how environmentally friendly they perceive it to be. This implies that businesses might boost their earnings by highlighting the advantages of their products for the environment and raising pricing.

6. RESEARCH METHODS

The influence of green marketing on customer behavior was investigated using a quantitative research methodology. 200 consumers who had already purchased an ecologically friendly item or service made up the sample for the poll. The poll includes inquiries on customer purchasing patterns, brand loyalty, and willingness to pay extra for organic goods. Descriptive statistics and regression analysis were used to analyze the data that had been obtained.

The survey's open-ended questions were intended to gauge respondents' demographics, awareness of and perceptions of green marketing, purchase habits for environmentally friendly goods and services, and brand loyalty to green businesses. willingness to pay more for goods and services that protect the environment. Before being given to a larger sample of customers, the questionnaire underwent a small-scale pre-test to assess its validity and reliability. The gathered data were examined using descriptive statistics including frequency, percentage, mean, and standard deviation. The link between green marketing and consumer behavior—specifically, the willingness to pay extra for green goods and services—was investigated using regression analysis.

This study's research approach offers a robust and thorough investigation of the influence of green marketing on customer behavior. An in-depth knowledge of the link between green marketing and customer behavior, particularly purchasing behavior, loyalty, and readiness to pay extra for green goods and services, is made possible by the combination of descriptive and regression analysis.

Table 1 shows that the sample was diverse in age, gender, and education, with a high proportion of participants between the ages of 25 and 34, women and those with a bachelor's degree.

Table 2 shows that the majority of participants are aware of the term "green marketing", consider it important, and prefer to buy from "green" companies.

Table 3 shows that a significant proportion of participants regularly purchase environmentally friendly goods or services, are willing to pay a premium for them, and that concern for the environment is the main reason for their purchase.

Table 1. Demographic characteristics of participants

DEMOGRAPHY	FREQUENCY	PERCENT
Age in year (s)		
18-24	30	15%
25-34	80	40%
35-44	50	25%
45-54	25	12.5%
over 55	15	7.5%
Sex		
Male	90	45%
women	105	52.5%
another	5	2.5%
Education		
high school	30	15%
baccalaureate	120	60%
mastery	40	20%
Ph.D.	10	5%

Table 2. Perceptions and perceptions of green marketing

Awareness and Recognition of Green Marketing	Frequency	Percentage
Do you know the term “green marketing”?	175	87.5%
think green marketing is important	180	90%
prefer to buy from environmentally friendly companies	185	92.5%

Table 3. Behavior when purchasing biological products or services

Buying Behavior	Frequency	Percent
Regularly purchase environmentally friendly products and services	155	77.5%
Willingness to pay extra for environmentally friendly products and services	125	62.5%
Main reasons to buy environmentally friendly products or services		
Environmental problems	80	40%
health problems	50	25%
Social responsibility	40	20%
price	20	10%
another	10	10%

Table 4 shows that the majority of participants indicated loyalty to eco-friendly brands, while a minority of participants wanted to switch to another eco-friendly brand.

Table 4. Green brand loyalty

Loyalty to Eco-Friendly Brands	Frequency	Percent
Loyalty to eco-friendly brands	145	72.5%
I want to switch to another sustainable brand	55	27.5%

Table 5 demonstrates that the majority of participants were willing to pay up to 10% more for environmentally friendly goods or services, while individuals were willing to pay 10%–20% more. A sizeable proportion refused to pay more for goods and services that were more ecologically friendly.

These tables show that participants have a favorable attitude toward green marketing and are prepared to consistently pay more for green goods and services. The vast majority of participants also showed an affinity for green brands.

Table 5. Willingness to pay more for environmentally friendly products or services

Willingness to Pay a High Price	Frequency	Percent
Willingness to pay up to 10% more for environmentally friendly goods and services	90	45%
Willing to pay 10-20% more for environmentally friendly goods and services	35	17.5%
Willingness to pay 20% or more for environmentally friendly goods or services	0	0%
I don't want to pay too much for environmentally friendly products and services	75	37.5%

Results

Some important conclusions concerning the influence of green marketing on customer behavior were drawn from a study of the survey data.

Green marketing awareness and perception: 90% of respondents believe that green marketing is significant, and the majority of respondents (87.5%) are aware of the term "green marketing." In addition, 92.5% of respondents stated they prefer to patronize eco-friendly businesses.

Environmentally friendly product or service purchasing habits: 62.5% of respondents said they would be ready to pay extra for environmentally friendly goods or services, while 77.5% of Respondents said they routinely purchase environmentally friendly products or services. The top three motivations for purchasing green goods or services were social responsibility (20%), health concerns (25%), and environmental conservation (40%) respectively.

Brand loyalty to eco-friendly companies: 27.5% of respondents indicated they would move to another eco-friendly brand, while 72.5% said they were loyal to eco-friendly brands.

Willingness to pay more for goods and services that are ecologically friendly: For environmentally friendly products or services, 45% of respondents indicated they would be prepared to pay up to 10% more, while 17.5% said they would be willing to spend an additional 10% to 20%. 37.5% of respondents said they would not be willing to spend too much on products and services that are ecologically friendly.

Green marketing and the desire to pay extra for ecologically friendly goods or services are significantly positively correlated, according to regression analysis (r = 0.618, p 0.001). This shows that customers are more likely to pay extra for green goods and services as green marketing grows.

The findings demonstrate that green marketing significantly influences customer behavior, specifically purchase decisions, brand loyalty, and readiness to pay extra for environmentally friendly goods and services. For businesses looking to attract customers with green goods and services, this has significant ramifications.

Table 6. Perceptions and perceptions of green marketing

Awareness and Recognition of Green Marketing	Percentage
Do you know the term "green marketing"?	87.5%
We think green marketing is important	90%
Prefer to buy from environmentally friendly companies	92.5%

The high level of knowledge and belief in the importance of green marketing and the preference for green businesses highlights the potential for businesses to use green marketing strategies to reach green consumers.

Table 7. Purchase of environmentally friendly goods or services

Purchasing Behavior for Environmentally Friendly Products and Services	Percent
Regularly purchase environmentally friendly products and services	77.5%
Willingness to pay extra for environmentally friendly products and services	62.5%
Reasons to buy environmentally friendly products and services	
Environmental problems	40%
health problems	25%
Social responsibility	20%

A significant proportion of respondents who regularly purchase green goods or services and are willing to pay extra for them believe that companies do not offer green goods or services that meet consumer needs and values. differentiate, provide.

Table 8. Green brand loyalty

Loyalty to Eco-Friendly Brands	Percent
Claimed loyalty to the brand	72.5%
I want to switch to another sustainable brand	27.5%

A high percentage of respondents who report being loyal to green brands are more likely to connect with long-term green consumers through companies that offer reliable, high-quality green products and services. This suggests that you can build meaningful relationships.

Table 9. Willingness to pay more for environmentally friendly products or services

Willingness to Pay Extra for Environmentally Friendly Products and Services	Percent
Willingness to pay up to 10% more for environmentally friendly goods and services	45%
Willing to pay 10-20% more for environmentally friendly goods and services	17.5%
I don't want to pay too much for environmentally friendly products and services	37.5%

A significant proportion of respondents are willing to pay more for environmentally friendly products and services, while a significant minority is opposed. This highlights the importance for companies to find the right balance between offering environmentally friendly products and services at high prices and remaining competitive in the market.

Table 10. Results of regression analysis

Variable	Factor (β)	p-Value
green marketing	0.618	< 0.001
R squared (degree of fit)	0.539	
Fitted R-square (goodness of fit)	0.535	
F-statistic (overall importance of the model)	129.8	< 0.001

Companies are likely to pay more for green goods and services, according to a strong positive association between green marketing and readiness to pay more for them.

Table 11. Perception of respondents on organic products

Statement	North India	D.	NOT	A	South India	Mean
Green foods are good for the health	0%	0%	8%	43%	49%	4.41
Green products are good for the environment	0%	0%	2%	37%	61%	4.59
Good quality green products	0%	4%	18%	40%	38%	4.12
Green products are better than standard products	3%	7%	23%	36%	31%	3.85
Green products are affordable	17%	57%	14%	9%	3%	2.24
Green products are readily available in stores	13%	21%	25%	31%	10%	3.04
Green products are well advertised	13%	23%	22%	35%	7%	3.00
The price of organic products influences the purchasing decision	2%	10%	13%	45%	30%	3.91

The Likert scale is used in this table to display respondents' impressions of organic goods. SA = strongly agree, SD = strongly disagree, D = disagree, N = neutral, A = agree. To establish how each sentence was perceived overall, an average score was also computed. In general, respondents firmly concur that organic goods are healthier (mean = 4.41) and better for the environment (average = 4.59) than conventional goods. They are less inclined to concur, nevertheless, that organic goods are reasonably priced (mean=2.24) and easily accessible in retailers (mean=3.04).

Green Retail

The practice of selling organic goods in an ecologically responsible manner is known as "green retailing." The need to lessen the damaging effects of retail on the environment and the rising awareness of environmental concerns gave rise to the idea of "green" retail. Green retailing is a tactic used by merchants to satisfy the market's rising demand for organic goods and gain a competitive edge.

Green retailing involves integrating sustainability principles into various aspects of the retail process, such as product design, sourcing, packaging, transportation, and disposal. Retailers can promote green retailing by selling products made from sustainable materials, promoting sustainable packaging, reducing waste, and adopting sustainable transportation methods. Retailers can also provide consumers with information about the environmental impact of their products, helping them make informed choices.

Green retailing has a number of benefits such as reduced environmental impact, improved brand image, increased customer loyalty, and reduced costs. By adopting sustainable practices, retailers can reduce their carbon footprint and contribute to environmental conservation efforts. Green retailing also helps retailers attract and retain environmentally conscious customers who pay more for organic products.

In conclusion, green retailing is an important strategy for retailers who want to meet the growing demand for sustainable products and reduce their environmental impact. By adopting sustainable practices, retailers can create a competitive advantage in the marketplace and enhance their brand image while contributing to their environmental efforts.

Figure 1. Respondents' attitude towards green retail (authors' contribution)

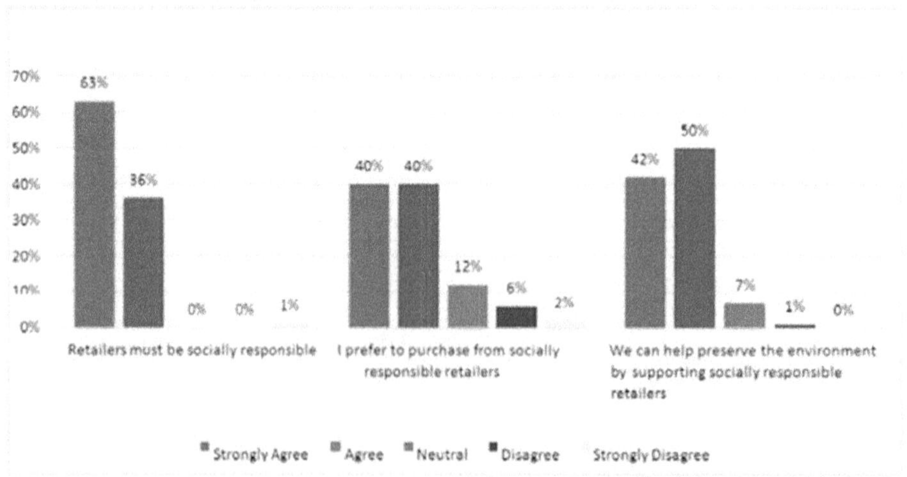

7. IMPLICATIONS

The findings have several implications for marketers and retailers.

- First, it is important for retailers to promote the sustainability of their products in order to attract environmentally conscious consumers. As shown in Table 5, consumers perceive organic products as environmentally friendly, healthy, and of good quality. Therefore, marketers should focus on promoting these properties of organic products in their advertising and advertising campaigns.
- Second, retailers can improve their green retail practices by providing consumers with sustainable packaging, reducing waste, and adopting sustainable transportation methods. As shown in Table 7, consumers value information on product packaging and often read labels before purchasing. Therefore, retailers must provide clear information on the environmental impact of their products and the sustainability of their packaging so that consumers can make an informed choice.
- Third, it is important that retailers place a reasonable value on organic products so that consumers can make rational buying decisions. As shown in Table 5, consumers consider green products to be of good quality but not affordable. Therefore, retailers need to set competitive prices to encourage consumers to choose organic products over standard products.
- Finally, it is important that traders and retailers conduct effective environmental advertising campaigns to raise awareness of environmental issues and promote organic products. Effective green advertising can raise awareness of environmental issues and motivate consumers to protect the environment by purchasing green products, as shown in Table 7. Therefore, merchants and retailers must create cost-effective and attractive green advertising campaigns to attract green consumers.

The significance of this study lies in the importance of promoting environmental considerations in marketing and retail, implementing sustainable practices, and creating effective environmental promotion campaigns to attract environmentally conscious consumers.

8. CONCLUSION

The purpose of this study was to examine the impact of green marketing on consumer behavior such as purchasing decisions, loyalty, and willingness to pay higher prices. The results show that consumers perceive organic products as environmentally friendly, healthy, and of good quality. However, they do not consider them affordable and the price of organic products influences their purchasing decisions.

The study also showed that green marketing practices such as green retailing and effective green promotions can have a significant impact on consumer behavior. Retailers can improve their green retail practices by offering sustainable packaging, reducing waste, and adopting sustainable transportation practices. Merchants promote the sustainability of their products to attract environmentally conscious consumers, conduct effective environmental promotion campaigns to raise awareness of environmental issues, and promote environmentally friendly products.

The implications of this research are to attract environmentally conscious consumers by promoting environmental considerations in marketing and retail, implementing sustainable practices, and creating effective environmental advertising campaigns, suggesting that 'it can be used to encourage sustainable purchasing decisions. The results are valuable for marketers and retailers to understand consumer behavior towards organic products and help develop effective green marketing strategies.

In conclusion, this study highlights the importance of green marketing practices to promote sustainability and positively influence consumer behavior. For marketers and retailers, implementing sustainable practices and encouraging sustainability is key to attracting green consumers and encouraging smart purchasing decisions.

9. DIRECTION FOR FUTURE RESEARCH

This study shed some light on how green marketing affects consumer behavior, but there is still more to learn about this topic. Future studies might go in the following directions:

- **Examine how demographic considerations affect the population:** The study indicated that customers' willingness to spend more on organic products is significantly influenced by their age and wealth. Future studies may examine how additional demographic variables like gender, education level, and employment affect how consumers behave toward organic goods.
- **Examine the effects of green certification**: Consumer behavior toward green products can be influenced by green certifications like the Forest Stewardship Council (FSC) and Leadership in Energy and Environmental Design (LEED). Future studies might examine how green certification affects customer behavior as well as how well various certifications work to persuade consumers to make certain purchases.
- **Find out how green marketing affects a consumer's loyalty to a brand:** This study demonstrated how green marketing might enhance consumer brand loyalty. Future studies may examine how brand loyalty and green marketing are related, as well as any moderating factors that may play a role.
- **Find out more about how social media affects green marketing**: social media is being utilized more and more for green marketing. Future studies should examine how social media affects how consumers behave toward organic items and how well different social media platforms work to promote organic goods.
- Analyze the impact of greenwashing: Greenwashing is a false or misleading claim about a product's environmental benefits. Future research could explore the impact of greenwashing on consumer behavior towards organic products and the effectiveness of various anti-greenwashing strategies.

These are just some of the possible future directions of research in this area. Businesses and politicians will find it even more crucial to comprehend how green marketing affects consumer behavior as sustainability and environmental problems gain popularity with consumers.

ACKNOWLEDGMENT

This research has not received any particular grant from any funding agency in the public, commercial, or not-for-profit organizations.

REFERENCES

Ahmed, R. R., Streimikiene, D., Qadir, H., & Streimikis, J. (2023). Effect of green marketing mix, green customer value, and attitude on green purchase intention: Evidence from the USA. *Environmental Science and Pollution Research International*, *30*(5), 11473–11495.

Chekima, B., Wafa, S. A. W. S. K., Igau, O. A., Chekima, S., & Sondoh, S. L. Jr. (2016). Examining green consumerism motivational drivers: Does premium price and demographics matter to green purchasing? *Journal of Cleaner Production*, *112*, 3436–3450. doi:10.1016/j.jclepro.2015.09.102

Das, S., Mishra, B. K., Panda, N., & Badawy, H. R. (2024). Sustainable Marketing Mix Strategies of Millets: A Voyage of Two Decades. In The Role of Women in Cultivating Sustainable Societies Through Millets (pp. 113-127). IGI Global.

Das, S., Saibabu, N., & Pranaya, D. (2023). Blockchain and Intelligent Computing Framework for Sustainable Agriculture: Theory, Methods, and Practice. In Intelligent Engineering Applications and Applied Sciences for Sustainability (pp. 208-228). IGI Global.

Galati, A., Thrassou, A., Christofi, M., Vrontis, D., & Migliore, G. (2023). Exploring travelers' willingness to pay for green hotels in the digital era. *Journal of Sustainable Tourism*, *31*(11), 2546–2563.

González-Rodríguez, M. R., Díaz-Fernández, M. C., & Font, X. (2020). Factors influencing willingness of customers of environmentally friendly hotels to pay a price premium. *International Journal of Contemporary Hospitality Management*, *32*(1), 60–80.

González-Viralta, D., Veas-González, I., Egaña-Bruna, F., Vidal-Silva, C., Delgado-Bello, C., & Pezoa-Fuentes, C. (2023). Positive effects of green practices on the consumers' satisfaction, loyalty, word-of-mouth, and willingness to pay. *Heliyon*, *9*(10). Advance online publication. doi:10.1016/j.heliyon.2023.e20353

Kanwal, N. D. S., Panda, T., Patro, U. S., & Das, S. (2024). Societal Sustainability: The Innovative Practices of the 21st Century. In Sustainable Disposal Methods of Food Wastes in Hospitality Operations (pp. 193-213). IGI Global.

Majeed, M. U., Aslam, S., Murtaza, S. A., Attila, S., & Molnár, E. (2022). Green marketing approaches and their impact on green purchase intentions: Mediating role of green brand image and consumer beliefs towards the environment. *Sustainability*, *14*(18), 11703.

Martinez, P. (2015). Customer loyalty: Exploring its antecedents from a green marketing perspective. *International Journal of Contemporary Hospitality Management*, *27*(5), 896–917.

Moser, A. K. (2015). Thinking green, buying green? Drivers of pro-environmental purchasing behavior. *Journal of Consumer Marketing*, *32*(3), 167–175.

Narayanan, S., & Singh, G. A. (2023). Consumers' willingness to pay for corporate social responsibility: Theory and evidence. *International Journal of Consumer Studies*, *47*(6), 2212–2244.

Panda, J., Das, S., Panda, M., & Pattnaik, D. (2023). Sustainable Intelligence: Navigating the Rise of Green Technologies for a Greener Environment. In Sustainable Science and Intelligent Technologies for Societal Development (pp. 464-474). IGI Global.

Sharma, A. P. (2021). Consumers' purchase behaviour and green marketing: A synthesis, review and agenda. *International Journal of Consumer Studies*, *45*(6), 1217–1238.

Tsai, P. H., Lin, G. Y., Zheng, Y. L., Chen, Y. C., Chen, P. Z., & Su, Z. C. (2020). Exploring the effect of Starbucks' green marketing on consumers' purchase decisions from consumers' perspective. *Journal of Retailing and Consumer Services*, *56*, 102162.

Venugopal, K., & Das, S. (2023). Entrepreneurial cluster branding influencing sustainable cashew market: A case study. *Parikalpana KIIT Journal of Management*, *19*(2), 83–96.

Venugopal, K., Das, S., & Badawy, H. R. H. (2023). Prediction Analysis of Gen Zers' Attitudes on Ecological Consciousness. In Sustainable Science and Intelligent Technologies for Societal Development (pp. 342-357). IGI Global.

Venugopal, K., Das, S., & Vakamullu, G. (2023). Critical Factors for the Upscale of Online Shopping: A Rural Perspective. In Influencer Marketing Applications Within the Metaverse (pp. 254-262). IGI Global.

Venugopal, K., Pranaya, D., Das, S., & Jena, S. K. (2023). Handloom Weaving: Critical Factors influencing the Satisfaction-The Socio & Economic Context. *Economic Affairs*, *68*(04), 1979–1988.

Waghray, A., Das, S., & Ahmed, S. (2024). An Assessment on Marketing Promotions and Strategies Adopted by Retailers Towards Millet-Based Products in Hyderabad. In *The Role of Women in Cultivating Sustainable Societies Through Millets* (pp. 143–155). IGI Global.

Zaidi, N., Dixit, S., Maurya, M., & Dharwal, M. (2022). Willingness to pay for green products and factors affecting Buyer's Behaviour: An empirical study. *Materials Today: Proceedings*, *49*, 3595–3599. doi:10.1016/j.matpr.2021.08.123

Zhang, B., Fu, Z., Huang, J., Wang, J., Xu, S., & Zhang, L. (2018). Consumers' perceptions, purchase intention, and willingness to pay a premium price for safe vegetables: A case study of Beijing, China. *Journal of Cleaner Production*, *197*, 1498–1507.

Zhang, Y., Xiao, C., & Zhou, G. (2020). Willingness to pay a price premium for energy-saving appliances: Role of perceived value and energy efficiency labeling. *Journal of Cleaner Production*, *242*, 118555.

Chapter 4
IoT Driven by Machine Learning (MLIoT) for the Retail Apparel Sector

Kutubuddin Sayyad Liyakat Kazi
https://orcid.org/0000-0001-5623-9211
BMIT, Solapur, India

ABSTRACT

Despite the challenges faced, the future of the apparel retail industry looks promising, with endless opportunities for growth and development. Automated body measurements and size suggestions for customers is a game-changer in the world of online shopping. It offers convenience, accuracy, inclusivity, and sustainability, benefiting both customers and retailers. With the constant advancements in technology, it is safe to say that this system will continue to evolve and improve, making the online shopping experience even more seamless and personalized in the future. MLIoT is transforming the retail apparel sector by providing retailers with real-time insights, automation, and personalization.

INTRODUCTION

The apparel retail industry is a dynamic and ever-evolving sector that caters to the growing demand for clothing, accessories, and footwear. This industry plays a significant role in the global economy, with the revenue generated by retail sales reaching a staggering $2 trillion in 2019. The sector includes a broad spectrum of companies, from independent small businesses to major global conglomerates. all of which contribute to the diverse landscape of the apparel retail market by Vahida(2023), K Kutubuddin(2023).

The apparel retail industry is constantly adapting to changing consumer preferences and trends, making it a highly competitive and complex market. One of the key drivers of this industry is the rise of fast fashion, where retailers produce and sell inexpensive clothing that follows the latest fashion trends. This has led to an increase in demand for affordable clothing, resulting in a high volume of sales and significant revenue for retailers K S(2022).

DOI: 10.4018/979-8-3693-3049-4.ch004

The growing influence of technology has also had a significant impact on the apparel retail industry. Online shopping has become increasingly popular, with consumers now having the option to purchase clothing from the comfort of their own homes. This has forced traditional brick-and-mortar retailers to adapt and create an online presence to stay relevant in the market. Social media platforms have additionally developed into an essential tool over merchants to market their goods and connect with their target market.

In recent years, sustainability has become a major concern for consumers, and this has also affected the apparel retail industry. With increased awareness about the environmental impact of fast fashion, consumers are now looking for more sustainable and ethical alternatives. This has led to the rise of eco-friendly and ethical fashion brands that focus on utilising eco-friendly materials, cutting waste, and encouraging ethical hiring procedures by Sherin(2021).

The retail apparel industry additionally remains highly fragmented, with a large number of small and medium-sized enterprises participating in the market. Due to the fierce competition that has resulted, retailers must constantly innovate and provide new goods and services in order to stay one step ahead of their rivals. This has also resulted in a diverse range of options for consumers, catering to different tastes and preferences.

The COVID-19 pandemic's effects are one of the main issues facing the retail clothing business. The closure of physical retail stores and disruptions in the supply chain have severely affected the industry, resulting in a decline in sales and revenue. However, the pandemic has also accelerated the shift to online shopping, with retailers investing in e-commerce and digital marketing to reach their customers.

To stay competitive in the market, retailers are constantly investing in technology and data analytics to better understand consumer behavior and preferences. This has led to the use of artificial intelligence-AI and ML-machine learning in areas such as inventory management, supply chain optimization, and personalized marketing by K Kutubuddin(2022).

Convenience as well as effectiveness are the primary elements that propel our daily lives in the fast-paced world of today. With the rise of e-commerce, shopping has become more accessible and convenient than ever before. However, one challenge that many customers face when shopping online is finding the right size and fit for their bodies. This is where the concept of an automatic customer's body measurements and size recommendation system comes into play.

Gone are the days when customers had to rely solely on size charts and their own estimation to determine the right size for their clothing. This traditional method often leads to inaccurate size selection and ultimately, dissatisfaction with the product. Thanks to technological advancements, retailers can now provide their customers with a more precise and customised sizing experience by utilising an automated system that takes customers' body measurements and recommends a size.

So, how does this system work? The process typically involves the use of a body scanning technology. Customers can either visit a physical store where the technology is available or use a virtual body scanning tool on the retailer's website. The body scanning technology captures the customer's body measurements in a matter of seconds, providing accurate data on their height, weight, body shape, and other relevant measurements.

Once the customer's body measurements are captured, the data is then used by the size recommendation system to suggest the most suitable size for the customer. The system takes into account the brand's specific size chart and compares it with the customer's body measurements to provide personalized size recommendations. This not only saves the customer time and effort but also eliminates the frustration of purchasing the wrong size.

Apart from the convenience and accuracy, an automatic customer's body measurements and size recommendation system also offers a more inclusive shopping experience for customers. With the traditional method of size selection, customers who fall outside the standard size range often face difficulty finding the right size for their bodies. However, with an automatic system, retailers can offer a wider range of sizes to cater to customers of all body types and sizes.

Moreover, this system also benefits retailers by reducing the number of returns and exchanges due to incorrect sizing. Returns and exchanges can be costly for retailers, not to mention the negative impact it may have on their brand reputation. By implementing an automatic size recommendation system, retailers can reduce the number of returns and exchanges, leading to more satisfied customers and cost savings for the business.

The use of an automatic customer's body measurements and size recommendation system is also a step towards sustainability in the fashion industry. With the rise of fast fashion, there has been an increase in the production and disposal of clothing, leading to environmental damage. By providing customers with accurate size recommendations, the chances of purchasing the wrong size and contributing to the problem of clothing waste are reduced.

The retail apparel industry has consistently been a leader in implementing new technology to improve customer experience and increase efficiency. With the rise of e-commerce and the growing demand for personalized shopping experiences, retailers are now turning to the Internet of Things (IoT) and Machine Learning (ML) to drive innovation in their operations by Altaf (2023).

IoT and ML technologies have been making waves in various industries, and now they are coming together to create a powerful force in the retail apparel sector. This combination, often referred to as 'MLIoT', is revolutionizing the way retailers operate and interact with their customers. In simple terms, MLIoT is the integration of IoT devices and sensors with Machine Learning algorithms to collect, analyze, and act upon data in real-time. This means that devices such as RFID tags, beacons, and cameras are used to gather data from the physical world, and ML algorithms are applied to this data to make predictions, recommendations, and automate processes.

MLIoT TRANSFORMING THE RETAIL APPAREL SECTOR

1. Streamlining Inventory Management

One of the biggest challenges for retailers is managing their inventory effectively. With the help of MLIoT, retailers can now get real-time insights into their inventory levels, identify slow-moving products, and make data-driven decisions on restocking and pricing. RFID tags and beacons attached to products can track their movement throughout the store, providing retailers with accurate inventory counts and reducing the chances of overstocking or stockouts.

2. Personalized Shopping Experience

With MLIoT, retailers can gather data on customer behavior, preferences, and purchase history to create personalized shopping experiences. For example, a customer trying on a shirt in a fitting room equipped with RFID technology can be recommended with complementary products or different sizes and colors based on their previous purchases. This boosts the likelihood of closing a deal in addition to improving the shopping experience.

3. Efficient Supply Chain Management

MLIoT can also be used to improve supply chain management in the retail apparel sector. Retailers may locate bottlenecks, optimize routes, and raise overall operational efficiency by tracking items all through their supply chain. This can lead to cost savings and faster delivery times, which are crucial in the competitive retail industry.

4. Smart Store Layouts

The layout of a store plays a significant role in influencing customer behavior and purchasing decisions. With the help of MLIoT, retailers can analyze customer movement and behavior within the store to optimize store layouts. For example, if a particular section of the store is frequently visited but has low sales, retailers can adjust the layout or product placement to increase sales.

5. Fraud Detection and Prevention

Retailers are also using MLIoT to detect and prevent fraudulent activities. ML algorithms are able to examine data from a variety of sources, including customer behavior and transaction history, to identify suspicious activities. This can help retailers prevent fraudulent returns and reduce losses due to theft.

We suggest a system for measuring and recommending the size of the human body in real time. Our system can quickly retrieve a user's full body measurements from just two images. To achieve normalization, our method doesn't need any specific background or clothing color. Rather, it makes use of computer vision and deep learning neural networks. Our system recommends the user's clothing size based on their complete body measurements, matching the brand's size chart that they wish to buy from.

IOT-INTERNET OF THINGS (IOT) AND ITS APPLICATIONS

In recent times, the term "IoT" has gained popularity in the tech sector. It relates to an interconnection between physical devices, cars, structures, as well as other objects ingrained using sensors, electronics, software, and network connectivity, enabling these objects acquire and exchange data(Figure 1). The aforementioned technology possesses an opportunity to change how we conduct our affairs, causing our daily activities to be simpler, more effective, and connected by K S (2023), Kazik (2022), & Kutub (2022).

IoT has a wide range of applications, from smart cities and homes to the industrial as well as healthcare sectors. Let's examine several of those most popular and cutting-edge IoT applications in more detail.

1. *Smart Homes:* The concept of a smart home, where all devices and appliances are connected and can be controlled remotely, has become a reality with IoT. From smart thermostats and lighting systems to security cameras and voice assistants, IoT enables us to automate and control our homes for optimal comfort and convenience.

2. *Smart Cities:* IoT is also being used to make our cities smarter and more efficient. With sensors and connectivity, Cities are able to gather data in real time about air quality, traffic, and energy usage to improve infrastructure and services. Smart traffic lights have the ability to modify their timings in response to traffic flow, which can alleviate congestion and enhance commute times.
3. *Industrial Internet of Things (IIoT):* In the industrial sector, IoT is revolutionizing processes and operations. By connecting machines and equipment, IIoT makes production process optimization, predictive maintenance, as well as real-time monitoring possible. This results in increased efficiency, reduced downtime, and cost savings for businesses.
4. *Healthcare:* IoT has immense potential in the healthcare sector, from remote patient monitoring to smart medication management. With wearable devices and sensors, patients can track their health parameters and share data with their doctors for better diagnosis and treatment. IoT is also being used for tracking medical equipment and inventory management in hospitals by Kzai K (2025=4).
5. *Agriculture:* In this, IoT is being used to improve crop yield, optimize resource usage, and monitor soil conditions. Farmers can use sensor data for creating data-driven decisions during the crops they grow by gathering information on temperature, moisture content, and nutrient levels. This technology can help reduce waste and increase sustainability in the agriculture industry by S Sayyad (2023).
6. *Transportation:* IoT has also found its way into the transportation sector, enabling connected and autonomous vehicles. With sensors and connectivity, cars can communicate with each other and with infrastructure, making roads safer and reducing accidents. IoT is also being used in logistics and supply chain management to track goods and optimize delivery routes, reducing costs and improving efficiency by Karale (2023).
7. *Wearables:* The popularity of wearable devices, such as fitness trackers and smartwatches, is a testament to the potential of IoT in the healthcare and personal wellness industry. These devices can monitor activity levels, sleep patterns, and heart rate, providing users with valuable insights into their health and wellness by Divya(2022).

Figure 1. IoT structure

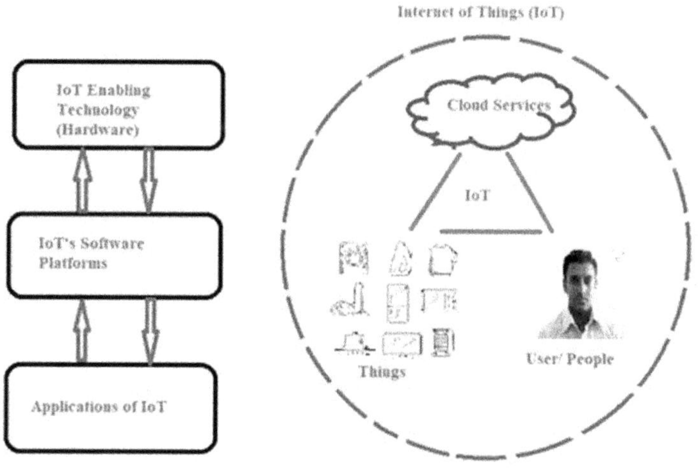

The above are just some of the many applications of IoT, and this technology continues to evolve and find new use cases. However, with all the benefits, IoT also poses some challenges, such as data privacy and security concerns. Computer hacking and data breaches are becoming more likely as an ever more devices are connected. To protect sensitive data, it is imperative that appropriate security measures are put in place.

Figure 2. IoT application scenario in 2023

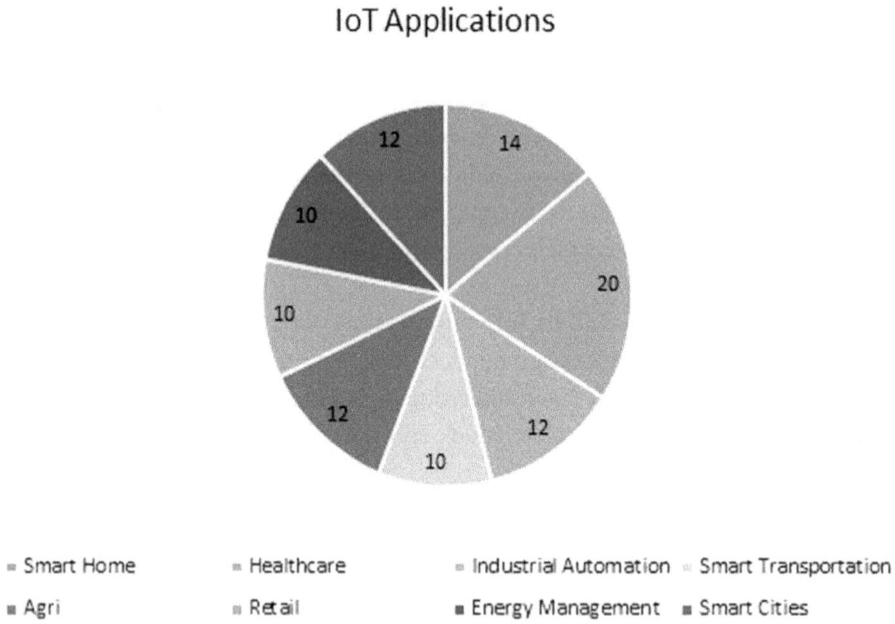

Figure 2 shows the application scenario in IoT for Year 2023. In all, IoT has the potential to revolutionize various industries and make our lives more convenient and connected. As this technology continues to develop, it is essential to address any concerns and ensure its responsible and ethical use. With the right approach, IoT can truly transform the way we live and work.

ML: MACHINE LEARNING

This ground-breaking technology is sweeping the globe. It has made its way into various industries and has significantly impacted the way we live, work, and interact with technology. ML has the potential to change and enhance a number of industries, from self-driving cars to personalized recommendations upon video streaming services. our lives by Dixit (2014), (2015a,b), Mulani(2019).

So, what exactly is ML? In simple terms, it is a subset of Artificial Intelligence (AI) that enables machines for learning via data with no becoming specifically programmed. This means that instead of following a set of predefined rules, machines can analyze data and make decisions or predictions based on patterns and trends. This ability to learn and adapt makes ML a powerful tool that has found widespread applications in various fields by Gouse (2018), K S L (2018), K S (2017). Figure 3 shows the scenario of application of AI in 2023.

Figure 3. ML applications scenario in 2023

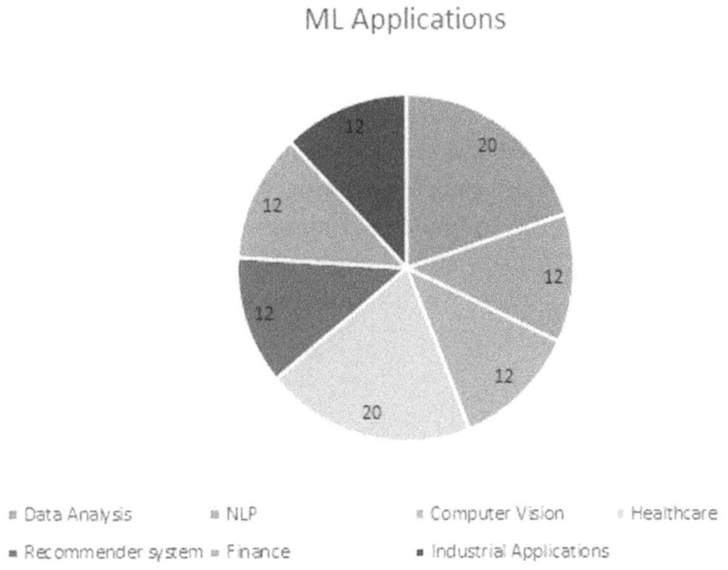

One of the most notable applications of ML is in the field of healthcare. Medical practitioners are able to examine enormous volumes of patient data and spot trends that could go unnoticed by human doctors. This can aid in early detection and diagnosis of diseases, leading to a more accurate and timely treatment. Additionally, ML can assist in creating individualized therapies for patients according to their medical histories, thereby improving the effectiveness and efficiency of healthcare by Sultana (2023).

Another area where ML has shown significant impact is in the financial sector. ML algorithms can analyze market trends, customer behavior, and other data to predict stock prices, identify frauds, and make investment decisions. This has not only made processes more efficient but has also reduced the risk associated with financial transactions by Karale (2023).

ML has also transformed how we engage with technology, particularly in the form of virtual assistants. These intelligent assistants, such as Siri, Alexa, and Google Assistant, use ML to understand and respond to human voice commands. They constantly learn from user interactions and become more personalized, making our lives easier and more convenient.

In the field of transportation, ML has enabled the development of self-driving cars. These cars use sensors and ML algorithms to analyze their surroundings and make decisions in real-time. This technology has the likelihood to lower human error-related accidents, improve the effectiveness of transportation, and eco-friendly by Mardanali (2023).

ML has also found its way into the world of e-commerce Shreya (2022). Online retailers use ML algorithms to analyze customer data and provide tailored product recommendations. Customers' shopping experiences are improved by this, and it also helps businesses increase their sales and revenue.

The use of ML is not limited to these industries; it has also made its way into education, agriculture, manufacturing, and many other fields. Its potential to automate processes, reduce errors, and make accurate predictions has made it a valuable asset for businesses and organizations by Vinay (2022), Sultanabanu (2023) Ravi(2022), Liyakat(2023),(2024), Sayyad(2023) K K(2022) Kutubuddin SL(2022) K Kazi(2022).

However, like any other technology, ML also has its challenges. One of the major concerns is the bias in data that can lead to biased decisions. For example, if a hiring algorithm is trained on data that is biased against a certain gender or race, it can result in biased hiring decisions. To tackle this issue, it is essential to have diverse and unbiased data sets and continuously monitor and evaluate ML systems.

In all, the applications of ML are vast and ever-growing. Its ability to learn, adapt, and with data to inform decisions possesses a possibility to transform industries and make our lives more efficient and convenient. However, it is crucial to make ethical and responsible use of this technology in order to maximize its benefits to society as a whole. With continuous advancements and improvements, ML is set to play a significant role in shaping our future.

LITERATURE SURVEY

The body platform for data called "3DLook" makes it easy for businesses to share measurement as well as shape data with one another. Regretfully, this application lacks a user interface and is solely intended for business use. Furthermore, it brings up some security issues regarding the location of user data, which includes images and their measurements. The majority of users will be at ease having their data saved solely locally on their gadgets. Furthermore, the app was very expensive to use for just one person.

The "MTAILOR" app is another similar system that promises 20% greater accuracy than a human tailor. Though users prefer not to deal with it, there are security concerns because consumers upload pictures to the cloud while certain field specialists independently review videos. Additionally, the app is limited to the vendor store's inventory.

Seventy-three percent of Millennials want clothing that is sustainable from both an environmental and socioeconomic standpoint, based to the Nielsen survey by Company, (2015). The fashion industry's digitalization fosters the development of resilient, creative, sustainable, as well as real-time facilities which is adapted to consumer needs for comfort, adaptability, and sustainability in a sustainable way. Research has shown that the implementation of digital technology can significantly aid in the achievement of sustainability. The capacity to examine current information regarding intelligent clothing as well as other articles of clothing on an online platform has been rendered feasible by digitalization. It does, in fact, assist in the analysis of data and in applying different analytics techniques to get the required insights out of it.

Bhagyashree et al. (2023), explains Heart Healthcare system utilizes ML. Recently, cardiovascular diseases (CVD) have surpassed all other causes of death in both developed and developing countries. Lowering the death rate can be achieved by early identification of cardiac illnesses and ongoing expert therapeutic supervision. However, because of the increased intelligence, effort, and expertise required, precise identification of cardiac problems under any situation and 24-an hour physician consultation remain unfeasible. This study presented the fundamental idea for a machine learning (ML)-based system that predicts the likelihood of developing heart disease by employing ML techniques to detect heart disease in the near future. There are fewer synthesized research articles in this field, despite the growing number of empirical studies on the subject, especially from developing nations. Predictive analytics is becoming an increasingly vital tool for human protection and heart welfare services in an era when data availability is rapidly growing. This cutting-edge technology helps heart-care agencies make more informed choices regarding how they can best assist their clients by using data gathered from past events to forecast future patterns and outcomes. Predictive analytics, like every other data-driven technology, must be utilized properly to ensure morally and practically sound business practices. The included studies in this study concentrate on using machine learning algorithms to forecast the heart healthcare system (HHS). For registration as well as notification, they used the K-means Elbow technique; for HHS, they used a decision tree; and for immunization reminders, they used MySQL.

Sunita et al. (2023), explain ML and IoT for Food and Fruit quality in food safety. This article describes a machine learning as well as IoT-based approach for monitoring perishable goods. The proposed system entails using Internet of Things (IoT) devices to upload images taken with high-resolution cameras to a cloud server. K-means clustering is used to segment these images before they are uploaded onto a cloud server. After principal component analysis is used to extract attributes from the images, the trained ML method have been utilized to classify the pictures. This suggested method uses machine learning, image processing, and the Internet of Things for tracking perishable food.

Mulani et al. (2019), utilizes Ml for Hand Gesture recognition system. Human-computer interaction that is intuitive and natural can be achieved through hand gestures. To maximize recognition of hand gestures for mouse operation, our new approach combines established methods of Viola-Jones-Haar-like feature-based recognition of objects and skin color-based ROI segmentation. A mouse operation consists of moving the cursor along with clicking with either the left or right mouse button. This paper first defines a Region of Interest (ROI) using color as a robust feature. Then, using the AdaBoost learning algorithm and Haar-like features, hand postures are detected within this ROI. By combining a series of poor classifiers, the AdaBoost learning algorithm dramatically improves performance and creates an accurate cascaded classifier.

Pradeepa et al. (2022), explains the use of ML & IoT for students Health perdition. As more students live independently and are spread out over wide geographic areas, it is now necessary to keep an eye on their health status. This study proposes an IoT-based approach to student health management that continuously monitors students' vital signs and uses cutting-edge medical technology to identify biological and behavioral changes. In this concept, the IoT module collects vital data, and NN models have been employed to evaluate the data and identify potential risks to children's physiological and behavioral changes. The results of the experiment indicate that the proposed model is a reliable and accurate way to assess the pupils' states. After evaluating the suggested model, the SVM achieved an optimal performance of 99.1%, which is satisfactory for our goals. The outcomes also outperformed algorithms for random forests, decision trees, and multilevel perceptron neural systems.

Kazi (2018), explains the use of ML in Aquatic study. By using color matching, the color correction over the whole sequence is lessened as well as the color differences between neighboring images. In aquatic image applications, we apply linear correction and gamma correction, respectively, for the brightness and chrominance elements in the original images (marine). The problem of color consistency in 360-degree panoramic photos is addressed by color correspondence and color difference distribution techniques. This article integrates the stitching approach into a panoramic imaging system to generate high-resolution and high-quality panoramic photographs to cellphones.

Nikita (2020), explains use of IoT for ITS. Within intelligent transportation systems (ITS), vehicle tracking data is essential for fleet managers who wish to track vehicles for logistics and transportation as well as for drivers and passengers who want to know where they are to cross or obtain location-relevant data. For the purpose of conducting rescue operations, the ability to identify a car that is in danger and locate illegal cars or vehicles carrying hazardous chemicals is essential to government authorities. Information technology and communication are necessary for ITS to operate. Some of these tools, like loop detectors, are well known to individuals in the transportation sector. However, an assortment of less well-known systems and technologies are necessary for ITS to function. While communication and control technologies form the foundation of ITS, human factors are equally important and can present difficulties. This paper outlines the most significant technological solutions for ITS and clarifies how human factors specialists should be included from the start in the network and instrument design of ITS. The study used the example of an Indian transportation scenario center to discuss how to find IoT solutions for ITS and evaluate them inside the corporate design.

Ravi et al (2022), explain use of IoT on LOVE. A system is needed to demonstrate the love and closeness to one another as well as their remembrance. Even today, the only ways to express closeness are still by phone or mail. We will therefore demonstrate our love and remembrance through the use of contemporary methodology and the IoT. There has never been a system or concept like this before. We present this system using the Internet of Things and sensors.

Sunil Kumar et al. (2022), explains Deep Learning for diseases identification in Plants. Plant diseases are the focus of this research because they seriously jeopardize the food production and livelihoods of small-scale farmers. In traditional farming, each row is visually inspected by trained personnel to detect plant diseases. Because it is labor-intensive and time-consuming, this task is flawed by nature because it is done by humans. The goal of this research is to combine image recognition and deep learning techniques (Faster R-CNN+ResNet50) to assess real-time photos in order to develop an automated identification algorithm for three of the most common diseases of maize plants: Northern Leaf Blight, Cercospora Spot, and Frequent Rust. The proposed system achieved a 93.5% reliability rate in effectively identifying three diseases of maize.

IOT IN FASHION

IoT is a revolutionary technology that has transformed the manner in which we work, live, and engage with the world. IoT has permeated many industries, including fashion, and is now present in everything from smart houses to internet-connected cars. IoT integration in the fashion industry has created a plethora of new opportunities and improved efficiency, personalization, and sustainability. The influence of IoT on the clothing sector as well as how it is influencing fashion's future will be discussed in this article.

To put it simply, IoT in fashion refers to the incorporation of connected devices and sensors in clothing and accessories. These devices collect and transmit data, which can be used to improve the overall experience of consumers. The apparel sector could undergo a revolution thanks to such technology, which offers real-time information and insights. leading to better decision-making and enhancing the overall customer experience.

Smart Clothing and Wearables

One of the most significant applications of IoT in fashion is the development of smart clothing and wearables. These are garments and accessories embedded with sensors, microchips, and other electronics that can collect and transmit data. For example, smart fitness trackers and smartwatches have become popular among consumers, helping them track their health and fitness goals. Similarly, there are smart shoes that can analyze your gait and posture, and even adjust the fit accordingly.

In addition to fitness and health, smart clothing can also enhance the fashion experience. For example, there are smart handbags that can charge your phone wirelessly, and smart jewelry that can track your daily activity and sleep patterns. These innovations not only add convenience but also make a fashion statement.

Personalization and Data Collection

IoT in fashion has enabled the collection of real-time data, which can be used to personalize the shopping experience for consumers. For example, smart mirrors in fitting rooms can recognize the garments a customer is trying on and suggest complementary items or accessories. This not only saves time but also provides a more personalized shopping experience. Retailers can also use data collected from IoT devices to analyze consumer behavior and preferences, leading to better inventory management and more targeted marketing strategies. This can also help reduce waste and overproduction in the fashion industry, making it more sustainable.

Improving Supply Chain and Inventory Management

The use of IoT in fashion can also improve supply chain and inventory management for retailers. By tracking the movement of products Retailers can guarantee that the correct items arrive in the correct location at the correct moment by using the supply chain. This can reduce the risk of overstocking or stockouts, ultimately leading to cost savings and a more efficient supply chain. In addition, IoT can also help in tracking product authenticity and preventing counterfeiting, which is a major issue in the fashion industry. By using RFID tags and sensors, retailers can track the journey of a product from production to the hands of the customer, ensuring its authenticity.

Challenges and Future of IoT in Fashion

Even though IoT has an opportunity to revolutionize the fashion industry, there are also some challenges that need to be addressed. One of the major concerns is data privacy and security. As more and more data is collected through connected devices, there is a risk of this data falling into the wrong hands. Therefore, it is essential for fashion brands to ensure the security of their IoT devices and the data they collect. Another challenge is the high cost of implementing IoT technology in fashion. For small and medium-sized fashion brands, the cost of incorporating IoT devices and sensors in their products may be prohibitive. However, as the technology advances and becomes more widespread, the cost is expected to decrease, making it more accessible for all fashion brands.

In all, IoT has the capacity to change the fashion industry, making it more personalized, efficient, and sustainable. The integration of connected devices in clothing and accessories is just the beginning, and we can expect to see more innovations in the future. As consumers become more tech-savvy, the demand for smart fashion is only going to increase, and fashion brands that embrace IoT will have a competitive edge in the market.

ML IN FASHION

ML has become a fashion industry buzzword, and for good reason. From predicting fashion trends to enhancing the customer experience, ML is revolutionizing the fashion industry in ways that were unimaginable just a few years ago.

So, what exactly is ML and how is it being used in the fashion industry? In simple terms, ML is a subset of AI that enables computers gain knowledge and grow to encounter with no getting explicitly programmed. Within the framework of fashion, this means that computers are able to learn and analyze large amounts of data, such as customer preferences and fashion trends, to make accurate predictions and recommendations.

One of the most prominent uses of ML in the fashion industry is trend forecasting. Fashion trends are constantly changing and it can be a daunting task for designers and retailers to keep up. However, with the help of ML, companies are able to analyze data from social media, online searches, and sales data to identify emerging trends and make informed decisions about their collections. This not only saves time and resources, but also ensures that fashion brands are producing designs that are in demand.

ML is also being applied to customize the shopping experience for customers. Through the examination of client information, such as previous purchases and browsing history, ML algorithms can make recommendations for products that are tailored to the individual's style and preferences. This raises the possibility of closing a deal while also improving the client experience. Companies like Stitch Fix and Amazon have successfully implemented this technology, leading to increased customer satisfaction and loyalty.

In addition to trend forecasting and personalization, ML is also being used in supply chain management. Fashion brands and retailers have to deal with a vast and complex network of suppliers, manufacturers, and logistics providers. By using ML algorithms, companies are able to optimize their supply chains by predicting demand and managing inventory levels more efficiently. This results in cost savings and a more streamlined supply chain process.

Sustainability is another field in which machine learning is having a big influence. The fashion industry is known for its environmental impact, with fast fashion and overproduction contributing to waste and pollution. ML algorithms can analyze data from production processes and supply chains to determine what aspects of sustainability need to be strengthened. This can lead to more sustainable practices, such as reducing waste and using eco-friendly materials.

Like any kind of technology, machine learning has its share of drawbacks. The bias within algorithms is one of the main issues. ML algorithms have the ability to reinforce prejudice and discrimination because they undergo training upon historical data. For example, an algorithm may produce proposals that aren't inclusive if the dataset used for training it is biased towards a specific physique or skin tone. Fashion brands and businesses need to make confident that the information utilized for teaching the algorithms is accurately reflecting every demographic in order to address this.

All things considered, ML has the power to revolutionize the fashion sector by enhancing customer satisfaction, sustainability, personalization, and efficiency. To prevent biases from being reinforced, it is crucial that businesses use this technology in an ethical and responsible manner. We may anticipate seeing even more cutting-edge applications of machine learning in the fashion sector as technology develops further, creating a more efficient and data-driven fashion scene.

MLIoT IN FASHION

Machine Learning Internet of Things (MLIoT) is the combination of two powerful technologies – machine learning and Internet of Things (IoT). AI includes ML-machine learning, which gives computers the ability to acquire knowledge and generate decisions with no explicit programming. Contrarily, IoT- Internet of Things is a network of actual physical objects, including cars and other items, that are embedded with software, sensors, and connectivity to allow them to communicate with one another and share data.

When both of these technologies work together, they produce a potent system that can analyze data, spot patterns, and decide without the need for human input. This enables automation and decision-making in real-time, improving the effectiveness and efficiency of processes.

The fashion industry has always been at the forefront of innovation and is no stranger to technology. From design and manufacturing to retail and marketing, technology has played a significant role in shaping the industry. With the emergence of MLIoT, the fashion industry is once again embracing new technology to enhance its processes and deliver a better experience to its customers.

One of the main areas where MLIoT is being used in the fashion industry is in supply chain management. With the help of IoT sensors, companies can track their products throughout the entire supply chain, from production to delivery. This not only improves efficiency but also allows for better inventory management and reduces the risk of counterfeiting.

MLIoT is also being used in customer experience and personalization. Through the assistance of ML algorithms, apparel manufacturers can analyze consumer information and tastes to offer personalized recommendations and suggestions. This improves customer satisfaction while also assisting businesses in better understanding their target market and developing products that speak to them.

Another field in which MLIoT is having a big influence is in sustainability. With the help of IoT sensors, companies can track the environmental impact of their products throughout their lifecycle. This enables them to make more informed decisions and take steps towards reducing their carbon footprint. Fashion brands are also using MLIoT to improve their marketing strategies. Businesses can create tailored and targeted marketing campaigns by analyzing customer data and behavior with the aid of ML algorithms. This helps to decrease resource waste while also boosting the efficacy of marketing campaigns.

CHALLENGES AND FUTURE OF MLIoT IN FASHION

While the potential of MLIoT in the fashion industry is immense, furthermore, there are certain issues that must be resolved. Data security and privacy is one of the major issues. There is a chance of breaches of data and improper utilization of identifiable information because of the volume of data being gathered and processed. Therefore, it is crucial for fashion companies to have robust data protection measures in place to ensure the security of customer data.

Another challenge is the high cost of implementing MLIoT technology. For smaller fashion companies, the cost of implementing this technology may be prohibitive, making it difficult for them to compete with larger brands. But as the technology is used more extensively, costs should come down, making it more affordable for smaller businesses.

The future of MLIoT in the fashion industry looks promising. As technology continues to advance, we can expect to see even more innovative uses of MLIoT in the fashion world. From smart clothing that can adjust to the wearer's body temperature to virtual fitting rooms that use machine learning to recommend the perfect outfit, the possibilities are endless.

In all, MLIoT has the potential to transform the fashion industry in ways that we could have never imagined. By combining the power of machine learning and IoT, fashion companies can improve their processes, enhance the customer experience, and contribute towards a more sustainable future. As this technology continues to evolve, we can expect to see even more exciting developments in the world of fashion.

METHODOLOGY

Figure 4 depicts our proposed system ML part, which consists of four primary steps:

Figure 4. Our suggested pipeline for body part measurement prediction

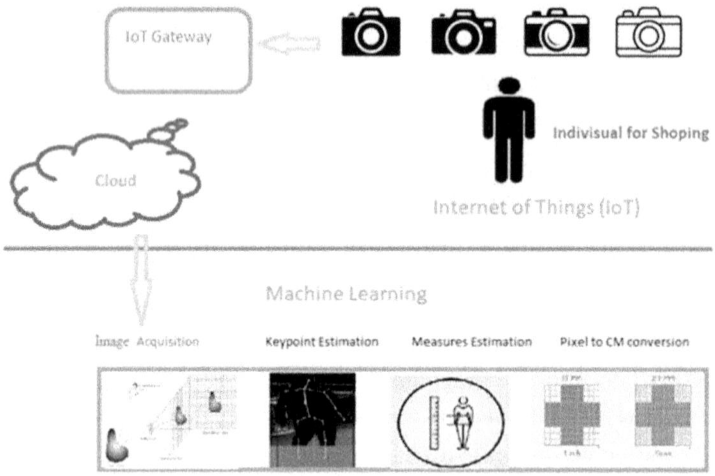

- Acquisition of images,
- Estimating Key points,
- Estimating body measurements, and
- Converting pixels to centimeters.

Below is a detailed description of each step.

Image Acquisition

We require the frontal and side images for every user. The subject of the frontal image stands with their arms apart and their limbs straight. The distance between the legs is about 15 cm. The user needs to keep his or her arms and legs closed for the side image. An illustrative example of the required images is provided in Figure 4.

Estimating Key Points

To the most effective of our understanding, the body measurement methods currently in use locate body feature points using heuristics. For instance, the hip is thought to be the largest and the waist to be the smallest middle portion of the body. Nevertheless, this isn't always the case. For instance, an obese person may have a paunch, which causes their waist to be bigger than their hips.

Estimating Body Measurements

In order to recommend a garment size, we estimate the seven body part measurements (shoulder width, waist, chest, hip, natural waist, sleeve length, along with pant length). Our voices employ every particular combination of indicates in the frontal as well as side images for acquire the horizontal as well as vertical measurements. For instance, to estimate the length of a shoulder, we use two frontal horizontal key points on the shoulder, whereas two vertical points—the waist or natural waist and ankle—are needed to determine the length of a pair of trousers. We obtain all of our vertical measurements from the side view picture.

Converting Pixels to Centimeters

In order to recommend a garment size, we estimate the seven body part measurements (shoulder width, waist, chest, hip, prior to that we determine the transformation, we employ Mask RCNN on a input frontal image for computing a subject height within pixels, h. For the subject, Mask R-CNN produces a masked output and a bounding box. Next, we request the user's height, L, in centimeters so that we can compute a ratio, R, which represents the pixel-to-cm ratio. Equation (1) can be used to calculate R by dividing the number of pixels (n) that represent a person by his height (L). By calculating this ratio, we can resolve the issue where a person appears small when they are far away from the camera or large when they are close to it. In order to recommend a garment size, we estimate the seven body part measurements (shoulder width, waist, chest, hip, Nevertheless, perspective effects can appear in some images, which could compromise the precision of the measured values. Lastly, using Equation (2), the predicted true measurements for the subject, M, are calculated by dividing the vertical or girth measurements (K) from R's earlier step.

$$R= n/L \tag{1}$$

$$M =K/R \tag{2}$$

We use a voting algorithm to recommend the best fitting size for size prediction. We run this voting algorithm after extracting the user's body measurements and adding the size chart provided by the retailer the user is considering. Every measurement on the size chart has been removed from the user's matching measurement (e.g., the user's waist measurement is subtracted compared to the size chart's waist XS). After sorting the results, we determine which size produces the smallest positive difference. Repeat this procedure for each measurement that is required for the particular piece of fabric. Every size will cast a vote to determine the entire cloth size which the user will ultimately be recommended.

RESULTS AND DISCUSSION

Two datasets are used by our system: one of them to feed measurements prediction and the other for key point estimation. Frontal and side views photos from the People snapshot dataset and the Fashion (DeepFashion) dataset are combined to create the key point estimation dataset. We used data augmentation through rotating the chosen images by 45,-45 degrees in order to expand the dataset.

Table I shows three randomly chosen subjects from our internal dataset, varying in age, gender, and shape, with samples predicted measurements (PM) compared to Actual Measurements (AM) and error in cm (Er). The average error in centimeters for our system after testing it on the entire dataset is also shown in the table.

Table 1. Results of estimation of body measurements

Measurements of Body Part in cm	Person 1 (Female)			Person 2 (Male)			Person 3(Child 18 Months)		
	AM	PM	Er in cm	AM	PM	Er	AM	PM	Er
Shoulder	36.7	36.2	0.5	42.5	41.4	1.1	8.25	7.2	1.05
Chest	96	94.5	1.5	96.4	97	1.4	19	17	2
Neck	33.4	31.3	2.1	38.1	36	2.1	3.25	2	2.25
Sleeve	79.1	77	2.0	81.4	80.1	1.3	7.5	6.5	1.0
Height(Shirt)	82.1	80	2.1	82.3	80	2.3	7.5	6.5	1.0
Waist	91.3	90	1.3	76.3	75	1.3	5.25	4.5	0.75
Hip	102.3	100	2.3	94.2	92	2.2	19.5	18	1.5
Height(Pant)	82	80	2.0	84	81.5	2.5	10	9	1.0

Our method yields a computed measurement between 0.5 and 2.5 cm in error. This implies greater potential for improvement down the road. Because there isn't a standardized dataset, we tested our method on limited internally dataset.

A deeper comprehension of body shape can improve the current results. As a result, we are creating improved mathematical formulas to depict body forms. Redesigned formulas will lower error and yield more precise measurements for a few human body parts that account for the largest percentage of error at present. It was extremely difficult to test the system with a larger group of participants because of the COVID-19 pandemic.

CONCLUSION

A system that automatically determines a customer's size and takes their body measurements is revolutionary in the realm of online shopping. Customers and retailers alike gain from its convenience, accuracy, inclusivity, and sustainability. It is reasonable to assume that this system will continue to develop and get better due to the ongoing advances in technology, making future online shopping even more smooth and customized. Retail apparel is being revolutionized by MLIoT, which offers retailers automation, personalization, and real-time insights. As this technology develops further, we should anticipate more creative applications and breakthroughs in the retail sector. Retailers that adopt MLIoT will be able to optimize their operations and offer a better shopping experience at a competitive advantage. MLIoT has the potential to transform the fashion industry in ways that we could have never imagined. By combining the power of machine learning and IoT, fashion companies can improve their processes, enhance the customer experience, and contribute towards a more sustainable future. We may anticipate even more fascinating advancements in the fashion industry as this technology keeps developing. Using a voting method, we determine the customer's ideal clothing size by precisely estimating ten body measurements that are used to predict clothing size. A completely autonomous key points forecasting will be taken into consideration for future work. For upcoming research, a bigger standardized body measurement dataset is also taken into consideration.

REFERENCES

3DLook. (n.d.). https://3dlook.me

Aavula, R., & Deshmukh, A. (2022). Design and Implementation of sensor and IoT based Remembrance system for closed one. *Telematique, 21*(1), 2769–2778.

Dhaware, B. U. (2023). Predictive Data Analytics Framework Based on Heart Healthcare System (HHS) Using Machine Learning. *Journal of Advanced Zoology, 44*(2).

Kalmkar, S., Mujawar, A., & Liyakat, D. K. K. S. (2022). 3D E-Commers using AR. *International Journal of Information Technology & Computer Engineering, 2*(6), 18–27. doi:10.55529/ijitc.26.18.27

Karale Aishwarya, A. (2023). Smart Billing Cart Using RFID, YOLO and Deep Learning for Mall Administration. *International Journal of Instrumentation and Innovation Sciences, 8*(2).

Kazi. (2022). *Systematic Survey on Alzheimer (AD) Diseases Detection.* Academic Press.

Kazi. (2022). *A Review paper Alzheimer.* Academic Press.

Kazi K. (2022). Model for Agricultural Information system to improve crop yield using IoT. *Journal of Open Source Development, 9*(2), 16 – 24.

Kazi, K. (2022). Smart Grid energy saving technique using Machine Learning. *Journal of Instrumentation Technology and Innovations, 12*(3), 1–10.

Kazi, K. (2024). AI-Driven IoT (AIIoT) in Healthcare Monitoring. In T. Nguyen & N. Vo (Eds.), *Using Traditional Design Methods to Enhance AI-Driven Decision Making* (pp. 77–101). IGI Global. doi:10.4018/979-8-3693-0639-0.ch003

Kazi, K. S. (2017). Significance And Usage Of Face Recognition System. *Scholarly Journal For Humanity Science and English Language*, *4*(20), 4764–4772.

Kazi, K S. (2022). Business Mode and Product Life Cycle to Improve Marketing in Healthcare Units. *E-Commerce for Future & Trends, 9*(3), 1-9.

Kazi, K. S. (2023). Detection of Malicious Nodes in IoT Networks based on Throughput and ML. *Journal of Electrical and Power System Engineering*, *9*(1), 22–29.

Kazi, K. S. L. (2018). Significance of Projection and Rotation of Image in Color Matching for High-Quality Panoramic Images used for Aquatic study. *International Journal of Aquatic Science*, *09*(02), 130–145.

Kazi & Shaikh. (2023). Machine Learning in the Production Process Control of Metal Melting. *Journal of Advancement in Machines*, *8*(2).

Kazi, S. (2023). Fruit Grading, Disease Detection, and an Image Processing Strategy. *Journal of Image Processing and Artificial Intelligence*, *9*(2), 17–34.

Kazi, S. S. L. (2023). ML in the Electronics Manufacturing Industry. *Journal of Switching Hub*, *8*(3), 9–13.

Kazi, V. (2023). Deep Learning, YOLO and RFID based smart Billing Handcart. *Journal of Communication Engineering & Systems*, *13*(1), 1–8.

Kazi Kutubuddin, S. L. (2022). Predict the Severity of Diabetes cases, using K-Means and Decision Tree Approach. *Journal of Advances in Shell Programming*, *9*(2), 24–31.

Kazi. (2023). Electronics with Artificial Intelligence Creating a Smarter Future: A Review. *Journal of Communication Engineering and Its Innovations*, *9*(3), 38–42.

Kosgiker, G. M. (2018). Machine Learning- Based System, Food Quality Inspection and Grading in Food industry. *International Journal of Food and Nutritional Sciences*, *11*(10), 723–730.

Kutub, K. (2022). Detection of Malicious Nodes in IoT Networks based on packet loss using ML. *Journal of Mobile Computing, Communication & mobile. Networks*, *9*(3), 9–16.

Kutubuddin, K. (2022). Big data and HR Analytics in Talent Management: A Study. *Recent Trends in Parallel Computing*, *9*(3), 16–26.

Liyakat, K. K. S. (2023). Detecting Malicious Nodes in IoT Networks Using Machine Learning and Artificial Neural Networks. *2023 International Conference on Emerging Smart Computing and Informatics (ESCI),* 1-5. 10.1109/ESCI56872.2023.10099544

Liyakat, K. K. S. (2023). Machine Learning Approach Using Artificial Neural Networks to Detect Malicious Nodes in IoT Networks. In P. K. Shukla, H. Mittal, & A. Engelbrecht (Eds.), *Computer Vision and Robotics. CVR 2023. Algorithms for Intelligent Systems*. Springer. doi:10.1007/978-981-99-4577-1_3

Liyakat, K. K. S. (2024). Machine Learning Approach Using Artificial Neural Networks to Detect Malicious Nodes in IoT Networks. In S. K. Udgata, S. Sethi, & X. Z. Gao (Eds.), *Intelligent Systems. ICMIB 2023. Lecture Notes in Networks and Systems* (Vol. 728). Springer. doi:10.1007/978-981-99-3932-9_12

Liyakat, S. (2023). ML in the Electronics Manufacturing Industry. *Journal of Switching Hub*, *8*(3), 9–13. doi:10.46610/JoSH.2023.v08i03.002

Mulani, A. O., & Patil, R. M. (2023). Discriminative Appearance Model for Robust Online Multiple Target Tracking. *Telematique*, *22*(1), 24–43.

Nerkar & Shinde. (2023). Monitoring Fresh Fruit and Food Using Iot and Machine Learning to Improve Food Safety and Quality. *Tuijin Jishu/Journal of Propulsion Technology*, *44*(3), 2927 – 2931.

Nikita, K. (2020). Design of Vehicle system using CAN Protocol. *International Journal for Research in Applied Science and Engineering Technology*, *8*(V), 1978–1983. doi:10.22214/ijraset.2020.5321

Pradeepa, M. (2022). Student Health Detection using a Machine Learning Approach and IoT. *2022 IEEE 2nd Mysore Sub Section International Conference (MysuruCon).*

Ravi, A. (2022). *Pattern Recognition- An Approach towards Machine Learning. Lambert Publications.*

Sayyad Liyakat. (2022). Nanotechnology Application in Neural Growth Support System. *Nano Trends: A Journal of Nanotechnology and Its Applications, 24*(2), 47 – 55.

Sherin Aly. (2021). *Toward Smart Internet Of Things (Iot) For Apparel Retail Industry: Automatic Customer's Body Measurements And Size Recommendation System Using Computer Vision Techniques.* Academic Press.

Sunil Kumar, Ganesh, Turukmane, & Batta. (2022). Deep Convolution Neural Network based solution for detecting plant Diseases. *Journal of Pharmaceutical Negative Results*, *13*(1), 464-471.

Swami. (2022). Sending notification to someone missing you through smart watch. *International Journal of Information Technology & Computer Engineering, 2*(8), 19 – 24.

Chapter 5
Navigating the Landscape of Green Marketing Trends and Identifying Greenwashing Red Flags

Pournima Somesh
Christ University, India

M. Ritika
Christ University, India

Harmandeep Singh
Christ University, India

ABSTRACT

Through this chapter, the authors intend to provide information to the fashion and retail industry about the latest trends and their drawbacks, further increasing the awareness of environmentally conscious consumers. The objective of the study is first to examine the prevalent green marketing strategies adopted by fashion and retail businesses. Further, it also evaluates the actual reality and effectiveness behind the strategies used by brands to understand if they are creating an illusion of sustainability or are genuinely committed through case studies of various retail brands. Lastly it investigates consumer attitudes and perceptions of green marketing in fashion and retail. This research employs an approach to explore driving factors for green marketing in the fashion and retail industry. Utilizing secondary data, a comprehensive review of existing literature on sustainable practices, consumer behaviour, and industry trends was done.

DOI: 10.4018/979-8-3693-3049-4.ch005

I. INTRODUCTION

Clothing production and consumption have increased steadily over the last few decades because of rising global incomes, rapid population expansion, and living standards. Clothing is made and designed to quickly change trends through early obsolescence and disposal (Shirvanimoghaddam et al.,2020).

The fashion industry has recently experienced a notable shift due to the surge in consumer consciousness regarding environmental concerns and sustainability. The fashion industry is gradually embracing a green revolution in response to the escalating concerns over climate change, resource depletion, and ethical sourcing. This paradigm shift is encapsulated in the concept of "green marketing," which seeks to integrate sustainability into the core of fashion business practices (Alexa et al., 2022). With the rise of environmental consciousness and worries about the ecological impact of different industries, the 1970s were a watershed year. As a result, there was a paradigm shift in the fashion and retail industries toward more environmentally friendly and sustainable practices. Ottman, J. (1998) demand for fashion products made sustainably and ethically increased along with customer awareness. Companies began using eco-friendly procedures in all aspects of their business, from procurement of raw materials to production and delivery. The 21st century has witnessed a rise in environmentally conscious fashion initiatives, with businesses using green marketing techniques more frequently to highlight their dedication to sustainability.

Given that a company's standing has a big influence on customers' perceptions and propensity to purchase, the idea of "Greenwashing," first introduced by Jay Westerveld in 1986, emerged in tandem with green marketing. Greenwashing is defined as "a phenomenon that includes poor environmental performance and positive communication about it," (de Freitas Netto et al). For instance, the greenwashing case of Patagonia urged consumers to buy fewer things and choose more sustainably by running an anti-consumerist campaign but "At the same time they are supporting customers in improving their behavior by urging them to make more thoughtful purchases (Allchin, 2014) Still, the reality is that only less than 1% of it can be recycled and in Europe, leftover textiles account for 15–25% of the total, of which half are recycled. The other half is utilized to make used apparel in underdeveloped nations. The remaining 80–85% of textiles made in Europe are burned or dumped in landfills if they are not recovered (Sandin & Peters, 2018).

II. GREEN MARKETING TRENDS IN RETAIL

SHIEN

The most downloaded app in the US in 2021 (even surpassing Amazon), Shein is a well-known Chinese brand with competitive prices and $10 billion in revenue that obliterates everything in its way. Chinese retailer SHEIN recently appointed a Chief Governance, Social, and Environmental Officer (also known as an Industry ESG Director) as part of its most recent effort to meet rising business and fashion standards (Srauturier, 2024). Customers can return leftover products to Shein for coupons, according to the brand's website. Shein advertises itself as a vegan company that doesn't use any fur or leather on its website (Kenk, 2022). Shein introduced its "Our Products/Our Planet" campaign in response to mounting negative publicity. The campaign states that Shein produces 50–100 pieces for each product and will only make big quantities of a product when there is a great demand for it. (Lai, 2024)

Greenwashing

Employing ESG officers and others in comparable positions seems like a good idea. However, this announcement sounds false since the fast-fashion brand wants to appear as though it is "concerned" about sustainability, even though its entire business model is based on environmental and labor abuse. (Srauturier, 2024) Shein employs a large number of subcontractors, which creates a control vacuum that invites abuse. These are small, unofficial factories with closed windows and subpar construction. There is also a considerable risk of fire. Because there are no contracts, employees must work 11–12 hours a day, 75 hours a week, without overtime compensation, and with only one day off a month, among other consequences. Naturally, the returned item is thrown away because recycling is more expensive for them. However, overconsumption and obsessive buying are the outcomes of this marketing strategy. Shein not using fur and leather isn't to defend the rights of animals. This is because the aforementioned materials are expensive; therefore, polyester is used for the fur, and polyurethane is used for the leather. However, these materials are harmful to the environment because they cannot be recycled (Kenk, 2022). Shein debuted its "Our Products/Our Planet" campaign, promising to produce 50–100 pieces for each product and to only go into large-scale production when the product is highly demanded. However, the campaign does not specify the high demand threshold or commit to using sustainable fabrics and materials. The Chinese online retailer also recently falsely stated on its website that conditions in the factories it uses were certified by international labor standards bodies, which has prompted many labor watchdogs to question how it produces its clothing at such low prices (Lai, 2024).

UNIQLO

Having grown to be a worldwide fashion giant with over 2,000 outlets in 25 countries, Uniqlo has gone a long way. One of the biggest retails holding businesses globally, Fast Retailing Co., Ltd., is the brand's owner and CEO, Tadashi Yanai. Uniqlo's sales approach revolves around the notion of "LifeWear," which emphasizes cost, simplicity, and usefulness so you may look fashionable without compromising comfort or breaking the bank. Nonetheless, people become a little more aware when the terms "high-quality clothing" and "affordable" are used together in the same phrase. Is Uniqlo ultimately a sustainable and ethical brand or is it just another rapid fashion outlet? (Antoniadou, 2023) In addition to creating energy-efficient infrastructure and supporting the Setouchi Olive Foundation, which works to preserve and restore the islands and coastal regions of Japan's Seto Inland Sea, Uniqlo has adopted several sustainable practices. The goal of Uniqlo has been sustainability for more than 20 years. We are dedicated to a healthy earth, society, and people as a worldwide company making ethical clothes, according to the firm's website. Uniqlo makes investments in energy-saving technology to lessen its carbon footprint. It has shifted to renewable energy sources and put energy-saving measures in place in its warehouses and retail locations. The organization has put in place a Supplier Code of Conduct to encourage ethical procurement and enhance working conditions for laborers in its supply chain. Uniqlo has put in place a program to cut down on wasteful packaging. In addition to employing reusable bags made of recycled materials, it has shrunk the size of its shopping bags. Customers who own lightly used Uniqlo clothing can bring it in to be recycled as part of the company's recycling program. Since its inception in Japan in 2006, the program has spread to the US, UK, and Australia, among other nations. Last but not least, a few fast-fashion retailers in Japan are offering free repairs for their apparel. Additionally, they have a programme called "Repair Service Voucher" that allows clients to mail in their damaged items for a free repair (Antoniadou, 2023).

Greenwashing

The Japanese store Uniqlo is a well-known fast fashion brand, so it's not surprising to see them on the list of greenwashing fashion brands. Numerous complaints and breaches of labor rights have been made against Uniqlo. The firm isn't known for its sustainability, either, despite having over 3,000 locations worldwide and producing a lot of inexpensive synthetic materials, such as rayon, polyester, nylon, and elastane, and selling them at extremely low prices. Nevertheless, a survey published by the Changing Markets Foundation indicates that many of Uniqlo's sustainability claims are overstated or incorrect. For example, Uniqlo advertised that 30% of the materials used to make its fleece products were recycled, but the actual number was closer to 1%. For their textiles, Uniqlo does not display any certifications. The true problem, though, is that the Japanese company still doesn't provide implementation settings or report on its progress towards its climate change aim of reducing emissions in its supply chain. Its environmental aims have also not been validated by science, making it very difficult to assess whether or not they align with international and national climate policies. Surprisingly, Uniqlo doesn't reveal its carbon footprint or environmental effect, which makes it challenging for customers to assess the sustainability of the company. This lack of openness calls into doubt the business's sustainability commitment. It has been alleged that Uniqlo uses dangerous chemicals throughout the clothes manufacturing process, which could endanger the workers. In a report titled "Toxic Threads: The Big Fashion Stitch-Up," published by Greenpeace in 2013, the fast-fashion companies Uniqlo and others were charged with employing dangerous chemicals throughout the clothes production process (Antoniadou, 2023).

BOOHOO

Boohoo is a fast fashion business that was founded in the UK in 2006 and has only recently reached unprecedented production levels. The brand's prices sit around the midrange, with one garment tending to cost between $20 and $90. Its sizes range from 2 to 28, but most garments only feature around seven of these sizes each It creates apparel for various events, including formal, informal, and night out. As they strive to become a more sustainable company, the READY FOR THE FUTURE line incorporates recycled materials like polyester. These classic loungewear pieces, matching tracksuit sets, and warm puffer coats are must-haves for the chilly months. It's never been simpler to dress more sustainably. According to Boohoo, half of their synthetic cellulosic and all of their cotton will come from more sustainably derived sources by 2025. Boohoo aims to map its raw materials supply chain for essential fibers by 2023 and promises to provide significant information about the raw material supply chain by 2025. Last but not least, Boohoo and the reGAIN app have teamed to enable customers to trade in their worn goods for vouchers so they may be recycled. Additionally, it states that it will be "looking at our resale and recycling offers to extend the life of our products and make sure that they don't end up in landfills" and that textile waste is a "big focus".

Greenwashing

Upon examining the products marked as "sustainable," it was discovered that a few of them were composed of acrylic, a kind of plastic. There isn't much evidence to support the brand's claim that this material can be recycled. Furthermore, a few of these products are less than £10 as the quality is bad and can't be worn for a long period. Further, the salary of the garment workers in the supply chain of Boohoo is also not mentioned. In addition to deceiving customers, Boohoo is not making any efforts to lessen its influence on the environment and its residents (Srauturier, 2024) Boohoo claims that by 2025, half of their synthetic cellulosic and all of their cotton and polyester will come from more sustainably sourced materials. It says that while it will continue to use wool, down, feathers, and leather, those materials will be sourced in line with industry best practices. We had anticipated seeing Boohoo utilizing sustainable alternatives because the factory farming sectors are major contributors to our changing climate and equivalent items are already available to replace them. The use of these materials has already been ceased by numerous rival companies (Boohoo Breakdown: The Fast Fashion Brand's Sustainability, n.d.).

Lululemon

Known by its common name, Lululemon, Lululemon Athletica Inc. is an international retailer of sports apparel with Canadian and American roots. In addition to yoga pants and other yoga gear, the firm has expanded since its foundation in 1998 to provide athletic, and lifestyle clothes, accessories, and personal care products (Wikipedia authors, 2024). By 2030, it wants to cut greenhouse gas emissions from owned businesses and supply chains by 60%. They are also devoted to adapting infrastructure to take back products after first use and recycle materials into a valuable next life, including fiber-to-fiber.

Greenwashing

There isn't much proof that it has made any significant efforts to reduce the impact of microplastics or preserve biodiversity in its supply chain. Lululemon's largest materials sourced by weight are polyester and nylon, two non-biodegradable polymers obtained from fossil fuels that have the potential to release toxic microfibres that pollute the environment. Studies conducted in the Arctic have revealed that over 75% of microplastic contamination originates from polyester. Therefore, large corporations that continue to heavily utilize polyester while professing to be sustainable bear a great deal of accountability for addressing their usage. Moreover, Lululemon's efforts to switch from virgin materials to better alternatives like recycled polyester and nylon are still insufficient (Elliott, 2023). Although it's admirable that Lululemon talks about ways to minimize its impact on the environment, this doesn't amount to much action. Which programs are they altering? What time is this happening? What is a "valuable next life"? A multinational company such as Lululemon has no excuse to ignore its environmental obligations (Lululemon - Sustainability Rating - Good on You, n.d.).

III. IMPACT OF FAST FASHION ON THE ENVIRONMENT

The apparel sector has seen a shift because of fast fashion, which provides customers with stylish items at reasonable rates and with quick turnover. But beneath the low prices and frequent design changes, there's a grim reality to fast fashion: it has a big environmental impact. This study explores the complex environmental consequences of the fast fashion industry's activities.

Pollution of Air and Water: A major component of fast fashion is the use of synthetic fabrics like polyester, which are produced using a lot of energy and are sourced from petrochemicals. Pollutants from the production process are released into the atmosphere and waterways, adding to pollution in both. In addition to contaminating water sources, toxic chemicals used in fabric dyeing, such as heavy metals and azo dyes, also pose a threat to human health and aquatic ecosystems.

Excessive Resource Consumption: Excessive resource consumption is a result of the unrelenting drive for quick production. Water shortage in areas where textile manufacturing is concentrated is exacerbated by fast fashion businesses' massive water use for fabric dyeing and finishing procedures. Furthermore, the industry's dependence on inexpensive labor and fossil fuels for transportation raises carbon emissions, which exacerbates climate change and degrades the environment.

Waste Generation and Landfill Overflow: The "throwaway culture" of fast fashion encourages the purchase of disposable apparel, which leads to an astounding volume of textile waste. Every year, millions of tons of unsold goods and unwanted clothing are dumped in landfills, where they slowly break down and release greenhouse gases like methane. Furthermore, when synthetic fibers are washed, they release microplastics into the water, further polluting aquatic environments and marine life.

Effects on Society and Economy: Even though this study focuses on the effects on the environment, it is important to recognize how social and environmental issues are intertwined. The fast fashion business continues to violate human rights and maintain subpar working conditions and low wages by using cheap labor from developing nations.

To address environmental sustainability, a comprehensive strategy that takes social justice and moral labor practices into account is required. Fast fashion has significant and wide-ranging negative effects on the environment, including waste production, pollution, resource depletion, and social inequities. To change the fashion industry and move toward a more ethical and sustainable model that puts long-term viability, social responsibility, and environmental stewardship first, immediate action is required. It is possible to lessen the negative consequences of rapid fashion and create the conditions for a more sustainable future by increasing awareness, putting creative solutions into practice, and holding stakeholders accountable.

The constant consumption of cheap clothing is necessary for fast fashion to exist. Compared to 2000, consumers bought 60% more clothes on average in 2014, but they only maintained them for half as long (Remy et al., 2016; Cobbing & Vicaire, 2016). Waste produced by fast fashion is massive. It is estimated that every second, the equivalent of one garbage truck's worth of textiles is incinerated or landfilled (Ellen MacArthur Foundation, 2021). Textile waste collection rates are extremely low. In Europe, only about 15% to 20% are collected. The remaining 80–85% are either burned or dumped in landfills (Sandin & Peters, 2018). The fashion sector uses a lot of carbon. The entire textile life cycle—from manufacturing to consumption and transportation—is impacted by it in terms of climate. The fashion industry is now heavily reliant on fossil fuels due to the 1990s' rapid expansion in the use of inexpensive synthetic fibres in textile manufacture. Globalisation of the textile supply chain: Clothes are produced, and they move through each stage of the process. In particular, Europe depends on textile imports to meet demand from consumers. Since synthetic plastic fibres already account for roughly 69% of all textile production, the fast fashion sector has grown innately dependent on their low-cost production (Changing Markets Foundation, 2021). In order to get fibres for textile manufacture, excessive resource exploitation is involved, which places a heavy reliance on non-renewable resources and hazardous materials like chemicals and pesticides in huge quantities (e.g., for dyeing). Pollution of rivers and streams, soil erosion, depletion of resources, drying up of water resources, pollution from microplastics, global warming, and the disposal of massive garbage mounds are examples of negative environmental effects. More than the European Union, the fashion industry is said to be responsible for 10% of global carbon emissions, according to a Business Insider analysis. Although 85% of textiles are disposed of in landfills annually, this depletes water resources and contaminates rivers and streams. The act of washing clothes releases 50 billion plastic bottles, or 500,000 tonnes of microfibres, into the ocean every year. The manufacture of fibre (15%), yarn preparation (28%) and dyeing and finishing (36%) are the three main variables influencing the industry's global environmental consequences, according to the 2018 Quantis International report. The study also discovered that because cotton farming involves energy-intensive processes that rely on fossil fuel energy, the phases of dyeing and finishing, yarn preparation, and fibre manufacturing have the greatest effects on resource depletion. On the other hand, freshwater withdrawal—water that is taken out of or diverted from a surface water or groundwater source—and ecosystem quality are most impacted by the stages of fiber production. According to UNFCCC projections, the textile sector alone will account for 60% of global emissions by 2030. The term "lead time" describes how long it takes for a product to go from design to purchase in the supply chain. In 2012, Zara could design, develop, and deliver a new outfit in two weeks, Forever 21 in six weeks, and H&M in eight weeks. Consequently, the fashion industry produced ridiculous amounts of waste. (Maiti, 2024). The fashion industry uses the second most water—2,000 gallons are required to make a single cotton shirt, while a pair of trousers requires 10,000 gallons. The 2015 documentary The True Cost claims that the world consumes 400% more new apparel annually—nearly 80 billion pieces—than it did twenty years ago. The average American now generates 82 pounds of textile waste per year (Pick a Slow Fashion Season, 2019). Consequently, manufactured textiles are the primary producers of plastic microfibres that end up in our oceans. Precisely 35% of all microplastics come from these artificial substances. As of 2019, 62 million metric tonnes of clothing were consumed globally, according to the latest figures. Over the past few decades, there has been a significant growth in the quantity that our society consumes. Though it may benefit the economy, more clothes wind up in landfills because cheap clothing wears out quickly and requires more washings, which raises the demand for new clothes. The two largest issues are burning clothing and clothing mounds in landfills, though there are other issues as well. In addition, a great deal of material is wasted because the quantity of cutouts for the garment prevents it from being employed in another type of manufacturing. 57% of all discarded clothing ends up in landfills, where it gathers before being taken out and burned. Burning landfills emit a lot of dangerous gases or dangerous substances that might be dangerous for the local population's health and the environment (Psci, 2020).

IV. CONSUMER BEHAVIOUR ON SUSTAINABLE MARKETING

Fashion companies have a strong enthusiasm for fashion and are aware of the value of sustainable techniques in marketing. For the entire fashion sector to explicitly focus on the Sustainable Development Goals (SDGs), a green marketing strategy that satisfies their demands is essential. Overproduction and unethical manufacturing practices are frequently encouraged by unsustainable fashion enterprises, as has been discussed for several years. While many European consumers of clothing are now more cognizant of the gravity of the situation and some of them anticipate greater transparency from fashion brands about the entire system of operations and marketing strategy, the majority of consumers do not demonstrate this awareness in their purchasing behavior. The clear difference between what people believe they need and what is needed is the definition of waste in consumption. Two primary consequences may result from this: either excessive purchases of goods or inefficient use of those items. Economic Growth (2020) agrees on and expands on this concept of wasteful consumption, which includes paying for any kind of products and services. Because human needs are boundless and our ability to satisfy them is finite, the disparity between what we buy and what we utilize is just waste (Aalto University School of Business, 2021). People in Europe buy more garments than they need, and the textile sector is the main source of pollution in the continent. The data provided by the European Parliament (2020) also demonstrate that, since the early 2000s, the amount of clothing purchased per person in Europe has nearly doubled. Forty percent of used clothing is thrown away within a year of purchase and is either shipped to Africa or is disposed of in landfills and burned. People typically purchase clothing with the goal of either stating their emotional need to conform and fit into an environment or showcasing their personalities and forging an identity, as was previously discussed while reading the literature on fashion consumption ideas (LAB University of Applied Sciences, 2021). According to a lot of research, women actively seek out and purchase clothing from more ethical apparel manufacturers, indicating that they are more ecologically sensitive than males. After housing, food, and other expenses, the fashion sector is currently ranked as the fourth-largest consumer of primary raw materials and water. The method used in the production of textiles is the cause of the high consumption. The consumer perspective is another crucial element that needs to be taken into account. Because of the way that social and cultural elements have changed people's lifestyles, retailers are continuously having to adjust to the demands of their customers (Bringé, 2023). Consequently, fast fashion emerged as the primary business model for a whole sector, with merchants vying with one another to provide the market with low-priced, highly customizable products. Because of this, the primary deterrent for students to buy sustainable fashion products is their expensive cost. Therefore, consumers' desire for sustainable fashion products may rise in response to the low price. As a result, fast fashion became the dominant business model for the whole industry, with retailers competing to provide the market with inexpensive, highly customized goods. As a result, the main obstacle preventing students from purchasing sustainable fashion items is their high price (Tryphena & Aram, 2023).

V. RECOMMENDATION

To the Companies

We are recommending a few ways through which clothing brands can achieve sustainability not only through their advertisements but also in reality.

- To promote the purchase of high-quality garments over inexpensive ones, and maximize product durability through design specifications, consumer education, and warranty programs.
- Promotes garment recovery programs and connects second-hand customers and sellers to facilitate textile reuse.
- Clothing firms should tell suppliers as well as the public about their production sites, the source of their raw materials, and the effects each stage of the production process has on the environment.

- Determine and set criteria for material claims; for instance, set a minimum level of sustainability for a product before it can be marketed as such. Encourage the use of reputable, independent labels to attest to material utilization.
- Information about the use of chemicals disclosed: Application of Product Passport Number.
- Use deadstock fabric rolls, make secondary fibres financially interesting and limit the use of blended fibres.
- Encourage a more sustainable mindset among consumers through educational material and transparency

TO THE CONSUMERS

Even though you got rid of that hot fashion trend from last season, its effects are still felt because of the energy required in its manufacture and the fact that it's still in one of the country's landfills. Because we're wearing and discarding more garments than ever before due to the rise of so-called fast fashion, there is rising worry about the overall environmental impact of our wardrobe choices. The apparel produced by many merchants doesn't last any longer, despite their claims to be addressing sustainability. Here are a few questions to ask before purchasing new clothes through which consumers can choose long-lasting clothing.

- **Am I Going To Re-Wear It?**

Consider this question before choosing a blouse or a pair of shoes: Do I enjoy it? Does it fit properly? Is it adaptable? For example, Winter boots are the best option if you're looking to get boots for the upcoming cold weather. You shouldn't go out and spend $2,000 on a pair of opulent Chanel winter boots because you won't want to wear them in the snow. Although it appears like a winter boot, it's not. It would be wiser for you to purchase boots that are made to trundle through the snow and are waterproof and insulated

- **Is It Comfortable To The Touch?**

Something won't feel comfortable on your body if it feels abrasive to the touch. This holds for any clothing, but it is particularly true for undergarments like bras. You will get rid of anything faster if it doesn't feel cozy. Don't buy wool sweaters if they itch you.

- **Is My Hand Visible Through It?**

Thick fabrics generally have a longer lifespan than thin ones. Putting your hand between the top and bottom layers of the T-shirt is a simpler method. It's too thin if you can see through it. Sweaters and button-down shirts are also subject to the hand rule. Thick materials also provide shoes greater resilience, which helps explain why men's shoes often last longer than women's.

- **Does It Hold Up Under Pulling?**

It's crucial to check the quality of the sewing on your clothing. When it comes to bras, make sure your stitches are uniform, free of loose threads, skipped stitches, or areas where you can already feel the stitching coming apart. The standard for other products, such as shirts, is around eight stitches per inch. Pulling on buttons and stitching is advised because measuring that while shopping would be difficult. Gently tug on it to ensure it doesn't collapse, without being very forceful.

- **Are The Pockets Square?**

A helpful tip when purchasing a patterned shirt is to make sure the design matches the body and the pocket. Additionally, notice if the fabric extends a few centimetres beyond the stitching. Mismatched pockets may seem like little things, but they indicate that the maker places more emphasis on quantity than quality. Additionally, a small amount of extra fabric in a seam or hem allows a tailor room to adjust a garment if you put on a few pounds or to sew up a tear, enabling you to restore a piece or prolong its life rather than throwing it out. "If the fabric was less costly, they would simply flip it to one side and run the overlocker through it; but, if the cloth is more costly, they would be on either side of the seam.

- **Is The Blend Satisfactory?**

When used appropriately, a lining can significantly extend the life of an item of clothing. A wool pair of lined formal pants. Tencel fabric is recommended for work trousers because of its strength, durability, and comfort. Plucking is a big worry when selecting a jumper since nobody wants to be coated in those little balls of ugly fluff. Loose knits pill more than tighter knits, while synthetic fibers and blends pill more than natural fibers like cotton or wool. Pima cotton and other long-fiber, cotton tend to be more expensive but also more durable when it comes to clothing. Purchasing shirts that are strengthened with a blend of polyester and short-blend fibers is a third alternative.

- **Can I Keep It Up?**

Investing in well-made clothing is the first step in making sure your ensembles last. You have to take care of them once they're in your closet. For example, fine textiles like silk need a lot more care and attention. Additionally, they must to be hung to dry because using a dryer on your pants is not recommended since heat damages the elastic. If you are concerned about sustainability, you must learn how to take care of your clothes because they may come loose from their seams or buttons. This general concept also applies to other elastic products, such as sports equipment and even T-shirts and jeans.

The sustainability of the fast-fashion business model is one of the most frequent topics of discussion and inquiry. How can these companies become sustainable when their core business strategy is to encourage excessive consumption? It appears that fast fashion companies have adopted sustainability and circularity as their go-to strategies during this discourse. Sadly, a lot of people see this as a ploy to play on consumer's environmental sensitivity to boost consumption, which is more akin to greenwashing than green marketing. Global fashion brands with their extensive customer and employment base, are obligated to take the lead in bringing about change since the pursuit of sustainability and circularity necessitates collaboration from both businesses and consumers. In addition, despite advocating for sustainability and taking action in this regard majority of the brand's communication is noticeably opaque and unclear, casting doubt on the veracity and coherence of their actions. Specifically, it is unclear how much of their claims are supported by evidence and how much is the result of greenwashing. Ultimately, it is hard to disregard the misleading green claims made by the fashion industry. Especially in light of their significant environmental impact. Fashion firms need to ensure that their consumers are receiving accurate and verified information for them to make informed selections. National action is required in this case. Laws requiring the fashion industry to verify green claims will also encourage businesses to adopt a more circular business model by requiring them to disclose information about the social and environmental impacts of their production methods. Take action against the fashion industry's growing "greenwashing" problem and put in place the required rules and regulations to stop fast fashion brands from spreading misleading information about the environmental credentials of their products.

REFERENCES

Aalto University School of Business. (2021, March 30). *Sustainable marketing in the fashion industry*. https://aaltodoc.aalto.fi/server/api/core/bitstreams/86348b6a-3b0f-46d6-8fc0-15d60eb70da6/content

Abbate, S., Centobelli, P., Cerchione, R., Nadeem, S. P., & Riccio, E. (2023). Sustainability trends and gaps in the textile, apparel and fashion industries. *Environment, Development and Sustainability*, *26*(2), 2837–2864. Advance online publication. doi:10.1007/s10668-022-02887-2 PMID:36788931

Alexa, L., Apetrei, A., & Pîslaru, M. (2022). Fast Fashion – An Industry at the Intersection of Green Marketing with Greenwashing. In Sciendo eBooks (pp. 263–268). doi:10.2478/9788366675735-042

Allchin, J. (2014, October 17). Case study: Patagonia's 'Don't buy this jacket' campaign. *Marketing Week*. https://www.marketingweek.com/case-study-patagonias-dont-buy-this-jacket-campaign/

Antoniadou, K. (2023, November 20). *Is Uniqlo ethical, sustainable, or fast fashion?* IndieGetup. https://indiegetup.com/is-uniqlo-ethical-sustainable-or-fast-fashion/

Bringé, A. (2023, January 2). The state of sustainability in the fashion industry (And what it means for brands). *Forbes*. https://www.forbes.com/sites/forbescommunicationscouncil/2023/01/02/the-state-of-sustainability-in-the-fashion-industry-and-what-it-means-for-brands/?sh=515fc2b1c827

Chan, E. (2019, July 24). 5 ways the fashion industry can achieve a greener future. *Vogue India*. https://www.vogue.in/fashion/content/5-ways-the-fashion-industry-can-achieve-a-greener-future

Choose a slow fashion season. (2019, December 9). Sustainability - University of Queensland. https://sustainability.uq.edu.au/projects/recycling-and-waste-minimisation/choose-slow-fashion-season

Cudlínová, E., Buchtele, R., & Dušek, R. (2022). The Fashion Industry and its Problematic Consequences in the Green Marketing Era a Review. *SHS Web of Conferences, 135*, 01011. https://doi.org/10.1051/shsconf/202213501011

EE Editorial Team. (2024, January 20). Is Patagonia greenwashing? A breakdown! *Ethically Engineered.* https://www.ethicallyengineered.com/is-patagonia-greenwashing/

Kenk, K. (2022, April 5). *Greenwashing in fast fashion: the case of Shein - Let's Do It foundation.* Let's Do It Foundation. https://letsdoitfoundation.org/2022/04/05/greenwashing-in-fast-fashion-the-case-of-shein/

LAB University of Applied Sciences. (2021). *Consumer Awareness on Sustainable Fashion.* https://www.theseus.fi/

Lai, O. (2024, January 5). *7 Fast fashion companies responsible for environmental pollution.* Earth.Org. https://earth.org/fast-fashion-companies/

Maiti, R. (2024, March 4). *Fast fashion and its environmental impact in 2024 | Earth.Org.* Earth.Org. https://earth.org/fast-fashions-detrimental-effect-on-the-environment/

Psci. (2020, July 20). *The Impact of fast fashion on the Environment — PSCI.* PSCI. https://psci.princeton.edu/tips/2020/7/20/the-impact-of-fast-fashion-on-the-environment

Ray, S., & Nayak, L. (2023). Marketing Sustainable Fashion: Trends and future directions. *Sustainability (Basel), 15*(7), 6202. doi:10.3390/su15076202

Shirvanimoghaddam, K., Motamed, B., Ramakrishna, S., & Naebe, M. (2020). Death by waste: Fashion and textile circular economy case. *Science of the Total Environment.* https://doi.org/ doi:10.1016/j.scitotenv.2020.137317

Srauturier. (2024, January 8). *Greenwashing examples: 8 Notorious fast fashion claims and campaigns - Good on you.* Good on You. https://goodonyou.eco/greenwashing-examples/

Tryphena, R., & Aram, I. A. (2023). Consumer perception on sustainable clothing among urban Indians. *Journal of Engineered Fibers and Fabrics, 18.* doi:10.1177/15589250231168964

Woo, E. (2021). The Relationship between Green Marketing and Firm Reputation: Evidence from Content Analysis. *Journal of Asian Finance, Economics and Business, 8*(4), 455–463. doi:10.13106/jafeb.2021.vol8.no4.0455

KEY TERMS AND DEFINITIONS

Circularity: Closed-loop systems, sustainable supply chains, waste reduction, product life extension, resource efficiency.

Fast Fashion: The quick turnover of clothing lines by fashion companies, often results in environmental and social consequences

Fossil Fuel: Fuels derived from ancient organic matter, such as coal, oil, and natural gas, contribute to environmental degradation and climate change.

Green Marketing: Strategies companies use to promote environmentally friendly products and practices.

Greenwashing: Techniques businesses employ to falsely portray their products or services as environmentally friendly.

Micro Plastics: Tiny plastic particles, environmental contamination, marine pollution, nanoplastics, ecological impact.

Recycling: Waste management, resource recovery, material reclamation, environmental stewardship.

Sustainability: Environmental conservation, social responsibility, economic viability, green practices, sustainable development.

Chapter 6
Purchase Intention of Sustainable Fashion:
The Relationship With Price

Paulo Botelho Pires
https://orcid.org/0000-0003-3786-6783
Porto Business School, Portugal

Cláudia Morais
School of Economics and Management, University of Porto, Portugal

Catarina Delgado
https://orcid.org/0000-0002-1494-0517
School of Economics and Management, University of Porto, Portugal

José Duarte Santos
https://orcid.org/0000-0001-5815-4983
CEOS.PP, ISCAP, Polytechnic of Porto, Portugal

ABSTRACT

In today's world, the idea of sustainable fashion is gaining traction. Finding a link between pricing and the purchase of sustainable clothes is the aim of this study. Regression models and t-tests of two independent samples (two-tailed tests) were applied by means of the application of a questionnaire. The study found that consumers' willingness to pay for price increases is related with non-linear (quadratic or exponential) product pricing. The results of this study suggest that consumers are willing to pay higher prices for sustainable clothing. Through an understanding of the relationship between price and consumer behavior, businesses can more effectively align their pricing strategies with the demands of environmentally conscious consumers.

DOI: 10.4018/979-8-3693-3049-4.ch006

1. INTRODUCTION

The growing awareness of environmental and social concerns in the fashion industry has brought considerable attention to the idea of sustainable fashion in recent years. One way to lessen the fashion industry's negative environmental effects is through sustainable fashion, which is one of the most polluting sectors of the global economy. The fashion industry needs to comprehend customer perceptions of sustainable fashion and the influence of pricing on sustainable fashion purchases to progress towards sustainability (Dropulić & Krupka, 2020). Recognizing and responding to consumer attitudes towards sustainable fashion and the impact of pricing on their purchasing decisions is essential for the industry to make progress towards sustainability. By taking these factors into account and responding to them, fashion brands can make informed decisions that not only benefit the environment but also appeal to their target market. This move towards sustainable fashion is not just a trend, but a necessary step towards creating a more ethical and environmentally conscious industry. While sustainable fashion is important for reducing environmental impact, it may not be enough to address all of the industry's issues, such as labor exploitation and overconsumption. Additionally, focusing solely on customer perceptions and pricing may overlook other crucial factors in achieving true sustainability in the fashion industry. Some of these factors include supply chain transparency, fair labor practices, and the use of eco-friendly materials. Without addressing these aspects, the fashion industry may struggle to make significant progress towards sustainability. Industry stakeholders must consider a holistic approach to sustainability that encompasses all aspects of production and consumption, not just customer perceptions and pricing strategies. By taking a comprehensive approach, the fashion industry can truly make a positive impact on both the environment and society as a whole. Nevertheless, a specific and unambiguous definition of sustainable fashion is required, particularly concerning consumer behavior (C. F. Morais et al., 2023). Additionally, for a variety of reasons, sustainable fashion is typically priced higher than traditional fashion (Haines & Lee, 2022). The cost of producing organic and natural materials like cotton, linen, or silk is higher than that of producing synthetic materials like polyester. Additionally driving up costs are investments made by sustainable fashion brands in premium materials and production techniques. Costs associated with sustainable fashion are also higher due to fair trade practices, which guarantee workers' rights to fair wages and moral working conditions (Goworek, 2011; Shaw et al., 2006). Yet, compared to fast fashion alternatives, sustainable fashion items may be more high-quality and long-lasting, which could eventually translate into a reduced price per wear. Prices are also anticipated to decrease as more brands use eco-friendly procedures and technology in response to the growing consumer demand for sustainable fashion. It is becoming more and more crucial to transform into a purpose-driven brand or business that understands the significance of creating value beyond profit to win over customers and prevent reputational harm (Rolland, 2023).

Prior studies have looked at a variety of criteria, including social responsibility, product quality, and brand reputation, that affect consumers' decisions to buy sustainable fashion. Nevertheless, little research has been done on how much price matters when making decisions, particularly how price affects consumers' decisions between conventional and sustainable fashion. This study attempts to close this knowledge gap by investigating the relationship between price and the decision to purchase sustainable fashion. There is also a strong link between the elements of sustainable fashion and the perceived value that customers place on them. This study aims to shed light on customers' price sensitivity toward sustainable fashion and determine the ideal price range for incentivizing purchases of sustainable clothing.

Because of this, the following is the research question: "How does pricing affect consumers' intention to buy sustainable fashion?".

The other sections are organized as follows: (i) an overview of the available research on sustainable fashion and how pricing relates to it; (ii) the methodology, which describes the techniques and experiments used; and (iii) a discussion of the results.

2. LITERATURE REVIEW

2.1. The Sustainable Fashion

Throughout a fashion product's whole life cycle, sustainable fashion techniques seek to reduce environmental effects and increase social responsibility (Henninger et al., 2016; Mukendi et al., 2020). It involves taking into account the socially, ecologically, and ethically responsible sourcing, manufacture, distribution, use, and disposal of clothes. Sustainable fashion, which is frequently linked to the slow fashion movement, emphasizes sustainability principles including improving working conditions and lowering pollution. Key components of sustainable fashion include using eco-friendly materials, cutting back on pesticide usage, encouraging recycling and upcycling projects, and placing a strong emphasis on supply chain transparency and traceability (Henninger et al., 2016). Overall, it is a holistic approach to fashion production that considers long-term economic, social, and environmental impacts.

According to Shen et al. (2013), the sustainable fashion construct is composed of eight dimensions: recycled, vintage, artisan, made-to-measure, fair trade, locally produced, organic and vegan. Other factors often highlighted are minimized environmental impact, moral labor practices, durability and quality, and circular economy. Regarding Jung and Jin (2014), they linked the notion of slow fashion to sustainable fashion, citing the following aspects: conserving the environment for sustainable living by supporting local communities and producers (equity and localism); preserving the historical significance of the product for sustainable perceived value (authenticity); pursuing diversity for the sustainable fashion industry (exclusivity); and optimizing product life and efficiency for a sustainable environment (functionality). These principles emphasize the importance of not only creating environmentally friendly fashion items but also prioritizing ethical production methods and supporting local economies. By focusing on the longevity and value of products, slow fashion encourages consumers to invest in pieces that will last, rather than constantly buying new items. Ultimately, by adhering to these principles, the fashion industry can work toward a more sustainable and responsible future. Slow fashion brands can use locally sourced organic materials to create a limited-edition collection, ensuring exclusivity while supporting the community. In addition, by designing versatile and timeless pieces that are made to last, the brands promote sustainability and encourage consumers to make conscious purchasing decisions. While it is true that investing in quality pieces can lead to a more sustainable wardrobe, the high price point of slow fashion brands can exclude lower-income individuals from participating in this trend. In addition, the constant pressure to stay on trend and relevant in the fashion industry may still drive consumers to buy.

There is a noticeable negative environmental impact associated with traditional fashion. Studies have demonstrated that the textile sector, encompassing clothing manufacture, processing, usage, and disposal, is a contributing factor to the deterioration of the environment (Karpova et al., 2022). These impacts are further compounded by dress standards and intentional obsolescence in fashion, both of which follow a dominant capitalist logic (Gonzalez et al., 2023). Fast fashion companies often prioritize profit over sustainability, leading to the exploitation of natural resources and the generation of significant amounts of waste. The demand for cheap, trendy clothing has resulted in the release of harmful chemicals into the environment during the production process, further exacerbating the industry's negative impact. As consumers become more aware of these issues, there is a growing movement towards sustainable and ethical fashion alternatives that prioritize environmental and social responsibility. The traditional fashion industry has a significant social impact, including labor exploitation, poor working conditions, and insufficient wages, particularly in developing countries (Crinis, 2019). The 'working poor' are often paid below subsistence wages, leading to cardiovascular risk factors and inadequate dietary support. Pregnant women in the industry are also vulnerable to exploitation, including abuse, discrimination, forced abortions, unpaid overtime, and unfair working conditions (Dobos, 2019). Strengthening labor laws and regulations is crucial to protecting workers' rights and ensuring fair working conditions (Barnes & Kozar, 2008). The clothing and textiles industry, which generates significant global revenue, faces challenges such as resource depletion, dependence on cheap labor, and environmental sustainability. It contributes to climate change, CO2 emissions, and pollution (Papamichael et al., 2022). Social and economic sustainability issues include forced labor, low wages, and inadequate worker representation (Fan & Zhou, 2020). The industry faces production cost disadvantages in developed countries, leading to a decline in domestic production. These issues call for a new circular business model that promotes resource-efficient production, natural materials, and fair labor practices (Doeringer & Crean, 2006; Connell & Kozar, 2017). Implementing a circular business model in the fashion industry would not only address the environmental impacts of the current linear production system but also help in tackling the social issues prevalent in the apparel industry. By promoting sustainable practices such as recycling and upcycling, companies can reduce their reliance on virgin resources and minimize waste generation. Additionally, adopting fair labor practices and ensuring worker representation can lead to improved working conditions and better livelihoods for garment workers around the world. Ultimately, a shift towards a circular business model in the fashion industry is essential for ensuring the long-term sustainability and ethical integrity of the apparel supply chain.

2.2. Fundamentals of Sustainable Fashion

The ideas of sustainable fashion encompass environmentally conscious production and distribution techniques, as well as ideals like as upcycling, veganism, recycling, fair trade, women-owned businesses, zero waste, and animal welfare (Kim & Suh, 2022). The design of sustainable clothing is impacted by customer, design, and corporate factors (Fan & Chang, 2023). Making the shift to a circular economy is critical; it calls for education, capital, and consumer spending power (Bartkutė et al., 2023). Slow fashion, in particular, empowers women and serves as an eco-marketplace and community value (Lee & Weder, 2021). The transition to sustainable fashion is good for society overall as well as the environment. Through endorsing brands that follow sustainable practices, customers may make purchases that are consistent with their ideals. An industry that is more responsible and conscientious is emerging as a result of the shift towards ethical and environmentally concerned fashion.

To address the environmental effects of the fashion business and promote ethical behavior, sustainable materials are crucial. Natural materials offer a safe substitute for synthetic colors, such as organic wool and natural colorants (Almalki & Tawfiq, 2023; Lin et al., 2022). Sustainable textiles can benefit from novel materials like bacterial cellulose and bio-based textiles (Rognoli et al., 2022; Wood et al., 2023). These materials support ethical manufacturing methods in addition to having a smaller environmental impact. Fashion firms may lessen their water and carbon emissions by using sustainable materials, which will ultimately result in a more environmentally friendly supply chain. Transparency and accountability in manufacturing processes are critical for businesses to embrace as the fashion industry moves toward sustainability. The fashion industry may contribute to a future that is more morally and ecologically conscientious by using sustainable materials and encouraging ethical business practices. By making a commitment to ethical manufacturing methods, fashion firms can help ensure that workers are treated fairly and paid a living wage. This not only benefits the workers themselves but also creates a more positive image for the company. Additionally, by prioritizing sustainability and transparency, fashion brands can attract a growing number of environmentally conscious consumers who are seeking out ethical and sustainable options. Ultimately, by embracing these practices, the fashion industry can play a significant role in creating a more sustainable and socially responsible future. Transparency, fair labor practices, safe working conditions, and ethical production are crucial components of sustainable fashion (Aakanksha & Aravendan, 2023). Companies need to take moral stands and screen suppliers beforehand according to several criteria. Subsidies, tax breaks, and public or nonprofit certifying bodies can all promote sustainable manufacturing (Nandkeolyar & Chen, 2023). Enhancing sustainability and ethical behaviors in the supply chain requires traceability and transparency (Peleg Mizrachi & Tal, 2022).

Therefore, sustainable fashion is produced in a way that minimizes its negative effects on the environment, including the use of used clothing, recycling clothing, using recycled resources, manufacturing it in an environmentally friendly manner, making it last for more time than traditional fashion, adhering to equitable trading ideals, using recycled materials, producing it from natural sources, and promoting a decrease in the usage of clothing.

2.3. Main Determining Factors for Buying Sustainable Fashion

Several studies have examined the factors that influence the purchase of sustainable clothes. There are several proven determinants, however they are not usually reported consistently or methodically. Environmental consciousness, perceived value, perceived risk, motivation, opportunity, ability, personal standards, societal norms, and environmental awareness are the primary factors that influence purchases of sustainable fashion (Hassan et al., 2022; Lin & Chen, 2022). According to other writers, the factors include consumer education, desire to pay a higher price, moral responsibility, understanding of the repercussions, prior sustainable purchasing behavior, fashion preference, conspicuous consumption, and environmental awareness (Floriano & Matos, 2022; Mehta et al., 2023; Tian et al., 2022). Affordability, ecological concerns, and the assigning of responsibility are among the economic, cognitive, and ecological aspects that have been identified by other research (Tandon et al., 2023). Consumers' intentions to purchase sustainable garments are also influenced by motivation, opportunity, and ability (Hasbullah et al., 2022). These factors all play a role in shaping consumers' decisions when it comes to purchasing sustainable garments. Affordability is a key consideration for many, as well as the ecological impact of their choices. Consumers also need to feel a sense of responsibility for their purchasing habits, and having the motivation, opportunity, and ability to make sustainable choices can further influence their behavior. Ultimately, a combination of economic, cognitive, and ecological factors come into play when consumers are making decisions about sustainable fashion. Consumers who are motivated to make sustainable choices may prioritize brands that align with their values and beliefs, even if it means paying a slightly higher price. This sense of responsibility can drive individuals to seek out information about a brand's supply chain and production practices before making a purchase. Additionally, having the ability to access sustainable options, whether through online shopping or local retailers, can make it easier for consumers to incorporate eco-friendly fashion into their wardrobe. By considering all of these factors, consumers can make more informed decisions that have a positive impact on both the environment and the fashion industry as a whole.

2.4. Availability to Pay More

Given that customers care about sustainability but do not always convert their intentions into sustainable purchasing behavior, price is one of the main determinants of the differences between attitudes and actions toward sustainable fashion (Wiederhold & Martinez, 2018). However, some consumers choose to buy more items at a lower cost rather than care about ethical difficulties in the creation of clothing, and they do not take these factors into account while making fashion purchases (Joergens, 2006). Fashion shoppers, on the other hand, are unlikely to purchase sustainable items if they believe the price is too high (Chan & Wong, 2012). Accordingly, Roberts (1996) claims that if customers think green items are excessively expensive, they won't purchase them. In fact, McNeill and Moore (2015) claimed that even while customers expressed a desire to be more sustainable and participate in sustainable design, they cited the high cost of sustainable fashion labels as a significant deterrent to buying sustainable clothes. Additional evidence that consumers are prepared to pay extra for sustainable fashion comes from Davari and Strutton (2014), and Henninger et al. (2016). However, there are other studies suggesting that consumers are willing to pay a premium for sustainable fashion items, indicating that price may not always be the primary factor influencing purchasing decisions. Additionally, consumers are more likely to purchase sustainable fashion items if they perceive them as high quality and durable, regardless of price. This suggests that consumers place value on the longevity and quality of sustainable fashion items, viewing them as an investment rather than a disposable purchase. These findings highlight the importance of effectively communicating the sustainability and durability of fashion products to consumers to drive demand and justify higher price points.

2.5. The Impact of Price on Sustainable Fashion Purchases

There is a complex link between pricing and purchases of sustainable fashion. Value-based pricing is common for slow and circular fashion firms, which cater to middle-class to upper-class consumers (Hapsari & Belgiawan). However, there is a complex link between price and quality in sustainable fashion. According to research, inexpensive clothing—which is frequently connected to fast fashion—is thought to be of worse quality and durability, which causes it to be thrown away after only a little use (Wakes et al., 2020). Although consumers are generally pleased with fashion businesses' sustainability, sustainability is not one of the most critical criteria that influences their purchasing decisions (Mandarić et al., 2022). The important lesson here is that although sustainability may be valued by customers, it could not be the main factor influencing their purchase decisions. On the other hand, contrary findings have been shown by studies. In fact, studies reveal that when making judgments about what to buy, customers of sustainable fashion put fashion, environmental concerns, and perceived consumer effectiveness ahead of price (Blas Riesgo, Codina, & Sádaba, 2023; Blas Riesgo, Lavanga, & Codina, 2023). This highlights the complexity of consumer behavior and the various factors that can influence purchasing decisions. While sustainability is important to some customers, others may prioritize fashion or environmental concerns. Ultimately, businesses must consider a combination of factors when developing sustainable fashion products to appeal to a wide range of consumers. By understanding the diverse motivations behind purchasing decisions, companies can better tailor their marketing strategies and product offerings to meet the needs of their target audience.

The following comments underline even more the evident lack of consensus among researchers. Customers' perceived value of the product and their environmental concerns both affect their willingness to pay more for sustainable fashion goods (Dangelico et al., 2022). However, there is a negative link between purchase intentions and sustainable pricing, and environmental concern, sustainable behavior, and sustainable pricing all pose challenges to the survival of eco-fashion firms (D'Souza et al., 2015). Even though some customers are ready to pay more for sustainable solutions, the literature indicates that price sensitivity is still a major obstacle to their general adoption. Contradictions exist in consumer behavior as well. For instance, despite their awareness of environmental issues, Gen Z customers don't always act by their principles while making purchases. This implies a discrepancy between their judgments and values, which might be impacted by advertising tactics and brand characteristics (Palomo-Domínguez et al., 2023). Additionally, luxury fashion consumers have contradictory views, demonstrating a desire for eco-friendly apparel yet a hesitancy to buy sustainable fashion items (Delieva & Eom, 2019). Overall, there are major obstacles linked to price sensitivity (D'Souza et al., 2015) and discrepancies between consumer values and behavior (Palomo-Domínguez et al., 2023), even though there is a segment of consumers who are willing to pay more for sustainable fashion due to their perceived value and environmental concerns (Dangelico et al., 2022). These results imply that even as the market for eco-friendly clothing is growing, issues with cost and customer perceptions still need to be resolved (Delieva & Eom, 2019). To address these issues and encourage broader adoption of sustainable fashion techniques, it could be necessary to develop specialized marketing plans and get a better grasp of customer behavior. As a result, companies must comprehend how customers respond to price adjustments in a sustainable way (Tascioglu et al., 2019). This understanding can help businesses tailor their pricing strategies to appeal to environmentally conscious consumers while still maintaining profitability. Additionally, companies may need to invest in educating consumers about the benefits of sustainable fashion to shift perceptions and increase their willingness to pay. By focusing on customer behavior and implementing targeted marketing efforts, the fashion industry can continue to expand its sustainable offerings and attract a larger audience of conscious consumers.

Further specialized research yields further insights. Customers are prepared to spend an additional 20% of their budget on eco-friendly apparel (Ciasullo et al., 2017). A proportion of 25 to 30 percent over the premium price was regarded as undesirable, according to Chan and Wong (2012), who asserted that consumers of fashion would purchase sustainable fashion goods if the premium price was no more than 10% of the normal price. Furthermore, consumers who plan to buy slow-fashion items are prepared to spend more than they would for other goods (Şener et al., 2019). Nonetheless, price continues to be the most significant consideration for the typical customer when making a purchase; 31.9% of the sample consistently choose the lowest price, independent of other considerations (Shen, 2023). The importance and urgency of strengthening the connection between customer willingness to pay and sustainable fashion items are well demonstrated by this most recent research. Consumers are becoming increasingly aware of the impact their purchasing decisions have on the environment and are willing to pay a premium for sustainable fashion items. However, most customers still prioritize price when making a purchase, showing that there is still work to be done in educating and encouraging consumers to choose sustainable options. Brands and retailers must bridge the gap between customer willingness to pay and sustainable fashion to drive positive change in the industry. The link between price and desire to pay more for sustainable fashion will be examined, with the following propositions made considering the literature's several research with contradictory findings: The price and willingness to pay extra for sustainable fashion are correlated.

3. METHODOLOGY

The methodology must specify the procedures to be followed for data collecting and analysis since it describes the intervention program that will be developed. To address the research questions and evaluate the research hypotheses developed on which the literature review is based, this study will be exploratory and quantitative in nature.

This study aims to investigate the purchasing behaviors of customers, male or female, who are eighteen years of age or older. All these people who buy fashion goods are included in the target population. From this population, a representative sample has been selected; this sample is a subset of the population (Portuguese residents) that was chosen to be surveyed. To make inferences about the overall population, this sample will be used. Snowball sampling and non-probabilistic convenience were used to create the study sample. The convenience sampling technique chooses participants who are easy to reach and convenient for the researcher to interview. On the other hand, snowball sampling grows the sample size like a snowball rolling down a hill by depending on current research participants to find new volunteers among their friends. In this instance, respondents are usually picked because they were in the right place at the appropriate time. Participants who were contacted through digital social media platforms including Facebook, Instagram, WhatsApp, LinkedIn, and others, as well as those who subscribed to newsletters, make up the sample that was chosen. Using the digital channels indicated in the preceding paragraph, all interview subjects were asked to take part in the study. Responses from participants were obtained in April and May of 2023. Primary data, obtained through a structured questionnaire survey, will make up the data gathered for this study. Using a series of preset questions, the questionnaire is a useful tool for getting pertinent information from responders. We will be able to collect precise and trustworthy data with this method, which is crucial to the accomplishment of this study endeavor. Utilizing primary data will guarantee that the information gathered is pertinent to the study issue and will offer a deeper comprehension of the phenomena being studied. A questionnaire with the structure shown in Table 1 was created to answer the research hypotheses.

4. RESULTS

Included in the study sample were 434 individuals. In addition, a query was created to find out if the respondents purchased sustainable clothing. Out of the 434 members, 79% are women, 18.4% are men, and 2.5% would rather remain anonymous. Women may be more interested in the fashion industry, which might account for the high proportion of female members. The age group of 18 to 30 makes up the biggest population, accounting for 68.9% of the total. The age group of 31–40 comes in second at 19.8%, followed by the age group of 41–50 at 9.2%, and the age group of 51–59 at 2.1%. The age distribution of participants displays a significantly declining pattern consistent with the trends observed in fashion purchasing. The gross monthly wage of the household is allocated as follows: 20.5% earn less than €1000, 24% make between €1001 and €1500, 19.5% are paid between €1501 and €2000, 13.4% are paid between €2001 and €2500, 10.1% are paid between €250 and €3000, 5.1% are paid between €300 and €3500, and 7.8% are paid more than €3500. Furthermore, the sample is typical of the Portuguese population in terms of income.

Table 1. Questionnaire structure and supporting references

Section	Items	References
How much do consumers value sustainable fashion?	Consider that you pay €50 for a t-shirt that has been produced in a conventional way. How much would you be willing to pay for a t-shirt produced under sustainable conditions?	Author's own work (ratio scale)
	Consider that you pay €90 for a pair of trousers produced under conventional conditions. How much would you be willing to pay for a pair of trousers produced under sustainable conditions?	
	Consider that you pay €150 for a pair of shoes produced under conventional conditions. How much are you willing to pay for a pair of shoes produced under sustainable conditions?	
	Consider that you pay €200 for a jacket produced under conventional conditions. How much would you be willing to pay for a jacket produced under sustainable conditions?	
How much do consumers value sustainable fashion?	Consider this: You paid €50 for a shirt produced under conventional conditions.	Author's own work (ratio scale)
	How much would you be willing to pay for this conventional shirt in a second-hand fashion shop?	
	How much would you be willing to pay for this conventional shirt made from recycled materials?	
	How much would you be willing to pay for this conventional shirt, but produced with organic materials?	
	How much would you be willing to pay for this conventional shirt, but produced to last longer than conventional fashion?	
	How much would you be willing to pay for this conventional shirt, but produced with a reduced environmental impact?	
	How much would you be willing to pay for this conventional shirt, but produced using fair trade principles?	
	How much would you be willing to pay for this conventional shirt, but produced in safe and suitable working environments?	
Demographic survey	Gender, age, gross monthly household income	

Source: authors

4.1. Results for Willingness to Pay How Much More?

There are four questions in the questionnaire designed to find out how much customers are prepared to spend on sustainable fashion items. The questions deal with various costs and goods, including a €200 jacket, a €90 pair of pants, a €150 pair of shoes, and a €50 T-shirt. Finding out how much extra buyers are ready to pay for identical items produced in sustainable ways is the aim. First, the average additional amount they are willing to pay is calculated (Table 2).

To compare the means of the four variables, three t-tests of two independent samples (a two-tailed test) were conducted. The results of each test rejected the hypothesis that the means were equal. This indicates that consumers are prepared to pay extra for things produced under sustainable conditions as long as the price of the product increases. A more thorough investigation was conducted considering the findings mentioned in the previous paragraph to determine the extra cost that customers are prepared to pay for products made sustainably. A quadratic regression and a graphical depiction were used to complete this investigation (Figure 1).

Table 2. The additional average value that they are willing to pay more

	€50 T-shirt	€90 pair of pants	€150 pair of shoes	€200 jacket
Total	€17.09	€19.67	€25.34	€38.31

Source: Authors

Figure 1. The additional average value of willingness to pay more

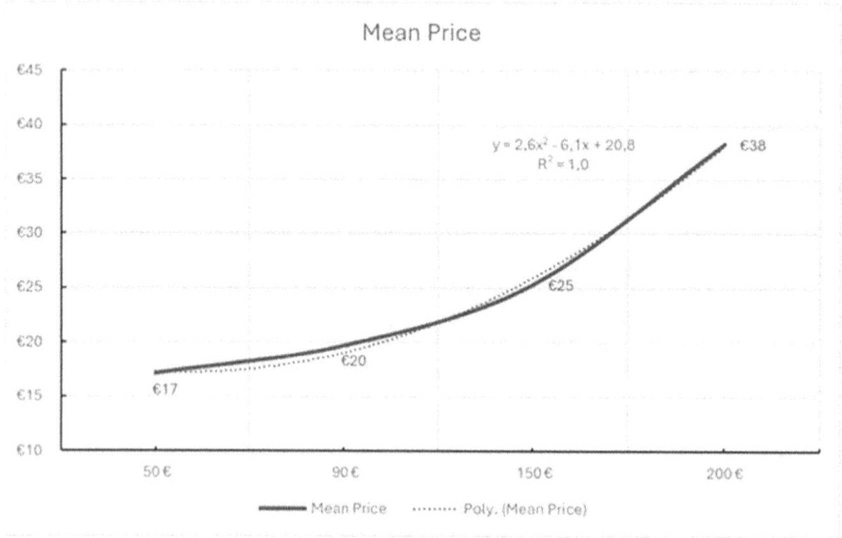

The price of the items and the rise they are prepared to pay do not have a linear relationship, that much is certain. As seen in the image, a quadratic regression provides a better representation of it (an exponential regression is another choice). This indicates that as the price of the items increases, the rise people are willing to pay for them also increases at a non-linear rate. This could be due to various factors such as brand loyalty, perceived value, or scarcity of the items. By utilizing a quadratic regression model, businesses can better understand and predict consumer behavior concerning pricing strategies.

Finding out how much of a price rise consumers are prepared to accept varies as a percentage of the product's price is the next stage. Like the previous technique, this one also employed a graphic to show the average increases that people are prepared to pay as a percentage for each of the four options. The results are displayed in Figure 2.

Some pertinent inferences can also be made in this case. The following is a description of the pattern: As the price of the products rises, the percentage increase that customers are prepared to pay for fashion items made in sustainable practices falls. One might speculate as to whether the last product represents a U-shaped pattern or a negative exponential, as it is an outlier.

Figure 2. Willingness to pay more as a percentage

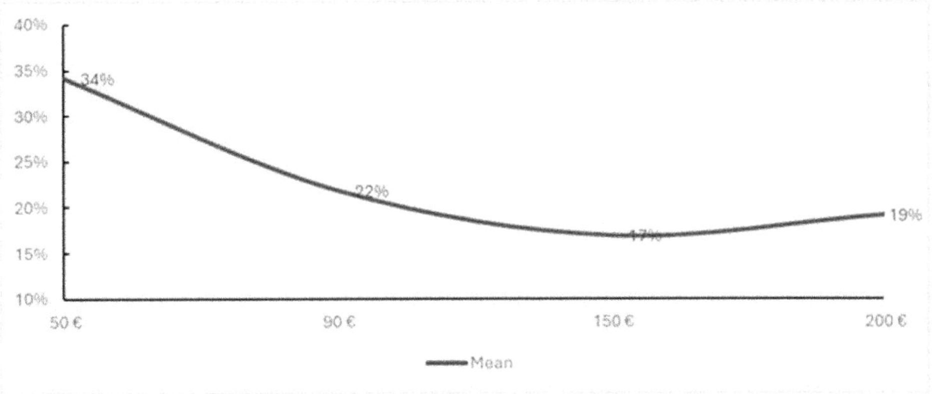

4.2. Results for How Much Do Consumers Value Sustainable Fashion?

The question of how much customers are willing to pay for the many elements that make up sustainable fashion is still open for discussion. Customers gave each item in Table 3 a monetary value to achieve this aim.

Table 3. The additional average value that they are willing to pay more

You paid €50 for a shirt produced under conventional conditions	Mean	Groups			Total
How much would you be willing to pay for this conventional shirt, but produced in safe and suitable working environments?	€67.61				35%
How much would you be willing to pay for this conventional shirt, but produced to last longer than conventional fashion?	€65.97				32%
How much would you be willing to pay for this conventional shirt, but produced using fair trade principles?	€65.67				31%
How much would you be willing to pay for this conventional shirt, but produced with a reduced environmental impact?	€65.15				30%
How much would you be willing to pay for this conventional shirt, but produced with organic materials?	€62.04				24%
How much would you be willing to pay for this conventional shirt made from recycled materials?	€59.13				18%
How much would you be willing to pay for this conventional shirt in a second-hand fashion shop?	€24.08				-52%

Source: authors

The table's items are arranged according to average financial value assignment in decreasing order. The items groups without statistically significant mean differences are represented by the gray regions. The two items were compared sequentially using a two-tailed independent samples t-test. The average difference between the first four items is hence zero. Customers therefore place equal importance on goods made in conditions that are safe and suitable for working in, made to last longer than traditional fashion, made following fair trade standards, and made with less of an impact on the environment. Parts made of organic materials and parts made of recycled materials come next. Since the value assigned to the final item is in the opposite direction of the scale of the other components, it was deemed unnecessary to compare them and was not considered for grouping.

Finally, we went on to examine the problem of purchasing at secondhand shops. Customers often estimate the value of used clothing to be around half (52%) that of new clothing. One possible reason for this perception is the wear and tear that may come with used clothing, leading customers to believe it is worth less than new items. Another factor to consider is the potential stigma attached to buying secondhand, which could affect how customers view the value of these products compared to new ones.

5. DISCUSSION, CONCLUSIONS, LIMITATIONS, AND CONTRIBUTIONS

Regarding the willingness to pay how much more, this study represents a significant advancement in our comprehension of the relationship between price and the factors that comprise sustainable fashion, as well as the price at which this kind of clothing is willing to be purchased. The results of this investigation do not agree with those of previous studies; there might be several reasons for this disagreement. A plausible rationale might be because the scope and accuracy of this inquiry are greater, including not only the costs of different items but also the financial evaluation of the elements that make up the concept of sustainable fashion. Additionally, the sample size used in this study was much larger than in previous research, providing a more comprehensive overview of consumer behavior towards sustainable fashion. Furthermore, the methodology employed in this investigation is more rigorous and thorough, ensuring that the results are reliable and valid. This study sheds new light on the complexities of pricing in sustainable fashion and offers valuable insights for both researchers and industry professionals.

It is important to note that the study's findings refuted the idea that there is a set amount or percentage that represents the price that customers are prepared to pay for sustainable fashion. As a result, the 20% (Ciasullo et al., 2017) or 10% (Chan & Wong, 2012) claims were not verified. According to the study, customer's willingness to pay a higher price in absolute terms for sustainable fashion is not constant and cannot be expressed by a linear relationship. An exponential or quadratic can be used to approximate the connection instead. Regarding percentage levels, the research found no evidence to back up Chan and Wong (2012)'s 25–30% restriction. The study's findings challenge commonly held beliefs about the correlation between customer willingness to pay and sustainable fashion pricing, suggesting a more complex relationship than previously thought. By using exponential or quadratic models to analyze the data, researchers were able to better understand how customers' willingness to pay for sustainable fashion fluctuates based on various factors. Contrary to previous research that suggested a specific percentage range for sustainable fashion pricing, this study found no evidence to support such restrictions, indicating a more nuanced approach is needed. The implications of these findings could have significant impacts on the marketing and pricing strategies of sustainable fashion brands, as they navigate consumer preferences and behaviors in the market. Further research may be necessary to delve deeper into understanding how consumers perceive value in sustainable fashion products and how that influences their purchasing decisions beyond traditional linear models of price sensitivity.

Upon closer inspection of the elements that comprise the concept of sustainable fashion, the emphasis on purchasing secondhand apparel stands out as very significant. Customers think that used clothing needs to be marked down by more than half. The remaining components are further divided into three categories: the highest-valued group consists of four components, while the lowest-valued groups include the addition of organic and recycled materials.

Notwithstanding its noteworthy accomplishments, this study has several shortcomings that should be acknowledged. Convenience sampling and snowballing approaches were used in the study, but these are not usually thought of as the most rigorous sample strategies. Furthermore, the sample was constrained to a somewhat small geographic area. However, it is important to emphasize that these limitations should not be interpreted as a significant barrier, but rather as a starting point for more investigation into the notion of sustainable fashion and the connection between cost and sustainable fashion.

REFERENCES

Aakanksha, L., & Aravendan, M. (2023). Impacts of Transparency and Traceability on Fashion Supply Chain System. *Intelligent Information Management*, *15*(3), 100–119. doi:10.4236/iim.2023.153006

Almalki, D. K., & Tawfiq, W. A. (2023). Implementation of a Sustainable Apparel Design Framework for Felted Women's Garments Made of Local Wool. *Fashion Practice*, *15*(3), 1–23. doi:10.1080/17569370.2023.2186033

Barnes, W. D., & Kozar, J. M. (2008). The exploitation of pregnant workers in apparel production. *Journal of Fashion Marketing and Management*, *12*(3), 285–293. doi:10.1108/13612020810889254

Bartkutė, R., Streimikiene, D., & Kačerauskas, T. (2023). Between fast and sustainable fashion: The attitude of young Lithuanian designers to the circular economy. *Sustainability (Basel)*, *15*(13), 9986. doi:10.3390/su15139986

Blas Riesgo, S., Codina, M., & Sádaba, T. (2023). Does Sustainability matter to fashion consumers? Clustering fashion consumers and their purchasing behavior in Spain. *Fashion Practice*, *15*(1), 36–63. doi:10.1080/17569370.2022.2051297

Blas Riesgo, S., Lavanga, M., & Codina, M. (2023). Drivers and barriers for sustainable fashion consumption in Spain: A comparison between sustainable and non-sustainable consumers. *International Journal of Fashion Design, Technology and Education*, *16*(1), 1–13. doi:10.1080/17543266.2022.2089239

Chan, T. Y., & Wong, C. W. (2012). The consumption side of sustainable fashion supply chain: Understanding fashion consumer eco-fashion consumption decision. *Journal of Fashion Marketing and Management*, *16*(2), 193–215. doi:10.1108/13612021211222824

Ciasullo, M. V., Maione, G., Torre, C., & Troisi, O. (2017). What about sustainability? An empirical analysis of consumers' purchasing behavior in fashion context. *Sustainability (Basel)*, *9*(9), 1617. doi:10.3390/su9091617

Crinis, V. (2019). Corporate social responsibility, human rights and clothing workers in Bangladesh and Malaysia. *Asian Studies Review*, *43*(2), 295–312. doi:10.1080/10357823.2019.1588850

D'Souza, C., Gilmore, A. J., Hartmann, P., Apaolaza Ibanez, V., & Sullivan-Mort, G. (2015). Male eco-fashion: A market reality. *International Journal of Consumer Studies*, *39*(1), 35–42. doi:10.1111/ijcs.12148

Dangelico, R. M., Alvino, L., & Fraccascia, L. (2022). Investigating the antecedents of consumer behavioral intention for sustainable fashion products: Evidence from a large survey of Italian consumers. *Technological Forecasting and Social Change*, *185*, 122010. doi:10.1016/j.techfore.2022.122010

Davari, A., & Strutton, D. (2014). Marketing mix strategies for closing the gap between green consumers' pro-environmental beliefs and behaviors. *Journal of Strategic Marketing*, *22*(7), 563–586. doi:10.1080/0965254X.2014.914059

Delieva, D., & Eom, H. J. (2019). Consumers' attitude toward socially responsible consumerism in the sustainable fashion market. *Business and Management Studies*, *5*(1), 59–67. doi:10.11114/bms.v5i1.4173

Dobos, N. (2019). Exploitation, working poverty, and the expressive power of wages. *Journal of Applied Philosophy*, *36*(2), 333–347. doi:10.1111/japp.12314

Doeringer, P., & Crean, S. (2006). Can fast fashion save the US apparel industry? *Socio-economic Review*, *4*(3), 353–377. doi:10.1093/ser/mwl014

Dropulić, B., & Krupka, Z. (2020). Are consumers always greener on the other side of the fence? Factors that influence green purchase intentions–the context of Croatian and Swedish consumers. *Market-Tržište*, *32*(Special Issue), 99–113. doi:10.22598/mt/2020.32.spec-issue.99

Fan, K.-K., & Chang, Y.-T. (2023). Exploring the Key Elements of Sustainable Design from a Social Responsibility Perspective: A Case Study of Fast Fashion Consumers' Evaluation of Green Projects. *Sustainability (Basel)*, *15*(2), 995. doi:10.3390/su15020995

Fan, K.-K., & Zhou, Y. (2020). The influence of traditional cultural resources (TCRs) on the communication of clothing brands. *Sustainability (Basel)*, *12*(6), 2379. doi:10.3390/su12062379

Floriano, M. D. P., & Matos, C. A. d. (2022). Understanding Brazilians' Intentions in Consuming Sustainable Fashion. *Brazilian Business Review (English Edition)*, *19*(5).

Gonzalez, V., Lou, X., & Chi, T. (2023). Evaluating environmental impact of natural and synthetic fibers: A life cycle assessment approach. *Sustainability (Basel)*, *15*(9), 7670. doi:10.3390/su15097670

Goworek, H. (2011). Social and environmental sustainability in the clothing industry: A case study of a fair trade retailer. *Social Responsibility Journal*, *7*(1), 74–86. doi:10.1108/17471111111114558

Haines, S., & Lee, S. H. (2022). One size fits all? Segmenting consumers to predict sustainable fashion behavior. *Journal of Fashion Marketing and Management*, *26*(2), 383–398. doi:10.1108/JFMM-08-2020-0161

Hapsari, P. D. N., & Belgiawan, P. F. (n.d.). *The Impact of Slow and Circular Fashion Concept on Consumers Purchase Intention*. Academic Press.

Hasbullah, N. N., & Sulaiman, Z. (1945). Drivers of sustainable apparel purchase intention: An empirical study of Malaysian millennial consumers. *Sustainability (New Rochelle, N.Y.)*, *14*(4).

Hassan, S. H., Yeap, J. A., & Al-Kumaim, N. H. (2022). Sustainable fashion consumption: Advocating philanthropic and economic motives in clothing disposal behaviour. *Sustainability (Basel)*, *14*(3), 1875. doi:10.3390/su14031875

Henninger, C. E., Alevizou, P. J., & Oates, C. J. (2016). What is sustainable fashion? *Journal of Fashion Marketing and Management*, *20*(4), 400–416. doi:10.1108/JFMM-07-2015-0052

Hiller Connell, K. Y., & Kozar, J. M. (2017). *Introduction to special issue on sustainability and the triple bottom line within the global clothing and textiles industry* (Vol. 4). Springer.

Joergens, C. (2006). Ethical fashion: Myth or future trend? *Journal of Fashion Marketing and Management*, *10*(3), 360–371. doi:10.1108/13612020610679321

Jung, S., & Jin, B. (2014). A theoretical investigation of slow fashion: Sustainable future of the apparel industry. *International Journal of Consumer Studies*, *38*(5), 510–519. doi:10.1111/ijcs.12127

Karpova, E. E., Reddy-Best, K. L., & Bayat, F. (2022). The fashion system's environmental impact: Theorizing the market's institutional actors, actions, logics, and norms. *Fashion Theory*, *26*(6), 799–820. doi:10.1080/1362704X.2022.2027680

Kim, Y., & Suh, S. (2022). The core value of sustainable fashion: A case study on "Market Credit". *Sustainability (Basel)*, *14*(21), 14423. doi:10.3390/su142114423

Lee, E., & Weder, F. (2021). Framing sustainable fashion concepts on social media. An analysis of# slowfashionaustralia Instagram posts and post-COVID visions of the future. *Sustainability (Basel)*, *13*(17), 9976. doi:10.3390/su13179976

Lin, L., Jiang, T., Xiao, L., Pervez, M. N., Cai, X., Naddeo, V., & Cai, Y. (2022). Sustainable fashion: Eco-friendly dyeing of wool fiber with novel mixtures of biodegradable natural dyes. *Scientific Reports*, *12*(1), 21040. doi:10.1038/s41598-022-25495-6 PMID:36470929

Lin, P.-H., & Chen, W.-H. (2022). Factors that influence consumers' sustainable apparel purchase intention: The moderating effect of generational cohorts. *Sustainability (Basel)*, *14*(14), 8950. doi:10.3390/su14148950

Mandarić, D., Hunjet, A., & Vuković, D. (2022). The impact of fashion brand sustainability on consumer purchasing decisions. *Journal of Risk and Financial Management*, *15*(4), 176. doi:10.3390/jrfm15040176

McNeill, L., & Moore, R. (2015). Sustainable fashion consumption and the fast fashion conundrum: Fashionable consumers and attitudes to sustainability in clothing choice. *International Journal of Consumer Studies*, *39*(3), 212–222. doi:10.1111/ijcs.12169

Mehta, P., Kaur, A., Singh, S., & Mehta, M. D. (2023). "Sustainable attitude"–a modest notion creating a tremendous difference in the glamourous fast fashion world: Investigating moderating effects. *Society and Business Review*, *18*(4), 549–571. doi:10.1108/SBR-10-2021-0205

Morais, C. F., Pires, P. B., Delgado, C., & Santos, J. D. (2023). Intention to Purchase Sustainable Fashion: Influencer and Worth-of-Mouth Determinants. In T. Tarnanidis, E. Papachristou, M. Karypidis, & V. Ismyrlis (Eds.), *Social Media and Online Consumer Decision Making in the Fashion Industry* (pp. 160–185). IGI Global. doi:10.4018/978-1-6684-8753-2.ch010

Morais, C. F. S., Pires, P. B., & Delgado, C. (2023). Determinants of Purchase Intention for Sustainable Fashion: Conceptual Model. In *Promoting Organizational Performance Through 5G and Agile Marketing* (pp. 75–95). IGI Global.

Mukendi, A., Davies, I., Glozer, S., & McDonagh, P. (2020). Sustainable fashion: Current and future research directions. *European Journal of Marketing*, *54*(11), 2873–2909. doi:10.1108/EJM-02-2019-0132

Nandkeolyar, O., & Chen, F. (2023). Credibility, transparency, and sustainability in fashion: A game-theoretic perspective. *Agricultural and Resource Economics Review*, *52*(1), 43–70. doi:10.1017/age.2022.24

Palomo-Domínguez, I., Elías-Zambrano, R., & Álvarez-Rodríguez, V. (2023). Gen Z's motivations towards sustainable fashion and eco-friendly brand attributes: The case of Vinted. *Sustainability (Basel)*, *15*(11), 8753. doi:10.3390/su15118753

Papamichael, I., Chatziparaskeva, G., Pedreño, J. N., Voukkali, I., Candel, M. B. A., & Zorpas, A. A. (2022). Building a new mindset in tomorrow fashion development through circular strategy models in the framework of waste management. *Current Opinion in Green and Sustainable Chemistry*, *36*, 100638. doi:10.1016/j.cogsc.2022.100638

Peleg Mizrachi, M., & Tal, A. (2022). Sustainable Fashion—Rationale and Policies. *Encyclopedia*, *2*(2), 1154–1167. doi:10.3390/encyclopedia2020077

Roberts, J. A. (1996). Green consumers in the 1990s: Profile and implications for advertising. *Journal of Business Research*, *36*(3), 217–231. doi:10.1016/0148-2963(95)00150-6

Rognoli, V., Petreca, B., Pollini, B., & Saito, C. (2022). Materials biography as a tool for designers' exploration of bio-based and bio-fabricated materials for the sustainable fashion industry. *Sustainability: Science. Sustainability*, *18*(1), 749–772. doi:10.1080/15487733.2022.2124740

Rolland, M. L. (2023). *Sustainability in Luxury and Fashion: Time for Action*. Euromonitor.

Şener, T., Bişkin, F., & Kılınç, N. (2019). Sustainable dressing: Consumers' value perceptions towards slow fashion. *Business Strategy and the Environment*, *28*(8), 1548–1557. doi:10.1002/bse.2330

Shaw, D., Hogg, G., Wilson, E., Shiu, E., & Hassan, L. (2006). Fashion victim: The impact of fair trade concerns on clothing choice. *Journal of Strategic Marketing*, *14*(4), 427–440. doi:10.1080/09652540600956426

Shen, D., Richards, J., & Liu, F. (2013). Consumers' awareness of sustainable fashion. *Marketing Management Journal*, *23*(2), 134–147.

Shen, Z. (2023). Mining sustainable fashion e-commerce: Social media texts and consumer behaviors. *Electronic Commerce Research*, *23*(2), 949–971. doi:10.1007/s10660-021-09498-5

Tandon, A., Sithipolvanichgul, J., Asmi, F., Anwar, M. A., & Dhir, A. (2023). Drivers of green apparel consumption: Digging a little deeper into green apparel buying intentions. *Business Strategy and the Environment*, *32*(6), 3997–4012. doi:10.1002/bse.3350

Tascioglu, M., Eastman, J., Bock, D., Manrodt, K., & Shepherd, C. D. (2019). The impact of retailers' sustainability and price on consumers' responses in different cultural contexts. *International Review of Retail, Distribution and Consumer Research*, *29*(4), 430–455. doi:10.1080/09593969.2019.1611619

Tian, Z.-B., Zhang, Y., & Yu, N. (2022). Evaluating factors for sustainable design of products in the apparel industry using DANP technique. International Conference on Statistics, Applied Mathematics, and Computing Science (CSAMCS 2021), Wakes, S., Dunn, L., Penty, D., Kitson, K., & Jowett, T. (2020). Is price an indicator of garment durability and longevity? *Sustainability*, *12*(21), 8906.

Wiederhold, M., & Martinez, L. F. (2018). Ethical consumer behaviour in Germany: The attitude-behaviour gap in the green apparel industry. *International Journal of Consumer Studies*, *42*(4), 419–429. doi:10.1111/ijcs.12435

Wood, J., Redfern, J., & Verran, J. (2023). Developing textile sustainability education in the curriculum: Pedagogical approaches to material innovation in fashion. *International Journal of Fashion Design, Technology and Education*, *16*(2), 141–151. doi:10.1080/17543266.2022.2131913 PMID:38098645

KEY TERMS AND DEFINITIONS

Consumer Knowledge: Consumer knowledge refers to the information and understanding that individuals have about products, services, and businesses available in the market. This knowledge can include details about pricing, quality, features, and the reputation of different brands.

Environmental Beliefs: An individual's attitudes, values, and perceptions towards the natural world and the importance of protecting it. These beliefs may stem from a variety of sources, including personal experiences, cultural upbringing, education, and exposure to environmental issues. People with strong environmental beliefs often advocate for sustainability, conservation, and environmental protection in their personal lives and communities.

Intention to Purchase: A consumer's willingness and desire to buy a specific product or service. It is often influenced by various factors such as personal preferences, brand loyalty, advertising, and peer recommendations.

Perceived Price: The value that a consumer places on a product or service based on their perceptions of its quality, brand reputation, and other factors. It is not necessarily the same as the actual price of the product, as consumers may be willing to pay more for something they perceive as higher quality.

Perceived Quality: A consumer's subjective judgment of a product's overall excellence or superiority. It encompasses both the tangible aspects of a product, such as its durability and performance, as well as the intangible aspects, such as brand reputation and customer service.

Sustainable Fashion: Sustainable fashion refers to clothing that is produced with minimal environmental impact and ethical labor practices. This includes using eco-friendly materials, reducing waste in the production process, and ensuring fair wages for workers.

Willingness to Pay More: Refers to the maximum amount of money that a consumer is willing to spend on a particular product or service. The willingness is influenced by various factors such as the perceived value of the item, personal preferences, and the individual's financial situation.

Chapter 7
The Consumer in the Fashion Industry:
An Empirical Study to Understand if It Is Sustainable

Francesco Pacchera
https://orcid.org/0000-0002-5809-392X
Tuscia University, Italy

Cecilia Silvestri
https://orcid.org/0000-0003-2528-601X
Tuscia University, Italy

Alessandro Ruggieri
Tuscia University, Italy

ABSTRACT

The production and consumption of textile products worldwide generate severe environmental impacts as well as economic and social repercussions. Companies are embarking on a new path towards sustainable production and consumption patterns to respond to increasingly environmentally conscious consumers. This study aims to investigate the characteristics of a sustainable consumer in the fashion industry and their level of awareness regarding sustainability at the time of purchase. To this end, a questionnaire was developed to analyse consumer behaviour in the fashion sector, while various statistical techniques were used to analyse the data. The results show that a cluster of consumers can be defined as sustainable, and that socio-demographic variables and price influence the purchase of sustainable products. Sustainability knowledge is also crucial for adopting sustainable consumption behaviour.

DOI: 10.4018/979-8-3693-3049-4.ch007

INTRODUCTION

The production and consumption of textile products worldwide generate high environmental impacts related to water consumption, energy consumption and air emissions, and economic and social repercussions (Sinha et al., 2023). The production of textile products is continuously increasing with products that have an increasingly shorter life cycle. This production model aimed at the overproduction and overconsumption of clothing products is known as fast fashion (Yang et al., 2017). According to this logic, consumers buy lower quality and cheaper clothing to keep up with the fashion of the moment. This model has several critical points related to resource consumption and waste management. To respond to increasing environmentally and socially aware consumers, several companies are embarking on a new path towards sustainable production models (Thorisdottir & Johannsdottir, 2019).

Sustainable fashion can be defined as 'clothing that incorporates one or more aspects of social and environmental sustainability' (Su et al., 2019, p. 1141). It is, therefore, based on fair trade principles, anti-exploitation and the use of materials that do not cause harm to the environment, as pointed out by (Goworek et al., 2012; Su & Chang, 2018). From a consumer perspective, sustainable fashion has been presented as a response to the overconsumption of clothing products. This perspective aims to address the socio-environmental issues that characterise the industry, including pollution, energy conservation, fair trade principles and exploitation-free labour (Diddi et al., 2019; L. McNeill & Venter, 2019; Su et al., 2019). Fashion represents a key sector for the circular transition at the European level. The industry comprises more than 160,000 companies with a workforce of 1.5 million people and a turnover of EUR 162 billion (EURATEX, 2020). Clothing in Europe generates over 57 million tonnes of waste per year (European Environmental Agency, 2020). European policies, particularly the EU Strategy for Sustainable and Circular Textiles, encourage the development of sustainable production and consumption patterns. They also position Europe as a forerunner of sustainable and circular value chains.

One of the critical points on which the sustainable fashion sector is developing at the European level concerns traceability and transparency of information along the production chain. This combines the production of sustainable products that at the same time respect ethical principles related to the welfare of workers further essential point is upstream in the production chain (Mukherjee, 2015). The use of sustainable raw materials that derive from renewable sources significantly reduces the environmental impacts related to the production of clothing materials (Cimatti et al., 2017). Technological innovation is also fundamental in the sector as through the use of new production techniques and technologies, production processes are more optimised and have a lower environmental impact (Nayak et al., 2020; Papahristou & Bilalis, 2017).

Consumers across Europe are becoming increasingly involved in the consumption of sustainable fashion products. Driven by the awareness of environmental issues and stimulated by new fashions triggered by sustainability, the consumption of sustainable fashion products is continuously growing (Mukendi et al., 2020). Sustainability issues and the circular economy are now familiar themes for consumers. Their knowledge towards sustainable consumption of clothing products does not justify an awareness of their behaviour (Busalim et al., 2022). Several studies in the literature explore consumer behaviour in sustainable fashion, as illustrated by studies such as that of (Jacobs et al., 2018) and (Koszewska, 2016). Still, no studies investigate the gap between consumers' attitudes towards sustainable consumption and their purchasing behavior towards sustainable products. Against this background, this study aims to examine the characteristics of a sustainable consumer in the fashion industry and their level of awareness in terms of sustainability at the time of purchase.

This research, therefore, aims to answer the following research questions:

RQ1 What are the characteristics of a sustainable consumer in the fashion industry?
RQ2 What is the level of consumer awareness at the time of purchase in the fashion industry?

BACKGROUND

The consumption of products from the fashion industry is changing (McQueen et al., 2022). Today, the figure of the sustainable consumer is becoming increasingly influential and environmental and social awareness are shaping society and behaviour (Domingos et al., 2022). Consumers no longer rely solely on aesthetics and trendiness but consider additional sustainability-related aspects (Busalim et al., 2022). Environmental responsibility, ethics and social awareness are references (Blazquez et al., 2020). To compete in the market, a fashion company will have to offer sustainable and fashionable products (Khandual & Pradhan, 2019).

In the fashion industry, the sustainable consumer can be defined as seeking out clothing products that respect sustainability principles(Mukendi et al., 2020). One example is the consumption of clothing products made from eco-friendly materials, i.e. from renewable sources or recycled raw materials (Daukantienė, 2023). Several brands now produce products that limit their environmental impact through sustainable production processes (Thorisdottir & Johannsdottir, 2019). Upcycling is one of the most widely used techniques (Bhatt et al., 2019).

Another aspect considered when buying clothes is related to the social impact of the fashion production chain (Cerchia & Piccolo, 2019). Consumers look for products that have been produced by ethical principles and workers' conditions (Clube & Tennant, 2022).

Consumers pay attention to the product life cycle and are interested in products with a longer life cycle (Jung & Jin, 2016). To counteract the fast fashion phenomenon, several consumers are inclined to buy more durable products made from quality materials (Fletcher, 2012; Gwilt, 2020). This is also leading to the growth of the secondary market, where second-hand products are consolidating as an excellent alternative to combat the industry's environmental impacts (Machado et al., 2019; Strähle & Gräff, 2017).

In this context, the communication of information on the production of the product starts to represent a fundamental element of the sector (Pereira et al., 2021; SanMiguel et al., 2021). Companies, through information campaigns, labels and websites, must, with maximum transparency, guarantee access to the information that consumers are interested in (Turunen & Halme, 2021). All this is aimed at avoiding the misinformation that results in greenwashing and alerts consumers to consume products that are not always sustainable (Adamkiewicz et al., 2022; Lu et al., 2022).

Moreover, the sustainability of products is not directly perceivable to the end consumer (Kaczorowska et al., 2019). Therefore, certification and control systems emerge as the main tools that can assure the consumer of specific qualities and respect for the environment and workers' rights (Lee et al., 2020). The sustainable consumer is a well-informed individual whose level of awareness has been shaped through the media with a focus on sustainability education (Zhang et al., 2021). Sustainability is seen as a competitive advantage in a company's strategic approach and contributes to the strengthening of reputation and brand image, crucial elements in the fashion industry (Brooksworth et al., 2022). Sustainable behavior becomes the basis of the relationship between business and customer/consumer (Pedersen et al., 2018). Thus, consumer interest drives the industry towards greater sustainability (Busalim et al., 2022).

METHODOLOGY

The study aims to investigate the characteristics of a sustainable consumer in the fashion industry and their level of awareness regarding sustainability at the time of purchase. For this purpose, a questionnaire was drawn up to analyze consumer behaviour in the fashion industry, while various statistical techniques were used to anazyse the data. A non-probabilistic sampling scheme, specifically an accidental sampling, was adopted to identify the customer population, as widely used in market research (Bracalente et al., 2009). The questionnaire analyze in the following two sections:

1. The consumer analysis contains information on consumers' perceptions of sustainable products in the fashion industry.
2. Consumer profile: contains information on socio-demographic characteristics.

The Likert scale measured consumer perception of sustainable products in the fashion industry. The scale assigned respondents a score ranging from "strongly disagree" (value 1) to "strongly agree" (value 6) (Likert, 1932). The data sample collected through the administration of the questionnaire was 230 persons, analyzed with the statistical software "STATA 12 Data Analysis and Statistical Software".

This study used a sample of Italian consumers as a reference. The fashion industry is one of the leading sectors in Italy. It is the third largest manufacturing sector in terms of companies (almost 45,000) and employees (over 397 thousand). Moreover, Italy is the world's second-largest exporter of clothing articles (Italian Trade Agency, 2023). Italy boasts a consolidated position on the world fashion scene, and therefore, investigating consumer perceptions in such a fashion-conscious country is an essential first step to extending the study (Silvestri et al., 2020). The sample analyzed consisted of 157 females and 73 males. The age of the consumers interviewed is as follows: 2% are over 20 years old, 17% are over 60 years old, 33% are between 20 and 29 years old, 17% are between 30 and 39 years old, 13% are between 40 and 49 years old, and 17% are between 50 and 59 years old. Descriptive and multivariate analyses were used to answer the research questions. Factor analysis and cluster analysis were used to understand which characteristics define sustainable consumers in the fashion industry and their level of awareness in purchasing sustainable products. The results of the statistical analyses carried out on the sample are reported in the next section. In the first step, descriptive analyses are reported that allow us to highlight the characteristics that influence and describe consumer behavior in the fashion industry. In the second step, multivariate analyses are reported to identify the types of consumers in the fashion industry and assess their purchasing awareness.

DATA ANALYSIS AND RESULTS

Factor Analysis

Factor analysis (FA) is used in market research to investigate consumers who display differential opinions regarding product characteristics or behavioral perceptions. FA allows consumer behavior analysis in this study, offering valuable data to test hypotheses (Bracalente et al., 2009). Factor analysis was used to address the challenges related to multicollinearity, which emerged from the correlation matrix (Tab.2). Table 1 presents a descriptive analysis of the variables examined.

Table 1. Descriptive statistics of sustainability factors

Items	Var.	Obs	Mean	Std. Dev.	Min	Max
Product life	var1	230	4.53	1.5	1	6
Price	var2	230	4.58	1.41	1	6
Recycled Product Awareness	var3	230	3.87	1.55	1	6
Presence of recycled components	var4	230	3.75	1.52	1	6
Awareness of sustainable choices	var5	230	4.08	1.56	1	6
Reduced environmental impact	var6	230	4.29	1.53	1	6
Reduced social impact	var7	230	4.07	1.57	1	6
Presence of environmental certifications	var8	230	3.66	1.62	1	6
Presence of quality certifications	var9	230	3.69	1.58	1	6
Made in	var10	230	4.2	1.51	1	6
Presence of eco-friendly fibers	var11	230	4.1	1.59	1	6
Possibility of cold washing	var12	230	3.73	1.78	1	6
Possibility of ironing at low temperatures	var13	230	3.53	1.81	1	6

Source: our elaboration on the dataset.

In Table 1, the items 'Price' (with an average of 4.58) and 'Product life' (with an average of 4.18) emerges as the most decisive. These categories are closely linked to the product's value, highlighting their importance in the consumer's purchasing decision. In contrast, the item 'Ability to iron at low temperatures' shows less influence, with an average of 3.53. This suggests the opportunity to focus on these aspects to increase consumer awareness.

A correlation study of the observed variables was employed (Table 2) to assess the presence of any redundancies that might confuse or reduce the significance of the statistical analysis results.

Correlation coefficients are instruments that measure the existence of a linear link between two quantitative variables, providing details on the intensity and sign of this relationship. The data presented in Table 2 show a robust connection between the variables under investigation, especially those related to 'Presence of recycled components', 'awareness of sustainable choices', 'reduction of environmental impact', the presence of environmental and quality certifications, and the presence of ecological fibers.

Although, in some cases, the linear link between some variables is not exceptionally high, it is considered appropriate to proceed with the component analysis of all variables. In the context of FA, each linear combination represents a function of all original variables but correlates specifically with some of them. On the other hand, the components are uncorrelated and, therefore, contribute to differentiating information content. The correlation matrix between the variables is the input for this technique, where a higher mean correlation indicates a higher synthesis capacity of the factor analysis. Consequently, correlations between the various observed variables are crucial to starting a market segmentation analysis with a classical approach. In the segmentation process, the initial step involves factor analysis to identify the fundamental dimensions of a phenomenon described by a set of quantitative variables. Using the principal component method, it was possible to select a limited number of 'new variables' (factors), $q<p$, that efficiently represent the main characteristics of the phenomenon, minimizing information loss. Before conducting the factorial analysis, the items' internal consistency was checked using Cronbach's

Table 2. Correlation matrix

	Product life	Price	Recycled Product Awareness	Presence of recycled components	Awareness of sustainable choices	Reduced environmental impact	Reduced social impact	Presence of environmental certifications	Presence of quality certifications	Made in	Presence of eco-friendly fibers	Possibility of cold washing	Possibility of ironing at low temperatures
Product life	1												
Price	0.67	1											
Recycled Product Awareness	0.48	0.42	1										
Presence of recycled components	0.48	0.41	0.92	1									
Awareness of sustainable choices	0.55	0.42	0.85	0.86	1								
Reduced environmental impact	0.50	0.42	0.85	0.84	0.90	1							
Reduced social impact	0.44	0.40	0.73	0.72	0.76	0.84	1						
Presence of environmental certifications	0.52	0.41	0.73	0.72	0.74	0.77	0.72	1					
Presence of quality certifications	0.53	0.41	0.70	0.70	0.73	0.76	0.72	0.94	1				
Made in	0.51	0.36	0.56	0.55	0.59	0.59	0.60	0.63	0.63	1			
Presence of eco-friendly fibers	0.48	0.36	0.74	0.75	0.75	0.76	0.67	0.73	0.72	0.63	1		
Possibility of cold washing	0.46	0.34	0.56	0.58	0.54	0.53	0.54	0.65	0.64	0.55	0.63	1	
Possibility of ironing at low temperatures	0.41	0.35	0.48	0.52	0.47	0.47	0.48	0.57	0.58	0.52	0.54	0.88	1

Source: our elaboration on the dataset.

α-index, as suggested by (Namukasa, 2013) and (Hair et al., 2006). This index, with values above 0.6 as a reliability criterion, was applied to check the internal consistency of the items. The results shown in Table 3 confirm the presence of good internal consistency.

Factorial analysis was employed to condense the information in the variables into factors, and the criterion used to identify new factors was based on eigenvalues > 1. A 'rotation' was applied to the initial factorial solution to facilitate interpretation. The orthogonal rotation of the factors was performed using Kaiser's varimax method. This type of rotation ensures that the rotated factors remain uncorrelated. Table 4 presents the factors' principal component matrix (eigenvectors) and shows that the first three factors have eigenvalues greater than 1. These three factors also contain approximately 81% of the information initially present in the dataset. For this reason, it was decided to consider only these first three factors to identify the new variables.

Table 3. Cronbach α test

Items	Var.	Obs	Sign	alpha
Product life	var1	230	+	0.95
Price	var2	230	+	0.96
Recycled Product Awareness	var3	230	+	0.95
Presence of recycled components	var4	230	+	0.95
Awareness of sustainable choices	var5	230	+	0.95
Reduced environmental impact	var6	230	+	0.95
Reduced social impact	var7	230	+	0.95
Presence of environmental certifications	var8	230	+	0.95
Presence of quality certifications	var9	230	+	0.95
Made in	var10	230	+	0.95
Presence of eco-friendly fibers	var11	230	+	0.95
Possibility of cold washing	var12	230	+	0.95
Possibility of ironing at low temperatures	var13	230	+	0.95
Test scales				0.95

Source: our elaboration of the data set.

Table 4. Rotation orthogonal Varimax (Kaiser off)

Factor	Variance	Difference	Proportion	Cumulative
Factor1	5.86	3.12	0.45	0.45
Factor2	2.74	0.76	0.21	0.66
Factor3	1.98	.	0.15	0.81

Source: our elaboration of the data set. Notes: Number of obs = 230; Retained factors = 3; Number of params = 36.

The saturation matrix was used to understand how the various factors can synthesize the different variables. Within this table, the correlations between the original variables and the factors were identified. Each variable is associated with the others according to the highest correlation factor, and then this factor is interpreted based on the variables associated with it. Table 5 shows that Factor 1 brings together aspects related to product sustainability (e.g. Presence of recycled components, Reduced environmental impact, and Presence of environmental certifications). Factor 2 summarizes the variables concerning energy saving (The presence of environmental certifications and the Possibility of ironing at low temperatures). Finally, Factor 3 summarizes the variables relating to product value (Price and Product Life).

Table 5. Saturation matrix (factor loadings)

Items	Variable	Factor1	Factor2	Factor3	Uniqueness	New Variables
Recycled Product Awareness	var3	0.87			0.15	Product sustainability - FA1
Presence of recycled components	var4	0.86			0.16	
Awareness of sustainable choices	var5	0.88			0.12	
Reduced environmental impact	var6	0.90			0.09	
Reduced social impact	var7	0.79			0.26	
Presence of environmental certifications	var8	0.73			0.21	
Presence of quality certifications	var9	0.71			0.22	
Made in	var10	0.51			0.44	
Presence of eco-friendly fibers	var11	0.74			0.26	
Possibility of cold washing	var12		0.86		0.09	Energy saving - FA2
Possibility of ironing at low temperatures	var13		0.90		0.10	
Price	var1			0.82	0.18	Value for money - FA3
Product life	var2			0.89	0.15	

Source: our elaboration of the data set.

Cluster Analysis (CA)

Whereas factor analysis summarises aspects of macro dimensions, clustering analysis allows individuals to be grouped according to shared characteristics, thus forming groups or segments characterised by considerable homogeneity (Bracalente et al., 2009). In the context of this research, Ward's hierarchical method (Brito et al., 2021; Majeed et al., 2022) is employed for market analysis when marketing actions influence the identification of consumer groups. The following tools were jointly used to define the number of groups: dendrogram analysis and the Calinski/Harabasz indicator (Bracalente et al., 2009; Gerdt et al., 2019).

Table 6 shows the socio-demographic variables of this study sample.

According to the Calinski/Harabasz indicator, the appropriate number depends on the value of the pseudo-F. Typically, one opts for the number of clusters associated with the highest pseudo-F. In this context, the highest value of pseudo-F corresponds to several factors, all converging on three as the highest number.

Table 6. Socio-demographic characteristics of the analyzed sample

Variable	Items
Gender	M/F
Age	<20;20-29;30-39;40-49;50-59;>60
Profession	Student; Employee; Freelancer; Laborer; Entrepreneur; Housewife; Entrepreneur; Unemployed; Retired; Other

Source: our elaboration of the data set.

Table 7. Calinski/Harabasz pseudo-F

Number of Clusters	Calinski/Harabasz Pseudo-F
3	130.52
4	116.51
5	97.24
6	85.13
7	77.43

Source: our elaboration

Using the Calinski-Harabasz index (Calinski&Harabasz, 1974) (Table 7), together with the dendrogram analysis, four groups can be identified sufficiently clear, and Table 8 analyses the three identified clusters based on the correlation link intensity.

The first cluster is distinctive due to the variable FA1, while the FA2characterises the second cluster. On the contrary, the third cluster shows no blatant discrimination related to any of the three factors.

Table 8. Cluster analysis: Correlation link intensity

Cluster	Product Sustainability - FA1	Energy Saving - FA2	Value for Money - FA3
CL1 - Sustainable consumer	0.8	-0.23	0.1
CL2 - Saving consumer	-0.35	0.65	0.14
CL3 - Indifferent consumer	-1.4	-0.21	-0.38
Total	-6.72×10^{-10}	8.89×10^{-10}	8.10×10^{-12}

Source: our elaboration of the data set.

Table 9 summarizes the socio-behavioral characteristics of the three clusters. The largest cluster is Cluster 1 (51.3%), followed by Cluster 2 (25.65%), and finally, Cluster 3 (23.04%).

Cluster 1 comprises women aged 30-39, 40-49 and over 60. They are primarily office workers, housewives and pensioners. They prefer an evergreen fashion style. They are interested in sustainability and are therefore willing to pay more for a sustainable product. They consider reducing consumption, buying environmentally friendly products, and extending the product life cycle to be central aspects of sustainable consumption (score given on Likert scale 5-6). They buy new products more when clothes are worn out, on promotion, or for novelty (score given on a Likert scale of 5-6).

Cluster 2 consists mainly of women under 20 and between 20 and 29. They are primarily students, unemployed, and engaged in other types of work not included in the questionnaire. They prefer a fashion style that is in step with current trends. They have little interest in sustainability and are unwilling to pay more for a sustainable product. They consider extending the product life cycle as a central aspect of sustainable consumption (score given on Likert scale 5) followed by buying environmentally friendly products (score given on Likert scale 4). They buy more new products when clothes are no longer in fashion (score given on Likert scale 4) or for novelty (score given on Likert scale 5-6).

Cluster 3 is mainly composed of men aged 50-59. They are mainly self-employed and blue-collar workers. They prefer a fashion style in step with current trends. They are not interested in sustainability and are, therefore, not willing to pay more for a sustainable product. On average, they consider extending the product life cycle an important aspect of sustainable consumption (score given on Likert scale 4). They are not conditioned to buy new products.

Table 9. Clusters' characteristics

Variable	CL1 - Sustainable Consumer	CL2 - Saving Consumer	CL3 - Indifferent Consumer
Dimension	51.31%	25.65%	23.04%
Gender	F	F	M
Age	30-39/40-49/>60	<20;20-29	50-59
Job	Office workers, Homemakers, Retired	Student; Unemployed; Other Employment	Freelancers; Workman
Fashion style	Evergreen	Trend	Trend
Willingness to pay	Yes	No	No
Interested in sustainable fashion	High (score 5-6)	Low - Medium (score 1;4)	Low (score 1-2)
Reduction of consumption	High (score 5-6)	Low - Medium (score 1;4)	Low (score 2-3)
Purchase of eco-sustainable products	High (score 5-6)	Medium (score 4-5)	Low (score 1;3)
Extend the product life cycle	High (score 5-6)	High (score 5)	Low - Medium (score 1;4)
Purchase used products	Medium (score 4-5)	Low (score 1-2)	Low (score 1;3)
Focus on quality	High (score 5-6)	Medium (score 4-5)	Low - Medium (score 1;4)
Purchase for wear of clothes	High (score 5-6)	Low-Medium (score 2;5)	Low - Medium (score 1;4)
Purchase for fashion trends	Low - High (score 3; 5-6)	Medium (score 4)	Low (score 1-2)
Purchase for promotion and sales	High (score 5-6)	Low - Medium (score 1; 4-5)	Low - Medium (score 2; 4)
Purchase for novelty	High (score 5-6)	High (score 5-6)	Low - Medium (score 1;4)
Purchase for advice	Medium-High (score 4-6)	Low- Medium (2-3;5)	Low (score 1)

Source: our elaboration of the data set.

DISCUSSION

This survey reveals important considerations regarding consumer behavior in the fashion industry. The objective of the study is to understand the characteristics of the sustainable consumer in the fashion industry and their level of awareness of sustainability.

The research aims to answer the following research questions:

RQ1 What are the characteristics of a sustainable consumer in the fashion industry?
RQ2 What is the level of consumer awareness at the time of purchase in the fashion industry?
RQ1 What are the characteristics of a sustainable consumer in the fashion industry?

The cluster analysis results indicate that, of the three clusters identified, only one (CL 1 - sustainable consumers) consists of individuals demonstrating a commitment to sustainability in the fashion industry. These individuals are interested in sustainability issues in fashion and actively inform themselves about related environmental problems (score 5-6 Likert scale). A higher level of consumer information is often associated with a better understanding of ecological issues, influencing consumer awareness and consideration of these aspects as relevant when shopping (Turunen & Halme, 2021). Another relevant aspect is the correlation between sustainability and demographic variables such as gender and age, which are considered crucial when analysing consumer behaviour (Jegethesan et al., 2012; Zelezny et al., 2000). Cluster 1 is predominantly composed of women, suggesting that the female gender shows a greater propensity for sustainability than the male gender. Previous studies on sustainable consumer behavior have shown a strong 'gender effect', with women tending to express more significant concern for consumption's environmental impacts and adopt more sustainable behaviour (Luchs & Mooradian, 2012). Women, therefore, are shown to be more sensitive to social and environmental issues, which is in line with findings in the literature (Luchs & Mooradian, 2012).

Cluster 2 (CL 2 - Saving consumer) consists of individuals who consider energy and money-saving aspects in their purchases. These individuals are unwilling to pay more to buy a product because their spending power is low. This is in line with the age of the members of the second group, who are either under 20 or between 20 and 29 years old. Young people consider the economic aspect when purchasing a product (Pena-cerezo et al., 2019). It is highlighted in the literature that price is one of the main obstacles in this context (Sheoran & Kumar, 2022). In the fashion industry, price is synonymous with quality (Wani, 2022). A study showed that young people are unwilling to pay more for a fashion product made from recycled materials as, according to them, the price increase is not justified by the quality of the materials (Fani et al., 2023). Cluster 2 considers the extension of the product's life cycle as an essential aspect of sustainability. They prefer a product with good quality and a good durability/price ratio. Young people usually show more interest in the aesthetic aspects of a product and do not want to choose a sustainable product that is not also fashionable (Pencarelli et al., 2020). Cluster 2 appears to follow fashion trends and is more interested in buying new products for novelty.

Cluster 3 (CL 3 - Indifferent consumer) consists of individuals who do not consider environmental aspects in their purchases. These individuals are unwilling to pay more to buy a fashion product as they are not interested in sustainability. They are indifferent to sustainable fashion and do not identify any critical factors that define the concept of sustainable fashion. This shows a lack of knowledge of the topic, which results in difficulty in recognising a product's sustainability(Heinl et al., 2021). A lack of information and understanding of the topic leads to an irresponsible consumer, where responsibility is a critical factor in sustainable consumption choices (Balderjahn et al., 2020).

RQ2 What is the level of consumer awareness at the time of purchase in the fashion industry?

The second research question seeks to investigate consumer awareness of sustainability issues. An analysis of the data shows that consumer awareness is linked to knowledge of the topic. An informed consumer has sustainable purchasing behavior. CL 1 consists of individuals informed about sustainability in the fashion industry. This is evident from the scores given to the questions defining the concept of sustainable fashion. In contrast, CL 3 appears to have no clear idea of sustainable fashion, and CL 2 is entirely unaware of the topic. A gap exists between attitude and behaviour in the sustainable consumption of clothing products (Dhir et al., 2021).Several studies have attempted to identify the drivers and associations present (Jacobs et al., 2018). Our study reveals how sustainable behavior can be improved through an increase in environmental knowledge. This aspect also appears in studies present in the literature on sustainable fashion product consumption (Dhir et al., 2021). Social media use can positively impact consumers' green behavior by informing them and increasing their awareness towards the consumption of fashion products (Salem & Alanadoly, 2021). Social media can engage the consumer, improve the transparency of information, and share experiences and opinions that increase awareness (Strähle & Gräff, 2017).

Educating consumers about sustainability is the basis for change in consumption behavior (Jeong & Ko, 2021). The study shows that consumers educated sustainably are conscious of their consumption. Therefore, media such as brands or certifications can educate consumers in their purchases by making them genuinely conscious (Mandarić et al., 2022). Companies, thus, should act as active promoters of environmental awareness by communicating the benefits and risks of irresponsible consumption (Marc et al., 2022).

This level of knowledge is also reflected in purchasing behavior. According to (Domingos et al., 2022), sustainable consumers, irrespective of their generation, tend to buy timeless clothes, even though they strongly need to feel up-to-date by purchasing fashionable products. This aspect also emerges in CL1, within which it is possible to identify consumers who buy new clothes when their old clothes are worn out. However, they are not entirely indifferent to novelty and, thus, to fashion trends. This latter aspect is very characteristic of the members of the CL2 predominantly composed of young people, thus the leading target group of fast fashion. One of the main drivers of young people's consumption habits is the desire to conform to the social norm and gain recognition from their peers; therefore, social pressure and identity play an important role in shaping young people's attitudes towards consumption (Yalkin & Elliott, 2006). Chasing fashion trends is important for young people to differentiate themselves and stand out from the crowd (L. S. McNeill et al., 2020; L. McNeill & Venter, 2019). Young people are part of a social circle and often need to express their individuality and gain peer approval by wearing fashionable clothes and using popular items (Eriko, 2012). In addition, fashion trends change quickly, which generates difficulties in the choice of purchase for a consumer who wants to be fashionable but simultaneously complies with sustainability principles (Anisah et al., 2024). However, according to (DeLong et al., 2019), young people can also have sustainable behaviors, and this focus comes from an external influence from a place with an eco-conscious culture that leads to involvement in more sustainable purchases.

Among sustainable behaviours is undoubtedly the purchase of second-hand products (Borusiak et al., 2020). According to the 3R concept, there are three basic types of sustainable consumption behavior: Reduce, Reuse, and Recycle. Reuse includes the use of goods previously used by other people. Second-hand purchase is acquiring used items through often specific retail formats and exchange venues, both offline and online, giving goods a second life.

Among the three clusters, only cluster 1 considers the purchase of second-hand products as an essential factor for sustainable fashion. The purchase of second-hand products is stimulated by a pro-environmental attitude and, therefore, by a social context in which information is an essential tool to increase consumers' awareness of the environment by inducing similarly sustainable behaviour (Colasante et al., 2023). Environmental concerns prompt consumers to adopt behaviours that can affect overproduction and prevent it from negatively affecting their living conditions (Cervellon et al., 2012). However, studies have shown that despite environmental awareness, individuals tend to be reluctant to buy second-hand clothes. Among the main criticisms is the perceived poor quality of second-hand clothes (Colasante & D'Adamo, 2021).

CL2 members do not show a predisposition to buy second-hand products; however, it is also true that young people play a crucial role in bringing about real change. The environmental concern of young people and their ability to become agents of change seem to be vital for the future state of the natural environment.

Socio-demographic variables also influence awareness of sustainability in the fashion industry. Such gender differences also emerge in other studies, where females are more aware than men (Mandarić et al., 2022).

CONCLUSION

The study aimed to analyze and identify the characteristics of sustainable consumers in the fashion industry and to consider their level of awareness at the time of purchase. Through descriptive and multivariate statistical analyses, it was possible to identify three main clusters. Of these, only one cluster (CL1 Sustainable Consumer) was identified as a cluster composed of sustainable individuals. The other two clusters are instead composed of individuals uninterested in sustainability (CL 2 - Saving consumer; CL 3 - Indifferent consumer). The analysis also shows how socio-demographic variables (gender and age) influence the purchase of sustainable products in the fashion industry while price is a barrier to purchasing sustainable garments. Finally, the study highlights how knowledge of sustainability is fundamental for adopting sustainable consumption behavior.

On a managerial level, the study implies that companies need to invest more in communication and strengthen their marketing strategies to make consumers more aware of sustainable fashion and, thus, more inclined to buy sustainable clothing.

At the research level, aspects of consumer awareness should be investigated in greater depth, and analyses should be strengthened on the information to be conveyed so that the consumer is informed and truly aware of their choices.

At the policy level, it is necessary to invest in consumer environmental education to better guide them in recognizing the characteristics of a sustainable product and choosing the product according to their own knowledge on the subject.

However, the study has some limitations. The limitations relate mainly to the limited number of participants and the method of participant selection (not accidentally probabilistic).

Future steps of the research include analyzing the relationship between knowledge on the topic of sustainable fashion and information conveyed by companies on labels and information sites to understand how this information can strengthen knowledge on the topic and make consumers aware of their choices.

REFERENCES

Adamkiewicz, J., Kochańska, E., Adamkiewicz, I., & Łukasik, R. M. (2022). Greenwashing and sustainable fashion industry. *Current Opinion in Green and Sustainable Chemistry*, *38*, 100710. doi:10.1016/j.cogsc.2022.100710

Anisah, T. N., Andika, A., Wahyudi, D., & Harnaji, B. (2024). Fast fashion revolution: Unveiling the path to sustainable style in the era of fast fashion. *E3S Web of Conferences, 475*, 2005.

Balderjahn, I., Lee, M. S. W., Seegebarth, B., & Peyer, M. (2020). A Sustainable Pathway to Consumer Wellbeing. The Role of Anticonsumption and Consumer Empowerment. *The Journal of Consumer Affairs*, *54*(2), 456–488. doi:10.1111/joca.12278

Bhatt, D., Silverman, J., & Dickson, M. A. (2019). Consumer interest in upcycling techniques and purchasing upcycled clothing as an approach to reducing textile waste. *International Journal of Fashion Design, Technology and Education*, *12*(1), 118–128. doi:10.1080/17543266.2018.1534001

Blazquez, M., Henninger, C. E., Alexander, B., & Franquesa, C. (2020). Consumers' knowledge and intentions towards sustainability: A Spanish fashion perspective. *Fashion Practice*, *12*(1), 34–54. doi: 10.1080/17569370.2019.1669326

Borusiak, B., Szymkowiak, A., Horska, E., Raszka, N., & Żelichowska, E. (2020). Towards building sustainable consumption: A study of second-hand buying intentions. *Sustainability (Basel)*, *12*(3), 875. doi:10.3390/su12030875

Bracalente, B., Cossignani, M., & Mulas, A. (2009). *Statistica Aziendale*. McGraw-Hil.

Brito, K. D. S., Filho, R. L. C. S., & Adeodato, P. J. L. (2021). A Systematic Review of Predicting Elections Based on Social Media Data: Research Challenges and Future Directions. *IEEE Transactions on Computational Social Systems*, *8*(4), 819–843. doi:10.1109/TCSS.2021.3063660

Brooksworth, F., Mogaji, E., & Bosah, G. (2022). *Brand, consumer and sustainability perspectives in fashion marketing: Conclusion and research agenda. In Fashion Marketing in Emerging Economies* (Vol. I). Brand, Consumer and Sustainability Perspectives.

Busalim, A., Fox, G., & Lynn, T. (2022). Consumer behavior in sustainable fashion: A systematic literature review and future research agenda. *International Journal of Consumer Studies*, *46*(5), 1804–1828. doi:10.1111/ijcs.12794

Cerchia, R. E., & Piccolo, K. (2019). The ethical consumer and codes of ethics in the fashion industry. *Laws*, *8*(4), 23. doi:10.3390/laws8040023

Cervellon, M., Carey, L., & Harms, T. (2012). Something old, something used: Determinants of women's purchase of vintage fashion vs second-hand fashion. *International Journal of Retail & Distribution Management, 40*(12), 956–974. doi:10.1108/09590551211274946

Cimatti, B., Campana, G., & Carluccio, L. (2017). Eco design and sustainable manufacturing in fashion: A case study in the luxury personal accessories industry. *Procedia Manufacturing, 8*, 393–400. doi:10.1016/j.promfg.2017.02.050

Clube, R. K. M., & Tennant, M. (2022). Social inclusion and the circular economy: The case of a fashion textiles manufacturer in Vietnam. *Business Strategy & Development, 5*(1), 4–16. doi:10.1002/bsd2.179

Colasante, A., & D'Adamo, I. (2021). The circular economy and bioeconomy in the fashion sector: Emergence of a "sustainability bias.". *Journal of Cleaner Production, 329*, 129774. doi:10.1016/j.jclepro.2021.129774

Colasante, A., D'Adamo, I., Rosa, P., & Morone, P. (2023). How consumer shopping habits affect willingness to embrace sustainable fashion. *Applied Economics Letters*, •••, 1–6. doi:10.1080/13504851.2023.2290578

Daukantienė, V. (2023). Analysis of the sustainability aspects of fashion: A literature review. *Textile Research Journal, 93*(3–4), 991–1002. doi:10.1177/00405175221124971

DeLong, M. R., Bang, H., & Gibson, L. (2019). Comparison of patterns of dressing for two generations within a local context. *Fashion, Style & Popular Culture, 6*(1), 99–117. doi:10.1386/fspc.6.1.99_1

Dhir, A., Sadiq, M., Talwar, S., Sakashita, M., & Kaur, P. (2021). Why do retail consumers buy green apparel? A knowledge-attitude-behaviour-context perspective. *Journal of Retailing and Consumer Services, 59*, 102398. doi:10.1016/j.jretconser.2020.102398

Diddi, S., Yan, R.-N., Bloodhart, B., Bajtelsmit, V., & McShane, K. (2019). Exploring young adult consumers' sustainable clothing consumption intention-behavior gap: A Behavioral Reasoning Theory perspective. *Sustainable Production and Consumption, 18*, 200–209. doi:10.1016/j.spc.2019.02.009

Domingos, M., Vale, V. T., & Faria, S. (2022). Slow fashion consumer behavior: A literature review. *Sustainability (Basel), 14*(5), 2860. doi:10.3390/su14052860

Eriko, Y. (2012). Accumulating Japanese popular culture: Media consumption experiences of Malaysian young adults. *Media Asia, 39*(4), 199–208. doi:10.1080/01296612.2012.11689938

EURATEX. (2020). Facts & Key Figure: Of The European textile and clothing industry. *Euratex*, 1–36. https://euratex.eu/wp-content/uploads/EURATEX-Facts-Key-Figures-2020-LQ.pdf

European Environmental Agency. (2020). *Textiles in Europe's circular economy Key messages*. 1–17. https://www.eea.europa.eu/themes/waste/resource-efficiency/textiles-in-europe-s-circular-economy

Fani, V., Mazzoli, V., & Acuti, D. (2023). 'I wanna be sustainable, but I don't wanna show it!': The effect of sustainability cues on young adult consumers' preferences. *Business Strategy and the Environment, 32*(6), 3344–3358. doi:10.1002/bse.3303

Fletcher, K. (2012). Durability, fashion, sustainability: The processes and practices of use. *Fashion Practice*, *4*(2), 221–238. doi:10.2752/175693812X13403765252389

Gerdt, S. O., Wagner, E., & Schewe, G. (2019). The relationship between sustainability and customer satisfaction in hospitality: An explorative investigation using eWOM as a data source. *Tourism Management*, *74*(March), 155–172. doi:10.1016/j.tourman.2019.02.010

Goworek, H., Fisher, T., Cooper, T., Woodward, S., & Hiller, A. (2012). The sustainable clothing market: An evaluation of potential strategies for UK retailers. *International Journal of Retail & Distribution Management*, *40*(12), 935–955. doi:10.1108/09590551211274937

Gwilt, A. (2020). Fashion and sustainability: Repairing the clothes we wear. In *Fashion theory* (pp. 188–200). Routledge. doi:10.4324/9781315099620-21

Hair, J., Black, W. C., Babin, B. J., Anderson, R. E., & Tatham, R. (2006). Multivariate data analysis. (Pearson Ed).

Heinl, L. T., Baatz, A., Beckmann, M., & Wehnert, P. (2021). Investigating sustainable NGO–firm partnerships: An experimental study of consumer perception of co-branded products. *Sustainability (Basel)*, *13*(22), 12761. doi:10.3390/su132212761

Italian Trade Agency. (2023). *L'italia nell'economia internazionale*. Author.

Jacobs, K., Petersen, L., Hörisch, J., & Battenfeld, D. (2018). Green thinking but thoughtless buying? An empirical extension of the value-attitude-behaviour hierarchy in sustainable clothing. *Journal of Cleaner Production*, *203*, 1155–1169. doi:10.1016/j.jclepro.2018.07.320

Jegethesan, K., Sneddon, J. N., & Soutar, G. N. (2012). Young Australian consumers' preferences for fashion apparel attributes. *Journal of Fashion Marketing and Management*, *16*(3), 275–289. doi:10.1108/13612021211246044

Jeong, D., & Ko, E. (2021). The influence of consumers' self-concept and perceived value on sustainable fashion. *Journal of Global Scholars of Marketing Science*, *31*(4), 511–525. doi:10.1080/21639159.2021.1885303

Jung, S., & Jin, B. (2016). From quantity to quality: Understanding slow fashion consumers for sustainability and consumer education. *International Journal of Consumer Studies*, *40*(4), 410–421. doi:10.1111/ijcs.12276

Kaczorowska, J., Rejman, K., Halicka, E., Szczebyło, A., & Górska-Warsewicz, H. (2019). Impact of food sustainability labels on the perceived product value and price expectations of urban consumers. *Sustainability (Basel)*, *11*(24), 7240. doi:10.3390/su11247240

Khandual, A., & Pradhan, S. (2019). Fashion brands and consumers approach towards sustainable fashion. *Fast Fashion, Fashion Brands and Sustainable Consumption*, 37–54.

Koszewska, M. (2016). Understanding consumer behavior in the sustainable clothing market: Model development and verification. *Green Fashion*, *1*, 43–94. doi:10.1007/978-981-10-0111-6_3

Lee, E. J., Bae, J., & Kim, K. H. (2020). The effect of sustainable certification reputation on consumer behavior in the fashion industry: Focusing on the mechanism of congruence. *Journal of Global Fashion Marketing*, *11*(2), 137–153. doi:10.1080/20932685.2020.1726198

Likert, R. (1932). A technique for the measurement of attitudes. *Archives de Psychologie*, *140*, 1–55.

Lu, X., Sheng, T., Zhou, X., Shen, C., & Fang, B. (2022). How does young consumers' greenwashing perception impact their green purchase intention in the fast fashion industry? An analysis from the perspective of perceived risk theory. *Sustainability (Basel)*, *14*(20), 13473. doi:10.3390/su142013473

Luchs, M. G., & Mooradian, T. A. (2012). Sex, Personality, and Sustainable Consumer Behaviour: Elucidating the Gender Effect. *Journal of Consumer Policy*, *35*(1), 127–144. doi:10.1007/s10603-011-9179-0

Machado, M. A. D., de Almeida, S. O., Bollick, L. C., & Bragagnolo, G. (2019). Second-hand fashion market: Consumer role in circular economy. *Journal of Fashion Marketing and Management*, *23*(3), 382–395. doi:10.1108/JFMM-07-2018-0099

Majeed, A., Ahmed, I., & Rasheed, A. (2022). Investigating influencing factors on consumers' choice behavior and their environmental concerns while purchasing green products in Pakistan. *Journal of Environmental Planning and Management*, *65*(6), 1110–1134. doi:10.1080/09640568.2021.1922995

Mandarić, D., Hunjet, A., & Vuković, D. (2022). The impact of fashion brand sustainability on consumer purchasing decisions. *Journal of Risk and Financial Management*, *15*(4), 176. doi:10.3390/jrfm15040176

Marc, I., Kušar, J., & Berlec, T. (2022). Decision-Making Techniques of the Consumer Behaviour Optimisation of the Product Own Price. *Applied Sciences (Basel, Switzerland)*, *12*(4), 2176. doi:10.3390/app12042176

McNeill, L., & Venter, B. (2019). Identity, self-concept and young women's engagement with collaborative, sustainable fashion consumption models. *International Journal of Consumer Studies*, *43*(4), 368–378. doi:10.1111/ijcs.12516

McNeill, L. S., Hamlin, R. P., McQueen, R. H., Degenstein, L., Garrett, T. C., Dunn, L., & Wakes, S. (2020). Fashion sensitive young consumers and fashion garment repair: Emotional connections to garments as a sustainability strategy. *International Journal of Consumer Studies*, *44*(4), 361–368. doi:10.1111/ijcs.12572

McQueen, R. H., McNeill, L. S., Kozlowski, A., & Jain, A. (2022). Frugality, style longevity and garment repair–environmental attitudes and consumption behaviour amongst young Canadian fashion consumers. *International Journal of Fashion Design, Technology and Education*, *15*(3), 371–384. doi:10.1080/17543266.2022.2072958

Mukendi, A., Davies, I., Glozer, S., & McDonagh, P. (2020). Sustainable fashion: Current and future research directions. *European Journal of Marketing*, *54*(11), 2873–2909. doi:10.1108/EJM-02-2019-0132

Mukherjee, S. (2015). Environmental and social impact of fashion: Towards an eco-friendly, ethical fashion. *International Journal of Interdisciplinary and Multidisciplinary Studies*, *2*(3), 22–35.

Namukasa, J. (2013). The influence of airline service quality on passenger satisfaction and loyalty: The case of Uganda airline industry. *The TQM Journal*, *25*(5), 520–532. doi:10.1108/TQM-11-2012-0092

Nayak, R., Panwar, T., & Nguyen, L. V. T. (2020). Sustainability in fashion and textiles: A survey from developing country. *Sustainable Technologies for Fashion and Textiles*, 3–30.

Papahristou, E., & Bilalis, N. (2017). Should the fashion industry confront the sustainability challenge with 3D prototyping technology. *International Journal of Sustainable Engineering*, *10*(4–5), 207–214. doi:10.1080/19397038.2017.1348563

Pedersen, E. R. G., Gwozdz, W., & Hvass, K. K. (2018). Exploring the relationship between business model innovation, corporate sustainability, and organisational values within the fashion industry. *Journal of Business Ethics*, *149*(2), 267–284. doi:10.1007/s10551-016-3044-7

Pena-cerezo, M. A., Artaraz-minon, M., & Tejedor-nunez, J. (2019). *Analysis of the Consciousness of University Undergraduates for Sustainable Consumption*. Academic Press.

Pencarelli, T., Ali Taha, V., Škerháková, V., Valentiny, T., & Fedorko, R. (2020). Luxury products and sustainability issues from the perspective of young Italian consumers. *Sustainability (Basel)*, *12*(1), 245. doi:10.3390/su12010245

Pereira, L., Carvalho, R., Dias, Á., Costa, R., & António, N. (2021). How does sustainability affect consumer choices in the fashion industry? *Resources*, *10*(4), 38. doi:10.3390/resources10040038

Salem, S. F., & Alanadoly, A. B. (2021). Personality traits and social media as drivers of word-of-mouth towards sustainable fashion. *Journal of Fashion Marketing and Management*, *25*(1), 24–44. doi:10.1108/JFMM-08-2019-0162

SanMiguel, P., Pérez-Bou, S., Sádaba, T., & Mir-Bernal, P. (2021). How to communicate sustainability: From the corporate Web to E-commerce. The case of the fashion industry. *Sustainability (Basel)*, *13*(20), 11363. doi:10.3390/su132011363

Sheoran, M., & Kumar, D. (2022). Benchmarking the barriers of sustainable consumer behaviour. *Social Responsibility Journal*, *18*(1), 19–42. doi:10.1108/SRJ-05-2020-0203

Silvestri, C., Aquilani, B., Piccarozzi, M., & Ruggieri, A. (2020). Consumer Quality Perception in Traditional Food: Parmigiano Reggiano Cheese. *Journal of International Food & Agribusiness Marketing*, *32*(2), 141–167. doi:10.1080/08974438.2019.1599754

Sinha, P., Sharma, M., & Agrawal, R. (2023). A systematic review and future research agenda for sustainable fashion in the apparel industry. *Benchmarking*, *30*(9), 3482–3507. doi:10.1108/BIJ-02-2022-0142

Strähle, J., & Gräff, C. (2017). *The Role of Social Media for a Sustainable Consumption BT - Green Fashion Retail*. Springer Singapore. doi:10.1007/978-981-10-2440-5_12

Su, J., & Chang, A. (2018). Factors affecting college students' brand loyalty toward fast fashion: A consumer-based brand equity approach. *International Journal of Retail & Distribution Management*, *46*(1), 90–107. doi:10.1108/IJRDM-01-2016-0015

Su, J., Watchravesringkan, K., Zhou, J., & Gil, M. (2019). Sustainable clothing: Perspectives from US and Chinese young Millennials. *International Journal of Retail & Distribution Management*, *47*(11), 1141–1162. doi:10.1108/IJRDM-09-2017-0184

Thorisdottir, T. S., & Johannsdottir, L. (2019). Sustainability within fashion business models: A systematic literature review. *Sustainability (Basel), 11*(8), 2233. doi:10.3390/su11082233

Turunen, L. L. M., & Halme, M. (2021). Communicating actionable sustainability information to consumers: The Shades of Green instrument for fashion. *Journal of Cleaner Production, 297*, 126605. doi:10.1016/j.jclepro.2021.126605

Wani, N. S. (2022). Factors Influencing Price Perception for Fashion: Study of Millennials in India. *Vision (Basel), 26*(3), 300–313. doi:10.1177/0972262920984856

Yalkin, C., & Elliott, R. (2006). *Female teenagers' friendship groups and fashion brands: A group socialization approach*. ACR Gender and Consumer Behavior.

Yang, S., Song, Y., & Tong, S. (2017). Sustainable retailing in the fashion industry: A systematic literature review. *Sustainability (Basel), 9*(7), 1266. doi:10.3390/su9071266

Zelezny, L. C., Chua, P.-P., & Aldrich, C. (2000). New Ways of Thinking about Environmentalism: Elaborating on Gender Differences in Environmentalism. *The Journal of Social Issues, 56*(3), 443–457. doi:10.1111/0022-4537.00177

Zhang, B., Zhang, Y., & Zhou, P. (2021). Consumer attitude towards sustainability of fast fashion products in the UK. *Sustainability (Basel), 13*(4), 1646. doi:10.3390/su13041646

Chapter 8
The Influence of Environmentally Mindful Marketing Tactics on the Perceptual Framework and Predispositions of Generation Z Shoppers in the Indian App

Sanjana S. Hothur
Christ University, India

Mallika Sankar
https://orcid.org/0000-0002-9296-8478
Christ University, India

Senthilmurugan Paramasivan
https://orcid.org/0000-0003-3249-8088
Christ University, India

Shikha Bhagat
https://orcid.org/0000-0001-8745-5558
Christ University, India

Roshna Thomas
Christ University, India

ABSTRACT

Green marketing decisively helps businesses distinguish themselves from their competition, strengthen their image, and obtain the attention of consumers who increasingly prefer environmentally conscious businesses. By elevating a business's reputation and image, green marketing creates an effect on how people consider a brand and enhances customer loyalty and retention. The "green generation," or Generation Z, is well-known for its sustainable product preferences and ecological concerns. The study analysed how green marketing techniques relate to and affect Gen Z customers' purchasing habits in India's garment industry. The study targeted 300+ Gen Z consumers through an online cross-sectional survey to get information on their perceptions of green brands, green marketing tactics, purchase intentions, and buying patterns. This study found that green marketing tactics used by fashion firms have a favorable impact and the ability to affect various aspects of customer behavior.

DOI: 10.4018/979-8-3693-3049-4.ch008

1. INTRODUCTION

The marketing industry has changed dramatically to incorporate green marketing as a fundamental idea and to react to the company's shift in perspective. As a result, diverse disciplines have been fast to adopt environmentally friendly behaviours and apply them to various elements of their activities (Smith, J., 2020). Green marketing, defined as the promotion and sale of environmentally friendly products or services, has gained increasing attention in recent years (Chen & Chang, 2013). While many businesses have adopted green marketing practices, there are still several challenges that need to be addressed, such as new concept development, cost factors, attitudes towards green products, appropriateness of green marketing strategies, non-cooperation among stakeholders, and avoiding green myopia (Peattie & Crane, 2005).

To further investigate the impact of green marketing on consumer behaviour, this study aims to examine the relationship between green marketing and the buying behaviour of Generation Z consumers in India, with a focus on the apparel sector. The research question is "What is the impact of green marketing on consumer behaviour determinants in the Indian apparel sector?" By responding to this query, the research hopes to shed light on how the Indian apparel industry responds to consumer behavior and establish the strength and direction of the correlation between green marketing and consumer behavior (Sharma & Banwet,2018).

The use of green marketing by marketers should be done for five major reasons: possibilities or competitive advantages; government pressure; competitive pressure; cost or profit challenges; and corporate social responsibilities (CSR) (Keller, 2021). There is a knowledge gap on the contribution of each of these aspects to the adoption of green marketing strategies. Although some study has looked at each of these components' independent effects on the adoption of green marketing, more analysis that weighs the relative importance of each aspect is required. To quantify the relative importance of each component in promoting the adoption of green marketing among a sample of marketers, a quantitative survey or experiment might be conducted. It will be possible to create more effective strategies for promoting environmentally sustainable practices in the marketing industry and gain a deeper understanding of the elements that drive the adoption of green marketing by filling in this research gap.

2. REVIEW OF PREVIOUS STUDY

Although it has emerged as a popular issue, the idea of "green marketing" was first identified as ecological marketing in the late 1970s (Henion, 1976). Three historical periods can be distinguished in the development of the green marketing idea (Hunt, 2011). The first stage began in the 1970s with a number of marketing initiatives targeting environmental problems like pesticide use and air pollution.. The second stage of this notion occurred in the following decade when marketers met opposition from environmental groups and consumers. The third stage of green marketing began in 2000, when modern technology, the introduction of more substantial government restrictions, and environmental consciousness promoted interest in the green marketing idea among academics and practitioners alike (Punitha and Rasdi, 2013).

Consumer awareness and brand goals are the primary motivators for businesses to go green (Ahuja2021) by integrating environmentally-friendly activities to marketing activities (Troumbis, 1991). Studies have shown that an increasing number of the general population have altered their behaviour to accommodate issues that matter to them (Rosenberger, 2001). There seems to be a shift in the behaviour pattern in companies to match that of their customers (Lotf,2018). Green marketing has led to many positive outlooks such as positive brand image and reduction in production costs due to reusability of materials (Durmaz, 2016). Green marketing has gained popularity over time due to the growing concern for environmental preservation (Mintel, 2006). Green marketing provides an opportunity for organizations to understand the customer's purchase patterns, purchase intention, all while associating their brand to the green products and services that they provide in order to rightfully position themselves in the upcoming green market (Cronin, 2011).

Consumer Behaviour: The study of consumer behaviour focuses on how people make decisions. Consumers have become more conscious of the importance of using products they buy (Kotler 1994). Making an ecologically friendly product is not enough to ensure a long-term future (Bello, 2008). Consumers and those in charge of marketing operations have critical responsibilities in this regard. The term "green consumer" refers to engaging in environmentally friendly habits or choosing green items over traditional alternatives (John Grant, 2008). Green consumers are less dogmatic about new items and ideas and more open-minded or accepting of them. As a result, they believe that protecting the environment is an essential duty (Shamdasani, 1993).

***Purchase intention*:** Purchase intention refers to a customer's desire to purchase a product or service (Shah,2012). Consumers' purchase behaviour is critical in gaining access to and evaluating a specific product (Keller, 2001). The selection of a brand is dependent on the

brand's group cohesiveness (Moschis, 1976). Customers believe that purchasing low-cost, simple-packaging, and unknown goods is a risk because the quality of these products is suspect (Gogoi, 2013). Awareness, knowledge, interest, preference, persuasion, and purchase are the six stages that a customer goes through before buying a product (Kotler & Armstrong, 2010). Other elements influencing purchase intention include customer knowledge, consumer perceptions, product packaging or design, and celebrity endorsement (Kawa, 2013).

Purchase Pattern-There are two sorts of purchases in Purchase Behaviour: "trial purchases" and "repeat purchases" whose lives have been affected due to globalization's influence on purchasing patterns (Schiffman & Kanuk, 2008). There appears to be a trend among customers to purchase and consume environmentally friendly products (Mishra and Sharma, 2010). Environmental knowledge, green product attributes, green promotion and green prices favourably influenced consumers' green purchasing behaviour (Mainieri, 1997). Organizations use green marketing strategies such as green branding, eco-labelling, and green packaging to influence consumers' buying patterns (Nik Abdul Rashid, 2009). As a result of the aforementioned aspects, we can see that various factors influence green consumers' purchasing patterns (Delafrooz, 2014). The green apparel perceived effectiveness and green apparel knowledge have significance impact on Indian consumers' green apparel purchase behavior. Consumer independent judgment making and novelty-seeking behavior have no impact on green apparel purchase behavior (Arpita and Pradeep, 2021)

Brand perception- Customers need to be exposed to the brand to form this association. What the customer views and experiences while interacting with the brand will shape their concept of it and, ultimately, their perception of the brand (Brown, 1992). Consumer perception refers to a person's feelings about a brand or product, influenced by past experiences, attitudes and beliefs, habits, preferences, and feelings (Dixit, 2020). Consumers' views of a brand as a reflection of brand/product features in their minds are influenced by a variety of factors, including marketing communication (Hsieh & Lindridge, 2005). Nonetheless, a consumer's emotional connection to a brand is based on his/her own experience (Keller, 2001, 2009). Consumer perception research is critical for developing marketing strategies, and a simple concern about environmental and ethical issues could prompt fashion brands to invest heavily in minimizing their environmental effect while increasing their social consciousness (Armstrong, 2015). Even though fast fashion firms have been blamed for producing different environmental issues, they are gradually working to create sustainable fashion that emphasizes social responsibility and awareness (Lohr. S.W.,2015). In response to these shifting consumption patterns, fast fashion labels such as H&M and Zara have introduced sustainable apparel collections aimed at a generation of consumers that value ethical consumption (Poulsson and Kale,2004). Consumers' perception influences the outcomes of firms' efforts to boost their brand value. As a result, as fast fashion firms participate in various marketing activities, it will be beneficial to explain consumers' genuine perceptions of the brands' sustainability efforts (Kinner and Taylor,1973). Buyers' ecological concerns had an apparent effect on their opinion of the brands (Patrick,2005) and customers' perceptions of green brand positioning had a beneficial effect on the brand (Koll and von Wallpach,2009). Consumers' perceptions of a brand influence their reactions to future interactions with the brand (Hartman and Spiro, 2005). The associative memory network model frequently captures brand association, representing the consumer's understanding of the brand (Chang. P.L, 2006). The structure of brand association memory in customers' minds is described by this model in consumers' minds. The green image equates to the brand's sustainable fashion regarding environmental pledges and environmental challenges from a fashion standpoint. According to the literature on the subject, green branding affects consumers' perceptions (Cherain and Jacob,2012).

Green Marketing Mix

Product is the main element surrounding green marketing strategies (Gosavi, 2013). The aspect of a product being environmentally friendly is not the same as a green product as they convey two different messages (Fan and Zeng, 2011). A green product refers to the various elements used to obtain the finished item in question (Steiner, 2015). These elements insinuate green products as it comes down to the materials used, the packaging, the production process, among other factors (Cherian & Jacob, 2012).

Another critical element that is determinantal in the profitability and generation of revenue is the price (Eric, 2007). It also determines if the product is positioned in the market and is targeting the right demographics (Sharma, 2011). The product's price must be fixed based on the value that the product carries for the customer, and there are certain factors taken into consideration to help evaluate the value of the product (Singh, 2013). Visual appeal, efficiency in performance, design and packaging and brand value are a few of the factors taken into account in the discussion of green marketing. Another critical aspect that is considered in this scenario is that of environmental value and quality of the product (Solvalier, 2010). It leads to the belief that there is legitimacy concerning the green aspect of the product, which may attract the right customer. This leads to the development of green confidence necessary in driving the customer towards the organization's desired intent (Dehghanan & Bakhshandeh, 2014).

Promotion plays as significant role in relay of accurate information to customers to keep them engaged with the company and its ongoing activities (Shirsavar and Fashkhamy, 2013). A green promotion initiative refers to certain information that paints the brand in green light and relays information that denotes the green practices undertaken by the company to produce products (Ankit and Mayur, 2013). The promotion of products is said to be in tune with the brand's image and builds credibility if the practices and techniques used to promote are environmentally sustainable product (Mohajan, 2012).

Place refers to the conscious effort on the part of the company that deliberates all the details of the operations of production and logistics (Garg & Sharma, 2017). The main aim of this element of the marketing mix in the green marketing context is to put extra emphasis on reducing carbon footprint by strategically managing the logistics involved (Shil, 2012). It need not echo the extra incurrence of costs as numerous strategies can be applied to turn the outcomes into revenue (Awan, 2011).

Psychological Factors

Perceived quality: Customer perceptions of the general quality or superiority of one product or service concerning other alternatives can be described as the customer's impression of one product or service's general quality or superiority in light of its projected goal case (Kia,2012). Perceived quality is a vague and intangible impression of a brand (Keller, 2008). The perceived quality, which refers to the relationship between the product and the consumers, determines purchase intention. (Payneand Holt, 2001) It is a continuous improvement process in which continuous modifications improve product performance and, as a result, customer satisfaction. (Tariq,2013) The perceived quality of a product comprises both tangible and intangible qualities. (Snoj et al. 2004). The eventual conclusion is that higher perceived quality leads to a higher buying intention. (Nah Hong, 2007.) The empirical studies revealed that a higher quality product results in a higher purchasing intention. (Tsiotsou,2006)

***Brand loyalty*:** A brand is a combination of a name and a symbol. Branding has a critical role in retaining a company's market share and attracting loyal customers. (Erics, 2012) Customers loyal to a brand will pay more for it than for equal things and are more likely to repurchase and suggest it to others. (Molla & Licker, 2001). There is a strong link between brand equity and the likelihood of recommending a product to others. (Azizi & Ajini, 2012). The majority of prior studies looked at the impact of brand image on consumer purchase intent and found that it had a substantial impact. On these variables (Arslan & Altuna, 2010)

Belief and attitude: based on extensive studies conducted on consumer buying behaviour, it has been observed by various consumer behaviourists that beliefs and attitude of a consumer does have an impact on their buying behaviour, where the attitudes and beliefs stem from a number of situational factors or internal and external attributes. (Fazio and Zanna, 1981). Over time various theories have been used to accurately describe the predictive processes that can be used to track the behaviours which are behind a person's attitude and beliefs. (Ajzen and Fishbein, 1977). Another connotation to measure attitudes and beliefs along with the theory is the set notion that certain conditions such as the factor of perception tend to be consistent which is then used to study the behaviour patterns of individual in by applying theories such as theory of reasoned. (Fazio,1989). The optimism and pessimism do not have a direct impact on the intention to purchase sustainable clothing (Antunes and Sofia,2022)

Values and Norms: values and norms tend to influence the lifestyle of an individual which greatly impact the choices that they make. This in turn tends to affect their behaviour which may be novelty seeking in nature as well as their perception about innovation and attitude towards switching to green products (Haanpaa, 2007). Norms and values have been studied as prevalent factors that influence the consumer's purchase habits and have shown that these do in turn determine their willingness to buy and consumer green products. (Jansson,2011)

Consumers' perceptions on environmental concerns and beliefs: Environmental behaviour of consumers: there have been numerous problems regarding the environment including global warming, deforestation, environmental pollution among other factors that are caused by organisations and in a few aspects' consumers alike (Papadopoulos, 2010). Organizations took this need as a way to create a new market to appease these consumers. However, the consumer base which bought the green products did not necessarily comprise of the same individuals who indulge in environmentally friendly behaviours and practices (Hoyer,2004). There have been past studies that have been conducted on similar lines which show that the relationship of consumers buying green products and them simultaneously indulging in environmentally friendly practises have been found in a very small percentage of the consumer base with this information in question, we can state that every research helps determine the cause of this behaviour as well as what causes the consumer base to purchase and consume green products (Pickett-Baker,2008) The internal locus control of consumers is a vital predictor of purchase behavior towards sustainable apparel products (Nupur and Parul,2021) Green purchase intention is directly influenced by Attitude towards green products, Environmental concern and Perceived consumer effectiveness directly and indirectly influenced through the mediating the role of attitude through Green products (Deepak and Rishi, 2018)

***Influence of social groups*:** green purchase behaviour, social standards, personal environmental norms, and self-monitoring influence green purchasing behaviour (Jansson, Marell, & Nordlund, 2010). It is a personality trait that describes a person's tendency to follow social standards, be influenced by others, and connect with groups (Bearden, 1989) The Theory of Planned Behaviour has been used in research on green buying behaviour better to understand the impact 25 of social norms on green purchasing. (Kalafatis, 1999) the influence of peers and society in general on that of an individual's consumer behaviour has been a widely discussed topic over different research disciplines. (Lee,2009)

3. STATEMENT PROBLEM

Businesses, especially in the apparel industry, are adopting green marketing strategies more frequently in an effort to stand out from the competition and satisfy consumers' increased desire for ethical and sustainable goods (Jain & Kaur, 2020). Peattie and Crane (2005) argue that the value of green marketing is found in its capacity to assist businesses in standing out from the competition, improving their image, and catering to the shifting tastes of their clientele. Thus, companies can improve customer service and make well-informed judgments about their marketing strategy by recognizing the significance of green marketing. According to Chen and Chang (2013), green marketing has a substantial effect on how consumers consider a brand since it enhances a company's reputation and image and increases customer loyalty and retention. The "green generation," or Generation Z, is recognized for its environmental sensitivity and recognition for sustainable goods (Gupta & Pooja, 2021). Businesses aiming to reach this demographic must have a thorough understanding of the preferences, brand perception, and purchasing intention of this market segment and improve their sales.

To sum up, the aim of this study is to fill the knowledge gap about how green marketing impacts customer behavior in the Indian garment industry. Businesses in the fashion sector can make more informed decisions about their marketing strategies and provide better customer service by comprehending the import of green marketing in the current market, the degree of Generation Z's preference for green marketing products, the impact of green marketing on brand perception, the relationship between green marketing and purchase intention, and the relationship between green marketing and purchase pattern.

4. RESEARCH GAP AND METHODOLOGY

To fully comprehend the impact of green marketing on customer behavior, further research is required, even with its increasing popularity. By studying how green marketing affects customer behavior in the Indian garment industry, this study seeks to close that gap. The study focuses the vital elements that characterize marketing, such as purchase intention, brand perception, and consumer preferences, while investigating many facets of green marketing to provide a comprehensive and nuanced viewpoint. In particular, this study looks into how Generation Z consumer purchases are influenced by green marketing in India's retail sector. Therefore, the following goals were planned for the study:

1. To ascertain the extent of preference among Gen Z for green marketing products in the apparel sector.
2. To identify the relationship between green marketing strategies, brand perception, purchase intention and purchasing pattern.
3. To understand the influence of green marketing strategies on brand perception, purchase intention and purchasing pattern.

Based on the objectives of the study, the following hypotheses are proposed

H_{01}: There is no relationship between green marketing and brand perception
H_{02}: there is no relationship between green marketing and purchase intention
H_{03}: there is no relationship between green marketing and purchase pattern

Research Design Adopted for the Study

The research design adopted for this study is descriptive research design as none of the variables in the study is altered throughout the research process. This research was conducted using both primary and secondary data. An online survey using google form questionnaire was used to gather the primary data for this investigation while secondary data was compiled from periodicals, online-published research papers and articles, and textbooks. The data collected was analysed using a variety of approaches. Statistical analysis such as Correlation Analysis, Regression Analysis and ANOVA has been carried out using SPSS software. The population for this study encompasses of the generation Z of India and the population of the study is infinite. The sample size for this study report is merely 300 participants, the data gained is invaluable. Sampling technique for this study, non-probability judgement sampling was chosen as the sampling method.

5. ANALYSIS OF THE STUDY

Demographic profile of respondents: According to the data 18 percent of respondents are between the ages of 12 and 16, 48 percent are between the ages of 17 and 21, and 34 percent are between the ages of 22 and 26. The majority of the people that responded were between the ages of 17 and 21. 38 percent of respondents are males, 51 percent of respondents are females, and 11 percent of respondents would rather not divulge their gender. The profiling of the data assist in determining the consumer's ability to prioritize the environment and sets a precedent for their view on green marketing. The respondents' data revealed that majority of the respondents strongly agree that Destruction of Forests is the most harmful factor while in the other criteria's, the respondents are majorly inclined towards agreeing that the other factors take equal blame. Though most of the consumers are neutral about their willingness to be inconvenienced in order to take actions that are more environmentally friendly. They seem to share equal consideration and concern with regards to the other aspects of the environment.

Inferential Statistical Analysis

The reliability value, α for all the study variables ranged from 0.71 to 0.8 suggests that the data is very consistent and reliable. To identify the relationship among green marketing strategies (GMS) with brand perception (BP), purchase intention (PI) and purchasing pattern (PP) a correlation analysis has been carried out with the following hypothesis:

H_{01}: There is no relationship between green marketing strategies, brand perception, purchase intention and purchasing pattern

H_{11}: There is a relationship between perception of green marketing, brand perception, purchase intention and purchasing pattern

Table 1. Correlations

	Pearson Correlation Value	**Sig. Value**
GMS and **BP**	**0.674**	**<.001**
GMS and PI	**0.529**	**<.001**
GMS and PP	**0.604**	**<.001**

The results reveal that there is significant relationship exists between green marketing strategies, brand perception, purchase intention and purchasing pattern. These results indicate that, increases or decreases in perception on green marketing strategies do significantly relate to increases or decreases in the brand perception, purchase intention and purchasing pattern. Green marketing strategies have a statistically significant positive linear relationship with brand perception ($r = 0.674$., at $p < .001$), purchase intention ($r = 0.529$., at $p < .001$) and purchasing pattern ($r = 0.604$., at $p < .001$)

Regression Analysis

A regression analysis was conducted to identify the influence of green marketing strategies on brand perception, purchase intention and purchasing pattern.

Model 1 predicts, 45.4 percent of the change in the dependent variable with the p value of 0.000

Table 2. Regression analysis and ANOVA

Model	R	R Square	Adjusted R Square	Std. Error of the Estimate	R Square Change	F Change	Sig. F Change
1	.674	.454	.452	.52536	.454	247.564	<.001

Regression Model 2

Model 2 predicts, 27.8 percent of the change in the dependent variable with the p value of 0.000

Table 3. Regression analysis and ANOVA

Model	R		R Square	Adjusted R Square	Std. Error of the Estimate	R Square Change	F Change	Sig. F Change
2	.529		.280	.278	.912	.280	113.290	<.001

Regression Model 3

Model 3 predicts, 27.8 percent of the change in the dependent variable with the p value of 0.000

Table 4. Regression analysis

Model	R	R Square	Adjusted R Square	Std. Error of the Estimate	R Square Change	F Change	Sig. F Change
3	.604	.365	.363	.58688	.365	171.107	<.001

a. Dependent Variable: purchase pattern
b. Predictors: (Constant), green marketing variable

6. FINDINGS OF THE STUDY

The study summarizes that green marketing strategies adopted by an apparel company seems to have a moderately positive effect and influences the different factors of consumer behaviour to varying degree. The study has briefly implored the behaviour of generation Z where respondents that lie between the ages of 12-26 have taken part in this study. With these set of consumers having different level of education and occupation in the related sense are all bound by the common fact of sharing similar degrees of environmental concerns and though they may not necessarily categories themselves are environmentally conscious consumers who will go out of their way to consume only green products, the study through a series of green marketing question revealed that generation z consumers are to an extent conscious about the environment and are inclined towards companies that are putting in the effort to adopt green marketing strategy. The study deliberately considered previously controversial fast fashion brands that were known to harm the environment and asked respondents if they were aware of the green making practices adopted by the brands and this awareness had changed their view of the brand. Based on the responses gathered and analysed, the paper can state that they were in fact aware of the strategies adopted and their view of the brands had improved due to the same. As the era of digitalization has changed the process of shopping, the paper briefly wondered and explored if the efforts made by apparel online line platforms in the direction of green marketing was noticed by the respondents. The respondents have indeed taken these actions into account thus father establishing the aspect of the study that green marketing strategies adopted by apparel brands will help them grow and are appreciated by the consumers. Other aims of the study were to understand from the perspective of the consumers as to what were the most important factors that need to be taken into consideration by organizations with respect to green marketing strategies and the results revealed that the respondents selected environmentally friendly packaging above all the other options given to them as the most 64 essential strategies followed by ensuring that the process of manufacturing was as eco-friendly as possible. When imploring the aspect of various factors that affect the consumers reasons to purchase green apparel which may also double up as the causes for them to not purchase said green products, the results from the analysis revealed that the major factor was that of availability that influenced their decision followed by the price of green apparel. The results of this hypothesis testing revealed that there was infect a positively moderate influence of green make ring strategies that is the independent variable on the three dependent variables of brand perception, purchase intention and purchase pattern.

Figure 1. Research framework

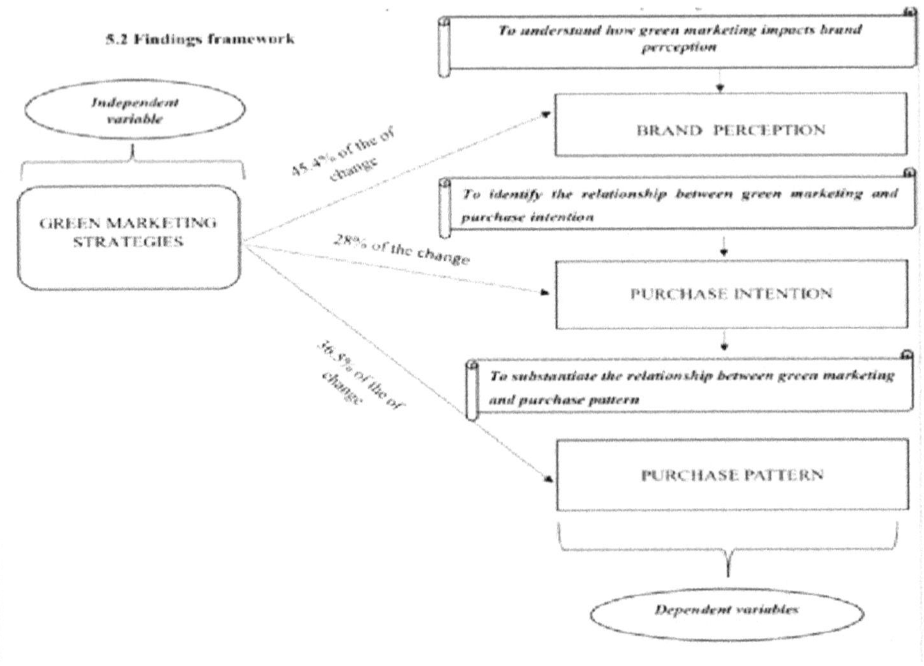

Managerial Implications

The aim of this research paper is to contribute to the vast pool of existing knowledge in the marketing segment and in particular the green marketing segment. This will make it easier for the different societal bodies to follow and utilize the findings of this particular research for their use including the development of green marketing strategies, for other academic purposes and also help the researcher of the paper to enhance their knowledge and research skills. The government has authority and the power to ensure that there are regulations, grants and opportunities for organizations to practice environmentally friendly practices and may utilize the findings of research to formulate regulations based on current use of strategies and the lack of results as shown in the paper. The academics is another obvious yet important discipline that utilizes the findings of research in order to update the current teachings, make use of findings for further research in the discipline as well as aid in the contribution of the knowledge pool in the discipline that will ultimately lead to innovation and further growth.

7. CONCLUSION

This study 'an analysis on the impact of green marketing strategies on the brand perception and preferences among Indian buyers of the apparel sector' was aimed at examining and understanding the extent to which various factors of consumer behaviour are influenced by the green marketing strategies. In this era of being environmentally conscious, it is only essential for companies to take accountability and change their practices to better suit the society and the environment alike. To succeed in the Indian market, the research stressed the need of understanding the behaviour of the upcoming shopper bracket of generation z and their buying behaviour with respect to the apparel category.

Suggestions and scope for future study- There lies an apparent gap in the current patterns of consumers to that in the near future and as the study of consumer behaviour is an ever-evolving complex process, it is essential to examine the current purchase intention with the developments that are due in the near future. As there is a clear difference between willingness and actual purchase, this factor may be considered as a limitation of the study but also as an opportunity for further research in this regard. As the study was conducted on a comparatively smaller scale with various limitations and by one mode of data collection, it is essential to substantiate the results by conducting the study on a global scale so as to understand consumer behaviour without geographic constraints.

REFERENCES

Ajzen, I., & Fishbein, M. (1977). Attitude-behaviour relations: A theoretical analysis and review of the research. *Psychological Bulletin*, *84*(5), 888–918. doi:10.1037/0033-2909.84.5.888

Ankit, G., & Mayur, R. (2013). *Green marketing: Impact of green advertising on consumer*. Academic Press.

Armstrong, C. M., Niinimäki, K., Kujala, S., Karell, E., & Lang, C. (2015). Sustainable product service systems for clothing: Exploring consumer perceptions of consumption alternatives in Finland. *Journal of Cleaner Production*, *97*, 30–39. doi:10.1016/j.jclepro.2014.01.046

Arnett, D. B., & Wittmann, C. M. (2014). Improving marketing success: The role of tacit knowledge exchange between sales and marketing. *Journal of Business Research*, *67*(3), 324–331. doi:10.1016/j.jbusres.2013.01.018

Arslan, F. M., & Altuna, O. K. (2010). The effect of brand extensions on product brand image. *Journal of Product and Brand Management*, *19*(3), 170–180. doi:10.1108/10610421011046157

Auty, S., & Elliott, R. (1998). Fashion involvement, self-monitoring and the meaning of brands. *Journal of Product and Brand Management*, *7*(2), 109–123. doi:10.1108/10610429810216874

Awan U (2011). *Green marketing: Marketing strategies for the Swedish energy companies*. Academic Press.

Bearden, W. O., Netemeyer, R. G., & Teel, J. E. (1989). Measurement of consumer susceptibility to interpersonal influence. *The Journal of Consumer Research*, *15*(4), 473–481. doi:10.1086/209186

Bello L. (2008). *Consumer Behaviour, National Open University of Nigeria, Ahmadu Bello Way Victoria Island Lagos*. Academic Press.

Brown, T. D., Baker, K. J., & Brand, R. A. (1992). Structural consequences of subchondral bone involvement in segmental osteonecrosis of the femoral head. *Journal of Orthopaedic Research*, *10*(1), 79–87. doi:10.1002/jor.1100100110 PMID:1727938

Chang, P. L., & Chieng, M. H. (2006). Building consumer–brand relationship: A cross-cultural experiential view. *Psychology and Marketing*, *23*(11), 927–959. doi:10.1002/mar.20140

Chen, Y. S., & Chang, C. H. (2013). Green marketing and its impact on supply chain management in industrial markets. *Industrial Marketing Management*, *42*(4), 657–669.

Chen, Y. S., & Chang, C. H. (2013). Greenwash and green trust: The mediation effects of green consumer confusion and green perceived risk. *Journal of Business Ethics*, *114*(3), 489–500. doi:10.1007/s10551-012-1360-0

Cherian, J., & Jacob, J. (2012). *Green Marketing: A Study of Consumers' Attitude towards Control* (8th ed.). Prentice-H.

Coronin, J., Gleim, M., Smith, J., & Ramires, E. (2011). Green Marketing Strategies: An Examination of Stakeholders and the Opportunities They Present. *Journal of the Academy of Marketing Science*, *39*(1), 158–174. doi:10.1007/s11747-010-0227-0

Deepak, J., & Rishi, K. (2018). Green purchasing behaviour: A conceptual framework and empirical investigation of Indian consumers, Journal of Retailing and Consumer Services. *Journal of Retailing and Consumer Services*, *41*, 60–69. doi:10.1016/j.jretconser.2017.11.008

Dehghanan, H., & Bakhshandeh, G. (2014). The impact of green perceived value and green perceived risk on green purchase behaviour of Iranian consumers. *International Journal of Management and Humanity Sciences*, *3*(2), 1349–1357.

Delafrooz, N., Taleghani, M., & Nouri, B. (2014). *Effect of green marketing on consumer purchase behaviour*. http://www.qscience.com/doi/pdf/10.5 339/connect.2014.5

Dixit, J. S., Alavi, S., & Ahuja, V. (2020). Measuring consumer brand perception for green apparel brands. *International Journal of E-Business Research, 16*(1), 28–46. doi:10.4018/IJEBR.2020010102

Dixit, J. S., Alavi, S., & Ahuja, V. (2021). Why apparel companies go green? *International Journal of Green Economics, 15*(1), 20–32. doi:10.1504/IJGE.2021.117666

Durmaz, Y., & Yaşar, V. (2016). Green Marketing and Benefits to Business. *Business and Management Studies, 2*(2), 2374-5916. doi:10.11114/bms.v2i2.1624

Eneizan, B. M., & Obaid, T. F. (2016). Prior research on green marketing and green marketing strategy: Critical analysis. Singaporean Journal of Business. *Economics and Management Studies, 51*(3965), 1–19.

Environment Friendly Products. (n.d.). *Asian Social Science, 8*(12). Advance online publication. doi:10.5539/ass.v8n12p117

Eric, K. (2007). *Green marketing practices by Kenya petroleum refineries: A study of the perception of the management of oil marketing companies in Kenya*. Ph.D. Dissertation, University of Nairobi, Kenya.

Erics, A., Ulna, S., & Candan. (2012). The effect of brand satisfaction, trust and brand commitment on loyalty and repurchase intentions. *Social and Behavioural Sciences, 58*, 1395 – 1404.

Fan, H., & Zeng, L. (2011). *Implementation of green marketing strategy in China: A study of the green food industry*. M.Sc. Thesis, University of GAVLE, China.

Fazio, R. H., & Zanna, M. P. (1981). Direct experience and attitude-behaviour consistency. In L. Berkowitz (Ed.), Advances in Experimental Social Psychology: Vol. 14. *Academic Press*.

Garg, S., & Sharma, V. (2017). Green Marketing: An Emerging Approach to Sustainable Development. *International Journal of Applied Agricultural Research, 12*(2), 177–184. doi:10.4108/eai.14-2-2017.152283

Gogoi, B. (2013). Study of antecedents of purchase intention and its effect on brand loyalty of private label brand of apparel. *International Journal of Sales & Marketing, 3*(2), 73–86.

Gosavi, P. S. (2013). Gaining competitive advantage through green marketing of cell phone. *ASM's International E-Journal of Ongoing Research in Management and IT, 13*(1), 1–11.

Grant, J. (2008). Green Marketing. *Strategic Direction, 24*(6), 25–27. doi:10.1108/02580540810868041

Gupta, S., & Pooja. (2021). Marketing to the green generation: How Generation Z's eco-consciousness is changing the game. *Journal of Management Research*.

Haanpaa, L. (2007). Consumers' green commitment: Indication of a postmodern lifestyle? *International Journal of Consumer Studies, 31*(5), 478–486. doi:10.1111/j.1470-6431.2007.00598.x

Hartman, K. B., & Spiro, R. L. (2005). Recapturing store image in customer-based store equity: A construct conceptualization. *Journal of Business Research, 58*(8), 1112–1120. doi:10.1016/j.jbusres.2004.01.008

Henion, K. E., & Kinnear, T. C. (1976b). A Guide to Ecological Marketing. In K. E. Henion & T. C. Kinnear (Eds.), *Ecological Marketing*. American Marketing Association.

Hoyer, W., & MacInnis, D. (2004). *Consumer Behaviour* (3rd ed.). CENGAGE.

Hsieh, M. H., & Lindridge, A. (2005). Universal appeals with local specifications. *Journal of Product and Brand Management*, *14*(1), 14–28. doi:10.1108/10610420510583716

Hunt, S. D. (2011). Sustainable marketing, equity, and economic growth: A resource-advantage, economic freedom approach. Journal of the Academy of Marketing Science. *International Journal of Industrial Marketing*, *1*(2), 1–19.

James, F. P. (2002). Experience use History as a segmentation tool to examine golf travelers' satisfaction, perceived value and repurchased intention. *Journal of Vacation Marketing*, *8*(4), 332–342. doi:10.1177/135676670200800404

Jansson, J. (2011). Consumer eco-innovation adoption: Assessing attitudinal factors and perceived product characteristics. *Business Strategy and the Environment*, *20*(3), 192–210. doi:10.1002/bse.690

Jansson, J., Marell, A., & Nordlund, A. (2010). Green consumer behaviour: Determinants of curtailment and eco-innovation adoption. *Journal of Consumer Marketing*, *27*(4), 358–370. doi:10.1108/07363761011052396

Kalafatis, S., Pollard, M., East, R., & Tsogas, M. H. (1999). Green marketing and Ajzen's theory of planned behaviour: A cross-market examination. *Journal of Consumer Marketing*, *16*(5), 441–460. doi:10.1108/07363769910289550

Kawa, L. W., Rahmadiani, S. F., & Kumar, S. (2013). Factors Affecting Consumer Decision Making: A Survey of Young-Adults on Imported Cosmetics in Jabodetabek, Indonesia. The SIJ Transactions on Industrial, Financial & Business Management, 1(5).

Keller, K. L. (2001). Building customer-based brand equity: Creating brand resonance requires carefully sequenced brand-building efforts. *Marketing Management*, *10*(2), 15–19.

Keller, K. L. (2008). Strategic Brand Management. Building, Measuring, and Managing Brand Equity. Pearson Education International.

Keller, K. L. (2009). Building strong brands in a modern marketing communications environment. *Journal of Marketing Communications*, *15*(2–3), 139–155. doi:10.1080/13527260902757530

Khare, A., & Kautish, P. (2022). Antecedents to green apparel purchase behavior of Indian consumers. *Journal of Global Scholars of Marketing Science*, *32*(2), 222–251. doi:10.1080/21639159.2021.1885301

Khare, A., & Sadachar, A. (2017). Green apparel buying behaviour: A study on Indian youth. *International Journal of Consumer Studies*, *41*(5), 558–569. doi:10.1111/ijcs.12367

Kim, W. E., & Thinavan Periyayya, V. (2013). The Beauty of Green Branding: Kinnear, T.C. and Taylor, J.R. (1973) 'The effect of ecological concern on brand perceptions'. *JMR, Journal of Marketing Research*, *10*(2), 191. doi:10.2307/3149825

Kiya, R. (2012). A study of the effects of firm ability association and brand awareness on repurchase intention and the mediator role of product quality and brand association in buying decision making process. *Marketing Management*, 14.

Koll, O., & von Wallpach, S. (2009). One brand perception? Or many? The heterogeneity of intrabrand knowledge. *Journal of Product and Brand Management, 18*(5), 338–345. doi:10.1108/10610420910981819

Kotler, P. (1994). Marketing Management: Analysis, Planning, Implementation and Lee, K. (2008), "Opportunities for green marketing: young consumers. *Marketing Intelligence & Planning, 26*(6), 573–586.

Kotler, P., & Armstrong, G. (2010). *Principles of Marketing*. Pearson Prentice Hall.

Lee, K. (2009). Gender differences in Hong Kong adolescent consumers' green purchasing behaviour. *Journal of Consumer Marketing, 26*(2), 87–96. doi:10.1108/07363760910940456

Lohr, S. W. (2015, June 21). *H&M's "Conscious" Collection? Don't Buy Into the Hype*. HuffPost. https://www.huffpost.com/entry/hms-conscious-collection-_b_7107964

Lotf, M., Yousef, A., & Jafari, S. (2018). The Effect of Emerging Green Market on Green Entrepreneurship and Sustainable Development in Knowledge-Based Companies. *Sustainability (Basel), 10*(7), 2308. doi:10.3390/su10072308

Mainieri, T., Barnett, E. G., Valdero, T. R., Unipan, J. B., & Oskamp, S. (1997). Green buying: The influence of environmental concern on consumer behaviour. *The Journal of Social Psychology, 137*(2), 189–204. doi:10.1080/00224549709595430

Mainieri, T., Barnett, E. G., Valdero, T. R., Unipan, J. B., & Oskamp, S. (1997). Green buying: The influence of environmental concern of consumer behaviour. *Journal of Social Psychology, 137*, 189–204.

Mintel. (2006). *Green living*. US Marketing Research Report.

Mishra, P., & Sharma, P. (2010). Green Marketing in India: Emerging Opportunities and Challenges. *Journal of Engineering, Science & Management in Education, 3*, 9–14.

Mohajan, H. (2012). Green Marketing Is A Sustainable Marketing System In The Twenty First Century. *International Journal of Management and Transformation, 6*(2), 23–39.

Molla, A., & Licker, P. (2001). E-commerce systems success: an attempt to extend and respecify the DeLone and McLean model of IS success. *Journal of Electronic Commerce Research, 2*(4), 131– 141.

Moschis, P. G. (1976). Social Comparison and Informal Group Influence. *JMR, Journal of Marketing Research, 13*(3), 237–244. doi:10.1177/002224377601300304

Nah-Hong, LN. (2007), The Effect of Brand Image and Product Knowledge on Purchase Intention Moderated by Price Discount. *J. Int. Manage. Stud., 2*.

Niinimaki, K. (2010). Eco-clothing, consumer identity and ideology. *Sustainable Development (Bradford), 18*(3), 150–162. doi:10.1002/sd.455

Nik Abdul Rashid, N. R. (2009). Awareness of eco-label in Malaysia's green marketing initiative. *International Journal of Business and Management, 4*(8), 132–141.

Nupur, A., & Parul, M. (2021). Investigating the relationship between Internal Environmental Locus of control and Behaviour towards sustainable apparel: The mediating role of intention to purchase. *Transnational Marketing Journal*, (3), 539–552.

Papadopoulos, I., Karagouni, G., Trigkas, M., & Platogianni, E. (2010). Green marketing: The case of Greece in certified and sustainably managed timber products. *EuroMed Journal of Business*, *5*(2), 166–190. doi:10.1108/14502191011065491

Patrick, A. I. (2005). Green branding effects on attitude: Functional versus emotional positioning strategies. *Marketing Intelligence & Planning*, *23*(1), 9–29. doi:10.1108/02634500510577447

Peattie, S., & Crane, A. (2005). Green marketing: legend, myth, farce, or prophesy? The Greening of Business. Springer.

Pickett-Baker, J., & Ozaki, R. (2008). Pro-environmental products: Marketing influence on consumer purchase decision. *Journal of Consumer Marketing*, *25*(5), 281–293. doi:10.1108/07363760810890516

Polonsky, M. J. (1994). An introduction to green marketing. *Electronic Green Journal*, *1*(2). Advance online publication. doi:10.5070/G31210177

Polonsky, M. J. (2011, December). Transformative green marketing: Impediments and opportunities. *Journal of Business Research*, *64*(12), 1311–1319. doi:10.1016/j.jbusres.2011.01.016

Polonsky, M. J. (2011). *Transformative green marketing: Impediments and opportunities*. Academic Press.

Polonsky, M. J., & Rosenberger, P. J. III. (2001). Reevaluating green marketing: A strategic approach. *Business Horizons*, *44*(5), 21–30. doi:10.1016/S0007-6813(01)80057-4

Poulsson, S. H. G., & Kale, S. H. (2004). The experience economy and commercial experiences. *The Marketing Review*, *4*(3), 267–277. doi:10.1362/1469347042223445

Punitha, S., & Rasdi, R. M. (2013). Corporate Social Responsibility: Adoption of Green Marketing by Hotel Industry. *Asian Social Science*, *9*(17), 79. doi:10.5539/ass.v9n17p79

Shah, H., Aziz, A., Jaffari, A. R., Waris, S., Ejaz, W., Fatima, M., & Sherazi, K. (2012). The Impact of Brands on Consumer Purchase Intentions. *Asian Journal of Business Management*, *4*(2), 105–110.

Shamdasani, Chon-Lin, & Richmond. (1993). Exploring Green Consumers In An Oriental Culture: Role Of Personal And Marketing Mix Factors. *Advances in Consumer Research. Association for Consumer Research (U. S.)*, *20*, 491.

Sharma, A., & Banwet, D. K. (2018). Green marketing and consumer behavior: The case of Generation Z in India's apparel sector. *Journal of Fashion Marketing and Management*, *22*(3), 384–401.

Sharma, Y. (2011). Changing consumer behaviour with respect to green marketing–a case study of consumer durables and retailing. *International Journal of Multidisciplinary Research*, *1*(4), 152–162.

Sheth, J. N., & Sisodia, R. S. (2015). *Does marketing need reform?: Fresh perspectives on the future*. Routledge. doi:10.4324/9781315705118

Shil, P. (2012). Evolution and future of environmental marketing. *Asia Pacific Journal Of Marketing and Management Review*, *1*(3), 74–81.

Shirsavar, H. A., & Fashkhamy, F. (2013). Green marketing: A new paradigm to gain competitive advantage in contemporary business. *Trends in Advanced Science and Engineering*, *7*(1), 12–18.

Shrikanth, R., & Raju, D. S. N. (2012). Contemporary green marketing-brief reference to Indian scenario. *International Journal of Social Sciences & Interdisciplinary Research, 1*(1), 26–39.

Singh, G. (2013). Green: The new colour of marketing in India. ASCI Journal of Smith, J. (2020). The impact of green marketing on the marketing industry. *JMR, Journal of Marketing Research, 57*(2), 87–94.

Snoj, B., Korda, P. A., & Mumel, D. (2004). The relationships among perceived quality, perceived risk and perceived product value. *Journal of Product and Brand Management, 13*(3), 156–167. doi:10.1108/10610420410538050

Solvalier, I. (2010). *Green marketing strategies case study about ICA group AB*. M.Sc.

Steiner, A. (2015). *Sustainable Consumption and Production*. United Nations Environment Programme UNAB.

Tariq, M., Nawaz, M., Butt, H., & Nawaz, M. (2013). Customer Perceptions about Branding and Purchase Intention:A Study of FMCG in an Emerging Market. *Journal of Basic and Applied Scientific Research, 3*(2), 340–347.

Thomas, J. B., & Peters, C. L. O. (2009). Silver seniors: Exploring the selfconcept, lifestyles, and apparel consumption of women over age 65. *International Journal of Retail & Distribution Management, 37*(12), 1018–1040. doi:10.1108/09590550911005001

Troumbis, A. Y. (1991). *Environmental Labelling on Services: The Case of Tourism*. Academic Press.

Tsiotsou, R. (2006). The role of perceived product quality and overall satisfaction on purchase intention. *International Journal of Consumer Studies, 30*(2), 207–217. doi:10.1111/j.1470-6431.2005.00477.x

Tung-Zong, C., & And Albert, R. W. (1994). Prices, Product information, and purchase intention: An empirical study. *Journal of the Academy of Marketing Science, 22*(1), 16–27. doi:10.1177/0092070394221002

Witt, E. B., & Bruce, D. G. (1972). Group Influence & Brand Choice Congruence. *JMR, Journal of Marketing Research, 9*(4), 440–443. doi:10.1177/002224377200900415

Chapter 9
The Role of Social Responsibility on Consumer Engagement Through Fashion Brands' Instagram

Sara Santos
https://orcid.org/0000-0002-3581-6478
Research Centre in Digital Services, Portugal

Paulo Silva
https://orcid.org/0000-0002-9955-9706
Research Centre in Digital Services, Portugal

Margarida Caramelo Lopes
ESEV, Instituto Politécnico de Viseu, Portugal

ABSTRACT

At a time when consumers are becoming more aware of social and environmental responsibility, they are increasingly recognising the fashion industry's impact on the world. Based on this growing awareness, the response from fashion brands is to strategically use digital platforms to highlight their commitment to the issue of sustainability. Brands that consciously share this content on online platforms adopt an effective communication strategy, attracting greater engagement with their audience. In particular, the analysis in this study focuses on the Instagram presence of three notable brands: Naz, Isto, and Tentree. The results of this study affirm the positive impact of social responsibility on consumer engagement when it comes to the Instagram accounts of these fashion brands. This underlines the significant role that social responsibility plays in influencing consumer perceptions and interactions in the digital sphere.

DOI: 10.4018/979-8-3693-3049-4.ch009

1. INTRODUCTION

With the advance of technology, social networks have become part of consumer's daily lives, where behaviour and lifestyles are undergoing transformations influenced by how brands communicate their content on digital platforms. In response to this change, digital marketing has achieved a paradigm shift, bringing together the values of traditional marketing with the dynamic characteristics of digital. In today's fashion industry, it is necessary to address the current environmental crisis and adopt new sustainable practices, as well as how brands communicate and articulate their commitment to sustainability. Digital platforms have become a prominent medium for showcasing sustainability-related initiatives and establishing a meaningful and authentic connection with consumers. However, although there have been several significant advances in understanding the relationship between social responsibility and digital marketing, the research scenario highlighted by Diez-Martin, Blanco-Gonzalez and Prado-Roman (2019) suggests that there is still a need to explore and investigate this crucial intersection more deeply today.

Furthermore, the observations of Khanal, Akhtaruzzaman and Kularatne (2021) highlight a notable gap in the existing body of information research. The predominant focus is on big brands and companies. This leaves small brands largely unexplored in the context of the impact of social media on social responsibility engagement. Underlining the need to broaden the research to cover a more diverse range of companies, it is necessary to recognise that social responsibility and social media engagement dynamics can vary according to companies' different scales and structures. Thus, this study aims to understand the dynamics of social responsibility as fashion brands share content on Instagram to attract and maintain consumer interest. This underlines a crucial and timely call for expanding research efforts regarding social responsibility and social media engagement, aiming for a comprehensive understanding that considers industry giants and smaller entities in this evolving landscape.

2. LITERATURE REVIEW

The progression of technologies and the emergence of Web 2.0 have fueled the expansion of online communication and social networks. Digital platforms provide users diverse opportunities, allowing them to create content and share information on various topics, fostering positive relationships and interactions with brands (Muntinga, Moorman, & Smit, 2011). In order to respond to this changing environment, brands must be prepared to navigate the ever-changing digital landscape. The potent role of social media in forming consumer perceptions and behaviour patterns demands a more proactive brand approach. By joining and adapting to digital, brands can take full advantage of user-generated content and keep in line with their audience's expectations, thus helping their success in the crowded online space. Social networks influence consumers' purchasing behaviour by enabling them to express opinions about products and share their experiences with brands (Mason, Narcum, & Mason, 2021). The research conducted by Majeed, Owusu-Ansah, and Ashmond (2021) indicates a positive correlation between social media marketing strategies and the growing trend of online interaction, stimulating user engagement on digital platforms through brand-related content. In today's digital landscape, where social media has become a permanent part of everyday life, brands increasingly recognise the value of developing a significant online presence.

The fashion industry relies heavily on social and environmental responsibility, underlining the importance of adopting practices and initiatives that guide us towards a more sustainable future. Implementing ethical and responsible production methods mitigates a brand's environmental footprint and promotes a sustainable reputation among consumers, thus contributing to a positive brand image (Thorisdottir & Johannsdottir, 2020). The future of fashion depends on its ability to balance style and sustainability. Adopting social and environmental responsibility is not just a trend but a shift that aligns fashion companies with consumer values. Social networks also serve as a platform to convey social responsibility and sustainability messages, influencing conscientious practices and actions that encourage user participation and positive electronic Word-of-Mouth (eWOM) (Khanal et al., 2021).

Consequently, digital platforms have become a critical success factor, acting as a tool to establish brand attachment by sharing initiatives related to social responsibility and fostering a connection between the consumer and the brand. Through the power of social media, consumers stay informed about a brand's content, participate in dialogues, share their experiences, and contribute to the ethical and responsible narrative. The nature of social media communication increases the impact of socially responsible initiatives, converting them into positive action.

2.1. Social Media and Fashion Brands

In today's world, the fashion industry is working hard to meet the diverse demands of consumers, including cultural, social, personality, influence and prestige factors. Understanding society's trends and consumption habits is crucial, and digital marketing tools, especially social media, play a key role in shaping consumer decisions and fostering brand loyalty (Ananda et al., 2019). In addition, the globalisation and, therefore, connectivity offered by the internet have broadened the boundaries of the fashion industry. Brands can now generate content and reach their audience in real-time, giving consumers instant access to the latest news.

Beyond its primary purpose, fashion represents an expression of authenticity on the brand's part, helping consumers establish a sense of attachment and identity with its brand. Many fashion brands, focusing on younger audiences, use social media to promote their brand, strengthen values, and build a solid reputation (Voorveld, 2019). Interaction on social media enables brands to engage with their audience in real-time, building a sense of inclusion and community beyond the simple consumption of fashion.

Social networks wield significant influence over consumer culture, transforming consumption into an exchange of information. Fashion companies have rapidly embraced social media, drawn by the potential benefits of new marketing channels, such as swift trend identification and direct customer engagement (Ananda et al., 2019). Fashion brands recognise the transformative nature of digital and have adopted social networks as a marketing and co-creation tool with their audience. Real-time feedback allows brands to quickly refine their strategies as the expectations of their follower base evolve. Castillo-Abdul et al. (2022) underscore the direct impact of content on brand reputation, emphasising positive engagement, particularly in the case of luxury fashion brands. The authors recommend that the fashion industry continues developing brand-related posts and content on social media to enhance relationships and engagement with consumers.

The fashion industry's profitable transformation in its relationship with the public stems from profound changes in online projection, distribution, positioning, and consumption processes. This evolution has prompted innovative marketing strategies, empowering users to transition from passive observers to active consumers and content creators (Castillo-Abdul et al., 2022). This change in brand communication is a departure from the traditional model, ushering in an era in which the fashion industry thrives on the collaborative involvement of the digital age.

Given the dynamic nature of fashion trends and the constant quest for novelty, digital platforms continually adapt to various fashion markets and the preferences of online content consumers (Quiles-Soler, Martínez-Sala, & Monserrat-Gauchi, 2022). Recognising that social networks serve as a means for brands to engage users and cultivate trust, it becomes imperative for fashion brands to utilise these platforms for conveying messages related to environmental and social issues, influencing followers to adopt actions that contribute to the betterment of the environment. With consumers increasingly looking for authenticity and initiatives that brands support, using digital platforms to convey messages related to environmental and social issues is becoming a powerful tool. For fashion brands, it is a way of staying fashionable and positively contributing to the dialogue on responsible and sustainable behaviour.

2.2. Social and Environmental Responsibility in the Fashion Industry

Fueled by a widespread push for sustainability, the urgent need to confront ecological challenges has made fashion consumers more informed and demanding. Despite this, some consumers still prioritise quantity over sustainable practices, posing a challenge to a more environmentally friendly transition (Niinimäki et al., 2020). Scholars have scrutinised fashion companies' social and environmental responsibility behaviour from various perspectives. Brewer (2019) examines the fashion industry's environmental impact, advocating for ethical improvements and proposing slow fashion as an alternative to the fast fashion model. Thorisdottir and Johannsdottir's (2020) literature review highlights how social responsibility contributes to the fashion industry's sustainability, emphasising the reduction of negative impacts through environmental commitments. This change implies reassessing production processes, the supply of materials and waste management strategies, recognising their role in environmental management.

Niinimäki et al. (2020) specifically focus on environmental impacts throughout the textile value cycle, highlighting issues such as water use, chemical pollution, $CO2$ emissions, and textile waste. These studies underscore the imperative to address the environmental crisis, particularly within the fashion sector, which ranks among the world's top polluters. Initiatives led by the UN aim to promote clothing awareness, recycling, and sustainability (United Nations, 2019). Notably, several fashion brands have received recognition from the UN, earning the Champions of the Earth award for initiatives dedicated to environmental protection (Quiles-Soler et al., 2022).

Both principal and smaller fashion companies are integrating sustainability into their core business models, acknowledging the global concern surrounding the environmental crisis (United Nations, 2019). Practices aligning with sustainability standards often emphasise increased transparency in production process reporting (Thorisdottir & Johannsdottir, 2020). These measures include raising awareness among producers, consumers, and influencers and advocating for labelling laws to inform consumers about production origins (Quiles-Soler et al., 2022). Consumers thus exert considerable leverage by making conscious choices that emphasise environmentally friendly and ethically produced fashion items. In addition, including influencers in the awareness-raising process can increase the reach and impact of sustainability messages, taking advantage of their platforms to defend responsible consumption.

Brands' social and environmental responsibility shapes their relationship with society, reflecting behaviours and actions that address both internal and external environmental concerns. Ethical and responsible production practices help maintain the brand's image by addressing environmental impacts and cultivating a reputation for sustainability with consumers (Thorisdottir & Johannsdottir, 2020). However, it is essential to note that some brands engage in social responsibility primarily for image-building and financial gain (Chaffee, 2017). Incorporating social and environmental responsibility plays a crucial role in defining the trajectory of the fashion industry. This commitment is not only a moral must but also a strategic one. Brands want to succeed in the long term in an era when consumers increasingly demand sustainable practices from brands. In conclusion, social and environmental responsibility is pivotal in the fashion industry, emphasising the necessity of adopting practices and measures that propel us towards a more sustainable future.

2.3. The Role of Social Media Engagement in Publicising Social and Environmental Issues

Most consumers have integrated social media seamlessly into their daily routines, shaping their lifestyles and behaviours. This greater user engagement on social media has increased the relevance of brands communicating successfully on digital media platforms (Schivinski, Christodoulides, & Dabrowski, 2016). The brands continuously scale up their social media presence to accommodate and embrace this evolving reality, promoting online engagement with consumers and planning for more interactivity (Shahbaznezhad, Dolan, & Rashidirad, 2021). As a result, social media makes it easier for users and brands to collaborate and share content, offering an opportunity to develop relationships where interaction is the main goal (Ebrahim, 2019). Social media marketing relies heavily on social media as its principal tool, emphasising establishing bidirectional communication between brands and their audiences. User engagement is one of the main advantages of social networks, allowing interaction and raising brand awareness (Desai, 2019). In addition, consumer interest is encouraged by exchanging content and relevant information (Ebrahim, 2019). Zhu and Chen (2015) believe that two types of social media characteristics exist: the nature of the connections, which is based on the profile compared to the actual content, and the level of customisation of the messages, i.e. the degree to which the message is personalised according to the preferences of the consumer (Zhu & Chen, 2015). These two factors lead to the four categories of the social network: 1) Profile-based social networks, consisting of relationships in the context of personalised messages formulated by brands, as is the situation on various social media platforms such as Facebook and LinkedIn; 2) Self-media networks, such as Twitter, which are also profile-based. However, there is the option of managing one's communication on social media; 3) Social platforms, known as creative outlets, are based on the sharing of ideas and interests of individuals through the creation of content, such as YouTube and Instagram; 4) Collaborative social networks are also based on content, but people can ask and participate (Voorveld, Noort, Muntinga, & Bronner, 2018). Muntinga et al. (2011) propose the COBRAs model, which aims to understand the motivations and behaviours of consumers' online brand activities. In this way, it is possible to understand the factors that motivate the public to use social networks and engage with the brand. Consumption, contribution and creation are the levels of involvement analysed in the study, which are related to the various motivations. Consumption represents participation without active contribution, i.e. users consume the brand's activity but do not participate directly. Examples are watching and listening to videos and audio related to brands and reading comments on social networks. In the case of contribution, this refers to the user's interactions with the content and with other users, where the most common examples are the evaluation of products or brands and actions such as liking, commenting or sharing content related to brands. Finally, creation represents the development and publication of content related to the brand and includes examples such as the publication of videos, audio and images related to the brand. This study concludes how consumer interest in online brand activities improves brand intentions and purchase motivation. The interaction between users and brands is of greater importance to brands, as social media users depend on recommendations from other users, stimulating the decision-making process (Majeed, Owusu-Ansah, & Ashmond, 2021). Consumers seek information and advice from other users, while consumers with high levels of opinion gather influence over the attitudes and behaviours of other users (Ananda, Hernández-García, Acquila-Natale, & Lamberti, 2019). Social networks provide tools that allow users to express their reactions and respond to content shared on the platforms. These tools include various plugins, such as "like", "retweet", "share", and "comment" (Ananda et al., 2019, p. 402). This way, users can share their interest in the content, and the brand receives feedback immediately. There are various metrics for evaluating the responses, such as the number of likes, favourites and comments. These metrics can also serve as eWoM indicators that tend to increase the number of shares on social media, in which a positive transmission can be an important indicator of the quality of the relationship with the brand (Ananda et al., 2019). Therefore, interactions on social media reflect user engagement with brand content, helping to strengthen a positive relationship with the brand. The potential to measure and analyse metrics such as the number of likes, shares and comments enables brands to understand the feedback on their content. Positive reactions become a key factor in reinforcing the relationship between users and the brand, creating a feeling of community and developing a positive relationship.

Social networks have transformed how we communicate, and as the focus on social and environmental issues intensifies, brands are under increasing pressure to showcase their efforts in these areas. There is a heightened awareness of sharing content that promotes brand engagement to underscore environmental and social concerns, aligning with user expectations and facilitating communication with stakeholders (Giacomini, Zola, Paredi, & Mazzoleni, 2020). However, a gap exists between societal behaviour and market values regarding social responsibility and sustainability (Diez-Martin et al., 2019). It becomes the responsibility of companies to leverage social media as a potent tool for promoting environmentally conscious behaviour. In this way, strategic social media campaigns can be designed to inspire and educate the public about the environmental impact of their actions. In the process, brands contribute to closing the gap between social values and market trends and position themselves as positive drivers of change in the broader socio-economic scene.

Recognising the social credibility of platforms such as Instagram is pivotal in shaping user attitudes and decisions regarding sustainable products and services (Jalali & Khalid, 2019). The intense dissemination of information in social media enables consumers to swiftly grasp ethical imperatives in the fashion industry. Ethical codes in digital marketing strategies attract fashion consumers by addressing critical issues like workers' rights and sustainability. However, distinguishing genuinely ethical companies from those merely projecting such values becomes crucial (Cerchia & Piccolo, 2019). As a result, brands are increasingly emphasising communicating their social and environmental responsibility actions while maintaining an active presence on digital platforms. This allows for disseminating their most conscientious and responsible messages on social media. By addressing social and environmental concerns, brands foster loyalty and capture users' attention and engagement.

3. METHODOLOGY

The research employs a qualitative methodology utilising an exploratory approach to establish a framework for analysing social media engagement, focusing on three sustainable fashion brands: Naz, Isto, and Tentree. The primary objective is to examine how users interact with posts related to social and environmental responsibility. The selection of these specific brands was driven by their consistent sharing of content regarding social responsibility and sustainability across various digital platforms.

Within this study, publications of the three sustainable fashion brands were scrutinised to compare the engagement rate of posts related to social responsibility with those featuring unrelated content. The chosen brands include two Portuguese brands, Naz and Isto, and one international brand, Tentree. Research on various sustainable brands on social networks showed that most brands refrain from publishing content related to social and environmental responsibility. Consequently, the three brands selected for the study were chosen as they regularly share content relevant to the specified topic. Naz is a clothing brand that focuses on fair and sustainable fashion, emphasising the importance of respecting natural resources and people (Naz, 2023). Isto, another clothing brand, aims to create enduring collections from organic and natural materials while advocating for price transparency throughout the production of its articles (Isto, 2023). Lastly, Tentree, a clothing brand, prioritises fair working conditions and utilises only recycled and sustainably sourced materials—notably, the brand plants ten trees for every garment purchased (Tentree, 2023). The social network chosen for the analysis is Instagram, where the last 50 posts from each brand were thoroughly examined. This analysis focuses on scrutinising the publications of these three sustainable fashion brands with the primary objective of comparing the engagement rate of posts related to social responsibility with posts featuring unrelated content. The range of posts analysed was selected from the latest posts made by the brands, considering the starting point of the analysis to be April 28, 2023 (Table 1).

Table 1. Period of analysis of the brands' social networks

	Start of Analysis Period	**End of the Analysis Period**
Naz	**January 30**	**April 28**
Isto	February 21	April 28
Tentree	February 14	April 28

The framework utilised in this study is derived from Vries et al. (2012) and encompasses the following components: date, indicating the publication date; content, denoting the type of content featured in the publication; format, representing the medium through which the publication was disseminated; the count of likes garnered by the publication; the number of positive comments, negative comments, and neutral comments, along with the total number of comments; the engagement rate of the publication; and the level of interactivity. To evaluate the content type of each publication, the table of contents outlined by Eriksson, Sjöberg, Rosenbröijer, and Fagerstrøm (2019) was referenced. This approach facilitates the characterisation of the content type in each brand's posts based on criteria such as inspiration, entertainment, transactional, cooperative and others (Table 2). Additionally, the SR (Social Responsibility) category was incorporated into the analysis grid to encompass the content related to social responsibility and sustainability.

In order to characterise the format of the publications under analysis and their level of interactivity, the criteria in Table 3 by Vries et al. (2012) were used.

Table 2. Type of publication content

Type of Content	Description
Inspiration	Selection of inspiring products and models, arrival of new products and other inspiring calls to action (e.g. take a look at this, get inspired)
Entertainment	Contests to win prizes, fun events and questions for fans.
Transactional	Price promotions, offers and other sales-related details.
Cooperative	Share or co-produce content with bloggers, stylists, magazines, television programs, etc.
Other	Content that does not fall under other characteristics (e.g. advertisements and general updates).

Source: adapted from Eriksson et al. (2019)

Table 3. Level of interactivity and format of publications

Level of Interactivity	Format
Low	Photography/image
Medium	Call-to-action (CTA)
High	Videos

Source: adapted from Vries et al. (2012)

The engagement rate is calculated using the formula from Putranto et al. (2022).

(number of likes+number of comments)/(number of followers) X 100

In this way, all the tools used to analyse the tables of the three fashion brands have been compiled and are presented in detail in the next chapter. Each table consists of date, content, format, number of likes, total number of comments, engagement rate and level of interactivity.

4. RESULTS

As mentioned above, the research aims to understand how social and environmental responsibility works as content shared on fashion brands' Instagram platforms to attract and maintain consumer interest. The following results comprise the data collected from each brand to answer this. Table 4 shows the characteristics and engagement rate of the 50 posts analysed from the Naz brand on its Instagram page @naz.fashion, which has 19,500 followers. Various factors, such as content, format and level of interaction, influence the level of interaction with posts. After analysing the posts, it is possible to see transactional content (such as topics related to sales and promotions), inspirational content (such as images, products and phrases), cooperative content (sharing posts or products from users and influencers), entertainment content (such as questions in the description) and social responsibility content (such as content on the theme of social responsibility and sustainability). In terms of format, there are image posts (low level of interactivity), video posts (high level of interactivity), image/CTA posts (low/medium level of interactivity) and CTA/video posts (medium/high level of interactivity). Overall, the engagement rate of the posts is low, with the highest figure being 0.77%, corresponding to the post on April 7, with 146 likes and four comments featuring inspirational content, a CTA/video format and a medium/high level of interactivity.

Table 4. Naz brand analysis grid

@naz.fashion (19 500 Followers)						
Date	**Content**	**Format**	**Likes**	**Total Comments**	**Engagement Rate**	**Level of Interactivity**
January 30	SR	Image/CTA	71	3	0,38%	Low/medium
February 1	Transactional	Image/CTA	47	0	0,24%	Low/medium
February 2	SR	Image	40	0	0,21%	Low
February 3	SR	Video	51	0	0,26%	High
February 5	Transactional	CTA/video	25	3	0,14%	Medium/high
February 9	Inspiration	Image/CTA	31	1	0,16%	Low/medium
February 10	Cooperative	Video	50	3	0,27%	High
February 13	Transactional	CTA/video	18	1	0,10%	Medium/high
February 15	Inspiration	CTA/video	38	2	0,21%	Medium/high
February 17	Transactional	CTA/video	38	0	0,19%	Medium/high
February 20	SR	Image	46	0	0,24%	Low
February 22	Transactional	Image/CTA	38	0	0,19%	Low/medium
February 23	Transactional	Image/CTA	24	0	0,12%	Low/medium
February 24	Transactional	Video	30	0	0,15%	High
February 26	Transactional	Image/CTA	19	0	0,10%	Low/medium
February 28	Entertainment	Image/CTA	20	2	0,11%	Low/medium
March 8	Entertainment	Vídeo	43	3	0,24%	High
March 10	SR	Image/CTA	49	1	0,26%	Low/medium
March 12	SR	CTA/video	31	2	0,17%	Medium/high
March 13	Inspiration	Image/CTA	23	0	0,12%	Low/medium
March 15	Inspiration	CTA/video	40	4	0,23%	Medium/high
March 16	Cooperative	Image/CTA	96	2	0,50%	Low/medium
March 20	Inspiration	CTA/video	40	0	0,21%	Medium/high
March 21	Inspiration	CTA/video	34	1	0,18%	Medium/high
March 23	Inspiration	Image/CTA	55	5	0,31%	Low/medium
March 24	SR	Image/CTA	54	3	0,29%	Low/medium
March 26	Inspiration	CTA/video	31	1	0,16%	Medium/high
March 28	SR	Image/CTA	28	2	0,15%	Low/medium
March 30	SR	Image/CTA	58	2	0,31%	Low/medium
March 31	Inspiration	Image/CTA	44	0	0,23%	Low/medium
April 2	Inspiration	Video	34	0	0,17%	High
April 3	Entertainment	Imagem/CTA	41	3	0,23%	Low/medium
April 5	Entertainment	CTA/video	46	4	0,26%	Medium/high
April 6	SR	Image	46	2	0,25%	Low
April 7	Inspiration	CTA/video	146	4	0,77%	Medium/high
April 10	Inspiration	CTA/video	78	1	0,41%	Medium/high

Table 4 continues

@naz.fashion (19 500 Followers)						
Date	**Content**	**Format**	**Likes**	**Total Comments**	**Engagement Rate**	**Level of Interactivity**
April 11	Inspiration	Image/CTA	25	0	0,13%	Low/medium
April 12	Inspiration	Image/CTA	24	0	0,13%	Low/medium
April 13	Entertainment	Image/CTA	81	8	0,46%	Low/medium
April 13	Entertainment	Video	36	1	0,19%	High
April 14	Inspiration	Image/CTA	67	4	0,36%	Low/medium
April 16	Cooperative	CTA/video	85	3	0,45%	Medium/high
April 18	Inspiration	Image/CTA	50	4	0,28%	Low/medium
April 19	SR	Image/CTA	111	0	0,57%	Low/medium
April 21	Inspiration	CTA/video	49	0	0,25%	Medium/high
April 23	Inspiration	CTA/video	84	5	0,46%	Medium/high
April 24	Inspiration	Image/CTA	29	0	0,15%	Low/medium
April 26	Inspiration	Image/CTA	62	1	0,32%	Low/medium
April 27	SR	Image/CTA	87	2	0,46%	Low/medium
April 28	Inspiration	Image/ CTA	47	0	0,24%	Low/medium

The characteristics and engagement rate of the 50 posts analysed from the Isto brand on the Instagram page @isto.pt, with 50,100 followers, can be seen in Table 5. After analysing the posts, it is possible to see inspirational content (such as images, articles and phrases), cooperative content (sharing posts or products from users and/or influencers), entertainment content (such as questions in the description), miscellaneous content (informative content and brand updates) and social responsibility content (such as content on the theme of social responsibility and sustainability). About the type of format, we can see that there are image posts (low level of interactivity), video posts (high level of interactivity) and image/CTA posts (low/medium level of interactivity). Various factors, such as the content, the format, and the level of interaction, can influence the level of interaction of posts. In general, the engagement rate of the posts is low, the highest figure being 1.06%, corresponding to the post on April 6, with 520 likes and ten comments, featuring diverse content, an Image format and a low level of interactivity.

Table 6 shows the characteristics and engagement rate of the 50 posts analysed from the Tentree brand on its Instagram page @tentree, with a total of 2.100.000 followers. As mentioned above, the level of interaction with posts is influenced by various factors, such as content, format and level of interaction. After analysing the posts, it is possible to see inspirational content (such as images, products and phrases), entertainment content (such as questions in the description), miscellaneous content (such as informative content and general updates) and social responsibility content (such as content on the subject of social responsibility and sustainability). About the type of format, there are image publications (low level of interactivity), video publications (high level of interactivity), image/CTA publications (low/medium level of interactivity) and CTA/video publications (medium/high level of interactivity). The engagement rate of the posts is generally low. However, one post stands out with 2.95%, corresponding to the post of March 3, with a total of 61.818 likes and 154 comments, featuring social responsibility content, video format and a high level of interactivity.

Table 5. Isto brand analysis grid

@isto.pt (50 100 Followers)						
Date	**Content**	**Format**	**Likes**	**Total Comments**	**Engagement Rate**	**Level of Interactivity**
February 21	Inspiration	Image/CTA	263	2	0,53%	Low/medium
February 22	Inspiration	Image	211	1	0,42%	Low
February 24	Inspiration	Image	82	0	0,16%	Low
February 26	Inspiration	Image/CTA	72	0	0,14%	Low/medium
February 26	Entertainment	Video	127	2	0,26%	High
February 28	SR	Image	306	3	0,62%	Low
March 2	Inspiration	Image/CTA	59	0	0,12%	Low/medium
March 3	SR	Video	52	0	0,10%	High
March 4	Inspiration	Image/CTA	136	0	0,27%	Low/medium
March 7	Inspiration	Video	83	1	0,17%	High
March 9	Inspiration	Video	62	1	0,13%	High
March 11	Inspiration	Video	73	0	0,15%	High
March 12	Inspiration	Image/CTA	248	0	0,50%	Low/medium
March 13	Inspiration	Image/CTA	61	0	0,12%	Low/medium
March 14	Inspiration	Image/CTA	81	1	0,16%	Low/medium
March 15	SR	Image/CTA	91	1	0,18%	Low/medium
March 15	SR	Image/CTA	64	0	0,13%	Low/medium
March 15	SR	Image/CTA	103	0	0,21%	Low/medium
March 16	Inspiration	CTA/Video	65	0	0,13%	Medium/high
March 17	Inspiration	Image/CTA	77	1	0,16%	Low/medium
March 18	Inspiration	Image/CTA	53	1	0,11%	Low/medium
March 20	Inspiration	Image	113	1	0,23%	Low
March 21	Inspiration	Image/CTA	101	2	0,21%	Low/medium
March 22	Inspiration	Image	457	3	0,92%	Low
March 24	Inspiration	Video	147	1	0,30%	High
March 26	SR	Video	425	1	0,85%	High
March 28	Other	Video	60	0	0,12%	High
March 31	Inspiration	Image/CTA	180	0	0,36%	Low/medium
April 1	Inspiration	Image/CTA	91	0	0,18%	Low/medium
April 2	Inspiration	Image	215	2	0,43%	Low
April 4	Other	Video	348	20	0,73%	High
April 6	Other	Image	520	10	1,06%	Low
April 9	Other	Image	161	0	0,32%	Low
April 12	SR	Image/CTA	119	1	0,24%	Low/medium
April 12	SR	Image/CTA	88	0	0,18%	Low/medium
April 12	SR	Image/CTA	74	1	0,15%	Low/medium
April 13	Inspiration	Image/CTA	75	1	0,15%	Low/medium

Table 5 continues

@isto.pt (50 100 Followers)						
Date	**Content**	**Format**	**Likes**	**Total Comments**	**Engagement Rate**	**Level of Interactivity**
April 14	Inspiration	Image/CTA	68	1	0,14%	Low/medium
April 15	Inspiration	Image/CTA	61	0	0,12%	Low/medium
April 16	SR	Image/CTA	67	0	0,13%	Low/medium
April 16	SR	Image/CTA	38	0	0,08%	Low/medium
April 16	SR	Image/CTA	84	1	0,17%	Low/medium
April 17	SR	Video	118	1	0,24%	High
April 18	SR	Video	74	0	0,15%	High
April 19	SR	Video	82	3	0,17%	High
April 20	SR	Video	63	0	0,13%	High
April 23	Cooperative	Video	113	4	0,23%	High
April 24	SR	Image	51	0	0,10%	Low
April 26	Inspiration	Image/CTA	64	0	0,13%	Low/medium
April 28	Inspiration	Image	105	0	0,21%	Low

A comparison of the engagement rates of the three brands in terms of social responsibility and publications not related to social responsibility can be seen in Table 7. In the case of the Naz brand, the average engagement rate for publications on social responsibility is 0.30%. In contrast, for publications not related to the topic, it is 0.25%. Therefore, the engagement rate is higher for social responsibility and sustainability publications. About the Isto brand, the average engagement rate for social responsibility publications is 0.23%, and for unrelated publications, it is 0.28%. In the case of the Isto brand, unrelated publications have a higher average engagement rate than publications related to social responsibility. Finally, the Tentree brand has an average engagement rate of 0.14% for publications on social responsibility and 0.06% for publications unrelated to the topic.

When examining the performance of the Naz and Tentree brands, it becomes clear that their commitment and communication about social responsibility resonated positively with their audience. The average engagement rate for posts associated with these brands exceeds the baseline established by unrelated content. This suggests greater public appreciation and interest in content that aligns with sustainability and social awareness values.

On the other hand, in the case of the Isto brand, the trend follows a slightly different trajectory. Despite the general trend towards higher engagement rates for socially responsible content, the average engagement rate for This brand's posts on this topic is comparatively lower. This variation can be attributed to several factors, such as brand positioning, messaging strategy or the specific nature of its sustainability initiatives.

As a result, the average engagement rate for posts on the topic of sustainability and social responsibility is higher than the average engagement rate for unrelated posts. Compared to unrelated posts, the average engagement rate for posts related to social responsibility is higher for the Naz and Tentree brands and lower for the Isto brands.

Table 6. Tentree brand analysis grid

@tentree (2 100 000 Followers)						
Date	**Content**	**Format**	**Likes**	**Total Comments**	**Engagement Rate**	**Level of Interactivity**
February 14	SR	Image	456	5	0,02%	Low
February 15	SR	Image/CTA	1894	2	0,09%	Low/medium
February 16	SR	Video	426	1	0,02%	High
February 17	SR	Image	663	4	0,03%	Low
February 19	Inspiration	Image	867	7	0,04%	Low
February 20	Inspiration	CTA/video	457	3	0,02%	Medium/high
February 21	SR	Image	556	0	0,03%	Low
February 22	Inspiration	Image/CTA	395	1	0,02%	Low/medium
February 23	SR	CTA/video	286	1	0,01%	Medium/high
February 24	SR	CTA/video	2541	23	0,12%	Medium/high
February 26	Inspiration	Image/CTA	566	3	0,03%	Low/medium
February 27	Inspiration	Image/CTA	369	0	0,02%	Low/medium
February 28	Inspiration	Image/CTA	533	2	0,03%	Low/medium
March 1	SR	Image/CTA	474	1	0,02%	Low/medium
March 2	Inspiration	Image/CTA	593	1	0,03%	Low/medium
March 3	SR	Video	61 818	154	2,95%	High
March 4	Entertainment	Image	738	0	0,04%	Low
March 6	Entertainment	Video	1092	5	0,05%	High
March 7	SR	Image/CTA	3364	36	0,16%	Low/medium
March 8	SR	Video	613	1	0,03%	High
March 9	Inspiration	Video	3823	11	0,18%	High
March 10	SR	Image	855	6	0,04%	Low
March 12	SR	Image/CTA	1333	12	0,06%	Low/medium
March 13	SR	Image	2259	5	0,11%	Low
March 14	SR	Image/CTA	663	5	0,03%	Low/medium
March 15	SR	Image/CTA	2067	4	0,10%	Low/medium
March 17	SR	Image	885	6	0,04%	Low
March 19	SR	Image	738	1	0,04%	Low
March 21	SR	Image/CTA	2553	18	0,12%	Low/medium
March 25	SR	Image	1069	5	0,05%	Low
March 27	SR	Image/CTA	881	1	0,04%	Low/medium
March 29	SR	Image/CTA	556	6	0,03%	Low/medium
March 31	Other	Image	1474	0	0,07%	Low
March 31	Entertainment	Image	1305	0	0,06%	Low
April 3	SR	Video	564	1	0,03%	High
April 5	SR	Image/CTA	456	1	0,02%	Low/medium

Table 6 continues

@tentree (2 100 000 Followers)						
Date	**Content**	**Format**	**Likes**	**Total Comments**	**Engagement Rate**	**Level of Interactivity**
April 8	SR	CTA/video	1475	6	0,07%	Medium/high
April 10	SR	CTA/video	860	4	0,04%	Medium/high
April 11	Inspiration	Image	1716	2	0,08%	Low
April 12	Inspiration	Image/CTA	523	1	0,02%	Low/medium
April 13	SR	CTA/Video	660	7	0,03%	Medium/high
April 16	SR	Image/CTA	987	4	0,05%	Low/medium
April 18	SR	CTA/Video	478	3	0,02%	Medium/high
April 20	Inspiration	Image	573	2	0,03%	Low
April 22	SR	Image/CTA	1626	16	0,08%	Low/medium
April 22	SR	Video	882	10	0,04%	Alto
April 25	Entertainment	Image	1039	36	0,05%	Low
April 26	Inspiration	Image	465	0	0,02%	Low
April 27	SR	Image	680	6	0,03%	Low
April 28	Entertainment	Image/CTA	7107	48	0,34%	Low/medium

Table 7. Average engagement rate

Sustainable Fashion Brand	**Average Engagement Rate**	
	Publications Related to Social Responsibility	**Non-Related Publications**
Naz	0,30%	0,25%
Isto.	0,23%	0,28%
Tentree	0,14%	0,06%

5. DISCUSSION AND CONCLUSION

In an era of digital connectivity, brands increasingly recognise the key role of a well-executed social media strategy in building consumer perceptions and promoting meaningful connections. This is made particularly apparent in the actions of the three brands, each highlighting the value of engaging the audiences seamlessly throughout the consumer journey. They highlighted the critical role of user engagement in building a community and fostering brand recall. Tailoring content to their audience, the brands aimed to generate interest and establish a strong connection with their audience. Communication strategies, particularly during product launches on social platforms, were geared towards increasing interaction and driving sales. Positive user experiences, mainly during uncertain times, significantly impacted purchasing decisions.

Brands' focus on supplying exceptional high-quality information has shown to be a crucial factor in capturing the public's attention. Their skilful promotion of green awareness has significantly increased consumer enthusiasm for sustainable labels. This transformation goes beyond pure consumer interest and plays a crucial role in building trust in sustainable brands and driving the adoption of eco-conscious behaviours among the public. This evolution emphasises the powerful impact of brand strategic communication and engagement strategies on forming consumer behaviour, particularly in sustainability. The power of socially aware generations, actively seeking out brands in line with their values, further amplifies this influence. Brands' willingness to supply high-quality items and stand up for environmental causes has now become a key driving force in fostering a more sustainable and responsible consumer behaviour culture. These changes, in particular, highlight the relationship between brand actions, consumer awareness and society's general tendency to adopt more sustainable consumption patterns.

These findings align with the conclusions drawn in the study by Castillo-Abdul et al. (2022), highlighting the effectiveness of using branded content related to social responsibility on Instagram. Such content publicises the brand and elicits more reactions from the page's followers. When examining the engagement rates of three brands concerning publications related to social responsibility versus those unrelated to the topic (refer to Table 7), distinct patterns become evident. For the Naz brand, publications centred on social responsibility exhibited a higher average engagement rate of 0.30%, surpassing the 0.25% rate for unrelated content. This suggests a trend towards greater engagement for publications tied to social responsibility. Conversely, the Isto brand witnessed a shift, with publications unrelated to social responsibility showing a higher average engagement rate of 0.28%, compared to 0.23% for content related to social responsibility. In contrast, the Tentree brand saw publications addressing social responsibility achieve an average engagement rate of 0.14%, notably surpassing the 0.06% rate for unrelated content.

This outcome aligns with the findings of the study by Gilal et al. (2020), indicating that consumers' perception of a brand's social responsibility actions significantly enhances their attachment to the brand. Similarly, the study by Romano et al. (2023) highlighted that social responsibility contributes to increased brand attachment, especially when messages contain content about responsible and conscious actions. Additionally, Neumann, Martinez, and Martinez (2021) research established that perceptions of social responsibility directly impact consumer attitudes towards fashion brands, influencing consumer trust and attachment. This underscores a notably higher engagement rate for publications related to sustainability.

In summary, engagement rates reveal varying audience preferences among brands. Naz and Tentree experienced higher engagement with content related to social responsibility, whereas Isto's audience appeared more engaged with content unrelated to social responsibility. This divergence underscores the differentiated nature of audience interests and the effectiveness of brand messages in different sustainability-oriented content. This study significantly contributes to digital marketing research by addressing the limited number of studies on social responsibility and its connection to fashion brands through social media engagement. Focusing on sustainable fashion within the fashion sector adds substantial value to the literature. The findings reveal a positive impact of social responsibility on consumer engagement within fashion brands' social networks, enriching the literature on these topics. Emphasising responsible brand practices emerges as a strategic approach to capturing and engaging users on social platforms. Remarkably, this study explores the online presence of Portuguese sustainable fashion brands, bridging the gap in research predominantly centred on international brands. Examining social networks has deepened our comprehension of fashion brands' sustainable strategies and practices, allowing for meaningful comparisons with global counterparts. Notably, the study underscores that posts addressing social responsibility and sustainability yield higher engagement rates, signifying consumer and brand followers' heightened interest and involvement. Recognising the characteristics of Portuguese users and their inclination towards sustainable fashion becomes a pivotal insight for fashion companies.

This study provides practical guidelines for brands seeking to involve users sustainably, underlining the fundamental role of social responsibility initiatives in retaining and attracting customers. It also urges brands to prioritise communicating sustainable actions on social media, promoting greater consumer awareness and sustained interest. Implementing conscious initiatives is crucial in significantly boosting social media engagement. While the literature review covered various themes, there needed to be more substantial content related to fashion, especially concerning sustainable practices in small-scale businesses. The intersection of fashion with brand attachment remains a less-explored area that warrants further investigation. Expanding the research scope to include diverse sectors such as footwear, cosmetics, and accessories could provide valuable insights. Additionally, exploring the applicability of this study across different cultures and regions while considering alternative statistical methodologies holds the potential to yield more comprehensive findings.

ACKNOWLEDGMENT

This work is funded by National Funds through the FCT—Foundation for Science and Technology, I.P., within the scope of the project Refª UIDB/05583/2020. Furthermore, we would like to thank the Research Centre in Digital Services (CISeD) and the Polytechnic of Viseu for their support.

REFERENCES

Brewer, M. K. (2019). Slow Fashion in a Fast Fashion World: Promoting Sustainability and Responsibility. *Laws*, *8*(4), 24. doi:10.3390/laws8040024

Cerchia, R. E., & Piccolo, K. (2019). The Ethical Consumer and Codes of Ethics in the Fashion Industry. *Laws*, *8*(4), 23. doi:10.3390/laws8040023

Chaffee, E. C. (2017). The Origins of Corporate Social Responsibility. *University of Cincinnati Law Review*, *85*, 347–373. https://ssrn.com/abstract=2957820

Desai, V., & Vidyapeeth, B. (2019). Digital Marketing: A Review. *International Journal of Trend in Scientific Research and Development*, *5*(5), 196–200. doi:10.31142/ijtsrd23100

Diez-Martin, F., Blanco-Gonzalez, A., & Prado-Roman, C. (2019). Research Challenges in Digital Marketing: Sustainability. *Sustainability (Basel)*, *11*(10), 2839. doi:10.3390/su11102839

Ebrahim, R. S. (2019). The Role of Trust in Understanding the Impact of Social Media Marketing on Brand Equity and Brand Loyalty. *Journal of Relationship Marketing*, *19*(3), 1–22. doi:10.1080/15332667.2019.1705742

Eriksson, N., Sjöberg, A., Rosenbröijer, C. J., & Fagerstrøm, A. (2019). Consumer brand post engagement on Facebook and Instagram – A study of three interior design brands. *Proceedings of The 19th International Conference on Electronic Business*, 116-124. https://hdl.handle.net/11250/3057617

Giacomini, D., Zola, P., Paredi, D., & Mazzoleni, M. (2020). Environmental disclosure and stakeholder engagement via social media: State of the art and potential in public utilities. *Corporate Social Responsibility and Environmental Management*, *27*(4), 1552–1564. doi:10.1002/csr.1904

Gilal, F. G., Channa, N. A., Gilal, N. G., Gilal, R. G., Gong, Z., & Zhang, N. (2020). Corporate social responsibility and brand passion among consumers: Theory and evidence. *Corporate Social Responsibility and Environmental Management*, *27*(5), 2275–2285. doi:10.1002/csr.1963

Isto. (2023). *About*. Consulted on June 28, 2023, at Isto: https://isto.pt/pages/about

Jalali, S. S., & Khalid, H. (2019). Understanding Instagram Influencers Values in Green Consumption Behaviour: A Review Paper. *Open International Journal of Informatics*, *7*(1), 47-58. https://oiji.utm.my/index.php/oiji/article/view/115

Khanal, A., Akhtaruzzaman, M., & Kularatne, I. (2021). The influence of social media on stakeholder engagement and the corporate social responsibility of small businesses. *Corporate Social Responsibility and Environmental Management*, *28*(6), 1921–1929. doi:10.1002/csr.2169

Kim, Y. K., & Sullivan, P. (2019). Emotional branding speaks to consumers' hearts: The case of fashion brands. *Fashion and Textiles*, *6*(1), 1–16. doi:10.1186/s40691-018-0164-y

Majeed, M., Owusu-Ansah, M., & Ashmond, A.-A. (2021). The influence of social media on purchase intention: The mediating role of brand equity. *Cogent Business & Management*, *8*(1), 1944008. doi:10.1080/23311975.2021.1944008

Mason, A. N., Narcum, J., & Mason, K. (2021). Social media marketing gained importance after Covid-19. *Cogent Business & Management*, *8*(1), 1870797. doi:10.1080/23311975.2020.1870797

Muntinga, D. G., Moorman, M., & Smit, E. G. (2011). Introducing COBRAs: Exploring motivations for brand-related social media use. *International Journal of Advertising*, *30*(1), 13–46. doi:10.2501/IJA-30-1-013-046

Naz. (2023). *About us*. Consulted on June 28, 2023, at Naz: https://naz.pt/pages/about-us

Neumann, H. L., Martinez, L. M., & Martinez, L. F. (2021). Sustainability efforts in the fast fashion industry: Consumer perception, trust and purchase intention. *Sustainability Accounting. Management and Policy Journal*, *12*(3), 571–590. doi:10.1108/SAMPJ-11-2019-0405

Niinimäki, K., Peters, G., Dahlbo, H., Perry, P., Rissanen, T., & Gwilt, A. (2020). The environmental price of fast fashion. *Nature Reviews. Earth & Environment*, *1*(4), 189–200. doi:10.1038/s43017-020-0039-9

Putranto, H. A., Rizaldi, T., Riskiawan, H. Y., Setyohadi, D. P. S., Atmadji, E. S. J., & Nuryanto, I. H. (2022). Measurement of Engagement Rate on Instagram for Business Marketing (Case Study: MSME of Dowry in Jember). *International Conference on Electrical and Information Technology (IEIT)*, 317-321. 10.1109/IEIT56384.2022.9967851

Quiles-Soler, C., Martínez-Sala, A.-M., & Monserrat-Gauchi, J. (2022). The fashion industry's environmental policy: Social media and corporate websites are vehicles for communicating corporate social responsibility. *Corporate Social Responsibility and Environmental Management*, 1–12. doi:10.1002/csr.2347

Romano, F. M., Devine, A., Tarabashkina, L., Soutar, G., & Quester, P. (2023). Specificity of CSR Ties That (Un)Bind Brand Attachment. *Australasian Marketing Journal*, *31*(1), 71–80. doi:10.1177/18393349211030699

Schivinski, B., Christodoulides, G., & Dabrowski, D. (2016). Measuring consumers' engagement with brand-related social-media content: Development and validation of a scale that identifies levels of social-media engagement with brands. *Journal of Advertising Research*, *56*(1), 64–80. doi:10.2501/JAR-2016-004

Shahbaznezhad, H., Dolan, R., & Rashidirad, M. (2021). The role of social media content format and platform in users' engagement behaviour. *Journal of Interactive Marketing*, *53*(1), 47–65. doi:10.1016/j.intmar.2020.05.001

Tentree (2023). *About*. Consulted on June 28, 2023, at Tentree: https://www.tentree.com/pages/about

Thorisdottir, T. S., & Johannsdottir, L. (2020). Corporate Social Responsibility Influencing Sustainability within the Fashion Industry. A Systematic Review. *Sustainability (Basel)*, *12*(21), 9167. doi:10.3390/su12219167

Voorveld, H. A. (2019). Brand Communication in Social Media: A Research Agenda. *Journal of Advertising*, *48*(1), 14–26. doi:10.1080/00913367.2019.1588808

Voorveld, H. A., Noort, G. V., Muntinga, D. G., & Bronner, F. (2018). Engagement with Social Media and Social Media Advertising: The Differentiating Role of Platform Type. *Journal of Advertising*, *47*(1), 38–54. doi:10.1080/00913367.2017.1405754

Vries, L. D., Gensler, S., & Leeflang, P. S. (2012). Popularity of brand posts on brand fan pages: An investigation of the effects of social media marketing. *Journal of Interactive Marketing*, *26*(2), 83–91. doi:10.1016/j.intmar.2012.01.003

Zhu, Y.-Q., & Chen, H.-G. (2015). Social media and human need satisfaction: Implications for social media marketing. *Business Horizons*, *58*(3), 335–345. doi:10.1016/j.bushor.2015.01.006

Chapter 10
Treating Textile Effluents for Sustainable Fashion and Green Marketing

Michael Karypidis
https://orcid.org/0000-0003-1076-4787
International Hellenic University, Greece

Theodore Tarnanidis
https://orcid.org/0000-0002-4836-3906
International Hellenic University, Greece

Evridiki Papachristou
International Hellenic University, Greece

ABSTRACT

One of the main causes of water pollution is the textile industry, which involves dyeing and finishing processes. Aquatic life and human health can be threatened by the variety of chemicals and dyes contained in the effluent generated by these processes. The impact of these effluents on the environment has been minimized by the development of several effluent treatments. This presentation discloses the available solutions for liquid effluent treatment from textile dyeing and finishing providing a fast, clear, and deep understanding of methods such as the physicochemical and biological treatments as well as the recent advanced oxidation processes. Thus, utilizing a combination of these technologies in a treatment plant can frequently lead to more effective outcomes. Ultimately, this investigation will assist researchers and academic practitioners in enhancing and aligning green marketing models with sustainability trends in the textile, apparel, and fashion industries.

DOI: 10.4018/979-8-3693-3049-4.ch010

1. INTRODUCTION

Water pollution is a major issue in the textile industry, and dyeing and finishing processes are the main culprits. Aquatic life may be harmed, and human health may be significantly threatened by the variety of chemicals and dyes contained in the effluent generated by these processes. To lessen the impact of these effluents on the environment, several effluent treatments have been developed over the years. This chapter discloses the available solutions for effluent treatment from textile dyeing and finishing methods. Furthermore, sustainable practices and technologies that minimize water usage in textile processes can contribute to environmental conservation efforts. Incorporating effluent treatment practices into green marketing enhances a brand's environmental credentials and aligns with the growing consumer demand for sustainable and ethically produced fashion. By emphasizing these efforts, brands can build a positive image and attract a broader base of conscious consumers. This research presents the data and findings collected from the relevant literature relating to sustainable fashion and textile production by further analyzing the impact of these eco-friendly methods on the consumption of textile products and the internal-organization marketing strategies.

2. EFFICIENT SOLUTIONS FOR TREATING TEXTILES

Water pollution is exacerbated by the textile industry, which is primarily responsible for dyeing and finishing processes. These processes generate effluent that has various chemicals and dyes that can harm aquatic life and pose a significant threat to human health. To reduce the environmental impact of these effluents, several treatments have been developed. This section discloses the available solutions for liquid effluent treatment from textile dyeing and finishing providing a fast, clear and deep understanding of methods such as the Physicochemical and Biological treatments as well as the recent Advanced Oxidation Processes.

The initial method utilizes chemical and physical processes to eliminate pollutants like suspended solids, color, and organic matter from wastewater. The addition of coagulation-flocculation to wastewater destabilizes the suspended particles, causing them to clump together. This can then be removed by settling or filtration. The addition of a flocculant (flocculation) helps the formed particles to aggregate and settle more efficiently removing color, suspended solids, and organic matter from textile effluent. Alternatively, the adsorption method involves the use of adsorbents such as activated carbon, zeolites, and clays which remove pollutants from wastewater by attracting and binding pollutants onto their surfaces which decolorizes and removes organic matter from dye house effluent. Similarly, membrane filtration uses membranes of different pore sizes such as microfiltration, ultrafiltration, nanofiltration, and reverse osmosis, to achieve the removal of the pollutant.

The Biological treatment uses microorganisms to remove pollutants from wastewater, such as the activated sludge process, biological aerated filter, and sequencing batch reactor. In the activated sludge process, wastewater is mixed with sludge and aerated to give oxygen to microorganisms that break down organic matter, then the sludge is separated and reused. In the biological aerated filter method, wastewater is passed through a bed of media that is populated with microorganisms that break down organic matter. Similarly, the sequencing batch reactor method also involves introducing wastewater in an aerating tank for a control time providing oxygen to the microorganisms which in stages decompose the organic matter, settle the suspended solids, and eventually decant the treated water.

Advanced oxidation processes (AOPs) are a group of chemical treatment methods that involve the generation of highly reactive hydroxyl radicals to oxidize and degrade organic pollutants in the effluent. The treatments performed by these processes are effective in tackling dye, chemical oxygen demand (COD), and total organic carbon (TOC) in textile effluent. AOPs are advantageous because they don't need chemicals, which can create sludge and can be combined with other treatment methods to achieve the desired treatment clarity level. The Fenton reaction process involves adding hydrogen peroxide and ferrous ions to wastewater, which produces hydroxyl radicals that oxidize and degrade organic pollutants. Similarly, the Photo-Fenton process uses ultraviolet (UV) light to provide additional energy to the system activating the hydrogen peroxide and ferrous ions which liberates the oxidizing hydroxyl radicals. Ozonation is an alternative AOP which uses ozone to liberate the hydroxyl radicals, which oxidize and decompose the pollutants of the wastewater. In electrochemical oxidation, wastewater passes through cells with an electric current without the addition of external chemicals. Oxidation takes place at the surface of the anode which degrades the organic pollutants in the wastewater.

Advanced oxidation/coagulation processes involve the combination of AOPs with coagulation-flocculation processes to remove pollutants. The AOPs provide oxidation and degradation of the pollutants, while the coagulation-flocculation processes remove the formed particles. Hybrid AOPs involve combining two or more AOPs (e.g. ozonation and UV irradiation) to improve treatment efficiency and reduce treatment time. The selection of the appropriate AOP depends on the nature and concentration of pollutants present in the effluent.

3. THE METHODS USED TO TREAT TEXTILE EFFLUENT

The textile industry's significant water consumption and pollution make it crucial to treat textile effluents to mitigate its environmental impact (Kallawar & Bhanvase, 2024; Periyasamy, 2024). Dyes, heavy metals, and organic compounds are common pollutants found in textile effluents. Additionally, substances derived from the auxiliaries used in the processes such as dispersants, levelling agents, salts, carriers, acids, alkalis (Velusamy *et al.*, 2021) including heavy metals, elements of nitrates, nitrites and phosphates create a hazard due to toxicity, carcinogenicity and low biodegradability leads to eutrophication, as they disturb the photosynthesis of marine plants (Berradi *et al.*, 2019) (Verma *et al.*, 2012). Furthermore, halophilic microbes can hydrolyze effluent and convert it into highly persistent/mutagenic byproducts (Rawat *et al.*, 2018). Included in this are the treatment methods available for textile effluent based on their type (Karypidis *et al.*, 2023):

Biological Treatment: This method uses microorganisms to remove pollutants from wastewater, such as the activated sludge process, biological aerated filter, and sequencing batch reactor (Madhav *et al.*, 2018)

- The process of activated sludge involves the addition of microorganisms to decompose organic matter.
- The biological aerated filter method uses air to provide oxygen to the microorganisms which decompose organic matter. (Birch *et al.*, 1989)
- The sequencing batch reactor method works in a similar manner, using aerating tanks for a control time in stages to decompose the organic matter, settle the suspended solids from the effluent water.

Physical Treatment: this method uses chemical and physical processes to remove pollutants such as suspended solids, color, and organic matter from wastewater.

- Filtration involves removing suspended particles by passing water through various filters.
- Adsorption is the method where active adsorbents possessing very large surface area per unit mass, attract and binding pollutants onto their surfaces.
- Sedimentation permits solids to settle at the bottom and separate them from the water.

Membrane Technologies: In this method the effluent is filtered through a membrane of specific pore size, such as microfiltration, ultrafiltration, nanofiltration, and reverse osmosis (Velusamy *et al.*, 2021):

- Microfiltration (MF) removes mainly solids while the rest of contaminants go through the membrane.
- Ultrafiltration (UF) uses a fine membrane that separates particles and microorganisms from water.
- Nanofiltration (NF) allows only monovalent species to pass through the membrane.
- Reverse Osmosis (RO) involves passing water through a semi-permeable membrane to remove almost all contaminants.

Adsorption:

- The adsorption method involves the use of adsorbents such as activated carbon, zeolites, and clays which remove pollutants from wastewater by attracting and binding pollutants onto their surfaces which decolorizes and removes organic matter and heavy metals (like Cd, Pb, Cr, Zn, Cu, Co, Hg and As) from dyehouse effluents
- There are different methods to obtain to produce active carbon such as the traditional pyrolytic method or the alternative hydrothermal carbonization method which is advantageous due to reduced contaminating gas production and less hazardous method of carbonizing raw material from waste such as glucose, starch, fructose or lignocellulosic materials, beer and livestock waste, swine manure or chitin from prawn shells, at temperatures up to 300°C instead of 700°C, followed by an activation stage (Zhao *et al.*, 2016; Hao *et al.*, 2014).

Chemical Treatment: At its simplest form the method involves addition of Coagulation-flocculation agents to the wastewater as described below:

- The addition of chemicals causes particles to destabilize from the suspension in the effluent, enabling them to clump together and settle.
- Certain chemicals are added to cause impurities to precipitate, which can then be separated. (Verma *et al.*, 2012)
- Advanced Oxidation Processes (AOPs) uses chemicals generating hydroxyl radicals that oxidize and degrade organic pollutants in the effluent at high speeds through hydrogen abstraction, electron transfer, and radical addition. (Zhang *et al.*, 2021). These are the most recent methods, and they are analyzed separately.

Advanced oxidation processes:

- Advanced oxidation processes (AOPs) are a group of chemical treatment methods that involve the generation of highly reactive hydroxyl radicals to oxidize and degrade organic pollutants in effluent. Hydrogen peroxide and ferrous ions are added to the wastewater during the Fenton reaction process, which produces hydroxyl radicals that oxidize and degrade organic pollutants (Rather *et al.*, 2019)
- Ozonation is employed to oxidize either directly or via hydroxyl radical liberation and decompose organic and color compounds. (Zhang *et al.*, 2021)
- Peroxidation is the process of adding H_2O_2 to ozonation to increase the decomposition rates of oxidation (Zhang *et al.*, 2021)
- UV radiation can also be used to provide additional energy to the system to achieve better decomposition rates and efficiency which can be cost effective when using UV from sun light. (Zepp *et al.*, 1992)
- Electrochemical oxidation is the process where the wastewater passes through cells of an electric current with no addition of external chemicals. H_2O_2 is produced in the cell starting the AOPs reactions.

Combined methods:

- Advanced oxidation/coagulation processes combine oxidation and coagulation processes to oxidize and clean effluent and the formed particles are removed by the coagulation-flocculation processes. Hybrid AOPs are formed by combining two or more AOPs (e.g., ozonation and UV irradiation) are combined for faster decomposition.

Today, there are many wastewater treatments available, but some need to improve their efficiency to become more commercially attractive. There is a lot of information that has already been published, and new ones are presented every day. The objective is to provide a comprehensive but straightforward comprehension of these technologies for all members of the textile industry chain, with a particular emphasis on fashion that is not proficient in this field. Nonetheless, they are the driving force behind the total sustainability strategy. A clean and sustainable fashion requires synergistic action to succeed. Often sacrifices have to be made in comfort and other properties. Use of sustainable materials and methods can affect mechanical behavior causing strictures to be rigid and harder and less comfortable. Additionally, increase in bending stiffness and fabric strength affect needle penetration, sewability and the ease of garment process manufacturing (Karypidis, 2018; Karypidis & Savvidis, 2018). Figure1 presents a sample of sustainably producing trouser with the use of hemp fibers which requires less water but exerts a more rigid structure. (Karypidis *et al*, 2023). The selection of treatment method is influenced by factors like the effluent's composition, local regulations, and the size of the textile industry operation. The use of a combination of these technologies in a treatment plant can often result in more effective results (Raza *et al.*, 2024). In addition, the use of sustainable practices and technologies that reduce water usage in textile processes can help to conserve the environment overall.

Figure 1. Trouser designed and made up from the hemp canvas fabric (Karypidis et al., 2023)

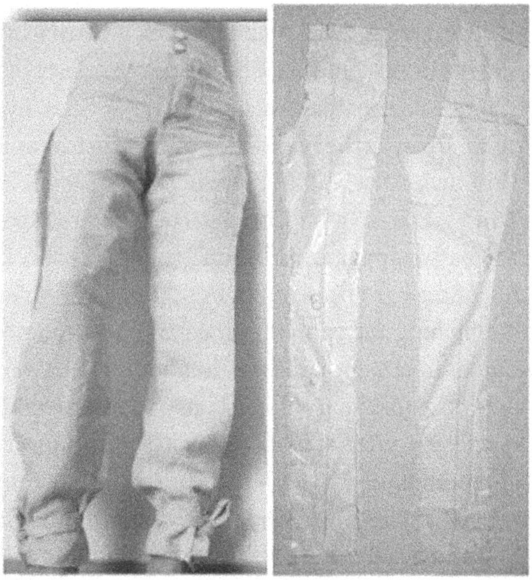

Each of the methods mentioned above has its own advantages and disadvantages. In textile wastewater treatment, a combination of the methods mentioned above is frequently employed to achieve the best results possible at a lower cost. Bioreactors that are effective in a wider range of dye types and produce smaller quantities of sludge can be produced when biological methods are combined with membranes. Membrane filtration (microfiltration and ultrafiltration) follows the use of a biological method as a post-treatment (referred as Membrane BioReactors) at high pollutant concentrations or at inadequate biological treatment yield (Robeson, 2012).

Advanced oxidation/coagulation processes combine oxidation and coagulation processes to remove pollutants. The AOPs oxidize and degrade the pollutants, while the coagulation-flocculation processes remove the formed particles. Hybrid Advanced Oxidation Processes (HAOPs) involve the combination of a series of Advanced Oxidation Processes (e.g., ozonation and UV irradiation are used to improve treatment efficiency and reduce treatment time. The selection of the appropriate AOP depends on the nature and concentration of pollutants present in the effluent.(Chakma *et al.,* 2015) Solar-assisted Photo-Fenton processes have been described in the literature and are a promising treatment for countries with abundant sunshine.(Yasar & Yousaf, 2013).

4. GREEN MARKETING ACTIONS AND TREATMENT

Textile effluent treatment is a crucial aspect of the sustainable fashion journey, and integrating this process into green marketing strategies can enhance a brand's image and appeal to environmentally conscious consumers (Singh & Pandey, 2012).For example, considerations for treating textile effluents for sustainable fashion can position effluent treatment as a responsible and essential practice within the brand's commitment to sustainability. The environmental impact of their garments can be traced by consumers through this. Additionally, fashion retailers can Launch campaigns to educate consumers about the environmental impact of traditional textile processes and how the brand's effluent treatment practices are contributing to positive change., i.e. feature relevant certifications prominently on product labels and marketing materials to build trust and credibility, develop a recognizable eco-label specific to the brand's commitment to effluent treatment and sustainable practices, highlight the use of innovative and eco-friendly technologies in reinforcing the brand's commitment to staying at the forefront of sustainable practices (Ottman, 2017; Polonsky *et al.*, 2001; Omar Zaki & Rosli, 2024; Yildirim et al., 2024).

What is more, organizations, can take advantage of the use of interactive platforms where consumers can learn about the brand's effluent treatment efforts and provide feedback on sustainability initiatives like the integration of circular economy fashion practices and up cycling efforts, by using eco-friendly packaging materials and communicating the eco-conscious choices made throughout the entire product lifecycle. By incorporating effluent treatment practices into green marketing, brands can enhance their environmental credentials and align with the growing consumer demand for sustainable and ethically produced fashion. By highlighting these efforts, brands can establish a positive image and attract a wider range of conscious consumers. Implementing strategies and practices that minimize environmental impact and promote sustainability throughout the supply chain, production processes, and marketing efforts is part of green marketing in the fashion industry. Green marketing within the fashion industry often uses these common actions and treatments. Fashion brands can show their sustainability commitment by implementing these actions and treatments and appealing to environmentally conscious consumers who prioritize ethical and eco-friendly products (Wang *et al.*, 2024).

Green washing can cause harm to corporate reputation and decrease the effectiveness of green marketing as a whole. It's unfortunate that companies can't avoid common green washing missteps due to the absence of set standards for marketing a product as environmentally friendly. Brands need to establish internal standards and best practices for their green marketing efforts, which is why it is crucial. Transparent and specific advertising should be the focus of these standards, as it builds trust with customers and contributes to positive brand perception (Pavan *et al.*, 2024).

Green marketing can have its disadvantages, such as the initial increase in costs and the need for many resources to develop and implement new advertising strategies. Organizations are required to invest in new technologies and raw materials that may be more expensive. Recognizing that these initial investments usually yield long-term savings through increased sales and more sustainable operations is important for the organization (Roy *et al.*, 2024).

5. DIGITAL COMMUNICATIONS IN FASHION

The emergence of Internet marketing, which involves promoting services and products through the Internet, was brought about by the use of the Internet in marketing. The classical perception of advertising and promotion has been dramatically altered by the use of the Internet as a marketing tool. The receiver of advertising is considered to be a passive participant in the communication process. This view is overturned by the technological characteristics of the Internet, particularly by its interactive environment. Using these technical characteristics, advertisements can now be interactive and contain valuable and useful content for consumers (Oklander & Kudina, 2021). The role of the advertising message receiver and Internet user is becoming more active and important. Business sustainability may be jeopardized if you don't use the Internet and don't take advantage of the opportunities and possibilities provided by online applications. In numerous countries, it is still viewed as complementary to traditional marketing methods and is not thought to decrease the advertising revenues of print and electronic media.

The internet's specific nature and function may be the cause of this. Young people are often communicated with through it, which has an anarchist structure without any central control. The majority of users are highly educated and economically well-educated, which suggests that those who make these arguments are likely disregarding the results of several studies that indicate they have purchasing power (Chaffey *et al.*, 2009). To sum up, Internet Marketing is a powerful way to advertise and promote. According to different scholars (Patil & Khathuria, 2020; Murphy (1998) the following are the primary advantages for a fashion business:

- Geographical coverage worldwide
- Low cost
- Promotes direct sales by involving new customers in an interactive dialogue
- Access to unexplored markets
- Measurable results
- Regardless of their size, businesses are provided with equal access to web access.
- Businesses can provide online customer support through it
- Enhances communication between the company and corporate entities.
- Enhances the business's flexibility by facilitating personalized promotions and sales to customers.
- Facilitates the creation of brand names.
- Public relations can benefit from this efficient tool.
- Enhancement of the competitiveness of the business.
- Developing an image of a company that is responsive to technological advancements.
- Establishing a channel for customers to give feedback to the business.
- Helps customers acquire data more easily.
- Enhances the process of conducting market research and analysis.

Businesses and the public benefit from the elimination of impersonal mass communication through the Internet. Many traditional advertising methods cannot support the elements of interaction and feedback, which are favored. The main form of promotion for a business in the near future will be internet marketing, which will be a necessary condition for sustainability and business development. Although the Internet and its technologies are not new or revolutionary, their scope and impact have expanded to encompass all spheres of human life, including professional, private, family, and other sectors. The internet and mobile digital technologies are not just technology, they are also more than that. It is a set of social relationships that integrate the use of technologies with various outcomes" (Miller, 2020).

One of the most important impacts of digital environments is the creation and proliferation of social networks, which have brought about profound shifts in cultures around the world, changing forms of taste, norms, products, communication styles and consumption patterns, both symbolic and material (McLean, 2016). It's understandable to assume that digital environments have an effect on consumer behavior in multiple ways, with two main directions being identified (Tarnanidis, 2024).

First, they influence social media behavior (Lamberton *et al.*, 2013; Norton *et al.*, 2013). As an example, being exposed to opinions. Reviews or options (e.g. offers in online auctions) of other consumers, or even simply to the lives of their friends through social media, can influence consumer behavior. Second, digital environments influence behavior in other, unrelated environments, a fact that was evident in research done by Wilcox and Stephen (2013) which showed that when exposed to closer friends on Facebook, consumers subsequently demonstrate lower self-control over choices related to healthy behaviors.

The promotion of sustainability and responsible consumption requires the use of green marketing in the fashion and clothing industry. Increased packaging waste and carbon emissions from transportation have been caused by the transition to e-commerce in the fashion industry. The challenge for brands is to balance the convenience of online shopping with the environmental impact of packaging materials and delivery logistics. E-commerce operations can reduce their environmental footprint by using sustainable packaging solutions and optimizing transportation routes. Overconsumption and fast fashion culture are often caused by digital marketing campaigns in the fashion industry (Tarnanidis *et al.*, 2023). The use of social media platforms and influencer marketing campaigns leads to the constant consumption and rapid turnover of clothing items, which causes excessive waste and environmental degradation (Chan *et al.*, 2022; Guedes & Soares, 2005; Rana, 2024). To promote sustainable consumption patterns, brands must rethink their digital marketing strategies and promote durable, versatile, and circularity.

6. CONCLUSION

The fashion industry is considered one of the most polluting industries in the world due to its major contribution to environmental and human health. Conventional textiles are made using toxic chemicals, which can cause toxic effects or slow decomposition rates, resulting in excessive water and energy consumption during processing and contributing to greenhouse gas emissions. Increasingly, people are interested in more sustainable and eco-friendly alternatives to conventional textiles in recent years. The fashion industry is facing numerous challenges and problematic consequences during the green marketing era that need to be addressed. Overconsumption has been caused by fast fashion due to brands producing cheap, disposable clothing at a rapid pace. Frequent purchasing is encouraged by this culture, which leads to increased waste generation and environmental degradation. The fashion industry is a major contributor to global pollution, resulting in significant environmental impacts. Fashion has a significant ecological footprint, from water pollution caused by textile dyeing and finishing processes to carbon emissions from transportation and production. The clothing industry is a dynamic and multifaceted sector that constantly adapts to technological advancements, market trends, and societal changes. For stakeholders across the industry, balancing economic growth with environmental sustainability and social responsibility is a crucial challenge.

7. CURRENT AND FUTURE CHALLENGES

Fashion has a strong dependence on finite resources such as water, land, and energy. Resource depletion and ecosystem destruction are caused by unsustainable practices like intensive cotton farming and deforestation for textile production. Labor exploitation has been associated with the fashion industry for many years, particularly in low-cost manufacturing regions. Garment factory workers frequently have to deal with poor working conditions, low wages, and lack of labor rights (Mukendi *et al.*, 2020). Despite increased scrutiny, ethical concerns about fair wages, worker safety, and child labor persist.

Some fashion brands engage in green washing, which involves exaggerating or misrepresenting their environmental efforts to appeal to eco-conscious consumers. The industry's trust and credibility may be eroded and consumers may be misled if they are looking for genuinely sustainable options. Fashion production produces huge amounts of waste at all stages of the supply chain, ranging from textile scraps during manufacturing to unsold inventory and discarded garments by consumers. The accumulation of landfills and environmental pollution are caused by this waste. Consumers may find it difficult to make informed choices about the environmental and social impact of the products they purchase due to the fashion industry's lack of transparency in supply chain practices. Lack of transparency causes accountability to be hindered and sustainability progress to be impeded (Štefko & Steffek, 2018).

Promoting sustainable fashion requires significant changes in consumer behavior. Although there is more awareness of environmental issues, many consumers still prioritize price, convenience, and trends over sustainability when making purchasing decisions. In order to adopt sustainable practices, the fashion industry must make significant investments in infrastructure and technology innovation. To develop and implement eco-friendly materials, processes, and supply chain solutions, it is necessary to collaborate and invest across the industry. The sustainability landscape of the fashion industry is shaped by government policies and regulations. The lack of enforcement mechanisms and regulatory frameworks that vary widely between countries can create challenges for global sustainability efforts. Collective action from fashion brands, consumers, policymakers (Patwary, 2020; Kumari, 2024), and other stakeholders is necessary to address these problematic consequences. By adopting transparent practices, investing in sustainable innovation, promoting ethical labor standards, and fostering consumer education, the fashion industry can move toward a more environmentally and socially responsible future in the green marketing era.

REFERENCES

Agustini, M. H., Athanasius, S. S., & Retnawati, B. B. (2020). Identification of green marketing strategies: Perspective of a developing country. *Innovative Marketing*, *15*(4), 42–56. doi:10.21511/im.15(4).2019.04

Alagarsamy, S., Mehrolia, S., & Mathew, S. (2021). How Green Consumption Value Affects Green Consumer Behaviour: The Mediating Role of Consumer Attitudes Towards Sustainable Food Logistics Practices. *Vision (Basel)*, *25*(1), 65–76. doi:10.1177/0972262920977986

Berradi, M., Hsissou, R., Khudhair, M., Assouag, M., Cherkaoui, O., El Bachiri, A., & El Harfi, A. (2019). Textile finishing dyes and their impact on aquatic environs. *Heliyon*, *5*(11), e02711. doi:10.1016/j.heliyon.2019.e02711 PMID:31840123

Birch, R. R., Biver, C., Campagna, R., Gledhill, W. E., Pagga, U., Steber, J., Reust, H., & Bontinck, W. J. (1989). Screening of chemicals for anaerobic biodegradability. *Chemosphere*, *19*(10–11), 1527–1550. doi:10.1016/0045-6535(89)90498-0

Chaffey, D., Ellis-Chadwick, F., & Mayer, R. (2009). *Internet marketing: strategy, implementation and practice*. Pearson Education.

Chakma, S., Das, L., & Moholkar, V. S. (2015). Dye decolorization with hybrid advanced oxidation processes comprising sonolysis/Fenton-like/photo-ferrioxalate systems: A mechanistic investigation. *Separation and Purification Technology*, *156*, 596–607. doi:10.1016/j.seppur.2015.10.055

Chan, T. J., Li, Y., Hashim, N. H., & Ibrahim, A. N. I. (2022). Online promotional communication attributes and company competitiveness of a Malaysian fast fashion clothing company. *International Journal of Technology*, *13*(6), 1344–1353. doi:10.14716/ijtech.v13i6.5955

Guedes, G., & Soares, P. (2005). Branding of fashion products: A communication process, a marketing approach. *Proceedings of The Association for Business Communication,* 7.

Hao, W., Björkman, E., Lilliestråle, M., & Hedin, N. (2014). Activated Carbons for Water Treatment Prepared by Phosphoric Acid Activation of Hydrothermally Treated Beer Waste. *Industrial & Engineering Chemistry Research*, *53*(40), 15389–15397. doi:10.1021/ie5004569

Kallawar, G. A., & Bhanvase, B. A. (2024). A review on existing and emerging approaches for textile wastewater treatments: Challenges and future perspectives. *Environmental Science and Pollution Research International*, *31*(2), 1748–1789. doi:10.1007/s11356-023-31175-3 PMID:38055170

Karypidis, M. (2018). Sewability interdependence on rigid structures. *IOP Conference Series. Materials Science and Engineering*, *459*(1), 012048. doi:10.1088/1757-899X/459/1/012048

Karypidis, M., Papadaki, A. I., & Stalika, A. (2023a). An overview of the available water textile effluent treatments. *Journal of International Scientific Publications: Materials. Metals Technology*, *17*(1), 178–188. doi:10.62991/MMT1996371718

Karypidis, M., Papadaki, A. I., & Stalika, A. (2023b). A critical evaluation of the use of hemp as a sustainable solutions in garment making treatments. *Journal of International Scientific Publications: Materials. Metals Technology*, *17*, 189–201. doi:10.62991/MMT1996373709

Karypidis, M., & Savvidis, G. (2018). *Analysis of Factors Influencing Needle Penetration Force through Woven Fabrics*. Academic Press.

Kell, K. (2021, December 22). *Hemp Fabric: What is it and is it Sustainable?* Going Zero Waste. https://www.goingzerowaste.com/blog/hemp-fabric-what-is-it-and-is-it-sustainable

Kumari, A. (2024). Transforming Business for a Sustainable Future Using Green Marketing. *Multidisciplinary Approach to Information Technology in Library and Information Science*, 132-150.

Lamberton, C. P., Naylor, R. W., & Haws, K. L. (2013). Same destination, different paths: When and how does observing others' choices and reasoning alter confidence in our own choices? *Journal of Consumer Psychology*, *23*(1), 74–89. doi:10.1016/j.jcps.2012.01.002

Liu, M., Fernando, D., Daniel, G., Madsen, B., Meyer, A. S., Ale, M. T., & Thygesen, A. (2015). Effect of harvest time and field retting duration on the chemical composition, morphology and mechanical properties of hemp fibers. *Industrial Crops and Products*, *69*, 29–39. doi:10.1016/j.indcrop.2015.02.010

Madhav, S., Ahamad, A., Singh, P., & Mishra, P. K. (2018). A review of textile industry: Wet processing, environmental impacts, and effluent treatment methods. *Environmental Quality Management*, *27*(3), 31–41. doi:10.1002/tqem.21538

McLean, P. (2016). *Culture in Networks*. Wiley.

Miller, V. (2020). *Understanding Digital Culture* (2nd ed.). Sage.

Muchenje, C., Tapera, M. C., Katsvairo, H. T., & Mugoni, E. (2023). Green Marketing Strategies and Consumer Behavior: Insights for Achieving Sustainable Marketing Success. In R. Masengu, S. Bigirimana, O. Chiwaridzo, R. Bensson, & C. Blossom (Eds.), *Sustainable Marketing, Branding, and Reputation Management: Strategies for a Greener Future* (pp. 465–484). IGI Global. doi:10.4018/979-8-3693-0019-0.ch024

Mukendi, A., Davies, I., Glozer, S., & McDonagh, P. (2020). Sustainable fashion: Current and future research directions. *European Journal of Marketing*, *54*(11), 2873–2909. doi:10.1108/EJM-02-2019-0132

Murphy, R. (1998). The Internet: A viable strategy for fashion retail marketing? *Journal of Fashion Marketing and Management*, *2*(3), 209–216. doi:10.1108/eb022529

Norton, D. A., Lamberton, C. P., & Naylor, R. W. (2013). The devil you (don't) know: Interpersonal ambiguity and inference making in competitive contexts. *The Journal of Consumer Research*, *40*(2), 239–254. doi:10.1086/669562

Oklander, M., & Kudina, A. (2021). Channels for promotion of fashion brands in the online space. *Baltic Journal of Economic Studies*, *7*(2), 179–187. doi:10.30525/2256-0742/2021-7-2-179-187

Omar Zaki, H., & Rosli, N. (2024). A Bibliometric Citation Analysis on Green Marketing and Waste Management. *International Journal of Management Studies*, *31*(1), 235–268. doi:10.32890/ijms2024.31.1.9

Ottman, J. (2017). *The new rules of green marketing: Strategies, tools, and inspiration for sustainable branding*. Routledge. doi:10.4324/9781351278683

Patil, K., & Khathuria, D. (2020). *Digital Marketing in Fashion Industry*. Academic Press.

Patwary, S. (2020). Clothing and textile sustainability: Current state of environmental challenges and the ways forward. *Textile & Leather Review*, *3*(3), 158–173. doi:10.31881/TLR.2020.16

Pavan, M., Samant, L., Mahajan, S., & Kaur, M. (2024). Role of Chemicals in Textile Processing and Its Alternatives. In *Climate Action Through Eco-Friendly Textiles* (pp. 55–72). Springer Nature Singapore. doi:10.1007/978-981-99-9856-2_5

Periyasamy, A. P. (2024). Recent Advances in the Remediation of Textile-Dye-Containing Wastewater: Prioritizing Human Health and Sustainable Wastewater Treatment. *Sustainability (Basel)*, *16*(2), 495. doi:10.3390/su16020495

Polonsky, M. J., & Rosenberger, P. J. III. (2001). Reevaluating green marketing: A strategic approach. *Business Horizons*, *44*(5), 21–21. doi:10.1016/S0007-6813(01)80057-4

Rana, N. (2024). Ethical AI Integration in Marketing Strategies for Sustainable E-Commerce Fashion Designing. In *Contemporary Management and Global Leadership for Sustainability* (pp. 218–233). IGI Global. doi:10.4018/979-8-3693-1273-5.ch013

Rather, L. J. (2019). 'Advances in the sustainable technologies for water conservation in textile industries. In *Water in Textiles and Fashion* (pp. 175–194). Elsevier. doi:10.1016/B978-0-08-102633-5.00010-5

Rawat, D., Sharma, R. S., Karmakar, S., Arora, L. S., & Mishra, V. (2018). Ecotoxic potential of a presumably non-toxic azo dye. *Ecotoxicology and Environmental Safety*, *148*, 528–537. doi:10.1016/j.ecoenv.2017.10.049 PMID:29125956

Raza, N., Rizwan, M., & Mujtaba, G. (2024). Bioremediation of real textile wastewater with a microalgal-bacterial consortium: An eco-friendly strategy. *Biomass Conversion and Biorefinery*, *14*(6), 7359–7371. doi:10.1007/s13399-022-03214-5

Reddy, K. P., Chandu, V., Srilakshmi, S., Thagaram, E., Sahyaja, C., & Osei, B. (2023). Consumers perception on green marketing towards eco-friendly fast moving consumer goods. *International Journal of Engineering Business Management, 15*. doi:10.1177/18479790231170962

Robeson, L. M. (2012). Polymer Membranes. In *Polymer Science: A Comprehensive Reference* (pp. 325–347). Elsevier. doi:10.1016/B978-0-444-53349-4.00211-9

Roy, R., Chavan, P. P., Rajeev, Y., Praveenraj, T., & Kolazhi, P. (2024). Sustainable Manufacturing Practices in Textiles and Fashion. In *Sustainable Manufacturing Practices in the Textiles and Fashion Sector* (pp. 1–22). Springer Nature Switzerland. doi:10.1007/978-3-031-51362-6_1

Sharma, A. P. (2021). Consumers' purchase behaviour and green marketing: A synthesis, review and agenda. *International Journal of Consumer Studies*, *45*(6), 1217–1238. doi:10.1111/ijcs.12722

Singh, P. B., & Pandey, K. K. (2012). Green marketing: Policies and practices for sustainable development. *Integral Review*, *5*(1), 22–30.

Štefko, R., & Steffek, V. (2018). Key issues in slow fashion: Current challenges and future perspectives. *Sustainability (Basel)*, *10*(7), 2270. doi:10.3390/su10072270

Tarnanidis, T. (2024). Exploring the Impact of Mobile Marketing Strategies on Consumer Behavior: A Comprehensive Analysis. *International Journal of Information, Business and Management*, *16*(2), 1–17.

Tarnanidis, T., Papachristou, E., Karypidis, M., & Ismyrlis, V. (Eds.). (2023). *Social Media and Online Consumer Decision Making in the Fashion Industry*. IGI Global. doi:10.4018/978-1-6684-8753-2

Velusamy, S., Roy, A., Sundaram, S., & Kumar Mallick, T. (2021). A Review on Heavy Metal Ions and Containing Dyes Removal Through Graphene Oxide-Based Adsorption Strategies for Textile Wastewater Treatment. *Chemical Record (New York, N.Y.)*, *21*(7), 1570–1610. doi:10.1002/tcr.202000153 PMID:33539046

Verma, A. K., Dash, R. R., & Bhunia, P. (2012). A review on chemical coagulation/flocculation technologies for removal of colour from textile wastewaters. *Journal of Environmental Management*, *93*(1), 154–168. doi:10.1016/j.jenvman.2011.09.012 PMID:22054582

Wang, Y., Shi, Y., Xu, X., & Zhu, Y. (2024). A Study on the Efficiency of Green Technology Innovation in Listed Chinese Water Environment Treatment Companies. *Water (Basel)*, *16*(3), 510. doi:10.3390/w16030510

Wilcox, K., & Stephen, A. T. (2013). Are close friends the enemy? Online social networks, self-esteem, and self-control. *The Journal of Consumer Research*, *40*(1), 90–103. doi:10.1086/668794

Yasar, A., & Yousaf, S. (2013). Solar assisted photo Fenton for cost effective degradation of textile effluents in comparison to AOPS. *Global NEST Journal*, *14*(4), 477–486. doi:10.30955/gnj.000804

Yazdanifard, R., & Yan, Y. K. (2014). The Concept of Green Marketing and Green Product Development on Concsumer Buying Approach. *Global Journal of Commerce & Management Perspective*, *3*(2), 33–38.

Yıldırım, S., Sevik, N., Kandpal, V., & Yıldırım, D. C. (2024). The Role of Green Brands on Achieving 2030 Sustainable Development Goals (2030 SDGs). In *Contemporary Management and Global Leadership for Sustainability* (pp. 141–162). IGI Global. doi:10.4018/979-8-3693-1273-5.ch009

Zepp, R. G., Faust, B. C., & Hoigne, J. (1992). Hydroxyl radical formation in aqueous reactions (pH 3-8) of iron(II) with hydrogen peroxide: The photo-Fenton reaction. *Environmental Science & Technology*, *26*(2), 313–319. doi:10.1021/es00026a011

Zhao, Y., Nzihou, A., Ren, B., Lyczko, N., Shen, C., Kang, C., & Ji, B. (2021). Waterworks Sludge: An Underrated Material for Beneficial Reuse in Water and Environmental Engineering. *Waste and Biomass Valorization*, *12*(8), 4239–4251. doi:10.1007/s12649-020-01232-w

KEY TERMS AND DEFINITIONS

Effluent Treatment: Is one type of waste water treatment method which is particularly designed to purify industrial waste water for its reuse and its aim is to release safe water to environment from the harmful effect caused by the effluent.

Fashion Green Marketing: In the context of the fashion industry refers to products that are produced with respect to working conditions and the environment, and to the possibility of finding a compromise between business objectives and environmental issues.

Fashion Industry: Encompasses the design, manufacturing, distribution, marketing, and sale of clothing and accessories.

Sustainable Fashion: Is a way in which brands create clothing that not only reduces the impact on the environment but is also mindful of the people who work to produce the garments.

Chapter 11
Unveiling the Viral Thread:
A Comprehensive Analysis of Virality Coefficients in Indian Fashion Brand Dynamics

N. Ravi Kumar
https://orcid.org/0000-0002-9308-7461
Presidency College, India

Prasad Kulkarni
Euclea Business School, UAE

V. Kalaiarasai
PSG College of Arts and Science, India

ABSTRACT

The research examined and clarified the complex dynamics that underlie the virality of Indian fashion brands. It also quantified and analyzed virality coefficients, exploring the elements and processes that facilitated the expansion of these brands' reach across various channels. The study used bibliometric analysis, classifying academic papers on the dynamics of Indian fashion brands by year, nation, and subject area by using data from the Scopus database. The basis for further research into the virality coefficients was laid by the visual mapping of keyword co-occurrences, the identification of clusters, and the extraction of variables using the VOSviewer software. Advanced textual analysis techniques were used for topic modeling at the same time, including lemmatization, TF-IDF matrix generation, and latent Dirichlet allocation (LDA). The Python programming language made it easier to see hidden motifs in the literature.

DOI: 10.4018/979-8-3693-3049-4.ch011

INTRODUCTION

Virality is a powerful force that can spread ideas and content among a wide range of people at a never-before-seen speed in the dynamic world of digital marketing and brand dynamics. In the dynamic and ever expanding Indian fashion market, knowing the subtleties of virality is critical for companies hoping to make an impression that will last into the future.

The rate at which current users adopt a product is gauged by its virality coefficient. It is a measure of the extent to which the user base expands through viral channels and can be computed using formal methods. The coefficient can also be used to indicate the average number of users that each user is likely to bring to the product. Spreadsheet modeling of virality can aid in comprehending and forecasting its effects. Adding virality to a product means putting certain plans in place to make it easier for people to use (Seufert, Benjamin, Eric, 2014). In contrast, a metric used in the study of gases and their behavior is the second virial coefficient. It is computed using formulas and contrasted with experimental data to determine how the coefficient varies with temperature for various materials (Umirzakov, I., H., 2013). The study of dense gases and their thermodynamic characteristics also makes use of the virial coefficient. Changes in the temperature dependence of the coefficient may result from the creation of connected states between interacting particles (Khomkim, A.L., Mulenko, V.B., Solovey, I.A., 1998). The computation of thermodynamic functions and virus coefficients in a system of charge and neutral particles with a specific form pseudopotential. The mass of tiny galaxy groupings is also estimated using the virial coefficient. It is based on the dynamic evolution of galaxies and is susceptible to estimating process uncertainties and oscillations (Niyati, Aggrawal, Ponnurangam, Kumaraguru, Anuja, Arora, 2017). Virality analysis of YouTube lesson videos with several metrics enabled.

This study explores the core of the issue by doing a thorough examination of the virality coefficients connected to Indian fashion labels. As a quantitative statistic, the virality coefficient allows for a more in-depth investigation of the variables that impact the distribution and amplification of material related to brands. This study aims to offer important insights into the tactics used by Indian fashion brands to leverage the power of social sharing, user engagement, and online visibility by dissecting the mechanics of virality.

A thorough investigation of virality coefficients in the context of Indian fashion will not only advance scholarly knowledge of modern marketing dynamics but also provide useful insights for practitioners in the field as the digital sphere continues to transform consumer behavior and brand narratives. We hope that our research will provide more insight into the patterns, trends, and factors that influence the virality of content in the Indian fashion industry and help consumers better understand how companies may use the digital space to their advantage.

Network Theory

Network theory serves as a methodological cornerstone inside the context of our study on the virality coefficient analysis of Indian fashion brands, providing a nuanced perspective on the complexities of digital interconnection. The following network theory applications are important contributions in the effort to understand the dynamics of fashion-related content diffusion online:

Identification of Key Influencers: The application of network theory makes it easier to identify important nodes in the digital environment that are significant to Indian fashion. By examining the topologies of social networks, prominently central elements can be identified, which can be used to identify people or things that act as catalysts for the spread of content. Determining the function of these influencers is critical to a thorough comprehension of information flow in the network.

Analysis of Network Topology

Analyzing network topology allows for a deeper understanding of the structural factors that determine how viral material becomes. The differentiation between highly interconnected clusters and more dispersed configurations offers important new perspectives on the complex dynamics governing the transmission of fashion-related content. This analytical method advances our knowledge of how the structure of the digital environment affects the spread of communications that are focused on brands.

Propagation Pathways: Network theory enables the methodical mapping of propagation paths, defining the orderly distribution of content via shares and retweets, for example. Deciphering the mechanics behind the virality of Indian fashion brand content depends on this detailed investigation of the pathways that information takes on the digital landscape.

Community Detection: Finding groups of people that have similar interests to oneself becomes important when explaining why something goes viral. The identification of these communities is made easier by network theory, which provides a more in-depth analysis of the ways in which various subgroups operating in the digital sphere contribute to the propagation of fashion brand messaging. Tailored marketing techniques that connect with the distinctive qualities of varied online communities are informed by this analytical approach.

Vulnerability and Resilience Analysis: A strong foundation for evaluating the digital network's resistance to changes and susceptibility to disturbances is provided by network theory. A thorough knowledge of the nodes that are most vulnerable to the spread of viral content, in comparison to their more robust counterparts, informs strategic choices that maximize the virality coefficient. This study also helps predict future nodes of influence or bottlenecks.

Dynamic Analysis over Time: Since networks are inherently dynamic, network theory makes it easier to analyze changes in the virality coefficient over time. Network evolution tracking over time provides insights into trends, seasonal patterns, or particular events that impact the spread of fashion-related content. A comprehensive grasp of the dynamic changes inherent in the digital realm is informed by this temporal perspective.

Research Objectives

1. Examine online network topologies to determine how they affect Indian fashion brands' virality coefficients.
2. Determine and evaluate how important influencers affect the virality coefficient of content on fashion in the online community.
3. Map content propagation paths through the digital network methodically in order to identify unique pathways that impact Indian fashion companies' virality coefficient.
4. Examine community dynamics and engagement patterns centered around fashion in the digital sphere to comprehend their influence on the virality coefficient.
5. Analyze how the virality coefficient for Indian fashion businesses has changed over time, keeping notice of shifts in community structures, influencer impact, and network dynamics.

LITERATURE REVIEW

Bibliographic Analysis

The graph demonstrates that during the previous ten years, there has been a steady growth in the quantity of papers published on viral marketing. This implies that study and interest in viral marketing are expanding. The rise in the quantity of papers on viral marketing that have been published can be attributed to several factors. It's possible that companies are growing increasingly eager to use viral marketing initiatives to connect with their target markets. Another theory is that people are becoming more and more aware of the elements that go into creating effective viral marketing campaigns. The graph also demonstrates how, in 2020, there was a particularly notable spike in the quantity of papers published on viral marketing. This is probably because of the COVID-19 epidemic, which caused a notable rise in the usage.

Figure 1. Documents by year (Scopus)

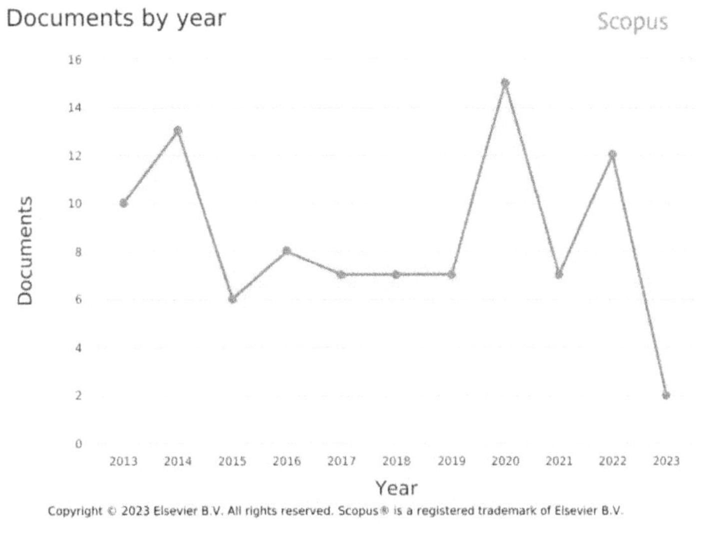

The graph indicates that business, management, and decision sciences account for 60.3% of the articles published on viral marketing. Social sciences (4.5%), computer science (11.5%), psychology (1.3%), agricultural and biological sciences (0.6%), engineering (0.6%), arts and humanities (0.6%), economics and econometrics (6.4%), and other (0.6%) are among the other subject areas that are covered.

This pie chart indicates that the majority of research in the subject of viral marketing is business-oriented. This is probably due to the fact that viral marketing efforts are mostly used by corporations. Viral marketing initiatives are used by businesses to expand their consumer base, raise brand awareness, and boost revenue. The pie chart indicates that interest in the social and psychological facets of viral marketing is also rising. This is probably because viral marketing initiatives depend on individuals disseminating information to others. Businesses must comprehend why individuals share content and what inspires them to do so in order to develop viral marketing strategies that are effective.

Figure 2. Documents by subject area (Scopus)

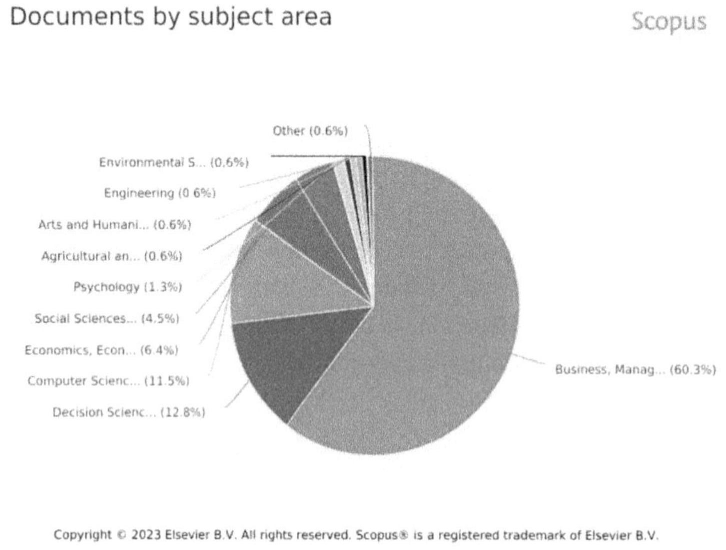

Figure 3. Documents by country or territory (Scopus)

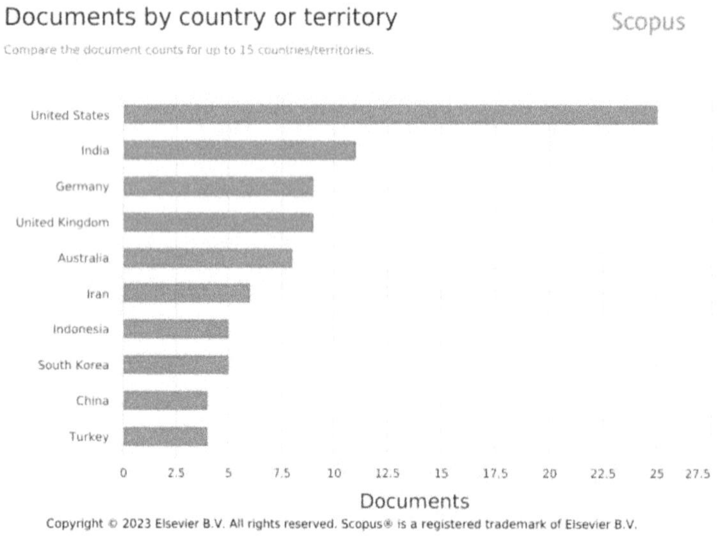

According to the barchart, the United States leads the world in searches for viral marketing, followed by the United Kingdom, Canada, Australia, and India. According to this barchart, industrialized nations are more likely than developing nations to be interested in viral marketing. This is perhaps because viral marketing strategies need a lot of online activity and are frequently expensive to execute. Developed nations are more desirable markets for viral marketing initiatives since they often have greater income levels and better internet penetration rates than developing nations. Additionally, the barchart demonstrates that English-speaking nations are more likely than non-English-speaking nations to be interested in viral marketing. This is probably because the vast majority of data regarding viral

The graphic depiction outlines the relationships between different ideas that are fundamental to viral marketing and includes components like word-of-mouth advertising, social media, social contagion, and peer pressure. The map has multiple ways to interpret its latitude. One interpretation that makes sense is as an example of the variety of elements that go into viral marketing efforts. Interestingly, word-of-mouth marketing's prominence suggests that it plays a crucial part in the viral marketing paradigm. Concurrently, social media's prominence highlights its importance as an additional important factor in the planning of viral marketing campaigns.

Figure 4. Relationships between ideas of viral marketing

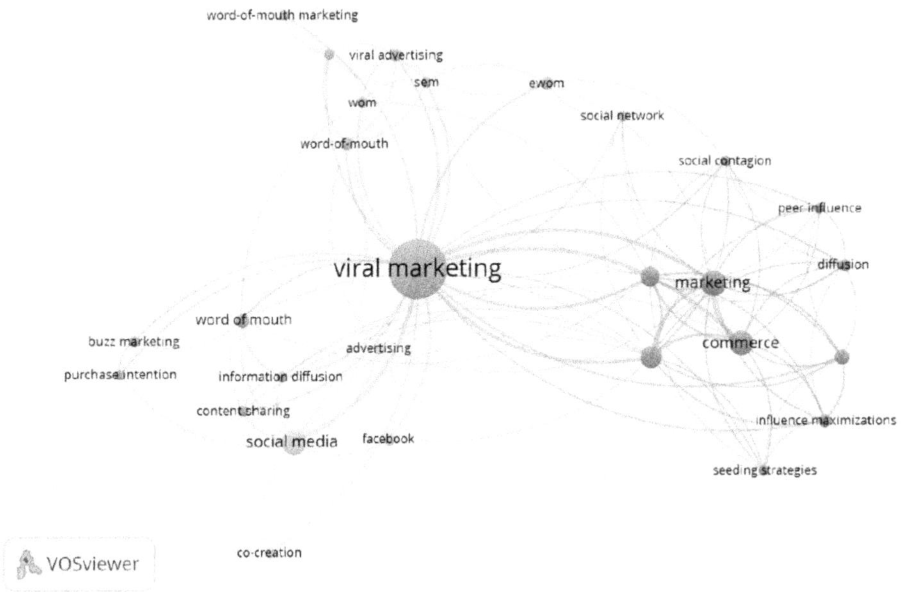

Another way to interpret the map is to see it as a representation of several stages in a viral advertising campaign. One way to think about seeding tactics is that their placement near the nadir of the map suggests that they are early-stage activities. On the other hand, the positioning of buy intention at the peak suggests that it is related to a later phase of a viral marketing effort.

When taken as a whole, the graphic illustration provides a thorough synopsis of ideas related to viral marketing. It's a useful tool for understanding the complex elements that go into viral marketing efforts and for outlining the steps that these initiatives take in order.

Word-of-mouth marketing, or WOM, is a type of advertising in which customers promote a good or service through unofficial channels including social media, online reviews, and discussions. Since word-of-mouth (WOM) is inherently credible and trustworthy, it is widely regarded as one of the most effective marketing channels.

Viral advertising is a type of advertising whereby users spread promotional content to other users. Ad campaigns that go viral frequently use comedy, mystery, or shock value to encourage audience members to share the content widely.

Social contagion is the process by which people are impacted by the deeds and mannerisms of others. Social contagion plays a crucial role in viral marketing by enabling the quick and easy spread of information about a good or service.

Peer influence is the power people have over the attitudes and actions of their peers. Peer influence becomes important in viral marketing since it encourages people to try new products and services because their peers recommend them and have positive experiences with them.

Diffusion: The process by which information spreads among a population is known as diffusion. Diffusion is a crucial component of viral marketing because it makes it possible for communications about a good or service to spread widely.

Social media: Facebook, Twitter, Instagram, and other social media platforms are important platforms for viral marketing campaigns because they facilitate quick and extensive information sharing between individuals and their networks.

Buzz marketing is a type of advertising where the goal is to create buzz and interest about a product or service. Buzz marketing initiatives are purposefully created to convey exclusivity and urgency.

Information Diffusion: The process through which knowledge spreads among a population. Information dispersion is essential for viral marketing initiatives since it helps make sure that communications about a product or service are seen by as many people as possible.

Content sharing is the process of sharing information with other people. A crucial aspect of viral marketing, content sharing enables people to spread knowledge about a good or service within their social networks.

Influence Maximization: The strategic process of locating and pursuing the most powerful people in a network is known as "influence maximization." Influence maximizing is a useful strategy for viral marketing campaigns that helps companies reach the people who are most likely to spread the word about their goods or services.

1. Viral Coefficient in Fashion Branding

Examining the viral coefficient in the context of fashion branding reveals its significance in measuring the rapid dissemination of marketing content through social media platforms (Jutéus, 2010). Social identification, ingroup/outgroup perceptions, materialism, and opinion leadership contribute to consumers' responses and their willingness to engage with fashion products (Jin, 2019). The success of fast-fashion brands, exemplified by Zara, emphasizes the importance of unique brand identification in a competitive market (Yin, 2022). Sustainable development in fast fashion has emerged as a crucial consideration due to environmental concerns (Giri, 2018).

2. Influencers and Online Content

Influencers, as key players in online content dissemination, significantly impact the viral coefficient (Himelboim, 2019; Sumith, 2017). The influence maximization problem underscores the importance of selecting the right users for viral marketing (Hu, 2015). Metrics and properties related to online social influence aid in the qualitative assessment of user-generated content, facilitating a nuanced understanding of influential content dynamics.

3. Community Dynamics and Engagement

Community dynamics and engagement emerge as influential factors in the viral coefficient, especially in online consumer communities (Alon, 2007). Effective engagement in these micro-social groups can mitigate stigma, disseminate messages, and inform interventions (Kpokiri, 2022). Community structures, such as reciprocal ties and specific triadic structures, significantly impact social contagion (Harrigan, 2012). Early spreading patterns of memes across communities serve as predictors of their future popularity (Weng, 2013).

Theoretical Model

Influencers play a crucial role in the field of social influence and community dynamics. These people or organizations, distinguished by their capacity to exert significant influence over others, present as well-known personalities, respected authorities, or persons with a sizable fan base. Influencers have an impact because they have the power to mold community members' behavior patterns. The community's network structure, which represents the complex web of relationships between its members, is crucial to comprehending the dynamics of information distribution. A society with a high degree of interconnectivity is more likely to have a quick content explosion since knowledge may flow easily from one person to another.

Figure 5. Theoretical model

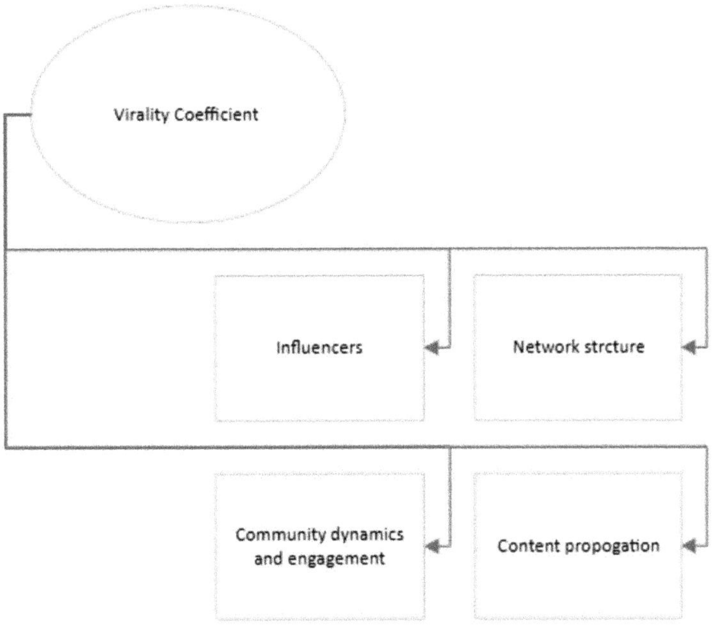

The essential component of engagement, which captures the general degree of activity and interaction within the community, is central to the discussion of community dynamics. Communities with high levels of engagement are more likely to actively share and consider content, which increases the chance that the content may go viral. The idea of content propagation, which includes the various ways in which knowledge is shared throughout the community, is essential to the process of content proliferation. These techniques include email forwarding conventions, the amplification effect enabled by social media platforms, and word-of-mouth distribution. Understanding and being aware of different modes of propagation makes a significant contribution to a thorough awareness of the dynamics controlling the flow of information within a particular community.

Research Methodology

Bibliometric Analysis: The research methodologically anchored itself in bibliometric analysis, undertaking a thorough examination of the virality coefficients inherent in the dynamics of Indian fashion brands. The main source of information used was the Scopus database, which provides a comprehensive collection of academic articles about the rise of Indian fashion firms. After a thorough bibliometric analysis, the literature was classified according to the subject domain, the geographical origin of publications, and the temporal dimension. This analysis provided a basis for further research as well as a more sophisticated knowledge of the changing trends in scholarly contributions. The bibliometric technique was enhanced by the use of VOSviewer software, which visually mapped keyword co-occurrences, identified clusters, and extracted crucial characteristics that were crucial in deciphering the intricate dynamics of viral

Topic Modeling: To find latent topics buried in the corpus of literature, the research explored the field of topic modeling, building on the knowledge gained from bibliometric analysis. Using cutting-edge methods including TF-IDF matrix generation, lemmatization, and Latent Dirichlet Allocation (LDA) analysis, the text of a few chosen journal articles was carefully examined. The subsequent topic modeling attempts were to pinpoint and describe the main ideas that were striking a chord in the conversation. Python programming was used to visualize these highlighted subjects, providing an understandable and nuanced depiction of the subtle layers inherent to the dynamics of viral coefficients in the context of Indian fashion brand dissemination. By using a combined bibliometric and topic modeling technique, the study offers insightful information to researchers, and marketers.

One important measure for fashion brands is the viral coefficient, which shows how likely it is that consumers will tell others about a brand. This measure is essential to the expansion of clientele and the boosting of revenue in the fashion sector. Two graphs that explain the key elements influencing fashion brands' viral coefficients are included in the graphic that is provided. The first graph shows that there is a positive relationship between sustainability and the viral coefficient, which indicates that consumers are more likely to promote firms that they believe to be sustainable. The second graph shows a positive relationship between the viral coefficient and content popularity, suggesting that brands that create viral content are more likely to be suggested. The picture elaborates more on the complex dynamics of fashion brands' viral coefficient. Important components include influencers, or people with large social media followings, whose recommendations have a big effect on a brand's virality index. Micro-influencers—individuals with smaller but nonetheless considerable social media followings—play a major role in elevating brands to a recommended level. When they endorse a company, opinion leaders—who are seen as authorities in their industry—have a significant impact on the brand's viral coefficient. User engagement is a crucial factor that measures how much a brand's content is interacted with; brands that have high levels of engagement are more likely to receive recommendations from customers. Furthermore, brands' online content quality and quantity become significant considerations; those that provide high-quality material are more likely to receive recommendations from customers. Ultimately, the examination of the viral coefficient and its determinants highlights the strategic significance of this metric for fashion firms. The graphs' positive connections and the detailed insights they offer shed light on the complex nature of consumer recommendations in the digital age, providing useful advice for firms looking to boost their viral impact and broaden their market reach.

Table 1. Topic modeling

Term	TF-IDF Category	Analysis
High TF-IDF:		
Viral coefficient	High	Central theme in various contexts (central theme)
Network structure	High	Influences viral coefficient (influences viral coefficient)
Influencers	High	Role in online content propagation (role in online content propagation)
Content propagation	High	Measurement and analysis in online networks (measurement and analysis in online networks)
Moderate TF-IDF:		
Community dynamics	Moderate	Influences viral coefficient (influences viral coefficient)
Fashion brands	Moderate	Viral coefficient in the fashion industry (viral coefficient in the fashion industry)
Eigenvalue	Moderate	Network structure and viral prevalence (network structure and viral prevalence)
Low TF-IDF:		
Sustainable development	Low	Specific context of fast fashion (specific context of fast fashion)
Osmotic second viral coefficient	Low	Niche application (niche application)

LDA Coherence Score: 0.425

The amount of thematic coherence is commendable, as indicated by the LDA coherence score of 0.425 for the explanation offered on the viral coefficient of fashion brands. This measure is used as an evaluation tool to appraise the topics' logical connections and organizational structure inside the explanation. A breakdown of the score range is necessary in order to clarify the score and maximize the explanatory quality:

Coherence levels are categorized according to the following scale, which runs from 0.0 to 1.0:

0.0-0.1: Denoting issues that lack a distinct theme structure and are not cohesive.
0.1–0.2: Reflecting subjects with a certain degree of thematic connectedness but not enough clarity.
0.2–0.3: Showing subjects that are reasonably coherent and whose themes are recognizable but could use more emphasis.
0.3–0.4: Showing strong coherence, with subjects being distinct and easy to understand.

0.4–0.5: Showing excellent coherence and strong topical links between the themes.
0.5-1.0: Showing exceptionally well-organized and regularly themed information, with outstanding coherence.

The explanation in this case is positioned within the "good coherence" range with a given score of 0.425. This suggests that there are observable basic themes about the viral coefficient and its determinants. Still, there is room for improvement, especially in terms of strengthening the theme links and improving the explanation's overall coherence. Thus, a more careful arrangement of the material and strengthening of thematic connections could improve the coherence of the explanation that is given even more.

Figure 6. Viral coefficient

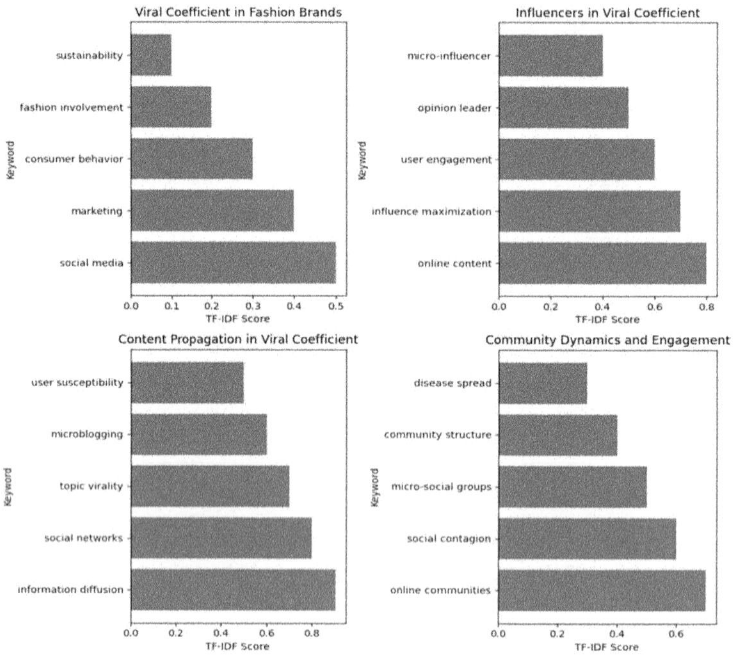

CONCLUSION

Managerial Implications

Strategic Influencer Engagement: In order to effectively manage in the digital environment, important influencers must be strategically identified and engaged. Understanding network structure and key nodes is necessary to maximize the virality coefficient, which allows for focused partnerships that have a big influence on brand awareness. It is recommended that managers foster connections with influencers who are positioned strategically to facilitate the distribution of material linked to brands.

Tailored Promotion for Virtual Communities: Success in management requires recognition of the existence of unique virtual communities. It is imperative to customize marketing techniques to correspond with the distinct interests of these communities. To boost engagement and increase the chance of content becoming viral in these micro-social groups, managers should tailor their content to resonate with certain community dynamics.

Dynamic Campaign Adaptation: Because online networks are dynamic, managers must maintain constant watchfulness. It is crucial to track variations in the virality coefficient over time. This entails the dynamic modification of marketing efforts in response to changing network dynamics, influencer impact, and community structures. Managers can leverage real-time modifications to capitalize on new trends and prevent future drops, so maintaining continued brand visibility.

Integrating Eco-Friendly Practices into Viral Marketing tactics: Managers should include eco-friendly practices into viral marketing tactics in response to the fast-fashion industry's growing concern for sustainability. Consumers that care about the environment may find resonance in viral content that emphasizes sustainable development, which could lead to favorable brand perceptions and enduring brand loyalty.

Resilience and Vulnerability Mitigation: By employing resilience and vulnerability assessments, managers can pinpoint weak points within the digital network. It is possible to use strategic interventions to increase resilience and reduce vulnerabilities, which will guarantee a more robust and efficient spread of viral material. With this proactive strategy, managers are better equipped to use their strategic acumen and vision to handle the complexity of the digital environment.

Research Implications

Progressing with Virality Coefficient Models: Scholars are urged to improve and develop models that quantify virality coefficients. These models will be more accurate and useful if network theory ideas are added, and specifics about the Indian fashion market—like cultural influences—are taken into account. Furthermore, the field would benefit greatly from the creation of predictive models for variations in virality across time.

Investigating Cross-Disciplinary Approaches: Because viral marketing research is interdisciplinary, cross-disciplinary approaches may offer deeper insights. Working together, the social sciences, computer science, and business can provide us a more thorough knowledge of the intricate dynamics determining virality. Multidisciplinary approaches are necessary to produce comprehensive and complex research results.

Longitudinal Studies on Viral Trends: To learn more about the changing trends and patterns of virality coefficients in the Indian fashion business, researchers should carry out longitudinal studies. This entails looking into the effects of long-term changes in customer behavior, seasonal variations, and outside events. A thorough understanding of the dynamic nature of digital virality is provided by longitudinal investigations.

Future Scope

Integration of developing Technologies: To improve the predictive power of virality coefficients, future research endeavors should investigate the integration of developing technologies, such as machine learning and artificial intelligence. Modern tools for dynamic campaign management can be given to managers by automated technologies, which can help with real-time monitoring and decision-making for marketing initiatives.

International Comparative Studies: An expanded understanding of virality coefficients can be obtained by conducting comparative analyses between the Indian fashion market and its international counterparts.

Comprehending the subtleties of culture and their impact on virality is crucial for both domestic and global brands. For companies that operate in a variety of international marketplaces, these studies can provide insightful information.

Ethics in Influencer Marketing: Future studies should examine the moral issues related to influencer collaborations since influencer marketing is still very important. By establishing best practices and norms, influencer partnerships in the digital sphere will be transparent and accountable, building consumer and brand confidence.

Consumer Behavior Analysis: A promising direction for future research is to examine in-depth consumer behavior in online communities. More efficient and focused marketing tactics can be developed by investigating the psychological elements influencing engagement and comprehending the causes of content resonance within particular audiences.

REFERENCES

Amin, M. A., Eltomey, M. A., & Abdelazeem, M. A. (2014). *Diffusion weighted MRI in chronic viral hepatitis C: Correlation between apparent diffusion coefficient values and histopathological scores.* Elsevier. https://www.sciencedirect.com/science/article/pii/S0378603X14000412

Bellemans, A., & Janssens, M. (1974). *On the Osmotic Second Viral Coefficient of Athermal Polymer Solutions. Macromolecules.* ACS Publications. > doi:10.1021/ma60042a022

Eric, B. (2014). Chapter 7 – Virality. doi:10.1016/B978-0-12-416690-5.00007-5

Forster, J. E. (2004). *Using varying-coefficient models to analyze the longitudinal relationship between CD4+ cell count and viral load in HIV-1 infected patients.* University of Colorado.

Han, Y., Long, X.P., Huang, Y.M., & Jiang, Z.H. (2009). Effect of LJ or Exp-6 Potential Function on Calcula tion of Reduced Second Viral Coefficient. *Chin. J. Energ. Mater.*

Huang, J. S., Huang, J. M., & Zhang, W. (2021). Semicovariance Coefficient Analysis of Spike Proteins from SARS-CoV-2 and Other Coronaviruses for Viral Evolution and Characteristics Associated with Fatality. *Entropy.* https://www.mdpi.com/1099-4300/23/5/512

Keesom, W. H. (1915). The second viral coefficient for rigid spherical molecules, whose mutual attraction is equivalent to that of a quadruplet placed at their centre. *Proc. R. Acad. Sci.* https://dwc.knaw.nl/DL/publications/PU00012540.pdf

Kobayashi, H. (1959). *Molecular weight dependence of intrinsic viscosity, diffusion constant, and second viral coefficient of polyacrylonitrile. Journal of Polymer Science.* > doi:10.1002/pol.1959.1203913530

Lednev, V. V. (1968). Method of determining the second viral coefficient for dilute solutions of biopolymers by the method of low-angle X-ray scatter. *Biophysics.* https://elibrary.ru/item.asp? id=30915903

Maillols, H., & Maillols, J. (1976). *Relation between 2nd viral coefficient a2 and molecular mass in polystyrene-benzene system.* Elsevier.

Miroshnichenko, V. P., Arshinov, P. S., & Petrov, V. M. (1989). *The bile cholate-cholesterol coefficient for assessing the causes of a protracted convalescence in patients with viral hepatitis*. https://europepmc.org/article/med/2629293

Moroz, L. V., & Bondaruk, I. Y. (2019). Direct (hyaluronic acid) and indirect (alanine aminotransferase, aspartate aminotransferase, de Rithis coefficient of liver fibrosis markers in patients with chronic viral.... *Journal of Education, Health and Sport*. https://apcz.umk.pl/JEHS/article/view/7379

Niyati, A., Anuja, A., & Ponnurangam, K. (2017). *Multiple metric aware YouTube tutorial videos virality analysis*. doi:10.1504/IJSNM.2017.10012952

Patz, R, & Ratzsch, M.T. (1989). *The Kerr Effect in real gases. 2. the 2nd Kerr viral coefficient of noble-gases*. Verlagsgesellsch Geest.

Salminen, J., & Hytönen, A. (2012). *Viral coefficient–Unveiling the Holy Grail of online marketing*. http://taac.org.ua/files/a2012/proceedings/FI-2-Salminen-Hytonen-238.pdf>

Smirnov, Y. A., Fomina, N. V., & Kaverin, N. V. (1973). A correlation between the buoyant density and the sedimentation coefficient of EMC viral polyribosomes. *FEBS Letters*. https://core.ac.uk/download/pdf/82695955.pdf

UmirzakovI. H. (2013). Some comments on 'Equation for the second virial coefficient'. doi:10.1109/PLASMA.1998.677937

Valente, J. J. (2006). Application of Self-interaction Chromatography as a Rational Approach to Measuring the Osmotic Second Viral Coefficient (B) for Protein Formulation. Colorado State University.

Chapter 12
Virtual Try-On Application and Fashion Purchase Intentions Among Gen Z Consumers in Malaysia

Logaiswari A. P. Indiran
Universiti Teknologi Malaysia, Malaysia

Afifi Alifia Salsabila Putri
Universiti Teknologi Malaysia, Indonesia

Chen Fu
https://orcid.org/0009-0006-4768-6865
Universiti Teknologi Malaysia, Malaysia

Jadel Autor Dungog
Iligan Institute of Technology, Mindanao State University, Philippines

ABSTRACT

Online shopping, integral to modern life, lacks the tactile experience of physical retail, a significant shortfall in fashion. This gap is being addressed by incorporating virtual reality (VR) and augmented reality (AR) technologies to meld the digital and in-store experiences. This research critically examines the impact of virtual try-on (VTO) applications on Gen Z's fashion purchasing intentions in Malaysia, assessing factors like virtual presence and perceived ease of use. A quantitative approach, involving a survey with 94 participants, was taken. The study presents a novel model merging the technology acceptance model (TAM) with virtual presence. Results indicate Gen Z's overwhelming endorsement of VTO, with perceived usefulness as their main buying intention driver. These insights offer valuable direction for VTO developers, marketing strategists, and policymakers aiming to promote VTO in fashion retail.

DOI: 10.4018/979-8-3693-3049-4.ch012

1. INTRODUCTION

As the technology business trend propels the transition from 2D to 3D innovation, marketers are keen to broaden their horizons, and the use of Virtual Reality (VR) and Augmented Reality (AR) technologies continues to flourish. This surge is attributed to the fact that 3D E-commerce produces superior-quality images, enabling customers to observe product specifications, thereby mitigating the occurrence of returns. It surpasses 2-dimensional platforms like traditional E-commerce, yielding higher product match rates through improved visual search features (Billewar and colleagues, 2021). Customers can leverage the Virtual Try-on application to generate virtual models based on their measurements, facial characteristics, hair color, and body shape. Additionally, they can zoom in, rotate the product, and examine it from various angles. This technology also facilitates information retrieval (Kim & Forsythe, 2008).

Since virtual try-on technology displays items that can be worn or referred to as "garments," it is very similar to online shopping. Many Malaysians have a strong desire to go shopping. According to E-commerce DB Country Reports 2021, 44 percent of Malaysia's population makes online purchases, with 14 million E-commerce users referred to as "e-consumers," the most popular categories purchased are apparel, food & beverages, and shoes. With a wealth background of 31 percent of e-consumers, this online shopping habit is compelling. Furthermore, based on public attitudes towards online shopping, the research predicts that the number of Malaysian e-consumers will increase by 27 percent to 18 million by 2025 (Eden et al., 2021).

The juxtaposition of virtual try-on technology and online shopping appears especially appropriate concerning Generation Z, a younger demographic leading the way in embracing and assimilating contemporary advancements. Generation Z, also known as Gen Z, is distinguished by its technological prowess. According to Utami (2021), Generation Z includes people born between 1998 and 2010 who began using the internet and the web as they grew older. Parents guided and encouraged their children to use social networking sites from an early age. Generation Z has grown up in a world that has always relied on technology (Murad et al., 2019). This generation has a natural affinity for quick adaptation to cutting-edge technologies, as evidenced by their embrace of innovations such as virtual try-ons.

In a nutshell despite E-commerce's pervasive market influence, it still falls short of replacing immersive on-site shopping experiences (Lu & Smith, 2008) due to the limitations inherent in 2-dimensional platforms. Nonetheless, the virtual try-on application is emerging as a critical point of convergence for both realms, to bridge the existing gap. At the same time, Malaysia has a plethora of online shopping platforms, but only a few incorporate features that provide customers with a three-dimensional experience or collaborate with virtual try-on companies and designers to enhance benefits. This study aims to investigate the relationship between the potential of virtual try-on applications (VTO) components; (i) virtual presence (VP), (ii) perceived ease of use (PEOU), (iii) perceived enjoyment (PE), and (iv) perceived of usefulness (POU) towards purchase intention from the perspective of tech-savvy Gen Z while also serving as a valuable reference for online shopping businesses and E-commerce entities. To achieve this purpose, the remainder of the article is structured as follows: it begins with a review of relevant literature and then presents our conceptualization of the research. Following that, it describes the methods used and the data collected. The article then presents the findings and analysis and discusses their significance. The article concludes with a section on limitations and future research directions.

2. LITERATURE REVIEW

In an era where technology seamlessly integrates into daily life, Generation Z takes the lead regarding digital literacy. The critical task is to understand how the convergence of virtual presence, ease of use, enjoyment, and perceived usefulness shapes their purchasing decisions. As this generation embraces innovation and easily navigates the digital landscape, our research aims to shed light on the intricate relationships between these Virtual Try-On (VTO) components and the likelihood of converting digital engagements into tangible transactions. The inclusion of Virtual Try-On applications in the e-commerce domain represents a paradigm shift in consumer engagement, particularly for the technologically savvy Generation Z. This study seeks to understand the dynamics of key VTO components, specifically (i) virtual presence (VP), (ii) perceived ease of use (PEOU), (iii) perceived enjoyment (PE), and (iv) perceived usefulness (POU), and their collective influence on purchase intention within this distinct demographic.

2.1. Virtual Try-On (VTO) Application

As online shopping grows in popularity and developments in Internet technology improve the consumer experience, virtual try-on (VTO) technology is being employed by online merchants to drive sales (Zhang et al., 2019). Users benefit from a more dynamic and engaging experience using virtual try-on applications, enabling them to see things realistically. This improved user experience may impact the product's impression and boost the chance of purchase (Kim et al., 2006). According to Bhattacherjee (2002), using virtual try-on technology may aid in developing trust between customers and online shops. Trust is an essential component influencing purchasing intent. Providing tools that promote openness and involvement may aid in developing trust. Customers' perceptions regarding VTO technology influence their propensity to buy apparel online, and this willingness is influenced by perceived utility, pleasure, and privacy risk (Zhang et al., 2019). According to studies, VTO significantly affects online shoppers' purchase choices (Merle et al., 2012). According to Celik (2016), the online consumer purchase decision-making process consists of five steps: issue identification, information search, assessment, decision-making, and post-buy behavior. VTO technology is introduced by online shops, allowing online shoppers to pick matching apparel from online stores, freely test numerous combinations, and view the clothing on the screen, allowing them to assess the clothing (Fiore et al., 2005). As a result, this technology is significant in the assessment stage, impacting consumers' purchase choices (Merle et al., 2012; Kim, 2016).

Engagement with VTO delivers a pleasant purchasing experience for clients and reflects its hedonic worth. This technology enables online shoppers to expand or rotate apparel, modify virtual models using their own physique data (Pachoulakis & Kapetanakis, 2012), and even upload images of their own faces to make models appear like them (Merle et al., 2012). VTO apps may also give social value by enabling users to poll their friends' views by sharing clothing styles on custom models (Kang & Johnson, 2013). Interactions between online customers and shopping help software might impact their purchase intention selections in the online environment (Kim, 2016). The term "online purchase intention" refers to whether online customers expect to make online purchases in the near future (Law & Ng, 2016), which is influenced by consumers' sentiments regarding shopping help software (Noordin et al., 2017). According to Yu & Damhorst (2015), both the hedonic and utilitarian features of virtual fitting have a role in deciding purchase intention. Another research looked at the hedonic value of interaction in virtual fitting room pictures and how it affects online approach reactions. It assesses the impact of picture interaction (limited to the mix-and-match function) and finds that it provides a stimulating experience, predicts emotional arousal, and leads to pleasure, buy intention, and intent to visit an online business. This indicates that combining information and entertaining components is essential for triggering emotions and generating good attitudes in VTO (Fiore et al., 2005).

2.2. Virtual Presence and Purchase Intention

Online interactions with consumers may impact brand assessment and purchase intent, social media may improve corporate brand sales (Chung et al., 2015; Stephen & Galak, 2012). According to Keng et al. (2011), engagement and intimacy are the criteria for categorizing virtual. According to Gefen & Straub (2004), a feeling of virtual presence on internet sites may boost client trust, which leads to increased purchase intent. The Internet not only promotes network-based communication, but it also promotes integration. People are more inclined to purchase a thing if a significant number of people enjoy or share it, consumer purchasing intentions are favorably impacted by willingness and compliance (Keng et al., 2018). According to Naylor et al. (2012), consumers will infer the preferences of others based on language, and consumers will have higher brand affinity if they see others promoting a given brand, enhancing brand assessment and buy intention. Lin et al. (2021) argues that pleasant social interactions and recommendations from virtual peers or influencers may significantly affect users' purchase intentions by creating a sense of community and trust.

According to Naylo et al. (2012), the perceived presence of a brand's online supporters can be influenced by the social influence of virtual brand communities, which in turn influences target consumers' brand evaluation and purchase intention, even when experienced in a passive and virtual environment. According to Gefen & Straub (2004), improving pure virtual presence on e-commerce websites may boost client confidence and, as a result, purchase intention. Keng (2016) agrees with this position and believes that buyers have stronger purchase inclinations in the context of pure virtual presence and product experience. Virtual presence may make customers feel more engaged and connected, increasing trust in products and online platforms, and affecting purchase intent (Sousa, 2020). Thus, the hypotheses developed is:

H1: *There is a significant relationship between Virtual Try-On Application's virtual presence and purchase intention among Gen-Z E-Consumers in Malaysia*

2.3. Perceived Ease of Use and Purchase Intention

In information systems and technology adoption, the link between perceived ease of use and purchase intention has been extensively researched (Amor & Yahia, 2022). The customer's intention to make online purchases via online businesses or websites is referred to as online purchase intention. (1) intention to buy things online, (2) time available for online purchase, (3) intention to purchase online within a short period of time, and (4) considerations for online shopping are the aspects of online purchase intention (Hong & Cha, 2013). Perceived ease of use is a notion in the Technology Acceptance Model (TAM) that relates to customers' belief that the Internet is more effective than in-person shopping in facilitating purchases (Wicaksono & Maharani, 2020; Rahmiati & Yuannita, 2019). A user-friendly system is more likely to inspire favorable views, raising purchasing intentions (Primanda et al., 2020). According to Zuelseptia (2018), perceived ease of use clearly and substantially influences customers' views about online purchase. Purchasing interest is also a useful technique for anticipating the purchase process, according to Septialana & Kusumastuti (2017). Purchasing interest is often linked to customer behavior, perceptions, and attitudes. According to Chelvarayan et al. (2023), perceived ease of use has a favorable and substantial influence on students' attitudes about accessing digital libraries. According to the findings of Oentario et al. (2017), perceived ease of use has a favorable and substantial influence on customer attitudes, and consumer attitudes positively impact online purchase intention. One of the Technology Acceptance Model's two principles is that perceived ease of use has been demonstrated to affect customer attitudes about online buying, consumers' good attitude toward online purchasing activities stems from their perception that internet shopping is simple (Zuelseptia, 2018).

Several other studies have found that perceived utility influences online purchase intentions as well as online users' actions and attitudes (Ventre & Kolbe, 2020; Harrigan et al., 2021). People may be more willing to accept online shopping if it offers benefits (Rahmiati & Yuannita, 2019), but they may be hesitant to switch from offline to online purchasing (Lu et al., 2011), influencing attitudes and online purchasing intentions. According to Shah et al. (2012), purchase intention is a decision based on a person's motivations for purchasing a brand of their choice. Its ease of use and usefulness influences people's intentions to use the system. Websites that are easy to use and provide useful information will increase e-commerce purchase intentions (Chen & Ching, 2013). Several studies have found that ease of use and usefulness increase purchase intent for online purchases (Tiwari & Joshi, 2020; Phetnoi et al., 2021). Therefore, the following hypothesis is proposed.

H2: *There is a significant relationship between Virtual Try-On Application's perceived ease of use and purchase intention among Gen-Z E-Consumers in Malaysia*

2.4. Perceived Enjoyment and Purchase Intention

Perceived enjoyment is associated with the fun and excitement of consumers' online purchases, as well as the hedonic component of online purchases, which assists customers in overcoming boredom, finding amusement, and seeking happiness and fulfilment (Bhalerao & Gujar, 2019). Previous research took a utilitarian hedonic approach, emphasizing the role of perceived pleasure in explaining future intentions to use e-commerce platforms (Akdim et al., 2022). Previous research has also shown that consumers are more likely to buy when having fun, leading people to believe that online shopping services are fun and exciting. Positive emotions may thus encourage consumers to use online shopping services (Chen et al., 2022). Although the quality of e-commerce website design does not directly influence purchase intention, it does increase perceived pleasure, which directly influences purchase intention, as Patel et al. (2020) demonstrated. Perceived pleasure, according to Mustika and Wahyudi (2022), is critical in mediating the link between website quality and purchase intention.

In marketing, virtual reality has been shown to positively impact emotions and induce positive customer reactions, influencing purchase intentions (Martnez-Navarro et al., 2019; Pizzi et al., 2019). Several studies have found that using the environment as a marketing tactic can influence customer feelings such as pleasure, excitement, and contentment, as well as consumer behaviors such as purchase intention (Azmi et al., 2022; Brengman et al., 2019; Karney et al., 2019). Azmi et al. (2023) hypothesized that the virtual environment's atmosphere would influence prospective home buyers' contentment, thereby influencing their purchase intention. In addition, perceived pleasure is defined as the degree to which a virtual reality experience is deemed pleasurable (Shuhaiber & Mashal, 2019). According to previous investigations, perceived pleasure is a significant driver of customer behavior that influences purchase intent (Li et al., 2021; Jang & Park, 2019). Therefore, the following hypotheses have been formulated:

H3: *There is a significant relationship between Virtual Try-On Application's perceived enjoyment and purchase intention among Gen-Z E-Consumers in Malaysia*

2.5. Perceived Usefulness and Purchase Intention

In 1989, Davis proposed the technology acceptance model, which contends that perceived utility can significantly influence users' attitudes and behavioral intentions towards adopting new technologies, eventually influencing their actual use behavior. Internet ratings and reviews have become a reliable source for online purchases (Gavilan et al., 2018). Consumer reviews can help businesses by providing value through online forums, communities, reviews, and recommendations (Marshall et al., 2012). The perceived usefulness of online reviews influences the buying effect of online reviews for Korean and American customers, according to Ventre and Kolbe (2020). Previous research has shown that the quantity and quality of online reviews influence consumer behavior and positively affect product sales (Chong et al., 2018; Luo & Ye, 2019). Cheung and Thadani (2012) discovered that the number of online reviews is strongly related to product sales.

According to Kusyanti et al. (2018), perceived usefulness in social media is the degree to which users believe using specific social media sites helps them achieve their purchasing goals. According to Hajli (2014), perceived usefulness is an essential concept in the context of e-commerce, and there is a positive relationship between a website's perceived usefulness and the desire to buy among social media users. In the Harrigan et al. (2021) study, the perceived utility of a website was defined as system and information quality. As a result, the higher the system and information quality, the higher the buy intent on social media. Perceived usefulness refers to customers' perceptions that online shopping is more effective than in-person shopping in increasing purchases (Rahmiati & Yuannita, 2019). There are several indicators of shopping website perceived utility, such as (1) improved work performance, (2) increased productivity, (3) increased efficiency, and (4) system usefulness (Venkatesh & Davis, 2000). Several studies have found that perceived usefulness influences online purchasing intentions as well as online consumer behavior and attitudes (Kripesh et al., 2020; Rahmiati & Yuannita, 2019). Simultaneously, Rahmiati and Yuannita (2019) demonstrated that perceived utility influences purchase intention rather than customer opinions. Therefore, the following hypotheses have been developed:

H4: *There is a significant relationship between Virtual Try-On Application's perceived usefulness and purchase intention among Gen-Z E-Consumers in Malaysia*

2.6. Research Framework

The research framework is depicted in the diagram Figure 1 below, which consists of four independent variables: virtual presence (VP), perceived ease of use (PEOU), perceived enjoyment (PE), and perceived usefulness (POU). Furthermore, the dependent variable is e-consumers' purchase intention (PI).

Figure 1. Research framework

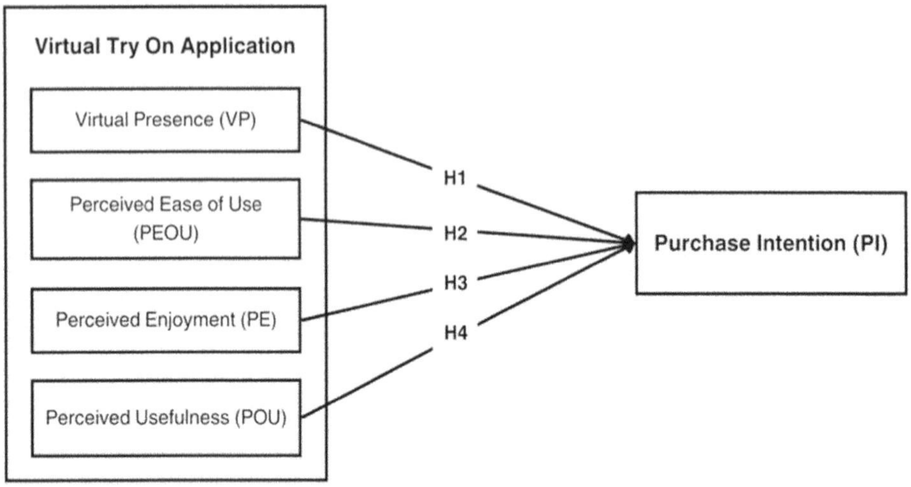

3. METHODOLOGY

This study used a quantitative method to collect opinions from many people to represent the general population. Notably, Malaysia has seen a significant increase in online shopping, with 44% of the population making purchases via internet platforms. In 2021, the recorded number of Malaysian e-consumers reached 14 million (Eden et al., 2021). This research focuses on Malaysian Gen Z e-consumers, specifically those aged 18 to 24. Individuals in this age range constituted 24 percent of e-commerce consumers in 2018, making them the second-largest user group (Online shopping in Malaysia 2019). The rationale for choosing e-consumers, particularly those using platforms such as Shopee, Lazada, Mudah.my, and others, stems from the fact that these platforms command the highest expenditure and frequency of visits among Malaysian online shoppers (Eden et al., 2021). Participants in this study had to meet certain requirements, including:

a) prior experience with online shopping on Malaysian e-commerce platforms.
b) Knowledge of 3D environments requires familiarity with the provided virtual try-on (VTO) application.

The questionnaire contained 36 questions ranging from Section A to Section F. Respondents were instructed to begin the survey by using the VTO application Wanna Kicks, a sneaker try-on app that uses augmented reality to allow users to explore both new releases and classic sneakers. Section A, which consisted of ten questions, sought demographic information from respondents. Sections B through E, each with five questions and a total of twenty, were designed to assess respondents' perceptions of various aspects of the virtual try-on (VTO) application. The questionnaire items were adapted from previous literature (Kim and Choo, 2021; Liu et al., 2020; Annie Jin and Bolebruch, 1970; Marelli et al., 2022; Zulkifli et al., 2016; Gupta & Nair, 2021; Leonnard et al., 2019; Richter & Raka, 2017; Mendonça, 2021; Hwangbo et al., 2020).

Finally, Part F included four questions to elicit information about respondents' purchase intentions for the virtual try-on application. These questions were adapted from previous research (Richter and Raka, 2017; Kim and Choo, 2021; Liu et al., 2020; Hwangbo et al., 2020). The Likert scale, a five-point scale ranging from 1 (Strongly Disagree) to 5 (Strongly Agree), was used to allow respondents to express their level of agreement or disagreement with the questionnaire statements.

4. FINDINGS

4.1. Demographic Profile

Table 1 in the document presents the demographic profile of the respondents who participated in the study on online shopping behavior in Malaysia. The table is structured to provide insights into various demographic factors such as gender, academic level, location, internet usage, and online shopping experience, including the platforms used. The study included 57 male respondents, which accounts for 60.6% of the total, and 37 female respondents, making up 39.4%. This indicates a higher participation rate among males in this study. Besides, the educational background of the participants is skewed towards higher education, with 81.9% holding a bachelor's degree. There are also 11 respondents with a Foundation/Diploma (11.7%) and 5 with a Secondary School education (5.3%). Most respondents are from Johor, with 76.6% of the total. Other locations such as Kedah, Kelantan, and Melaka have minimal representation, each with 2.1%. Some areas like Negeri Sembilan, Pahang, Perlis, Pulau Pinang, Sabah, Sarawak, Selangor, and W.P. Kuala Lumpur have a presence between 1.1% and 4.3%. All respondents use the internet, with varying frequencies. A significant majority, 77.7%, use the internet several times a day, indicating a high level of internet engagement among the participants. 18.1% use it once a day, and a small fraction, 3.2%, use it 2-3 times a week. Finally, response regarding online shopping experience; When asked if they have ever experienced online shopping in Malaysia, all respondents indicated that they have. The table also lists the online shopping platforms frequented by the respondents. Shopee is the most visited platform, with 93 mentions (48.7%), followed by Lazada with 37 mentions (39.4%). Other platforms like Carousell, Mudah.my, eBay, Amazon, Zalora, and others have lower frequencies, ranging from 1.1% to 24.5%.

4.2. Assessment of Measurement Model

The results of the descriptive analysis (Table 2) in this study revealed mean scores ranging from 3.90 to 4.47 on a model scale running from 1 (strongly disagree) to 5 (strongly agree). These scores suggest that the VTO application factors are widely accepted as representative of the independent variables. Hair et al. (2010) assert that assessing convergent validity involves evaluating factor loadings, composite reliability, and average variance extracted. In this study, all item loadings exceeded the recommended value of 0.5. The average variance extracted, reflecting the overall variance in the indicators accounted for by the latent construct, ranged from 0.599 to 0.748, surpassing the recommended threshold of 0.5 (Hair et al., 2010). As depicted in Table IV, the composite reliability (CR) values for all constructs ranged from 0.881 to 0.937, significantly exceeding the recommended level of 0.70. Therefore, the measurement model exhibits satisfactory convergent validity.

Table 1. Demographic profile

Profile	Description	Number of Respondents	Percentage (%)
Gender	Male Female	57 37	60.6 39.4
What is your highest academic level?	No Formal Education Primary School Secondary School Foundation/Diploma Bachelor's degree Master PhD	0 0 1 5 11 77 0	00 0 1.1 5.3 11.7 81.9 0
What is your location?	Johor Kedah Kelantan Melaka Negeri Sembilan Pahang Perak Perlis Pulau Pinang Sabah Sarawak Selangor Trengganu W.P. Kuala Lumpur W.P Labuan W.P Putrajaya	72 2 2 1 0 3 2 0 2 2 1 4 0 3 0 0	76.6 2.1 2.1 1.1 0 3.2 2.1 0 2.1 2.1 1.1 4.3 0 3.2 0 0
What is your average internet usage?	Several times a month 2 -3 times a week Once a day Several times a day Many times in a day	3 1 0 17 73	3.2 1.1 0 18.1 77.7
Have you ever experienced online shopping in Malaysia?	Yes No	94 0	100 0
What is Shopping platform you frequently visited?	Shopee Lazada Carousell Mudah.my eBay Amazon Zalora Others	93 37 13 15 1 4 23 5	48.7 39.4 13.8 16 1.1 4.3 24.5 5.3

Discriminant validity is ascertained through the Fornell-Lacker Criterion. Moreover, Table 3 indicates that the model exhibits good discriminant validity. The assessment of the Fornell-Lacker Criterion suggests that the square root of each construct's Average Variance Extracted (AVE) with its own construct should be higher than its correlations with other constructs (Hair et al., 2011). While most of the data indicates that the correlation between each construct is consistent, it is noteworthy to observe that Perceived Enjoyment (PEOU) shows a slightly lower value within its own construct (0.848) compared to its correlation with Perceived Usefulness (POU), which is 0.850. This suggests that PE and POU exhibit a relatively low correlation.

Table 2. Results of average variance extracted (AVE) and convergent validity (CR)

Construct	Item	Loading	AVE	CR
Virtual Presence	VP1 VP2 VP3 VP4 VP5	0.752 0.757 0.894 0.725 0.728	0.599	0.881
Perceived Ease of Use	PEOU1 PEOU2 PEOU3 PEOU4 PEOU5	0.893 0.854 0.696 0.886 0.878	0.713	0.925
Perceived Enjoyment	PE1 PE2 PE3 PE4 PE5	0.906 0.847 0.879 0.877 0.719	0.719	0.927
Perceived Usefulness	POU1 POU2 POU3 POU4 POU5	0.873 0.852 0.843 0.883 0.871	0.748	0.937
Purchase Intention	PI1 PI2 PI3 PI4	0.842 0.881 0.854 0.786	0.709	0.907

Table 3. Discriminant validity of the study

Construct	1	2	3	4	5
1. Purchase Intention	0.842				
2. Virtual Presence	0.686	0.774			
3. Perceived Ease of Use	0.681	0.759	0.845		
4. Perceived Enjoyment	0.745	0.764	0.812	0.848	
5. Perceived Usefulness	0.791	0.735	0.805	0.850	0.865

4.3. Assessment of Structural Model

Figure 2 below presents this study's Partial Least Squares (PLS) model, depicting the inner model path coefficients, while the outer model includes loadings with construct R2. In Figure 2, the R2 is 0.657, considered indicative of a moderate to substantial model (Hair et al., 2010), indicating that the model is considered good. The path coefficients depicting the relationship between each construct and purchase intention are shown in Table 4. The R2 value for the model is 0.656, which is considered moderate to substantial (Hair et al., 2010), indicating that the model is considered good. Path coefficients elucidate all latent construct variables' relationships and effects. The path coefficient for virtual presence (VP) is 0.182, the path coefficient for perceived ease of use (PEOU) is -0.027, the path coefficient for perceived enjoyment (PE) is 0.184, and the path coefficient for perceived usefulness (POU) is 0.522. Except for

Perceived Ease of Use, all variables in this model have positive path coefficients, as explained in the interpretation of these results (PEOU).

Table 4 also presents the results of the hypotheses testing. To test the hypothesis, we use path coefficient (β), t value, and p-value <0.05 which the result of t value supposed to be greater than 1.96.The structural model testing showed that Virtual Presence (VP) was not significantly related (β = 0.182, t = 1.363, p<0.05) to Purchase Intention (PI) followed by Perceived Ease of Use was not significantly related (β = -0.027, t = 0.155, p<0.05) to Purchase Intention (PI), Perceived Enjoyment was not significantly related (β = 0.184, t = 1.009, p<0.05) and Perceived of Usefulness was significantly related (β = 0.522, t = 3.514, p<0.05). Thus, H1, H2 and H3 were not supported while H4 was not supported.

Figure 2. Structural result model of PLS-SEM

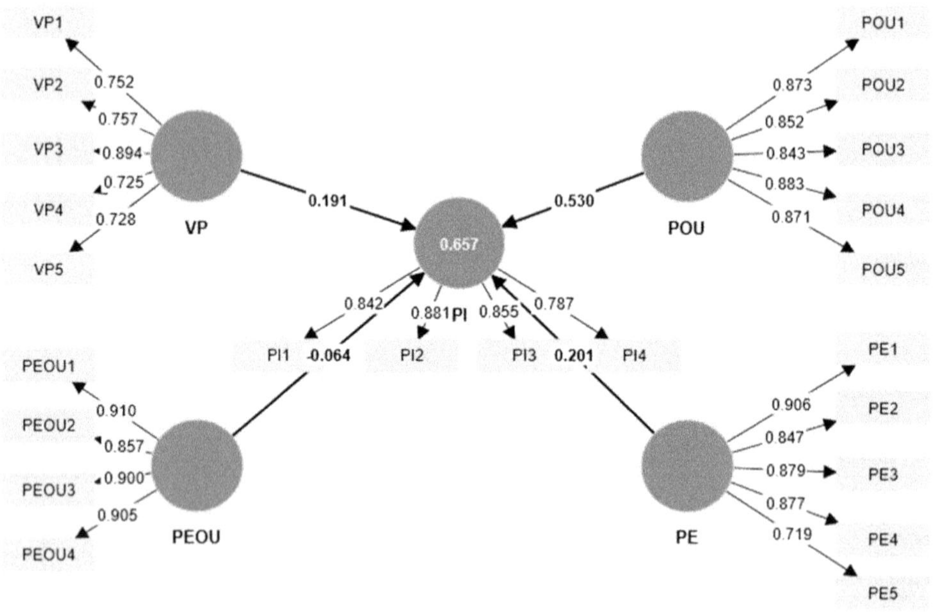

Table 4. Examining results of hypothesized direct effects of the factors in structural model

Hypothesis	Path	Path Coefficient	T-value	Std. Beta	Decision
H1	VP PI	0.182	1.363	0.174	Not Supported
H2	PEOU PI	-0.027	0.155	-0.039	Not Supported
H3	PE PI	0.184	1.009	0.523	Not Supported
H4	POU PI	0.522	3.514	0.212	Supported

5. DISCUSSION

The main objective of this research was to determine the statistical significance of the relationship between four independent variables: virtual presence, perceived ease of use, perceived enjoyment, and perceived usefulness toward purchase intention. Based on the results, it is possible to conclude that the measurement or scale is reliable and valid. The discriminant validity test reveals that the latent constructs PE and POU have a weak correlation. A descriptive analysis was also performed, demonstrating a statistically significant mean ranging from 3.90 to 4.47. This suggests that most respondents answered the questionnaire on a scale of 3 to 5, indicating agreement with questions about virtual presence, perceived ease of use, perceived enjoyment, perceived usefulness, and their association with the desire to purchase the product.

Although three of the four hypotheses had favorable path coefficients (> 0.100), their t-values are relatively low, as revealed by examining the path coefficients. As a result, three of the four hypotheses are dismissed. Hypothesis 1 shows that Virtual Presence has no significant relationship with purchase intention among Malaysian Generation Z e-consumers (t = 1.363, M=3.90 to 4.38). This suggests that, while e-consumers experience a sense of "virtuality" when using VTO applications, like the experience of shopping in a physical store, Gen Z e-consumers are not motivated to make a purchase. Hypothesis 2 statistical analysis shows that there is no statistically significant relationship between Perceived Ease of Use and purchase intention (t=0.155, M=3.98 to 4.39). This implies that, even if Gen Z e-consumers find the VTO application simple to use, facilitating their ability to try products, this ease of use is insufficient to entice them to make purchases.

Furthermore, Hypothesis 3 shows no statistically significant relationship between perceived enjoyment and purchase intent (t=1.009/M=4.24 to 4.47). As a result, Generation Z in Malaysia finds the VTO app enjoyable and the capabilities provided intriguing; however, they are not influenced to purchase the product. Nonetheless, hypothesis 4 shows a statistically significant relationship between perceived usefulness and purchase intention (t=3.514, M=4.19 to 4.33). This demonstrates that Generation Z is interested in purchasing a product when they perceive an application to be beneficial, such as providing comprehensive product information, saving them time, and serving as a tool for their consideration before purchasing the goods.

According to the previous analysis's findings, the Virtual Try-On (VTO) application features were deemed adequate for respondents to interact with them. However, when it comes to purchase intentions (PI), Generation Z e-consumers are more likely to do so if they perceive the application to be useful. We believe that various factors, including Generation Z's cautious approach to purchasing, contribute to this. Compared to previous age groups such as millennials and Gen Y, Generation Z, which includes people aged 18 to 24, has a diverse financial situation and frequently relies on parental support. As a result, Generation Z tends to spend less than older age groups such as millennials and Generation Y.

Furthermore, the rejection of several hypotheses (H1, H2, and H3) due to low t-values does not necessarily imply that the variables are insignificant. When a variable has a significant relationship with the outcome variable, but the sample size is small, a low t-value with a significant path coefficient may occur. In studies with small sample sizes, the t-value may not be sensitive enough to detect the true relationship. Previous research has found correlations between the four variables (Leonard et al., 2019; Kim & Forsythe, 2008; Zhang et al., 2019; Qin et al., 2021), but none have specifically targeted Generation Z e-consumers. This study adds to previous research by indicating that different age groups may have different responses.

6. CONCLUSION

This study examines the factors derived from Virtual Try-On (VTO) applications that influence Generation Z e-consumers' purchase intentions. The goal was to investigate the impact of factors like Virtual Presence (VP), Perceived Ease of Use (PEOU), Perceived Enjoyment (PE), and Perceived Usefulness (POU) on Purchase Intention (PI). The goal was to gain insight into the behavior of Gen Z e-consumers while using VTO applications, as well as their proclivity to purchase. We expanded Davis' (1989) Electronic Technology Acceptance Model (TAM) by incorporating the Virtual Presence factor from Leonard et al. (2019). According to the findings, the VTO application has a positive impact on e-consumers by providing them with a sense of ease of use, virtual presence, and enjoyment. This suggests that the VTO application effectively bridges the gap to the physical store but has little influence on purchase intent. However, in their purchasing decisions, Generation Z emphasizes the importance of perceived usefulness. Other factors, such as financial independence among some respondents or unexplored variables not considered in this study, may influence their purchase intention. This study's notable contributions include providing a new perspective among young people (Gen Z), as well as enriching the literature on technology acceptance and purchase intention. According to the study, future research should consider a larger sample size to uncover deeper correlations between variables and to broaden the geographical distribution of respondents in order to better predict purchase intention and VTO application adoption.

REFERENCES

Ai-Lim Lee, E., Wong, K. W., & Fung, C. C. (2010). How does desktop virtual reality enhance learning outcomes? A structural equation modeling approach. *Computers & Education*, *55*(4), 1424–1442. doi:10.1016/j.compedu.2010.06.006

Akdim, K., Casaló, L. V., & Flavián, C. (2022). The role of utilitarian and hedonic aspects in the continuance intention to use social mobile apps. *Journal of Retailing and Consumer Services*, *66*, 102888. doi:10.1016/j.jretconser.2021.102888

Annie Jin, S.-A., & Bolebruch, J. (1970). Virtual commerce (V-commerce) in second life: The roles of physical presence and brand-self connection. *Journal of Virtual Worlds Research*, *2*(4). Advance online publication. doi:10.4101/jvwr.v2i4.867

Azmi, A., Ibrahim, R., Abdul Ghafar, M., & Rashidi, A. (2022). Smarter real estate marketing using virtual reality to influence potential homebuyers' emotions and purchase intention. *Smart and Sustainable Built Environment*, *11*(4), 870–890. doi:10.1108/SASBE-03-2021-0056

Azmi, A., Ibrahim, R., Ghafar, M. A., & Rashidi, A. (2023). *Metaverse for Real Estate Marketing: The Impact of Virtual Reality on Satisfaction*. Perceived Enjoyment and Purchase Intention.

Ben Amor, N., & Ben Yahia, I. (2022). Investigating blockchain technology effects on online platforms transactions: Do risk aversion and technophilia matter? *Journal of Internet Commerce*, *21*(3), 271–296. doi:10.1080/15332861.2021.1961188

Bhalerao, J. V., & Gujar, R. V. (2019). Impacting factors for online shopping: A literature review. *International Journal of Innovative Science and Research Technology*, *4*(1), 444–448.

Bhattacherjee, A. (2002). Individual trust in online firms: Scale development and initial test. *Journal of Management Information Systems*, *19*(1), 211–241. doi:10.1080/07421222.2002.11045715

Billewar, S. R., Jadhav, K., Sriram, V. P., Arun, D. A., Mohd Abdul, S., Gulati, K., & Bhasin, D. N. (2021). The rise of 3D E-commerce: The online shopping gets real with virtual reality and augmented reality during COVID-19. *World Journal of Engineering*, *19*(2), 244–253. doi:10.1108/WJE-06-2021-0338

Brengman, M., Willems, K., & Van Kerrebroeck, H. (2019). Can't touch this: The impact of augmented reality versus touch and non-touch interfaces on perceived ownership. *Virtual Reality (Waltham Cross)*, *23*(3), 269–280. doi:10.1007/s10055-018-0335-6

Celik, H. (2016). The functionality of online shopping site within the customer service life cycle: a literature review. Encyclopedia of E-Commerce Development, Implementation, and Management, 791-803. doi:10.4018/978-1-4666-9787-4.ch055

Chelvarayan, A., Yi, C. X., & Fern, Y. S. (2023). Online Shopping During Covid 19 Pandemic: The Students' Perception in Malaysia. *Global Business and Management Research*, 15.

Chen, J. V., Ruangsri, S., Ha, Q. A., & Widjaja, A. E. (2022). An experimental study of consumers' impulse buying behaviour in augmented reality mobile shopping apps. *Behaviour & Information Technology*, *41*(15), 3360–3381. doi:10.1080/0144929X.2021.1987523

Chen, M. Y., & Teng, C. I. (2013). A comprehensive model of the effects of online store image on purchase intention in an e-commerce environment. *Electronic Commerce Research*, *13*(1), 1–23. doi:10.1007/s10660-013-9104-5

Cheung, C. M., & Thadani, D. R. (2012). The impact of electronic word-of-mouth communication: A literature analysis and integrative model. *Decision Support Systems*, *54*(1), 461–470. doi:10.1016/j.dss.2012.06.008

Chin, L. P., & Ahmad, Z. A. (2015). Perceived enjoyment and Malaysian consumers' intention to use a single platform e-payment. *SHS Web of Conferences, 18*, 01009. 10.1051/shsconf/20151801009

Chong, A. Y. L., Lacka, E., Boying, L., & Chan, H. K. (2018). The role of social media in enhancing guanxi and perceived effectiveness of E-commerce institutional mechanisms in online marketplace. *Information & Management*, *55*(5), 621–632. doi:10.1016/j.im.2018.01.003

Chung, N., Han, H., & Koo, C. (2015). Adoption of travel information in user-generated content on social media: The moderating effect of social presence. *Behaviour & Information Technology*, *34*(9), 902–919. doi:10.1080/0144929X.2015.1039060

Ciaramitaro, B. L. (2010, August 31). Virtual Worlds and E-Commerce. In Technologies and Applications for Building Customer Relationships. Academic Press.

Davis, F. D. (1989). Perceived usefulness, perceived ease of use, and user acceptance of Information Technology. *Management Information Systems Quarterly*, *13*(3), 319. doi:10.2307/249008

Davis, F. D., Bagozzi, R. P., & Warshaw, P. R. (1992). Extrinsic and intrinsic motivation to use computers in the workplace. *Journal of Applied Social Psychology*, *22*(14), 1111–1132. doi:10.1111/j.1559-1816.1992.tb00945.x

Eden, S., Hoyer, A. L., Niemeier, D., & Peters, L. (2021). *E-commerce*. DB Country Reports: E-commerce in Malaysia 2021.

Fiore, A. M., Jin, H. J., & Kim, J. (2005). For fun and profit: Hedonic value from image interactivity and responses toward an online store. *Psychology and Marketing*, *22*(8), 669–694. doi:10.1002/mar.20079

Gavilan, D., Avello, M., & Martinez-Navarro, G. (2018). The influence of online ratings and reviews on hotel booking consideration. *Tourism Management*, *66*, 53–61. doi:10.1016/j.tourman.2017.10.018

Gefen, D., & Straub, D. W. (2004). Consumer trust in B2C e-Commerce and the importance of social presence: Experiments in e-Products and e-Services. *Omega*, *32*(6), 407–424. doi:10.1016/j.omega.2004.01.006

Guo, G., & Elgendi, M. (2013). A new recommender system for 3D E-commerce: An EEG based approach. *Journal of Advanced Management Science*, *1*(1), 61–65. doi:10.12720/joams.1.1.61-65

Hair, J.F., Black, W.C., Babin. B.J., & Anderson. R. E. (2010). Multivariate data analysis. Prentice Hall.

Hair, J., Hult, G. T. M., Ringle, C., & Sarstedt, M. (2014). *A Primer on Partial Least Squares Structural Equation Modeling (PLS-SEM)*. SAGE Publications, Incorporated.

Hajli, M. N. (2014). A study of the impact of social media on consumers. *International Journal of Market Research*, *56*(3), 387–404. doi:10.2501/IJMR-2014-025

Hamid, A. A., Razak, F. Z., Bakar, A. A., & Abdullah, W. S. (2016). The effects of perceived usefulness and perceived ease of use on continuance intention to use E-government. *Procedia Economics and Finance*, *35*, 644–649. doi:10.1016/S2212-5671(16)00079-4

Harrigan, M., Feddema, K., Wang, S., Harrigan, P., & Diot, E. (2021). How trust leads to online purchase intention founded in perceived usefulness and peer communication. *Journal of Consumer Behaviour*, *20*(5), 1297–1312. doi:10.1002/cb.1936

Hong, I. B., & Cha, H. S. (2013). The mediating role of consumer trust in an online merchant in predicting purchase intention. *International Journal of Information Management*, *33*(6), 927–939. doi:10.1016/j.ijinfomgt.2013.08.007

Jang, Y., & Park, E. (2019). An adoption model for virtual reality games: The roles of presence and enjoyment. *Telematics and Informatics*, *42*, 101239. doi:10.1016/j.tele.2019.101239

Kang, J. Y. M., & Johnson, K. K. (2013). How does social commerce work for apparel shopping? Apparel social e-shopping with social network storefronts. *Journal of Customer Behaviour*, *12*(1), 53–72. doi:10.1362/147539213X13645550618524

Karney, T., Vize, R., & Gong, T. (2019). *Digitally Engaged Consumers: A Multi-Level Perspective of Higher Education Actors and Their Technology Readiness*. Academic Press.

Keng, C. J., Chang, W. H., Chen, C. H., & Chang, Y. Y. (2016). Mere virtual presence with product experience affects brand attitude and purchase intention. *Social Behavior and Personality*, *44*(3), 431–444. doi:10.2224/sbp.2016.44.3.431

Keng, C. J., Chen, Y. H., & Huang, Y. H. (2018). The influence of mere virtual presence with product experience and social virtual product experience on brand attitude and purchase intention: Conformity and social ties as moderators. *Corporate Management Review*, *38*(2), 57–94.

Keng, C. J., Liao, T. H., & Yang, Y. I. (2012). The effects of sequential combinations of virtual experience, direct experience, and indirect experience: The moderating roles of need for touch and product involvement. *Electronic Commerce Research*, *12*(2), 177–199. doi:10.1007/s10660-012-9093-9

Kim, D. E. (2016). Psychophysical testing of garment size variation using three-dimensional virtual try-on technology. *Textile Research Journal*, *86*(4), 365–379. doi:10.1177/0040517515591782

Kim, J., & Forsythe, S. (2008). Adoption of virtual try-on technology for Online Apparel Shopping. *Journal of Interactive Marketing*, *22*(2), 45–59. doi:10.1002/dir.20113

Kim, M., Kim, J. H., & Lennon, S. J. (2006). Online service attributes available on apparel retail web sites: An E-S-QUAL approach. *Managing Service Quality*, *16*(1), 51–77. doi:10.1108/09604520610639964

Kripesh, A. S., Prabhu, H. M., & Sriram, K. V. (2020). An empirical study on the effect of product information and perceived usefulness on purchase intention during online shopping in India. *International Journal of Business Innovation and Research*, *21*(4), 509–522. doi:10.1504/IJBIR.2020.105982

Kusyanti, A., Catherina, H. P. A., Puspitasari, D. R., & Sari, Y. A. L. (2018). Teen's social media adoption: An empirical investigation in Indonesia. *International Journal of Advanced Computer Science and Applications*, *9*(2). Advance online publication. doi:10.14569/IJACSA.2018.090252

Law, M., & Ng, M. (2016). Age and gender differences: Understanding mature online users with the online purchase intention model. *Journal of Global Scholars of Marketing Science*, *26*(3), 248–269. doi:10.1080/21639159.2016.1174540

Leonnard, L., Paramita, A. S., & Maulidiani, J. J. (2019). The effect of augmented reality shopping applications on purchase intention. *Esensi: Jurnal Bisnis Dan Manajemen*, *9*(2), 131–142. doi:10.15408/ess.v9i2.9724

Li, X., Loahavilai, P. O., & Naktnasukanjn, N. (2021, December). Predictors of online buying behavior in social commerce. In *2021 3rd International Conference on E-Business and E-commerce Engineering* (pp. 1-6). 10.1145/3510249.3510250

Lin, C. A., Crowe, J., Pierre, L., & Lee, Y. (2021). Effects of parasocial interaction with an instafamous influencer on brand attitudes and purchase intentions. *The Journal of Social Media in Society*, *10*(1), 55–78.

Lu, Y., & Smith, S. (2008). Augmented reality E-commerce: How the technology benefits people's lives. *Human-Computer Interaction*. Advance online publication. doi:10.5772/6301

Luo, Y., & Ye, Q. (2019). The effects of online reviews, perceived value, and gender on continuance intention to use international online outshopping website: An elaboration likelihood model perspective. *Journal of International Consumer Marketing*, *31*(3), 250–269. doi:10.1080/08961530.2018.1503987

Marshall, G. W., Moncrief, W. C., Rudd, J. M., & Lee, N. (2012). Revolution in sales: The impact of social media and related technology on the selling environment. *Journal of Personal Selling & Sales Management, 32*(3), 349–363. doi:10.2753/PSS0885-3134320305

Martínez-Navarro, J., Bigné, E., Guixeres, J., Alcañiz, M., & Torrecilla, C. (2019). The influence of virtual reality in e-commerce. *Journal of Business Research, 100*, 475–482. doi:10.1016/j.jbusres.2018.10.054

Merle, A., Senecal, S., & St-Onge, A. (2012). Whether and how virtual try-on influences consumer responses to an apparel web site. *International Journal of Electronic Commerce, 16*(3), 41–64. doi:10.2753/JEC1086-4415160302

Murad, Hussin, Yusof, Miserom, & Ya'acob. (2019). *A Conceptual Foundation for Smart Education Driven by Gen Z.* . doi:10.6007/IJARBSS/v9-i5/6226

Mustika, D. V., & Wahyudi, L. (2022). Does the Quality of Beauty E-commerce Impact Online Purchase Intention? The Role of Perceived Enjoyment and Perceived Trust. International Journal of Economics. *Business and Management Research, 6*(04), 199–218.

Naylor, R. W., Lamberton, C. P., & West, P. M. (2012). Beyond the "like" button: The impact of mere virtual presence on brand evaluations and purchase intentions in social media settings. *Journal of Marketing, 76*(6), 105–120. doi:10.1509/jm.11.0105

Noordin, S., Ashaari, N. S., & Wook, T. S. M. T. (2017, November). Virtual fitting room: The needs for usability and profound emotional elements. In *2017 6th International Conference on Electrical Engineering and Informatics (ICEEI)* (pp. 1-6). IEEE.

Oentario, Y., Harianto, A., & Irawati, J. (2017). Pengaruh Usefulness, Ease of Use, Risk Terhadap Intentionto Buy Onlinepatisserie Melalui Consumer Attitude Berbasis Media Sosial Di Surabaya. *Jurnal Manajemen Pemasaran, 11*(1), 26–31. doi:10.9744/pemasaran.11.1.26-31

Online shopping in Malaysia. Bargain Hunting. (2019, December 6). Retrieved January 6, 2023, from https://www.picodi.com/my/bargain-hunting/online-shopping-in-malaysia

Pachoulakis, I., & Kapetanakis, K. (2012). Augmented reality platforms for virtual fitting rooms. *The International Journal of Multimedia & Its Applications, 4*(4), 35–46. doi:10.5121/ijma.2012.4404

Patel, V., Das, K., Chatterjee, R., & Shukla, Y. (2020). Does the interface quality of mobile shopping apps affect purchase intention? An empirical study. *Australasian Marketing Journal, 28*(4), 300–309. doi:10.1016/j.ausmj.2020.08.004

Phetnoi, N., Siripipatthanakul, S., & Phayaphrom, B. (2021). Factors affecting purchase intention via online shopping sites and apps during COVID-19 in Thailand. Journal of Management in Businesss. *Health Care Education, 1*(1), 1–17.

Pizzi, G., Scarpi, D., Pichierri, M., & Vannucci, V. (2019). Virtual reality, real reactions?: Comparing consumers' perceptions and shopping orientation across physical and virtual-reality retail stores. *Computers in Human Behavior, 96*, 1–12. doi:10.1016/j.chb.2019.02.008

Primanda, R., Setyaning, A. N., Hidayat, A., & Ekasasi, S. R. (2020). The role of trust on perceived usefulness and perceived ease of use toward purchase intention among Yogyakarta's students. *INOBIS: Jurnal Inovasi Bisnis dan Manajemen Indonesia, 3*(3), 316-326.

Qin, H., Peak, D. A., & Prybutok, V. (2021). A virtual market in your pocket: How does mobile augmented reality (MAR) Influence Consumer Decision Making? *Journal of Retailing and Consumer Services, 58*,102337. doi:10.1016/j.jretconser.2020.102337

Rahmiati, R., & Yuannita, I. I. (2019). The influence of trust, perceived usefulness, perceived ease of use, and attitude on purchase intention. *Jurnal Kajian Manajemen Bisnis*, *8*(1), 27–34. doi:10.24036/jkmb.10884800

Resources, A., & Resources, A. (2022, April 7). *V-commerce is a cut above the rest –the next big thing*. Apparel Resources. Retrieved June 25, 2022, from https://apparelresources.com/technology-news/retail-tech/V-commerce-cut-rest-next- big-thing/

Sam, M., Fazli, M., & Tahir, M. N. H. (2009). Website quality and consumer online purchase intention of air ticket. *International Journal of Basic and Applied Sciences*, *9*(10), 1–8.

Septialana, M. K., & Kusumastuti, A. E. (2017). Pengaruh faktor intrinsik, faktor ekstrinsik dan sikap konsumen terhadap minat menjadi mitra laku pandai (Studi pada masyarakat kota Pekalongan, Semarang, dan Yogyakarta). *EBBANK*, *8*(2), 1–16.

Shuhaiber, A., & Mashal, I. (2019). Understanding users' acceptance of smart homes. *Technology in Society*, *58*, 101110. doi:10.1016/j.techsoc.2019.01.003

Sousa, F. P. D. (2020). *The impact of social virtual presence agents and content-based product recommendation system on on-line customer purchase intention* (Master's thesis).

Stephen, A. T., & Galak, J. (2012). The effects of traditional and social earned media on sales: A study of a microlending marketplace. *JMR, Journal of Marketing Research*, *49*(5), 624–639. doi:10.1509/jmr.09.0401

Tiwari, P., & Joshi, H. (2020). Factors influencing online purchase intention towards online shopping of Gen Z. *International Journal of Business Competition and Growth*, *7*(2), 175–187. doi:10.1504/IJBCG.2020.111944

Utami, R. T. (2021). *Generation Z Consumer Satisfaction in Online Shopping*. https://doi.org/http://dx.doi.org/10.33603/jshr.v1i1.5878

Venkatesh, V., & Davis, F. D. (2000). A theoretical extension of the technology acceptance model: Four longitudinal field studies. *Management Science*, *46*(2), 186–204. doi:10.1287/mnsc.46.2.186.11926

Ventre, I., & Kolbe, D. (2020). The impact of perceived usefulness of online reviews, trust and perceived risk on online purchase intention in emerging markets: A Mexican perspective. *Journal of International Consumer Marketing*, *32*(4), 287–299. doi:10.1080/08961530.2020.1712293

Wicaksono, A., & Maharani, A. (2020). The effect of perceived usefulness and perceived ease of use on the technology acceptance model to use online travel agency. *Journal of Business and Management Review*, *1*(5), 313–328. doi:10.47153/jbmr15.502020

Xiao, M., Wang, R., & Chan-Olmsted, S. (2018, July 3). Factors affecting YouTube influencer marketing credibility: A heuristic-systematic model. *Journal of Media Business Studies, 15*(3), 188–213. doi: 10.1080/16522354.2018.1501146

Yu, U. J., & Damhorst, M. L. (2015). Body satisfaction as antecedent to virtual product experience in an online apparel shopping context. *Clothing & Textiles Research Journal, 33*(1), 3–18. doi:10.1177/0887302X14556150

Zhang, T., Wang, W. Y., Cao, L., & Wang, Y. (2019). The role of Virtual Try-on technology in online purchase decision from consumers' aspect. *Internet Research, 29*(3), 529–551. doi:10.1108/IntR-12-2017-0540

Zuelseptia, S., Rahmiati, R., & Engriani, Y. (2018, July). The Influence of Perceived Risk and Perceived Ease of Use on Consumer's Attitude and Online Purchase Intention. In *First Padang International Conference On Economics Education, Economics, Business and Management, Accounting and Entrepreneurship (PICEEBA 2018)* (pp. 550-556). Atlantis Press.

KEY TERMS AND DEFINITIONS

Perceived Ease of Use (PEOU): A user's belief that using a particular system or technology will be free of effort. In this study, it relates to how effortlessly consumers can navigate and interact with the Virtual Try-On (VTO) application.

Perceived Enjoyment (PE): The extent to which the act of using a technology is perceived to be enjoyable, aside from any performance outcomes that may be anticipated. This term in the research refers to the fun or pleasure derived from using the VTO application.

Perceived Usefulness (POU): The degree to which a person believes that using a particular system or technology will enhance their job performance or shopping experience. In the context of this research, it is the consumer's belief that the VTO application will improve their online shopping experience.

Purchase Intention (PI): The likelihood that a consumer will plan to buy a product or service. In this study, it is the measure of the probability that Gen Z consumers will purchase products after using the VTO application.

Technology Acceptance Model (TAM): A theoretical model that explains how users come to accept and use a technology. It suggests that perceived usefulness and perceived ease of use predict users' intention to use a technology, which in turn, predicts actual usage.

Virtual Presence (VP): The sense of being in a virtual environment, often using Virtual Reality (VR) or Augmented Reality (AR) technologies. In the context of e-commerce, it refers to the consumer's perception of being present in a 3D shopping environment.

Virtual Try-On (VTO) Application: A software application that allows users to virtually try on products, such as clothing or footwear, using AR or VR technologies. In this research, the VTO application Wanna Kicks is used to study its impact on the purchase intentions of Gen Z consumers.

Chapter 13
Exploring Contemporary Green Marketing Theories:
Insights From the Research

Ashish Ashok Uikey
https://orcid.org/0000-0002-8905-2717
Symbiosis International University (Deemed), India

ABSTRACT

This chapter offers an in-depth exploration and analysis of various theories underpinning green marketing research to understand and predict consumer behavior towards environmentally friendly products and services. The discussion navigates through diverse theoretical frameworks like the theory of planned behavior, theory of reasoned action, attitude-behavior-context theory, value-belief-norm theory, etc. While these theories offer valuable perspectives, they also exhibit limitations in predicting and comprehensively explaining green consumer actions. To bridge these gaps, future research directions propose integrating theories; accounting for cultural, social, and economic influences; exploring emerging technological advancements to refine green marketing strategies. The integration and exploration of these theories offer a robust foundation for businesses to develop effective strategies aligning with diverse consumer motivations and contexts, fostering sustainable consumption patterns for a greener future.

1. INTRODUCTION

Sustainability holds significant societal importance, as an increasing number of consumers are becoming mindful and inquisitive about their choices and how these choices affect the environment (Sharma et al., 2022). With the escalation of global environmental concerns, there's a noticeable uptick in public consciousness regarding environmental preservation and sustainability (Gilal et al., 2020). The idea of green consumption is gaining momentum (Fan et al., 2022), making the shift towards sustainable development a paramount goal for businesses (Ghosh, 2019). More companies are embracing green marketing strategies to offer eco-friendly goods and services (Gelderman et al., 2021). The primary focus of

DOI: 10.4018/979-8-3693-3049-4.ch013

green marketing lies in meeting needs of environmentally conscious consumers through the provision of eco-friendly products (Liu et al., 2012). Many businesses have acknowledged the significance of green marketing and the crucial role of environmentally friendly strategies in meeting customer demands and fostering competitiveness among companies (Schubert et al., 2010). As more consumers express concerns about environmental harm caused by certain products, the concept of green marketing, encompassing eco-friendly products, pricing, distribution, and advertising, has emerged as a vital solution to address these worries and cater to the growing demand for sustainable purchases. Companies are now actively pursuing strategies such as eliminating hazardous materials from production, minimizing waste, and leveraging eco-friendly channels and promotions to offer competitive prices, all integral aspects of green marketing (Rivas et al., 2022). Even service industries are adopting innovative measures to cut down on energy consumption (Sohail, 2017).

This article is an extensive resource tailored for researchers studying the intersection of green marketing and consumer behavior within eco-conscious markets. Its primary goal is to meticulously outline and analyze the array of theories applied in green marketing research. By doing so, it aims to shed light on how these theoretical frameworks not only contribute to understanding consumer behavior, but also play a pivotal role in crafting effective marketing strategies and fostering sustainable consumption patterns. The core aim of this article is to serve as a compass, offering researchers a comprehensive understanding of the theories underpinning green marketing research. This understanding acts as a robust foundation, empowering researchers to explore and grasp the intricate nuances of consumer behavior in the realm of environmentally sustainable products and services. By exploring these theoretical foundations, scholars can gain profound insights into the catalysts, hurdles, and influential factors steering consumers' choices within green markets.

2. DEFINING GREEN MARKETING

Defining Green Marketing involves integrating fundamental marketing aspects like price and promotion with the primary aim of lessening environmental impact (Oyewole, 2001). It's important to note that this approach doesn't necessarily advocate for reduced consumption. Instead, its objective lies in encouraging consumers to buy eco-friendly products and services (Hartmann & Apaolaza Ibáñez, 2006; Leonidou et al., 2013). The concept initially known as "ecological marketing" emerged in 1976, defined by Hennion and Kinnear as encompassing marketing activities contributing to environmental issues and offering potential solutions (Dangelico & Vocalelli, 2017). Over time, various definitions surfaced. Fuller (1999) expanded on the notion, highlighting that green marketing not only prioritizes environmental friendliness but also involves strategic planning, execution, and oversight. This encompasses pricing, promotion, and distribution of products, aiming to meet consumer needs and organizational objectives while respecting and aligning with different ecosystems (Dangelico & Vocalelli, 2017). The American Marketing Association (AMA) defined green marketing as development and promotion of products presumed to be safe for environment. This includes designing products to minimize negative environmental impacts or enhance environmental quality. It involves efforts in production, promotion, packaging, and product reclamation, all tailored to address ecological concerns (Jaworski et al., 2019).

3. THEORIES USED IN GREEN MARKETING RESEARCH

3.1 Theory of Planned Behavior (TPB)

Ajzen (1991) proposed that intention serves as the primary psychological motivator for behavior. The Theory of Planned Behavior (TPB) incorporates three key consumer traits: perceived behavioral control, attitudes, and norms (Albayrak et al., 2011). TPB merges the Theory of Reasoned Action (TRA) while emphasizing the aspect of control. For instance, the decision to adopt environmentally friendly practices, such as choosing e-bills, relies on perceived control, positive environmental attitudes, and strong subjective norms (Albayrak et al., 2011). Studies utilizing TPB have underscored cultural differences in perceived behavioral control and subjective norms (Kalafatis et al., 1999). Critics argue that TPB may not comprehensively explain environmental behavior and advocate for the Values-Beliefs-Norms model (VBN), which encompasses internal values and external norms (Eagly & Chaiken, 1993). Adjustments to TPB have been suggested, such as integrating consumer confidence in actual green impact or highlighting the significance of green issues in an individual's self-identity (Gabler et al., 2013; Shaw et al., 2000). Research like that of Tarkiainen and Sundqvist (2005) suggests that health consciousness significantly influences attitudes towards purchasing organic food, indicating potential oversimplification of green consumer behavior by TPB. To address this limitation, future studies should delve into additional factors like belief importance, habitual behaviors, self-efficacy, moral norms, and emotional beliefs when employing TPB to comprehend individual green behaviors (Conner & Armitage, 1998).

3.2 Theory of Reasoned Action (TRA)

The Theory of Reasoned Action (TRA) proposes that an individual's actions are influenced by both internal beliefs and external factors (Fishbein & Ajzen, 2011). Personal convictions and the opinions of others significantly impact how consumers approach environmentally friendly practices (Osterhus, 1997). Particularly concerning behaviors influenced by group norms, subjective norms are essential and may lead to consequences for those who don't comply (Biswas et al., 2000). When individuals decide to buy recycled or easily recyclable items, their decisions are shaped by a blend of their beliefs and the concern for negative reactions based on subjective norms (Biswas et al., 2000). Multiple studies highlight different factors affecting attitudes towards eco-conscious purchases, including environmental knowledge (Polonsky et al., 2012), cultural norms (Chan, 2001), subjective norms, and environmental concern (Smith & Paladino, 2010). Environmental norms serve as a mediator between general environmental beliefs and attitudes towards green purchasing (Gadenne et al., 2011). However, the Theory of Reasoned Action has faced criticism for inconsistently linking behavioral attitude with actual behavior (Kim & Damhorst, 1998). While it asserts a strong association between attitude and action, this doesn't always align with the connection between environmental attitude and behavior (Roberts, 1996). Some research suggests that an environmental attitude might not significantly predict the intention to make green purchases (Ramayah et al., 2010). Therefore, solely relying on TRA to explain green marketing behavior might not be adequate. Other theories, such as the Theory of Planned Behavior, which takes into account perceived behavioral control (Bandura, 1997), offer more comprehensive explanations. Numerous personal and situational factors, like the range of choices available, also play crucial roles in influencing environmentally friendly purchasing behaviors (Mainieri et al., 1997; Sheppard et al., 1988).

3.3 Attitude-Behavior-Context Theory

The ABC Theory posits that the context in which individuals find themselves plays a crucial role in connecting their attitudes to their behaviors (Peattie, 2010). Simply put, when it comes to a particular environmental concern, one's attitude towards that specific issue better predicts their behavior regarding it, rather than their general attitude towards the entire natural environment (Fielding et al., 2008). This specific link between attitude, behavior, and context isn't consistent across individuals or cultures, making it challenging for marketers and researchers to generalize results in green marketing (Zhao et al., 2014), including across different racial groups (Johnson et al., 2004). A more comprehensive classification system that considers multiple dimensions of environmental attitudes and behaviors would enhance our understanding of how individual-level green consumerism connects with the ABC framework. One model previously used was the New Environmental/Ecological Paradigm scale developed by Dunlap and Van Liere (1978), known for its multidimensional approach (Albrecht et al., 1982). However, some concerns have been raised about its accuracy in predicting specific green behaviors, potentially measuring generalized green beliefs rather than specific actions. Consequently, this scale hasn't been widely employed in recent studies (Stern et al., 1995).

3.4 Value-Belief-Norm Theory

The Values-Beliefs-Norms (VBN) theory suggests a link between personal values and beliefs, which in turn shape societal norms. In the context of green marketing, altruistic values prompt a belief that human actions have a negative impact on the environment. This belief then fosters pro-environmental norms at an individual level, influencing behavior that supports environmental conservation (Stern et al., 1993). The VBN theory sheds light on how environmental norms develop across different consumer groups, going beyond just those who are environmentally conscious (Stern et al., 1995). Studies using the VBN framework have shown that skepticism toward corporations' environmental claims reduces consumers' inclination toward green behavior (Albayrak et al., 2011). Additionally, the levels of individualism or collectivism significantly influence environmental beliefs and commitment (Cho et al., 2013).

Researchers have applied the VBN theory to understand various aspects such as energy consumption patterns (Testa et al., 2016), the gap between attitudes and actions in sustainable tourism (Juvan & Dolnicar, 2014), trends in green consumption (Nyborg et al., 2006), and global pro-environmental behavior (Oreg & Katz-Gerro, 2006). However, VBN alone may not fully account for green behavior; the Theory of Planned Behavior (TPB) might provide more accurate predictions in this regard (Kaiser et al., 2005). Instances where consumers hold in both environmentally friendly and non-green behaviors pose a challenge to the VBN theory (McDonald et al., 2012; Peattie, 1999).

3.5 Cognition–Affect–Behavior

According to the CAB model, the process of making decisions begins with cognitions, which involve personal beliefs, thoughts, perceptions, or attitudes about a specific issue or object. Next comes affect, which includes the emotions or feelings that individuals have towards that same issue or object. This process ultimately leads to behaviors, whether it involves intentions to act or actual actions (Babin & Harris, 2010; Solomon, 2011; Wan-Ling Hu & Ming-Hone Tsai, 2009). The order of these elements - cognitions, affects, and behaviors - can vary depending on the type of decision being made (Babin &

Harris, 2010; Solomon, 2011). Nguyen et al. (2019) used the C-A-B model to explore the link between green skepticism and Green Purchase Intention (GPI) while taking into account the negative effects of greenwashing. Their research showed how the increasing prevalence of greenwashing in the food industry shapes consumers' cognitive awareness. This heightened awareness raises doubts about the credibility of claims regarding green foods, ultimately impacting their intention to make green purchases.

3.6 Norm Activation Theory

Schwartz (1977) developed the Norm Activation Model (NAM) centered on altruistic behavior, emphasizing personal norms distinct from intentions. This model underscores the significance of personal norms, rooted in a sense of moral obligation, which is differentiated from mere intentions. NAM defines personal norms through an individual's awareness of the consequences associated with performing or not performing a specific behavior. This concept also includes the responsibility tied to executing a particular action (Schwartz, 1977). In the NAM model, personal norms refer to feeling a moral duty to act or refrain from certain actions (Schwartz & Howard, 1980), while awareness of consequences involves the ability to understand the outcomes of not taking these actions (De Groot & Steg, 2009). Ascribing responsibility means acknowledging that one must take responsibility for non-environmentally friendly behavior (De Groot & Steg, 2009). Personal norms play a crucial role in predicting pro-environmental intentions, as they lead individuals to feel compelled to engage in environmentally friendly behaviors once activated (Schwartz, 1977). The awareness of consequences and the acknowledgment of responsibility contribute to the formation of personal norms (Hopper & Nielsen, 1991). Conversely, if awareness of consequences and responsibility acknowledgment diminish, behavior is less likely to align with current personal norms. The NAM theory holds significant importance in the realm of social psychology when exploring altruistic behavior. It is extensively used to examine intentions and actions related to environmental conservation. Within NAM, the primary variables encompass personal norms, understanding consequences, and assigning responsibility (Schwartz, 1977). NAM has served as a pivotal theoretical framework for anticipating environmentally conscious behavior, as evidenced by its application in studies by Ebreo et al. (2003), Harland et al. (2007), Matthies et al. (2012), Steg et al. (2014), and Zhang et al. (2013).

3.7 Stimulus-Organism-Response Theory

The S-O-R model, extensively recognized in multiple studies (Russell & Mehrabian, 1974; Chang et al., 2011; Choi & Kandampully, 2019), serves as a crucial framework for understanding how people react to different triggers. This theory aims to deepen our understanding of how external factors (S) affect how consumers perceive things (O), leading to emotional responses that influence how consumers react (Siebert et al., 1963; Gambetti et al., 2012; Goi et al., 2018). Although commonly used in traditional marketing and consumer behavior studies, the S-O-R model hasn't been widely applied to environmental issues and the acceptance of environmentally friendly products (Chang et al., 2015). The limited exploration in this area might be due to the complexity of environmental stimuli, making analysis challenging (Choi & Kandampully, 2019). There's an urgent need to examine how environmental cues impact consumer involvement. The term "organism" refers to an internal process that can influence how external stimuli link to individual responses (Chang et al., 2015; Stern et al., 1999). It's a reasonable assumption that stimuli can affect consumer responses by interacting with this internal process. Uikey and Baber (2023) tested the S-O-R model in their study which tries to find out the effect of Green Transparency and Green Perceived Value on the Green Brand Loyalty.

3.8 Acquisition-Transaction Utility Theory

ATUT is a concept that helps explain why individuals choose certain products and their intentions to buy them. ATUT suggests that when people evaluate a product, they consider its overall cost, the perceived value, and the difference between the reference price (received value) and the selling price (purchase cost) as key factors (Thaler, 1983). This theory indicates that consumer behavior in purchasing is influenced by how they perceive these differences. Researchers Bei and Simpson (1995) used ATUT as a foundation to explore what drives consumers to purchase recycled products. Their study found that factors like price, perceived quality, and psychological benefits contribute to the decision to buy such products. While some studies in green marketing have referred to ATUT, very few have actively applied it. Since the research of Bei and Simpson's (1995), the landscape of green products has evolved significantly, becoming more diverse and commonplace. New product attributes, such as eco-labeling, ties to carbon footprints, and considerations of food miles, might affect a product's perceived utility compared to similar products lacking these features.

4. DISCUSSION

The study discusses the intricate landscape of green marketing theories, emphasizing their impact on consumer behavior and the promotion of environmentally conscious choices. The multifaceted discussion revolves around various theoretical frameworks such as the Theory of Planned Behavior (TPB), Theory of Reasoned Action (TRA), Attitude-Behavior-Context Theory, Value-Belief-Norm Theory (V-B-N), Cognition–Affect–Behavior, Norm Activation Theory (NAM), Stimulus-Organism-Response Theory (S-O-R) and Acquisition-Transaction Utility Theory (ATUT). Each theory provides a unique lens to comprehend and predict consumer behavior towards eco-friendly products. While TPB amalgamates psychological drivers like attitudes and norms, critics highlight its potential oversimplification of green consumer behavior. TRA, focusing on internal beliefs and external norms, faces challenges in consistent prediction of green purchase intentions. The VBN theory links values, beliefs, and norms, shedding light on how altruistic values influence environmentally friendly actions. The ABC Theory explores the intricate relationship between attitudes, behaviors, and context, emphasizing the importance of specific attitudes towards certain environmental issues. Theories like Cognition–Affect–Behavior, NAM, S-O-R and ATUT elucidate diverse aspects influencing green consumer behavior, from cognitive awareness and emotional responses to perceived utility, motivations, and internal and external influences. Each theory presents limitations and potential gaps, prompting the need for comprehensive investigations, considering additional factors like belief salience, habitual behaviors, and moral norms. The complex interplay between these theories underscores the necessity for a holistic approach in understanding and promoting sustainable consumption patterns. Further research integrating these theories could offer deeper insights into the nuanced dynamics between consumer behavior and environmental consciousness, guiding businesses towards more effective green marketing strategies that resonate with diverse consumer motivations and contexts.

5. THEORETICAL INTEGRATION AND FUTURE RESEARCH DIRECTIONS

The diverse range of theories presents opportunities for integration to create a more holistic understanding of green consumer behavior. Future research should explore the interplay between these theories and consider additional factors such as belief salience, habitual behaviors, and the influence of marketing strategies on shaping green consumerism. Investigating the impact of cultural, social, and economic factors on these theories' applicability across diverse consumer segments is imperative for developing effective green marketing strategies. The evolving nature of consumer preferences and the dynamic market landscape necessitate continual exploration and adaptation of theoretical frameworks in green marketing research. A deeper examination of emerging concepts and technological advancements, such as blockchain's role in validating sustainability claims or AI-driven personalized marketing for sustainable products, can enrich the understanding and application of theories in contemporary green marketing practices. The convergence of various theoretical perspectives in green marketing research provides a robust foundation for comprehending consumer behavior towards sustainability. Integrating these theories, alongside addressing their limitations through empirical studies, will further enhance the efficacy of green marketing strategies and contribute to fostering a more sustainable future.

6. CONCLUSION

The discourse on green marketing theories illuminates the intricate tapestry of factors shaping consumer behavior toward environmentally conscious choices. Each theory, from TPB and TRA to V-B-N, ABC, C-A-B, NAM, S-O-R and ATUT, offers a distinct viewpoint into understanding and predicting consumer responses to eco-friendly products. TPB integrates psychological elements but risks oversimplification, while TRA emphasizes beliefs and norms but struggles with consistent predictions. VBN highlights how values influence actions, while the ABC Theory emphasizes specific attitudes toward environmental issues. Theories like C-A-B, NAM, S-O-R and ATUT delve into cognitive, emotional, and motivational aspects. They all have limitations, necessitating further exploration considering factors like belief salience and habitual behaviors. The complexity inherent in these theories emphasizes the need for a holistic approach to comprehend and promote sustainable consumption patterns. Future research should aim at integrating these theories, considering cultural and economic influences, exploring emerging concepts and technologies like blockchain and AI-driven marketing, and addressing empirical gaps to refine green marketing strategies and pave the way for a more sustainable future.

REFERENCES

Ajzen, I. (1991). The theory of planned behavior. *Organizational Behavior and Human Decision Processes*, *50*(2), 179–211. doi:10.1016/0749-5978(91)90020-T

Albayrak, T., Caber, M., Moutinho, L., & Herstein, R. (2011). The Influence of Skepticism on Green Purchase Behavior. *International Journal of Business and Social Science*, *2*(13), 189–197. https://doi.org/http://ijbssnet.com/journals/Vol._2_No._13_Special_Issue_July_2011/20.pdf

Albrecht, D., Bultena, G., Hoiberg, E., & Nowak, P. (1982). Measuring environmental concern: The new environmental paradigm scale. *The Journal of Environmental Education*, *13*(3), 39–43. doi:10.1080/00958964.1982.9942647

Babin, B., & Harris, E. (2010). *CB 2*. Cengage Learning.

Bandura, A. (1997). *Self-Efficacy: The exercise of control*. Macmillan.

Bei, L.-T., & Simpson, E. M. (1995). The Determinants of Consumers' Purchase Decisions For Recycled Products: An Application of Acquisition-Transaction Utility Theory. *Advances in Consumer Research. Association for Consumer Research (U. S.)*, *22*, 257–261. https://doi.org/https://www.acrwebsite.org/volumes/7711/volumes/v22/NA%201322#:~:text=Based%20on%20Thaler's%20acquisition%2Dtransaction,buy%20this%20particular%20recycled%20product

Biswas, A., Licata, J. W., McKee, D., Pullig, C., & Daughtridge, C. (2000). The recycling cycle: An empirical examination of consumer waste recycling and recycling shopping behaviors. *Journal of Public Policy & Marketing*, *19*(1), 93–105. doi:10.1509/jppm.19.1.93.16950

Chan, R. Y. K. (2001). Determinants of Chinese consumers' green purchase behavior. *Psychology and Marketing*, *18*(4), 389–413. doi:10.1002/mar.1013

Chang, H. J., Cho, H. J., Turner, T., Gupta, M., & Watchravesringkan, K. (2015). Effects of store attributes on retail patronage behaviors. *Journal of Fashion Marketing and Management*, *19*(2), 136–153. doi:10.1108/JFMM-03-2014-0019

Chang, H.-J., Eckman, M., & Yan, R.-N. (2011). Application of the Stimulus-Organism-Response model to the retail environment: The role of hedonic motivation in impulse buying behavior. *International Review of Retail, Distribution and Consumer Research*, *21*(3), 233–249. doi:10.1080/09593969.2011.578798

Cho, Y.-N., Thyroff, A., Rapert, M. I., Park, S.-Y., & Lee, H. J. (2013). To be or not to be green: Exploring individualism and collectivism as antecedents of environmental behavior. *Journal of Business Research*, *66*(8), 1052–1059. doi:10.1016/j.jbusres.2012.08.020

Choi, H., & Kandampully, J. (2019). The effect of atmosphere on customer engagement in upscale hotels: An application of S-O-R paradigm. *International Journal of Hospitality Management*, *77*, 40–50. doi:10.1016/j.ijhm.2018.06.012

Conner, M., & Armitage, C. J. (1998). Extending the Theory of Planned Behavior: A review and avenues for further research. *Journal of Applied Social Psychology*, *28*(15), 1429–1464. doi:10.1111/j.1559-1816.1998.tb01685.x

Dangelico, R. M., & Vocalelli, D. (2017). "Green Marketing": An analysis of definitions, strategy steps, and tools through a systematic review of the literature. *Journal of Cleaner Production*, *165*, 1263–1279. doi:10.1016/j.jclepro.2017.07.184

De Groot, J. I. M., & Steg, L. (2009). Morality and prosocial behavior: The role of awareness, responsibility, and norms in the norm activation model. *The Journal of Social Psychology*, *149*(4), 425–449. doi:10.3200/SOCP.149.4.425-449 PMID:19702104

Dunlap, R. E., & Van Liere, K. D. (1978). The "new environmental paradigm.". *The Journal of Environmental Education, 9*(4), 10–19. doi:10.1080/00958964.1978.10801875

Eagly, A. H., & Chaiken, S. (1993). *The Psychology of Attitudes*. Cengage Learning.

Ebreo, A., Vining, J., & Cristancho, S. (2003). Responsibility for environmental problems and the consequences of waste reduction: A test of the norm-activation model. *Journal of Environmental Systems, 29*(3), 219–244. doi:10.2190/EQGD-2DAA-KAAJ-W1DC

Fan, M., Khalique, A., Qalati, S. A., Gillal, F. G., & Gillal, R. G. (2022). Antecedents of sustainable e-waste disposal behavior: The moderating role of gender. *Environmental Science and Pollution Research International, 29*(14), 20878–20891. doi:10.1007/s11356-021-17275-y PMID:34741741

Fielding, K. S., McDonald, R., & Louis, W. R. (2008). Theory of planned behaviour, identity and intentions to engage in environmental activism. *Journal of Environmental Psychology, 28*(4), 318–326. doi:10.1016/j.jenvp.2008.03.003

Fishbein, M., & Ajzen, I. (2011). *Predicting and changing behavior: The reasoned action approach*. Psychology Press. doi:10.4324/9780203838020

Fuller, D. A. (1999). *Sustainable marketing*. SAGE.

Gabler, C. B., Butler, T. D., & Adams, F. G. (2013). The environmental belief-behaviour gap: Exploring barriers to green consumerism. *Journal of Customer Behaviour, 12*(2), 159–176. doi:10.1362/147539213X13832198548292

Gadenne, D., Sharma, B., Kerr, D., & Smith, T. (2011). The influence of consumers' environmental beliefs and attitudes on energy saving behaviours. *Energy Policy, 39*(12), 7684–7694. doi:10.1016/j.enpol.2011.09.002

Gambetti, R. C., Graffigna, G., & Biraghi, S. (2012). The grounded theory approach to consumer-brand engagement: The practitioner's standpoint. *International Journal of Market Research, 54*(5), 659–687. doi:10.2501/IJMR-54-5-659-687

Gelderman, C. J., Schijns, J., Lambrechts, W., & Vijgen, S. (2021). Green marketing as an environmental practice: The impact on green satisfaction and green loyalty in a business-to-business context. *Business Strategy and the Environment, 30*(4), 2061–2076. doi:10.1002/bse.2732

Ghosh, M. (2019). Determinants of green procurement implementation and its impact on firm performance. *Journal of Manufacturing Technology Management, 30*(2), 462–482. doi:10.1108/JMTM-06-2018-0168

Gilal, F. G., Gilal, N. G., Channa, N. A., Gilal, R. G., Gilal, R. G., & Tunio, M. N. (2020). Towards an integrated model for the transference of environmental responsibility. *Business Strategy and the Environment, 29*(6), 2614–2623. doi:10.1002/bse.2524

Goi, M.-T., Kalidas, V., & Yunus, N. (2018). Mediating roles of emotion and experience in the stimulus-organism-response framework in higher education institutions. *Journal of Marketing for Higher Education, 28*(1), 90–112. doi:10.1080/08841241.2018.1425231

Harland, P., Staats, H., & Wilke, H. A. M. (2007). Situational and personality factors as direct or personal norm mediated predictors of pro-environmental behavior: Questions derived from norm-activation theory. *Basic and Applied Social Psychology*, *29*(4), 323–334. doi:10.1080/01973530701665058

Hartmann, P., & Apaolaza Ibáñez, V. (2006). Green value added. *Marketing Intelligence & Planning*, *24*(7), 673–680. doi:10.1108/02634500610711842

Hopper, J. R., & Nielsen, J. M. (1991). Recycling as altruistic behavior normative and behavioral strategies to expand participation in a community recycling program. *Environment and Behavior*, *23*(2), 195–220. doi:10.1177/0013916591232004

Jaworski, B., Lutz, R., Marshall, G. W., Price, L., & Varadarajan, R. (2019, February 22). *What is Marketing?* American Marketing Association. https://www.ama.org/the-definition-of-marketing-what-is-marketing/

Johnson, C. Y., Bowker, J. M., & Cordell, H. K. (2004). Ethnic variation in environmental belief and behavior. *Environment and Behavior*, *36*(2), 157–186. doi:10.1177/0013916503251478

Juvan, E., & Dolnicar, S. (2014). The attitude–behaviour gap in sustainable tourism. *Annals of Tourism Research*, *48*, 76–95. doi:10.1016/j.annals.2014.05.012

Kaiser, F. G., Hubner, G., & Bogner, F. X. (2005). Contrasting the theory of planned behavior with the value-belief-norm model in explaining conservation behavior1. *Journal of Applied Social Psychology*, *35*(10), 2150–2170. doi:10.1111/j.1559-1816.2005.tb02213.x

Kalafatis, S. P., Pollard, M., East, R., & Tsogas, M. H. (1999). Green marketing and Ajzen's theory of planned behaviour: A cross-market examination. *Journal of Consumer Marketing*, *16*(5), 441–460. doi:10.1108/07363769910289550

Kim, H.-S., & Damhorst, M. L. (1998). Environmental concern and apparel consumption. *Clothing & Textiles Research Journal*, *16*(3), 126–133. doi:10.1177/0887302X9801600303

Leonidou, C. N., Katsikeas, C. S., & Morgan, N. A. (2013). "Greening" the marketing mix: Do firms do it and does it pay off? *Journal of the Academy of Marketing Science*, *41*(2), 151–170. doi:10.1007/s11747-012-0317-2

Liu, S., Kasturiratne, D., & Moizer, J. (2012). A hub-and-spoke model for multi-dimensional integration of green marketing and sustainable supply chain management. *Industrial Marketing Management*, *41*(4), 581–588. doi:10.1016/j.indmarman.2012.04.005

Mainieri, T., Barnett, E. G., Valdero, T. R., Unipan, J. B., & Oskamp, S. (1997). Green buying: The influence of environmental concern on consumer behavior. *The Journal of Social Psychology*, *137*(2), 189–204. doi:10.1080/00224549709595430

Matthies, E., Selge, S., & Klöckner, C. A. (2012). The role of parental behaviour for the development of behaviour specific environmental norms – The example of recycling and re-use behaviour. *Journal of Environmental Psychology*, *32*(3), 277–284. doi:10.1016/j.jenvp.2012.04.003

McDonald, S., Oates, C. J., Alevizou, P. J., Young, C. W., & Hwang, K. (2012). Individual strategies for sustainable consumption. *Journal of Marketing Management, 28*(3–4), 445–468. doi:10.1080/0267257X.2012.658839

Nguyen, T. T. H., Yang, Z., Nguyen, N., Johnson, L. W., & Cao, T. K. (2019). Greenwash and green purchase intention: The mediating role of green skepticism. *Sustainability (Basel), 11*(9), 2653. doi:10.3390/su11092653

Nyborg, K., Howarth, R. B., & Brekke, K. A. (2006). Green consumers and public policy: On socially contingent moral motivation. *Resource and Energy Economics, 28*(4), 351–366. doi:10.1016/j.reseneeco.2006.03.001

Oreg, S., & Katz-Gerro, T. (2006). Predicting proenvironmental behavior cross-nationally. *Environment and Behavior, 38*(4), 462–483. doi:10.1177/0013916505286012

Osterhus, T. L. (1997). Pro-Social consumer influence strategies: When and how do they work? *Journal of Marketing, 61*(4), 16–29. doi:10.1177/002224299706100402

Oyewole, P. (2001). Social Costs of Environmental Justice Associated with the Practice of Green Marketing. *Journal of Business Ethics, 29*(3), 239–251. doi:10.1023/A:1026592805470

Peattie, K. (1999). Trappings versus substance in the greening of marketing planning. *Journal of Strategic Marketing, 7*(2), 131–148. doi:10.1080/096525499346486

Peattie, K. (2010). Green consumption: Behavior and norms. *Annual Review of Environment and Resources, 35*(1), 195–228. doi:10.1146/annurev-environ-032609-094328

Polonsky, M. J., Vocino, A., Grau, S. L., Garma, R., & Ferdous, A. S. (2012). The impact of general and carbon-related environmental knowledge on attitudes and behaviour of US consumers. *Journal of Marketing Management, 28*(3–4), 238–263. doi:10.1080/0267257X.2012.659279

Ramayah, T., Lee, J. W. C., & Mohamad, O. (2010). Green product purchase intention: Some insights from a developing country. *Resources, Conservation and Recycling, 54*(12), 1419–1427. doi:10.1016/j.resconrec.2010.06.007

Rivas, A. A., Liao, Y.-K., Vu, M.-Q., & Hung, C.-S. (2022). Toward a comprehensive model of green marketing and innovative green adoption: Application of a stimulus-organism-response model. *Sustainability (Basel), 14*(6), 3288. doi:10.3390/su14063288

Roberts, J. A. (1996). Green consumers in the 1990s: Profile and implications for advertising. *Journal of Business Research, 36*(3), 217–231. doi:10.1016/0148-2963(95)00150-6

Russell, J. A., & Mehrabian, A. (1974). Distinguishing anger and anxiety in terms of emotional response factors. *Journal of Consulting and Clinical Psychology, 42*(1), 79–83. doi:10.1037/h0035915 PMID:4814102

Schubert, F., Kandampully, J., Solnet, D., & Kralj, A. (2010). Exploring consumer perceptions of green restaurants in the US. *Tourism and Hospitality Research, 10*(4), 286–300. doi:10.1057/thr.2010.17

Schwartz, S. H. (1977). Normative influences on altruism. In Advances in Experimental Social Psychology (pp. 221–279). Elsevier. doi:10.1016/S0065-2601(08)60358-5

Schwartz, S. H., & Howard, J. A. (1980). Explanations of the moderating effect of responsibility denial on the personal norm-behavior relationship. *Social Psychology Quarterly*, *43*(4), 441. doi:10.2307/3033965

Sharma, K., Aswal, C., & Paul, J. (2023). Factors affecting green purchase behavior: A systematic literature review. *Business Strategy and the Environment*, *32*(4), 2078–2092. doi:10.1002/bse.3237

Shaw, D., Shiu, E., & Clarke, I. (2000). The contribution of ethical obligation and self-identity to the theory of planned behaviour: An exploration of ethical consumers. *Journal of Marketing Management*, *16*(8), 879–894. doi:10.1362/026725700784683672

Sheppard, B. H., Hartwick, J., & Warshaw, P. R. (1988). The theory of reasoned action: A meta-analysis of past research with recommendations for modifications and future research. *The Journal of Consumer Research*, *15*(3), 325. doi:10.1086/209170

Siebert, F., Peterson, T., & Schramm, W. (1963). *Four theories of the press: The authoritarian, libertarian, social responsibility, and Soviet Communist concepts of what the press should be and do*. University of Illinois Press. doi:10.5406/j.ctv1nhr0v

Smith, S., & Paladino, A. (2010). Eating clean and green? Investigating consumer motivations towards the purchase of organic food. *Australasian Marketing Journal*, *18*(2), 93–104. doi:10.1016/j.ausmj.2010.01.001

Sohail, M. S. (2017). Green marketing strategies: How do they influence consumer-based brand equity? *J. for Global Business Advancement*, *10*(3), 229. doi:10.1504/JGBA.2017.084607

Solomon, M. R. (2011). *Consumer behavior: Buying, having, and being*. Prentice Hall.

Steg, L., Perlaviciute, G., van der Werff, E., & Lurvink, J. (2014). The significance of hedonic values for environmentally relevant attitudes, preferences, and actions. *Environment and Behavior*, *46*(2), 163–192. doi:10.1177/0013916512454730

Stern, P., Dietz, T., Abel, T., Guagnano, G., & Kalof, L. (1999). A Value-Belief-Norm theory of support for social movements: The case of environmentalism. *Human Ecology Review*, *6*(2), 81–97.

Stern, P. C., Dietz, T., & Kalof, L. (1993). Value orientations, gender, and environmental concern. *Environment and Behavior*, *25*(5), 322–348. doi:10.1177/0013916593255002

Stern, P. C., Kalof, L., Dietz, T., & Guagnano, G. A. (1995). Values, beliefs, and proenvironmental action: Attitude formation toward emergent attitude objects1. *Journal of Applied Social Psychology*, *25*(18), 1611–1636. doi:10.1111/j.1559-1816.1995.tb02636.x

Tarkiainen, A., & Sundqvist, S. (2005). Subjective norms, attitudes and intentions of Finnish consumers in buying organic food. *British Food Journal*, *107*(11), 808–822. doi:10.1108/00070700510629760

Testa, F., Cosic, A., & Iraldo, F. (2016). Determining factors of curtailment and purchasing energy related behaviours. *Journal of Cleaner Production*, *112*, 3810–3819. doi:10.1016/j.jclepro.2015.07.134

Thaler, R. (1983). Transaction Utility Theory. *Advances in Consumer Research. Association for Consumer Research (U. S.)*, *10*, 229–232. https://doi.org/https://www.acrwebsite.org/volumes/6118/volumes/v10/NA%20-%2010

Uikey, A. A., & Baber, R. (2023). Exploring the Factors that Foster Green Brand Loyalty: The Role of Green Transparency, Green Perceived Value, Green Brand Trust and Self-Brand Connection. *Journal of Content Community and Communication*, *17*(9), 155–170. doi:10.31620/JCCC.09.23/13

Wan-Ling Hu, A., & Ming-Hone Tsai, W. (2009). An empirical study of an enjoyment-based response hierarchy model of watching MDTV on the move. *Journal of Consumer Marketing*, *26*(2), 66–77. doi:10.1108/07363760910940438

Zhang, Y., Wang, Z., & Zhou, G. (2013). Antecedents of employee electricity saving behavior in organizations: An empirical study based on norm activation model. *Energy Policy*, *62*, 1120–1127. doi:10.1016/j.enpol.2013.07.036

Zhao, H., Gao, Q., Wu, Y., Wang, Y., & Zhu, X. (2014). What affects green consumer behavior in China? A case study from Qingdao. *Journal of Cleaner Production*, *63*, 143–151. doi:10.1016/j.jclepro.2013.05.021

Chapter 14
Analyzing the Impact of Digital Fashion, Gaming, and the Metaverse on Social Presence in Digital Worlds Through a Literature Review

Tia Bilali
International Hellenic University, Greece

Evridiki Papahristou
International Hellenic University, Greece

ABSTRACT

This research explores the concept of social presence in the context of the evolving relationship between technology, fashion, and digital environments, specifically focusing on the intersections of fashion in the metaverse and fashion in gaming. The study employs a scoping literature review methodology, utilising desk research to gather and synthesise evidence. The convergence of the physical and digital realms, facilitated by technologies of metaverse and gaming, have brought a new way of social presence and more materials to support it. The methodology used is a systematic literature review with the concept based on the reality virtuality continuum and the concept of social presence, with effects on user experience, engagement, and purchase behaviour. This research provides information and attempts to deepen the meaning of the existence of digital fashion in games and metaverse through by measuring it with social presence response.

DOI: 10.4018/979-8-3693-3049-4.ch014

1. INTRODUCTION

A comprehensive, educational, user-friendly, and enjoyable shopping experience for the customer forms the cornerstone for all brands and merchants. In addition to being required, it should be comprehensive and involve a variety of functions and activities that come together to create the final product that customers see on their laptop or mobile device screens. Prior to the 2019 pandemic, retailers and brands have been utilizing internet platforms to cater to the purchasing needs of their clientele (Torok, 2020). With the projection of rise of e-commerce in the coming years, with evidence from North American market, by 2027 the sales revenue will have doubled as of that of 2023 (Statista, 2024). Even though this forecast only applies to North America, mobile commerce accounts for 65,7% of all retail e-commerce sales worldwide (Statista, 2024). It is vital to at least note that customers can now access practically any type of goods or service through their phones and through a plethora of options. Online retailers are always encouraged to develop new concepts and innovate through their channels by this allure. The present paper focuses on an industry that derives from a series of human decisions as well as a sociological idea (Kawamura, 2005). The fashion industry encompasses not only apparel but also accessories, makeup, other systems and activities, and entertainment (Kawamura, 2005); a retail industry that might profit from virtual reality in the current global economy. Improving the user experience is largely dependent on the fashion industry's usage of retail technologies. Out of the variety of aspects to be researched for enhancing user experience, this research focuses on the psychological aspect that is created during the user's navigation in digital immersive environments, such as gaming, online retail stores and the metaverse. Although the aforementioned are consisted of a multidimensional building system with different modalities and interfaces, they are all closing up to factors that become common to all of them. By synthesizing them all and finding common grounds, their digital environments conclude in using common tools and/or terms with virtual reality being one example. In fact, virtual reality (VR) is among the most intriguing options for next-generation e- commerce and may allow companies to enhance the consumer experience (Morotti et al. 2020; Park et al. 2018).

The fashion industry has undergone numerous significant instances of digital revolution. Examples include the use of 3D virtual prototyping and visualization tools to reduce resource consumption and waste generation (Papahristou & Bilalis, 2017); incorporating wearable antennas into everyday clothing (Papachristou & Anastassiu, 2022); utilizing machine learning to transform fashion design into actionable planning (Papachristou et al., 2020); and providing personalized services through VR and AR technologies (Lau & Ki, 2021; K. & Panakaje, 2022; Dwivedi et al., 2015; Virtanen et al., 2017; Sengupta, 2021; Tora Northman, 2021; Breiter & Siegfried, 2022; Guzzetti et al., 2023; Alexander, 2019; Batista da Silva Oliveira & Chimenti, 2021). Fashion brands are being pushed by numerous variables and studies to investigate new and creative ways to reach their target audience and sell or promote their products. News ways of approach though do not only reach the target audience but can also create new ones (Virtualinfocom, 2023). However, where there is progress and improvement on certain aspects of e-commerce and online retail, it is natural for less improved (older technics) to stay out of date. Social media helps fashion break free from the fashion industry by fostering the growth of "social fashion," which is technology used to promote creativity (Tarnanidis et al., 2023). Wu et al. (2019) found out that older interaction strategies increase customer's effort in completing a task that should be satisfying and entertaining. The rise of the cognitive load may have a negative effect on the shopping experience (e.g., presence, immersion, and attractiveness) (Peukert et al. 2019). Examples of strategies that are less innovative can be scrolling through navigation, depicting images and text to show a product instead of more advanced virtual environments such as immersive ones (Wu et al., 2019). Conversely, immersive environments such as games, SNS and the metaverse, have several potential benefits, especially for fashion retail (Ricci et al., 2023). Digital technologies facilitate the production of fashion by individuals and serve as a means of interacting with the industry to obtain financial and cultural capital, as has been widely underlined in the context of fashion blogging (Tarnanidis et al., 2023; Rocamora, 2018).

The aim was to organize and classify all the features for structuring the research's foundation. Thus, the virtual environment and the user were distinguished as separate entities. The virtual environment, representing virtual reality in this study, was examined based on its inherent nature. This paper revolves around the fundamental idea of a direct connection between inputs, outputs, and environments, affecting the end-user through defined processes. Through a systematic literature review guided by specific selection criteria rooted in the conceptual framework, this study seeks to explore recent research on online fashion retail, particularly focusing on the integration of VR/AR elements within immersive environments. The study aims to investigate how these advancements influence end-users and their sense of social presence, as manifested through emotional responses. Therefore, the paper aims to address the research questions below:

RQ1: How has social presence been defined previously? In what terms and within what context?
RQ2: In what aspects has social presence been previously measured?
- **2.1:** In terms of digital environment design and immersion?
- **2.2:** In terms of forms of interaction within the digital environment?
- **2.3:** In terms of consumer behavior and user experience?
- **2.4:** In terms of product distribution and perception degree?

2. CONCEPTUAL FRAMEWORK

This research began with two key definitions: digital environments and user experience, with a focus on social presence. It aims to create a model explaining how immersive environments affect the user's presence and to highlight decisions made during the interaction. Conceptual framework includes the major and most generalized aspects that open the first set search criteria in literature. One is the digital environments that include the modalities and strategies used in non-physical products. The second is the user experience factor that is being translated from a set of psychological variables which consist of the term of social presence. The current study proposes an integrative model to understand the functional mechanism by which immersive environments influence the user's social presence and proposes a set of similarities/differences between the different digital environments.

The idea of the particular study developed naturally from user perceptions of characters in gaming environments through individual desk research. Ultimately, this investigation produced the major findings that are reported here. In order to more fully capture the idea, the research expanded its focus beyond gaming settings and digital fashion products to immersive worlds. The end-user was recast in terms of user experience and consumer behavior, which shifted the focus of the study to the integration of mixed reality and its effects on the end user.

Reality and virtuality combine to form mixed reality (Kim et al., 2023; Milgram & Kishino, 1994). Milgram and Kishino (1994) established the concept of Reality-Virtuality to describe the flow from a completely physical to a purely digital environment with mixed reality situations. A variety of techniques, instruments, and ideas that are influenced by the communication between the transmitter and the recipient are used to make this shift from reality to virtuality (see Figure 1). These two parties are the user and the interface/AR/VR modality being used in this study as it stands right now. A combination of organisms and services act as a distributor between the merchandiser/brand and its market, determining the outcome that users view on their screens. The right side of the RV continuum describes a virtual environment produced by computer simulations in which the viewer observes only computer-generated data (often referred to as virtual reality). According to Yuen et al. (2011), the left side of the continuum represents the real world, where a physical scene is witnessed. On opposing ends of the RV spectrum are AR and VR. Augmented reality is situated adjacent to true reality on the continuum (Kim et al., 2023; Yuen et al., 2011).

The second key definition this paper is based on is a set of emotions, extracted from social presence. According to several studies (Kim et al., 2023; Kim, 2015; Kühn and Petzer, 2018; Morone et al., 2018), environment cues affect consumer's states such as presence and perception (Kim et al., 2023; Kim, 2015; Kuhn and Petzer, 2018; Morone et al., 2018). Eventually the states affected, influence the behaviors of the user resulting in impacting purchase behavior, digital social interaction, and perception. Hence, the influenced behavior is translated through the general presence of the user in the immersive environments, also known as social presence (Ming et al., 2021).

Figure 1. Linear graph of mixed reality: Designed by author, according to original graph

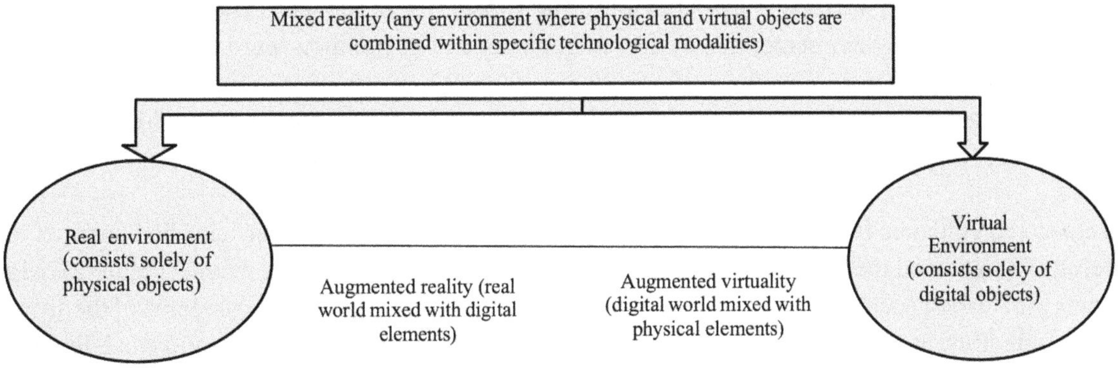

3. METHODOLOGY

The methodology used is a systematic literature review and the selection criteria for the search of articles were categorized based on the conceptual framework. The set of indicators were set according to the different elements that are integrated in the reality virtuality continuum and the s-o-r model. A comprehensive search was conducted across academic databases, more specifically, Google Scholar, Scopus, ACM, IEE, ResearchGate, Springer/ Elsevier, and with a wide selection of journals and reports. The conceptual framework set a base for the first criteria for search of terms. The Mixed reality concept specified the nature of virtual environments which were to be selected and researched on, while the concept of social presence identified preferred research results scoping impacts on user experience, identification and purchase behavior. This baseline of research created a continuous flow of thinking with a starting point the computer – human interaction and ending point the dimensions of social presence in virtual environments through a set of modalities and activities.

Set of indicators – keywords based on Reality Virtuality continuum applications:

The first set of indicators was sourced through the Reality Virtuality continuum modalities Like AR and VR applications. The integration of such medium creates immersion. Immersion can be applied in many types of environments in the virtual worlds, hence the research first started with sets of keywords 1 and 2:

S1: Virtual reality; Augmented reality; immersive environments; technology; modality; fashion retail; digital fashion; immersive virtual environments

Through S1, articles that focused on fashion retail in combination with immersive environments such as the metaverse and games, were identified and stored for research, while assisted in the sourcing of the 2nd set of keywords.

S2: metaverse; gaming environments; games; digital fashion; visual store; virtual agent; e-commerce; immersive virtual reality; virtual try-ons

Set of indicators – keywords based on computer human interaction and social presence:

In order to cover the second part of the concept of this research the indicators were within the context of the computer human interaction and emotions. The experience of the users and the impact on their purchase decisions and their perception of the environment and its products were identified through:

S3: virtual reality; digital fashion; user experience; interaction; immersive environments; social presence; emotions; purchase behavior consumer behavior; behavioral intention

Due to the guidance from the first two sets, a lot of criteria regarding the articles had been set and therefore S3 tightened the boundaries without the need to create a 4th set. The graph (Figure 2) below presents the flow for each set of indicators – keywords. S1, S2, S3, S4 assisted on the search of the articles in digital libraries, and with advanced research on specific terms, came the identification and discard of articles. During the identification process the abstracts, purpose and results of the selected articles were inserted in a spreadsheet for further assessment and final selection. The last part is the analysis, where the final selection in articles was formed in a list searching on the methodology and results respectively.

4. LITERATURE REVIEW

Social Presence Definitions Through Literature

"The degree of salience of the other person in a mediated communication and the consequent salience of their inter-personal interactions'' is what Short et al., (1976) quoted as first approach of the term social presence (Whiteside, 2015). Short, Williams and Christie between the 1960s to 70s studied the psychological state of a human being and its perceived presence in a social environment (''real'' and ''there'') with mediated communication (Whiteside, 2015; Calefato & Lanubile, 2010; Gonçalves et

al., 2023). Due to the fact that early telecommunications had just appeared (Whiteside, 2015) the term grew wider covering communication environments of the mixed reality that was developed through the years, but the presence of an individual stayed as the main stable variable in a dynamic environment. As the media of communication evolves, so does the variety of aspects that affect social presence, which lead to research that have conceptualized dimensions of social presence in a mediated communicational environment delving deeper into an individual's existence in a virtual environment (Whiteside, 2015). Rettie (2003) splits early social presence research into two very different categories: research that "refers to the perceptions, behaviors, or attitudes of the participants in a mediated interaction" and research that "focuses on social presence as a property of a medium in mediated communication." With the expansion of communication and social lives created in virtual environments as well, the sense of belonging from the physical world is transferred and translated in the virtual worlds through the scope of social presence (Howard, 2010). The research by Howard examined storyboards and storytelling techniques specifically designed to create the sense of belonging and sharing a bond between communicators (Howard, 2010).

Figure 2. Systematic literature review process (search – identification – analysis)

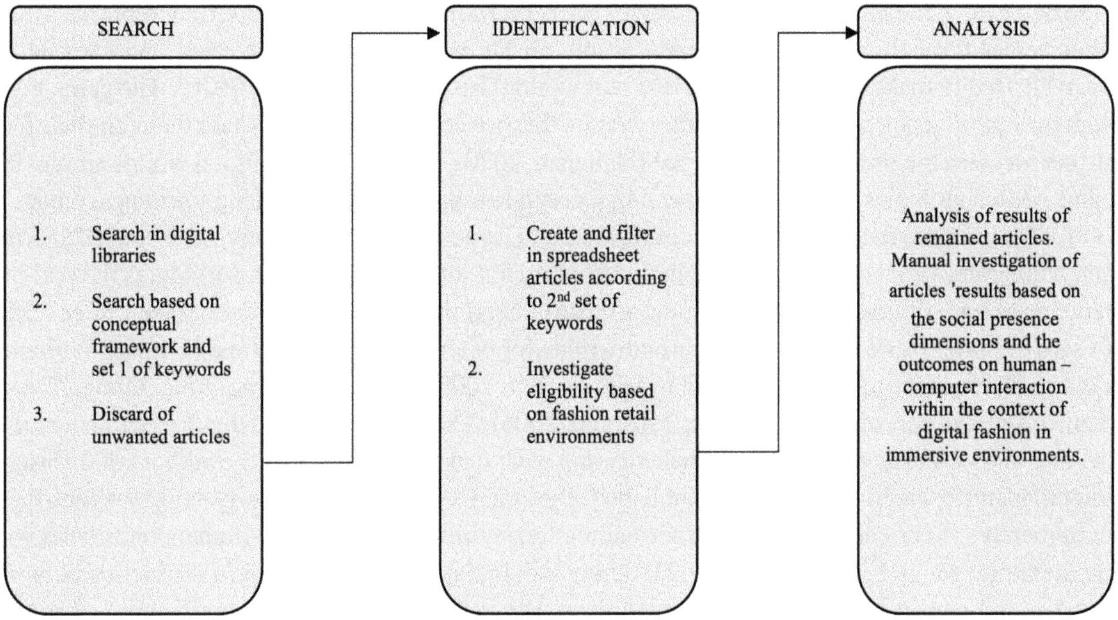
SEARCH
1. Search in digital libraries
2. Search based on conceptual framework and set 1 of keywords
3. Discard of unwanted articles
IDENTIFICATION
1. Create and filter in spreadsheet articles according to 2nd set of keywords
2. Investigate eligibility based on fashion retail environments
ANALYSIS
Analysis of results of remained articles. Manual investigation of articles 'results based on the social presence dimensions and the outcomes on human – computer interaction within the context of digital fashion in immersive environments.

Past Research on Social Presence as Multidimensional

Social presence is a mutli-dimensional designation because it is originated from a rather diverse set of researches. (Cui, Lockee & Meng, 2013). Researchers have linked social presence to important outcome and variables of online retail and promotion/ advertisement. Social presence has been defined as *"the ability of learners to project themselves socially and affectively in a community"* (Rourke, Anderson, Garrison and Archer, 2000), but also as the "measure of the feeling of belonging in a community through the eyes of the user" (Tu &McIsaac, 2002). Furthermore, social presence can be described as the *"degree to which a person is perceived as 'real person' in a mediated communication"* (Gunawardena & Zittle,

1997). Through the years and within variable context, social presence has been described in many ways making it difficult to actually measure it and define it. Social presence has been linked with sets of emotions such as satisfaction (Richardson, Maeda, Lv, and Caskurlu, 2017), individuality within a community (Garrison, 2009), and cohesion, acclimatation while having interpersonal relationships (Kreijns et al., 2004). However, even as unidimensional or multi- dimensional term, social presence is a factor that is sourced from the interaction between a human and a computer and affects directly the primer's emotions, experience and decision making bringing to the surface hedonistic and sense of presence feelings.

Immersive Environments: Definition and Characteristics

As stated in the Britannica Dictionary (2024), "immersion" refers to giving oneself entirely over to an activity or interest. Immersion virtual environments are increasingly evolving into brand-new "spaces of life" (Guitton, 2011). Scholars and researchers have investigated—and continue to investigate—the complexity of virtual worlds that are made and have a significant user base. Games have some of the most well-known immersive settings. People's lives have long been infused with interactive multimedia-based immersive game settings (Dwivedi et al., 2022). According to Lau and Ki's research from 2021, the TaoBao Life game is considered immersive. Users of TaoBao Life can build virtual representations for themselves through avatars, play games, communicate with other users' avatars, and earn points that can be used to make real purchases in the real world (Lau & Ki, 2021; You, 2020). The game gives players the option to snap images with other avatars that are actual people and share them on their feed to further increase the immersive experience (Hallanan, 2020). The goal of the digital worlds employing VR and AR technologies is to make immersion a crucial component of improving user engagement in the virtual environment and giving it a continuous feel (Jaynes et al., 2003; Dwivedi et al., 2022; Kim, 2021). Numerous social components are included in digital interactive settings, serving as the real immersive features (Guitton, 2011). According to researchers, these components are crucial in ensuring that users or players stay in the offered virtual worlds for extended periods of time (Caplan, Williams, & Yee, 2010; Ducheneaut et al., 2006; Hsu, Wen, & Wu, 2009; Williams, Ducheneaut, Xiong, Yee, & Nickell, 2006; Ducheneaut, Yee, Nickell, & Moore, 2006). Though there are many distinct factors that contribute to a virtual environment's complexity and what makes it immersive, the authors of this study attempt to identify, based on previously published research, the aspects that already exist that contribute to an immersive experience. Research on virtual reality environments and their immersion filled a void in the literature, which Kim and Choo (2023) addressed. In their study, they made a distinction between immersive and non-immersive environments (albeit VR tools are employed in both cases). A virtual environment can be created using a variety of methods, according to Mills and Noyes (1999), who define an immersive and non-immersive environment in this way. Simplifying this, a virtual reality- enabled digital environment is not fully immersive depending on factors like environment size, navigational aids, user movement responsiveness, system requirements, and perception level of the presented world (Park et al., 2018).

Immersive Environments in Fashion Retail

Over the past few years, there has been a significant increase in interest in integrating immersive environments, and the fashion sector is one of the industries at the forefront of this trend. There have been many motives that have driven the fashion industry in total, to turn into new challenges and grow inside the industry in order to keep its market share. Different factors, different situations and circumstances have built fashion's ways of contacting and engaging with its customers. The cases below were studied during the conduct of this paper and are consisted of studies from all around the world, with a main point of view on the analysis of integration of immersive environments, virtual reality, metaverse and digital fashion - with the aim to investigate their likeness and interaction with the consumer as well as the ways it affects the purchasing behavior of consumers.

Based on self- determination theory (SDT), Lau & Ki (2021) addressed the question of whether the immersive environments provided by VR fashion apps, fulfil customers' intrinsic needs. Based on the same theory, they investigated what motivates people to act while using the app TaoBao Life. Their findings showed that a consumer's intrinsic needs, when satisfied, lead to purchasing activities. By satisfying these needs in specific ways, the consumer is led to decisions for themselves and their avatar (Lau & Ki, 2021). 'The extent to which consumers feel their inherent needs for competence, autonomy, and relatedness are fulfilled is critical in motivating their behavioral intention to use VR fashion apps continuously and make in-app purchases' (Lau & Ki, 2021). In their research, they found out that when competence was satisfied with the sense of challenge and autonomy was satisfied through the freedom to personalize their own avatar (VR fashion app features), then they were more motivated to continue using VR fashion apps. Relatedness is satisfied with the sense of social presence and social support while using the VR fashion apps, but it wouldn't affect the purchasing behavior as much as autonomy and challenge (Lau & Ki, 2021). With respect to the intent of purchase, the strongest need that was fulfilled and led to being activities, was that of autonomy, meaning - in TaoBao Life - individuals dressing their own avatars (Lau & Ki, 2021).

Nowadays, fashion brands use social media to promote their products of clothing, cosmetics, accessories in the form of style, art, culture and tradition (K. & Panakaje, 2022; Dwivedi et al., 2015). Social media platforms now play a big role in spreading the word and reaching out to audiences, with whom fashion brands can keep a close touch, communicate and supply according to the customers' needs (Dwivedi et al., 2015). Instagram for example, is a social media platform belonging to the umbrella of Meta platforms, where fashion brands can be impacted on their commercial enterprise growth by the customers' capacity of likes and comments (Virtanen et al., 2017). Although there is a large possibility of addiction to simulated reality (Statista, 2022) metaverse environments offer a seamless transition from the real to the digital world with multimodal experiences and interactions. This transition brings possibilities unknown to people so far, making immersive environments growing more and more in the likes of many industries (Dick, 2021; Mystakidis, 2022), including that of fashion. Therefore, organizations are willing to adapt their business models and operational capacity according to the requirements of the metaverse (Dwivedi et al., 2022).

The metaverse channels, such as Instagram, TikTok, Facebook and other new immersive environments, will create new marketing strategies, seemingly starting with showcasing their products - if it is a fashion brand (Dwivedi et al., 2022). Sengupta (2021) mentions Nike's move in the metaverse by releasing virtual outfits and sneakers in the meta - ecosystem, making 3.1 million US dollars of sales in 7 minutes. Louis Vuitton on the other hand, known for its high - end products and luxury fashion has already engaged with metaverse and gaming environments, creating a digital game - 'Louis the Game' - in honors of its founder's birthday (Dwivedi et al., 2022; Tora Northman, 2021), making this move an 'example of digital branding exercise in the metaverse' (Harriet Lloyd- Smith, 2021). Because the metaverse presents different opportunities on how users socialize and interact with each other, it is inevitable for humans not to care and not want to be represented. This representation takes many forms either looking completely alike or not at all to the user (Dwivedi et al., 2022). Hence fashion brands with existing tangible products, are already expressing their interest in dressing virtual avatars, and brands with no tangible products (Dwivedi et al., 2022). On the other hand, The Fabricant, a fashion house of digital products, is already offering non-tangible fashion items to dress the individuals during their online presence in any form (Heng, 2022).

The channels and ways to purchase and dress oneself in immersive environments differ and many organizations have already built their own micro- economies. Roblox for example has its own digital community where users belong to and can create and distribute their creations using a simple developer toolkit which is provided by the platform (Stephens, 2023). With this move, Roblox has amassed in a short period of time millions of different games and experiences becoming its own small economy where users, gamers and creators, meet, create a community and exchange their goods (Stephens, 2023). It is not only the way that a digital product is distributed and makes the actual distribution different, but it is also the environments where it is used that make it differ as well; for example, the skins of players in League of Legends and the championship cup that Louis Vuitton designed, using the fashion house's logo but within the context of the games environment. Fashion brands have already penetrated the market of skins, marking their 'race' in them and claiming rights to representing one self's identity of their users (Reza et al., 2019). The cybernetic world is a social space, and Nakamura (2008) already examined the possibilities that users have in creating a representation of themselves according to their preferences, highlighting that 'performance— especially how people use speech and mannerisms to present their identities—is as important in cyberspace as it is in "real life.

In an attempt to make the users connect their virtual selves and match them with their real embodiment, game Fortnite and French fashion house Balenciaga, created exclusive set of apparel with some garments being the same in digital and real form, making users/ gamers dressed like their in-game virtual avatars (Breiter & Siegfried, 2022). Even though Balenciaga is a house that offers luxury products priced accordingly, in Fortnite, the digital garments of the brand had the same prices as those of non - luxurious brands (Breiter & Siegfried, 2022). On the other hand, the exploratory research by Guzzetti et al., (2023) states that there are mixed feelings that describe the perception of gamification activities coming from fashion houses, creating negative emotions, and eventually making the likeness falling in the mix of antecedents of brand hate. Through their content analysis, it was realized that many users/ gamers were against the appearance of fashion brands in games, due to the fact that the primer are targeting audiences which are sensitive and not grown enough to filter self- strengthen and contemplate a purchase (Guzzetti et al., 2023). That would be why a vast majority of users are young people, adolescents, and gamers with no real purchase power, other than that of their parents (Guzzetti et al., 2023).

However, and by moving far from the gaming industry and entering the social media world, come the virtual influencers (VI) with audiences reaching the number of millions and access from all genders, ages, and ethnicities. The companies that have developed these virtual influencers are already receiving investments of millions of dollars, with an example of Brud, the start-up that created the world's first virtual influencer, Lil Miquela (Alexander, 2019; Batista da Silva Oliveira & Chimenti, 2021). These VIs are human- like, with an AI system operating behind them. Because of their nature, the organizations that have developed them alongside the organizations that are selecting them for their advertisements (see Lil Miquela and Bella Hadid for Calvin Klein, Shudu Gram for Samsung, Imma Gram for IKEA, etc.) are making VIs interact with real models and post on their social media as a real -life person. Hence, there have been researches concerning the societal effect these influencers will have in the future (Batista da Silva Oliveira & Chimenti, 2021). In the research of Batista da Silva Oliveira and Chimenti (2021), there were 5 categories constructed through interviews, regarding the VIs, which can support the management decisions while choosing these influencers. These five categories came from interviews and interaction of the interviewees and the VIs, aiming to answer how the latter affect and drive the consumer/ user/ follower into certain interactions according to the context they are presented at. According to Batista da Silva Oliveira and Chimenti (2021) these are: attractiveness, authenticity, controllability, scalability, and anthropomorphism/ humanization. Attractiveness is related to the VIs appeal (behavioral/ physical) to followers therefore it is inherent to influence. Authenticity is about trust, reliability and transparency, factors that affect the public opinion if not followed. Controllability of the VI or the human influencer, differs between them and the organization. Although literature shows that VIs will be controlled easier than the human influencers, it is still uncertain whether other parameters such as contracts, engagement, and regulations avoid deficiencies that will harm the outcome. Finally, anthropomorphism/ humanization refers only to VIs and affects the content of the VI profile, its contacts with brands and finally its livability from the audience. However, these five technicalities can change the way advertisements are made and create new ways of promotion.

Examining the Aspects That Influence Purchase Behavior Based on Previous Studies

Due to the undeniable interaction between the end - user and the digital worlds - either with the environment or with the virtual entities included - a way to measure this interaction, and more specifically its effect in the human's behavior, is to quantify its degree.. Because the consumer is considered to be an 'intelligent, rational thinking and problem-solving organism' (Zaichkowsky, 1985; Markin & Narayana, 1975), there have been many studies concerning the idea of consumer behaviour and its types, as noted by Wright (1974), Lastovicka and Gardner (1978), and Clarke and Belk (1978), whose research was based on Zaichkowsky's findings:

Wright (1974) found out that when different varieties of media are used for the same product, the influence response was also different. Lastovicka and Gardner (1978) stated that the same product has different involvement across people, while Clarke and Belk (1978) found out that the different purchase situations of the same product, cause differences in its evaluation and in levels of involvement. However, in Zaichkowsky's attempt to create a category that would include all types of products, and affects the involvement, it was found out that personal involvement is a stable factor which can be analyzed. Laurent and Kapferer (1985) mention in their research that one product should be analyzed through all the facets of involvement. In their attempt to combine research and create a unified proposed method measuring the degree of involvement, and its types, by keeping stable the personal factor, Laurent and Kapferer (1985) measured different product in the below facets of involvement:

The product's personal meaning to the end- user (perceived importance), the decision of whether the product is purchased because of poor choice or by mistake (perceived risk), the functional or psychological risk (symbolic value given or signed by the end - user) and the pleasure it offers (hedonic value) are the facets developed and used for measuring the degree of involvement in consumer behavior (Laurent & Kapferer, 1985).

5. RESULTS

The analysis of the articles selected at the last stage of the systematic literature review is based on the scope of their research and the impact of immersive environments on social media, user experience and emotions and on purchase behavior, as shown in Table 1 below:

Table 1. Analytical presentation of all reviewed articles

Title	Year of publication	Scope of research	Impact on social presence	Impact on user experience and emotions	Impact on purchase behaviour
Connectedness, Awareness and Social Presence (Rettie, 2003)	2003	Discusses the relationship between connectedness and social presence. Connectedness is investigated to be a potentially key concept for the analysis and the development of communication technology.	Connectedness is related to social presence but not equivalent. The primer is an emotional experience that influences and is influenced by technology.	Awareness and connectedness affect overall user experience and interaction.	Not directly addressed.
Co – creation experiences: the next practice in value creation (Prahalad & Ramaswamy, 2004)	2004	Investigates the meaning of value and the process of value creation shifting their interest from product and firm to personalized consumer experiences.	Creates a sense of belonging and significantly enhances user interaction.	Delivers an emotionally rich experience that increases user attachment to the platform.	Influences positive purchasing behaviours due to enhanced emotional investments.
Augmented Reality: An Overview and Five Directions for AR in Education (Yuen et al., 2011)	2011	Reviews how augmented reality enhances user experience and learning outcomes by simulating immersive environments that increase emotional engagement and retention.	the continuing research in AR technologies, it is possible that AR will eventually lead to a complete and immersive VR (virtual reality), allowing humans to surround themselves with a convincing virtual environment in which they can interact with other humans, with computers, and with programs.	Not directly addressed.	

Table 1 continued

Title	Year of publication	Scope of research	Impact on social presence	Impact on user experience and emotions	Impact on purchase behaviour
Applied Games – In Search of a New Definition (Schmidt et al., 2015)	2015	Applying gaming experiences on environmtns other than entertainment and examining the effect on user experience and potential purchase intent.	Not directly addressed.	Focus on engaging and solving complex issues using game-like experiences. Impact on emotions is not directly addressed.	Game elements used to engage users and potentially influence behaviour.
Lost in Open Worlds: Design Patterns for Player Navigation in Virtual Reality Games (Liszio & Masuch, 2016)	2016	Evaluates most common design patterns by analysing user behaviour in gaming environments	Enhanced navigation aids impact positively social presence.	Improved user engagement and positive emotional response.	Purchase behaviour is not directly addressed.
To immerse or not? Experimenting with two virtual retail environments (Papagiannidis et al., 2017)	2017	Examines the determinants of user simulated experiences and their effect on user experience and enganement.	Builds a sense of real-time social interaction and presence in virtual meetings or events.	Improves the quality of interactions, leading to greater emotional fulfilment and user satisfaction.	Facilitates a higher inclination towards making purchases related to virtual event participation or related goods.
Sales impact of servicescape's rational stimuli: A natural experiment (Morone et al., 2018)	2018	Examines how physical elements in retail environments can simulate the effects of virtual elements by eliciting specific emotional responses that affect purchase behaviour.	Atmospheric stimuli can influence the consumer overall behaviour.	Consumers behave in certain ways according to the environment and its purposed design.	Purchase behaviour is directly affected by environmental stimuli.
Feasibility and user experience of virtual reality fashion stores (Park et al., 2018)	2018	Investigates the effectiveness of virtual reality in creating realistic fashion store environments to enhance customer experience and interaction.	VR environments improve social presence and user satisfaction.	There are positive behavioural intentions and emotions.	Enhances purchase behaviors
A personality-based emotional model for embodied conversational agents: Effects on perceived social presence and game experience of users (Sajjadi et al., 2019)	2019	Investigates the effect of the interaction with embodies conversational agents on the perceived social presence and game experience in VR social simulators.	Strengthens user presence and fosters interactions that mirror real-world social settings.	Enhances the user experience by providing sensory-rich environments that evoke strong emotional responses.	Leads to increased spending on virtual items that enhance the user's virtual lifestyle.

Table 1 continued

Title	Year of publication	Scope of research	Impact on social presence	Impact on user experience and emotions	Impact on purchase behaviour
Immersive Technologies in Retail: Practices of Augmented and Virtual Reality (Boletsis & Karahasanovic, 2020)	2020	Examines the value that immersive AR and VR technologies can bring to retailing.	AR and VR enhance customer engagement by integrating digital experiences with physical shopping.	Enhances retail experiences through immersive technologies; VR offers high immersion.	VR creates strong emotional engagement due to high immersion and influences through enhanced immersive shopping experiences
Fostering Purchase Intentions Toward Online Retailer Websites in an Emerging Market An S-O-R Perspective (Kühn & Petzer, 2018)	2020	Focuses on the impact of online environments on user engagement and purchase intentions, applying the Stimulus- Organism-Response model to explore how online features influence consumer behaviour.	Enhanced user interaction.	Improved website navigation.	Increased satisfaction and purchase intentions.
Fostering Fashion Retail Experiences Through Virtual Reality and Voice Assistants (Morotti et al., 2020)	2020	Virtual reality in fashion retail; integration of voice assistants	Enhances ease of use and enjoyment. VR applications enhance social shopping experience.	Increases comfort and appreciation.	Positively influences attitudes towards using VR for shopping.
How virtual reality affects consumer choice (Meißner et al., 2020)	2020	Application of AR and VR technologies in retail settings.	Augmented and virtual reality technologies enhance the shopping experience.	Increased user satisfaction.	Increased purchase intent.
Nike Acquired This Company That Makes Virtual Sneakers and NFTs for the Metaverse (Sengupta, 2021)	2021	Nike's acquisition of NFT company.	Enriches visitor experience and emotional connection with the site	Enhances feeling of presence and engagement	May increase sales of related products and services
Investigating the impact of shopper personality on behaviour in immersive Virtual Reality store environments (Schnack et al., 2021)	2021	Studies the ''Big Five'' personality traits: agreeableness, conscientiousness, extraversion, neuroticism and openness to experience.	Fosters deeper social bonds through shared virtual experiences.	Contributes to a heightened sense of excitement and emotional involvement.	Drives a higher rate of conversion from browsing to purchasing within the environment.
3D Tech Festival 2021: Executive summary (Alvanon, 2021)	2021	Explores digital fashion's impact on design and production, reducing resource use and on the user.	Social currency is shifting from regular social media posts to digital ownership of limited-edition virtual goods.	Enhanced user engagement through digital platforms.	The purchase decisions of the consumers are affected.

Table 1 continued

Title	Year of publication	Scope of research	Impact on social presence	Impact on user experience and emotions	Impact on purchase behaviour
A Classification of Internet Retail Stores (Spiller & Lohse, 1997)	2021	Highlights the difference of user experience and satisfaction between offline and online purchases.	Online retail presence and communication with consumer is considered more personal, or a good opportunity for decision making and profiling.	Online retail differs from offline and creates a more stable profile of the consumer enabling the retailer to enhance technical features for better user experience.	New interactive features in online shopping adds new dimensions in shopping and purchase.
Louis Vuitton's new game is better than "Fortnite" (Northman, 2021)	2021	Deployment of AR technologies in retail settings. Augmented reality's role in enhancing consumer retail experiences. The case og Louis Vuitton game *"Louis"*.	Improves shopping experience, increases engagement through the game envionemnt.	Augments the feeling of being in a real store environment, enhancing customer interactions, s, increasing engagement and emotional connection.	Positively affects purchase decisions through enhanced product visualization.
Head-hunting on the internet: Identity Tourism and Racial Passing on the Internet (Nakamura, 2002)	2022	Impact of multiplayer gaming on social interactions	Improves emotional wellbeing through engaging gameplay	Enhances sense of community and social interactions	Increases in-game purchases and subscriptions
Digital Transformation in Luxury Brands (Rangel & López, 2022)	2022	Digital strategies in luxury fashion affecting customer experiences.	The shift towards digital platforms has improved user experience.	Impacts customer retention.	Impacts purchase decisions.
Fashion's next metaverse opportunity: Turning real models into digital avatars (Schulz, 2022)	2022	Explores the development of digital avatars based on real models for use in the metaverse, focusing on both ethical considerations and practical applications.	Enhances social presence by linking virtual identities with real-life models	Enhanced social presence is positively affecting user engagement and perception.	The positive affection on engagement and perception can influence purchase decisions in digital spaces
Interrogating social presence in games with experiential vignettes (Hudson & Cairns, 2014)	2023	Explores the nature of social presence in digital games.	Increases users' feelings of connectedness and decreases social anxiety.	Leads to improved user retention through better emotional experiences.	Boosts economic engagement by enhancing the perceived value of virtual interactions and transactions.

Table 1 continued

Title	Year of publication	Scope of research	Impact on social presence	Impact on user experience and emotions	Impact on purchase behaviour
Fashion's New Ecosystem: The future of 3D, DPC and virtual try-on (Alvanon, 2023) ARTICLE 161	2023	Focuses on enhancing team-wide training and technical foundation in a virtual festival setting, impacting collaborative work and knowledge exchange across the fashion industry.	Digital entities cover social matters like diversity and inclusion in digital social spaces.	Enhanced user interactivity and positive emotions.	Digital applications in user experience enhance purchase decisions.
Immersive technologies and consumer behaviour: A systematic review of two decades of research (Ambika et al., 2023)	2023	Studies how virtual reality environments impact consumer emotions and purchasing behaviour through enhanced interactive experiences.	Social presence and social interactions can be positively and negatively affected in a digital environment.	Digital technologies allow the user to engage with the brand actively.	Purchase decisions are affected and the brand receives direct feedback enabling it to engage with the consumer.
Digital real estate in the metaverse: An empirical analysis of retail investor motivations (Ante et al., 2023)	2023	Analyses the growing trend of digital real estate within the metaverse and its influence on retail investors.	The immersive nature of the metaverse increases the perceived value of virtual properties.	The increased value is enhancing the user's emotional investment.	The increased value is driving purchase behaviours in virtual markets.
Blockchain for the metaverse: A Review (Huynh-The et al., 2023)	2023	Reviews how blockchain technology can be implemented in the metaverse to enhance security and user trust.	The integration of blockchain increases user confidence and safety, significantly improving the social presence.	Improved overall user experience within the metaverse.	Not directly addressed
Virtual Agents in Immersive Virtual Reality Environments: Impact of Humanoid Avatars and Output Modalities on Shopping Experience (Zhu et al., 2023)	2023	Examines the impact of humanoid avatars and output modalities on the shopping experience within virtual environments.	Finds that realistic avatars enhance user engagement and emotional connections.	Through the enhanced user engagement, the overall shopping satisfaction is improved.	The purchase behaviour is improved.
Exploring blockchain-based metaverses: Data collection and valuation of virtual lands using machine learning techniques (Casale-Brunet et al., 2023)	2023	Discusses the data collection and valuation of virtual lands using machine learning techniques in blockchain-based metaverses.	Demonstrates how advanced data analysis enhances user interaction with the environment.	Creates a more personalized and emotionally engaging user experience.	Not addressed direclty.
Artificial intelligence in fine arts: A systematic review of empirical research (Oksanen et al., 2023)	2023	Reviews empirical research on AI applications in the fine arts, focusing on user interaction and experience.	AI enhances the social presence in digital art galleries.	Improves user emotional response and engagement with art	Potentially influences purchasing decisions of digital art pieces.

Table 1 continued

Title	Year of publication	Scope of research	Impact on social presence	Impact on user experience and emotions	Impact on purchase behaviour
Documenting the next chapter in one of fashion's biggest, and fastest- developing, stories (Hanson, 2023)	2023	Exploration of fashion integration within metaverse platforms.	Immersive metaverse environments significantly affect social presence.	Immersive environments significantly affect emotional engagement.	Purchase behaviour is influenced.
The adoption of digital fashion as an end product: A systematic literature review of research foci and future research agenda (Chan et al., 2023)	2023	Virtual reality in fashion retail.	Enhanced through immersive shopping experiences.	Positive influence on user engagement and emotional responses	Increased willingness to make in-app purchases.
Immersive interactive technologies and virtual shopping experiences: Differences in consumer perceptions between augmented reality (AR) and virtual reality (VR) (Kim et al., 2023)	2023	Different impacts of the use of AR and VR on interactivity/ vividness, sense of presence, user experience, user attitude and behavioural intention.	Enhances user's sense of connection and presence within virtual settings.	Improves emotional engagement and overall satisfaction in the virtual environment.	Directly influences purchase decisions within the environment due to enhanced user engagement.
Why do not satisfied consumers show reuse behaviour? The context of online games (Tseng & Wang, 2013)	2023	Studies the potential factor that form the connection between satisfied consumers and reuse behaviour.	Strengthens feelings of being "there" and "real" among participants.	Increases enjoyment and reduces frustration, leading to a more pleasant user experience.	Motivates users to invest in virtual goods and services, enhancing economic activity within the platform.
Social gaming: A systematic review (Gonçalves et al., 2023)	2023	Studies gaming experiences (involving more than one person) and their effect on social elements among partakers.	Amplifies the feeling of personal interaction and reduces feelings of isolation.	Leads to higher user satisfaction and a greater emotional connection to the virtual world.	Increases user tendency to spend more time and money in virtual settings.
Developing scales for assessing metaverse characteristics (Boo & Suh, 2024)	2024	Focuses on creating reliable scales to measure various aspects of metaverse environments, including user experience and social presence.	Effective measurement tools help better understand how the metaverse impacts user emotions and social interactions, influencing overall experience and behavioural responses.	Metaverse's impact on a user's experiential value remains insignificant in the current metaverse platforms.	The experiential value affects the purchase behaviour in the metaverse.

Table 1 continued

Title	Year of publication	Scope of research	Impact on social presence	Impact on user experience and emotions	Impact on purchase behaviour
Would co-workers notice if you wore digital clothes on Zoom? (McDowell, 2024)	2024	Utilization of digital fashion in video calls like Zoom.	Digital fashion enhances user engagement during video calls by providing a unique way to express identity and enhance presence.	User engagement is enhanced through the unique way to express identity with digital fashion.	There is activity of purchased digital fashion items (accessories, clothing, make-up).
Examining the moderating effects of shopping orientation, product knowledge and involvement on the effectiveness of Virtual Reality (VR) retail environment (Zhang et al., 2024)	2024	Investigates the advantage of VR retailing as a continuous impactful factor on consumer product knowledge, shopping orientation and product involvement.	Enhances users' perception of being part of a dynamic, interactive community.	Provides a robust and emotionally engaging user experience, leading to high satisfaction rates.	Encourages more frequent and higher- value transactions in immersive marketplaces.
A Micro-foundation Perspective on Business Model Innovation in the Metaverse (Mancuso et al., 2024)	2024	Business model innovation in virtual environments like Roblox and Meta	Interactive platforms like Roblox enhance different immersive experiences from gaming to social hangouts.	VR applications create and capture value on an individual and relational level.	Potential to innovate value creation and capture in business models therefore influence user engagement and purchasing decisions.
Accessible Metaverse: A Theoretical Framework for Accessibility and Inclusion in the Metaverse (Othman et al., 2024)	2024	Examination of consumer behavior within metaverse platforms.	Enhances engagement and provides rich emotional experiences.	Strengthens social bonds and presence in digital communities.	Influences purchase ofvirtual goods and services.

6. DISCUSSION

The results of the wide range of research highlight the profound effects that immersive technologies—especially AR and VR—have on user experiences, feelings, and buying patterns in a variety of industries, such as fashion, retail, gaming, and digital surroundings. Numerous scholarly investigations underscore the advantageous consequences of immersive settings in augmenting social presence, emotional engagement, and aggregate user happiness. Park et al. (2018), for example, conducted research that shows how VR environments in fashion stores improve social presence and user pleasure, which in turn influences consumer behavior. Zhu et al. (2023) and Meißner et al. (2020) have conducted research that highlight the beneficial relationship between immersive technology and enhanced user experiences, which in turn lead to higher purchase intent and satisfaction.

Furthermore, integrating cutting-edge technologies like artificial intelligence (AI) and blockchain into immersive environments enhances user interactions, fosters trust, and improves overall user experience. Huynh-The et al. (2023) claim that integrating blockchain technology improves user safety and confidence, which boosts social presence and overall metaverse user experience. Similar to this, Oksanen et al. (2023) demonstrate how AI applications enhance social presence in digital galleries and impact user emotions, which benefits fine arts. Lau & Ki (2021) realized that the interaction of the avatars in the digital environment influenced the users' buying activities in the real world. Additionally, several studies point to the complexities of user interactions and the varying effects of immersive technologies across different user demographics and contexts, suggesting the need for more targeted research methodologies and analyses. Despite the evident benefits, there are limitations and areas for future research to consider. Many studies acknowledge the need for further investigation into the nuanced effects of immersive technologies on user behavior and perceptions.

7. LIMITATIONS AND FURTHER RESEARCH

Many of the research mainly examine the advantages of immersive technologies, allowing opportunity for investigation of any potential disadvantages or adverse consequences. Future research could look into things like virtual fatigue, ethical implication of safety and privacy matters, which is the other – negative side of the coin. Immersive settings can bring negative results and emotions to the users which is why the specific research can be decided as one sided or biased. To provide a balanced perspective on the usage of immersive environments research must leave space for the investigation of any potential disadvantages or adverse consequences. One drawback is that user-reported data may contain bias or subjectivity due to individual differences in social presence, emotional engagement, and purchasing behaviors. This is considered a limitation for many papers, as for this one, but sets the next step for more objective measures and further criteria of investig ation.

REFERENCES

Alexander, J. (2019, January 30). *Virtual creators aren't ai - but Ai is coming for them.* The Verge. https://www.theverge.com/2019/1/30/18200509/ai-virtual-creators-lil-miquela-instagram-artificial-intelligence

Alvanon, A. (2023, November 30). *New Report - Fashion's New Ecosystem: The future of 3D, DPC and Virtual Try-on.* https://alvanon.com/3d-tech-fest-2022-executive-report/

Alvanon. (2021, December 8). *3D Tech Festival 2021: Executive summary (EN/DE).* https://alvanon.com/new-report-the-3d-tech-fest-executive/

Ambika, A., Shin, H., & Jain, V. (2023). Immersive Technologies and consumer behavior: A systematic review of two decades of research. *Australian Journal of Management.* Advance online publication. doi:10.1177/03128962231181429

Ante, L., Wazinski, F.-P., & Saggu, A. (2023a). Digital Real Estate in the metaverse: An empirical analysis of retail investor motivations. *Finance Research Letters, 58*(Part A). doi:10.1016/j.frl.2023.104299

Batista da Silva Oliveira, A., & Chimenti, P. (2021). "humanized robots": A proposition of categories to understand virtual influencers. *AJIS. Australasian Journal of Information Systems*, *25*, 21–27. doi:10.3127/ajis.v25i0.3223

Bin Kim, W., & Jung Choo, H. (2023). How virtual reality shopping experience enhances consumer creativity: The mediating role of perceptual curiosity. *Journal of Business Research*, *154*(C), 113378. doi:10.1016/j.jbusres.2022.113378

Boletsis, C., & Karahasanovic, A. (2020). Immersive Technologies in Retail: Practices of Augmented and Virtual Reality. In *Proceedings of the 4th International Conference on Computer- Human Interaction Research and Applications (CHIRA 2020)* (pp. 281-290). SCITEPRESS – Science and Technology Publications, Lda. 10.5220/0010181702810290

Boo, C., & Suh, A. (2024). Developing scales for assessing metaverse characteristics and testing their utility. *Computers in Human Behavior Reports*, *13*, 100366. doi:10.1016/j.chbr.2023.100366

Breiter, D. and Siegfried, P. (2022). The Metaverse: Exploring consumer's expectations, their attitudes, and it's meaning to the fashion industry. *Tekstilna industrija*, *70*(2), 51–60. doi:10.5937/tekstind2202051B

Brunet, S. C., Mattavelli, M., & Chiariglione, L. (2023). Exploring the data of blockchain-based metaverses. In *2023 IEEE International Conference on Metaverse Computing, Networking and Applications (MetaCom)*. IEEE. 10.1109/MetaCom57706.2023.00031

Calefato, F., & Lanubile, F. (2010). Communication Media Selection for Remote Interaction of Ad Hoc Groups. *Advances in Computers*, *78*, 271–313. doi:10.1016/S0065-2458(10)78006-2

Caplan, S. E., & High, A. C. (2012). Online Social Interaction, Psychosocial Well-Being, and Problematic Internet Use. *Internet Addiction*, *1*, 35–53. doi:10.1002/9781118013991.ch3

Chevalier, S. (2024, February 6). *Global retail e-commerce sales 2014-2027*. Statista. https://www.statista.com/statistics/379046/worldwide-retail-e-commerce-sales/

Clarke, K., & Belk, R. W. (1979). The Effects of Product Involvement and Task Definition on Anticipated Consumer Effort. *Advances in Consumer Research*, *6*(1), 313–318. Available at: https://core.ac.uk/reader/4835200

Coppola, D. (2024). *Mobile retail e-commerce sales in the United States from 2019 to 2027*. Statista. Available at: https://www.statista.com/statistics/249855/mobile-retail- commerce-revenue-in-the-united-states/

Cowan, K., & Ketron, S. (2019). A dual model of product involvement for effective virtual reality: The roles of imagination, co-creation, telepresence, and interactivity. *Journal of Business Research*, *100*, 483–492. doi:10.1016/j.jbusres.2018.10.063

Cui, G., Lockee, B., & Meng, C. (2012). Building Modern Online Social Presence: A review of Social Presence Theory and its instructional design implications for future trends. *Education and Information Technologies*, *18*(4), 661–685. doi:10.1007/s10639-012-9192-1

Dick, E. (2021). *Public Policy for the Metaverse: Key Takeaways from the 2021 AR/VR Policy Conference*. Information Technology and Innovation Foundation.

Ducheneaut, N., Yee, N., Nickell, E., & Moore, R. J. (2006). Alone together? *Proceedings of the SIGCHI Conference on Human Factors in Computing Systems*. 10.1145/1124772.1124834

Dwivedi, Y. K., Hughes, L., Baabdullah, A. M., Ribeiro-Navarrete, S., Giannakis, M., Al-Debei, M. M., Dennehy, D., Metri, B., Buhalis, D., Cheung, C. M. K., Conboy, K., Doyle, R., Dubey, R., Dutot, V., Felix, R., Goyal, D. P., Gustafsson, A., Hinsch, C., Jebabli, I., ... Wamba, S. F. (2022a). Metaverse beyond the hype: Multidisciplinary perspectives on emerging challenges, opportunities, and agenda for research, practice and policy. *International Journal of Information Management*, *66*, 102542. doi:10.1016/j.ijinfomgt.2022.102542

Dwivedi, Y. K., Hughes, L., Baabdullah, A. M., Ribeiro-Navarrete, S., Giannakis, M., Al-Debei, M. M., Dwivedi, Y. K., Kapoor, K. K., & Chen, H. (2015). Social media marketing and advertising. *The Marketing Review*, *15*(3), 289–309. doi:10.1362/146934715X14441363377999

Dwivedi, Y. K., Kapoor, K. K., & Chen, H. (2015). Social media marketing and advertising. *The Marketing Review*, *15*(3), 289–309. doi:10.1362/146934715X14441363377999

Gonçalves, D., Pais, P., Gerling, K., Guerreiro, T., & Rodrigues, A. (2023a). Social Gaming: A systematic review. *Computers in Human Behavior*, *147*, 107851. doi:10.1016/j.chb.2023.107851

Guitton, M. J. (2012). Living in the Hutt Space: Immersive process in the star wars role-play community of second life. *Computers in Human Behavior*, *28*(5), 1681–1691. doi:10.1016/j.chb.2012.04.006

Gunawardena, C. N., & Zittle, F. J. (1997). Social presence as a predictor of satisfaction within a computer- mediated conferencing environment. *American Journal of Distance Education*, *11*(3), 8–26. doi:10.1080/08923649709526970

Guzzetti, A., Crespi, R., & Atwal, G. (2023). Gaming and luxury brands: Love and hate. *The Journal of Business Strategy*, *45*(3), 206–213. doi:10.1108/JBS-05-2023-0086

Hallanan, L. (2020, March 17). *Alibaba uses lockdown to promote its Virtual Avatar Game*. Jing Daily. https://jingdaily.com/posts/alibaba-uses-lockdown-to-promote-its-virtual-avatar-game

Hanson, B. (2023). Documenting the next chapter in one of fashion's biggest, and fastest- developing, stories. *The Interline*. Available at: https://www.theinterline.com/2023/12/13/digital-product-creation-report-2023-available- now/

Heng, E. (2022, April 12). *Digital fashion house the Fabricant paves the way for more innovation within the metaverse*. Vogue Singapore. https://vogue.sg/the-fabricant-metaverse-funding/

Howard, H. W. (2023). The adoption of digital fashion as an end product: A systematic literature review of research foci and future research agenda. *Journal of Global Fashion Marketing*, *15*(1), 1–26. doi:10.1080/20932685.2023.2251033

Howard, T. W. (2010). *Belonging*. Design to Thrive., doi:10.1016/B978-0-12-374921-5.00006-1

Hsu, S. H., Wen, M.-H., & Wu, M.-C. (2009). Exploring user experiences as predictors of MMORPG addiction. *Computers & Education*, *53*(3), 990–999. doi:10.1016/j.compedu.2009.05.016

Hudson, M., & Cairns, P. (2014). Interrogating social presence in games with experiential vignettes. *Entertainment Computing*, *5*(2), 101–114. doi:10.1016/j.entcom.2014.01.001

Huynh-The, T., Gadekallu, T. R., Wang, W., Yenduri, G., Ranaweera, P., Pham, Q.-V., da Costa, D. B., & Liyanage, M. (2023). Blockchain for the metaverse: A Review. *Future Generation Computer Systems*, *143*, 401–419. doi:10.1016/j.future.2023.02.008

K., M., & Panakaje, N. (2022). Customer perception in relationship between social-media and purchasing behavior of fashion products. *International Journal of Case Studies in Business, IT, and Education*, 67–98. doi:10.47992/IJCSBE.2581.6942.0185

Kawamura, Y. (2014). *Fashion-ology: An introduction to fashion studies*. Bloomsbury.

Kim, J.-H., Kim, M., Park, M., & Yoo, J. (2023). Immersive Interactive Technologies and virtual shopping experiences: Differences in consumer perceptions between augmented reality (AR) and virtual reality (VR). *Telematics and Informatics*, *77*, 101936. doi:10.1016/j.tele.2022.101936

Kreijns, K., Van Acker, F., Vermeulen, M., & Van Buuren, H. (2014). Community of Inquiry: Social Presence Revisited. *E-Learning and Digital Media*, *11*(1), 5–18. doi:10.2304/elea.2014.11.1.5

Kühn, S. W., & Petzer, D. J. (2018a). Fostering purchase intentions toward online retailer websites in an emerging market: An S-O-R perspective. *Journal of Internet Commerce*, *17*(3), 255–282. doi:10.1080/15332861.2018.1463799

Lastovicka, J. L., & Joachimsthaler, E. A. (1988). Improving the detection of personality-behaviour relationships in Consumer Research. *The Journal of Consumer Research*, *14*(4), 583–587. doi:10.1086/209138

Lau, O., & Ki, C.-W. (2021). Can consumers' gamified, personalized, and engaging experiences with VR fashion apps increase in-app purchase intention by fulfilling needs? *Fashion and Textiles*, *8*(1), 36. Advance online publication. doi:10.1186/s40691-021-00270-9

Laurent, G., & Kapferer, J.-N. (1985). Measuring consumer involvement profiles. *JMR, Journal of Marketing Research*, *22*(1), 41–53. doi:10.1177/002224378502200104

Liszio, S., & Masuch, M. (2016a). Lost in Open worlds. *Proceedings of the 13th International Conference on Advances in Computer Entertainment Technology*. 10.1145/3001773.3001794

Lloyd-Smith, H. (2021, August 3). *Louis Vuitton Marks 200th birthday with art video game*. https://www.wallpaper.com/art/louis-vuitton-video-game-200th-anniversary

Mancuso, I., Petruzzelli, A. M., Panniello, U., & Nespoli, C. (2024). A microfoundation perspective on business model innovation: The cases of Roblox and meta in metaverse. *IEEE Transactions on Engineering Management*, 1–14. doi:10.1109/TEM.2023.3275198

Mcdowell, M. (2024, January 9). *Would co-workers notice ifyou wore digital clothes onzoom?* Vogue Business.

Meißner, M., Pfeiffer, J., Peukert, C., Dietrich, H., & Pfeiffer, T. (2020). How virtual reality affects consumer choice. *Journal of Business Research*, *117*, 219–231. doi:10.1016/j.jbusres.2020.06.004

Milgram, P., Takemura, H., Utsumi, A., & Kishino, F. (1995). Augmented reality: a class of displays on the reality-virtuality continuum. *SPIE Proceedings*. 10.1117/12.197321

Mills, S., & Noyes, J. (1999). Virtual reality: An overview of user-related design issues. *Interacting with Computers*, *11*(4), 375–386. doi:10.1016/S0953-5438(98)00057-5

Ming, J., Jianqiu, Z., Bilal, M., Akram, U., & Fan, M. (2021). How social presence influences impulse buying behavior in live streaming commerce? the role of S-O-R theory. *International Journal of Web Information Systems*, *17*(4), 300–320. doi:10.1108/IJWIS-02-2021-0012

Morone, A., Nemore, F., & Schirone, D. A. (2018a). Sales impact of servicescape's rational stimuli: A natural experiment. *Journal of Retailing and Consumer Services*, *45*, 256–262. doi:10.1016/j.jretconser.2018.09.011

Morotti, E., Donatiello, L., & Marfia, G. (2020a). Fostering fashion retail experiences through virtual reality and voice assistants. *2020 IEEE Conference on Virtual Reality and 3D User Interfaces Abstracts and Workshops (VRW)*. 10.1109/VRW50115.2020.00074

Mystakidis, S. (2022). Metaverse. *Metaverse Encyclopedia*, *2*(1), 486–497. doi:10.3390/encyclopedia2010031

Nakamura, L. (2008). *Digitizing race: Visual cultures of the internet*. University of Minnesota.

Narayana, C. L., & Markin, R. J. (1975). Consumer behaviour and product performance: An alternative conceptualization. *Journal of Marketing*, *39*(4), 1–6. doi:10.1177/002224297503900401

Nezami, K., & Suen, C. Y. (2023). An unbiased artificial referee in beauty contests based on pattern recognition and ai. *Computers in Human Behavior: Artificial Humans*, *1*(2), 100025. doi:10.1016/j.chbah.2023.100025

Northman, T. (2021, August 11). *Louis Vuitton's new game is better than "fortnite."* Highsnobiety. https://www.highsnobiety.com/p/louis-vuitton-nft-game/

Oksanen, A., Cvetkovic, A., Akin, N., Latikka, R., Bergdahl, J., Chen, Y., & Savela, N. (2023). Artificial Intelligence in fine arts: A systematic review of Empirical Research. *Computers in Human Behavior: Artificial Humans*, *1*(2), 100004. doi:10.1016/j.chbah.2023.100004

Othman, A., Chemnad, K., Hassanien, A. E., Tlili, A., Zhang, C. Y., Al-Thani, D., Altınay, F., Chalghoumi, H. S., Al-Khalifa, H., Obeid, M., Jemni, M., Al-Hadhrami, T., & Altınay, Z. (2024). Accessible metaverse: A theoretical framework for accessibility and inclusion in the metaverse. *Multimodal Technologies and Interaction*, *8*(3), 21–38. doi:10.3390/mti8030021

Papachristou, E., & Anastassiu, H. T. (2022). Application of 3D Virtual Prototyping Technology to the Integration of Wearable Antennas into Fashion Garments. *Technologies*, *10*(3), 62. doi:10.3390/technologies10030062

Papagiannidis, S., Pantano, E., See-To, E. W. K., Dennis, C., & Bourlakis, M. (2017). To immerse or not? experimenting with two virtual retail environments. Information Technology &amp. *Information Technology & People*, *30*(1), 163–188. doi:10.1108/ITP-03-2015-0069

Papahristou, E., & Bilalis, N. (2017). Should the fashion industry confront the sustainability challenge with 3D prototyping technology. *International Journal of Sustainable Engineering*, *10*(4–5), 207–214. doi:10.1080/19397038.2017.1348563

Park, M., Im, H., & Kim, D. Y. (2018). Feasibility and user experience of virtual reality fashion stores. *Fashion and Textiles*, *5*(1), 32. Advance online publication. doi:10.1186/s40691-018-0149-x

Peukert, C., Pfeiffer, J., Meißner, M., Pfeiffer, T., & Weinhardt, C. (2019). Shopping in virtual reality stores: The influence of immersion on system adoption. *Journal of Management Information Systems*, *36*(3), 755–788. doi:10.1080/07421222.2019.1628889

Prahalad, C. K., & Ramaswamy, V. (2004). Co-creation experiences: The next practice in value creation. *Journal of Interactive Marketing*, *18*(3), 5–14. doi:10.1002/dir.20015

Rangel, C., & López, B. (2022). Digital transformation in luxury brands. Sustainable International Business Models in a Digitally Transforming World, 222–239. doi:10.4324/9781003195986-17

Rettie, R. (2003) Connectedness, awareness and social presence. *6th Annual International Workshop on Presence.*

Reza, A., Chu, S., Khan, Z., Nedd, A., Castillo, A., & Gardner, D. (2019). *Skins for sale: Linking player identity, representation, and purchasing practices.* Information in Contemporary Society. doi:10.1007/978-3-030-15742-5_11

Ricci, M., Evangelista, A., Di Roma, A., & Fiorentino, M. (2023). Immersive and desktop virtual reality in Virtual Fashion Stores: A comparison between shopping experiences. *Virtual Reality (Waltham Cross)*, *27*(3), 2281–2296. doi:10.1007/s10055-023-00806-y PMID:37360805

Richardson, J. C., Maeda, Y., Lv, J., & Caskurlu, S. (2017). Social presence in relation to students' satisfaction and learning in the online environment: A meta-analysis. *Computers in Human Behavior*, *71*, 402–417. doi:10.1016/j.chb.2017.02.001

Rocamora, A. (2018). The Labour of Fashion Blogging. In L. Armstrong & F. McDowell (Eds.), *Fashioning Professionals: Identity and Representation at Work in the Creative Industries* (pp. 65–81). doi:10.5040/9781350001879.ch-004

Rourke, L., Anderson, T., Garrison, D. R., & Archer, W. (2007). Assessing Social Presence In Asynchronous Text-based Computer Conferencing. *International Journal of E-Learning & Distance Education Revue Internationale Du E-Learning Et La Formation à Distance, 14*(2), 50–71. Retrieved from https://www.ijede.ca/index.php/jde/article/view/153

Sajjadi, P., Hoffmann, L., Cimiano, P., & Kopp, S. (2019). A personality-based emotional model for embodied conversational agents: Effects on perceived social presence and game experience of users. *Entertainment Computing*, *32*, 100313. doi:10.1016/j.entcom.2019.100313

Schmidt, R., Emmerich, K., & Schmidt, B. (2015). Applied games – in search of a new definition. *Entertainment Computing - ICEC 2015*, 100–111. doi:10.1007/978-3-319-24589-8_8

Schnack, A., Wright, M. J., & Elms, J. (2021). Investigating the impact of shopper personality on behaviour in immersive virtual reality store environments. *Journal of Retailing and Consumer Services*, *61*, 102581. doi:10.1016/j.jretconser.2021.102581

Schulz, M. (2022, September 7). *Fashion's next metaverse opportunity: Turning real models into digital avatars*. VOGUE Business. https://www.voguebusiness.com/technology/fashions-next- metaverse-opportunity-turning-real-models-into-digital-avatars#:~:text=Technology-

Sengupta, D. (2021, December 19). *Nike acquired this company that makes virtual sneakers and nfts for the metaverse*. Beebom. https://beebom.com/nike-acquired-company-makes-virtual- sneakers-nfts-metaverse/

Spiller, P., & Lohse, G. L. (1997). A classification of internet retail stores. *International Journal of Electronic Commerce*, *2*(2), 29–56. doi:10.1080/10864415.1997.11518307

Stephens, D. (2023, October 16). *The metaverse will radically change retail*. The Business of Fashion. https://www.businessoffashion.com/opinions/retail/the-metaverse-will-radically- change-retail/

Tarnanidis, T. K., Papachristou, E., Karypidis, M., & Ismyrlis, V. (2023). How Social Media Affects Consumer Behavior in the Fashion Industry. In *Social Media and Online Consumer Decision Making in the Fashion Industry* (pp. 324–337). IGI Global. Retrieved 2024, from https://www.igi-global.com/chapter/social-media-affects-consumer-behavior/327699

Torok, G. (2020, September 9). *Council post: Pandemic potential: Four app development trends in a post-covid-19 world*. Forbes. https://www.forbes.com/sites/forbestechcouncil/2020/09/10/pandemic-potential-four-app- development-trends-in-a-post-covid-19-world/

Tseng, F.-M., & Wang, C.-Y. (2013). Why do not satisfied consumers show reuse behavior? the context of online games. *Computers in Human Behavior*, *29*(3), 1012–1022. doi:10.1016/j.chb.2012.12.011

Tu, C.-H., & McIsaac, M. (2002). The relationship of social presence and interaction in online classes. *American Journal of Distance Education*, *16*(3), 131–150. doi:10.1207/S15389286AJDE1603_2

Virtanen, H., Björk, P., & Sjöström, E. (2017). Follow for follow: Marketing of a start-up company on Instagram. *Journal of Small Business and Enterprise Development*, *24*(3), 468–484. doi:10.1108/JSBED-12-2016-0202

Virtualinfocom, V. (2023b, May 14). *Unlocking new fashion frontiers: How to market garments through games*. LinkedIn. https://www.linkedin.com/pulse/unlocking-new-fashion-frontiers- how-market-garments-through/

Whiteside, A. L., & Dikkers, A. G. (2016). *Leveraging the social presence model*. Emotions, Technology, and Learning. doi:10.1016/B978-0-12-800649-8.00013-4

Wright, P. L. (1973). The cognitive processes mediating acceptance of advertising. *JMR, Journal of Marketing Research*, *10*(1), 53–62. doi:10.1177/002224377301000108

Wu, H., Luo, W., Pan, N., Nan, S., Deng, Y., Fu, S., & Yang, L. (2019). Understanding freehand gestures: A study of freehand gestural interaction for immersive VR shopping applications. *Human-Centric Computing and Information Sciences*, *9*(1), 43. Advance online publication. doi:10.1186/s13673-019-0204-7

Yuen, S. C.-Y., Yaoyuneyong, G., & Johnson, E. (2011a). Augmented reality: An overview and five directions for AR in education. *Journal of Educational Technology Development and Exchange*, *4*(1). Advance online publication. doi:10.18785/jetde.0401.10

Zaichkowsky, J. L. (1985). Measuring the involvement construct. *The Journal of Consumer Research, 12*(3), 341. doi:10.1086/208520

Zhang, X., Yang, D., Yow, C. H., Huang, L., Wu, X., Huang, X., Guo, J., Zhou, S., & Cai, Y. (2022). Metaverse for cultural heritages. *Electronics (Basel), 11*(22), 3730. doi:10.3390/electronics11223730

Zhang, Y., Shao, W., Quach, S., Thaichon, P., & Li, Q. (2024). Examining the moderating effects of shopping orientation, product knowledge and involvement on the effectiveness of virtual reality (VR) retail environment. *Journal of Retailing and Consumer Services, 78*, 103713. doi:10.1016/j.jretconser.2024.103713

Zhu, S., Hu, W., Li, W., & Dong, Y. (2023). Virtual agents in immersive virtual reality environments: Impact of humanoid avatars and output modalities on shopping experience. *International Journal of Human-Computer Interaction*, 1–23. doi:10.1080/10447318.2023.2241293

Compilation of References

3DLook. (n.d.). https://3dlook.me

Aakanksha, L., & Aravendan, M. (2023). Impacts of Transparency and Traceability on Fashion Supply Chain System. *Intelligent Information Management*, *15*(3), 100–119. doi:10.4236/iim.2023.153006

Aalto University School of Business. (2021, March 30). *Sustainable marketing in the fashion industry*. https://aaltodoc.aalto.fi/server/api/core/bitstreams/86348b6a-3b0f-46d6-8fc0-15d60eb70da6/content

Aavula, R., & Deshmukh, A. (2022). Design and Implementation of sensor and IoT based Remembrance system for closed one. *Telematique*, *21*(1), 2769–2778.

Abbate, S., Centobelli, P., Cerchione, R., Nadeem, S. P., & Riccio, E. (2023). Sustainability trends and gaps in the textile, apparel and fashion industries. *Environment, Development and Sustainability*, *26*(2), 2837–2864. Advance online publication. doi:10.1007/s10668-022-02887-2 PMID:36788931

Abrar, M., Sibtain, M. M., & Shabbir, R. (2021). Understanding purchase intention towards eco-friendly clothing for generation Y & Z. *Cogent Business & Management*, *8*(1), 1997247. doi:10.1080/23311975.2021.1997247

Adamkiewicz, J., Kochańska, E., Adamkiewicz, I., & Łukasik, R. M. (2022). Greenwashing and sustainable fashion industry. *Current Opinion in Green and Sustainable Chemistry*, *38*, 100710. doi:10.1016/j.cogsc.2022.100710

Agustini, M. H., Athanasius, S. S., & Retnawati, B. B. (2020). Identification of green marketing strategies: Perspective of a developing country. *Innovative Marketing*, *15*(4), 42–56. doi:10.21511/im.15(4).2019.04

Ahmad, W., & Zhang, Q. (2020). Green purchase intention: Effects of electronic service quality and customer green psychology. *Journal of Cleaner Production*, *267*, 122053. doi:10.1016/j.jclepro.2020.122053

Ahmed, R. R., Streimikiene, D., Qadir, H., & Streimikis, J. (2023). Effect of green marketing mix, green customer value, and attitude on green purchase intention: Evidence from the USA. *Environmental Science and Pollution Research International*, *30*(5), 11473–11495.

Ai-Lim Lee, E., Wong, K. W., & Fung, C. C. (2010). How does desktop virtual reality enhance learning outcomes? A structural equation modeling approach. *Computers & Education*, *55*(4), 1424–1442. doi:10.1016/j.compedu.2010.06.006

Ajzen, I. (1991). The theory of planned behavior. *Organizational Behavior and Human Decision Processes*, *50*(2), 179–211. doi:10.1016/0749-5978(91)90020-T

Ajzen, I., & Fishbein, M. (1977). Attitude-behaviour relations: A theoretical analysis and review of the research. *Psychological Bulletin*, *84*(5), 888–918. doi:10.1037/0033-2909.84.5.888

Ajzen, I., & Manstead, A. S. (2007). Changing health-related behaviors: An approach based on the theory of planned behavior. In M. Hewstone, H. Schut, J. De Wit, K. Van Den Bos, & M. Stroebe (Eds.), *The scope of social psychology: Theory and applications* (pp. 43–63). Psychology Press.

Akdim, K., Casaló, L. V., & Flavián, C. (2022). The role of utilitarian and hedonic aspects in the continuance intention to use social mobile apps. *Journal of Retailing and Consumer Services*, *66*, 102888. doi:10.1016/j.jretconser.2021.102888

Akter, M. M. K., Haq, U. N., Islam, M. M., & Uddin, M. A. (2022). Textile-apparel manufacturing and material waste management in the circular economy: A conceptual model to achieve sustainable development goals (SDG) 12 for Bangladesh. *Cleaner Environmental Systems, 4*. 100070.doi.org/10.1016/j.cesys.2022.100070

Alagarsamy, S., Mehrolia, S., & Mathew, S. (2021). How Green Consumption Value Affects Green Consumer Behaviour: The Mediating Role of Consumer Attitudes Towards Sustainable Food Logistics Practices. *Vision (Basel)*, *25*(1), 65–76. doi:10.1177/0972262920977986

Albayrak, T., Caber, M., Moutinho, L., & Herstein, R. (2011). The Influence of Skepticism on Green Purchase Behavior. *International Journal of Business and Social Science*, *2*(13), 189–197. https://doi.org/http://ijbssnet.com/journals/Vol._2_No._13_Special_Issue_July_2011/20.pdf

Albino, V., Balice, A., & Dangelico, R. M. (2009). Environmental strategies and green product development: An overview on sustainability-driven companies. *Business Strategy and the Environment*, *18*(2), 83–96. Advance online publication. doi:10.1002/bse.638

Albrecht, D., Bultena, G., Hoiberg, E., & Nowak, P. (1982). Measuring environmental concern: The new environmental paradigm scale. *The Journal of Environmental Education*, *13*(3), 39–43. doi:10.1080/00958964.1982.9942647

Alexa, L., Apetrei, A., & Pîslaru, M. (2022). Fast Fashion – An Industry at the Intersection of Green Marketing with Greenwashing. In Sciendo eBooks (pp. 263–268). doi:10.2478/9788366675735-042

Alexander, J. (2019, January 30). *Virtual creators aren't ai - but Ai is coming for them.* The Verge. https://www.theverge.com/2019/1/30/18200509/ai-virtual-creators-lil-miquela-instagram- artificial-intelligence

AlFarraj, O., Alalwan, A. A., Obeidat, Z. M., Baabdullah, A., Aldmour, R., & Al-Haddad, S. (2021). Examining the impact of influencers' credibility dimensions: Attractiveness, trustworthiness and expertise on the purchase intention in the aesthetic dermatology industry. *Review of International Business and Strategy*, *31*(3), 355–374. doi:10.1108/RIBS-07-2020-0089

Allchin, J. (2014, October 17). Case study: Patagonia's 'Don't buy this jacket' campaign. *Marketing Week*. https://www.marketingweek.com/case-study-patagonias-dont-buy-this-jacket-campaign/

Allport, G. W. (1961). Pattern and growth in personality. In Journal of the American Academy of Child Psychiatry. Holt, Rinehart & Winston.

Almalki, D. K., & Tawfiq, W. A. (2023). Implementation of a Sustainable Apparel Design Framework for Felted Women's Garments Made of Local Wool. *Fashion Practice*, *15*(3), 1–23. doi:10.1080/17569370.2023.2186033

Alvanon, A. (2023, November 30). *New Report - Fashion's New Ecosystem: The future of 3D, DPC and Virtual Try-on*. https://alvanon.com/3d-tech-fest-2022-executive-report/

Alvanon. (2021, December 8). *3D Tech Festival 2021: Executive summary (EN/DE)*. https://alvanon.com/new-report-the-3d-tech-fest-executive/

Ambika, A., Shin, H., & Jain, V. (2023). Immersive Technologies and consumer behavior: A systematic review of two decades of research. *Australian Journal of Management*. Advance online publication. doi:10.1177/03128962231181429

Amel, E. L., Manning, C. M., & Scott, B. A. (2009). Mindfulness and Sustainable Behavior: Pondering Attention and Awareness as Means for Increasing Green Behavior. *Ecopsychology, 1*(1), 14–25. doi:10.1089/eco.2008.0005

Amin, M. A., Eltomey, M. A., & Abdelazeem, M. A. (2014). *Diffusion weighted MRI in chronic viral hepatitis C: Correlation between apparent diffusion coefficient values and histopathological scores*. Elsevier. https://www.sciencedirect.com/science/article/pii/S0378603X14000412

Andrea, L. (2016). *How H&M Became The World's 2nd Largest Fashion Retailer*. Referralcandy.Com. https://www.referralcandy.com/blog/hm-word-of-mouth-marketing

Anisah, T. N., Andika, A., Wahyudi, D., & Harnaji, B. (2024). Fast fashion revolution: Unveiling the path to sustainable style in the era of fast fashion. *E3S Web of Conferences, 475*, 2005.

Ankit, G., & Mayur, R. (2013). *Green marketing: Impact of green advertising on consumer*. Academic Press.

Annamdevula, S., Nudurupati, S. S., Pappu, R. P., & Sinha, R. (2023). Moral obligation for recycling among youth: Extended models of the theory of planned behavior. *Young Consumers, 24*(2), 165–183. doi:10.1108/YC-05-2022-1520

Annie Jin, S.-A., & Bolebruch, J. (1970). Virtual commerce (V-commerce) in second life: The roles of physical presence and brand-self connection. *Journal of Virtual Worlds Research, 2*(4). Advance online publication. doi:10.4101/jvwr.v2i4.867

Ante, L., Wazinski, F.-P., & Saggu, A. (2023a). Digital Real Estate in the metaverse: An empirical analysis of retail investor motivations. *Finance Research Letters, 58*(Part A). doi:10.1016/j.frl.2023.104299

Antoniadou, K. (2023, November 20). *Is Uniqlo ethical, sustainable, or fast fashion?* IndieGetup. https://indiegetup.com/is-uniqlo-ethical-sustainable-or-fast-fashion/

Armitage, C. J., & Christian, J. (2003). From attitudes to behaviour: Basic and applied research on the theory of planned behaviour. Current Psychology. doi:10.1007/s12144-003-1015-5

Armstrong, C. M., Niinimäki, K., Kujala, S., Karell, E., & Lang, C. (2015). Sustainable product service systems for clothing: Exploring consumer perceptions of consumption alternatives in Finland. *Journal of Cleaner Production, 97*, 30–39. doi:10.1016/j.jclepro.2014.01.046

Arnett, D. B., & Wittmann, C. M. (2014). Improving marketing success: The role of tacit knowledge exchange between sales and marketing. *Journal of Business Research, 67*(3), 324–331. doi:10.1016/j.jbusres.2013.01.018

Arrigo, E. (2013). Corporate responsibility management in fast fashion companies: The Gap Inc. case. *Journal of Fashion Marketing and Management, 17*(2), 175–189. Advance online publication. doi:10.1108/JFMM-10-2011-0074

Arslan, F. M., & Altuna, O. K. (2010). The effect of brand extensions on product brand image. *Journal of Product and Brand Management, 19*(3), 170–180. doi:10.1108/10610421011046157

Auty, S., & Elliott, R. (1998). Fashion involvement, self-monitoring and the meaning of brands. *Journal of Product and Brand Management, 7*(2), 109–123. doi:10.1108/10610429810216874

Awan U (2011). *Green marketing: Marketing strategies for the Swedish energy companies*. Academic Press.

Azmi, A., Ibrahim, R., Abdul Ghafar, M., & Rashidi, A. (2022). Smarter real estate marketing using virtual reality to influence potential homebuyers' emotions and purchase intention. *Smart and Sustainable Built Environment, 11*(4), 870–890. doi:10.1108/SASBE-03-2021-0056

Azmi, A., Ibrahim, R., Ghafar, M. A., & Rashidi, A. (2023). *Metaverse for Real Estate Marketing: The Impact of Virtual Reality on Satisfaction*. Perceived Enjoyment and Purchase Intention.

Babin, B., & Harris, E. (2010). *CB 2*. Cengage Learning.

Bae, M. (2018). Understanding the effect of the discrepancy between sought and obtained gratification on social networking site users' satisfaction and continuance intention. *Computers in Human Behavior, 79*, 137–153. Advance online publication. doi:10.1016/j.chb.2017.10.026

Bairrada, C. M., Coelho, A. F. D. M., & Moreira, J. R. M. (2023). Attitudes towards ethical consumption in clothing: Comparing Peruvian and Portuguese consumers. *Journal of International Consumer Marketing*. 1-17.doi.org/10.1080/08961530.2023.2200221

Balakrishnan, B. K. P. D., Dahnil, M. I., & Yi, W. J. (2014). The Impact of Social Media Marketing Medium toward Purchase Intention and Brand Loyalty among Generation Y. *Procedia: Social and Behavioral Sciences, 148*, 177–185. doi:10.1016/j.sbspro.2014.07.032

Balderjahn, I., Lee, M. S. W., Seegebarth, B., & Peyer, M. (2020). A Sustainable Pathway to Consumer Wellbeing. The Role of Anticonsumption and Consumer Empowerment. *The Journal of Consumer Affairs, 54*(2), 456–488. doi:10.1111/joca.12278

Bandura, A. (1997). *Self-Efficacy: The exercise of control*. Macmillan.

Barnes, W. D., & Kozar, J. M. (2008). The exploitation of pregnant workers in apparel production. *Journal of Fashion Marketing and Management, 12*(3), 285–293. doi:10.1108/13612020810889254

Bartkutė, R., Streimikiene, D., & Kačerauskas, T. (2023). Between fast and sustainable fashion: The attitude of young Lithuanian designers to the circular economy. *Sustainability (Basel), 15*(13), 9986. doi:10.3390/su15139986

Batista da Silva Oliveira, A., & Chimenti, P. (2021). "humanized robots": A proposition of categories to understand virtual influencers. *AJIS. Australasian Journal of Information Systems, 25*, 21–27. doi:10.3127/ajis.v25i0.3223

Baumgardner, J., & Richards, A. (2004). Feminism and Femininity: Or How We Learned to Stop Worrying and Love the Thong. In All About the Girl: Power Culture and Identity (pp. 59–63). doi:10.4324/9780203492567

Bearden, W. O., Netemeyer, R. G., & Teel, J. E. (1989). Measurement of consumer susceptibility to interpersonal influence. *The Journal of Consumer Research, 15*(4), 473–481. doi:10.1086/209186

Becker-Leifhold, C. V. (2018). The role of values in collaborative fashion consumption - A critical investigation through the lenses of the theory of planned behavior. *Journal of Cleaner Production, 199*, 781–791. doi:10.1016/j.jclepro.2018.06.296

Bei, L.-T., & Simpson, E. M. (1995). The Determinants of Consumers' Purchase Decisions For Recycled Products: An Application of Acquisition-Transaction Utility Theory. *Advances in Consumer Research. Association for Consumer Research (U. S.), 22*, 257–261. https://doi.org/https://www.acrwebsite.org/volumes/7711/volumes/v22/NA%201322#:~:text=Based%20on%20Thaler's%20acquisition%2Dtransaction,buy%20this%20particular%20recycled%20product

Bellemans, A., & Janssens, M. (1974). *On the Osmotic Second Viral Coefficient of Athermal Polymer Solutions. Macromolecules*. ACS Publications. > doi:10.1021/ma60042a022

Bello L. (2008). *Consumer Behaviour, National Open University of Nigeria, Ahmadu Bello Way Victoria Island Lagos*. Academic Press.

Ben Amor, N., & Ben Yahia, I. (2022). Investigating blockchain technology effects on online platforms transactions: Do risk aversion and technophilia matter? *Journal of Internet Commerce, 21*(3), 271–296. doi:10.1080/15332861.2021.1961188

Benjamin, S., & Lee, D. (2022, October 11). *BoF Insights | Gen-Z and Fashion in the Age of Realism | BoF*. Business of Fashion. https://www.businessoffashion.com/reports/retail/gen-z-fashion-in-the-age-of-realism-bof-insights-social-media-report/

Berradi, M., Hsissou, R., Khudhair, M., Assouag, M., Cherkaoui, O., El Bachiri, A., & El Harfi, A. (2019). Textile finishing dyes and their impact on aquatic environs. *Heliyon*, *5*(11), e02711. doi:10.1016/j.heliyon.2019.e02711 PMID:31840123

Bhalerao, J. V., & Gujar, R. V. (2019). Impacting factors for online shopping: A literature review. *International Journal of Innovative Science and Research Technology*, *4*(1), 444–448.

Bhattacherjee, A. (2002). Individual trust in online firms: Scale development and initial test. *Journal of Management Information Systems*, *19*(1), 211–241. doi:10.1080/07421222.2002.11045715

Bhatt, D., Silverman, J., & Dickson, M. A. (2019). Consumer interest in upcycling techniques and purchasing upcycled clothing as an approach to reducing textile waste. *International Journal of Fashion Design, Technology and Education*, *12*(1), 118–128. doi:10.1080/17543266.2018.1534001

Bielawska, K., & Grebosz-Krawczyk, M. (2021). Consumers' Choice Behaviour Toward Green Clothing. *European Research Studies*, *24*(2), 238–256. doi:10.35808/ersj/2124

Billewar, S. R., Jadhav, K., Sriram, V. P., Arun, D. A., Mohd Abdul, S., Gulati, K., & Bhasin, D. N. (2021). The rise of 3D E-commerce: The online shopping gets real with virtual reality and augmented reality during COVID-19. *World Journal of Engineering*, *19*(2), 244–253. doi:10.1108/WJE-06-2021-0338

Bin Kim, W., & Jung Choo, H. (2023). How virtual reality shopping experience enhances consumer creativity: The mediating role of perceptual curiosity. *Journal of Business Research*, *154*(C), 113378. doi:10.1016/j.jbusres.2022.113378

Birch, R. R., Biver, C., Campagna, R., Gledhill, W. E., Pagga, U., Steber, J., Reust, H., & Bontinck, W. J. (1989). Screening of chemicals for anaerobic biodegradability. *Chemosphere*, *19*(10–11), 1527–1550. doi:10.1016/0045-6535(89)90498-0

Biswas, A., Licata, J. W., McKee, D., Pullig, C., & Daughtridge, C. (2000). The recycling cycle: An empirical examination of consumer waste recycling and recycling shopping behaviors. *Journal of Public Policy & Marketing*, *19*(1), 93–105. doi:10.1509/jppm.19.1.93.16950

Blas Riesgo, S., Codina, M., & Sádaba, T. (2023). Does Sustainability matter to fashion consumers? Clustering fashion consumers and their purchasing behavior in Spain. *Fashion Practice*, *15*(1), 36–63. doi:10.1080/17569370.2022.2051297

Blas Riesgo, S., Lavanga, M., & Codina, M. (2023). Drivers and barriers for sustainable fashion consumption in Spain: A comparison between sustainable and non-sustainable consumers. *International Journal of Fashion Design, Technology and Education*, *16*(1), 1–13. doi:10.1080/17543266.2022.2089239

Blazquez, M., Henninger, C. E., Alexander, B., & Franquesa, C. (2020). Consumers' knowledge and intentions towards sustainability: A Spanish fashion perspective. *Fashion Practice*, *12*(1), 34–54. doi:10.1080/17569370.2019.1669326

Bocken, N. M. P., & Short, S. W. (2016). Towards a sufficiency-driven business model: Experiences and opportunities. *Environmental Innovation and Societal Transitions*, *18*, 41–61. doi:10.1016/j.eist.2015.07.010

Boletsis, C., & Karahasanovic, A. (2020). Immersive Technologies in Retail: Practices of Augmented and Virtual Reality. In *Proceedings of the 4th International Conference on Computer- Human Interaction Research and Applications (CHIRA 2020)* (pp. 281-290). SCITEPRESS – Science and Technology Publications, Lda. 10.5220/0010181702810290

Boo, C., & Suh, A. (2024). Developing scales for assessing metaverse characteristics and testing their utility. *Computers in Human Behavior Reports*, *13*, 100366. doi:10.1016/j.chbr.2023.100366

Bornstein, M. H. (2018). *The SAGE Encyclopedia of Lifespan Human Development.* SAGE Publications, Inc. doi:10.4135/9781506307633

Borusiak, B., Szymkowiak, A., Horska, E., Raszka, N., & Żelichowska, E. (2020). Towards building sustainable consumption: A study of second-hand buying intentions. *Sustainability (Basel), 12*(3), 875. doi:10.3390/su12030875

Bracalente, B., Cossignani, M., & Mulas, A. (2009). *Statistica Aziendale.* McGraw-Hil.

Brandão, A., & da Costa, A. G. (2021). Extending the theory of planned behavior to understand the effects of barriers towards sustainable fashion consumption. *European Business Review, 33*(5), 742–774. doi:10.1108/EBR-11-2020-0306

Breiter, D. and Siegfried, P. (2022). The Metaverse: Exploring consumer's expectations, their attitudes, and it's meaning to the fashion industry. *Tekstilna industrija, 70*(2), 51–60. doi:10.5937/tekstind2202051B

Brengman, M., Willems, K., & Van Kerrebroeck, H. (2019). Can't touch this: The impact of augmented reality versus touch and non-touch interfaces on perceived ownership. *Virtual Reality (Waltham Cross), 23*(3), 269–280. doi:10.1007/s10055-018-0335-6

Brenot, A., Chuffart, C., Coste-Manière, I., Deroche, M., Godat, E., Lemoine, L., Ramchandani, M., Sette, E., & Tornaire, C. (2019). Water footprint in fashion and luxury industry. In *Water in Textiles and Fashion* (pp. 95–113). Elsevier. doi:10.1016/B978-0-08-102633-5.00006-3

Brewer, M. K. (2019). Slow Fashion in a Fast Fashion World: Promoting Sustainability and Responsibility. *Laws, 8*(4), 24. doi:10.3390/laws8040024

Brick, C., & Lewis, G. J. (2016). Unearthing the "Green" Personality: Core Traits Predict Environmentally Friendly Behavior. *Environment and Behavior, 48*(5), 635–658. Advance online publication. doi:10.1177/0013916514554695

Bringé, A. (2023, January 2). The state of sustainability in the fashion industry (And what it means for brands). *Forbes.* https://www.forbes.com/sites/forbescommunicationscouncil/2023/01/02/the-state-of-sustainability-in-the-fashion-industry-and-what-it-means-for-brands/?sh=515fc2b1c827

Brito, K. D. S., Filho, R. L. C. S., & Adeodato, P. J. L. (2021). A Systematic Review of Predicting Elections Based on Social Media Data: Research Challenges and Future Directions. *IEEE Transactions on Computational Social Systems, 8*(4), 819–843. doi:10.1109/TCSS.2021.3063660

Brodie, R. J., Ilic, A., Juric, B., & Hollebeek, L. (2013). Consumer engagement in a virtual brand community: An exploratory analysis. *Journal of Business Research, 66*(1), 105–114. doi:10.1016/j.jbusres.2011.07.029

Brooksworth, F., Mogaji, E., & Bosah, G. (2022). *Brand, consumer and sustainability perspectives in fashion marketing: Conclusion and research agenda. In Fashion Marketing in Emerging Economies* (Vol. I). Brand, Consumer and Sustainability Perspectives.

Brown, T. D., Baker, K. J., & Brand, R. A. (1992). Structural consequences of subchondral bone involvement in segmental osteonecrosis of the femoral head. *Journal of Orthopaedic Research, 10*(1), 79–87. doi:10.1002/jor.1100100110 PMID:1727938

Brunet, S. C., Mattavelli, M., & Chiariglione, L. (2023). Exploring the data of blockchain-based metaverses. In *2023 IEEE International Conference on Metaverse Computing, Networking and Applications (MetaCom).* IEEE. 10.1109/MetaCom57706.2023.00031

Buenstorf, G., & Cordes, C. (2008). Can sustainable consumption be learned? A model of cultural evolution. *Ecological Economics, 67*(4), 646–657. doi:10.1016/j.ecolecon.2008.01.028

Bulmer, S., Palakshappa, N., Dodds, S., & Harper, S. (2024). Sustainability, brand authenticity and Instagram messaging. *Journal of Business Research, 175*, 114547. doi:10.1016/j.jbusres.2024.114547

Busalim, A., Fox, G., & Lynn, T. (2022). Consumer behavior in sustainable fashion: A systematic literature review and future research agenda. *International Journal of Consumer Studies, 46*(5), 1804–1828. doi:10.1111/ijcs.12794

Buzzo, A., & Abreu, M. J. (2019). Fast fashion, fashion brands & sustainable consumption. In S. Muthu (Ed.), *Fast fashion, fashion brands, and sustainable consumption, textile science and clothing technology*. Springer. doi:10.1007/978-981-13-1268-7_1

Cachon, G. P., & Swinney, R. (2011). The value of fast fashion: Quick response, enhanced design, and strategic consumer behavior. *Management Science, 57*(4), 778–795. Advance online publication. doi:10.1287/mnsc.1100.1303

Calefato, F., & Lanubile, F. (2010). Communication Media Selection for Remote Interaction of Ad Hoc Groups. *Advances in Computers, 78*, 271–313. doi:10.1016/S0065-2458(10)78006-2

Caplan, S. E., & High, A. C. (2012). Online Social Interaction, Psychosocial Well-Being, and Problematic Internet Use. *Internet Addiction, 1*, 35–53. doi:10.1002/9781118013991.ch3

Carlson, J., Wyllie, J., Rahman, M. M., & Voola, R. (2019). Enhancing brand relationship performance through customer participation and value creation in social media brand communities. *Journal of Retailing and Consumer Services, 50*, 333–341. doi:10.1016/j.jretconser.2018.07.008

Carlson, L., Grove, S. J., & Kangun, N. (1993). A Content Analysis of Environmental Advertising Claims: A Matrix Method Approach. *Journal of Advertising, 22*(3), 27–39. doi:10.1080/00913367.1993.10673409

Celik, H. (2016). The functionality of online shopping site within the customer service life cycle: a literature review. Encyclopedia of E-Commerce Development, Implementation, and Management, 791-803. doi:10.4018/978-1-4666-9787-4.ch055

Cerchia, R. E., & Piccolo, K. (2019). The ethical consumer and codes of ethics in the fashion industry. *Laws, 8*(4), 23. doi:10.3390/laws8040023

Cervellon, M., Carey, L., & Harms, T. (2012). Something old, something used: Determinants of women's purchase of vintage fashion vs second-hand fashion. *International Journal of Retail & Distribution Management, 40*(12), 956–974. doi:10.1108/09590551211274946

Chaffee, E. C. (2017). The Origins of Corporate Social Responsibility. *University of Cincinnati Law Review, 85*, 347–373. https://ssrn.com/abstract=2957820

Chaffey, D., Ellis-Chadwick, F., & Mayer, R. (2009). *Internet marketing: strategy, implementation and practice*. Pearson Education.

Chakma, S., Das, L., & Moholkar, V. S. (2015). Dye decolorization with hybrid advanced oxidation processes comprising sonolysis/Fenton-like/photo-ferrioxalate systems: A mechanistic investigation. *Separation and Purification Technology, 156*, 596–607. doi:10.1016/j.seppur.2015.10.055

Chan, E. (2019, July 24). 5 ways the fashion industry can achieve a greener future. *Vogue India*. https://www.vogue.in/fashion/content/5-ways-the-fashion-industry-can-achieve-a-greener-future

Chang, H. J., Cho, H. J., Turner, T., Gupta, M., & Watchravesringkan, K. (2015). Effects of store attributes on retail patronage behaviors. *Journal of Fashion Marketing and Management, 19*(2), 136–153. doi:10.1108/JFMM-03-2014-0019

Chang, H. J., & Watchravesringkan, K. T. (2018). Who are sustainably minded apparel shoppers? An investigation of the influencing factors of sustainable apparel consumption. *International Journal of Retail & Distribution Management, 46*(2), 148–162. doi:10.1108/IJRDM-10-2016-0176

Chang, H.-J., Eckman, M., & Yan, R.-N. (2011). Application of the Stimulus-Organism-Response model to the retail environment: The role of hedonic motivation in impulse buying behavior. *International Review of Retail, Distribution and Consumer Research, 21*(3), 233–249. doi:10.1080/09593969.2011.578798

Chang, K. C., Hsu, C. L., Hsu, Y. T., & Chen, M. C. (2019). How green marketing, perceived motives, and incentives influence behavioral intentions. *Journal of Retailing and Consumer Services, 49*, 336–345. doi:10.1016/j.jretconser.2019.04.012

Chang, P. L., & Chieng, M. H. (2006). Building consumer–brand relationship: A cross-cultural experiential view. *Psychology and Marketing, 23*(11), 927–959. doi:10.1002/mar.20140

Chan, R. Y. K. (2001). Determinants of Chinese consumers' green purchase behavior. *Psychology and Marketing, 18*(4), 389–413. doi:10.1002/mar.1013

Chan, T. J., Li, Y., Hashim, N. H., & Ibrahim, A. N. I. (2022). Online promotional communication attributes and company competitiveness of a Malaysian fast fashion clothing company. *International Journal of Technology, 13*(6), 1344–1353. doi:10.14716/ijtech.v13i6.5955

Chan, T. Y., & Wong, C. W. (2012). The consumption side of sustainable fashion supply chain: Understanding fashion consumer eco-fashion consumption decision. *Journal of Fashion Marketing and Management, 16*(2), 193–215. doi:10.1108/13612021211222824

Charm, T., Dhar, R., Haas, S., Liu, J., Novemsky, N., & Teichner, W. (2020). *Understanding and shaping consumer behavior in the next normal | McKinsey*. https://www.mckinsey.com/business-functions/marketing-and-sales/our-insights/understanding-and-shaping-consumer-behavior-in-the-next-normal# doi:10.1080/0144929X.2019.1587001

Cheah, J.-H., Ting, H., Cham, T. H., & Memon, M. A. (2019). The effect of selfie promotion and celebrity endorsed advertisement on decision-making processes: A model comparison. *Internet Research, 29*(3), 552–577. doi:10.1108/IntR-12-2017-0530

Chekima, B., Wafa, S. A. W. S. K., Igau, O. A., Chekima, S., & Sondoh, S. L. Jr. (2016). Examining green consumerism motivational drivers: Does premium price and demographics matter to green purchasing? *Journal of Cleaner Production, 112*, 3436–3450. doi:10.1016/j.jclepro.2015.09.102

Chelvarayan, A., Yi, C. X., & Fern, Y. S. (2023). Online Shopping During Covid 19 Pandemic: The Students' Perception in Malaysia. *Global Business and Management Research*, 15.

Chen, J. V., Ruangsri, S., Ha, Q. A., & Widjaja, A. E. (2022). An experimental study of consumers' impulse buying behaviour in augmented reality mobile shopping apps. *Behaviour & Information Technology, 41*(15), 3360–3381. doi:10.1080/0144929X.2021.1987523

Chen, M. Y., & Teng, C. I. (2013). A comprehensive model of the effects of online store image on purchase intention in an e-commerce environment. *Electronic Commerce Research, 13*(1), 1–23. doi:10.1007/s10660-013-9104-5

Chen, Y. C., Shang, R. A., & Li, M. J. (2014). The effects of perceived relevance of travel blogs' content on the behavioral intention to visit a tourist destination. *Computers in Human Behavior, 30*, 787–799. Advance online publication. doi:10.1016/j.chb.2013.05.019

Chen, Y. S. (2010). The drivers of green brand equity: Green brand image, green satisfaction, and green trust. *Journal of Business Ethics, 93*(2), 307–319. Advance online publication. doi:10.1007/s10551-009-0223-9

Chen, Y. S., & Chang, C. H. (2013). Green marketing and its impact on supply chain management in industrial markets. *Industrial Marketing Management, 42*(4), 657–669.

Chen, Y. S., & Chang, C. H. (2013). Greenwash and green trust: The mediation effects of green consumer confusion and green perceived risk. *Journal of Business Ethics, 114*(3), 489–500. doi:10.1007/s10551-012-1360-0

Cherian, J., & Jacob, J. (2012). *Green Marketing: A Study of Consumers' Attitude towards Control* (8th ed.). Prentice-H.

Cheung, C. M., & Thadani, D. R. (2012). The impact of electronic word-of-mouth communication: A literature analysis and integrative model. *Decision Support Systems, 54*(1), 461–470. doi:10.1016/j.dss.2012.06.008

Chevalier, S. (2024, February 6). *Global retail e-commerce sales 2014-2027.* Statista. https://www.statista.com/statistics/379046/worldwide-retail-e-commerce-sales/

Chin, L. P., & Ahmad, Z. A. (2015). Perceived enjoyment and Malaysian consumers' intention to use a single platform e-payment. *SHS Web of Conferences, 18*, 01009. 10.1051/shsconf/20151801009

Chi, T., Gerard, J., Yu, Y., & Wang, Y. (2021). A study of US consumers' intention to purchase slow fashion apparel: Understanding the key determinants. *International Journal of Fashion Design, Technology and Education, 14*(1), 101–112. doi:10.1080/17543266.2021.1872714

Choi, H., & Kandampully, J. (2019). The effect of atmosphere on customer engagement in upscale hotels: An application of S-O-R paradigm. *International Journal of Hospitality Management, 77*, 40–50. doi:10.1016/j.ijhm.2018.06.012

Chong, A. Y. L., Lacka, E., Boying, L., & Chan, H. K. (2018). The role of social media in enhancing guanxi and perceived effectiveness of E-commerce institutional mechanisms in online marketplace. *Information & Management, 55*(5), 621–632. doi:10.1016/j.im.2018.01.003

Choose a slow fashion season. (2019, December 9). Sustainability - University of Queensland. https://sustainability.uq.edu.au/projects/recycling-and-waste-minimisation/choose-slow-fashion-season

Chow, P.-S., & Li, C. K. Y. (2018). Towards Closed-Loop Fashion Supply Chains—Reflections from Retailer-Facilitated Used Apparel Collection Programs. In *Contemporary Case Studies on Fashion Production, Marketing and Operations* (pp. 219–239). Springer. doi:10.1007/978-981-10-7007-5_13

Cho, Y.-N., Thyroff, A., Rapert, M. I., Park, S.-Y., & Lee, H. J. (2013). To be or not to be green: Exploring individualism and collectivism as antecedents of environmental behavior. *Journal of Business Research, 66*(8), 1052–1059. doi:10.1016/j.jbusres.2012.08.020

Chung, N., Han, H., & Koo, C. (2015). Adoption of travel information in user-generated content on social media: The moderating effect of social presence. *Behaviour & Information Technology, 34*(9), 902–919. doi:10.1080/0144929X.2015.1039060

Chu, S.-C., Chen, H.-T., & Gan, C. (2020). Consumers' engagement with corporate social responsibility (CSR) communication in social media: Evidence from China and the United States. *Journal of Business Research, 110*, 260–271. doi:10.1016/j.jbusres.2020.01.036

Ciaramitaro, B. L. (2010, August 31). Virtual Worlds and E-Commerce. In Technologies and Applications for Building Customer Relationships. Academic Press.

Ciasullo, M. V., Maione, G., Torre, C., & Troisi, O. (2017). What about sustainability? An empirical analysis of consumers' purchasing behavior in fashion context. *Sustainability (Basel), 9*(9), 1617. doi:10.3390/su9091617

Cimatti, B., Campana, G., & Carluccio, L. (2017). Eco design and sustainable manufacturing in fashion: A case study in the luxury personal accessories industry. *Procedia Manufacturing*, *8*, 393–400. doi:10.1016/j.promfg.2017.02.050

Clarke, K., & Belk, R. W. (1979). The Effects of Product Involvement and Task Definition on Anticipated Consumer Effort. *Advances in Consumer Research*, *6*(1), 313–318. Available at: https://core.ac.uk/reader/4835200

Claxton, S. M., & Kent, A. (2020). The management of sustainable fashion design strategies: An analysis of the designer's role. *Journal of Cleaner Production*, *268*, 122112. doi:10.1016/j.jclepro.2020.122112

Clube, R. K. M., & Tennant, M. (2022). Social inclusion and the circular economy: The case of a fashion textiles manufacturer in Vietnam. *Business Strategy & Development*, *5*(1), 4–16. doi:10.1002/bsd2.179

Colasante, A., & D'Adamo, I. (2021). The circular economy and bioeconomy in the fashion sector: Emergence of a "sustainability bias.". *Journal of Cleaner Production*, *329*, 129774. doi:10.1016/j.jclepro.2021.129774

Colasante, A., D'Adamo, I., Rosa, P., & Morone, P. (2023). How consumer shopping habits affect willingness to embrace sustainable fashion. *Applied Economics Letters*, ●●●, 1–6. doi:10.1080/13504851.2023.2290578

Conner, M., & Armitage, C. J. (1998). Extending the Theory of Planned Behavior: A review and avenues for further research. *Journal of Applied Social Psychology*, *28*(15), 1429–1464. doi:10.1111/j.1559-1816.1998.tb01685.x

Coppola, D. (2024). *Mobile retail e-commerce sales in the United States from 2019 to 2027*. Statista. Available at: https://www.statista.com/statistics/249855/mobile-retail- commerce-revenue-in-the-united-states/

Cowan, K., & Ketron, S. (2019). A dual model of product involvement for effective virtual reality: The roles of imagination, co-creation, telepresence, and interactivity. *Journal of Business Research*, *100*, 483–492. doi:10.1016/j.jbusres.2018.10.063

Cowan, K., & Kinley, T. (2014). Green spirit: Consumer empathies for green apparel. *International Journal of Consumer Studies*, *38*(5), 493–499. Advance online publication. doi:10.1111/ijcs.12125

Crinis, V. (2019). Corporate social responsibility, human rights and clothing workers in Bangladesh and Malaysia. *Asian Studies Review*, *43*(2), 295–312. doi:10.1080/10357823.2019.1588850

Cronin, J. J. Jr, Smith, J. S., Gleim, M. R., Ramirez, E., & Martinez, J. D. (2011). Green marketing strategies: An examination of stakeholders and the opportunities they present. *Journal of the Academy of Marketing Science*, *39*(1), 158–174. Advance online publication. doi:10.1007/s11747-010-0227-0

Cudlínová, E., Buchtele, R., & Dušek, R. (2022). The Fashion Industry and its Problematic Consequences in the Green Marketing Era a Review. *SHS Web of Conferences, 135*, 01011. https://doi.org/10.1051/shsconf/202213501011

Cui, G., Lockee, B., & Meng, C. (2012). Building Modern Online Social Presence: A review of Social Presence Theory and its instructional design implications for future trends. *Education and Information Technologies*, *18*(4), 661–685. doi:10.1007/s10639-012-9192-1

D'Souza, C., Gilmore, A. J., Hartmann, P., Apaolaza Ibáñez, V., & Sullivan-Mort, G. (2015). Male eco-fashion: A market reality. *International Journal of Consumer Studies*, *39*(1), 35–42. Advance online publication. doi:10.1111/ijcs.12148

Dangelico, R. M., Alvino, L., & Fraccascia, L. (2022). Investigating the antecedents of consumer behavioral intention for sustainable fashion products: Evidence from a large survey of Italian consumers. *Technological Forecasting and Social Change*, *185*, 122010. doi:10.1016/j.techfore.2022.122010

Dangelico, R. M., & Vocalelli, D. (2017). "Green Marketing": An analysis of definitions, strategy steps, and tools through a systematic review of the literature. *Journal of Cleaner Production*, *165*, 1263–1279. doi:10.1016/j.jclepro.2017.07.184

Danielle, W., & Forbes, C. A. (2021). *Influencer Marketing's Surprising Rise Of The 'Everyperson.'* Forbes. Com. https://www.forbes.com/sites/forbesagencycouncil/2021/02/04/influencer-marketings-surprising-rise-of-the-everyperson/?sh=7660272e3b23

Das, S., Mishra, B. K., Panda, N., & Badawy, H. R. (2024). Sustainable Marketing Mix Strategies of Millets: A Voyage of Two Decades. In The Role of Women in Cultivating Sustainable Societies Through Millets (pp. 113-127). IGI Global.

Das, S., Saibabu, N., & Pranaya, D. (2023). Blockchain and Intelligent Computing Framework for Sustainable Agriculture: Theory, Methods, and Practice. In Intelligent Engineering Applications and Applied Sciences for Sustainability (pp. 208-228). IGI Global.

Daukantienė, V. (2023). Analysis of the sustainability aspects of fashion: A literature review. *Textile Research Journal*, *93*(3–4), 991–1002. doi:10.1177/00405175221124971

Davari, A., & Strutton, D. (2014). Marketing mix strategies for closing the gap between green consumers' pro-environmental beliefs and behaviors. *Journal of Strategic Marketing*, *22*(7), 563–586. doi:10.1080/0965254X.2014.914059

Davis, F. D. (1989). Perceived usefulness, perceived ease of use, and user acceptance of Information Technology. *Management Information Systems Quarterly*, *13*(3), 319. doi:10.2307/249008

Davis, F. D., Bagozzi, R. P., & Warshaw, P. R. (1992). Extrinsic and intrinsic motivation to use computers in the workplace. *Journal of Applied Social Psychology*, *22*(14), 1111–1132. doi:10.1111/j.1559-1816.1992.tb00945.x

De Groot, J. I. M., & Steg, L. (2009). Morality and prosocial behavior: The role of awareness, responsibility, and norms in the norm activation model. *The Journal of Social Psychology*, *149*(4), 425–449. doi:10.3200/SOCP.149.4.425-449 PMID:19702104

de Lenne, O., & Vandenbosch, L. (2017). Media and sustainable apparel buying intention. *Journal of Fashion Marketing and Management*, *21*(4), 483–498. doi:10.1108/JFMM-11-2016-0101

De Vries, L., Gensler, S., & Leeflang, P. S. H. (2012). Popularity of Brand Posts on Brand Fan Pages: An Investigation of the Effects of Social Media Marketing. *Journal of Interactive Marketing*, *26*(2), 83–91. Advance online publication. doi:10.1016/j.intmar.2012.01.003

Deepak, J., & Rishi, K. (2018). Green purchasing behaviour: A conceptual framework and empirical investigation of Indian consumers, Journal of Retailing and Consumer Services. *Journal of Retailing and Consumer Services*, *41*, 60–69. doi:10.1016/j.jretconser.2017.11.008

Dehghanan, H., & Bakhshandeh, G. (2014). The impact of green perceived value and green perceived risk on green purchase behaviour of Iranian consumers. *International Journal of Management and Humanity Sciences*, *3*(2), 1349–1357.

Delafrooz, N., Taleghani, M., & Nouri, B. (2014). *Effect of green marketing on consumer purchase behaviour.* http://www.qscience.com/doi/pdf/10.5 339/connect.2014.5

Delieva, D., & Eom, H. J. (2019). Consumers' attitude toward socially responsible consumerism in the sustainable fashion market. *Business and Management Studies*, *5*(1), 59–67. doi:10.11114/bms.v5i1.4173

Deloitte. (2022). *The Deloitte Global 2022 Gen Z and Millennial Survey.* Author.

DeLong, M. R., Bang, H., & Gibson, L. (2019). Comparison of patterns of dressing for two generations within a local context. *Fashion, Style & Popular Culture*, *6*(1), 99–117. doi:10.1386/fspc.6.1.99_1

Deng, X. (2015). Understanding Chinese consumers' ethical purchasing decision-making process: A combination of qualitative and quantitative study. *Geoforum*, *67*, 204–213. doi:10.1016/j.geoforum.2015.03.018

Department of Statistics of Malaysia. (2023). *Population based on age group. Department of Statistics of Malaysia.* Retrieved at https://statsgeo.mycensus.gov.my/geostats/mapv2.php#

Desai, V., & Vidyapeeth, B. (2019). Digital Marketing: A Review. *International Journal of Trend in Scientific Research and Development*, *5*(5), 196–200. doi:10.31142/ijtsrd23100

Dhaware, B. U. (2023). Predictive Data Analytics Framework Based on Heart Healthcare System (HHS) Using Machine Learning. *Journal of Advanced Zoology, 44*(2).

Dhir, A., Sadiq, M., Talwar, S., Sakashita, M., & Kaur, P. (2021). Why do retail consumers buy green apparel? A knowledge-attitude-behaviour-context perspective. *Journal of Retailing and Consumer Services*, *59*, 102398. Advance online publication. doi:10.1016/j.jretconser.2020.102398

Dick, E. (2021). *Public Policy for the Metaverse: Key Takeaways from the 2021 AR/VR Policy Conference*. Information Technology and Innovation Foundation.

Diddi, S., Yan, R.-N., Bloodhart, B., Bajtelsmit, V., & McShane, K. (2019). Exploring young adult consumers' sustainable clothing consumption intention-behavior gap: A Behavioral Reasoning Theory perspective. *Sustainable Production and Consumption*, *18*, 200–209. doi:10.1016/j.spc.2019.02.009

Diez-Martin, F., Blanco-Gonzalez, A., & Prado-Roman, C. (2019). Research Challenges in Digital Marketing: Sustainability. *Sustainability (Basel)*, *11*(10), 2839. doi:10.3390/su11102839

Dixit, J. S., Alavi, S., & Ahuja, V. (2020). Measuring consumer brand perception for green apparel brands. *International Journal of E-Business Research*, *16*(1), 28–46. doi:10.4018/IJEBR.2020010102

Dixit, J. S., Alavi, S., & Ahuja, V. (2021). Why apparel companies go green? *International Journal of Green Economics*, *15*(1), 20–32. doi:10.1504/IJGE.2021.117666

Djafarova, E., & Bowes, T. (2021). 'Instagram made Me buy it': Generation Z impulse purchases in fashion industry. *Journal of Retailing and Consumer Services*, *59*, 102345. doi:10.1016/j.jretconser.2020.102345

Djafarova, E., & Foots, S. (2022). Exploring ethical consumption of generation Z: Theory of planned behavior. *Young Consumers*, *23*(3), 413–431. doi:10.1108/YC-10-2021-1405

Djafarova, E., & Rushworth, C. (2017). Exploring the credibility of online celebrities' Instagram profiles in influencing the purchase decisions of young female users. *Computers in Human Behavior*, *68*, 1–7. doi:10.1016/j.chb.2016.11.009

Dobos, N. (2019). Exploitation, working poverty, and the expressive power of wages. *Journal of Applied Philosophy*, *36*(2), 333–347. doi:10.1111/japp.12314

Doeringer, P., & Crean, S. (2006). Can fast fashion save the US apparel industry? *Socio-economic Review*, *4*(3), 353–377. doi:10.1093/ser/mwl014

Domingos, M., Vale, V. T., & Faria, S. (2022). Slow fashion consumer behavior: A literature review. *Sustainability (Basel)*, *14*(5), 2860. doi:10.3390/su14052860

Dropulić, B., & Krupka, Z. (2020). Are consumers always greener on the other side of the fence? Factors that influence green purchase intentions–the context of Croatian and Swedish consumers. *Market-Tržište*, *32*(Special Issue), 99–113. doi:10.22598/mt/2020.32.spec-issue.99

Ducheneaut, N., Yee, N., Nickell, E., & Moore, R. J. (2006). Alone together? *Proceedings of the SIGCHI Conference on Human Factors in Computing Systems*. 10.1145/1124772.1124834

Dunlap, R. E., & Van Liere, K. D. (1978). The “new environmental paradigm.”. *The Journal of Environmental Education, 9*(4), 10–19. doi:10.1080/00958964.1978.10801875

Durmaz, Y., & Yaşar, V. (2016). Green Marketing and Benefits to Business. *Business and Management Studies, 2*(2), 2374-5916. doi:10.11114/bms.v2i2.1624

Dwivedi, Y. K., Hughes, L., Baabdullah, A. M., Ribeiro-Navarrete, S., Giannakis, M., Al-Debei, M. M., Dennehy, D., Metri, B., Buhalis, D., Cheung, C. M. K., Conboy, K., Doyle, R., Dubey, R., Dutot, V., Felix, R., Goyal, D. P., Gustafsson, A., Hinsch, C., Jebabli, I., ... Wamba, S. F. (2022a). Metaverse beyond the hype: Multidisciplinary perspectives on emerging challenges, opportunities, and agenda for research, practice and policy. *International Journal of Information Management, 66*, 102542. doi:10.1016/j.ijinfomgt.2022.102542

Dwivedi, Y. K., Hughes, L., Baabdullah, A. M., Ribeiro-Navarrete, S., Giannakis, M., Al-Debei, M. M., Dwivedi, Y. K., Kapoor, K. K., & Chen, H. (2015). Social media marketing and advertising. *The Marketing Review, 15*(3), 289–309. doi:10.1362/146934715X14441363377999

Eagly, A. H., & Chaiken, S. (1993). *The Psychology of Attitudes*. Cengage Learning.

Ebrahim, R. S. (2019). The Role of Trust in Understanding the Impact of Social Media Marketing on Brand Equity and Brand Loyalty. *Journal of Relationship Marketing, 19*(3), 1–22. doi:10.1080/15332667.2019.1705742

Ebreo, A., Vining, J., & Cristancho, S. (2003). Responsibility for environmental problems and the consequences of waste reduction: A test of the norm-activation model. *Journal of Environmental Systems, 29*(3), 219–244. doi:10.2190/EQGD-2DAA-KAAJ-W1DC

Eden, S., Hoyer, A. L., Niemeier, D., & Peters, L. (2021). *E-commerce*. DB Country Reports: E-commerce in Malaysia 2021.

EE Editorial Team. (2024, January 20). Is Patagonia greenwashing? A breakdown! *Ethically Engineered*. https://www.ethicallyengineered.com/is-patagonia-greenwashing/

Eilert, M., & Nappier Cherup, A. (2020). The Activist Company: Examining a Company’s Pursuit of Societal Change Through Corporate Activism Using an Institutional Theoretical Lens. *Journal of Public Policy & Marketing, 39*(4), 461–476. Advance online publication. doi:10.1177/0743915620947408

Elisa, W., & Cecilia, H.-M. (2016). Relationship Marketing in Green Fashion—A Case Study of hessnatur. In S. S. Muthu & M. A. Gardetti (Eds.), *Green Fashion* (1st ed., pp. 21–47). Springer Singapore. doi:10.1007/978-981-10-0245-8

Eneizan, B. M., & Obaid, T. F. (2016). Prior research on green marketing and green marketing strategy: Critical analysis. Singaporean Journal of Business. *Economics and Management Studies, 51*(3965), 1–19.

Environment Friendly Products. (n.d.). *Asian Social Science, 8*(12). Advance online publication. doi:10.5539/ass.v8n12p117

Eric, B. (2014). Chapter 7 – Virality. doi:10.1016/B978-0-12-416690-5.00007-5

Eric, K. (2007). *Green marketing practices by Kenya petroleum refineries: A study of the perception of the management of oil marketing companies in Kenya*. Ph.D. Dissertation, University of Nairobi, Kenya.

Erics, A., Ulna, S., & Candan. (2012). The effect of brand satisfaction, trust and brand commitment on loyalty and repurchase intentions. *Social and Behavioural Sciences, 58*, 1395 – 1404.

Eriko, Y. (2012). Accumulating Japanese popular culture: Media consumption experiences of Malaysian young adults. *Media Asia, 39*(4), 199–208. doi:10.1080/01296612.2012.11689938

Eriksson, N., Sjöberg, A., Rosenbröijer, C. J., & Fagerstrøm, A. (2019). Consumer brand post engagement on Facebook and Instagram – A study of three interior design brands. *Proceedings of The 19th International Conference on Electronic Business*, 116-124. https://hdl.handle.net/11250/3057617

Erz, A., & Heeris Christensen, A.-B. (2018). Transforming Consumers Into Brands: Tracing Transformation Processes of the Practice of Blogging. *Journal of Interactive Marketing*, *43*, 69–82. doi:10.1016/j.intmar.2017.12.002

Esmaeelinezhad, O., & Afrazeh, A. (2018). Linking personality traits and individuals' knowledge management behavior. *Aslib Journal of Information Management*, *70*(3), 234–251. Advance online publication. doi:10.1108/AJIM-01-2018-0019

EURATEX. (2020). Facts & Key Figure: Of The European textile and clothing industry. *Euratex*, 1–36. https://euratex.eu/wp-content/uploads/EURATEX-Facts-Key-Figures-2020-LQ.pdf

European Environmental Agency. (2020). *Textiles in Europe's circular economy Key messages*. 1–17. https://www.eea.europa.eu/themes/waste/resource-efficiency/textiles-in-europe-s-circular-economy

Ewe, S. Y., & Tjiptono, F. (2023). Green behavior among Gen Z consumers in an emerging market: Eco-friendly versus non-eco-friendly products. *Young Consumers*, *24*(2), 234–252. doi:10.1108/YC-06-2022-1533

Fan, H., & Zeng, L. (2011). *Implementation of green marketing strategy in China: A study of the green food industry.* M.Sc. Thesis, University of GAVLE, China.

Fan, F., Chan, K., Wang, Y., Li, Y., & Prieler, M. (2023). How influencers' social media posts have an influence on audience engagement among young consumers. *Young Consumers*, *24*(4), 427–444. doi:10.1108/YC-08-2022-1588

Fang, W. T., Hassan, A. A., & LePage, B. A. (2022). Environmental ethics: Modelling for values and choices. In W. T. Fang, A. A. Hassan, & B. A. LePage (Eds.), The living environmental education: Sound Science towards a cleaner, safer, and healthier future (pp. 151–174). Academic Press.

Fani, V., Mazzoli, V., & Acuti, D. (2023). 'I wanna be sustainable, but I don't wanna show it!': The effect of sustainability cues on young adult consumers' preferences. *Business Strategy and the Environment*, *32*(6), 3344–3358. doi:10.1002/bse.3303

Fan, K.-K., & Chang, Y.-T. (2023). Exploring the Key Elements of Sustainable Design from a Social Responsibility Perspective: A Case Study of Fast Fashion Consumers' Evaluation of Green Projects. *Sustainability (Basel)*, *15*(2), 995. doi:10.3390/su15020995

Fan, K.-K., & Zhou, Y. (2020). The influence of traditional cultural resources (TCRs) on the communication of clothing brands. *Sustainability (Basel)*, *12*(6), 2379. doi:10.3390/su12062379

Fan, M., Khalique, A., Qalati, S. A., Gillal, F. G., & Gillal, R. G. (2022). Antecedents of sustainable e-waste disposal behavior: The moderating role of gender. *Environmental Science and Pollution Research International*, *29*(14), 20878–20891. doi:10.1007/s11356-021-17275-y PMID:34741741

Fazio, R. H., & Zanna, M. P. (1981). Direct experience and attitude-behaviour consistency. In L. Berkowitz (Ed.), Advances in Experimental Social Psychology: Vol. 14. *Academic Press.*

Fernández, P., Hartmann, P., & Apaolaza, V. (2022). What drives CSR communication effectiveness on social media? A process-based theoretical framework and research agenda. *International Journal of Advertising*, *41*(3), 385–413. Advance online publication. doi:10.1080/02650487.2021.1947016

Fielding, K. S., McDonald, R., & Louis, W. R. (2008). Theory of planned behaviour, identity and intentions to engage in environmental activism. *Journal of Environmental Psychology*, *28*(4), 318–326. doi:10.1016/j.jenvp.2008.03.003

Fiore, A. M., Jin, H. J., & Kim, J. (2005). For fun and profit: Hedonic value from image interactivity and responses toward an online store. *Psychology and Marketing*, *22*(8), 669–694. doi:10.1002/mar.20079

Fishbein, M., & Ajzen, I. (1975). *Belief, attitude, intention, and behavior: An introduction to theory and research*. Addison–Wesley.

Fishbein, M., & Ajzen, I. (2011). *Predicting and changing behavior: The reasoned action approach*. Psychology Press. doi:10.4324/9780203838020

Fletcher, K. (2010). Slow Fashion: An Invitation for Systems Change. *Fashion Practice*, *2*(2), 259–265. doi:10.2752/175693810X12774625387594

Fletcher, K. (2012). Durability, fashion, sustainability: The processes and practices of use. *Fashion Practice*, *4*(2), 221–238. doi:10.2752/175693812X13403765252389

Floriano, M. D. P., & Matos, C. A. d. (2022). Understanding Brazilians' Intentions in Consuming Sustainable Fashion. *Brazilian Business Review (English Edition)*, *19*(5).

Fornell, C., & Larcker, D. F. (1981). Structural equation models with unobservable variables and measurement error: Algebra and statistics. *JMR, Journal of Marketing Research*, *18*(3), 382–388. doi:10.1177/002224378101800313

Forster, J. E. (2004). *Using varying-coefficient models to analyze the longitudinal relationship between CD4+ cell count and viral load in HIV-1 infected patients*. University of Colorado.

Francois, F., John, B., & Leah, J. L. Z. (2023). *Selling Sustainability Means Decoding Consumers | Bain & Company*. Bain & Company. https://www.bain.com/insights/selling-sustainability-means-decoding-consumers-ceo-sustainability-guide-2023/

Frick, V., Gossen, M., Santarius, T., & Geiger, S. (2021). When your shop says #lessismore. Online communication interventions for clothing sufficiency. *Journal of Environmental Psychology*, *75*, 101595. doi:10.1016/j.jenvp.2021.101595

Fuller, D. A. (1999). *Sustainable marketing*. SAGE.

Gabler, C. B., Butler, T. D., & Adams, F. G. (2013). The environmental belief-behaviour gap: Exploring barriers to green consumerism. *Journal of Customer Behaviour*, *12*(2), 159–176. doi:10.1362/147539213X13832198548292

Gadenne, D., Sharma, B., Kerr, D., & Smith, T. (2011). The influence of consumers' environmental beliefs and attitudes on energy saving behaviours. *Energy Policy*, *39*(12), 7684–7694. doi:10.1016/j.enpol.2011.09.002

Galati, A., Thrassou, A., Christofi, M., Vrontis, D., & Migliore, G. (2023). Exploring travelers' willingness to pay for green hotels in the digital era. *Journal of Sustainable Tourism*, *31*(11), 2546–2563.

Gambetti, R. C., Graffigna, G., & Biraghi, S. (2012). The grounded theory approach to consumer-brand engagement: The practitioner's standpoint. *International Journal of Market Research*, *54*(5), 659–687. doi:10.2501/IJMR-54-5-659-687

Gandomi, A., & Haider, M. (2015). Beyond the hype: Big data concepts, methods, and analytics. *International Journal of Information Management*, *35*(2), 137–144. doi:10.1016/j.ijinfomgt.2014.10.007

Gannon, V., & Prothero, A. (2018). Beauty bloggers and YouTubers as a community of practice. *Journal of Marketing Management*, *34*(7-8), 592–619. Advance online publication. doi:10.1080/0267257X.2018.1482941

Garg, S., & Sharma, V. (2017). Green Marketing: An Emerging Approach to Sustainable Development. *International Journal of Applied Agricultural Research*, *12*(2), 177–184. doi:10.4108/eai.14-2-2017.152283

Gavilan, D., Avello, M., & Martinez-Navarro, G. (2018). The influence of online ratings and reviews on hotel booking consideration. *Tourism Management, 66*, 53–61. doi:10.1016/j.tourman.2017.10.018

Gefen, D., & Straub, D. W. (2004). Consumer trust in B2C e-Commerce and the importance of social presence: Experiments in e-Products and e-Services. *Omega, 32*(6), 407–424. doi:10.1016/j.omega.2004.01.006

Geiger, S. M., & Keller, J. (2018). Shopping for Clothes and Sensitivity to the Suffering of Others: The Role of Compassion and Values in Sustainable Fashion Consumption. *Environment and Behavior, 50*(10), 1119–1144. doi:10.1177/0013916517732109

Gelderman, C. J., Schijns, J., Lambrechts, W., & Vijgen, S. (2021). Green marketing as an environmental practice: The impact on green satisfaction and green loyalty in a business-to-business context. *Business Strategy and the Environment, 30*(4), 2061–2076. doi:10.1002/bse.2732

Gerdt, S. O., Wagner, E., & Schewe, G. (2019). The relationship between sustainability and customer satisfaction in hospitality: An explorative investigation using eWOM as a data source. *Tourism Management, 74*(March), 155–172. doi:10.1016/j.tourman.2019.02.010

Ghosh, M. (2019). Determinants of green procurement implementation and its impact on firm performance. *Journal of Manufacturing Technology Management, 30*(2), 462–482. doi:10.1108/JMTM-06-2018-0168

Giacomini, D., Zola, P., Paredi, D., & Mazzoleni, M. (2020). Environmental disclosure and stakeholder engagement via social media: State of the art and potential in public utilities. *Corporate Social Responsibility and Environmental Management, 27*(4), 1552–1564. doi:10.1002/csr.1904

Gil De Zuniga, H., Diehl, T., Huber, B., & Liu, J. (2017). Personality Traits and Social Media Use in 20 Countries: How Personality Relates to Frequency of Social Media Use, Social Media News Use, and Social Media Use for Social Interaction. *Cyberpsychology, Behavior, and Social Networking, 20*(9), 540–552. Advance online publication. doi:10.1089/cyber.2017.0295 PMID:28922034

Gilal, F. G., Channa, N. A., Gilal, N. G., Gilal, R. G., Gong, Z., & Zhang, N. (2020). Corporate social responsibility and brand passion among consumers: Theory and evidence. *Corporate Social Responsibility and Environmental Management, 27*(5), 2275–2285. doi:10.1002/csr.1963

Gilal, F. G., Gilal, N. G., Channa, N. A., Gilal, R. G., Gilal, R. G., & Tunio, M. N. (2020). Towards an integrated model for the transference of environmental responsibility. *Business Strategy and the Environment, 29*(6), 2614–2623. doi:10.1002/bse.2524

Gogoi, B. (2013). Study of antecedents of purchase intention and its effect on brand loyalty of private label brand of apparel. *International Journal of Sales & Marketing, 3*(2), 73–86.

Goi, M.-T., Kalidas, V., & Yunus, N. (2018). Mediating roles of emotion and experience in the stimulus-organism-response framework in higher education institutions. *Journal of Marketing for Higher Education, 28*(1), 90–112. doi:10.1080/08841241.2018.1425231

Goldsmith, E. B. E., Ronald, G., & Todd, B. (2015). Social Influence and Sustainable Behavior. In *Social Influence and Sustainable Consumption* (1st ed., pp. 127–154). Springer Cham. doi:10.1007/978-3-319-20738-4_8

Gonçalves, D., Pais, P., Gerling, K., Guerreiro, T., & Rodrigues, A. (2023a). Social Gaming: A systematic review. *Computers in Human Behavior, 147*, 107851. doi:10.1016/j.chb.2023.107851

Gong, W., & Li, X. (2017). Engaging fans on microblog: The synthetic influence of parasocial interaction and source characteristics on celebrity endorsement. *Psychology and Marketing, 34*(7), 720–732. doi:10.1002/mar.21018

González-Rodríguez, M. R., Díaz-Fernández, M. C., & Font, X. (2020). Factors influencing willingness of customers of environmentally friendly hotels to pay a price premium. *International Journal of Contemporary Hospitality Management, 32*(1), 60–80.

Gonzalez, V., Lou, X., & Chi, T. (2023). Evaluating environmental impact of natural and synthetic fibers: A life cycle assessment approach. *Sustainability (Basel), 15*(9), 7670. doi:10.3390/su15097670

González-Viralta, D., Veas-González, I., Egaña-Bruna, F., Vidal-Silva, C., Delgado-Bello, C., & Pezoa-Fuentes, C. (2023). Positive effects of green practices on the consumers' satisfaction, loyalty, word-of-mouth, and willingness to pay. *Heliyon, 9*(10). Advance online publication. doi:10.1016/j.heliyon.2023.e20353

Gorge, H., Herbert, M., Özçağlar-Toulouse, N., & Robert, I. (2015). What Do We Really Need? Questioning Consumption Through Sufficiency. *Journal of Macromarketing, 35*(1), 11–22. doi:10.1177/0276146714553935

Gosavi, P. S. (2013). Gaining competitive advantage through green marketing of cell phone. *ASM's International E-Journal of Ongoing Research in Management and IT, 13*(1), 1–11.

Goworek, H. (2011). Social and environmental sustainability in the clothing industry: A case study of a fair trade retailer. *Social Responsibility Journal, 7*(1), 74–86. doi:10.1108/17471111111114558

Goworek, H., Fisher, T., Cooper, T., Woodward, S., & Hiller, A. (2012). The sustainable clothing market: An evaluation of potential strategies for UK retailers. *International Journal of Retail & Distribution Management, 40*(12), 935–955. doi:10.1108/09590551211274937

Grant, J. (2008). Green Marketing. *Strategic Direction, 24*(6), 25–27. doi:10.1108/02580540810868041

Gräve, J.-F. (2017). Exploring the Perception of Influencers vs. Traditional Celebrities. *Proceedings of the 8th International Conference on Social Media & Society - #SMSociety, 17*, 1–5. 10.1145/3097286.3097322

Grazzini, L., Acuti, D., & Aiello, G. (2021). Solving the puzzle of sustainable fashion consumption: The role of consumers' implicit attitudes and perceived warmth. *Journal of Cleaner Production, 287*, 125579. doi:10.1016/j.jclepro.2020.125579

Guedes, G., & Soares, P. (2005). Branding of fashion products: A communication process, a marketing approach. *Proceedings of The Association for Business Communication,* 7.

Guercini, S., Milanesi, M., Mir-Bernal, P., & Runfola, A. (2020). Surfing the Waves of New Marketing in Luxury Fashion: The Case of Online Multi-brand Retailers. In Springer Proceedings in Business and Economics (pp. 203–210). doi:10.1007/978-3-030-47595-6_25

Guitton, M. J. (2012). Living in the Hutt Space: Immersive process in the star wars role-play community of second life. *Computers in Human Behavior, 28*(5), 1681–1691. doi:10.1016/j.chb.2012.04.006

Gunawardena, C. N., & Zittle, F. J. (1997). Social presence as a predictor of satisfaction within a computer- mediated conferencing environment. *American Journal of Distance Education, 11*(3), 8–26. doi:10.1080/08923649709526970

Guo, G., & Elgendi, M. (2013). A new recommender system for 3D E-commerce: An EEG based approach. *Journal of Advanced Management Science, 1*(1), 61–65. doi:10.12720/joams.1.1.61-65

Gupta, S., & Pooja. (2021). Marketing to the green generation: How Generation Z's eco-consciousness is changing the game. *Journal of Management Research.*

Gupta, S., Gwozdz, W., & Gentry, J. (2019). The Role of Style Versus Fashion Orientation on Sustainable Apparel Consumption. *Journal of Macromarketing, 39*(2), 188–207. Advance online publication. doi:10.1177/0276146719835283

Guzzetti, A., Crespi, R., & Atwal, G. (2023). Gaming and luxury brands: Love and hate. *The Journal of Business Strategy*, *45*(3), 206–213. doi:10.1108/JBS-05-2023-0086

Gwilt, A. (2020). Fashion and sustainability: Repairing the clothes we wear. In *Fashion theory* (pp. 188–200). Routledge. doi:10.4324/9781315099620-21

Haanpaa, L. (2007). Consumers' green commitment: Indication of a postmodern lifestyle? *International Journal of Consumer Studies*, *31*(5), 478–486. doi:10.1111/j.1470-6431.2007.00598.x

Haines, S., Fares, O. H., Mohan, M., & Lee, S. H. (2023, November 08). (Mark). (2023). Social media fashion influencer eWOM communications: Understanding the trajectory of sustainable fashion conversations on YouTube fashion haul videos. *Journal of Fashion Marketing and Management*, *27*(6), 1027–1046. Advance online publication. doi:10.1108/JFMM-02-2022-0029

Haines, S., & Lee, S. H. (2022). One size fits all? Segmenting consumers to predict sustainable fashion behavior. *Journal of Fashion Marketing and Management*, *26*(2), 383–398. doi:10.1108/JFMM-08-2020-0161

Hair, J.F., Black, W.C., Babin. B.J., & Anderson. R. E. (2010). Multivariate data analysis. Prentice Hall.

Hair, J. F. Jr, Matthews, L. M., Matthews, R. L., & Sarstedt, M. (2017). PLS-SEM or CB-SEM: Updated guidelines on which method to use. *International Journal of Multivariate Data Analysis*, *1*(2). 107–123.doi.org/10.1504/IJMDA.2017.087624

Hair, J., Black, W. C., Babin, B. J., Anderson, R. E., & Tatham, R. (2006). Multivariate data analysis. (Pearson Ed).

Hair, J., Hult, G. T. M., Ringle, C., & Sarstedt, M. (2014). *A Primer on Partial Least Squares Structural Equation Modeling (PLS-SEM)*. SAGE Publications, Incorporated.

Hajli, N. (2014). A study of the impact of social media on consumers. *International Journal of Market Research*, *56*(3), 387–404. Advance online publication. doi:10.2501/IJMR-2014-025

Hallanan, L. (2020, March 17). *Alibaba uses lockdown to promote its Virtual Avatar Game*. Jing Daily. https://jingdaily.com/posts/alibaba-uses-lockdown-to-promote-its-virtual-avatar-game

Hamid, A. A., Razak, F. Z., Bakar, A. A., & Abdullah, W. S. (2016). The effects of perceived usefulness and perceived ease of use on continuance intention to use E-government. *Procedia Economics and Finance*, *35*, 644–649. doi:10.1016/S2212-5671(16)00079-4

Han, Y., Long, X.P., Huang, Y.M., & Jiang, Z.H. (2009). Effect of LJ or Exp-6 Potential Function on Calcula tion of Reduced Second Viral Coefficient. *Chin. J. Energ. Mater.*

Hanson, B. (2023). Documenting the next chapter in one of fashion's biggest, and fastest- developing, stories. *The Interline*. Available at: https://www.theinterline.com/2023/12/13/digital-product-creation-report-2023-available- now/

Hao, W., Björkman, E., Lilliestråle, M., & Hedin, N. (2014). Activated Carbons for Water Treatment Prepared by Phosphoric Acid Activation of Hydrothermally Treated Beer Waste. *Industrial & Engineering Chemistry Research*, *53*(40), 15389–15397. doi:10.1021/ie5004569

Hapsari, P. D. N., & Belgiawan, P. F. (n.d.). *The Impact of Slow and Circular Fashion Concept on Consumers Purchase Intention*. Academic Press.

Harland, P., Staats, H., & Wilke, H. A. M. (2007). Situational and personality factors as direct or personal norm mediated predictors of pro-environmental behavior: Questions derived from norm-activation theory. *Basic and Applied Social Psychology*, *29*(4), 323–334. doi:10.1080/01973530701665058

Harrigan, M., Feddema, K., Wang, S., Harrigan, P., & Diot, E. (2021). How trust leads to online purchase intention founded in perceived usefulness and peer communication. *Journal of Consumer Behaviour*, *20*(5), 1297–1312. doi:10.1002/cb.1936

Hartman, K. B., & Spiro, R. L. (2005). Recapturing store image in customer-based store equity: A construct conceptualization. *Journal of Business Research*, *58*(8), 1112–1120. doi:10.1016/j.jbusres.2004.01.008

Hartmann, T. (2016). Mass Communication and Para-Social Interaction: Observations on Intimacy at a Distance. In Schlüsselwerke der Medienwirkungsforschung (pp. 75–84). Springer Fachmedien Wiesbaden. doi:10.1007/978-3-658-09923-7_7

Hartmann, P., & Apaolaza Ibáñez, V. (2006). Green value added. *Marketing Intelligence & Planning*, *24*(7), 673–680. doi:10.1108/02634500610711842

Hasan, M. M., Cai, L., Ji, X., & Ocran, F. M. (2022). *Eco-Friendly Clothing Market: A Study of Willingness to Purchase Organic Cotton Clothing in Bangladesh*. Sustainability. doi:10.3390/su14084827

Hasbullah, N. N., & Sulaiman, Z. (1945). Drivers of sustainable apparel purchase intention: An empirical study of Malaysian millennial consumers. *Sustainability (New Rochelle, N.Y.)*, *14*(4).

Hassan, S. H., Yeap, J. A., & Al-Kumaim, N. H. (2022). Sustainable fashion consumption: Advocating philanthropic and economic motives in clothing disposal behaviour. *Sustainability (Basel)*, *14*(3), 1875. doi:10.3390/su14031875

Hayes, A. F., & Preacher, K. J. (2013). Conditional processing modeling: Using structural equation modeling to examine contingent causal processes. In G. R. Hancock & R. O. Mueller (Eds.), *Structural equation modeling: A second course* (pp. 219–266). IAP Information Age Publishing.

Hayes, S. G., & Venkatraman, P. (Eds.). (2016). *Materials and Technology for Sportswear and Performance Apparel* (p. 370). CRC Press.

Heinl, L. T., Baatz, A., Beckmann, M., & Wehnert, P. (2021). Investigating sustainable NGO–firm partnerships: An experimental study of consumer perception of co-branded products. *Sustainability (Basel)*, *13*(22), 12761. doi:10.3390/su132212761

Heller Baird, C., & Parasnis, G. (2011). From social media to social customer relationship management. *Strategy and Leadership*, *39*(5), 30–37. doi:10.1108/10878571111161507

Heng, E. (2022, April 12). *Digital fashion house the Fabricant paves the way for more innovation within the metaverse*. Vogue Singapore. https://vogue.sg/the-fabricant-metaverse-funding/

Henion, K. E., & Kinnear, T. C. (1976b). A Guide to Ecological Marketing. In K. E. Henion & T. C. Kinnear (Eds.), *Ecological Marketing*. American Marketing Association.

Henninger, C. E., Alevizou, P. J., & Oates, C. J. (2016). What is sustainable fashion? *Journal of Fashion Marketing and Management*, *20*(4), 400–416. doi:10.1108/JFMM-07-2015-0052

Hiller Connell, K. Y., & Kozar, J. M. (2012). Social Normative Influence: An Exploratory Study Investigating its Effectiveness in Increasing Engagement in Sustainable Apparel-Purchasing Behaviors. *Journal of Global Fashion Marketing*. doi:10.1080/20932685.2012.10600847

Hiller Connell, K. Y., & Kozar, J. M. (2017). *Introduction to special issue on sustainability and the triple bottom line within the global clothing and textiles industry* (Vol. 4). Springer.

Hoffmann, S., & Lee, M. S. W. (2016). Consume Less and Be Happy? Consume Less to Be Happy! An Introduction to the Special Issue on Anti-Consumption and Consumer Well-Being. *The Journal of Consumer Affairs*, *50*(1), 3–17. doi:10.1111/joca.12104

Hollebeek, L. D., Glynn, M. S., & Brodie, R. J. (2014). Consumer Brand Engagement in Social Media: Conceptualization, Scale Development and Validation. *Journal of Interactive Marketing*, *28*(2), 149–165. doi:10.1016/j.intmar.2013.12.002

Hong, I. B., & Cha, H. S. (2013). The mediating role of consumer trust in an online merchant in predicting purchase intention. *International Journal of Information Management*, *33*(6), 927–939. doi:10.1016/j.ijinfomgt.2013.08.007

Hopper, J. R., & Nielsen, J. M. (1991). Recycling as altruistic behavior normative and behavioral strategies to expand participation in a community recycling program. *Environment and Behavior*, *23*(2), 195–220. doi:10.1177/0013916591232004

Horton, D., & Richard Wohl, R. (1956). Mass Communication and Para-Social Interaction. *Psychiatry*, *19*(3), 215–229. doi:10.1080/00332747.1956.11023049 PMID:13359569

Hosta, M., & Zabkar, V. (2021). Antecedents of environmentally and socially responsible sustainable consumer behavior. *Journal of Business Ethics*, *171*(2), 273–293. doi:10.1007/s10551-019-04416-0

Howard, H. W. (2023). The adoption of digital fashion as an end product: A systematic literature review of research foci and future research agenda. *Journal of Global Fashion Marketing*, *15*(1), 1–26. doi:10.1080/20932685.2023.2251033

Howard, T. W. (2010). *Belonging*. Design to Thrive., doi:10.1016/B978-0-12-374921-5.00006-1

Hoyer, W., & MacInnis, D. (2004). *Consumer Behaviour* (3rd ed.). CENGAGE.

Hsieh, M. H., & Lindridge, A. (2005). Universal appeals with local specifications. *Journal of Product and Brand Management*, *14*(1), 14–28. doi:10.1108/10610420510583716

Hsu, S. H., Wen, M.-H., & Wu, M.-C. (2009). Exploring user experiences as predictors of MMORPG addiction. *Computers & Education*, *53*(3), 990–999. doi:10.1016/j.compedu.2009.05.016

Huang, J. S., Huang, J. M., & Zhang, W. (2021). Semicovariance Coefficient Analysis of Spike Proteins from SARS-CoV-2 and Other Coronaviruses for Viral Evolution and Characteristics Associated with Fatality. *Entropy*. https://www.mdpi.com/1099-4300/23/5/512

Hudson, M., & Cairns, P. (2014). Interrogating social presence in games with experiential vignettes. *Entertainment Computing*, *5*(2), 101–114. doi:10.1016/j.entcom.2014.01.001

Hu, N., Bose, I., Koh, N. S., & Liu, L. (2012). Manipulation of online reviews: An analysis of ratings, readability, and sentiments. *Decision Support Systems*, *52*(3), 674–684. Advance online publication. doi:10.1016/j.dss.2011.11.002

Hung, K., Li, S. Y., & Tse, D. K. (2011). Interpersonal Trust and Platform Credibility in a Chinese Multibrand Online Community. *Journal of Advertising*, *40*(3), 99–112. doi:10.2753/JOA0091-3367400308

Hunt, S. D. (2011). Sustainable marketing, equity, and economic growth: A resource-advantage, economic freedom approach. Journal of the Academy of Marketing Science. *International Journal of Industrial Marketing*, *1*(2), 1–19.

Huynh-The, T., Gadekallu, T. R., Wang, W., Yenduri, G., Ranaweera, P., Pham, Q.-V., da Costa, D. B., & Liyanage, M. (2023). Blockchain for the metaverse: A Review. *Future Generation Computer Systems*, *143*, 401–419. doi:10.1016/j.future.2023.02.008

Hwang, C., Lee, Y., Diddi, S., & Karpova, E. (2016). "Don't buy this jacket": Consumer reaction toward anti-consumption apparel advertisement. *Journal of Fashion Marketing and Management*, *20*(4), 435–452. doi:10.1108/JFMM-12-2014-0087

Isto. (2023). *About*. Consulted on June 28, 2023, at Isto: https://isto.pt/pages/about

Italian Trade Agency. (2023). *L'italia nell'economia internazionale*. Author.

Jacobs, K., Petersen, L., Hörisch, J., & Battenfeld, D. (2018). Green thinking but thoughtless buying? An empirical extension of the value-attitude-behaviour hierarchy in sustainable clothing. *Journal of Cleaner Production*, *203*, 1155–1169. Advance online publication. doi:10.1016/j.jclepro.2018.07.320

Jalali, S. S., & Khalid, H. (2019). Understanding Instagram Influencers Values in Green Consumption Behaviour: A Review Paper. *Open International Journal of Informatics*, *7*(1), 47-58. https://oiji.utm.my/index.php/oiji/article/view/115

James, F. P. (2002). Experience use History as a segmentation tool to examine golf travelers' satisfaction, perceived value and repurchased intention. *Journal of Vacation Marketing*, *8*(4), 332–342. doi:10.1177/135676670200800404

Jang, Y., & Park, E. (2019). An adoption model for virtual reality games: The roles of presence and enjoyment. *Telematics and Informatics*, *42*, 101239. doi:10.1016/j.tele.2019.101239

Jansson, J. (2011). Consumer eco-innovation adoption: Assessing attitudinal factors and perceived product characteristics. *Business Strategy and the Environment*, *20*(3), 192–210. doi:10.1002/bse.690

Jansson, J., Marell, A., & Nordlund, A. (2010). Green consumer behaviour: Determinants of curtailment and eco-innovation adoption. *Journal of Consumer Marketing*, *27*(4), 358–370. doi:10.1108/07363761011052396

Jaworski, B., Lutz, R., Marshall, G. W., Price, L., & Varadarajan, R. (2019, February 22). *What is Marketing?* American Marketing Association. https://www.ama.org/the-definition-of-marketing-what-is-marketing/

Jegethesan, K., Sneddon, J. N., & Soutar, G. N. (2012). Young Australian consumers' preferences for fashion apparel attributes. *Journal of Fashion Marketing and Management*, *16*(3), 275–289. doi:10.1108/13612021211246044

Jeong, D., & Ko, E. (2021). The influence of consumers' self-concept and perceived value on sustainable fashion. *Journal of Global Scholars of Marketing Science: Bridging Asia and the World*. doi:10.1080/21639159.2021.1885303

Jermsittiparsert, K., Siam, M. R. A., Issa, M. R., Ahmed, U., & Pahi, M. H. (2019). Do consumers expect companies to be socially responsible? The impact of corporate social responsibility on buying behavior. *Uncertain Supply Chain Management*, 741–752. doi:10.5267/j.uscm.2019.1.005

Jestratijevic, I., Rudd, N. A., & Uanhoro, J. (2020). Transparency of sustainability disclosures among luxury and mass-market fashion brands. *Journal of Global Fashion Marketing*, *11*(2), 99–116. doi:10.1080/20932685.2019.1708774

Jin, S. V., Muqaddam, A., & Ryu, E. (2019). Instafamous and social media influencer marketing. *Marketing Intelligence & Planning*, *37*(5), 567–579. Advance online publication. doi:10.1108/MIP-09-2018-0375

Joergens, C. (2006). Ethical fashion: Myth or future trend? *Journal of Fashion Marketing and Management*, *10*(3), 360–371. doi:10.1108/13612020610679321

Johnson, C. Y., Bowker, J. M., & Cordell, H. K. (2004). Ethnic variation in environmental belief and behavior. *Environment and Behavior*, *36*(2), 157–186. doi:10.1177/0013916503251478

Jones, A., & Kang, J. (2020). Media technology shifts: Exploring millennial consumers' fashion-information- seeking behaviors and motivations. *Canadian Journal of Administrative Sciences / Revue Canadienne Des Sciences de l'Administration*, *37*(1), 13–29. doi:10.1002/cjas.1546

Joo, J., & Sang, Y. (2013). Exploring Koreans' smartphone usage: An integrated model of the technology acceptance model and uses and gratifications theory. *Computers in Human Behavior*, *29*(6), 2512–2518. Advance online publication. doi:10.1016/j.chb.2013.06.002

Jorgenson, S. N., Stephens, J. C., & White, B. (2019). Environmental education in transition: A critical review of recent research on climate change and energy education. *The Journal of Environmental Education*, *50*(3), 160–171. doi:10.1080/00958964.2019.1604478

Joy, A., Sherry, J. F. Jr, Venkatesh, A., Wang, J., & Chan, R. (2012). Fast fashion, sustainability, and the ethical appeal of luxury brands. *Fashion Theory*, *16*(3), 273–295. Advance online publication. doi:10.2752/175174112X13340749707123

Jung, S., & Jin, B. (2014). A theoretical investigation of slow fashion: Sustainable future of the apparel industry. *International Journal of Consumer Studies*, *38*(5), 510–519. doi:10.1111/ijcs.12127

Jung, S., & Jin, B. (2016). From quantity to quality: Understanding slow fashion consumers for sustainability and consumer education. *International Journal of Consumer Studies*, *40*(4), 410–421. doi:10.1111/ijcs.12276

Juvan, E., & Dolnicar, S. (2014). The attitude–behaviour gap in sustainable tourism. *Annals of Tourism Research*, *48*, 76–95. doi:10.1016/j.annals.2014.05.012

K., M., & Panakaje, N. (2022). Customer perception in relationship between social-media and purchasing behavior of fashion products. *International Journal of Case Studies in Business, IT, and Education*, 67–98. doi:10.47992/IJCSBE.2581.6942.0185

Kaczorowska, J., Rejman, K., Halicka, E., Szczebyło, A., & Górska-Warsewicz, H. (2019). Impact of food sustainability labels on the perceived product value and price expectations of urban consumers. *Sustainability (Basel)*, *11*(24), 7240. doi:10.3390/su11247240

Kaiser, F. G., Hubner, G., & Bogner, F. X. (2005). Contrasting the theory of planned behavior with the value-belief-norm model in explaining conservation behavior1. *Journal of Applied Social Psychology*, *35*(10), 2150–2170. doi:10.1111/j.1559-1816.2005.tb02213.x

Kalafatis, S., Pollard, M., East, R., & Tsogas, M. H. (1999). Green marketing and Ajzen's theory of planned behaviour: A cross-market examination. *Journal of Consumer Marketing*, *16*(5), 441–460. doi:10.1108/07363769910289550

Kallawar, G. A., & Bhanvase, B. A. (2024). A review on existing and emerging approaches for textile wastewater treatments: Challenges and future perspectives. *Environmental Science and Pollution Research International*, *31*(2), 1748–1789. doi:10.1007/s11356-023-31175-3 PMID:38055170

Kalmkar, S., Mujawar, A., & Liyakat, D. K. K. S. (2022). 3D E-Commers using AR. *International Journal of Information Technology & Computer Engineering*, *2*(6), 18–27. doi:10.55529/ijitc.26.18.27

Kamins, M. A. (1990). An investigation into the "match-up" hypothesis in celebrity advertising: When beauty may be only skin deep. *Journal of Advertising*, *19*(1), 4–13. Advance online publication. doi:10.1080/00913367.1990.10673175

Kang, J. Y. M., & Johnson, K. K. (2013). How does social commerce work for apparel shopping? Apparel social e-shopping with social network storefronts. *Journal of Customer Behaviour*, *12*(1), 53–72. doi:10.1362/147539213X13645550618524

Kang, J. Y. M., & Kim, J. (2017). Online customer relationship marketing tactics through social media and perceived customer retention orientation of the green retailer. *Journal of Fashion Marketing and Management*, *21*(3), 298–316. Advance online publication. doi:10.1108/JFMM-08-2016-0071

Kanwal, N. D. S., Panda, T., Patro, U. S., & Das, S. (2024). Societal Sustainability: The Innovative Practices of the 21st Century. In Sustainable Disposal Methods of Food Wastes in Hospitality Operations (pp. 193-213). IGI Global.

Karale Aishwarya, A. (2023). Smart Billing Cart Using RFID, YOLO and Deep Learning for Mall Administration. *International Journal of Instrumentation and Innovation Sciences, 8*(2).

Karavasilis, G., Nerantzaki, D.-M., Pantelidis, P., Paschaloudis, D., & Vrana, V. (2015). What Generation Y in Greece thinks about Green Hotels. *World Journal of Entrepreneurship, Management and Sustainable Development, 11*(4), 268–280. doi:10.1108/WJEMSD-02-2015-0010

Karimi Alavijeh, M. R., Esmaeili, A., Sepahvand, A., & Davidaviciene, V. (2018). The effect of customer equity drivers on word-of-mouth behavior with mediating role of customer loyalty and purchase intention. *The Engineering Economist, 29*(2). Advance online publication. doi:10.5755/j01.ee.29.2.17718

Karney, T., Vize, R., & Gong, T. (2019). *Digitally Engaged Consumers: A Multi-Level Perspective of Higher Education Actors and Their Technology Readiness*. Academic Press.

Karpova, E. E., Reddy-Best, K. L., & Bayat, F. (2022). The fashion system's environmental impact: Theorizing the market's institutional actors, actions, logics, and norms. *Fashion Theory, 26*(6), 799–820. doi:10.1080/1362704X.2022.2027680

Karypidis, M., & Savvidis, G. (2018). *Analysis of Factors Influencing Needle Penetration Force through Woven Fabrics*. Academic Press.

Karypidis, M. (2018). Sewability interdependence on rigid structures. *IOP Conference Series. Materials Science and Engineering, 459*(1), 012048. doi:10.1088/1757-899X/459/1/012048

Karypidis, M., Papadaki, A. I., & Stalika, A. (2023a). An overview of the available water textile effluent treatments. *Journal of International Scientific Publications: Materials. Metals Technology, 17*(1), 178–188. doi:10.62991/MMT1996371718

Karypidis, M., Papadaki, A. I., & Stalika, A. (2023b). A critical evaluation of the use of hemp as a sustainable solutions in garment making treatments. *Journal of International Scientific Publications: Materials. Metals Technology, 17*, 189–201. doi:10.62991/MMT1996373709

Katz, E., Haas, H., & Gurevitch, M. (1973). On the Use of the Mass Media for Important Things. *American Sociological Review, 38*(2), 164. Advance online publication. doi:10.2307/2094393

Kautish, P., Khare, A., & Sharma, R. (2021). Influence of values, brand consciousness and behavioral intentions in predicting luxury fashion consumption. *Journal of Product and Brand Management, 30*(4), 513–531. doi:10.1108/JPBM-08-2019-2535

Kawa, L. W., Rahmadiani, S. F., & Kumar, S. (2013). Factors Affecting Consumer Decision Making: A Survey of Young-Adults on Imported Cosmetics in Jabodetabek, Indonesia. The SIJ Transactions on Industrial, Financial & Business Management, 1(5).

Kawamura, Y. (2014). *Fashion-ology: An introduction to fashion studies*. Bloomsbury.

Kazi & Shaikh. (2023). Machine Learning in the Production Process Control of Metal Melting. *Journal of Advancement in Machines, 8*(2).

Kazi K. (2022). Model for Agricultural Information system to improve crop yield using IoT. *Journal of Open Source Development, 9*(2), 16 – 24.

Kazi Kutubuddin, S. L. (2022). Predict the Severity of Diabetes cases, using K-Means and Decision Tree Approach. *Journal of Advances in Shell Programming, 9*(2), 24–31.

Kazi, K S. (2022). Business Mode and Product Life Cycle to Improve Marketing in Healthcare Units. *E-Commerce for Future & Trends, 9*(3), 1-9.

Kazi. (2022). *A Review paper Alzheimer*. Academic Press.

Kazi. (2022). *Systematic Survey on Alzheimer (AD) Diseases Detection*. Academic Press.

Kazi. (2023). Electronics with Artificial Intelligence Creating a Smarter Future: A Review. *Journal of Communication Engineering and Its Innovations*, *9*(3), 38–42.

Kazi, K. (2022). Smart Grid energy saving technique using Machine Learning. *Journal of Instrumentation Technology and Innovations*, *12*(3), 1–10.

Kazi, K. (2024). AI-Driven IoT (AIIoT) in Healthcare Monitoring. In T. Nguyen & N. Vo (Eds.), *Using Traditional Design Methods to Enhance AI-Driven Decision Making* (pp. 77–101). IGI Global. doi:10.4018/979-8-3693-0639-0.ch003

Kazi, K. S. (2017). Significance And Usage Of Face Recognition System. *Scholarly Journal For Humanity Science and English Language*, *4*(20), 4764–4772.

Kazi, K. S. (2023). Detection of Malicious Nodes in IoT Networks based on Throughput and ML. *Journal of Electrical and Power System Engineering*, *9*(1), 22–29.

Kazi, K. S. L. (2018). Significance of Projection and Rotation of Image in Color Matching for High-Quality Panoramic Images used for Aquatic study. *International Journal of Aquatic Science*, *09*(02), 130–145.

Kazi, S. (2023). Fruit Grading, Disease Detection, and an Image Processing Strategy. *Journal of Image Processing and Artificial Intelligence*, *9*(2), 17–34.

Kazi, S. S. L. (2023). ML in the Electronics Manufacturing Industry. *Journal of Switching Hub*, *8*(3), 9–13.

Kazi, V. (2023). Deep Learning, YOLO and RFID based smart Billing Handcart. *Journal of Communication Engineering & Systems*, *13*(1), 1–8.

Keesom, W. H. (1915). The second viral coefficient for rigid spherical molecules, whose mutual attraction is equivalent to that of a quadruplet placed at their centre. *Proc. R. Acad. Sci.* https://dwc.knaw.nl/DL/publications/PU00012540.pdf

Kell, K. (2021, December 22). *Hemp Fabric: What is it and is it Sustainable?* Going Zero Waste. https://www.goingzerowaste.com/blog/hemp-fabric-what-is-it-and-is-it-sustainable

Keller, K. L. (2008). Strategic Brand Management. Building, Measuring, and Managing Brand Equity. Pearson Education International.

Keller, K. L. (2001). Building customer-based brand equity: Creating brand resonance requires carefully sequenced brand-building efforts. *Marketing Management*, *10*(2), 15–19.

Keller, K. L. (2009). Building strong brands in a modern marketing communications environment. *Journal of Marketing Communications*, *15*(2–3), 139–155. doi:10.1080/13527260902757530

Kelman, H. C. (2006). Interests, Relationships, Identities: Three Central Issues for Individuals and Groups in Negotiating Their Social Environment. *Annual Review of Psychology*, *57*(1), 1–26. doi:10.1146/annurev.psych.57.102904.190156 PMID:16318587

Keng, C. J., Chang, W. H., Chen, C. H., & Chang, Y. Y. (2016). Mere virtual presence with product experience affects brand attitude and purchase intention. *Social Behavior and Personality*, *44*(3), 431–444. doi:10.2224/sbp.2016.44.3.431

Keng, C. J., Chen, Y. H., & Huang, Y. H. (2018). The influence of mere virtual presence with product experience and social virtual product experience on brand attitude and purchase intention: Conformity and social ties as moderators. *Corporate Management Review*, *38*(2), 57–94.

Keng, C. J., Liao, T. H., & Yang, Y. I. (2012). The effects of sequential combinations of virtual experience, direct experience, and indirect experience: The moderating roles of need for touch and product involvement. *Electronic Commerce Research*, *12*(2), 177–199. doi:10.1007/s10660-012-9093-9

Kenk, K. (2022, April 5). *Greenwashing in fast fashion: the case of Shein - Let's Do It foundation*. Let's Do It Foundation. https://letsdoitfoundation.org/2022/04/05/greenwashing-in-fast-fashion-the-case-of-shein/

Khanal, A., Akhtaruzzaman, M., & Kularatne, I. (2021). The influence of social media on stakeholder engagement and the corporate social responsibility of small businesses. *Corporate Social Responsibility and Environmental Management*, *28*(6), 1921–1929. doi:10.1002/csr.2169

Khandual, A., & Pradhan, S. (2019). Fashion brands and consumers approach towards sustainable fashion. *Fast Fashion, Fashion Brands and Sustainable Consumption*, 37–54.

Khan, M. M., Fatima, F., Ranjha, M. T., & Akhtar, S. (2022). Willingness to Pay For Sustainable Green Clothing. *Indonesian Journal of Social and Environmental Issues*, *3*(2), 167–178. doi:10.47540/ijsei.v3i2.565

Khare, A. (2023). Green apparel buying: Role of past behavior, knowledge, and peer influence in the assessment of green apparel perceived benefits. *Journal of International Consumer Marketing*, *35*(1), 109–125. doi:10.1080/08961530.2019.1635553

Khare, A., & Kautish, P. (2021). Cosmopolitanism, self-identity, online communities and green apparel perception. *Marketing Intelligence & Planning*. Advance online publication. doi:10.1108/MIP-11-2019-0556

Khare, A., & Kautish, P. (2022). Antecedents to green apparel purchase behavior of Indian consumers. *Journal of Global Scholars of Marketing Science*, *32*(2), 222–251. doi:10.1080/21639159.2021.1885301

Khare, A., & Sadachar, A. (2017). Green apparel buying behaviour: A study on Indian youth. *International Journal of Consumer Studies*, *41*(5), 558–569. Advance online publication. doi:10.1111/ijcs.12367

Khare, A., Sadachar, A., & Chakraborty, S. (2022). Influence of celebrities and online communities on Indian consumers' green clothing involvement and purchase behavior. *Journal of Fashion Marketing and Management*, *26*(4), 676–699. Advance online publication. doi:10.1108/JFMM-02-2021-0033

Kim, A. J., & Johnson, K. K. P. (2016). Power of consumers using social media: Examining the influences of brand-related user-generated content on Facebook. *Computers in Human Behavior*, *58*, 98–108. doi:10.1016/j.chb.2015.12.047

Kim, B., Hong, S., & Lee, H. (2021). Brand Communities on Instagram: Exploring Fortune 500 Companies' Instagram Communication Practices. *International Journal of Strategic Communication*, *15*(3), 177–192. Advance online publication. doi:10.1080/1553118X.2020.1867556

Kim, D. E. (2016). Psychophysical testing of garment size variation using three-dimensional virtual try-on technology. *Textile Research Journal*, *86*(4), 365–379. doi:10.1177/0040517515591782

Kim, H.-S., & Damhorst, M. L. (1998). Environmental concern and apparel consumption. *Clothing & Textiles Research Journal*, *16*(3), 126–133. doi:10.1177/0887302X9801600303

Kim, J., & Forsythe, S. (2008). Adoption of virtual try-on technology for Online Apparel Shopping. *Journal of Interactive Marketing*, *22*(2), 45–59. doi:10.1002/dir.20113

Kim, J.-H., Kim, M., Park, M., & Yoo, J. (2023). Immersive Interactive Technologies and virtual shopping experiences: Differences in consumer perceptions between augmented reality (AR) and virtual reality (VR). *Telematics and Informatics*, *77*, 101936. doi:10.1016/j.tele.2022.101936

Kim, J., Kang, S., & Lee, K. H. (2020). How social capital impacts the purchase intention of sustainable fashion products. *Journal of Business Research*, *117*, 596–603. Advance online publication. doi:10.1016/j.jbusres.2018.10.010

Kim, K. H., & Kim, E. Y. (2020). Fashion marketing trends in social media and sustainability in fashion management. *Journal of Business Research, 117*, 508–509. doi:10.1016/j.jbusres.2020.06.001

Kim, M., Kim, J. H., & Lennon, S. J. (2006). Online service attributes available on apparel retail web sites: An E-S-QUAL approach. *Managing Service Quality, 16*(1), 51–77. doi:10.1108/09604520610639964

Kim, W. E., & Thinavan Periyayya, V. (2013). The Beauty of Green Branding: Kinnear, T.C. and Taylor, J.R. (1973) 'The effect of ecological concern on brand perceptions'. *JMR, Journal of Marketing Research, 10*(2), 191. doi:10.2307/3149825

Kim, Y. K., & Sullivan, P. (2019). Emotional branding speaks to consumers' hearts: The case of fashion brands. *Fashion and Textiles, 6*(1), 1–16. doi:10.1186/s40691-018-0164-y

Kim, Y., & Suh, S. (2022). The core value of sustainable fashion: A case study on "Market Credit". *Sustainability (Basel), 14*(21), 14423. doi:10.3390/su142114423

Kim, Y., Yun, S., Lee, J., & Ko, E. (2016). How consumer knowledge shapes green consumption: An empirical study on voluntary carbon offsetting. *International Journal of Advertising, 35*(1), 23–41. Advance online publication. doi:10.1080/02650487.2015.1096102

Kiya, R. (2012). A study of the effects of firm ability association and brand awareness on repurchase intention and the mediator role of product quality and brand association in buying decision making process. *Marketing Management*, 14.

Koay, K. Y., Cheung, M. L., Soh, P. C.-H., & Teoh, C. W. (2022). Social media influencer marketing: The moderating role of materialism. *European Business Review, 34*(2), 224–243. doi:10.1108/EBR-02-2021-0032

Kobayashi, H. (1959). *Molecular weight dependence of intrinsic viscosity, diffusion constant, and second viral coefficient of polyacrylonitrile. Journal of Polymer Science.* > doi:10.1002/pol.1959.1203913530

Koll, O., & von Wallpach, S. (2009). One brand perception? Or many? The heterogeneity of intrabrand knowledge. *Journal of Product and Brand Management, 18*(5), 338–345. doi:10.1108/10610420910981819

Kong, H. M., Ko, E., Chae, H., & Mattila, P. (2016). Understanding fashion consumers' attitude and behavioral intention toward sustainable fashion products: Focus on sustainable knowledge sources and knowledge types. *Journal of Global Fashion Marketing, 7*(2), 103–119. doi:10.1080/20932685.2015.1131435

Kong, H. M., Witmaier, A., & Ko, E. (2021). Sustainability and social media communication: How consumers respond to marketing efforts of luxury and non-luxury fashion brands. *Journal of Business Research, 131*, 640–651. doi:10.1016/j.jbusres.2020.08.021

Kosgiker, G. M. (2018). Machine Learning- Based System, Food Quality Inspection and Grading in Food industry. *International Journal of Food and Nutritional Sciences, 11*(10), 723–730.

Koszewska, M. (2021). Clothing labels: Why are they important for sustainable consumer behavior? *Journal of Consumer Protection and Food Safety, 16*. 1–3.doi.org/10.1007/s00003-021-01319-z

Koszewska, M. (2016). Understanding consumer behavior in the sustainable clothing market: Model development and verification. *Green Fashion, 1*, 43–94. doi:10.1007/978-981-10-0111-6_3

Kotler, P. (1994). Marketing Management: Analysis, Planning, Implementation and Lee, K. (2008), "Opportunities for green marketing: young consumers. *Marketing Intelligence & Planning, 26*(6), 573–586.

Kotler, P., & Armstrong, G. (2010). *Principles of Marketing*. Pearson Prentice Hall.

Kreijns, K., Van Acker, F., Vermeulen, M., & Van Buuren, H. (2014). Community of Inquiry: Social Presence Revisited. *E-Learning and Digital Media, 11*(1), 5–18. doi:10.2304/elea.2014.11.1.5

Kripesh, A. S., Prabhu, H. M., & Sriram, K. V. (2020). An empirical study on the effect of product information and perceived usefulness on purchase intention during online shopping in India. *International Journal of Business Innovation and Research*, *21*(4), 509–522. doi:10.1504/IJBIR.2020.105982

Kühn, S. W., & Petzer, D. J. (2018a). Fostering purchase intentions toward online retailer websites in an emerging market: An S-O-R perspective. *Journal of Internet Commerce*, *17*(3), 255–282. doi:10.1080/15332861.2018.1463799

Kumar, N., Garg, P., & Singh, S. (2022). Pro-environmental purchase intention towards eco-friendly apparel: Augmenting the theory of planned behavior with perceived consumer effectiveness and environmental concern. *Journal of Global Fashion Marketing*. doi:10.1080/20932685.2021.2016062

Kumari, A. (2024). Transforming Business for a Sustainable Future Using Green Marketing. *Multidisciplinary Approach to Information Technology in Library and Information Science*, 132-150.

Kusyanti, A., Catherina, H. P. A., Puspitasari, D. R., & Sari, Y. A. L. (2018). Teen's social media adoption: An empirical investigation in Indonesia. *International Journal of Advanced Computer Science and Applications*, *9*(2). Advance online publication. doi:10.14569/IJACSA.2018.090252

Kutub, K. (2022). Detection of Malicious Nodes in IoT Networks based on packet loss using ML. *Journal of Mobile Computing, Communication & mobile. Networks*, *9*(3), 9–16.

Kutubuddin, K. (2022). Big data and HR Analytics in Talent Management: A Study. *Recent Trends in Parallel Computing*, *9*(3), 16–26.

LAB University of Applied Sciences. (2021). *Consumer Awareness on Sustainable Fashion*. https://www.theseus.fi/

Lai, O. (2024, January 5). *7 Fast fashion companies responsible for environmental pollution*. Earth.Org. https://earth.org/fast-fashion-companies/

Lamberton, C. P., Naylor, R. W., & Haws, K. L. (2013). Same destination, different paths: When and how does observing others' choices and reasoning alter confidence in our own choices? *Journal of Consumer Psychology*, *23*(1), 74–89. doi:10.1016/j.jcps.2012.01.002

Lastovicka, J. L., & Joachimsthaler, E. A. (1988). Improving the detection of personality-behaviour relationships in Consumer Research. *The Journal of Consumer Research*, *14*(4), 583–587. doi:10.1086/209138

Lau, O., & Ki, C.-W. (2021). Can consumers' gamified, personalized, and engaging experiences with VR fashion apps increase in-app purchase intention by fulfilling needs? *Fashion and Textiles*, *8*(1), 36. Advance online publication. doi:10.1186/s40691-021-00270-9

Laurent, G., & Kapferer, J.-N. (1985). Measuring consumer involvement profiles. *JMR, Journal of Marketing Research*, *22*(1), 41–53. doi:10.1177/002224378502200104

Law, M., & Ng, M. (2016). Age and gender differences: Understanding mature online users with the online purchase intention model. *Journal of Global Scholars of Marketing Science*, *26*(3), 248–269. doi:10.1080/21639159.2016.1174540

Lednev, V. V. (1968). Method of determining the second viral coefficient for dilute solutions of biopolymers by the method of low-angle X-ray scatter. *Biophysics*. https://elibrary.ru/item.asp? id=30915903

Lee, E. J., Bae, J., & Kim, K. H. (2020). The effect of sustainable certification reputation on consumer behavior in the fashion industry: Focusing on the mechanism of congruence. *Journal of Global Fashion Marketing*, *11*(2), 137–153. doi:10.1080/20932685.2020.1726198

Lee, E. J., Choi, H., Han, J., Kim, D. H., Ko, E., & Kim, K. H. (2020). How to "Nudge" your consumers towards sustainable fashion consumption: An fMRI investigation. *Journal of Business Research, 117*, 642–651. doi:10.1016/j.jbusres.2019.09.050

Lee, E., & Weder, F. (2021). Framing sustainable fashion concepts on social media. An analysis of# slowfashionaustralia Instagram posts and post-COVID visions of the future. *Sustainability (Basel), 13*(17), 9976. doi:10.3390/su13179976

Lee, J. E., & Watkins, B. (2016). YouTube vloggers' influence on consumer luxury brand perceptions and intentions. *Journal of Business Research, 69*(12), 5753–5760. Advance online publication. doi:10.1016/j.jbusres.2016.04.171

Lee, K. (2009). Gender differences in Hong Kong adolescent consumers' green purchasing behaviour. *Journal of Consumer Marketing, 26*(2), 87–96. doi:10.1108/07363760910940456

Legere, A., & Kang, J. (2020). The role of self-concept in shaping sustainable consumption: A model of slow fashion. *Journal of Cleaner Production, 258*, 120699. doi:10.1016/j.jclepro.2020.120699

Leong, L. Y., Jaafar, N. I., & Sulaiman, A. (2017). Understanding impulse purchase in Facebook commerce: Does Big Five matter? *Internet Research, 27*(4), 786–818. Advance online publication. doi:10.1108/IntR-04-2016-0107

Leonidou, C. N., Katsikeas, C. S., & Morgan, N. A. (2013). "Greening" the marketing mix: Do firms do it and does it pay off? *Journal of the Academy of Marketing Science, 41*(2), 151–170. doi:10.1007/s11747-012-0317-2

Leonnard, L., Paramita, A. S., & Maulidiani, J. J. (2019). The effect of augmented reality shopping applications on purchase intention. *Esensi: Jurnal Bisnis Dan Manajemen, 9*(2), 131–142. doi:10.15408/ess.v9i2.9724

Leung, F. F., Gu, F. F., Li, Y., Zhang, J. Z., & Palmatier, R. W. (2022). Influencer Marketing Effectiveness. *Journal of Marketing, 86*(6), 93–115. doi:10.1177/00222429221102889

Li, X., Loahavilai, P. O., & Naktnasukanjn, N. (2021, December). Predictors of online buying behavior in social commerce. In *2021 3rd International Conference on E-Business and E-commerce Engineering* (pp. 1-6). 10.1145/3510249.3510250

Li, D., Zhao, L., Ma, S., Shao, S., & Zhang, L. (2019). What influences an individual's pro-environmental behavior? A literature review. *Resources, Conservation and Recycling, 146*, 28–34. doi:10.1016/j.resconrec.2019.03.024

Likert, R. (1932). A technique for the measurement of attitudes. *Archives de Psychologie, 140*, 1–55.

Lin, C. A., Crowe, J., Pierre, L., & Lee, Y. (2021). Effects of parasocial interaction with an instafamous influencer on brand attitudes and purchase intentions. *The Journal of Social Media in Society, 10*(1), 55–78.

Lin, L., Jiang, T., Xiao, L., Pervez, M. N., Cai, X., Naddeo, V., & Cai, Y. (2022). Sustainable fashion: Eco-friendly dyeing of wool fiber with novel mixtures of biodegradable natural dyes. *Scientific Reports, 12*(1), 21040. doi:10.1038/s41598-022-25495-6 PMID:36470929

Lin, M. T. B., Zhu, D., Liu, C., & Kim, P. B. (2022). A meta-analysis of antecedents of pro-environmental, behavioral intention of tourists and hospitality consumers. *Tourism Management, 93*, 104566. doi:10.1016/j.tourman.2022.104566

Lin, P.-H., & Chen, W.-H. (2022). Factors that influence consumers' sustainable apparel purchase intention: The moderating effect of generational cohorts. *Sustainability (Basel), 14*(14), 8950. doi:10.3390/su14148950

Liszio, S., & Masuch, M. (2016a). Lost in Open worlds. *Proceedings of the 13th International Conference on Advances in Computer Entertainment Technology*. 10.1145/3001773.3001794

Liu, F. (2022). Driving Green Consumption: Exploring Generation Z Consumers' Action Issues on Sustainable Fashion in China. *Studies in Social Science & Humanities, 1*(5), 25–49. doi:10.56397/SSSH.2022.12.03

Liu, M., Fernando, D., Daniel, G., Madsen, B., Meyer, A. S., Ale, M. T., & Thygesen, A. (2015). Effect of harvest time and field retting duration on the chemical composition, morphology and mechanical properties of hemp fibers. *Industrial Crops and Products*, *69*, 29–39. doi:10.1016/j.indcrop.2015.02.010

Liu, S., Kasturiratne, D., & Moizer, J. (2012). A hub-and-spoke model for multi-dimensional integration of green marketing and sustainable supply chain management. *Industrial Marketing Management*, *41*(4), 581–588. doi:10.1016/j.indmarman.2012.04.005

Liu, Y., Liu, M. T., Perez, A., Chan, W., Collado, J., & Mo, Z. (2021). The importance of knowledge and trust for ethical fashion consumption. *Asia Pacific Journal of Marketing and Logistics*, *33*(5), 1175–1194. doi:10.1108/APJML-02-2020-0081

Liyakat, K. K. S. (2023). Detecting Malicious Nodes in IoT Networks Using Machine Learning and Artificial Neural Networks. *2023 International Conference on Emerging Smart Computing and Informatics (ESCI),* 1-5. 10.1109/ESCI56872.2023.10099544

Liyakat, K. K. S. (2023). Machine Learning Approach Using Artificial Neural Networks to Detect Malicious Nodes in IoT Networks. In P. K. Shukla, H. Mittal, & A. Engelbrecht (Eds.), *Computer Vision and Robotics. CVR 2023. Algorithms for Intelligent Systems*. Springer. doi:10.1007/978-981-99-4577-1_3

Liyakat, K. K. S. (2024). Machine Learning Approach Using Artificial Neural Networks to Detect Malicious Nodes in IoT Networks. In S. K. Udgata, S. Sethi, & X. Z. Gao (Eds.), *Intelligent Systems. ICMIB 2023. Lecture Notes in Networks and Systems* (Vol. 728). Springer. doi:10.1007/978-981-99-3932-9_12

Liyakat, S. (2023). ML in the Electronics Manufacturing Industry. *Journal of Switching Hub*, *8*(3), 9–13. doi:10.46610/JoSH.2023.v08i03.002

Lloyd-Smith, H. (2021, August 3). *Louis Vuitton Marks 200th birthday with art video game.* https://www.wallpaper.com/art/louis-vuitton-video-game-200th-anniversary

Loehlin, J. C. (1998). *Latent variable models: An introduction to factor, path, and structural analysis*. Erlbaum.

Lohr, S. W. (2015, June 21). *H&M's "Conscious" Collection? Don't Buy Into the Hype*. HuffPost. https://www.huffpost.com/entry/hms-conscious-collection-_b_7107964

Lotf, M., Yousef, A., & Jafari, S. (2018). The Effect of Emerging Green Market on Green Entrepreneurship and Sustainable Development in Knowledge-Based Companies. *Sustainability (Basel)*, *10*(7), 2308. doi:10.3390/su10072308

Lou, C., & Yuan, S. (2019). Influencer Marketing: How Message Value and Credibility Affect Consumer Trust of Branded Content on Social Media. *Journal of Interactive Advertising*, *19*(1), 58–73. Advance online publication. doi:10.1080/15252019.2018.1533501

Luchs, M. G., & Mooradian, T. A. (2012). Sex, Personality, and Sustainable Consumer Behaviour: Elucidating the Gender Effect. *Journal of Consumer Policy*, *35*(1), 127–144. doi:10.1007/s10603-011-9179-0

Lucy, B. (2023). *Top 10 Sustainable Clothing Companies 2023.* Sustainability. https://sustainabilitymag.com/articles/top-10-sustainable-clothing-companies

Luo, Y., & Ye, Q. (2019). The effects of online reviews, perceived value, and gender on continuance intention to use international online outshopping website: An elaboration likelihood model perspective. *Journal of International Consumer Marketing*, *31*(3), 250–269. doi:10.1080/08961530.2018.1503987

Lu, X., Sheng, T., Zhou, X., Shen, C., & Fang, B. (2022). How does young consumers' greenwashing perception impact their green purchase intention in the fast fashion industry? An analysis from the perspective of perceived risk theory. *Sustainability (Basel)*, *14*(20), 13473. doi:10.3390/su142013473

Lu, Y., & Smith, S. (2008). Augmented reality E-commerce: How the technology benefits people's lives. *Human-Computer Interaction*. Advance online publication. doi:10.5772/6301

Lynn, T., Muzellec, L., Caemmerer, B., & Turley, D. (2017). Social network sites: Early adopters' personality and influence. *Journal of Product and Brand Management*, *26*(1), 42–51. doi:10.1108/JPBM-10-2015-1025

Machado, M. A. D., de Almeida, S. O., Bollick, L. C., & Bragagnolo, G. (2019). Second-hand fashion market: Consumer role in circular economy. *Journal of Fashion Marketing and Management*, *23*(3), 382–395. doi:10.1108/JFMM-07-2018-0099

MacKenzie, S. B., & Podsakoff, P. M. (2012). Common method bias in marketing: Causes, mechanisms, and procedural remedies. *Journal of Retailing*, *88*(4), 542–555. doi:10.1016/j.jretai.2012.08.001

Madhav, S., Ahamad, A., Singh, P., & Mishra, P. K. (2018). A review of textile industry: Wet processing, environmental impacts, and effluent treatment methods. *Environmental Quality Management*, *27*(3), 31–41. doi:10.1002/tqem.21538

Maillols, H., & Maillols, J. (1976). *Relation between 2nd viral coefficient a2 and molecular mass in polystyrene-benzene system*. Elsevier.

Mainieri, T., Barnett, E. G., Valdero, T. R., Unipan, J. B., & Oskamp, S. (1997). Green buying: The influence of environmental concern of consumer behaviour. *Journal of Social Psychology, 137*, 189–204.

Mainieri, T., Barnett, E. G., Valdero, T. R., Unipan, J. B., & Oskamp, S. (1997). Green buying: The influence of environmental concern on consumer behaviour. *The Journal of Social Psychology*, *137*(2), 189–204. doi:10.1080/00224549709595430

Maiti, R. (2024, March 4). *Fast fashion and its environmental impact in 2024 | Earth.Org*. Earth.Org. https://earth.org/fast-fashions-detrimental-effect-on-the-environment/

Majeed, A., Ahmed, I., & Rasheed, A. (2022). Investigating influencing factors on consumers' choice behavior and their environmental concerns while purchasing green products in Pakistan. *Journal of Environmental Planning and Management*, *65*(6), 1110–1134. doi:10.1080/09640568.2021.1922995

Majeed, M. U., Aslam, S., Murtaza, S. A., Attila, S., & Molnár, E. (2022). Green marketing approaches and their impact on green purchase intentions: Mediating role of green brand image and consumer beliefs towards the environment. *Sustainability*, *14*(18), 11703.

Majeed, M., Owusu-Ansah, M., & Ashmond, A.-A. (2021). The influence of social media on purchase intention: The mediating role of brand equity. *Cogent Business & Management*, *8*(1), 1944008. doi:10.1080/23311975.2021.1944008

Mancuso, I., Petruzzelli, A. M., Panniello, U., & Nespoli, C. (2024). A microfoundation perspective on business model innovation: The cases of Roblox and meta in metaverse. *IEEE Transactions on Engineering Management*, 1–14. doi:10.1109/TEM.2023.3275198

Mandarić, D., Hunjet, A., & Vuković, D. (2022). The impact of fashion brand sustainability on consumer purchasing decisions. *Journal of Risk and Financial Management*, *15*(4), 176. doi:10.3390/jrfm15040176

Marc, I., Kušar, J., & Berlec, T. (2022). Decision-Making Techniques of the Consumer Behaviour Optimisation of the Product Own Price. *Applied Sciences (Basel, Switzerland)*, *12*(4), 2176. doi:10.3390/app12042176

Marshall, G. W., Moncrief, W. C., Rudd, J. M., & Lee, N. (2012). Revolution in sales: The impact of social media and related technology on the selling environment. *Journal of Personal Selling & Sales Management*, *32*(3), 349–363. doi:10.2753/PSS0885-3134320305

Martínez-Navarro, J., Bigné, E., Guixeres, J., Alcañiz, M., & Torrecilla, C. (2019). The influence of virtual reality in e-commerce. *Journal of Business Research*, *100*, 475–482. doi:10.1016/j.jbusres.2018.10.054

Martinez, P. (2015). Customer loyalty: Exploring its antecedents from a green marketing perspective. *International Journal of Contemporary Hospitality Management*, *27*(5), 896–917.

Mason, A. N., Narcum, J., & Mason, K. (2021). Social media marketing gained importance after Covid-19. *Cogent Business & Management*, *8*(1), 1870797. doi:10.1080/23311975.2020.1870797

Matthies, E., Selge, S., & Klöckner, C. A. (2012). The role of parental behaviour for the development of behaviour specific environmental norms – The example of recycling and re-use behaviour. *Journal of Environmental Psychology*, *32*(3), 277–284. doi:10.1016/j.jenvp.2012.04.003

McDonald, S., Oates, C. J., Alevizou, P. J., Young, C. W., & Hwang, K. (2012). Individual strategies for sustainable consumption. *Journal of Marketing Management*, *28*(3–4), 445–468. doi:10.1080/0267257X.2012.658839

Mcdowell, M. (2024, January 9). *Would co-workers notice ifyou wore digital clothes onzoom?* Vogue Business.

McEachern, M. G., Middleton, D., & Cassidy, T. (2020). Encouraging sustainable behavior change via a social practice approach: A focus on apparel consumption practices. *Journal of Consumer Policy*, *43*(2), 397–418. doi:10.1007/s10603-020-09454-0

McKinsey & Company. (2020). *Survey: Consumer sentiment on sustainability in fashion | McKinsey*. Mckinsey.Com. https://www.mckinsey.com/industries/retail/our-insights/survey-consumer-sentiment-on-sustainability-in-fashion

McLean, P. (2016). *Culture in Networks*. Wiley.

McNeill, L. S., Hamlin, R. P., McQueen, R. H., Degenstein, L., Garrett, T. C., Dunn, L., & Wakes, S. (2020). Fashion sensitive young consumers and fashion garment repair: Emotional connections to garments as a sustainability strategy. *International Journal of Consumer Studies*, *44*(4), 361–368. doi:10.1111/ijcs.12572

McNeill, L., & Moore, R. (2015). Sustainable fashion consumption and the fast fashion conundrum: Fashionable consumers and attitudes to sustainability in clothing choice. *International Journal of Consumer Studies*, *39*(3), 212–222. doi:10.1111/ijcs.12169

McNeill, L., & Venter, B. (2019). Identity, self-concept and young women's engagement with collaborative, sustainable fashion consumption models. *International Journal of Consumer Studies*, *43*(4), 368–378. Advance online publication. doi:10.1111/ijcs.12516

McQueen, R. H., McNeill, L. S., Kozlowski, A., & Jain, A. (2022). Frugality, style longevity and garment repair–environmental attitudes and consumption behaviour amongst young Canadian fashion consumers. *International Journal of Fashion Design, Technology and Education*, *15*(3), 371–384. doi:10.1080/17543266.2022.2072958

Mehta, P., Kaur, A., Singh, S., & Mehta, M. D. (2023). "Sustainable attitude"–a modest notion creating a tremendous difference in the glamourous fast fashion world: Investigating moderating effects. *Society and Business Review*, *18*(4), 549–571. doi:10.1108/SBR-10-2021-0205

Meißner, M., Pfeiffer, J., Peukert, C., Dietrich, H., & Pfeiffer, T. (2020). How virtual reality affects consumer choice. *Journal of Business Research*, *117*, 219–231. doi:10.1016/j.jbusres.2020.06.004

Merle, A., Senecal, S., & St-Onge, A. (2012). Whether and how virtual try-on influences consumer responses to an apparel web site. *International Journal of Electronic Commerce*, *16*(3), 41–64. doi:10.2753/JEC1086-4415160302

Meyer, A. (2001). What's in it for the customers? Successfully marketing green clothes. *Business Strategy and the Environment*, *10*(5), 317–330. doi:10.1002/bse.302

Milanesi, M., Kyrdoda, Y., & Runfola, A. (2022). How do you depict sustainability? An analysis of images posted on Instagram by sustainable fashion companies. *Journal of Global Fashion Marketing*, *13*(2), 101–115. doi:10.1080/20932685.2021.1998789

Milgram, P., Takemura, H., Utsumi, A., & Kishino, F. (1995). Augmented reality: a class of displays on the reality-virtuality continuum. *SPIE Proceedings*. 10.1117/12.197321

Miller, V. (2020). *Understanding Digital Culture* (2nd ed.). Sage.

Mills, S., & Noyes, J. (1999). Virtual reality: An overview of user-related design issues. *Interacting with Computers*, *11*(4), 375–386. doi:10.1016/S0953-5438(98)00057-5

Ming, J., Jianqiu, Z., Bilal, M., Akram, U., & Fan, M. (2021). How social presence influences impulse buying behavior in live streaming commerce? the role of S-O-R theory. *International Journal of Web Information Systems*, *17*(4), 300–320. doi:10.1108/IJWIS-02-2021-0012

Mintel. (2006). *Green living*. US Marketing Research Report.

Miroshnichenko, V. P., Arshinov, P. S., & Petrov, V. M. (1989). *The bile cholate-cholesterol coefficient for assessing the causes of a protracted convalescence in patients with viral hepatitis*. https://europepmc.org/article/med/2629293

Mishra, P., & Sharma, P. (2010). Green Marketing in India: Emerging Opportunities and Challenges. *Journal of Engineering, Science & Management in Education*, *3*, 9–14.

Mohajan, H. (2012). Green Marketing Is A Sustainable Marketing System In The Twenty First Century. *International Journal of Management and Transformation*, *6*(2), 23–39.

Mohr, L. A., Webb, D. J., & Harris, K. (2001). Do Consumers Expect Companies to be Socially Responsible? The Impact of Corporate Social Responsibility on Buying Behavior. *The Journal of Consumer Affairs*, *35*(1), 45–72. doi:10.1111/j.1745-6606.2001.tb00102.x

Molla, A., & Licker, P. (2001). E-commerce systems success: an attempt to extend and respecify the DeLone and McLean model of IS success. *Journal of Electronic Commerce Research, 2*(4), 131– 141.

Montshiwa, V. T., & Moroke, N. D. (2014). Assessment of the reliability and validity of student-lecturer evaluation questionnaire: A case of Northwest University. *Mediterranean Journal of Social Sciences*, *5*(14), 352. doi:10.5901/mjss.2014.v5n14p352

Morais, C. F. S., Pires, P. B., & Delgado, C. (2023). Determinants of Purchase Intention for Sustainable Fashion: Conceptual Model. In *Promoting Organizational Performance Through 5G and Agile Marketing* (pp. 75–95). IGI Global.

Morais, C. F., Pires, P. B., Delgado, C., & Santos, J. D. (2023). Intention to Purchase Sustainable Fashion: Influencer and Worth-of-Mouth Determinants. In T. Tarnanidis, E. Papachristou, M. Karypidis, & V. Ismyrlis (Eds.), *Social Media and Online Consumer Decision Making in the Fashion Industry* (pp. 160–185). IGI Global. doi:10.4018/978-1-6684-8753-2.ch010

Morone, A., Nemore, F., & Schirone, D. A. (2018a). Sales impact of servicescape's rational stimuli: A natural experiment. *Journal of Retailing and Consumer Services*, *45*, 256–262. doi:10.1016/j.jretconser.2018.09.011

Morotti, E., Donatiello, L., & Marfia, G. (2020a). Fostering fashion retail experiences through virtual reality and voice assistants. *2020 IEEE Conference on Virtual Reality and 3D User Interfaces Abstracts and Workshops (VRW)*. 10.1109/VRW50115.2020.00074

Moroz, L. V., & Bondaruk, I. Y. (2019). Direct (hyaluronic acid) and indirect (alanine aminotransferase, aspartate aminotransferase, de Rithis coefficient of liver fibrosis markers in patients with chronic viral…. *Journal of Education, Health and Sport.* https://apcz.umk.pl/JEHS/article/view/7379

Morrison, M. A., Cheong, H. J., & McMillan, S. J. (2013). Posting, Lurking, and Networking: Behaviors and Characteristics of Consumers in the Context of User-Generated Content. *Journal of Interactive Advertising*, *13*(2), 97–108. doi:10.1080/15252019.2013.826552

Moschis, P. G. (1976). Social Comparison and Informal Group Influence. *JMR, Journal of Marketing Research*, *13*(3), 237–244. doi:10.1177/002224377601300304

Moser, A. K. (2015). Thinking green, buying green? Drivers of pro - Environmental purchasing behavior. *Journal of Consumer Marketing*, *32*(3), 167–175. Advance online publication. doi:10.1108/JCM-10-2014-1179

Moser, A. K. (2015). Thinking green, buying green? Drivers of pro-environmental purchasing behavior. *Journal of Consumer Marketing*, *32*(3), 167–175.

Muchenje, C., Tapera, M. C., Katsvairo, H. T., & Mugoni, E. (2023). Green Marketing Strategies and Consumer Behavior: Insights for Achieving Sustainable Marketing Success. In R. Masengu, S. Bigirimana, O. Chiwaridzo, R. Bensson, & C. Blossom (Eds.), *Sustainable Marketing, Branding, and Reputation Management: Strategies for a Greener Future* (pp. 465–484). IGI Global. doi:10.4018/979-8-3693-0019-0.ch024

Muk, A. (2013). What factors influence millennials to like brand pages? *Journal of Marketing Analytics*, *1*(3), 127–137. doi:10.1057/jma.2013.12

Mukendi, A., Davies, I., Glozer, S., & McDonagh, P. (2020). Sustainable fashion: Current and future research directions. *European Journal of Marketing*, *54*(11), 2873–2909. doi:10.1108/EJM-02-2019-0132

Mukherjee, S. (2015). Environmental and social impact of fashion: Towards an eco-friendly, ethical fashion. *International Journal of Interdisciplinary and Multidisciplinary Studies*, *2*(3), 22–35.

Mulani, A. O., & Patil, R. M. (2023). Discriminative Appearance Model for Robust Online Multiple Target Tracking. *Telematique*, *22*(1), 24–43.

Muntinga, D. G., Moorman, M., & Smit, E. G. (2011). Introducing COBRAs: Exploring motivations for brand-related social media use. *International Journal of Advertising*, *30*(1), 13–46. doi:10.2501/IJA-30-1-013-046

Murad, Hussin, Yusof, Miserom, & Ya'acob. (2019). *A Conceptual Foundation for Smart Education Driven by Gen Z.* . doi:10.6007/IJARBSS/v9-i5/6226

Murphy, R. (1998). The Internet: A viable strategy for fashion retail marketing? *Journal of Fashion Marketing and Management*, *2*(3), 209–216. doi:10.1108/eb022529

Mustika, D. V., & Wahyudi, L. (2022). Does the Quality of Beauty E-commerce Impact Online Purchase Intention? The Role of Perceived Enjoyment and Perceived Trust. International Journal of Economics. *Business and Management Research*, *6*(04), 199–218.

Muthu, S. S. (Ed.). (2019). *Consumer behavior and sustainable fashion consumption.* Springer. doi:10.1007/978-981-13-1265-6

Mystakidis, S. (2022). Metaverse. *Metaverse Encyclopedia*, *2*(1), 486–497. doi:10.3390/encyclopedia2010031

Nah-Hong, LN. (2007), The Effect of Brand Image and Product Knowledge on Purchase Intention Moderated by Price Discount. *J. Int. Manage. Stud., 2.*

Nakamura, L. (2008). *Digitizing race: Visual cultures of the internet*. University of Minnesota.

Namukasa, J. (2013). The influence of airline service quality on passenger satisfaction and loyalty: The case of Uganda airline industry. *The TQM Journal*, *25*(5), 520–532. doi:10.1108/TQM-11-2012-0092

Nandkeolyar, O., & Chen, F. (2023). Credibility, transparency, and sustainability in fashion: A game-theoretic perspective. *Agricultural and Resource Economics Review*, *52*(1), 43–70. doi:10.1017/age.2022.24

Narayana, C. L., & Markin, R. J. (1975). Consumer behaviour and product performance: An alternative conceptualization. *Journal of Marketing*, *39*(4), 1–6. doi:10.1177/002224297503900401

Narayanan, S., & Singh, G. A. (2023). Consumers' willingness to pay for corporate social responsibility: Theory and evidence. *International Journal of Consumer Studies*, *47*(6), 2212–2244.

Nayak, R., Panwar, T., & Nguyen, L. V. T. (2020). Sustainability in fashion and textiles: A survey from developing country. *Sustainable Technologies for Fashion and Textiles*, 3–30.

Naylor, R. W., Lamberton, C. P., & West, P. M. (2012). Beyond the "like" button: The impact of mere virtual presence on brand evaluations and purchase intentions in social media settings. *Journal of Marketing*, *76*(6), 105–120. doi:10.1509/jm.11.0105

Naz. (2023). *About us*. Consulted on June 28, 2023, at Naz: https://naz.pt/pages/about-us

Nerkar & Shinde. (2023). Monitoring Fresh Fruit and Food Using Iot and Machine Learning to Improve Food Safety and Quality. *Tuijin Jishu/Journal of Propulsion Technology*, *44*(3), 2927 – 2931.

Neuendorf, K. A. (2017). The Content Analysis Guidebook. In *The Content Analysis Guidebook* (2nd ed.). SAGE Publications, Inc., doi:10.4135/9781071802878.n1

Neumann, H. L., Martinez, L. M., & Martinez, L. F. (2021). Sustainability efforts in the fast fashion industry: Consumer perception, trust and purchase intention. *Sustainability Accounting. Management and Policy Journal*, *12*(3), 571–590. doi:10.1108/SAMPJ-11-2019-0405

Nezami, K., & Suen, C. Y. (2023). An unbiased artificial referee in beauty contests based on pattern recognition and ai. *Computers in Human Behavior: Artificial Humans*, *1*(2), 100025. doi:10.1016/j.chbah.2023.100025

Ng, P. M. L., & Cheung, C. T. Y. (2022). Why do young people do things for the environment? The effect of perceived values on pro-environmental behavior. *Young Consumers*, *23*(4), 539–554. doi:10.1108/YC-11-2021-1411

Nguyen, T. T. H., Yang, Z., Nguyen, N., Johnson, L. W., & Cao, T. K. (2019). Greenwash and green purchase intention: The mediating role of green skepticism. *Sustainability (Basel)*, *11*(9), 2653. doi:10.3390/su11092653

Nguyen, T. T., Dang, H. Q., & Le-Anh, T. (2023). Impacts of household norms and trust on organic food purchase behavior under adapted theory of planned behavior. *Journal of Agribusiness in Developing and Emerging Economies*. Advance online publication. doi:10.1108/JADEE-10-2022-0218

Niinimaki, K. (2010). Eco-clothing, consumer identity and ideology. *Sustainable Development (Bradford)*, *18*(3), 150–162. doi:10.1002/sd.455

Niinimäki, K., Peters, G., Dahlbo, H., Perry, P., Rissanen, T., & Gwilt, A. (2020). The environmental price of fast fashion. *Nature Reviews. Earth & Environment*, *1*(4), 189–200. doi:10.1038/s43017-020-0039-9

Nik Abdul Rashid, N. R. (2009). Awareness of eco-label in Malaysia's green marketing initiative. *International Journal of Business and Management*, *4*(8), 132–141.

Nikita, K. (2020). Design of Vehicle system using CAN Protocol. *International Journal for Research in Applied Science and Engineering Technology*, *8*(V), 1978–1983. doi:10.22214/ijraset.2020.5321

Niyati, A., Anuja, A., & Ponnurangam, K. (2017). *Multiple metric aware YouTube tutorial videos virality analysis*. doi:10.1504/IJSNM.2017.10012952

Noordin, S., Ashaari, N. S., & Wook, T. S. M. T. (2017, November). Virtual fitting room: The needs for usability and profound emotional elements. In *2017 6th International Conference on Electrical Engineering and Informatics (ICEEI)* (pp. 1-6). IEEE.

Northman, T. (2021, August 11). *Louis Vuitton's new game is better than "fortnite."* Highsnobiety. https://www.highsnobiety.com/p/louis-vuitton-nft-game/

Norton, D. A., Lamberton, C. P., & Naylor, R. W. (2013). The devil you (don't) know: Interpersonal ambiguity and inference making in competitive contexts. *The Journal of Consumer Research*, *40*(2), 239–254. doi:10.1086/669562

Nupur, A., & Parul, M. (2021). Investigating the relationship between Internal Environmental Locus of control and Behaviour towards sustainable apparel: The mediating role of intention to purchase. *Transnational Marketing Journal*, (3), 539–552.

Nyborg, K., Howarth, R. B., & Brekke, K. A. (2006). Green consumers and public policy: On socially contingent moral motivation. *Resource and Energy Economics*, *28*(4), 351–366. doi:10.1016/j.reseneeco.2006.03.001

Oentario, Y., Harianto, A., & Irawati, J. (2017). Pengaruh Usefulness, Ease of Use, Risk Terhadap Intentionto Buy Onlinepatisserie Melalui Consumer Attitude Berbasis Media Sosial Di Surabaya. *Jurnal Manajemen Pemasaran*, *11*(1), 26–31. doi:10.9744/pemasaran.11.1.26-31

Oklander, M., & Kudina, A. (2021). Channels for promotion of fashion brands in the online space. *Baltic Journal of Economic Studies*, *7*(2), 179–187. doi:10.30525/2256-0742/2021-7-2-179-187

Oksanen, A., Cvetkovic, A., Akin, N., Latikka, R., Bergdahl, J., Chen, Y., & Savela, N. (2023). Artificial Intelligence in fine arts: A systematic review of Empirical Research. *Computers in Human Behavior: Artificial Humans*, *1*(2), 100004. doi:10.1016/j.chbah.2023.100004

Oladayo, S. (2017). *Sustainable and Ethical Fashion Consumption: the role of Consumer Attitude and Behaviou*. Hamburg School of Business Administration.

Omar Zaki, H., & Rosli, N. (2024). A Bibliometric Citation Analysis on Green Marketing and Waste Management. *International Journal of Management Studies*, *31*(1), 235–268. doi:10.32890/ijms2024.31.1.9

Online shopping in Malaysia. Bargain Hunting. (2019, December 6). Retrieved January 6, 2023, from https://www.picodi.com/my/bargain-hunting/online-shopping-in-malaysia

Oreg, S., & Katz-Gerro, T. (2006). Predicting proenvironmental behavior cross-nationally. *Environment and Behavior*, *38*(4), 462–483. doi:10.1177/0013916505286012

Ortega-Egea, J. M., & García-de-Frutos, N. (2019). Greenpeace's Detox campaign: Towards a more sustainable textile industry. In M. M. Galen-Ladero & H. M. Alves (Eds.), *Case studies on social marketing. Management for professionals*. Springer. doi:10.1007/978-3-030-04843-3_4

Osterhus, T. L. (1997). Pro-Social consumer influence strategies: When and how do they work? *Journal of Marketing*, *61*(4), 16–29. doi:10.1177/002224299706100402

Othman, A., Chemnad, K., Hassanien, A. E., Tlili, A., Zhang, C. Y., Al-Thani, D., Altınay, F., Chalghoumi, H. S., Al-Khalifa, H., Obeid, M., Jemni, M., Al-Hadhrami, T., & Altınay, Z. (2024). Accessible metaverse: A theoretical framework for accessibility and inclusion in the metaverse. *Multimodal Technologies and Interaction*, *8*(3), 21–38. doi:10.3390/mti8030021

Ottman, J. (2017). *The new rules of green marketing: Strategies, tools, and inspiration for sustainable branding*. Routledge. doi:10.4324/9781351278683

Oyewole, P. (2001). Social Costs of Environmental Justice Associated with the Practice of Green Marketing. *Journal of Business Ethics*, *29*(3), 239–251. doi:10.1023/A:1026592805470

Pachoulakis, I., & Kapetanakis, K. (2012). Augmented reality platforms for virtual fitting rooms. *The International Journal of Multimedia & Its Applications*, *4*(4), 35–46. doi:10.5121/ijma.2012.4404

Paço, A., Leal Filho, W., Ávila, L. V., & Dennis, K. (2021). Fostering sustainable consumer behavior regarding clothing: Assessing trends on purchases, recycling, and disposal. *Textile Research Journal*, *91*(3-4), 373–384. doi:10.1177/0040517520944524

Palomo-Domínguez, I., Elías-Zambrano, R., & Álvarez-Rodríguez, V. (2023). Gen Z's motivations towards sustainable fashion and eco-friendly brand attributes: The case of Vinted. *Sustainability (Basel)*, *15*(11), 8753. doi:10.3390/su15118753

Pal, R., & Gander, J. (2018). Modelling environmental value: An examination of sustainable business models within the fashion industry. *Journal of Cleaner Production*, *184*, 251–263. doi:10.1016/j.jclepro.2018.02.001

Panda, J., Das, S., Panda, M., & Pattnaik, D. (2023). Sustainable Intelligence: Navigating the Rise of Green Technologies for a Greener Environment. In Sustainable Science and Intelligent Technologies for Societal Development (pp. 464-474). IGI Global.

Papachristou, E., & Anastassiu, H. T. (2022). Application of 3D Virtual Prototyping Technology to the Integration of Wearable Antennas into Fashion Garments. *Technologies*, *10*(3), 62. doi:10.3390/technologies10030062

Papadopoulos, I., Karagouni, G., Trigkas, M., & Platogianni, E. (2010). Green marketing: The case of Greece in certified and sustainably managed timber products. *EuroMed Journal of Business*, *5*(2), 166–190. doi:10.1108/14502191011065491

Papadopoulou, M., Papasolomou, I., & Thrassou, A. (2022). Exploring the level of sustainability awareness among consumers within the fast-fashion clothing industry: A dual business and consumer perspective. *Competitiveness Review*, *32*(3), 350–375. Advance online publication. doi:10.1108/CR-04-2021-0061

Papagiannidis, S., Pantano, E., See-To, E. W. K., Dennis, C., & Bourlakis, M. (2017). To immerse or not? experimenting with two virtual retail environments. Information Technology &amp. *Information Technology & People*, *30*(1), 163–188. doi:10.1108/ITP-03-2015-0069

Papahristou, E., & Bilalis, N. (2017). Should the fashion industry confront the sustainability challenge with 3D prototyping technology. *International Journal of Sustainable Engineering*, *10*(4–5), 207–214. doi:10.1080/19397038.2017.1348563

Papamichael, I., Chatziparaskeva, G., Pedreño, J. N., Voukkali, I., Candel, M. B. A., & Zorpas, A. A. (2022). Building a new mindset in tomorrow fashion development through circular strategy models in the framework of waste management. *Current Opinion in Green and Sustainable Chemistry*, *36*, 100638. doi:10.1016/j.cogsc.2022.100638

Park, H. J., & Lin, L. M. (2020). Exploring attitude–behavior gap in sustainable consumption: Comparison of recycled and upcycled fashion products. *Journal of Business Research*, *117*, 623–628. doi:10.1016/j.jbusres.2018.08.025

Park, M., Im, H., & Kim, D. Y. (2018). Feasibility and user experience of virtual reality fashion stores. *Fashion and Textiles*, *5*(1), 32. Advance online publication. doi:10.1186/s40691-018-0149-x

Patel, V., Das, K., Chatterjee, R., & Shukla, Y. (2020). Does the interface quality of mobile shopping apps affect purchase intention? An empirical study. *Australasian Marketing Journal*, *28*(4), 300–309. doi:10.1016/j.ausmj.2020.08.004

Patil, K., & Khathuria, D. (2020). *Digital Marketing in Fashion Industry*. Academic Press.

Patrick, A. I. (2005). Green branding effects on attitude: Functional versus emotional positioning strategies. *Marketing Intelligence & Planning*, *23*(1), 9–29. doi:10.1108/02634500510577447

Patwary, S. (2020). Clothing and textile sustainability: Current state of environmental challenges and the ways forward. *Textile & Leather Review*, *3*(3), 158–173. doi:10.31881/TLR.2020.16

Patz, R, & Ratzsch, M.T. (1989). *The Kerr Effect in real gases. 2. the 2nd Kerr viral coefficient of noble-gases*. Verlagsgesellsch Geest.

Pavan, M., Samant, L., Mahajan, S., & Kaur, M. (2024). Role of Chemicals in Textile Processing and Its Alternatives. In *Climate Action Through Eco-Friendly Textiles* (pp. 55–72). Springer Nature Singapore. doi:10.1007/978-981-99-9856-2_5

Peattie, S., & Crane, A. (2005). Green marketing: legend, myth, farce, or prophesy? The Greening of Business. Springer.

Peattie, K. (1999). Trappings versus substance in the greening of marketing planning. *Journal of Strategic Marketing*, *7*(2), 131–148. doi:10.1080/096525499346486

Peattie, K. (2010). Green consumption: Behavior and norms. *Annual Review of Environment and Resources*, *35*(1), 195–228. doi:10.1146/annurev-environ-032609-094328

Pedersen, E. R. G., Gwozdz, W., & Hvass, K. K. (2018). Exploring the relationship between business model innovation, corporate sustainability, and organisational values within the fashion industry. *Journal of Business Ethics*, *149*(2), 267–284. doi:10.1007/s10551-016-3044-7

Peeroo, S., Samy, M., & Jones, B. (2017). Facebook: A blessing or a curse for grocery stores? *International Journal of Retail & Distribution Management*, *45*(12), 1242–1259. doi:10.1108/IJRDM-12-2016-0234

Peleg Mizrachi, M., & Tal, A. (2022). Sustainable Fashion—Rationale and Policies. *Encyclopedia*, *2*(2), 1154–1167. doi:10.3390/encyclopedia2020077

Pena-cerezo, M. A., Artaraz-minon, M., & Tejedor-nunez, J. (2019). *Analysis of the Consciousness of University Undergraduates for Sustainable Consumption*. Academic Press.

Pencarelli, T., Ali Taha, V., Škerháková, V., Valentiny, T., & Fedorko, R. (2020). Luxury products and sustainability issues from the perspective of young Italian consumers. *Sustainability (Basel)*, *12*(1), 245. doi:10.3390/su12010245

Pereira, L., Carvalho, R., Dias, Á., Costa, R., & António, N. (2021). How does sustainability affect consumer choices in the fashion industry? *Resources*, *10*(4), 38. doi:10.3390/resources10040038

Pérez-Curiel, C., Jiménez-Marín, G., & García-Medina, I. (2021). The Role of Social Media in the Fashion Industry: The Case of Eco Luxury in Today's Consumption. In *Firms in the Fashion Industry* (pp. 97–115). Springer International Publishing. doi:10.1007/978-3-030-76255-1_7

Periyasamy, A. P. (2024). Recent Advances in the Remediation of Textile-Dye-Containing Wastewater: Prioritizing Human Health and Sustainable Wastewater Treatment. *Sustainability (Basel)*, *16*(2), 495. doi:10.3390/su16020495

Petersson McIntyre, M. (2021). Shame, Blame, and Passion: Affects of (Un)sustainable Wardrobes. *Fashion Theory*, *25*(6), 735–755. doi:10.1080/1362704X.2019.1676506

Peukert, C., Pfeiffer, J., Meißner, M., Pfeiffer, T., & Weinhardt, C. (2019). Shopping in virtual reality stores: The influence of immersion on system adoption. *Journal of Management Information Systems*, *36*(3), 755–788. doi:10.1080/07421222.2019.1628889

Phetnoi, N., Siripipatthanakul, S., & Phayaphrom, B. (2021). Factors affecting purchase intention via online shopping sites and apps during COVID-19 in Thailand. Journal of Management in Businesss. *Health Care Education*, *1*(1), 1–17.

Pickett-Baker, J., & Ozaki, R. (2008). Pro-environmental products: Marketing influence on consumer purchase decision. *Journal of Consumer Marketing*, *25*(5), 281–293. doi:10.1108/07363760810890516

Pizzi, G., Scarpi, D., Pichierri, M., & Vannucci, V. (2019). Virtual reality, real reactions?: Comparing consumers' perceptions and shopping orientation across physical and virtual-reality retail stores. *Computers in Human Behavior*, *96*, 1–12. doi:10.1016/j.chb.2019.02.008

Polonsky, M. J. (2011). *Transformative green marketing: Impediments and opportunities*. Academic Press.

Polonsky, M. J. (1994). An introduction to green marketing. *Electronic Green Journal*, *1*(2). Advance online publication. doi:10.5070/G31210177

Polonsky, M. J. (2011, December). Transformative green marketing: Impediments and opportunities. *Journal of Business Research*, *64*(12), 1311–1319. doi:10.1016/j.jbusres.2011.01.016

Polonsky, M. J., & Rosenberger, P. J. III. (2001). Reevaluating green marketing: A strategic approach. *Business Horizons*, *44*(5), 21–30. doi:10.1016/S0007-6813(01)80057-4

Polonsky, M. J., Vocino, A., Grau, S. L., Garma, R., & Ferdous, A. S. (2012). The impact of general and carbon-related environmental knowledge on attitudes and behaviour of US consumers. *Journal of Marketing Management*, *28*(3–4), 238–263. doi:10.1080/0267257X.2012.659279

Pornsrimate, K., & Khamwon, A. (2021). How to convert Millennial consumers to brand evangelists through social media micro-influencers. *Innovative Marketing*, *17*(2), 18–32. doi:10.21511/im.17(2).2021.03

Poulsson, S. H. G., & Kale, S. H. (2004). The experience economy and commercial experiences. *The Marketing Review*, *4*(3), 267–277. doi:10.1362/1469347042223445

Pradeep, K. (2016). Digital and Internet Marketing: Crucial Business Management Landscape. In *E-Governance in India: Problems, Prototypes and Prospects* (pp. 91–118). Nova Science Publishing. https://www.researchgate.net/publication/316137040_Digital_and_Internet_Marketing_Crucial_Business_Management_Landscape

Pradeepa, M. (2022). Student Health Detection using a Machine Learning Approach and IoT. *2022 IEEE 2nd Mysore Sub Section International Conference (MysuruCon).*

Prahalad, C. K., & Ramaswamy, V. (2004). Co-creation experiences: The next practice in value creation. *Journal of Interactive Marketing*, *18*(3), 5–14. doi:10.1002/dir.20015

Primanda, R., Setyaning, A. N., Hidayat, A., & Ekasasi, S. R. (2020). The role of trust on perceived usefulness and perceived ease of use toward purchase intention among Yogyakarta's students. *INOBIS: Jurnal Inovasi Bisnis dan Manajemen Indonesia, 3*(3), 316-326.

Psci. (2020, July 20). *The Impact of fast fashion on the Environment—PSCI*. PSCI. https://psci.princeton.edu/tips/2020/7/20/the-impact-of-fast-fashion-on-the-environment

Punitha, S., & Rasdi, R. M. (2013). Corporate Social Responsibility: Adoption of Green Marketing by Hotel Industry. *Asian Social Science*, *9*(17), 79. doi:10.5539/ass.v9n17p79

Putranto, H. A., Rizaldi, T., Riskiawan, H. Y., Setyohadi, D. P. S., Atmadji, E. S. J., & Nuryanto, I. H. (2022). Measurement of Engagement Rate on Instagram for Business Marketing (Case Study: MSME of Dowry in Jember). *International Conference on Electrical and Information Technology (IEIT)*, 317-321. 10.1109/IEIT56384.2022.9967851

Pymnts. (2023). *Gen Z Tops Millennials on Social Media Shopping and Spending*. Pymnts.Com. https://www.pymnts.com/news/social-commerce/2023/gen-z-tops-millennials-on-social-media-shopping-and-spending/

Qin, H., Peak, D. A., & Prybutok, V. (2021). A virtual market in your pocket: How does mobile augmented reality (MAR) Influence Consumer Decision Making? *Journal of Retailing and Consumer Services, 58*,102337. doi:10.1016/j.jretconser.2020.102337

Quach, S., & Thaichon, P. (2017). From connoisseur luxury to mass luxury: Value co-creation and co-destruction in the online environment. *Journal of Business Research*, *81*, 163–172. Advance online publication. doi:10.1016/j.jbusres.2017.06.015

Quan-Haase, A., & Young, A. L. (2010). *Uses and Gratifications of Social Media: A Comparison of Facebook and Instant Messaging*. doi:10.1177/0270467610380009

Quiles-Soler, C., Martínez-Sala, A.-M., & Monserrat-Gauchi, J. (2022). The fashion industry's environmental policy: Social media and corporate websites are vehicles for communicating corporate social responsibility. *Corporate Social Responsibility and Environmental Management*, 1–12. doi:10.1002/csr.2347

Rafie, S. K., Abu, R., Abdul, S. K. S., & Mutalib, A. Z. H. S. (2021). Environmental sustainability practices in rural libraries. *International Journal of Service Management and Sustainability*, *6*(1). 165–176.doi.org/10.24191/ijsms.v6i1.12885

Rahmiati, R., & Yuannita, I. I. (2019). The influence of trust, perceived usefulness, perceived ease of use, and attitude on purchase intention. *Jurnal Kajian Manajemen Bisnis*, *8*(1), 27–34. doi:10.24036/jkmb.10884800

Rajapaksa, D., Gifford, R., Torgler, B., Garcia-Valiñas, M., Athukorala, W., Managi, S., & Wilson, C. (2019). Do monetary and non-monetary incentives influence environmental attitudes and behavior? Evidence from an experimental analysis. *Resources, Conservation and Recycling*, *149*, 168–176. doi:10.1016/j.resconrec.2019.05.034

Ramayah, T., Lee, J. W. C., & Mohamad, O. (2010). Green product purchase intention: Some insights from a developing country. *Resources, Conservation and Recycling*, *54*(12), 1419–1427. doi:10.1016/j.resconrec.2010.06.007

Rana, N. (2024). Ethical AI Integration in Marketing Strategies for Sustainable E-Commerce Fashion Designing. In *Contemporary Management and Global Leadership for Sustainability* (pp. 218–233). IGI Global. doi:10.4018/979-8-3693-1273-5.ch013

Rangel, C., & López, B. (2022). Digital transformation in luxury brands. Sustainable International Business Models in a Digitally Transforming World, 222–239. doi:10.4324/9781003195986-17

Rather, L. J. (2019). 'Advances in the sustainable technologies for water conservation in textile industries. In *Water in Textiles and Fashion* (pp. 175–194). Elsevier. doi:10.1016/B978-0-08-102633-5.00010-5

Rausch, T. M., & Kopplin, C. S. (2021). Bridge the gap: Consumers' purchase intention and behavior regarding sustainable clothing. *Journal of Cleaner Production, 278*, 123882. doi:10.1016/j.jclepro.2020.123882

Ravi, A. (2022). *Pattern Recognition- An Approach towards Machine Learning. Lambert Publications.*

Rawat, D., Sharma, R. S., Karmakar, S., Arora, L. S., & Mishra, V. (2018). Ecotoxic potential of a presumably non-toxic azo dye. *Ecotoxicology and Environmental Safety*, *148*, 528–537. doi:10.1016/j.ecoenv.2017.10.049 PMID:29125956

Ray, S., & Nayak, L. (2023). Marketing Sustainable Fashion: Trends and future directions. *Sustainability (Basel), 15*(7), 6202. doi:10.3390/su15076202

Raza, N., Rizwan, M., & Mujtaba, G. (2024). Bioremediation of real textile wastewater with a microalgal-bacterial consortium: An eco-friendly strategy. *Biomass Conversion and Biorefinery, 14*(6), 7359–7371. doi:10.1007/s13399-022-03214-5

Razzaq, A., Ansari, N. Y., Razzaq, Z., & Awan, H. M. (2018). The impact of fashion involvement and pro-environmental attitude on sustainable clothing consumption: The moderating role of Islamic religiosity. *SAGE Open, 8*(2). doi:10.1177/2158244018774611

Reddy, K. P., Chandu, V., Srilakshmi, S., Thagaram, E., Sahyaja, C., & Osei, B. (2023). Consumers perception on green marketing towards eco-friendly fast moving consumer goods. *International Journal of Engineering Business Management, 15*. doi:10.1177/18479790231170962

Reich, B. J., & Soule, C. A. A. (2016). Green Demarketing in Advertisements: Comparing "Buy Green" and "Buy Less" Appeals in Product and Institutional Advertising Contexts. *Journal of Advertising, 45*(4), 441–458. doi:10.1080/00913367.2016.1214649

Remi, R. (2020). *Sustainability sells: Why consumers and clothing brands alike are turning to sustainability as a guiding light*. Business Insider, India. https://www.businessinsider.in/international/news/sustainability-sells-why-consumers-and-clothing-brands-alike-are-turning-to-sustainability-as-a-guiding-light/articleshow/73259499.cms

Rendtorff, J. D. (2020). Sustainability, basic ethical principles, and innovation. In J. D. Rendtorff (Ed.), *Handbook of business legitimacy: Responsibility, ethics, and society* (pp. 1631–1658). Springer International Publishing. doi:10.1007/978-3-030-14622-1_48

Resources, A., & Resources, A. (2022, April 7). *V-commerce is a cut above the rest –the next big thing*. Apparel Resources. Retrieved June 25, 2022, from https://apparelresources.com/technology-news/retail-tech/V-commerce-cut-rest-next- big-thing/

Rettie, R. (2003) Connectedness, awareness and social presence. *6th Annual International Workshop on Presence.*

Reza, A., Chu, S., Khan, Z., Nedd, A., Castillo, A., & Gardner, D. (2019). *Skins for sale: Linking player identity, representation, and purchasing practices*. Information in Contemporary Society. doi:10.1007/978-3-030-15742-5_11

Ricci, M., Evangelista, A., Di Roma, A., & Fiorentino, M. (2023). Immersive and desktop virtual reality in Virtual Fashion Stores: A comparison between shopping experiences. *Virtual Reality (Waltham Cross), 27*(3), 2281–2296. doi:10.1007/s10055-023-00806-y PMID:37360805

Richardson, J. C., Maeda, Y., Lv, J., & Caskurlu, S. (2017). Social presence in relation to students' satisfaction and learning in the online environment: A meta-analysis. *Computers in Human Behavior, 71*, 402–417. doi:10.1016/j.chb.2017.02.001

Rietveld, R., van Dolen, W., Mazloom, M., & Worring, M. (2020). What You Feel, Is What You Like Influence of Message Appeals on Customer Engagement on Instagram. *Journal of Interactive Marketing, 49*(1), 20–53. Advance online publication. doi:10.1016/j.intmar.2019.06.003

Rivas, A. A., Liao, Y.-K., Vu, M.-Q., & Hung, C.-S. (2022). Toward a comprehensive model of green marketing and innovative green adoption: Application of a stimulus-organism-response model. *Sustainability (Basel), 14*(6), 3288. doi:10.3390/su14063288

Roberts, J. A. (1996). Green consumers in the 1990s: Profile and implications for advertising. *Journal of Business Research, 36*(3), 217–231. doi:10.1016/0148-2963(95)00150-6

Robeson, L. M. (2012). Polymer Membranes. In *Polymer Science: A Comprehensive Reference* (pp. 325–347). Elsevier. doi:10.1016/B978-0-444-53349-4.00211-9

Rocamora, A. (2018). The Labour of Fashion Blogging. In L. Armstrong & F. McDowell (Eds.), *Fashioning Professionals: Identity and Representation at Work in the Creative Industries* (pp. 65–81). doi:10.5040/9781350001879.ch-004

Rognoli, V., Petreca, B., Pollini, B., & Saito, C. (2022). Materials biography as a tool for designers' exploration of bio-based and bio-fabricated materials for the sustainable fashion industry. *Sustainability: Science. Sustainability*, *18*(1), 749–772. doi:10.1080/15487733.2022.2124740

Rolland, M. L. (2023). *Sustainability in Luxury and Fashion: Time for Action*. Euromonitor.

Romani, S., Grappi, S., Zarantonello, L., & Bagozzi, R. P. (2015). The revenge of the consumer! How brand moral violations lead to consumer anti-brand activism. *Journal of Brand Management*, *22*(8), 658–672. doi:10.1057/bm.2015.38

Romano, F. M., Devine, A., Tarabashkina, L., Soutar, G., & Quester, P. (2023). Specificity of CSR Ties That (Un)Bind Brand Attachment. *Australasian Marketing Journal*, *31*(1), 71–80. doi:10.1177/18393349211030699

Roozen, I., Raedts, M., & Meijburg, L. (2021). Do verbal and visual nudges influence consumers' choice for sustainable fashion? *Journal of Global Fashion Marketing*, *12*(4), 327–342. doi:10.1080/20932685.2021.1930096

Rotimi, E. O. O., Johnson, L. W., Kalantari Daronkola, H., Topple, C., & Hopkins, J. (2023). Predictors of consumers' behavior to recycle end-of-life garments in Australia. *Journal of Fashion Marketing and Management*, *27*(2), 262–286. doi:10.1108/JFMM-06-2022-0125

Rourke, L., Anderson, T., Garrison, D. R., & Archer, W. (2007). Assessing Social Presence In Asynchronous Text-based Computer Conferencing. *International Journal of E-Learning & Distance Education Revue Internationale Du E-Learning Et La Formation à Distance, 14*(2), 50–71. Retrieved from https://www.ijede.ca/index.php/jde/article/view/153

Roy, R., Chavan, P. P., Rajeev, Y., Praveenraj, T., & Kolazhi, P. (2024). Sustainable Manufacturing Practices in Textiles and Fashion. In *Sustainable Manufacturing Practices in the Textiles and Fashion Sector* (pp. 1–22). Springer Nature Switzerland. doi:10.1007/978-3-031-51362-6_1

Rungruangjit, W. (2022). What drives Taobao live streaming commerce? The role of parasocial relationships, congruence and source credibility in Chinese consumers' purchase intentions. *Heliyon*, *8*(6), e09676. doi:10.1016/j.heliyon.2022.e09676 PMID:35756134

Rungruangjit, W., & Charoenpornpanichkul, K. (2022). Building Stronger Brand Evangelism for Sustainable Marketing through Micro-Influencer-Generated Content on Instagram in the Fashion Industry. *Sustainability (Basel)*, *14*(23), 15770. doi:10.3390/su142315770

Russell, J. A., & Mehrabian, A. (1974). Distinguishing anger and anxiety in terms of emotional response factors. *Journal of Consulting and Clinical Psychology*, *42*(1), 79–83. doi:10.1037/h0035915 PMID:4814102

Ryan, R. M., & Deci, E. L. (2000). Self-determination theory and the facilitation of intrinsic motivation, social development, and well-being. *The American Psychologist*, *55*(1), 68–78. Advance online publication. doi:10.1037/0003-066X.55.1.68 PMID:11392867

Sadiq, M., Bharti, K., Adil, M., & Singh, R. (2021). Why do consumers buy green apparel? The role of dispositional traits, environmental orientation, environmental knowledge, and monetary incentive. *Journal of Retailing and Consumer Services*, *62*, 102643. doi:10.1016/j.jretconser.2021.102643

Sajjadi, P., Hoffmann, L., Cimiano, P., & Kopp, S. (2019). A personality-based emotional model for embodied conversational agents: Effects on perceived social presence and game experience of users. *Entertainment Computing*, *32*, 100313. doi:10.1016/j.entcom.2019.100313

Salem, S. F., & Alanadoly, A. B. (2021). Personality traits and social media as drivers of word-of-mouth towards sustainable fashion. *Journal of Fashion Marketing and Management*, *25*(1), 24–44. Advance online publication. doi:10.1108/JFMM-08-2019-0162

Salminen, J., & Hytönen, A. (2012). *Viral coefficient–Unveiling the Holy Grail of online marketing*. http://taac.org.ua/files/a2012/proceedings/FI-2-Salminen-Hytonen-238.pdf>

Sam, M., Fazli, M., & Tahir, M. N. H. (2009). Website quality and consumer online purchase intention of air ticket. *International Journal of Basic and Applied Sciences*, *9*(10), 1–8.

Sandberg, M. (2021). Sufficiency transitions: A review of consumption changes for environmental sustainability. *Journal of Cleaner Production*, *293*, 126097. doi:10.1016/j.jclepro.2021.126097

SanMiguel, P., Pérez-Bou, S., Sádaba, T., & Mir-Bernal, P. (2021). How to communicate sustainability: From the corporate Web to E-commerce. The case of the fashion industry. *Sustainability (Basel)*, *13*(20), 11363. doi:10.3390/su132011363

Sann, R., Jansom, S., & Muennaburan, T. (2023). An extension of the theory of planned behavior in Thailand cycling tourism: The mediating role of attractiveness of sustainable alternatives. *Leisure Studies*, 1–15.doi.org/10.1080/02614367.2023.2182346

Saricam, C., & Okur, N. (2019). Analyzing the consumer behavior regarding sustainable fashion using the theory of planned behavior. *Consumer Behavior and Sustainable Fashion Consumption*, 1–37.doi.org/10.1007/978-981-13-1265-6_1

Sayyad Liyakat. (2022). Nanotechnology Application in Neural Growth Support System. *Nano Trends: A Journal of Nanotechnology and Its Applications, 24*(2), 47 – 55.

Schiffman, L. G., & Kanuk, L. L. (2007). *Consumer behavior* (9th ed.). Pearson Prentice Hall.

Schivinski, B., Christodoulides, G., & Dabrowski, D. (2016). Measuring consumers' engagement with brand-related social-media content: Development and validation of a scale that identifies levels of social-media engagement with brands. *Journal of Advertising Research*, *56*(1), 64–80. doi:10.2501/JAR-2016-004

Schmidt, R., Emmerich, K., & Schmidt, B. (2015). Applied games – in search of a new definition. *Entertainment Computing - ICEC 2015*, 100–111. doi:10.1007/978-3-319-24589-8_8

Schmuck, D., Matthes, J., & Naderer, B. (2018). Misleading Consumers with Green Advertising? An Affect–Reason–Involvement Account of Greenwashing Effects in Environmental Advertising. *Journal of Advertising*, *47*(2), 127–145. doi:10.1080/00913367.2018.1452652

Schnack, A., Wright, M. J., & Elms, J. (2021). Investigating the impact of shopper personality on behaviour in immersive virtual reality store environments. *Journal of Retailing and Consumer Services*, *61*, 102581. doi:10.1016/j.jretconser.2021.102581

Schouten, A. P., Janssen, L., & Verspaget, M. (2020). Celebrity vs. Influencer endorsements in advertising: The role of identification, credibility, and Product-Endorser fit. *International Journal of Advertising*, *39*(2), 258–281. doi:10.1080/02650487.2019.1634898

Schouten, A. P., Janssen, L., & Verspaget, M. (2021). Celebrity vs. Influencer endorsements in advertising: the role of identification, credibility, and Product-Endorser fit. In *Leveraged Marketing Communications* (1st ed., pp. 208–231). Routledge. doi:10.4324/9781003155249-12

Schubert, F., Kandampully, J., Solnet, D., & Kralj, A. (2010). Exploring consumer perceptions of green restaurants in the US. *Tourism and Hospitality Research*, *10*(4), 286–300. doi:10.1057/thr.2010.17

Schulz, M. (2022, September 7). *Fashion's next metaverse opportunity: Turning real models into digital avatars*. VOGUE Business. https://www.voguebusiness.com/technology/fashions-next- metaverse-opportunity-turning-real-models-into-digital-avatars#:~:text=Technology-

Schwartz, S. H. (1977). Normative influences on altruism. In Advances in Experimental Social Psychology (pp. 221–279). Elsevier. doi:10.1016/S0065-2601(08)60358-5

Schwartz, D., Milfont, T. L., & Hilton, D. (2019). The interplay between intrinsic motivation, financial incentives, and nudges in sustainable consumption. In K. Gangl & E. Kirchler (Eds.), *A research agenda for economic psychology* (pp. 87–103). Edward Elgar Publishing. doi:10.4337/9781788116060.00012

Schwartz, S. H., & Howard, J. A. (1980). Explanations of the moderating effect of responsibility denial on the personal norm-behavior relationship. *Social Psychology Quarterly*, *43*(4), 441. doi:10.2307/3033965

Şener, T., Bişkin, F., & Kılınç, N. (2019). Sustainable dressing: Consumers' value perceptions towards slow fashion. *Business Strategy and the Environment*, *28*(8), 1548–1557. doi:10.1002/bse.2330

Sengupta, D. (2021, December 19). *Nike acquired this company that makes virtual sneakers and nfts for the metaverse*. Beebom. https://beebom.com/nike-acquired-company-makes-virtual- sneakers-nfts-metaverse/

Septialana, M. K., & Kusumastuti, A. E. (2017). Pengaruh faktor intrinsik, faktor ekstrinsik dan sikap konsumen terhadap minat menjadi mitra laku pandai (Studi pada masyarakat kota Pekalongan, Semarang, dan Yogyakarta). *EBBANK*, *8*(2), 1–16.

Shahbaznezhad, H., Dolan, R., & Rashidirad, M. (2021). The role of social media content format and platform in users' engagement behaviour. *Journal of Interactive Marketing*, *53*(1), 47–65. doi:10.1016/j.intmar.2020.05.001

Shah, H., Aziz, A., Jaffari, A. R., Waris, S., Ejaz, W., Fatima, M., & Sherazi, K. (2012). The Impact of Brands on Consumer Purchase Intentions. *Asian Journal of Business Management*, *4*(2), 105–110.

Shamdasani, Chon-Lin, & Richmond. (1993). Exploring Green Consumers In An Oriental Culture: Role Of Personal And Marketing Mix Factors. *Advances in Consumer Research. Association for Consumer Research (U. S.)*, *20*, 491.

Shang, K.-C., Chao, C.-C., & Lirn, T.-C. (2016). The application of personality traits model on the freight forwarding service industry. *Maritime Business Review*, *1*(3), 231–252. doi:10.1108/MABR-09-2016-0021

Sharma, A. P. (2021). Consumers' purchase behaviour and green marketing: A synthesis, review and agenda. *International Journal of Consumer Studies*, *45*(6), 1217–1238.

Sharma, A., & Banwet, D. K. (2018). Green marketing and consumer behavior: The case of Generation Z in India's apparel sector. *Journal of Fashion Marketing and Management*, *22*(3), 384–401.

Sharma, K., Aswal, C., & Paul, J. (2023). Factors affecting green purchase behavior: A systematic literature review. *Business Strategy and the Environment*, *32*(4), 2078–2092. doi:10.1002/bse.3237

Sharma, Y. (2011). Changing consumer behaviour with respect to green marketing–a case study of consumer durables and retailing. *International Journal of Multidisciplinary Research*, *1*(4), 152–162.

Shaw, D., Hogg, G., Wilson, E., Shiu, E., & Hassan, L. (2006). Fashion victim: The impact of fair trade concerns on clothing choice. *Journal of Strategic Marketing*, *14*(4), 427–440. doi:10.1080/09652540600956426

Shaw, D., Shiu, E., & Clarke, I. (2000). The contribution of ethical obligation and self-identity to the theory of planned behaviour: An exploration of ethical consumers. *Journal of Marketing Management*, *16*(8), 879–894. doi:10.1362/026725700784683672

Sheldon, P., & Bryant, K. (2016). Instagram: Motives for its use and relationship to narcissism and contextual age. *Computers in Human Behavior*, *58*, 89–97. doi:10.1016/j.chb.2015.12.059

Shelley, W. (2023). [*Social Media Sites & Platforms*. Search Engine Journal. https://www.searchenginejournal.com/social-media/social-media-platforms/

Shen, B. (2014). Sustainable Fashion Supply Chain: Lessons from H&M. *Sustainability (Basel)*, *6*(9), 6236–6249. doi:10.3390/su6096236

Shen, B., Wang, Y., Lo, C. K. Y., & Shum, M. (2012). The impact of ethical fashion on consumer purchase behavior. *Journal of Fashion Marketing and Management*, *16*(2), 234–245. doi:10.1108/13612021211222842

Shen, B., Zheng, J.-H., Chow, P.-S., & Chow, K.-Y. (2014). Perception of fashion sustainability in online community. *Journal of the Textile Institute*, *105*(9), 971–979. doi:10.1080/00405000.2013.866334

Shen, D., Richards, J., & Liu, F. (2013). Consumers' awareness of sustainable fashion. *Marketing Management Journal*, *23*(2), 134–147.

Shen, Z. (2023). Mining sustainable fashion e-commerce: Social media texts and consumer behaviors. *Electronic Commerce Research*, *23*(2), 949–971. doi:10.1007/s10660-021-09498-5

Sheoran, M., & Kumar, D. (2022). Benchmarking the barriers of sustainable consumer behaviour. *Social Responsibility Journal*, *18*(1), 19–42. doi:10.1108/SRJ-05-2020-0203

Sheppard, B. H., Hartwick, J., & Warshaw, P. R. (1988). The theory of reasoned action: A meta-analysis of past research with recommendations for modifications and future research. *The Journal of Consumer Research*, *15*(3), 325. doi:10.1086/209170

Sherin Aly. (2021). *Toward Smart Internet Of Things (Iot) For Apparel Retail Industry: Automatic Customer's Body Measurements And Size Recommendation System Using Computer Vision Techniques*. Academic Press.

Sheth, J. N., & Sisodia, R. S. (2015). *Does marketing need reform?: Fresh perspectives on the future*. Routledge. doi:10.4324/9781315705118

Shil, P. (2012). Evolution and future of environmental marketing. *Asia Pacific Journal Of Marketing and Management Review*, *1*(3), 74–81.

Shirsavar, H. A., & Fashkhamy, F. (2013). Green marketing: A new paradigm to gain competitive advantage in contemporary business. *Trends in Advanced Science and Engineering*, *7*(1), 12–18.

Shirvanimoghaddam, K., Motamed, B., Ramakrishna, S., & Naebe, M. (2020). Death by waste: Fashion and textile circular economy case. *Science of the Total Environment*. https://doi.org/ doi:10.1016/j.scitotenv.2020.137317

Shrikanth, R., & Raju, D. S. N. (2012). Contemporary green marketing-brief reference to Indian scenario. *International Journal of Social Sciences & Interdisciplinary Research*, *1*(1), 26–39.

Shuhaiber, A., & Mashal, I. (2019). Understanding users' acceptance of smart homes. *Technology in Society*, *58*, 101110. doi:10.1016/j.techsoc.2019.01.003

Siebert, F., Peterson, T., & Schramm, W. (1963). *Four theories of the press: The authoritarian, libertarian, social responsibility, and Soviet Communist concepts of what the press should be and do.* University of Illinois Press. doi:10.5406/j.ctv1nhr0v

Silvestri, C., Aquilani, B., Piccarozzi, M., & Ruggieri, A. (2020). Consumer Quality Perception in Traditional Food: Parmigiano Reggiano Cheese. *Journal of International Food & Agribusiness Marketing*, *32*(2), 141–167. doi:10.1080/08974438.2019.1599754

Singh, G. (2013). Green: The new colour of marketing in India. ASCI Journal of Smith, J. (2020). The impact of green marketing on the marketing industry. *JMR, Journal of Marketing Research*, *57*(2), 87–94.

Singh, P. B., & Pandey, K. K. (2012). Green marketing: Policies and practices for sustainable development. *Integral Review*, *5*(1), 22–30.

Sinha, P., Sharma, M., & Agrawal, R. (2023). A systematic review and future research agenda for sustainable fashion in the apparel industry. *Benchmarking*, *30*(9), 3482–3507. doi:10.1108/BIJ-02-2022-0142

Siregar, Y., Kent, A., Peirson-Smith, A., & Guan, C. (2023). Disrupting the fashion retail journey: Social media and GenZ's fashion consumption. *International Journal of Retail & Distribution Management*, *51*(7), 862–875. Advance online publication. doi:10.1108/IJRDM-01-2022-0002

Smirnov, Y. A., Fomina, N. V., & Kaverin, N. V. (1973). A correlation between the buoyant density and the sedimentation coefficient of EMC viral polyribosomes. *FEBS Letters.* https://core.ac.uk/download/pdf/82695955.pdf

Smith, A. N., Fischer, E., & Yongjian, C. (2012). How Does Brand-related User-generated Content Differ across YouTube, Facebook, and Twitter? *Journal of Interactive Marketing*, *26*(2), 102–113. doi:10.1016/j.intmar.2012.01.002

Smith, S., & Paladino, A. (2010). Eating clean and green? Investigating consumer motivations towards the purchase of organic food. *Australasian Marketing Journal*, *18*(2), 93–104. doi:10.1016/j.ausmj.2010.01.001

Snoj, B., Korda, P. A., & Mumel, D. (2004). The relationships among perceived quality, perceived risk and perceived product value. *Journal of Product and Brand Management*, *13*(3), 156–167. doi:10.1108/10610420410538050

Sohail, M. S. (2017). Green marketing strategies: How do they influence consumer-based brand equity? *J. for Global Business Advancement*, *10*(3), 229. doi:10.1504/JGBA.2017.084607

Solomon, M. R. (2011). *Consumer behavior: Buying, having, and being.* Prentice Hall.

Solvalier, I. (2010). *Green marketing strategies case study about ICA group AB.* M.Sc.

Sonnenberg, N., Jacobs, B., & Momberg, D. (2014). The Role of Information Exposure in Female University Students' Evaluation and Selection of Eco-Friendly Apparel in the South African Emerging Economy. *Clothing & Textiles Research Journal*, *32*(4), 266–281. Advance online publication. doi:10.1177/0887302X14541542

Sousa, F. P. D. (2020). *The impact of social virtual presence agents and content-based product recommendation system on on-line customer purchase intention* (Master's thesis).

Spiller, P., & Lohse, G. L. (1997). A classification of internet retail stores. *International Journal of Electronic Commerce*, *2*(2), 29–56. doi:10.1080/10864415.1997.11518307

Srauturier. (2024, January 8). *Greenwashing examples: 8 Notorious fast fashion claims and campaigns - Good on you.* Good on You. https://goodonyou.eco/greenwashing-examples/

Stacy, D. J. (2023a). *Biggest social media platforms 2023.* Statista.Com. https://www.statista.com/statistics/272014/global-social-networks-ranked-by-number-of-users/

Stacy, D. J. (2023b). *Number of worldwide social network users 2027.* Statista.Com. https://www.statista.com/statistics/278414/number-of-worldwide-social-network-users/

Štefko, R., & Steffek, V. (2018). Key issues in slow fashion: Current challenges and future perspectives. *Sustainability (Basel), 10*(7), 2270. doi:10.3390/su10072270

Steg, L., Perlaviciute, G., van der Werff, E., & Lurvink, J. (2014). The significance of hedonic values for environmentally relevant attitudes, preferences, and actions. *Environment and Behavior, 46*(2), 163–192. doi:10.1177/0013916512454730

Steiner, A. (2015). *Sustainable Consumption and Production.* United Nations Environment Programme UNAB.

Stephen, A. T., & Galak, J. (2012). The effects of traditional and social earned media on sales: A study of a microlending marketplace. *JMR, Journal of Marketing Research, 49*(5), 624–639. doi:10.1509/jmr.09.0401

Stephens, D. (2023, October 16). *The metaverse will radically change retail.* The Business of Fashion. https://www.businessoffashion.com/opinions/retail/the-metaverse-will-radically- change-retail/

Stern, P. C., Dietz, T., & Kalof, L. (1993). Value orientations, gender, and environmental concern. *Environment and Behavior, 25*(5), 322–348. doi:10.1177/0013916593255002

Stern, P. C., Kalof, L., Dietz, T., & Guagnano, G. A. (1995). Values, beliefs, and proenvironmental action: Attitude formation toward emergent attitude objects1. *Journal of Applied Social Psychology, 25*(18), 1611–1636. doi:10.1111/j.1559-1816.1995.tb02636.x

Stern, P., Dietz, T., Abel, T., Guagnano, G., & Kalof, L. (1999). A Value-Belief-Norm theory of support for social movements: The case of environmentalism. *Human Ecology Review, 6*(2), 81–97.

Strähle, J., & Chantal, G. (2016). The Role of Social Media for a Sustainable Consumption. In *Green Fashion Retail* (1st ed., pp. 225–247). Springer Singapore. doi:10.1007/978-981-10-2440-5_3

Strähle, J., & Gräff, C. (2017). *The Role of Social Media for a Sustainable Consumption BT - Green Fashion Retail.* Springer Singapore. doi:10.1007/978-981-10-2440-5_12

Su, J., & Chang, A. (2018). Factors affecting college students' brand loyalty toward fast fashion: A consumer-based brand equity approach. *International Journal of Retail & Distribution Management, 46*(1), 90–107. doi:10.1108/IJRDM-01-2016-0015

Su, J., Watchravesringkan, K., Zhou, J., & Gil, M. (2019). Sustainable clothing: Perspectives from US and Chinese young Millennials. *International Journal of Retail & Distribution Management, 47*(11), 1141–1162. doi:10.1108/IJRDM-09-2017-0184

Sujood, S. S., Bano, N., & Al Rousan, R. (2023). Understanding intention of Gen Z Indians to visit heritage sites by applying the extended theory of planned behavior: A sustainable approach. *Journal of Cultural Heritage Management and Sustainable Development.* Advance online publication. doi:10.1108/JCHMSD-03-2022-0039

Sunil Kumar, Ganesh, Turukmane, & Batta. (2022). Deep Convolution Neural Network based solution for detecting plant Diseases. *Journal of Pharmaceutical Negative Results, 13*(1), 464-471.

Sussman, R., & Gifford, R. (2019). Causality in the theory of planned behavior. *Personality and Social Psychology Bulletin, 45*(6), 920–933. doi:10.1177/0146167218801363 PMID:30264655

Swami. (2022). Sending notification to someone missing you through smart watch. *International Journal of Information Technology & Computer Engineering, 2*(8), 19 – 24.

Tandon, A., Sithipolvanichgul, J., Asmi, F., Anwar, M. A., & Dhir, A. (2023). Drivers of green apparel consumption: Digging a little deeper into green apparel buying intentions. *Business Strategy and the Environment*, *32*(6), 3997–4012. doi:10.1002/bse.3350

Tapscott, D. (2008). *Grown up digital: How the net generation is changing your world*. McGraw Hill Professional.

Tariq, M., Nawaz, M., Butt, H., & Nawaz, M. (2013). Customer Perceptions about Branding and Purchase Intention:A Study of FMCG in an Emerging Market. *Journal of Basic and Applied Scientific Research*, *3*(2), 340–347.

Tarkiainen, A., & Sundqvist, S. (2005). Subjective norms, attitudes and intentions of Finnish consumers in buying organic food. *British Food Journal*, *107*(11), 808–822. doi:10.1108/00070700510629760

Tarnanidis, T. K., Papachristou, E., Karypidis, M., & Ismyrlis, V. (2023). How Social Media Affects Consumer Behavior in the Fashion Industry. In *Social Media and Online Consumer Decision Making in the Fashion Industry* (pp. 324–337). IGI Global. Retrieved 2024, from https://www.igi-global.com/chapter/social-media-affects-consumer-behavior/327699

Tarnanidis, T. (2024). Exploring the Impact of Mobile Marketing Strategies on Consumer Behavior: A Comprehensive Analysis. *International Journal of Information, Business and Management*, *16*(2), 1–17.

Tarnanidis, T., Papachristou, E., Karypidis, M., & Ismyrlis, V. (Eds.). (2023). *Social Media and Online Consumer Decision Making in the Fashion Industry*. IGI Global. doi:10.4018/978-1-6684-8753-2

Tascioglu, M., Eastman, J., Bock, D., Manrodt, K., & Shepherd, C. D. (2019). The impact of retailers' sustainability and price on consumers' responses in different cultural contexts. *International Review of Retail, Distribution and Consumer Research*, *29*(4), 430–455. doi:10.1080/09593969.2019.1611619

Tentree (2023). *About*. Consulted on June 28, 2023, at Tentree: https://www.tentree.com/pages/about

Terry, D. J., & O'Leary, J. E. (1995). The theory of planned behaviour: The effects of perceived behavioural control and self-efficacy. *British Journal of Social Psychology*, *34*(2), 199–220. Advance online publication. doi:10.1111/j.2044-8309.1995.tb01058.x PMID:7620846

Testa, D. S., Bakhshian, S., & Eike, R. (2021). Engaging consumers with sustainable fashion on Instagram. *Journal of Fashion Marketing and Management*, *25*(4), 569–584. doi:10.1108/JFMM-11-2019-0266

Testa, F., Cosic, A., & Iraldo, F. (2016). Determining factors of curtailment and purchasing energy related behaviours. *Journal of Cleaner Production*, *112*, 3810–3819. doi:10.1016/j.jclepro.2015.07.134

Thaler, R. (1983). Transaction Utility Theory. *Advances in Consumer Research. Association for Consumer Research (U. S.)*, *10*, 229–232. https://doi.org/https://www.acrwebsite.org/volumes/6118/volumes/v10/NA%20-%2010

Thomas, J. B., & Peters, C. L. O. (2009). Silver seniors: Exploring the selfconcept, lifestyles, and apparel consumption of women over age 65. *International Journal of Retail & Distribution Management*, *37*(12), 1018–1040. doi:10.1108/09590550911005001

Thorisdottir, T. S., & Johannsdottir, L. (2019). Sustainability within fashion business models: A systematic literature review. *Sustainability (Basel)*, *11*(8), 2233. doi:10.3390/su11082233

Thorisdottir, T. S., & Johannsdottir, L. (2020). Corporate Social Responsibility Influencing Sustainability within the Fashion Industry. A Systematic Review. *Sustainability (Basel)*, *12*(21), 9167. doi:10.3390/su12219167

Tian, Z.-B., Zhang, Y., & Yu, N. (2022). Evaluating factors for sustainable design of products in the apparel industry using DANP technique. International Conference on Statistics, Applied Mathematics, and Computing Science (CSAMCS 2021), Wakes, S., Dunn, L., Penty, D., Kitson, K., & Jowett, T. (2020). Is price an indicator of garment durability and longevity? *Sustainability*, *12*(21), 8906.

Tiwari, A., Kumar, A., Kant, R., & Jaiswal, D. (2023). Impact of fashion influencers on consumers' purchase intentions: Theory of planned behavior and mediation of attitude. *Journal of Fashion Marketing and Management*. Advance online publication. doi:10.1108/JFMM-11-2022-0253

Tiwari, P., & Joshi, H. (2020). Factors influencing online purchase intention towards online shopping of Gen Z. *International Journal of Business Competition and Growth*, *7*(2), 175–187. doi:10.1504/IJBCG.2020.111944

Todeschini, B. V., Cortimiglia, M. N., Callegaro-de-Menezes, D., & Ghezzi, A. (2017). Innovative and sustainable business models in the fashion industry: Entrepreneurial drivers, opportunities, and challenges. *Business Horizons*, *60*(6), 759–770. doi:10.1016/j.bushor.2017.07.003

Tommasel, A., Corbellini, A., Godoy, D., & Schiaffino, S. (2015). Exploring the role of personality traits in followee recommendation. *Online Information Review*, *39*(6), 812–830. Advance online publication. doi:10.1108/OIR-04-2015-0107

Tonglet, M., Phillips, P. S., & Read, A. D. (2004). Using the theory of planned behavior to investigate the determinants of recycling behavior: A case study from Brixworth, U K. *Resources, Conservation and Recycling*, *41*(3), 191–214. doi:10.1016/j.resconrec.2003.11.001

Torok, G. (2020, September 9). *Council post: Pandemic potential: Four app development trends in a post-covid-19 world*. Forbes. https://www.forbes.com/sites/forbestechcouncil/2020/09/10/pandemic-potential-four-app- development-trends-in-a-post-covid-19-world/

Tran, K., Nguyen, T., Tran, Y., Nguyen, A., Luu, K., & Nguyen, Y. (2022). Eco-friendly fashion among generation Z: Mixed-methods study on price, value image, customer fulfillment, and pro-environmental behavior. *PLoS One*, *17*(8), e0272789. doi:10.1371/journal.pone.0272789 PMID:35972928

Troumbis, A. Y. (1991). *Environmental Labelling on Services: The Case of Tourism*. Academic Press.

Tryphena, R., & Aram, I. A. (2023). Consumer perception on sustainable clothing among urban Indians. *Journal of Engineered Fibers and Fabrics*, *18*. doi:10.1177/15589250231168964

Tsai, P. H., Lin, G. Y., Zheng, Y. L., Chen, Y. C., Chen, P. Z., & Su, Z. C. (2020). Exploring the effect of Starbucks' green marketing on consumers' purchase decisions from consumers' perspective. *Journal of Retailing and Consumer Services*, *56*, 102162.

Tseng, F.-M., & Wang, C.-Y. (2013). Why do not satisfied consumers show reuse behavior? the context of online games. *Computers in Human Behavior*, *29*(3), 1012–1022. doi:10.1016/j.chb.2012.12.011

Tsiotsou, R. (2006). The role of perceived product quality and overall satisfaction on purchase intention. *International Journal of Consumer Studies*, *30*(2), 207–217. doi:10.1111/j.1470-6431.2005.00477.x

Tu, C.-H., & McIsaac, M. (2002). The relationship of social presence and interaction in online classes. *American Journal of Distance Education*, *16*(3), 131–150. doi:10.1207/S15389286AJDE1603_2

Tung-Zong, C., & And Albert, R. W. (1994). Prices, Product information, and purchase intention: An empirical study. *Journal of the Academy of Marketing Science*, *22*(1), 16–27. doi:10.1177/0092070394221002

Turker, D., & Altuntas, C. (2014). Sustainable supply chain management in the fast fashion industry: An analysis of corporate reports. *European Management Journal*, *32*(5), 837–849. doi:10.1016/j.emj.2014.02.001

Turunen, L. L. M., & Halme, M. (2021). Communicating actionable sustainability information to consumers: The Shades of Green instrument for fashion. *Journal of Cleaner Production*, *297*, 126605. doi:10.1016/j.jclepro.2021.126605

Uikey, A. A., & Baber, R. (2023). Exploring the Factors that Foster Green Brand Loyalty: The Role of Green Transparency, Green Perceived Value, Green Brand Trust and Self-Brand Connection. *Journal of Content Community and Communication*, *17*(9), 155–170. doi:10.31620/JCCC.09.23/13

UmirzakovI. H. (2013). Some comments on 'Equation for the second virial coefficient'. doi:10.1109/PLASMA.1998.677937

Utami, R. T. (2021). *Generation Z Consumer Satisfaction in Online Shopping*. https://doi.org/http://dx.doi.org/10.33603/jshr.v1i1.5878

Valente, J. J. (2006). Application of Self-interaction Chromatography as a Rational Approach to Measuring the Osmotic Second Viral Coefficient (B) for Protein Formulation. Colorado State University.

Velasco-Molpeceres, A., Zarauza-Castro, J., Pérez-Curiel, C., & Mateos-González, S. (2022). Slow Fashion as a Communication Strategy of Fashion Brands on Instagram. *Sustainability (Basel)*, *15*(1), 423. doi:10.3390/su15010423

Velusamy, S., Roy, A., Sundaram, S., & Kumar Mallick, T. (2021). A Review on Heavy Metal Ions and Containing Dyes Removal Through Graphene Oxide-Based Adsorption Strategies for Textile Wastewater Treatment. *Chemical Record (New York, N.Y.)*, *21*(7), 1570–1610. doi:10.1002/tcr.202000153 PMID:33539046

Venkatesh, V., & Davis, F. D. (2000). A theoretical extension of the technology acceptance model: Four longitudinal field studies. *Management Science*, *46*(2), 186–204. doi:10.1287/mnsc.46.2.186.11926

Ventre, I., & Kolbe, D. (2020). The impact of perceived usefulness of online reviews, trust and perceived risk on online purchase intention in emerging markets: A Mexican perspective. *Journal of International Consumer Marketing*, *32*(4), 287–299. doi:10.1080/08961530.2020.1712293

Venugopal, K., Das, S., & Badawy, H. R. H. (2023). Prediction Analysis of Gen Zers' Attitudes on Ecological Consciousness. In Sustainable Science and Intelligent Technologies for Societal Development (pp. 342-357). IGI Global.

Venugopal, K., Das, S., & Vakamullu, G. (2023). Critical Factors for the Upscale of Online Shopping: A Rural Perspective. In Influencer Marketing Applications Within the Metaverse (pp. 254-262). IGI Global.

Venugopal, K., & Das, S. (2023). Entrepreneurial cluster branding influencing sustainable cashew market: A case study. *Parikalpana KIIT Journal of Management*, *19*(2), 83–96.

Venugopal, K., Pranaya, D., Das, S., & Jena, S. K. (2023). Handloom Weaving: Critical Factors influencing the Satisfaction-The Socio & Economic Context. *Economic Affairs*, *68*(04), 1979–1988.

Verma, A. K., Dash, R. R., & Bhunia, P. (2012). A review on chemical coagulation/flocculation technologies for removal of colour from textile wastewaters. *Journal of Environmental Management*, *93*(1), 154–168. doi:10.1016/j.jenvman.2011.09.012 PMID:22054582

Viciunaite, V. (2022). Communicating Sustainable Business Models to Consumers: A Translation Theory Perspective. *Organization & Environment*, *35*(2), 233–251. doi:10.1177/1086026620953448

Virtanen, H., Björk, P., & Sjöström, E. (2017). Follow for follow: Marketing of a start-up company on Instagram. *Journal of Small Business and Enterprise Development*, *24*(3), 468–484. doi:10.1108/JSBED-12-2016-0202

Virtualinfocom, V. (2023b, May 14). *Unlocking new fashion frontiers: How to market garments through games*. LinkedIn. https://www.linkedin.com/pulse/unlocking-new-fashion-frontiers- how-market-garments-through/

Vita, G., Ivanova, D., Dumitru, A., García-Mira, R., Carrus, G., Stadler, K., Krause, K., Wood, R., & Hertwich, E. G. (2020). Happier with less? Members of European environmental grassroots initiatives reconcile lower carbon footprints with higher life satisfaction and income increases. *Energy Research & Social Science*, *60*, 101329. doi:10.1016/j.erss.2019.101329

Vladimirova, K., Henninger, C. E., Alosaimi, S. I., Brydges, T., Choopani, H., Hanlon, M., Iran, S., McCormick, H., & Zhou, S. (2023). Exploring the influence of social media on sustainable fashion consumption: A systematic literature review and future research agenda. *Journal of Global Fashion Marketing*, 1–22. doi:10.1080/20932685.2023.2237978

Voorveld, H. A. M. (2019). Brand Communication in Social Media: A Research Agenda. *Journal of Advertising*, *48*(1), 14–26. Advance online publication. doi:10.1080/00913367.2019.1588808

Voorveld, H. A., Noort, G. V., Muntinga, D. G., & Bronner, F. (2018). Engagement with Social Media and Social Media Advertising: The Differentiating Role of Platform Type. *Journal of Advertising*, *47*(1), 38–54. doi:10.1080/00913367.2017.1405754

Vredenburg, J., Kapitan, S., Spry, A., & Kemper, J. A. (2020). Brands Taking a Stand: Authentic Brand Activism or Woke Washing? *Journal of Public Policy & Marketing*, *39*(4), 444–460. doi:10.1177/0743915620947359

Waghray, A., Das, S., & Ahmed, S. (2024). An Assessment on Marketing Promotions and Strategies Adopted by Retailers Towards Millet-Based Products in Hyderabad. In *The Role of Women in Cultivating Sustainable Societies Through Millets* (pp. 143–155). IGI Global.

Wagner, M., Curteza, A., Hong, Y., Chen, Y., Thomassey, S., & Zeng, X. (2019). A design analysis for eco-fashion style using sensory evaluation tools: Consumer perceptions of product appearance. *Journal of Retailing and Consumer Services*, *51*, 253–262. Advance online publication. doi:10.1016/j.jretconser.2019.06.005

Wallace, E., Buil, I., & Catalán, S. (2020). Facebook and luxury fashion brands: Self-congruent posts and purchase intentions. *Journal of Fashion Marketing and Management*, *24*(4), 571–588. doi:10.1108/JFMM-09-2019-0215

Wang, P., & Huang, Q. (2023). Digital influencers, social power and consumer engagement in social commerce. *Internet Research*, *33*(1), 178–207. doi:10.1108/INTR-08-2020-0467

Wang, Y., Shi, Y., Xu, X., & Zhu, Y. (2024). A Study on the Efficiency of Green Technology Innovation in Listed Chinese Water Environment Treatment Companies. *Water (Basel)*, *16*(3), 510. doi:10.3390/w16030510

Wang, Y., Xiang, D., Yang, Z., & Ma, S. S. (2019). Unraveling customer sustainable consumption behaviors in sharing economy: A socio-economic approach based on social exchange theory. *Journal of Cleaner Production*, *208*, 869–879. doi:10.1016/j.jclepro.2018.10.139

Wani, N. S. (2022). Factors Influencing Price Perception for Fashion: Study of Millennials in India. *Vision (Basel)*, *26*(3), 300–313. doi:10.1177/0972262920984856

Wan-Ling Hu, A., & Ming-Hone Tsai, W. (2009). An empirical study of an enjoyment-based response hierarchy model of watching MDTV on the move. *Journal of Consumer Marketing*, *26*(2), 66–77. doi:10.1108/07363760910940438

Whiteside, A. L., & Dikkers, A. G. (2016). *Leveraging the social presence model.* Emotions, Technology, and Learning. doi:10.1016/B978-0-12-800649-8.00013-4

Whiting, A., & Williams, D. (2013). Why people use social media: A uses and gratifications approach. *Qualitative Market Research*, *16*(4), 362–369. doi:10.1108/QMR-06-2013-0041

Wicaksono, A., & Maharani, A. (2020). The effect of perceived usefulness and perceived ease of use on the technology acceptance model to use online travel agency. *Journal of Business and Management Review*, *1*(5), 313–328. doi:10.47153/jbmr15.502020

Wiederhold, M., & Martinez, L. F. (2018). Ethical consumer behaviour in Germany: The attitude-behaviour gap in the green apparel industry. *International Journal of Consumer Studies*, *42*(4), 419–429. Advance online publication. doi:10.1111/ijcs.12435

Wilcox, K., & Stephen, A. T. (2013). Are close friends the enemy? Online social networks, self-esteem, and self-control. *The Journal of Consumer Research*, *40*(1), 90–103. doi:10.1086/668794

Williams, A., & Hodges, N. (2022). Adolescent Generation Z and sustainable and responsible fashion consumption: Exploring the value-action gap. *Young Consumers*, *23*(4), 651–666. doi:10.1108/YC-11-2021-1419

Witt, E. B., & Bruce, D. G. (1972). Group Influence & Brand Choice Congruence. *JMR, Journal of Marketing Research*, *9*(4), 440–443. doi:10.1177/002224377200900415

Wood, J., Redfern, J., & Verran, J. (2023). Developing textile sustainability education in the curriculum: Pedagogical approaches to material innovation in fashion. *International Journal of Fashion Design, Technology and Education*, *16*(2), 141–151. doi:10.1080/17543266.2022.2131913 PMID:38098645

Woo, E. (2021). The Relationship between Green Marketing and Firm Reputation: Evidence from Content Analysis. *Journal of Asian Finance, Economics and Business*, *8*(4), 455–463. doi:10.13106/jafeb.2021.vol8.no4.0455

Wright, P. L. (1973). The cognitive processes mediating acceptance of advertising. *JMR, Journal of Marketing Research*, *10*(1), 53–62. doi:10.1177/002224377301000108

Wu, H., Luo, W., Pan, N., Nan, S., Deng, Y., Fu, S., & Yang, L. (2019). Understanding freehand gestures: A study of freehand gestural interaction for immersive VR shopping applications. *Human-Centric Computing and Information Sciences*, *9*(1), 43. Advance online publication. doi:10.1186/s13673-019-0204-7

Xiao, M., Wang, R., & Chan-Olmsted, S. (2018, July 3). Factors affecting YouTube influencer marketing credibility: A heuristic-systematic model. *Journal of Media Business Studies*, *15*(3), 188–213. doi:10.1080/16522354.2018.1501146

Xu, Y., & Chen, Z. (2006). Relevance judgment: What do information users consider beyond topicality? *Journal of the American Society for Information Science and Technology*, *57*(7), 961–973. Advance online publication. doi:10.1002/asi.20361

Yalkin, C., & Elliott, R. (2006). *Female teenagers' friendship groups and fashion brands: A group socialization approach*. ACR Gender and Consumer Behavior.

Yang, S., Song, Y., & Tong, S. (2017). Sustainable retailing in the fashion industry: A systematic literature review. *Sustainability (Basel)*, *9*(7), 1266. doi:10.3390/su9071266

Yasar, A., & Yousaf, S. (2013). Solar assisted photo Fenton for cost effective degradation of textile effluents in comparison to AOPS. *Global NEST Journal*, *14*(4), 477–486. doi:10.30955/gnj.000804

Yazdanifard, R., & Yan, Y. K. (2014). The Concept of Green Marketing and Green Product Development on Concsumer Buying Approach. *Global Journal of Commerce & Management Perspective*, *3*(2), 33–38.

Yıldırım, S., Sevik, N., Kandpal, V., & Yıldırım, D. C. (2024). The Role of Green Brands on Achieving 2030 Sustainable Development Goals (2030 SDGs). In *Contemporary Management and Global Leadership for Sustainability* (pp. 141–162). IGI Global. doi:10.4018/979-8-3693-1273-5.ch009

Yoo, J.-J., Divita, L., & Kim, H.-Y. (2018). Predicting consumer intention to purchase clothing products made from sustainable fabrics: Implications for the fast-fashion industry. *Clothing Cultures*, *5*(1), 47–60. doi:10.1386/cc.5.1.47_1

Yuen, S. C.-Y., Yaoyuneyong, G., & Johnson, E. (2011a). Augmented reality: An overview and five directions for AR in education. *Journal of Educational Technology Development and Exchange*, *4*(1). Advance online publication. doi:10.18785/jetde.0401.10

Yuriev, A., Dahmen, M., Paillé, P., Boiral, O., & Guillaumie, L. (2020). Pro-environmental behaviors through the lens of the theory of planned behavior: A scoping review. *Resources, Conservation and Recycling*, *155*, 104660. doi:10.1016/j.resconrec.2019.104660

Yu, U. J., & Damhorst, M. L. (2015). Body satisfaction as antecedent to virtual product experience in an online apparel shopping context. *Clothing & Textiles Research Journal*, *33*(1), 3–18. doi:10.1177/0887302X14556150

Zaichkowsky, J. L. (1985). Measuring the involvement construct. *The Journal of Consumer Research*, *12*(3), 341. doi:10.1086/208520

Zaidi, N., Dixit, S., Maurya, M., & Dharwal, M. (2022). Willingness to pay for green products and factors affecting Buyer's Behaviour: An empirical study. *Materials Today: Proceedings*, *49*, 3595–3599. doi:10.1016/j.matpr.2021.08.123

Zelezny, L. C., Chua, P.-P., & Aldrich, C. (2000). New Ways of Thinking about Environmentalism: Elaborating on Gender Differences in Environmentalism. *The Journal of Social Issues*, *56*(3), 443–457. doi:10.1111/0022-4537.00177

Zepp, R. G., Faust, B. C., & Hoigne, J. (1992). Hydroxyl radical formation in aqueous reactions (pH 3-8) of iron(II) with hydrogen peroxide: The photo-Fenton reaction. *Environmental Science & Technology*, *26*(2), 313–319. doi:10.1021/es00026a011

Zeren, D., & Gökdağlı, N. (2020). Influencer Versus Celebrity Endorser Performance on Instagram. In *Strategic Innvotive Marketing and Tourism* (pp. 695–704). Springer Science and Business Media B.V. doi:10.1007/978-3-030-36126-6_77

Zhang, B., Fu, Z., Huang, J., Wang, J., Xu, S., & Zhang, L. (2018). Consumers' perceptions, purchase intention, and willingness to pay a premium price for safe vegetables: A case study of Beijing, China. *Journal of Cleaner Production*, *197*, 1498–1507.

Zhang, B., Zhang, Y., & Zhou, P. (2021). Consumer attitude towards sustainability of fast fashion products in the UK. *Sustainability (Basel)*, *13*(4), 1646. doi:10.3390/su13041646

Zhang, T., Wang, W. Y., Cao, L., & Wang, Y. (2019). The role of Virtual Try-on technology in online purchase decision from consumers' aspect. *Internet Research*, *29*(3), 529–551. doi:10.1108/IntR-12-2017-0540

Zhang, X., & Choi, J. (2022). *The Importance of Social Influencer-Generated Contents for User Cognition and Emotional Attachment: An Information Relevance Perspective*. Sustainability. doi:10.3390/su14116676

Zhang, X., Yang, D., Yow, C. H., Huang, L., Wu, X., Huang, X., Guo, J., Zhou, S., & Cai, Y. (2022). Metaverse for cultural heritages. *Electronics (Basel)*, *11*(22), 3730. doi:10.3390/electronics11223730

Zhang, Y., Shao, W., Quach, S., Thaichon, P., & Li, Q. (2024). Examining the moderating effects of shopping orientation, product knowledge and involvement on the effectiveness of virtual reality (VR) retail environment. *Journal of Retailing and Consumer Services*, *78*, 103713. doi:10.1016/j.jretconser.2024.103713

Zhang, Y., Wang, Z., & Zhou, G. (2013). Antecedents of employee electricity saving behavior in organizations: An empirical study based on norm activation model. *Energy Policy*, *62*, 1120–1127. doi:10.1016/j.enpol.2013.07.036

Zhang, Y., Xiao, C., & Zhou, G. (2020). Willingness to pay a price premium for energy-saving appliances: Role of perceived value and energy efficiency labeling. *Journal of Cleaner Production*, *242*, 118555.

Zhao, H., Gao, Q., Wu, Y., Wang, Y., & Zhu, X. (2014). What affects green consumer behavior in China? A case study from Qingdao. *Journal of Cleaner Production*, *63*, 143–151. doi:10.1016/j.jclepro.2013.05.021

Zhao, L., Lee, S. H., & Copeland, L. R. (2019). Social media and Chinese consumers' environmentally sustainable apparel purchase intentions. *Asia Pacific Journal of Marketing and Logistics*, *31*(4), 855–874. Advance online publication. doi:10.1108/APJML-08-2017-0183

Zhao, L., Lee, S. H., Li, M., & Sun, P. (2022). *The Use of Social Media to Promote Sustainable Fashion and Benefit Communications: A Data-Mining Approach*. Sustainability. doi:10.3390/su14031178

Zhao, W., Lun, R., Gordon, C., Fofana, A. B. M., Espy, D. D., Reinthal, M. A., Ekelman, B., Goodman, G. D., Niederriter, J. E., & Luo, X. (2017). A Human-Centered Activity Tracking System: Toward a Healthier Workplace. *IEEE Transactions on Human-Machine Systems*, *47*(3), 343–355. Advance online publication. doi:10.1109/THMS.2016.2611825

Zhao, Y., Nzihou, A., Ren, B., Lyczko, N., Shen, C., Kang, C., & Ji, B. (2021). Waterworks Sludge: An Underrated Material for Beneficial Reuse in Water and Environmental Engineering. *Waste and Biomass Valorization*, *12*(8), 4239–4251. doi:10.1007/s12649-020-01232-w

Zheng, Y., & Chi, T. (2015). Factors influencing purchase intention towards environmentally friendly apparel: An empirical study of US consumers. *International Journal of Fashion Design, Technology and Education*, *8*(2), 68–77. Advance online publication. doi:10.1080/17543266.2014.990059

Zhu, S., Hu, W., Li, W., & Dong, Y. (2023). Virtual agents in immersive virtual reality environments: Impact of humanoid avatars and output modalities on shopping experience. *International Journal of Human-Computer Interaction*, 1–23. do i:10.1080/10447318.2023.2241293

Zhu, Y.-Q., & Chen, H.-G. (2015). Social media and human need satisfaction: Implications for social media marketing. *Business Horizons*, *58*(3), 335–345. doi:10.1016/j.bushor.2015.01.006

Zuelseptia, S., Rahmiati, R., & Engriani, Y. (2018, July). The Influence of Perceived Risk and Perceived Ease of Use on Consumer's Attitude and Online Purchase Intention. In *First Padang International Conference On Economics Education, Economics, Business and Management, Accounting and Entrepreneurship (PICEEBA 2018)* (pp. 550-556). Atlantis Press.

About the Contributors

Theodore K. Tarnanidis is a marketing scholar, Adjunct Lecturer at the International Hellenic University and Researcher in Applications of D.Sc. and MCDA. Theodore has six years experience as a marketing and decision making practitioner. He made his post-doc research in the area of sustainable entrepreneurship from the University of Macedonia. He obtained a Ph.D. from the University of London Met., UK. He received his M.B.A from Liverpool University, UK and is a graduate from the University of Macedonia (Business Administration) and Alexander Technological Educational Institute (Marketing). His research focuses on Decision-Making Processes in Sustainable Innovations and Entrepreneurship, Conjoint Models and preference measurement techniques, modelling of purchases and consumer behaviour. His work has been published in various internationally renowned scientific conferences (Academy of Marketing, European Marketing Academy, PROMETHEE Days, Hellenic Operational Research) and in journals (Journal of Business Ethics, World Review of Entrepreneurship, Management and Sustainable Development, Journal of Retailing and Consumer Services, Current Issues in Tourism, Marketing Science & Inspirations, Management Science Letters).

Evridiki Papachristou is an Assistant Professor at International Hellenic University, School of Design Sciences, Faculty of Creative Design and Clothing. She is also a research member of the CAD/CAM Lab (Technical University of Crete- School of Production Engineering & Management). Recent research projects involve a Conceptual Fashion Product Design Assisted by Artificial Intelligence - AI-CFPD, andi-mannequin a Digital Platform for the Design and Rapid Garment Prototyping - both co-financed by Greece and the EU. After many years spent researching and practicing the effective integration of 3D virtual prototype in the apparel industry, she is currently conducting applied research on the intersection of fashion and data mining and knowledge discovery, to further the technology and its adoption. Evridiki is also interested in the role of Industry 4.0 in creating institutional, social and cultural change towards more sustainable and circular practices. She is the scientific responsible for an Erasmus+ Capacity Building program, 3DGarT (3D Garment Training) and co-ordinator of Erasmus+ Capacity Building program 3D4U (3D for Ukraine). Her work has been published in various scientific journals (International Journal of Advanced Manufacturing Technologies, Journal of Textile Science & Engineering, Machines, Journal of Sustainable Engineering, Technologies, Journal of Textile Engineering & Fashion Technology) and in numerous international conferences (AUTEX, FAIM, PI APPAREL, SETN, 3DBodyTech, DFI, ICMI, DCAC). She has also appeared as a 3D expert in WhichPLM.com, a fashion technology editorial.

Michail Karypidis is a textile engineer, active both academically and in the textile industry for almost two decades. His orientation towards textiles emanates from his family textile business.His background is multicultural, having graduated from a public high school in Minnesota, USA. He pursued his undergraduate studies at UMIST (University of Manchester Institute of Science and Technology, UK) to receive a B.Sc. degree in Textile Science and Technology/Chemistry and a PhD in Textile Technology in 2001, sponsored by the EPSRC (Engineering and Physical Sciences Research Centre) and as a member of the University of Manchester's Total Technology Group. A subsequent M.B.A. (Executive) degree enhanced his interdisciplinary knowledge and enabled him to advance his professional career in the textile business of the medical and workwear sector for 19 years. He lectures since 2004, at the Faculty of Design and Production of Clothing of the Alexander Technological Educational Institute of Thessaloniki, taken over by the Technological University of Central Macedonia, Greece. In 2019 the institution merged with the International Hellenic University and the Faculty integrated in the Creative Design and Clothing of the School of Design Sciences, where he presently works as an Assistant Professor. His work has been presented at international scientific conferences and published in academic periodicals.

Vasileios Ismyrlis holds a position of Statistician at Greek Statistical Authority (EL.STAT) since the April of 2014. He had also been an administrative employee for eleven years, in the social insurance institute IKA-ETAM. He has also a two-years experience in a bank and an experience of teaching financial and statistical lessons in vocational post-secondary education and in universities. He graduated with a degree in "Statistics and Insurance sciences" from the University of Piraeus. His postgraduate studies are in the field of "Quality Assurance". He obtained his Ph.D. in "Quality management and Multidimensional statistics", from the Department of Business Administration of the University of Macedonia, Greece. He had authored eighteen journal articles and conference proceedings publications. Mr. Ismyrlis' current research interests include: Multidimensional statistics, Applied statistics, Social statistics, Biostatistics, Human resources management, Quality management, Time series. He has fluency in the written and spoken English language and an adequate knowledge of French.

* * *

Hassan Badawy have more than twenty years of industry and academic experience in the field of tourism, He held a number of positions in different professional, and academic entities including the Egyptian Ministry of Tourism, the British University in Egypt (BUE), The Faculty of Tourism and Hotels at Luxor University in Egypt, and a number of internationally funded tourism development projects. Graduated with a Bachelor's degree in tourism guidance, he then got a master and Ph.D. degrees in tourism, and then he got a Master degree in cultural heritage management from Sorbonne University where he specialized in cultural tourism marketing. As an acknowledgment of his contribution and effort in academia and community development, he was awarded the Fulbright Scholarship in 2022 in tourism and Heritage studies. He also won different scholarships from different international organizations where he attended a number of tourism training programs. Invited as a keynote speaker at a number of international scientific Conferences and Seminars centered around different topics especially sustainable development, cultural heritage management, Entrepreneurship, and heritage Tourism Marketing. Worked as a consultant and trainer for a number of international development projects funded by international organizations including USAID, UNDP, and UNWFP where he was responsible for developing a number of work plans to enhance employability in the tourism sector, he was also responsible for identifying training needs, developing training materials, and the delivery of the training. Supervised and evaluated a number of scientific researches in areas and topics related to tourism marketing and sustainable development. Active in community services such as working as a voluntary Start-ups Mentor with German development cooperation (GIZ), he also delivered different training programs on women's empowerment.

Shikha Bhagat is an Assistant Professor in School of Business and Management, Christ University, Bangalore, India.

Saumendra Das is presently working as an Associate Professor at the School of Management Studies, GIET University, Gunupur, Odisha. He has more than 20 years of teaching, research, and industry experience. He has published more than 57 articles in national and international journals, conference proceedings, and book chapters. He also authored and edited six books. Dr Das has participated and presented many papers in seminars, conferences, and workshops in India and abroad. He has organized many FDPs and workshops in his career. He is an academician, author, and editor. He has also published two patents. He is an active member of various professional bodies such as ICA, ISTE and RFI. In the year 2023, he was awarded as the best teacher by Research Foundation India.

Catarina Delgado, Ph.D., is an associate professor at the Faculty of Economics, University of Porto (FEP.UP), and a researcher at CEF.UP and LIAAD/ INESC TEC. Her research interests are primarily in the areas of responsible consumers, responsible e-commerce, sustainable and responsible supply chains, ecotourism, ESG/ CSR disclosure, quality management/ kaizen/ lean six sigma, and scientometrics. Her teaching focus is on Operations and Logistics (operations management, supply chain management, operational research), Quality Management and Continuous Improvement (Kaizen, Lean, Six Sigma), and Social Responsibility and Sustainability Reporting. Author of the book "Supply Chain Social Sustainability for Manufacturing" (Springer, 2020), her academic work has been published in several leading international scientific journals, such as Journal of Cleaner Production, International Journal of Production Economics, Sustainability, Journal of Manufacturing Technology Management, JASIST, Informetrics, Scientometrics, and Social Responsibility Journal.

Jadel Dungog is a distinguished economics student from Mindanao State University - Iligan Institute of Technology, with a remarkable academic record. Her professional journey is marked by a series of roles that leverage her strong foundation in economics and quantitative analysis, including her proficiency in tools such as SmartPLS, STATA, Python for Data Analytics, Tableau, and Excel Analytics. In 2024, Ms. Dungog furthers her experience in the field of economics through a research assistantship at the Faculty of Management, Universiti Teknologi Malaysia (UTM). This role is a testament to her ability to blend standard and innovative thinking, and it will allow her to apply her robust analytical skills and attention to detail in a research environment. Her work at UTM is expected to contribute significantly to her growth as an economist, building on her extensive experience as a writer and strategist in management, legal, finance, and marketing sectors across Asia, Europe, and the US.

Chen Fu is from Beijing, China. She studied as a graduate student at Capital University of Economics and Business, majoring in management. Since 2021, she has been focusing on getting a doctorate from University of Technology Malaysia, majoring in management. She is also a boss, running different types of businesses (including restaurant chains, electronic product sales, engineering projects, machinery and equipment sales etc.). In 2013, he founded Beijing Chenshi Lianchuang Technology Co., Ltd. to engage in the sales of HP printers, mainly through channel sales. With the rise of online sales, the online sales department and self-media department were established in 2016 and have been operating until today. I am a person who never stops. In the past ten years, I rarely let myself rest. I always feel that when you are young, you have to work hard, and if you set your goal, you must keep going unswervingly.

Sanjana Hothur is a student in Christ University Bangalore.

Logaiswari Indiran has successfully completed her doctoral degree in Management at the University Technology Malaysia (UTM) in 2018. Throughout her 21-year teaching career, she has made significant contributions to the Faculty of Management, focusing her research efforts on various areas including technology entrepreneurship, innovation, intellectual capital, business incubators, and start-ups.

Kutubuddin Kazi has completed his B.E., M.E., and Ph.D. in E&TC Engineering and is nowadays working as a Professor & Head in Electronics and Telecommunication Engineering Department and also as Dean R&D. He is Post Doctoral Fellow working on "IoT in Healthcare applications". He has published more than 110+ articles in various Journals. Also published 11 books in the field of Engineering. He has 15 Indian Patents, 2 Indian copyright patents, 2 South African Grant Patent, and 8 UK Grant Patent. All patents are in the field of IoT in Healthcare. He worked as a Reviewer for Scopus Conferences and Journal also reviewer for IGI Global. Also work as Editorial Board Member for various Journals.

Prasad Kulkarni is working as Assistant Professor in Presidency College, Bangalore, India.

Nurul Hidayana Mohd Noor, Ph.D., is Senior Lecturer in Faculty of Administrative Science and Policy Studies, Universiti Teknologi MARA (UiTM), Seremban, Negeri Sembilan, Malaysia (ORCID:). Her main research activity is entrepreneurship, environmental, nonprofit, organizational management, and youth studies. She has published widely on these subjects in publications such as the Journal of Entrepreneurship in Emerging Economies, Journal of Entrepreneurship and Public Policy, and Human Service Organizations: Management, Leadership & Governance.

Tapaswini Panda is presently working as Guest Faculty at Model Degree College, Rayagada, Odisha. She has completed Master of Business Administration from GIET University, Gunupur, India. Her research interest is on Work Life Balance, Quality of Work Life and Human Resource Information System. She has published three patents in India and abroad. She is a passionate researcher and a true academician teaches the subject such as Principles of Management, Human Resource Management, Organizational Development and Change. She has published one paper in National Journal and two book chapters.

Debasis Pani received MBA from Sambalpur University and PhD from Berhampur University. He has been working as an Assistant Professor at GIACR Rayagada, affiliated to Biju Patnaik University of Technology, Rourkela for the last 16 years. His research interest include consumer behaviour and rural entrepreneurship.

Senthilmurugan Paramasivam is an associate Professor and researcher working with Christ University.

Udaya Sankar Patro is presently working as a Lecturer at Rayagada Autonomous College, Rayagada, Odisha. He has completed a Master of Business Administration from GIET University, Gunupur, India. His research interest is on Workplace Spirituality, Work life Integrity and Human Resource Management. He has published three patents in India and abroad. He is a passionate researcher and a true academician who teaches the subjects such as Management and Theory Practices, Managerial Economics, and Human Resource Management. He has published one paper in National Journal and two book chapters.

Afifi Alifia Salsabila Putri earned her Bachelor's degree in Management (Technology) from Universiti Teknologi Malaysia in 2023, distinguished by the prestigious Dean's List Award. Her academic journey was marked by notable achievements, including the receipt of both the Best Paper Award and Best Presenter Award at the MoT Symposium UTM in 2023. Afifi's research pursuits focus on unraveling the intricate interplay between business strategies and technological advancements, mirroring her academic specialization. She is currently work as a Business Consultant at EY Indonesia, She leverages her expertise to address contemporary business challenges comprehensively. Afifi is also acknowledged as the author of Virtual Try-On Application and Fashion Purchase Intentions Among Gen Z Consumers in Malaysia.

Alessandro Ruggieri is Full Professor of Commodity Science at the Department of Economics and Management (DEIM) of University 'Tuscia' in Viterbo (Italy) where he holds the courses of Technology, Innovation and Quality, Quality Management and Certification and Quality Management Techniques. From 21st July 2011 to date is the Director of the Department of Economics and Management (DEIM) at the University of Tuscia. His research has developed mainly under the following guidelines: (i) Quality of goods, products and services. Studies and research on the quality according to the approaches of "Total Quality Management" and "Quality Certification" by "ISO 9000" standards; (i) The relationship between quality and consumer, with particular reference to customer satisfaction; (iii) Quality and innovation in the agro-food industry; (iv) Environmental issues, with particular reference to management and environmental certification; (v) Innovation and technology transfer, with particular attention to the role of innovation for regional development.

Nayan Deep S. Kanwal lays claim to almost 36 years of professional experience primarily in Communication, Scholarly Journal publishing and Research and Development Management & Administration. His research expertise is in the following areas: Languages, Linguistics, Management, Environmental sciences, etc. Nayan is an experienced senior Executive Editor, Editor-in-Chief, Author, Reviewer and a Professor, with a demonstrated history of working in the publishing industry. Skilled in Academic Publishing, Publications, Creative Writing, and Text Editing. Strong media and communication professional with substantial experience in Communications, Media, Print Design with a strong scholarly journal publishing background. He has written on a wide range of subjects beyond his area of study, agriculture. He has published articles in different publications as well as book chapters in his long academic and professional career. He has also authored and co-authored several research and development books. The subjects he has written on range from management and administration of research to information technology. Nayan is described as a man with conviction and commitment, responsible for the education of countless postgraduate students from all over the world. He is a brilliant and intelligent communicator who has devoted himself for the promotion of academic publications not only for Malaysia, but also for the developing world and for the entire humanity. There must be some method to his madness that single-handed he has created this mammoth publishing impact. He is full of surprises and his level of energy is very high and contagious". Professor Nayan Kanwal has authored and co-authored numerous academic books and journals, served as a reviewer to many SCOPUS-indexed journals. He has also served as an external examiner/ evaluator for PHD thesis with several universities around the globe. He has delivered countless lecturers, invited by universities in Malaysia, Thailand and Indonesia; attended copious Seminars/Workshops/Courses and has been invited as a Special Guest at more than a hundred Plenary/ Keynote/ Invited Talks. In addition, he has also been involved in research consultancies in Indonesia, Thailand, Vietnam and Malaysia. He is a Fellow of the Royal Society of Arts (FRSA), United Kingdom, a Life Member of the British Institute of Management (BIM), United Kingdom, an Associate Member of the Marketing Institute of Singapore (AMIS) and an Associate Member of the Australian Institute of Agricultural Science and Technology (AIAST).

Mallika Sankar is an Assistant Professor in School of Business and Management, Christ University, Bangalore, India.

José Duarte da Rocha Santos received his PhD in Management from Vigo University. He also holds MSc in Marketing and a bachelor's degree in Business Sciences. Between 1987 and 2002, he played various roles in sales, marketing, and management of companies in the information technology sector. From 2003 to 2018, he performed the functions of a management and marketing consultant. Since 1999, he has been a professor in higher education in Portugal in the fields of management and marketing. He is currently a marketing professor at the Accounting and Business School of the Polytechnic of Porto (ISCAP/P.PORTO). He is also a senior researcher at the CEOS.PP - Centre for Organizational and Social Studies of the Polytechnic of Porto, Portugal. His main areas of research are strategic marketing, relational marketing and digital relationship strategies.

Paulo Silva has a PhD in Communication Sciences - Communication in New Technological Environments from the Faculty of Arts and Humanities of the University of Coimbra, an MSc in eLearning Management Systems from the NOVA School of Social Sciences and Humanities, and a Graduation in Public Relations and Corporate Communication from the ESCS - School of Communication and Media Studies, Polytechnic Institute of Lisbon and also holds the Specialist Title in Marketing and Advertising of the Polytechnic Institute of Viseu. His full-time professional experience includes the activities of Account and Marketing Manager in an Advertising and Communication group from May 2010 to July 2021, General Manager in a multinational food safety group from March 2007 to April 2010 and Customer Service Manager in an Advertising and Communication Group from August 1998 to March 2007. Since March 2009, he has taught Marketing and Advertising at the Escola Superior de Educação de Viseu, Instituto Politécnico de Viseu, where he is currently a full-time lecturer. He is also a Portuguese Association of Communication Sciences - SOPCOM advertising working group member.

Cecilia Silvestri is Researcher of Commodity Science at the Department of Economics and Management (DEIM) at the University of Tuscia, Viterbo (Italy) where she held the course Quality and Customer Relationships. She had her PhD in 2011 in "Economics and local development" at the University of Tuscia. Consistent with carried out studies, her research has developed along the following guidelines: (i) Quality of goods, products and services. Studies and research on the quality according to the approaches of "Total Quality Management" and standards "ISO 9000", (ii) The relationship between quality and consumers, with particular reference to satisfaction and loyalty, (iii) Quality and innovation in the agro-food, (iv) Innovation and technology transfer, with particular attention to the role of technological innovation for territorial development.

Neetu Singh is a PhD in Fashion Management and Associate Professor at Symbiosis Institute of Design. Her areas of interest are Fashion Marketing, Fashion Branding, Retail Management, and supply chain management in fashion business.

Index

Milton Keynes UK
Ingram Content Group UK Ltd.
UKHW022011250624
444693UK00006B/138